ALSO BY LOIS W. BANNER

American Beauty
  (1983)

Elizabeth Cady Stanton
  (1979)

Women in Modern America
  (1974)

  coeditor
Clio's Consciousness Raised
  (1974)

IN FULL FLOWER

In Full Flower

Aging Women, Power, and Sexuality

A HISTORY

Lois W. Banner

ALFRED A. KNOPF

NEW YORK

1992

THIS IS A BORZOI BOOK
PUBLISHED BY ALFRED A. KNOPF, INC.

Copyright © 1992 by Lois W. Banner
All rights reserved under International and Pan-American Copyright
Conventions. Published in the United States by Alfred A. Knopf, Inc., New
York, and simultaneously in Canada by Random House of Canada Limited,
Toronto. Distributed by Random House, Inc., New York.

Library of Congress Cataloging-in-Publication Data
Banner, Lois W.
    In full flower : aging women, power, and sexuality / by Lois W.
Banner. — 1st ed.
        p.   cm.
    Includes bibliographical references and index.
    ISBN 0-394-57943-7
    1. Interpersonal relations—History.   2. Aged women—History.
    3. Young men—History.   I. Title.
    HM132.B335   1992
    305.3—dc20   91-4266
                    CIP

Manufactured in the United States of America
Published May 22, 1992
Second Printing, August 1992

To Gloria Feman Orenstein, who inspired it; to Helen Lefkowitz Horowitz, who validated it; to Elinor Accampo, who lived it with me; to Nikki Smith and Jane Garrett, who believed in it. And for Dominick, a presence.

CONTENTS

Acknowledgments   *ix*

INTRODUCTION   3

PART ONE
Sunset Boulevard: *The Movie, the People*   25

CHAPTER ONE   Sunset Boulevard   30

PART TWO
The Ancient World: From Prepatriarchal Times to the Early
  Medieval Era   57

CHAPTER TWO   *The Possibilities for Penelope*   61
CHAPTER THREE   *Goddesses Revealed and Obscured:*
                     The Story of Sappho and Phaon   91

PART THREE
Aging Women in Advance and Retreat: From the Medieval Period
  to the Eighteenth Century   125

CHAPTER FOUR   *The Wife of Bath as Historical Prototype*   129

CHAPTER FIVE   *Aging Women, Power, and Sexuality:*
From the Wife of Bath to the Witch   164

CHAPTER SIX   *The Eroticized Young Male and*
Women's Response   198

PART FOUR

From the Philosophes to Freud: Aging Women in More Modern Eras   233

CHAPTER SEVEN   *The Nineteenth Century: Margaret Fuller*
and Colette—Continental and
Anglo-American Comparisons   237

CHAPTER EIGHT   *The Twentieth Century: Menopause*
and Its Meaning   273

PART FIVE

The Contemporary Period   311

CHAPTER NINE   *Aging and Ethnicity: Goddesses Reconsidered*   315

EPILOGUE   353

Notes   359
Index   409

Illustrations follow page 160.

ACKNOWLEDGMENTS

THE INITIAL IMPULSE for this book proceeded from my own personal saga of aging and relationships. In addition, it grew out of my interest, as a scholar of women's studies, in feminist spirituality and the prepatriarchal goddesses. They seemed to me to symbolize a time of comity before the onset of those patriarchal arrangements which have profoundly molded the contours of Western society and of the modern world. The controversy over the existence and meaning of these ancient divine figures constituted one of the most intriguing research issues I had encountered, and I was drawn as a scholar to their investigation. And I was fortunate to have at the University of Southern California, in my colleagues Gloria Orenstein, Miriam Dexter Robbins, Savina Teubal, and Karen Segal, scholars versed in the literature concerning the ancient goddesses.

During the years of thought and research that ensued, many individuals aided my ongoing perceptions. Among others, I must acknowledge many colleagues at USC who gave so generously of their time and knowledge. In particular, Lloyd Moote presented me with bibliographies and insights. Without his urging I never would have attended the conference on aging at the University of Maryland in 1988 where I met the supportive group of humanists working to bring their insights within the field of gerontology. (This group especially includes, among others, Thomas Cole and Alison Lingo.) Paul Knoll gave me invaluable aid in understanding the medieval world, as did Elizabeth Perry for the Renaissance. Ronald Love shared with me his knowledge of early modern male dress.

Diana Meehan provided me with information from folklore, sharing with me her intellectual understanding and personal support. Susan Kneedler first introduced me to the "loathly lady." Geoffrey Henderson deepened my thinking with regard to women in ancient Greece, and Amy Richlin guided me through the mazes of classical scholarship. Without her critical ability, I would undoubtedly have made more errors than I have. And Betty Friedan provided me with many insights, not the least of which has been her own model, in her life, of triumphant aging.

I thank Harlan Hahn, who writes about "ugliness" as I write about "beauty," for many constructive agreements and disagreements. To Irene Diamond I am grateful for all the hours of conversation. To Harry Brod, my thanks for accepting with aplomb my criticisms of the men's studies movement which he played a role in founding, even as we together team-taught the truths of feminism to resisting undergraduates. And I also thank Thomas Cole and Marylin Arthur Katz for sharing their unpublished manuscripts with me.

I cannot sufficiently thank Gloria Orenstein, Helen Horowitz, and Elinor Accampo for their support through what was a long and arduous process of research, thought, and writing. Each in her own way led me to deeper conceptualizations; their individual readings of the final manuscript enriched it. In addition, my work on menopause in the modern period was particularly aided by the critical readings of Regina Morantz, Thomas Cole, and Barrie Thorne.

A number of students served as research assistants during the course of researching and writing this book. Chief among them are my daughter, Olivia Banner, and my co-daughter, Issa Lampe. Both are notable thinkers and writers; both supported me with aplomb through difficult times. I thank Issa, in particular, for the evenings we spent discussing the resonance of my themes within art history. To Olivia my thanks are endless: for teaching me literary theory, for writing a portion of the book when my energy flagged, for all those middle-of-the-night phone calls abroad to obtain illustrations. I have written little about mothers and daughters in this book, but it is with great pride that I watch my own daughter's aging and her successes. To my son Gideon I can only say that I appreciate his support and the patience with which he puts up with his mother's pursuit of writing and waits for his turn on the computer—always, at my house, in demand.

My thanks once again go to the University of Southern California, an institution which for the past seven years has been a home to me and which has provided me with my colleagues in the History Department and in the Program for the Study of Women and Men in Society. The latter group have, indeed, become my family. They have included Gloria Orenstein, Helen Horowitz, Barrie Thorne, Walter Williams, Roberta Seid, Michael Messner, Mark Kann, Harry Brod, Judith Stiehm, Carol Jacklin, Nancy Lutkehaus, Lila Karp, and Amy Richlin. After my twenty-year hegira within academia, it was perhaps fitting that I found a place among those USC Trojans who, in the 1930s, numbered my mother, in the 1960s my brother, and in the 1980s my daughter. USC has supported me in many ways, including the awarding of faculty research grants to complete this work.

Finally, to my literary agent, Nikki Smith, and my editor, Jane Garrett, I want to express my gratitude for their support. No one could ask for better literary and personal guidance than what they have provided.

Others aided me in ways they probably never knew. There was, for example, my class of students in American popular culture who informed me, after they had watched *Sunset Boulevard*, that I was wrong in viewing William Holden as appearing to be much younger than Gloria Swanson. To their eyes, attuned to the mentality of the 1980s, Swanson was appealing. Then there was the museum curator in England we called to track down a painting of Queen Elizabeth I. This individual provided a welcome moment of feminist humor in the middle of our pressured search. When informed that the manuscript being illustrated concerned the subject of relationships, especially those between older women and younger men, she expostulated: "Oh, my, they had boy toys then, too."

Finally, to Dominick, what can I say? Only he knows what we have meant to each other, for good and for ill.

IN FULL FLOWER

Introduction

*F*IVE YEARS AGO, when I was forty-eight, I chanced into a relationship with a man of thirty, eighteen years my junior. For a long time I did not know his age. His mature air, his height, and his black, bushy beard gave him the appearance of being older than he was. When I discovered the difference in our ages, my reaction surprised me. For I found myself thinking that something was wrong about our being together. He was young enough to be my son, and that bothered me. I felt that I ought to be with someone my own age and he with someone his age.

Perhaps there were understandable reasons for my unease. The only woman I knew who had become involved with a younger man had been ridiculed by her family and friends. How could a woman with grown children be involved with a man nearly half her age? It was undignified. She was denying him the opportunity to have children on his own. What could they have to talk about? They lived in different generations; their interests had to be different.

An inveterate moviegoer, I could recall numerous films starring aging actors like Cary Grant involved with younger women. When it came to the reverse situation, however, my recollections stopped with the witchlike portrait of Anne Bancroft, involved with Dustin Hoffman, in the 1967 film *The Graduate*. (In 1967 I was twenty-eight.) At the time it was released, this movie had seemed to capture the youthful, rebellious spirit of the 1960s. In retrospect, I could see, I had paid little attention to Hoffman's rejection of Bancroft for her daughter. Hoffman seemed young and vulnerable; I accepted the film's point of view that Bancroft deserved what she got. In my eyes the future belonged to rebellious youth and not to aging women who were materialistic and conventional.

Encountering on a personal level the issues occasioned by a cross-age relationship led me toward investigating the subject of aging more generally and toward examining matters of power and sexuality central to all relationships. As this book took shape, the subject of cross-age relationships, initially its sole focus, became a springboard toward scrutinizing aging more generally, especially women's aging. As I examined texts and contexts throughout the Western experience, I found that erotic and platonic associations between aging women and younger men unconnected by familial ties have often been both a subject of literature and a lived reality. I also found that they afford a perspective on understanding the historical meanings of both age and youth as stages of life. Throughout this work these two topics—that of age-disparate relationships and of aging—are interconnected. My investigation of one leads to an investigation of the other. Both subjects provide elucidation of the key matter of how, whether young or old, we make our way through the journey of life, to attain a respected, joyous maturity, to grow to the point that we are "in full flower."

As I initially thought about these subjects of aging and of asymmetrical age relationships between older women and younger men, I remembered that as recently as the late 1970s I had considered cross-age relationships a male prerogative unavailable to aging women. And so I had presented them over the years to my women's studies classes. The phenomenon had long seemed to me a quintessential example of sexism, a final ironic proof of the unequal access to privilege and power between men and women. For in addition to all their other privileges, men as they aged were still regarded as virile and attractive, even with bulging stomachs and balding heads. Young women were drawn to their power—whether monetary or personal—and deficiencies were overlooked. Older women, in contrast, were perceived as sexually neutral. Accordingly they became shapeless figures who cut their hair short, wore stout shoes, and clung to out-of-date polyester fashions as part of their automatic assumption of the grandmother role. So it had been for my own mother and grandmother.

"How many of you could visualize your fathers of forty or fifty involved with a woman of twenty?" I would ask my students. All would answer in the positive. None regarded such a relationship between an aging man and a younger woman as reprehensible or even as unusual. Every family had an example of it somewhere. But when I asked if they could visualize their mothers in a similar relationship, they would laugh. So preposterous to them was the idea of an aging woman with a young man that they regarded such a relationship as humorous. For it violated their notions of correct partnership: just as men should be taller in height than women so they should be older.

Yet in the past five years or so, such attitudes have changed. My students no longer laugh at such relationships. In fact, they are quick to point out the cases they know of from media examples or from among their family and friends. Many of my own middle-aged women friends have formed such relationships. They are joined in this behavior by well-known entertainment figures like Mary Tyler Moore and Olivia Newton-John, whose relationships with younger husbands and lovers have been emblazoned in gossip sheets and family magazines alike. For a time several years ago hardly a week went by without a story on the phenomenon in some mass-circulation magazine or on some television talk show. Popular writers cite statistics showing that cross-age relationships between older women and younger men are on the increase. Thus, for example, of the marriages that took place in 1983, more than 30 percent of the women aged twenty-five to thirty-four married younger men. In that year, among women aged thirty-five to forty-four, nearly 40 percent married younger men.[1]

I have suggested that the privilege of aging men to form relationships with younger women lies at the heart of patriarchal inequalities between the sexes. Can it be concluded then that women's seeming acquisition of this privilege symbolizes an overturning of patriarchy? As aging women form relationships with younger men, can we presume that a significant gain toward gender equality has been achieved? Or, alternatively, has the situation really changed? Are we rather witnessing a short-term trend in the history of gender relations? Further, does what seems a contemporary trend on the part of young men to form associations with aging women indicate an overturning of predominating ageism? Can we assume that the double discrimination of ageism and sexism directed toward aging women is now receding into the past to be replaced by an egalitarian future?

The attempt to answer these questions provided the genesis for this book. Yet they are not simple questions, and the answers to them are not simple answers. Nor are they questions, I discovered, which can be answered only by investigating the historical present, the time in which we now live. Like most matters concerning the interactions between women and men which on the surface appear without historical content, there is, in fact, a history involved. And it is a rich and multifaceted history.

But like many subjects concerning women and aging, it has been a forgotten history. Over the past fifteen years historians of women have produced a large body of work. They have detailed the dynamics of social structures and individual lives; they have woven a rich tapestry of the interactions of race, class, and gender. But the thread of aging has been overlooked. It has been overlooked because that generation of women historians in the 1960s and 1970s who reclaimed Clio, the Muse of history, and rewrote the past were young women, working out the dynamics of their own lives in their studies. (I draw on my own experience in making such a statement; I count myself among this group.) Aging remained obscure to us partly because we were in rebellion against older generations perceived as antifeminist. Moreover, reflecting traditional attitudes, we chose to look on old women as invisible and on our own youth as the real reality.

Had any of us who were reinventing the history of women during those decades written about aging, I suspect that our point of view would have resembled that of Simone de Beauvoir in her now-classic work *The Coming of Age,* published in 1970. (This work remains the major text on aging in women's history.) De Beauvoir's presentation of the subject is as a history of unrelieved oppression. A privileged few may have been cared for by their families or have preserved enough wealth for self-support. But they are the exception, not the rule. To be a woman other than young in Western culture is to be twice over "the other," to borrow the famous central concept of de Beauvoir's *The Second Sex,* her germinal book about women. For aging women suffer the double discrimination of being both women and aging at the same time.

Yet my knowledge of the general history of women makes me question these conclusions. The two decades we have now spent writing the history of women have shown us the varied ways in which women have resisted patriarchy, finding ways to get around its confines. If we accept the theoretical implications of de Beauvoir's volume, then aging women have had no history. Each era merely replicates the same unpleasant story.

I doubt that this is the case. I think that, as with women's history generally, there is a history for aging women to discover and to reclaim. Indeed, within the United States and among this nation's most oppressed group, namely black women, older women have played powerful roles. They were midwives and conjurors under slavery and after emancipation: they were the "grannies" who tended the children and preserved family continuity. The authority of aging women and the community respect they have engendered are apparent in such disparate personas as the "red-hot mamas" of the blues and jazz tradition as well as the strong, determined women who led local community activist organizations during the civil rights era. Is this experience of black women paradigmatic of the experience of all women? Or has their special seasoning in suffering shaped a personality unreplicated among others within the Western experience?

To reclaim this history of aging women, to find other stories hidden beneath the accepted narratives of the past, is the purpose of this book. I have attempted to decipher old material in new ways and to subject overlooked texts to more critical and creative readings. My goal has been to write a history of aging which, while sensitive to oppression, sees signposts of change and evidences of ambiguity. In many ways, I have written this book in dialogue with de Beauvoir. As well as oppression, I have been interested in subversion, in contestation, in contextualization. I do not believe that looking at subtexts or subcultures is an exercise in exposing only what is marginal and thus unimportant: the "dominant discourse" alone is not the sole focus of my concern. Underlying discourses evidence both what the dominant discourse lacks and what sort of discourses compete with it.[2] Nor do I think that exploring what might have been is a romantic gesture. For such exposés offer important lessons to the present, and what they tell us is that the truth of the past has never been simple. For personal empowerment and the ability to effect change, we need to know the multiple, variegated tales and themes of oppression, resistance, and independence that history reveals.

My story on one level is elementary. Aging women, like women more generally, have been historical actors. They have been queens and empresses, reigning like Elizabeth I of England or Catherine the Great of Russia until well into their sixties and seventies. They have, like the twelfth-century Hildegard of Bingen, managed great abbeys in the ages of Christian expansion. Or, like Mary Baker Eddy in a nineteenth-century age of secularism and science, they have founded new religions. They have, like Susan B. Anthony or Elizabeth Cady Stanton, led feminist crusades into their seventies, starting, like Stanton, new careers in their postmenopausal years. Like Sarah Bernhardt or Lillie Langtry, they have been acclaimed actresses, playing a variety of roles from the spectrum of age even when septuagenarians. They have been courtesans and mistresses of kings, like Diane de Poitiers in the sixteenth century, the lifetime paramour of Henry II, and the independent Ninon de Lenclos in the seventeenth century. These women preserved a reputation for sensual skill and physical grace well past the midpoint of their lives.

And aging women have consistently had relationships with younger men. In fiction, aging women and younger men have courted and loved and have been special friends. Penelope in the eighth-century B.C.E. *Odyssey* has a grown son and young suitors courting her. Much of the story of Geoffrey Chaucer's Wife of Bath in his fourteenth-century *Canterbury Tales* involves her relationship with her young fifth husband, Jenkin. Then there are Henry Fielding's eighteenth-century satiric presentations: Lady Bellaston involved with Tom Jones in *Tom Jones* and Lady Booby and Mrs. Slipslop pursuing Joseph Andrews in *Joseph Andrews*.

In real life Elizabeth I of England and Catherine the Great of Russia had a series of younger companions as they aged. Germaine de Staël, the famed early-nineteenth-century writer who brought German romanticism to France, had a long and eventually unhappy relationship with the younger writer Benjamin Constant. She spent the last years of her life happily with the young, adoring John Rocca. George Eliot married her young secretary, John Cross, after Henry Lewes, her longtime companion, died. The American Margaret Fuller, journalist, feminist, and friend of New England transcendentalists, when thirty-six journeyed to Italy and there met and married Count Giovanni Angelo Ossoli, ten years younger. (In the Middle East, Mohammed, Islam's founder, at the age of twenty-three, in 593 C.E., married a wealthy merchant widow fifteen years his senior. Financially secure, Mohammed was able to turn to religious studies.)[3]

This phenomenon of relationships between aging women and younger men in European regions was not confined to the elites. Especially in the early modern era, such associations could be found throughout the class structure. They existed in notable percentages among the peasantry and the working class, who usually formed families for economic reasons rather than romantic ones. Through inheritance as widows or through savings, some women possessed monetary resources; thus they became attractive marital prospects. In preindustrial Europe for aging women peasant proprietors to marry their laborers or for widows who had inherited businesses under the guild system to marry their workers was not peculiar.

When demographers write about cross-age relationships they regard them as a product of the relative numbers of men and women in populations. In their opinion, whenever what they call a "positive sex ratio" (more men than women) occurs within a population, men will often turn to older women in order to have sexual and marital partners. The return to a "negative sex ratio" (more women than men) will bring the reassertion of the normal patriarchal pattern of men choosing younger women. In contrast, scholars with an economic bent interpret these relationships as financially motivated, as a case in which young men with limited economic resources are drawn to women who have them. Conversely, Freudian analysts reason that the Oedipal fixation on the mother draws certain young men to act out fantasies of incest with their mothers by union with older women.

Freud himself initiated this analytic posture with his famous explanation of Hamlet's tie with his mother as Oedipal in intent. The interpretation assumed major importance in the 1950s, a decade when Freudianism was a strong cultural force, especially in the United States. Freudian analysts then reversed the equation focused on young men to argue that most menopausal women experienced a recrudescence of the Oedipal complex and desired younger men. This desire Freudians found so prurient that they implied it fell within the prohibitions of the incest taboo. They thereby illustrated that in this postwar age of intense family formation, the reversal of age and gender hierarchies was especially threatening. Such theorization, however, was rarely applied to older men with younger women.[4]

Each of these approaches—the demographic, the economic, the psychological—has some validity. Their individual influences will appear throughout this manuscript. But none alone does full justice to the complexity of this subject of age-disparate relationships or to those individual and cultural factors which played oscillatingly fixed and variant functions in producing them. Moreover, these perspectives fail to consider the appeal of aging women who have attained political or economic power. Power, it is said, functions as an aphrodisiac when attached to men. No less compelling, it might be said, is its allure when attached to women. Then there is the appeal of aging women who have gained wisdom and self-awareness. Developmental psychologists tell us that many women become more confident and poised as they age, that they lose the shyness and lack of self-esteem often characteristic of young women in Western culture.[5] To some men such ego integration is appealing.

Aging women in Western culture have been defined from a positive perspective not only in terms of power or self-awareness. Like Cleopatra of Egypt (especially as constructed in the later European imagination), they have also been objects of desire, with a vibrant sexuality acknowledged as appealing. Or aging women have been figures of wisdom, apart from sexuality. They have possessed, as does Plato's Diotima in the *Symposium,* special insights. And this wisdom, this understanding of life, can make them attractive to younger men for whom sacred or profane knowledge may be the key to life success. In feudal courts, young men clustered around older women, the wives of their lords, to learn courtesy and grace. The eighteenth-century philosophes frequented the salons of society women, often older, who supported their endeavors. In Lord Chester-field's famed eighteenth-century advice letters to his son, he stressed that young men should ingratiate themselves with aging women to learn social graces and gain entrance into aristocratic society.[6]

Yet under patriarchy, visualizations of aging women's authority and their sexuality can also threaten: thus occurs the personification of aging women as witches or shrews or their common definition as "invisible"; as persons so removed from youthful beauty that their beings become transparent, nonexistent. And, the oft-noted invisibility of aging women may in fact be a reaction against their actual power. How many men, even in contemporary culture and after twenty years of the women's movement, are in truth able to form relationships with women more powerful, wealthier, and more successful than they?

In the first decades of the nineteenth century the young George Gordon, Lord Byron, became what we would call a "cult" figure among women because of his beauty, his publicized romantic escapades, and his erotic epic poetry. In his poem *Don Juan* (a study of the prototypical European male seducer), he drew on strains of a vitriolic ageist sexism when he complained of aging women who were pursuing him. Remember, he wrote, the "raging" of the "desperate dowager" in her "dog days," stung by a young man's refusal of her offer of love. Citing the literary examples of Phaedra, of Greek legend; Potiphar's wife, of the biblical Old Testament; and Lady Booby, of Richardson's *Joseph Andrews,* he expressed his regret that "poets and tutors" did not make available even more examples to expose the pitfalls of these relationships to European young men.[7]

Benjamin Franklin, renowned among the eighteenth-century American Founding Fathers for his technological and political skill and for his writings counseling sobriety to young men, offered somewhat different advice than Byron on this subject of cross-age relationships. In passages which have gained a certain prurient notoriety, Franklin suggested that aging women's conversation was more interesting than that of younger women and that their diminution of beauty fostered in them a greater willingness to please. Years of experience taught them prudence in con-ducting affairs, and their sexual experience made them more interesting sexual partners.

Franklin spent a number of years as a diplomat in Paris, where he frequented female-managed salons and became something of a celebrity. This experience doubtless familiarized him with the sometime French appreciation of aging women. Franklin felt young men's "violent natural [sexual] inclinations" would best be contained through marriage to women of their own ages. But he feared unmarried young men's frequenting of prostitutes, and he concluded that if young men thought "Commerce with the sex [women] inevitable," they should always *"prefer old Women to young ones."* His advice ended with the celebrated statement: "in the dark all Cats are grey."[8]

Such male-centered predilections as those of Byron and Franklin add a needed element to my story. Yet they only too easily obscure not only the attractiveness of aging women but also women's own authority in the matter of choice. For, if any archetypal pattern lies behind these cross-age relationships, it may be that what the aging women involved in them desire in male partners is the gentleness of youth and not the aggressiveness of the ideal mature patriarchal male. Thus women flock after romantic figures like Byron, or Rudolph Valentino, or the "mati-née idol."

Moreover, the Adonis figure, the young adult male still preserving childhood feminine identifications, has been a consistent character in Western expression and perhaps in Western life. For within these relation-ships in which normal role expectations are often reversed may be con-tained—even if metaphorically—the felt need of many to reverse the expected gender conventions of power and mastery, of gentleness and maternalness, to accede alternating areas of control and nurturance. And this may be why, over the ages, they have been so denigrated.

Recent analysts of contemporary age-disparate relationships between older women and younger men discount any notions of power or perver-sity. In their interview-based studies, Joyce Sunila, Victoria Huston, and Arlene Derenski and Sally Landsburg all conclude that their subjects display ego-balanced personalities freed from fixed life-stage behavior. Their women subjects seem young in attitude and the men seem older than their chronological years. Both the women and the men are less prone to view their association in conventional family terms than couples in which the partners are closer in age or in which the man is older than the woman. In exploring their emotional partnering, the couples Joyce Sunila interviewed describe the emotional side of their relationships as permeated by "oceanic" feelings encompassing all the cycles of age. There is no hint of an Oedipal fixation. In fact, these age-disparate couplings, according to Sunila, were characterized by a lack of conventional expecta-tions and alignments.[9]

All of these analysts highlight studies of sexuality which demonstrate that men reach the high point of their sexual drive when still young, usually in their late teens or early twenties, and that they experience a decline thereafter. Women's cycle of sexuality is the reverse. Thus in terms of sexuality aging women and younger men may be suited to one another. Moreover, women live longer than men, on the average seven years longer. If women married younger men, they might avoid the common experience of outliving husbands, or of having to care for an older, ailing husband. Instead, they might have a healthy spouse to care for them when they are old.

Although these findings seem plausible, I think that these authors romanticize their subject. I am suspicious of conclusions that discount generational differences and internalized prohibitions for both young men and older women about crossing age barriers. Moreover, I question that childhood relationships and the working out of personalities constructed at early ages play no role in age-disparate relationships. But they also play a part, I would argue, in all relationships. The network of family and kin experienced in childhood and often continued in later life is the primary personal and social structure we possess and through which most of us live out our internal lives. Even as the old model family of mother and father and children living together and of mothers staying home to raise the children seems to be breaking down, we still symbolically speak in terms of mothers and fathers, daughters and sons, sisters and brothers. We thereby express our allegiance to primary social alliances.

Healthy relationships require nurturing and support, assertion and sensitivity: everyone, of every age, needs both mothering and fathering as well as the independence of aloneness and the support and camaraderie of brotherhood and sisterhood. But using these family referents does not mean that only in age-disparate relationships do individuals define their relationships in terms of the parent-child experience. Nor is it necessarily the case that the older woman will become the mother and the younger man the son; the positions can just as easily be reversed. Conversely, it is reductionist to assert that all individuals crossing age barriers to come together think in these terms.

Historically, the common convention has been that younger men will become involved with older women only for their money. The term "gigolo," first used in late nineteenth-century France, refers to a younger man who services an older woman sexually for pay. There is no similar term for a young woman prostitute with an aging man. The disparity in terminology indicates, first, that the latter kind of relationship is not considered exceptional, that the young woman/older man relationship is so usual that it does not require semantic notice. The difference also implies that all younger lovers of older women are gigolos, desirous only of access to their status or their money. The further connotation is that the power and sexuality of aging women is illusory, existing to be exploited.

Derived from the feminine "gigolette," the word "gigolo" also has within it the connotations of a negative masculinity, of a stereotypically homosexual "feminine" personality.[10] Consider its difference from the word "pimp," another masculine word within the culture of prostitution. This is an exploding word. Whatever its pejorative implications, its force connotes an ultimate male power over female sexuality. It stands at a remove from the femininity of the gigolo as a male type.

Methodology and Meaning: A Feminist Approach

*T*HIS BOOK has a presentist cast. For the motivation for writing it has proceeded as much from my more recent involvement in the field of women's studies as from my long-term involvement in the field of history. To be a feminist scholar, I have learned, is to possess an ethical commitment to individual autonomy and gender equality. I have come to believe, indeed, that "the personal is political." That aphorism, central to all discourse in women's studies, has been a rallying cry against the traditional criterion of supposed scholarly objectivity, a stance which often masked personal interest under a guise of anonymity.

Thus I am telling an ethical tale, as well as writing a history. I am trying to understand the moral meaning of a historical phenomenon, not merely to chart, over time and across European cultures, the development of that phenomenon. It is for this reason that this book, while focusing on aging women and their self-presentation, also takes up topics that deal with a variety of types of relationships. I cannot, for example, analyze age-disparate linkages—or the meaning of sexuality and power—without dealing with the young men involved in them. I cannot come to any final conclusion about the role these relationships played in women's lives without taking into account their analogue in the more frequent associations between aging men and younger women. Then there are the less obvious analogues: the couplings, for example, between aging women and younger women, or those between older men and younger men. Further, a major kind of association technically involves no "significant other," the relationship to one's self, the relationship of being alone.

And women, of course, have always lived alone. In many ways that has been the most variant of stances. For in a culture committed to relationships, to remain alone has been the most different. Its successful pursuit requires that individuals come to terms not only with the negative definitions of singleness within Western culture but also with the stages of life in their own emotional makeup.

Do not mistake my intent. For I think that I have found in this subject of age-disparate relationships in all its richness a major theme of Western literature and life. Its incidence waxes and wanes, and its disappearance as well as its appearance (either as a subject of literature or as real experience) provides illumination on many areas connected with what I might call the "history of the personal": love, sex, spirituality, power, autonomy, friendship, and, above all, the nature of gender construction and self-definition. What may appear on the surface to be trivial is actually profound, providing insight into that quest for personal fulfillment which has come to define much of modern history as well as the deepest yearning of most of our lives.

I cannot pretend to be all-inclusive in covering my topic. Like all subjects dealing with relationships, power, and sexuality, there is a "dark" side to it. There is a way in which partnership can become perversion, and empowerment can degenerate into control. For example, associations between age and youth can involve incest. Pederasty (the term dating from the Greeks for relationships between older and younger men) can become pedophilia, or the perverse sexual desire, especially on the part of men, for children. I do not mean to defend that European practice by which servants initiated their young charges into sexuality. I make no case for that nineteenth-century culture of prostitution which produced child brothels and accommodated the male compulsion to deflower virgins. All of these subjects await historical scrutiny, but I have not focused on them in this book. I have instead often (but not always) preferred to focus on the ways in which age and youth have more positively interacted.

A history of relationships lies at the core of this book. But, let me reiterate, so does the history of aging. And here let me clarify my definition of aging. From the outset I must emphasize that my understanding is supple and shifting. My preference is to regard aging as a continuum along which individuals move, often at differing speeds and with differing attitudes toward the process of aging itself. In this approach, I use a combination of "life-cycle" and "life-stage" theorization. The former opens up areas of ambiguity in the individual process of development and allows focus on continuity: a cycle implies unfolding, growth, change. The latter, although rigid, identifies common age plateaus that probably do exist, at least in cultural definitions.[11]

Throughout the European and American experience the idea has been paramount, from the Greeks to the present, that life is experienced as stages (although definitions of the chronological timing of these stages in the past has often differed from our present definitions). These stages in all these ages more or less correspond to our modern-day conceptions of youth, middle age, and old age. This simple point is important: in contradistinction to most previous histories of aging, I have included middle age as well as old age in my analysis. Extending these dimensions in such manner brings an enriched contextualization to the understanding of aging, underscoring even further its proportions both as a series of plateaus and as a process.

What I have found for women by cultural definition is a delineation between middle age and old age, between a period infused by positive possibility and one demarcated by negativity. Procreational ability seems to trigger the definitional difference, and menopause seems to stand in the middle as the gatekeeper from one to the other. Having noted these distinctions, I hasten to root them in ambiguity. Menopause (produced by hormonal changes) is a process lasting for a number of years. Cultural perceptions of individual aging are dependent on the look of face and body; healthy living or the use of cosmetics may enable aging women to pass as younger.

This issue of appearance, with all its ambiguities, is a central concern of my work. For appearance, more than any other factor, has occasioned the objectification of aging. We define someone as old because he or she looks old. Initially we overlook the subjectivity of their own reality. It is in this context that aging women especially become doubly "the other." Trivialized because they are not young, they are also derided because they stand outside of standard conventions of beauty. On the other hand, there is an alternative Western tradition—of ambiguity, of questioning the concept of "beauty" itself. At the very simplest, however, how people look and cultural constructions of the meaning of those looks offer a powerful entrance into understanding complexities and dualities as they apply to the meanings—both symbolic and real—of aging women's lives.

Because of my complex definition of aging, I have purposely not been rigorous in my definition of the age ranges involved in "disparate" or "cross-age" relationships (standard sociological terms I have employed throughout this manuscript). For the most part, age ranges greater than five years have caught my attention. Yet in a Euro-American culture constructed according to patriarchal standards from the earliest of times, the presumption has been that, particularly in proper heterosexual couplings, men should be older than women. Thus any deviation from this standard can be viewed as unusual, as troubling from the conventional point of view.

The Historical Context and the Importance of Patriarchy

My HISTORY of aging women begins in the ancient past, with prepatriarchal goddesses and their younger male consorts. The early existence of these divine partners provides a profound beginning to my story as well as an early location for investigating its manifold meanings. I also find the eventual privileging of the young male consorts to be a striking indication of the coming into existence of Western patriarchy— of that system of violence, division, and duality which has dominated the Western mentality since early times.

Moreover, I find that the centrality of goddesses in ancient mythologies extended their influence into later centuries in ways that historians have failed to recognize. This is especially the case for the Greek and Roman writings which so powerfully influenced later European literature. Renaissance scholars, for example, not only rediscovered Plato and other classical writers but also unearthed the ancient "mystery" religions and their palimpsest of powerful goddesses. As late as the mid-nineteenth century in *Woman in the Nineteenth Century,* Margaret Fuller built her system of gender interaction around the goddess–young god typology. To Fuller these goddesses—and the young gods—offered models of independence, empowerment, and comity.

My history continues from the pre-Greek period through the ages of Roman imperialism and of medieval localism. The medieval era was a time when, feminist historians tell us, the lack of centralized institutions allowed women a certain social and political leverage. I will chart the decrease in that importance and the special impacts of that decrease on aging women during the ages of European nation-state building, of the rise of capitalist enterprise, of religious upheaval and "reformation," and of the movement into the modern age.

More contemporary times also concern me. I will investigate nineteenth-century Victorianism and its impacts on aging women. And I will examine the cyclical nature of women's twentieth-century experience—those alternations between times of feminist activism and cultural advance and times of retrogression—through the lens of the lives of aging women, especially through their experience of menopause.

Several additional major themes inform this work. Important among these is the sharp break in the definition of women's nature which occurred in the eighteenth century. Since ancient times women had been defined as possessed by a voracious sexuality; the eighteenth century witnessed a redefinition of femaleness in terms of spirituality. This shift in definition applied especially to aging women. In combination with new patterns of family formation and a new popularity of affect in family relationships, this definitional shift produced the modern "grandmother" role for aging women. In previous ages women had not consistently played this role.

A second theme involves an emphasis on the power of patriarchy and an attempt to deconstruct its dimensions by investigating, over time, male roles and behavior. I access this investigation especially through an exploration of male clothing and body type. These topics are part of that subject of physical appearance which has informed my previous work. Focusing on male appearance has enabled me to construct a history of the eroticization of young men, of their appeal as sexual subjects both to older women and to older men. As well, I have been able to add a new dimension to the history of the nature of male "youth" as a life-stage category. I focus on this subject of male dress and body type where I find its historical meanings most manifest: in fifth-century B.C.E. Athens and in medieval and early modern Europe.

In contrast to most "new" gender scholars and to my men's studies colleagues, I have abandoned neither the term "patriarchy" nor the notion of continuity of historical structure on which it is based. In the recent emphasis on individual differences and "oppressions" and the questioning of the existence of fixed cultural structures or roles, we forget the protean nature of patriarchy, able to take on differing shapes in differing eras. Gender hierarchy based on the subordination of women often engages in a negativizing redefinition of images, idealizations, and stereotypes regarding women, especially when an improvement in women's position seems threatening. Such a reaction can be seen in the conflicting redefinitions of aging women's sexuality and of menopause over the centuries.

Moreover, raised to accept gender division, women have consistently been proponents and even enforcers of patriarchal attitudes, of the predominating masculine point of view. This phenomenon is evident in women accusing other women of witchcraft, or women enforcing nineteenth-century Victorianism, or women antisuffragists who were major opponents of women's suffrage in the United States. (In China, older women were the ones who enforced foot-binding on younger women; in those countries practicing clitoridectomy, older women perform the primitive operation.) Divided from other women by class and ethnicity, women of the elites have often functioned as agents of oppression with regard to other groups, as in employers patronizing servants. Indeed, patriarchy's greatest victimization may have been in fashioning women of all classes who, as shrews and harridans, practice their own version of gender manipulation.[12]

Yet in acknowledging female complicity and in stressing male sensitivity and pain, we easily relegate male privilege and power to a secondary position. We thereby forget patriarchal objectification, the reduction of women to sexualized beings whose purpose is to service men's needs for pleasure and power. Apparent in pornography and in underlying motivations for the double standard and for rape, women's objectification also existed in early European imaginings about witchcraft. Here the victimization applied especially to aging women. For these witchcraft fantasies fabricated a vast culture of inverted prostitution, under which all women, possessed of an overriding sexuality, were potential witches intent on controlling men. Aging women, their sexuality emboldened by menopause, were presumably witchcraft's instigators and leaders, just as, within the actual premodern culture of prostitution, aging women were often, as madams and "go-betweens," the primary procurers.

Behind objectification lies a power motivation. As well, it is connected to that glorification of violence which has always been central to definitions of Euro-American masculinity. This violence is apparent in the founding texts of the Western imaginative tradition, in those stylized and glorified battles in the *Iliad* as well as in Odysseus's ritualized slaying of his wife Penelope's suitors in the *Odyssey*. This violence has continued to the present in cultural models like the cowboy and the urban macho superhero. It is also apparent in continuing evidences in contemporary society of high rates of rape, wife battering, and male incest against female children.

"Manhood," David Leverenz has written, "begins as a battlefield code ... to transform fears of vulnerability into a desire for dominance."[13] In the *Iliad*, Achilles knows that if he fights he will die. But his desire for honor, for glory in battle prowess, is greater than his fear of death. In the *Odyssey,* Odysseus kills the suitors who have despoiled his land—even though his son, Telemachus, enters a plea against the violence and the suitors promise to make amends. I do not doubt, as Leverenz suggests, that the emotion of fear within the individual male psyche may generate machismo, whether this machismo is the product of vulnerability, or of the fear of women, or of a mother perceived as all-powerful, or even of a "castrating" father.

With regard to motherhood, Adrienne Rich has written that it is both an institution and an experience.[14] The same perception could be extended to the analysis of patriarchy. It also functions both as an institution and as a series of individual experiences. But the cultural impacts of patriarchy as an institution especially need deciphering, involved as they are in the production of systems of sexism, of racism, above all, of violence.

Gender—that collection of defining masculinities and femininities— is, as many scholars have noted, a cultural product which has changed over time.[15] And, as Susan Jeffords records in her admirable study of cultural representations of gender in the United States with regard to the Vietnam War, patriarchy has consistently been able to readjust itself to threats against its hegemony by reinventing idealizations of the masculine heroic.[16] Thus, for example, women's centuries-long assertion of the need to soften men's demeanor (beginning at least with the fifteenth-century Christine de Pizan) brought in the eighteenth century the reassertion of a principle of invigorated masculinity, especially on the part of Jean-Jacques Rousseau. One could argue that a similar redrawing occurred in the 1890s and that the process may be occurring in present times.

But beneath change lies continuity. Centuries of experience have not modified the existence of those notions of duality which abide at the heart of Western constructions of self and society and which have always underlain divisions of ethnicity, of class, of race, of age and youth, of maleness and femaleness, of ugliness and beauty. Our structures of subordination are inbuilt in our very thought processes which focus on division and function by creating harmful categories of "the other." This time-honored characteristic of our culture has rendered insurmountable the realization of holism, of an end to hierarchy and a predominating rationality. Our dualistic mode of thought has privileged technology above nature, war over peace, the power of patriarchy over the many examples of difference—of an alternative history—that can be offered.[17]

Or, patriarchy reconciles these dualisms in its own way to uphold its conventions of power and violence. Thus there is the long Western tradition of love upholding war. This tradition is evident in Spartan mothers gladly sending sons to battle. It is apparent in Hera, Aphrodite, and Athena of Greek mythology initiating a beauty contest which will result in the Trojan War. It is present in female cheerleaders, chosen for beauty, at male athletic games. It is evident, as Susan Jeffords suggests, in the identification of technology's products as articles of beauty and in the connection of both beauty and technology with the aesthetic of war, as the ultimate spectacle, as that which most fully crosses the boundaries between beauty and ugliness seen in terms of the ultimate dualism, that between life and death.[18]

Judith Bennett has written that the study of patriarchy is "as central to the study of women's history as capitalism is to labor history or racism is to Afro-American history."[19] I would extend her trenchant observation to the assertion that the loss of the concept of patriarchy may signal the end of the feminist history of women—and of men. Scholars positing the existence of structures that extend beyond the immediate have recently been charged with "essentialism." The deployment of this charge seems to imply that any theory recognizing any fixity of social or cultural structure ipso facto cannot recognize differences of race, or class, or internal difference within genders. But the charge itself fails to recognize its own failing: that the ideology of feminism when it emerged as a powerful political force in the 1960s was rooted in the idea of commonality among women. What provided feminism's moral and political force has been the concept of a female body and biology (albeit always culturally constructed) which is not the same as that of men.[20]

Sources and Influences

IN PLUMBING my subject, I have turned to the writings of social and family historians. I have examined narrative accounts of past events, published autobiographies, intellectual treatises, didactic works about behavior (what in the nineteenth century came to be termed "etiquette" books). I have looked at medical writings and analyses of life-cycle literature. And I have often used literary sources, with full realization that many historians may question such usage. Yet I would submit that as evidence of human consciousness, of cultural mentality, of mythic and collective representation of cultural belief systems about gender, literature offers a special window on reality. It affords a way of deepening the understanding of other kinds of texts.[21]

Thus Chaucer's Wife of Bath in *The Canterbury Tales,* in all her complexity, stands astride the ages as a representation of one sort of mythology, of cultural belief regarding aging women. She stands as an archetype—by that term I mean a transhistorical symbol of a certain kind of replicated individual reality. She can tell us much about who we have been historically. Read in connection with a variety of other kinds of historical sources, Chaucer's text provides an enriched context to the history which frames it. Reflexively, the understanding of the historical context deepens literary analysis.

As to this question of methodology, what has influenced me more than anything else is the cultural approach long characteristic of the field of American Studies. In this specialization, history and literature are combined in a variety of ways to provide insight into what is often called "character." This character is a broad conceptualization. It can involve the nature of a people, a culture, a group, even a gender. In a sense, by combining the reading of literary texts with more regular kinds of historical sources I might qualify as a "new historicist." But my training in a broad-based historical methodology involving the work of demographers and statisticians, of family and social historians, as well as my fascination for tracing historical narratives over long periods of time, makes me a maverick even in that camp. I stretch the "new historicism" far beyond any current definitional boundaries. If I fit into any camp, it may be that of the "new" cultural historians who, following Philippe Ariès and Norbert Elias, investigate "long-term trends in the human psyche."[22]

Beyond any initial influence lies my admiration for the work of Marina Warner, whose parallel approach focuses on the European experience (with art as her locus), especially in her works *Alone of All Her Sex: The Myth and the Cult of the Virgin Mary* and *Monuments and Maidens: The Allegory of the Female Form.*[23] Moreover, recently steeped in interdisciplinary women's studies, I have long wondered how a historian might replicate the broad theoretical approach adopted by political scientist Nancy Hartsock in *Money, Sex, and Power,* or by psychologist Dorothy Dinnerstein in *The Mermaid and the Minotaur,* or by poet Adrienne Rich in *Of Woman Born.*[24] In many ways this book represents my working out of that wonderment. Moreover, the attempt to be synthetic gave me, an American historian by identification, the nerve to delve into European sources.

What I discovered is perhaps obvious: historians deal with origins and with continuity and change over time. Chronology is key. But so is revisionism. As historians we engage in an ongoing process of refining our sources, of extending our theorizations, of interpreting the past both in terms of itself and in terms of present concerns. In our discipline no theory is ever final, no historical interpretation ever definitive. And revisionism itself can generate new approaches. Under this rubric of revisionism which defines the historical enterprise can be subsumed all those lessons about the past as a chorus of voices or a tapestry of interweaving threads which I have gleaned from literary critics and learned from the liberating intellectual experience that interdisciplinarity provides.

Thus interweaving a variety of sources, the past with the present, focusing in turn on central themes like power or sexuality that have their own chronology, my time line is not always linear and orderly. Indeed, my history of aging resembles a tapestry, a weaving together of many threads and colors in changing but also continuing patterns, its interweaving threads still affecting the presently forming design. The Fates, by Greek legend, weave the tapestry of life. Spider Woman, by Native American belief, weaves the web which entraps and empowers us all. Penelope in the *Odyssey,* in weaving a shroud for her dead father-in-law, unraveled each night what she had woven the day before, so that the tapestry would never be finished and she would never have to meet her fate. There can be tears in the fabric and dangling threads; it can be unraveled every night if Penelope is our model. Thus there can be breaks and ruptures, places where alternative discourses and models can reveal themselves, to show a palimpsest beneath the more obvious landscape; perhaps even alternative weavers at work.

More than this, I want to make clear that my reading of individuals, events, and texts is rooted in irony and ambiguity. It rests on my sense of good and evil, of male and female, of age and youth, of difference in all its fulsomeness, as each involved with the other, each, in a sense, generating the other. "Fair is foul, and foul is fair," the three witches in Shakespeare's *Macbeth* intone. As descendants of the triune prepatriarchal goddesses revived within Shakespeare's alchemical Renaissance imagination, they speak truth about life and about aging.

Aging women can be regarded as fair or as foul. Or, alternatively, they can be regarded as both. It all depends on cultural cues, on the disposition of the viewer, on whether carnality or spirituality is at issue, on a host of other factors. There is, as in everything I will investigate, a text and a countertext which both stand apart and interweave to create the stories we call history. And, because of human imagination and inbuilt desires to be different, individuals both resist, as well as replicate, dominant discourses. Irony and caprice as much as continuity are a central part of the character of Clio, the Muse of history.

But if "Fair is foul, and foul is fair" can be applied as an adage to aging women in many ways, both in the past and in the present, it can also be applied to young men. Thus in the end I make no brief for age-disparate relationships, or for heterosexuality, or for the privileging of any sort of relationship. I am interested in their existence and meaning and, beyond that, in their resonances over time, seen in kaleidoscopic variation, in intertwinings and in how they can take us beyond the ordinary. I want to investigate how, through understanding the past in the present and the present in the past, we can find contentment, empowerment, jubilation, as we age.

Within the Western experience, flower imagery has often been used as a metaphoric language for women's beauty. Within this botanic vocabulary, aging is often equated with decay. In *Twelfth Night,* Shakespeare drew on a virulent variation of this convention when he wrote, identifying women's beauty with youthful virginity, that "women are as roses, whose fair flower / Being once display'd, doth fall that very hour." I want to reverse this convention. I want to emphasize alternative traditions which celebrated aging women as exemplars of the generative earth or, drawing from imagery based on the four seasons, extolled aging women as partaking of a rich, autumnal period of life. The twentieth-century French writer Colette, among novelists a preeminent analyst of aging, drew on a venerable tradition dating as far back as Ovid when she called the autumnal years "the vintage time."[25] These years can, indeed, be abundant and rich, a time of continued blooming, of full flowering.

Because I wonder about what I have created; because like any ongoing tapestry my work may have loose ends; because I have found limited preexisting analysis of many of the themes regarding aging and youth I investigate, I have decided to call this work a "meditation" on history, rather than a history per se. The dialogue with de Beauvoir in which I have engaged has been long and arduous but deeply fulfilling. In the process I have come to respect her work on aging of which I was initially critical. I can only hope that others will profit from such dialogue with me, as they more deeply plumb the areas in which my history is sketchy, no more than a meditation. As such, it hopes to open up notions of the complexities of cultural codes to encompass the rich panoply of the subjects both of age and of disparate, not ordinary, relationships.

PART ONE

Sunset Boulevard:
The Movie, the People

I N ORDER TO locate my narrative in the American present while pointing to its roots in the European past, I begin my story with an analysis of the 1950 movie *Sunset Boulevard*. This film centers on the relationship between an aging actress, Norma Desmond (played by Gloria Swanson), and a younger screenwriter, Joe Gillis (played by William Holden). In this film American presentist values are posed against Old World symbolisms in the aftermath of World War II. Joe Gillis personifies American values. Norma Desmond, a film star of the 1920s, living as a recluse in aristocratic luxury, personifies the European symbolisms. In the richness of its characterizations and its cultural themes, *Sunset Boulevard* is a major American artistic creation, ranking with major literary texts in understanding the American character. As well, it resonates to the major realities and mythologies regarding aging women which inform the rest of this work.

As a cultural statement, *Sunset Boulevard* addresses many themes. These themes include the nature of Hollywood in the eras when it became a major producer of modern mass culture. They also include the nature of the post–World War II world in which the movie is set. The movie also confronts issues of gender and class and the meaning of the age-old male heroic and female romantic impulses. Whether consciously or unconsciously on the part of Billy Wilder, the movie's writer and director, it is filled with resonances to names and places long past, to a rich history of symbols and stories regarding women and relationships.

Sunset Boulevard confronts issues of how to live one's life in a world of deceit and despair. The deceit is intrinsic to a movie industry primarily interested in profits. The despair is inherent in the lives of those failing to succeed or discarded by Hollywood's relentless drive for new, younger faces. Further, deceit and despair permeate the lives of those who fail to approach aging nobly or with zest. The cultural disillusionment of the postwar years provides an analogue to the disillusionment of aging. The advent of a new movie industry, based on sound and big screen and eventually color, over against the artistry of silent films, also raises issues about the present and the past, about the valorization of what is new simply because it is new, not because it is necessarily better.

The film bears the artistic stamp of Billy Wilder. In many ways it was an outgrowth of his own experiences. He, too, was molded by an American present and a European past. He was born in Poland. His mother, long fascinated by the United States, named him after that American showman and sometime hero William F. Cody, popularly known as Buffalo Bill. As a young man, Wilder had moved to Germany, where he became a director of expressionist films. For a time before he achieved career success, he worked in a Berlin dance hall, partnering older women patrons. Thus he had firsthand knowledge of *Sunset Boulevard*'s subject. He moved to the United States in the late 1930s. According to his biographers, he had inherited his mother's love of the United States, and he possessed an encyclopedic knowledge of American mores.[1]

By using *Sunset Boulevard* as my opening statement, I do not mean to imply that this is a feminist film. I mean only to suggest that Wilder's portrayal of aging brilliantly depicts the complexities of growing older. I often use male authors in this book. I do so partly because of the relatively limited number of female authors before the eighteenth century. More important, what interests me are cultural signals which impact on the minds of authors and influence, through their voices, individual works. Culture is a mélange, a potpourri of messages which we both screen and by which we are shaped. Artists of substance both reflect and reshape those messages in epic ways, telling us what the world of images we inhabit is all about. Or, they give us the pleasure of receiving mixed messages with manifold, puzzling meanings, so that we can exercise our own minds and imaginations.[2]

When Wilder came to shoot *Sunset Boulevard,* he had only a minimal script. The movie partly developed on a day-to-day basis, shaped around the interactions of a group of actors, some of whom were playing not only the characters Wilder created but also themselves. Like Norma Desmond, Gloria Swanson was an aging actress, famed in the 1920s, whose film career had ended with the advent of sound. Erich von Stroheim, who plays Desmond's butler, Max, had been a famed actor and director in the 1920s whose career had also gone into eclipse. Cecil B. DeMille, Buster

Keaton, and Hedda Hopper all play themselves in the film. In *Sunset Boulevard* art mirrors life, and each character must confront not only a fictionalized experience of aging but also an actual experience of aging.

In terms of attitudes toward aging, *Sunset Boulevard* is composed of multivariant texts. My interpretation of it illustrates my mode of proceeding, one that probes beneath the surface, trying to expose additional layers of meaning—both within the text itself and through placing the text within a historical context of time, place, and culture. Thus I offer two interpretations of the film, based around a reading of Norma Desmond's meaning. The first is standard and views Desmond as decentered, as a fragmented, foolish aging woman. The second is more subtle. It explores her rationality and her autonomy and the possibility that these personality features could have sustained a different, more optimistic, ending.

The film *Sunset Boulevard* has not only provided a setting for my exploration; it has also provided a metaphorical, presentist rooting for my historical meanderings. I have, indeed, turned history on its head, reading the present before the past, seeing the past as a tapestry whose interweaving threads still affect the present design. Whether Wilder was cognizant of his meanings, *Sunset Boulevard* as text is filled with transhistorical symbolizations of aging and of relationships. This factor constitutes the film's virtuosity: it juxtaposes the commonplace with genius, the ordinary with the divine. The image of the sunset has often provided creative imaginations with a metaphor for aging. It is the time of day just before the sun goes down, when the sky often shines with a special radiance. But it inevitably precedes the night.

Sunset Boulevard as a title also refers to a street in the city of Los Angeles, where I was raised and where I now live. It is a long road, for those of you who do not know it, stretching from downtown Los Angeles to the sea. Following the path of an old Indian trail, it is often winding and narrow. The word "boulevard," with the Parisian connotation of a broad and straight street, does not exactly describe Sunset Boulevard. True, it passes through areas of wealth. The "Sunset Strip," filled with cabarets and comedy clubs, is still part of it. But the street, often narrow, twists and curves through areas of urban sprawl and homes of the less well-to-do. It is not an easy road to navigate, as any driver who lives in Los Angeles can tell you.

CHAPTER ONE

Sunset Boulevard

NORMA DESMOND slowly descends the grand staircase of her Sunset Boulevard mansion. Floodlights bathe her in light. Cameras roll, clutched by newsreel cameramen on the stairs and in the vestibule below. This scene constitutes one of the most famous moments in film. Norma Desmond, the aging film star, with a career long past, has shot and killed Joe Gillis, an impoverished younger screenwriter, mired in debt and with only "a couple of B pictures to his credit." The news of the slaying once again has brought her into the spotlight. The press has swarmed to her house to immortalize what they can of the aftermath of the lurid deed. Now they catch her on celluloid as she moves slowly down the stairs among them. The film, an extended flashback, details the events that led up to the slaying.[1]

Some months before Norma's fatal action, Joe had stumbled into Norma's mansion while eluding bill collectors attempting to repossess his car. He had wound up living with her. Desperate for money and fascinated by the charisma of her past fame, for months he had worked with her rewriting the screenplay based on the story of Salome and John the Baptist that she herself had previously written for a hoped-for screen comeback. A sometime romance had developed between Norma and Joe. But when he decided to leave her, she reacted with murderous rage and a seeming retreat into madness. Coming down the staircase, she thinks she is on her old movie set, descending the stairs of a great palace as the pagan princess Salome, the incarnation of the heroine of her hoped-for film.

Why does Norma kill Joe? Is *Sunset Boulevard* simply a movie about an aging woman who kills her younger lover because he is going to leave her? Is the message of the movie that aging for women is inescapable and its boundaries on beauty and desirability insurmountable? Does the movie conclude that Norma can neither recreate a career long ended nor succeed in a relationship which transcends age categories? One can give two answers to these questions, even as there are two possible interpretations of the film. One is negative, viewing the relationship as doomed from the beginning; the other is more positive, visualizing options for both Norma and Joe.

And one cannot fully comprehend either Norma or Joe without understanding the other characters in the film. Their possible significance decenters the narrative, giving an enriched contextualization to *Sunset Boulevard*'s presentation of aging.

Norma Desmond and Her Meaning as Negativity

FROM ONE POINT OF VIEW *Sunset Boulevard* seems to take a disapproving stance toward Norma Desmond. Because of Norma's age, there may be no way that her relationship with Joe can succeed, just as there may be no way she can regain either her acting career or her youthful beauty. For her Joe may be only a gigolo, a representative of that sort of young man who, for money, services older women sexually. Even Norma seems to acknowledge that that may be the case when she telephones Betty Schaefer, her putative younger rival, in a futile attempt to end Betty's interest in Joe. She alludes to Joe as nothing but a manipulator of older women. Love between Joe and Norma may be problematic; he seems angry with her throughout the film. A voice-over narrative by Joe provides a running commentary on the film's action. Throughout this narrative, Joe is critical of Norma. Most telling is his name: Joe Gillis. For this name, Joe Gillis, almost sounds out the word "gigolo."

In many ways Desmond is presented unsympathetically. The makeup that she wears underscores her theatrical, larger-than-life behavior. For the makeup is heavy, with oversized lips and eyes giving Norma the look of an overaged Kewpie doll. Or, alternatively, with her harsh face and dark, outlined eyes, she looks like the vamp character of her heyday in the 1920s gone to seed. With long, dark fingernails on hands clutching Joe or enfolding him in an embrace, she seems a vampire, feeding off Joe's youth to make it her own. So did Nosferatu, the vampire's nineteenth-century progenitor, who drank young blood to remain immortal. So, too, in one version of ancient myth, did female figures like Lamia,

Empusa, and the Sphinx. There is another resemblance in Norma Desmond's face. That is to the screen depiction of witches. In looks, her forebears are Margaret Hamilton in *The Wizard of Oz* and Walt Disney's witch in *Snow White*.

Periodically childlike in her dependence in scenes with Joe, Norma at these times gives the impression of Shirley Temple gone awry, of a child trying to act like an adult and not succeeding. Joe comments about her handwriting: "I wondered what a handwriting expert might make of that childish scrawl of hers." His parting words are to tell her to grow up. "There's nothing tragic about being fifty—not unless you try to be twenty-five."

Norma Desmond's very name has meaning. Names are important in *Sunset Boulevard,* for they give additional resonance to people and places. And Norma's name is steeped in tragedy. Her first name, Norma, seems related to Vincenzo Bellini's operatic Norma. This nineteenth-century Norma is a priestess of an ancient Druid cult whose discovery of her Roman husband's love for a younger priestess results in her death. Norma Desmond's name also seems related to that of Mabel Normand, preeminent in early American films as a comedienne and as one of Mack Sennett's bathing beauties, young women whose beauty posed a sharp, comic contrast to the often ugly male comedians with whom they cavorted in Sennett's films. Both the fictional Norma Desmond and the actual Gloria Swanson began their careers in Mack Sennett's troupe. In jest, Desmond tells Joe that in the Sennett chorus line, "Mabel Normand was always stepping on my feet." Normand's career was ruined by her suspected involvement in the 1922 murder of film director William Desmond Taylor, with whom she had probably been romantically involved.

The tragic naming of Norma extends to her surname, as well. For Norma is a Desmond, *de monde*, a "woman of the world." As such, she is fashioned in the French tradition of an older woman who can teach a younger man of indeterminate social roots how to maneuver in an upper-class world. But this tradition may be inappropriate in the post–World War II world of renewed commitment to traditional gender definitions, with domesticity as the proper role for women. In the film, Desmond's failure at life may be traceable to her denial of this maternalness, to her avoidance of any hint of playing a domestic role. On the other hand, the film may imply a critique of this view of women and of the traditional nuclear family in which it is encased.

Younger actresses like Hedy Lamarr or Dorothy Lamour (Desmond's 1940s contemporaries) could exist alone on tropical islands or with indeterminate personal lives as bargirls and singers in exotic foreign lands, favorite settings for forties films. But older women who attempted to continue the role of femme fatale in film easily became parodies of their former selves. For them, the confines of home and family were crucial. From that vantage they could function as self-sacrificing martyrs or prophets, like Irene Dunne in *I Remember Mama* or Ethel Barrymore in many of the movies that she made.

Even Norma's house, a reflection of her persona (as houses often are for women) seems of negative value. In his dialogue Joe describes Norma's house. It is huge, with eight master bedrooms. There is a sunken tub in every bathroom, a bowling alley in the basement, a swimming pool, and a tennis court. A large living room contains a pipe organ, which Max, Norma's mysterious butler, plays. A large screen is hidden behind a painting in that room, and Norma uncovers it in the evenings to show her twenties films to Joe.

Joe calls the house a "white elephant." It is a curiosity, a relic past its time of usefulness. It seems especially out of date in the post–World War II world which looked to the suburbs and the tract home as the new family nirvana. Norma's house is the sort of place that film stars built in the 1920s, when, in Joe's words, they were "making eighteen thousand dollars a week and [paying] no taxes." When Joe leaves the house, he goes to the milieu of his younger friends. They live in crowded, noisy apartments, sharing their space as they share their dreams. They group together with the balm of youth and its hope for the future around them. "There is nothing like being twenty-two," Joe says to Betty.

The house, however, is filled with significance for Norma. Houses are entities which have accompanied women throughout history, often as symbols of their hopes and fears. From Penelope in the *Odyssey,* avoiding the danger of her suitors by sequestering herself in her private quarters, to the medieval lady of the castle, listening in the great hall to her troubadours, to the eighteenth-century lady of the salon, whose largesse lured France's intellectuals to her parlor, the private world of the house was a female world. Men built palaces as architectural monuments to their greatness. Women decorated those palaces and filled their spaces with children, with gossip, with feminine graciousness.

Norma's house in *Sunset Boulevard* is gloomy and ornate. It has that Spanish flair often found in eclectic Los Angeles architecture. It suits Norma's style. If anything, however, it bears resemblance to those massive manses of Gothic fiction. And, *Sunset Boulevard* can be read as a classic of the Gothic tale which has been a staple of women's fiction since *The*

Castle of Otranto and *Jane Eyre.* The dark interiors, camera shots slightly off center, Erich von Stroheim's menacing butler—these features are reminiscent, as well, of the Dracula and Frankenstein horror films of the 1930s. They constitute perhaps a Grand Guignol of Norma Desmond's off-centered imagination.

Even more powerful are the connections in film with Alfred Hitchcock's 1940 screen adaptation of Daphne du Maurier's *Rebecca,* the most famed women's Gothic tale of the twentieth century. In this work du Maurier had resurrected the genre after it had been in eclipse for some decades. In *Rebecca,* as in *Sunset Boulevard*, there is a huge house, a menacing housekeeper, and a relationship which crosses age categories. But in *Rebecca,* the older partner is a man and the younger one a woman. And, although they encounter difficulties in the course of the story, in the end all is well between them.

Like Jane Eyre, the nineteenth-century prototypical Gothic heroine, the heroine of *Rebecca* matures through her experiences with life's problems and eventually brings strength to the older man who initially seemed to dominate her but whose vulnerability is revealed midway through the plot. Both can leave the dark house of their early life together, the massive manse that turns into a castle of horrors, for a cottage of domestic contentment.

For Norma Desmond, however, that kind of cottage can seemingly never exist. Her house is her museum and her mausoleum. On the one hand, it seems empty, devoid of the real life that a family might bring. It is a gilded cage which she has unwittingly created. It is a series of rooms as dramatic settings to mirror her mementos which evidence that she was a star. And, in contrast to the situations for Jane Eyre and for the heroine of *Rebecca,* there is neither a madwoman in the attic, nor a hidden room full of secrets, that proves the rest of the characters are sane. Norma may be it—the attic madwoman, I mean.

Desmond's overblown setting mirrors her curious personal relationships. Desmond has neither children nor family, the standard supports of aging women. She is an appropriate age to be a grandmother, but one could hardly visualize her in that role. What she has is a chimpanzee and her mysterious butler, Max. In addition, she has a group of elderly friends from her film days with whom she plays bridge. Joe calls them the "waxworks" in his voice-over narrative, and that is indeed what they resemble. They are pale; they project a waxen image. Deadpan Buster Keaton is among them, but he is not comic here.

For a moment there seems a different reality for Norma when Max turns out to have been her first husband, the director who discovered her. But this is no pleasant domestic ménage formed by two individuals who, having bonded for life, are happily growing old together. This is not Darby and Joan, those eighteenth-century ballad characters whose domestic felicity became a watchword for long, contented marriage. This is not Robert Browning wooing Elizabeth Barrett Browning with: "Grow old along with me!/The best is yet to be." Rather, Max is a combination of Norma's nurse, her flunky, and an impresario who supports her fantasies. For he writes her anonymous fan letters so that she can sustain the illusion that she is still a star, beloved by a public which has not forsaken her.

Then there is her monkey, perhaps the most graphic symbol of her barren life. When the movie begins, the animal has already died, and Desmond is preparing for the internment. On the monkey, Desmond has lavished her maternal drives. Watching the chimp burial from afar, Joe notes that it looks as though "she were laying to rest an only child." With sarcasm, he makes reference to King Kong, the massive monkey of the 1933 movie *King Kong*, whom entrepreneurs captured in his island Eden to exhibit to the American public. King Kong was an epic animal, symbolizing nature destroyed by civilization; he was not an aging woman's pet. Here Desmond becomes one of those lonely, middle-aged women who bestow their attention on pet poodles and parakeets and who have long been a butt of jokes and of the comedian's caustic wit.

More than this, Joe tells us that Norma is fifty years old. Thus we can presume that she is menopausal. The point is important. For by common belief menopausal women are difficult, hysterical, even crazy. Thus Desmond may be a product of her hormones, a middle-aged woman out of whack. Any child born to a menopausal woman runs a high risk of being deformed, a "monster" in shape. To seventeenth-century Puritans, the stillborn, misshapen child born to menopausal Anne Hutchinson soon after her conviction for heresy was ample proof that she was a witch. Thus a monkey (especially a chimpanzee, closest to humans in genetic makeup) is an appropriate offspring for Norma.

The dilemma of this middle-aged woman is further underscored by the confrontation between Norma Desmond and another character, director Cecil B. DeMille. DeMille plays himself in the film, and it is to DeMille that Desmond goes with an appeal to produce the screenplay of Salome and John the Baptist that Gillis is rewriting for her. Desmond interrupts DeMille on the studio set of a movie he is directing. She mistakenly believes that he has phoned her with an offer to back her projected Salome film.

It is a doubly tragic scene, with fantasy and reality thoroughly inter-mixed. For the real Gloria Swanson's major triumphs three decades before had been in a series of upper-class melodramas directed by DeMille; many contended that he had made her a star. Now twenty years later, DeMille remains a director, vigorous and commanding, still directing films starring seductive women. But younger women star in these films. Among them is Hedy Lamarr, a dark-haired Gloria Swanson descendant. Lamarr plays the siren of *Samson and Delilah,* the film onto the set of which Desmond/Swanson descends in *Sunset Boulevard.* The scene, filmographers tell us, was actually shot on the *Samson and Delilah* set in the midst of work in progress.

The tragic comparison between DeMille the director and his former star is deepened when we realize that DeMille is old enough to be Desmond's father. He is seventy; she is fifty. She calls him "the chief," her title for him in the twenties. She defers to him on the set, as in the old days. There is a rapport between them, but it is like a father with a daughter. With honeyed words he soothes her, but he tells her nothing.

Sunset Boulevard belongs to that genre of cinema known as Hollywood films. In these films a critique of the movie industry is a central purpose.[2] And what *Sunset Boulevard* as an example of this genre shows us is not only the clash between the old Hollywood and the new Hollywood, between the first generation of Hollywood filmmakers and those who followed them, but also the ways in which both Hollywoods, with their false commercial values, could warp individual lives. "The men in the front office," declaims Norma, "they took the idols and smashed them."

Hollywood created Norma Desmond, and it may have made her monstrous. "You cannot imagine how she was at seventeen," DeMille tells an assistant. "A dozen press agents working overtime can do terrible things to the human spirit." Through their efforts, Norma became a new person. Redrawn to their specifications, steeped in the narcissism of celebrity status, she did not know who she was. With her illusions shattered, Norma retreats into murderous rage.

The story of Salome, the role she wants to play, revolves around Salome's demand for the head of John the Baptist, the biblical prophet who scorned her love. Lacking power, Salome gained revenge through an execution which seems a symbolic castration. For if Joe is angry, Norma is also angry. The Hollywood patriarchy made her; the Hollywood patriarchy cast her aside. They "shot" her all those years with their cameras; now she must shoot them. Perhaps unfortunately, the victim of her murderous rage is only a minor screenwriter. Indeed, Joe had once told her that what she needed was someone of her own status, a "big shot." His words may have been only too true. Norma may have vented her rage at the wrong target, confusing love and power, sexuality and hierarchy.

But it is characteristic of women that they personalize their targets. Norma defers to DeMille, but he does not enter her house. Joe is in her house; he will do for the whole of Hollywood. That Joe's relationship with Norma will end disastrously is foreshadowed early in the film. When Joe stumbles into Norma's mansion after hiding his car in her garage, both Norma and Max mistake Joe for the undertaker come to bury her beloved monkey. There is a burial scene emblematic of what will happen to Joe. He will be the "chump" to replace her "chimp." He will also become the undertaker of her dreams: the person who will bury them.

On the gold cigarette case which Norma gives Joe she has had inscribed: "Mad About the Boy." Thus is indicated her infatuation and her need to possess. But eventually Joe will make her mad enough to kill him. Joe cannot be her child; he will not be her lover. Despite the lushness of her locale and the primitive chimp as pet, this is no Edenic paradise, no primeval Adamic retreat. From this perspective Desmond is no Eve, no original earth mother, but only a go-between, a conduit to power. The studio heads, the controlling patriarchs, are the real stars. Norma is a dragon whose powers of seduction are only temporary but the impact of whose actions is eternal.

Following one version of ancient myth, the young god must die when his yearly cycle of regeneration has ended. And so Norma kills Joe, propelling him by the force of her bullets into the swimming pool. As the movie opens—and as it closes—we see him lying in the pool. There he lies peacefully, floating in a state beyond consciousness, buoyed up by water, ever a symbol of women's maternal nature. There he lies peacefully, surrounded by that life-giving amniotic fluid which Norma's body has never produced. There he lies, asleep in a womb which in Norma is desiccated and dry.

After Norma has shot Joe and he lies in the pool, she looks to the sky and triumphantly declaims: "Stars are ageless. . . ." The look in her eyes, the shadings on her face, replicate a figure in an earlier frame of the film. This figure is from a clip of a film in her triumphant years which she has showed Joe in one of her living-room screenings. The figure is actually the young Gloria Swanson in her starring role in *Queen Kelly,* the last important film Swanson made before her career as a star in silent films went into decline.

The message is manifold. The aging Gloria Swanson becomes the young Gloria Swanson; in our eyes the two figures merge into the eternal star, radiant. Metaphorically, and for a moment, Norma Desmond joins the goddesses of myth and legend in several guises, both old and young. But stars, of course, only shine at night; in the light of day they seem to disappear. And so does Norma, advancing and retreating; sometimes powerful through her past fame and her own persona; often powerless, an aging woman yearning after a fame and a love she perhaps no longer can have.

The Production Background:
Real Life Embedding

FANTASY AND REALITY are intertwined in *Sunset Boulevard*. And so are age-disparate relationships. The one between Norma Desmond and Joe Gillis forms the central drama of the film. But these sorts of relationships are also intermixed in the history of the film's production and in the real lives of the people involved in that production.

Thus, for example, Wilder had difficulty casting the roles of Norma and Joe. Few actors seemed willing to expose themselves before the public in this dark romance between age and youth. Mae West, Wilder's initial choice for Norma, adamantly refused the role. She thought that playing the part would tarnish her image as a mocking femme fatale. She had created this image during the 1930s, and she maintained it in the 1940s in a successful nightclub act. In this act choruses of young men accompanied her singing and dancing as foils to her vamping. She wanted nothing to do with the role of an aging woman who could not control the young man in her life.[3] Wilder also approached Pola Negri and Mary Pickford to play the role of Norma, but both turned him down.

With regard to the role of Joe, Montgomery Clift initially accepted it and then backed out only a few weeks before production began. He contended that his fans would not like seeing him involved with an older woman. Yet this public reason for his refusal masked a private reality. For some time Clift had been involved with Libby Holman, a popular singer from the 1920s who was thirty years older than he. Many years before, Holman had shot and killed her wealthy husband. Although she had been acquitted of the crime, she did not want to relive the experience.

The pattern of male actors refusing the role of Joe continued. Fred MacMurray was the next to demur. He argued that he did not want to endanger his public image as a wholesome hero by playing the somewhat tarnished Joe. Yet he had previously portrayed the murderous insurance agent in Wilder's *Double Indemnity*. Even though William Holden's career at that point was in the doldrums, he was so reluctant to play the lover of an older woman that the head of Paramount studios, to which he was bound by contract, had to order him to take the part.

Gloria Swanson herself initially hesitated accepting the role of Norma Desmond. Swanson's career had been in eclipse for over a decade, but she did not want to begin the difficult task of trying to regain it with an unimportant role. She wanted a role that would have a striking impact, that would be a "bigger than life part." She had, after all, been a major star of the 1920s, and the decline of her Hollywood career seemed a caprice of the fate that had brought sound to the movies. There had been no problem with her voice, with her looks, with her movement. Perhaps the issue was her involvement with Joseph Kennedy, their estrangement, and the difficulties of filming *Queen Kelly* (never released in a full version). Perhaps she was deemed simply too old for the new medium of sound. But, in contrast to Norma, Swanson had not become a recluse. She had moved to New York and worked successfully in radio. Still, she had never forgotten Hollywood.[4]

In the end, Swanson was allowed liberty in delineating the character of Norma Desmond. In the original conception of the film, the character of Desmond was secondary in importance to that of Gillis. But the manic brilliance of Swanson's portrayal showed through in her screen test, and Wilder acceded to Swanson's demand that the Desmond role be expanded. Swanson's portrayal is compelling. For it seems driven by some core of rage in her being. The end to her film career may have engendered the rage. Or it may have proceeded from her reaction to the American fixation with youth, a fixation which rendered Swanson obsolete while her sense of a vigorous self was still strong.

To play the role of Norma's butler, Max, Wilder turned to Erich von Stroheim, with whom he had previously worked in Europe. In real life, von Stroheim's involvements with Gloria Swanson were considerable. Von Stroheim had had a career as conflicted as Swanson's. He had been a famed actor and director in the 1920s (second only to

D. W. Griffith in reputation). But in the 1930s he could find work only as an actor. The last major Hollywood film he had directed had been *Queen Kelly,* which starred Swanson. For von Stroheim, as for Gloria Swanson, *Sunset Boulevard* was a case of art mirroring life. But the fit may have been too close for him: he called the role of Max "that lousy butler part."[5]

Billy Wilder's own life was also interwoven with the film. A middle-aged man at the time of its making, he was involved with a younger woman. Some said that the character of Betty, the young woman in the film, was based on this woman. Yet, as I shall presently discuss, Betty's negative aspects might indicate a failing relationship. It is also possible that Wilder wrote aspects of himself into *Sunset Boulevard,* that Norma Desmond was partly Billy Wilder, a Wilder experiencing his own discomforts associated with aging and with the difficulty of operating as an artist in commercial Hollywood. Thus art may have mirrored life for Wilder as well as for his actors. In the figure of Norma, Wilder perhaps worked out his own feelings about his European past and his American present and the crass world of Hollywood. Perhaps he, too, wanted to shoot the big shots.

The movie had interesting impacts on the careers of all the individuals involved with it. Erich von Stroheim went back to Europe; he played no more roles in Hollywood. Billy Wilder went on to make more movies. But only *Some Like It Hot,* I would submit, matched the brilliance of *Sunset Boulevard.* For William Holden, *Sunset Boulevard* launched a distinguished career, a career accelerated by his success in a different role that same year. In *Born Yesterday,* he portrayed a journalist hired to instruct showgirl Judy Holliday in proper manners and speech.

Gloria Swanson was not so fortunate as Holden. She had hoped *Sunset Boulevard* would reinvigorate her career. In fact, after this success she was mostly offered similar roles involving aging, fading actresses. Nor did she win the Oscar for best actress at the 1951 Academy Awards. Bette Davis had also been nominated, for her role as another aging actress in *All About Eve,* and most analysts think that academy members' votes were split between Swanson and Davis, leaving Judy Holliday the prize for best actress in *Born Yesterday.*

Again it was youth triumphing over age: the young showgirl seemingly more important than Davis and Swanson, two aging actresses playing aging actresses. For the roles that Swanson and Davis played in *Sunset Boulevard* and *All About Eve* were similar: both were involved with men who seemed to prefer younger women. In *All About Eve,* Davis played a famous actress still vigorous in her career who decided to renounce her profession to keep her husband. Swanson as Desmond killed the younger man she loved who had rejected her. In 1960 Swanson told a writer for *Harper's* magazine: "All they care about here is the ghastly American worship of youth and that's why there is no mature actress on the screen today."[6] Yet her words, however prophetic, tell only a partial truth.

Norma Desmond *as Authoritative:*
Sunset Boulevard *as Historical Text*

A SECOND INTERPRETATION can be made of Norma Desmond and of her relationship with Joe Gillis, an interpretation at variance with the first. It is an interpretation in which Norma is determined and powerful, in which the blame for her behavior lies with others, in which her actions are not capricious and proceeding out of an overemotional woman's sense of unrequited love. Instead they follow from rational motives.

This second interpretation begins to be plausible when we consider the rest of the characters in the film. For all of them are flawed. Even Cecil B. DeMille, with his 1950s biblical epics, began making films of questionable quality. Max the butler as an aging individual is even more pathetic than Norma. Reduced to the status of servant in the home of his former wife, he panders to her fantasies. The message of Max seems to be that, for men, aging can be even more devastating than for women.

Nor is youth portrayed in the film as a golden time. Betty Schaefer, Joe's younger inamorata, attempts to use Joe for her own ends as much as Norma does. During the day with Norma, Joe rewrites the Salome script. In the evenings, secretly with Betty, Joe is writing another script about a male and a female schoolteacher sharing the same apartment. This script was Betty's idea. Betty is the only character in the movie whose background is thoroughly revealed. We learn little about the details of Joe's, Norma's, or Max's pasts, but we learn a great deal about Betty. She is a Hollywood child, born to a family whose members had worked in the studios in minor capacities.

Betty herself is driven to succeed in the industry. She had tried acting, she reveals, and had failed. Now, as a studio script reader, she sees some talent in Joe's work, and she attaches herself to him. Actress Nancy Olson plays Betty with touching sincerity, and Olson's blond looks seem to make this figure the ideal ingenue, innocent and genuine. Alone among *Sunset Boulevard*'s actors, Olson was a newcomer, first introduced in this film.

Still, something is wrong with Betty. In his voice-over narrative, Joe's first statement about her is a reference to her nose. "Something is smelly" about Betty, Joe seems to say. And we learn that in her drive to succeed as an actress, Betty has had her nose straightened: her use of artifice is as great as Norma's. There is more. Within Western popular tradition, the nose has often been symbolic of sexuality, and Betty's sexuality indeed is flawed. For some inexplicable reason, she has thrown over Artie, Joe's close friend and a film director beginning to succeed, and taken up with Joe. Perhaps her motivation stems from the fact that jug-eared, dog-faced Jack Webb plays Artie and handsome William Holden plays Joe. So it is in the genre of romance, where good looks carry great weight. Betty declares her love for Joe after one kiss. Not even the knowledge of his involvement with Norma dampens her ardor.

As a figure, Betty Schaefer is a parody of those heroines of romantic novels who reform rakes or who, through their innocence and youth, bring redemption and peace. In looks Nancy Olson resembles Joan Fontaine; one thinks of the heroine role in *Rebecca,* which Fontaine played. But in the world of *Sunset Boulevard,* unlike that of *Rebecca,* a young woman doesn't possess special magic just because she is young. Joe describes Norma as smelling of tuberoses, a lush floral scent reminiscent of funerals. Joe describes Betty in terms of aromas even less romantic: her smell reminds him of freshly laundered handkerchiefs and new cars. These are the smells of domesticity, of suburbia, of an anonymous, commercialized cleanliness.

More than anything else, the reality of Joe's love for Betty is our expectation, based on our experience of scores of films in which people who look like Nancy Olson and William Holden invariably wind up with one another. It is not surprising that, when Betty rushes to Norma's mansion to rescue Joe after she learns of his involvement with Norma, he refuses to go with her. Why would Joe want a younger version of Norma?

In fact, Wilder has no particular love for youth. This attitude is displayed in one key scene when, at a friend's party, Joe waits his turn to use the phone. Two adolescent girls are talking on it, softly giggling into it. The sound of their laughing initially seems a refreshing contrast to the solemnity of Norma's house. Yet on and on the giggling goes, reaching a crescendo. It becomes irritating, redolent of those mindless phone conversations characteristic of American adolescents. Joe's palpable annoyance with them lends a cynical glaze to the statement he makes to Betty about the glories of being twenty-two.

At this party in Artie's tiny apartment, Joe and Betty, their romance just beginning, are crowded into the bathroom. While Joe waits for the phone, the two of them playfully banter the kinds of lines of undying sentimental love to be found in any romantic script. Their playfulness with each other seems healthy, their irreverence about romance up-to-date. But the words they speak, given that they will soon act out the romantic narrative's central act of "falling in love," seem another indication that their relationship is meant to be a parody of Hollywood youth couples and of the conventions of romance. (The conversation is perhaps further parodied by its occurrence in a bathroom.)

If as a person Betty is flawed, so is Joe. Aside from moments of sensitivity in scenes with Norma and Betty, he is not nice. One could argue that he uses these women for his own ends as much as they use him. His most heroic act in the film, one might say, is his renunciation of both of them. Max calls him a stray dog. Artie characterizes him in jest as a "uranium smuggler" and asks him if he is the killer of the Black Dahlia, a woman luridly murdered in Los Angeles in the 1940s.

Just how talented a writer Joe is and the extent to which he could ever succeed in Hollywood is debatable. Joe scorns Norma's screenplay as a "hodgepodge of melodramatic plots." But his own screenplay about a baseball player hardly seems much better. Joe is only one of many young people seeking to succeed in Hollywood. The rooms he and his friends inhabit seem crowded. Even he comes to see his quest for fame and fortune as a failure. Before he meets Norma he is about to go back home to Dayton, Ohio, to reclaim his job as a copy editor at the *Dayton Evening Post*.

Nor is Joe all that young. During the course of the film the ages of the women characters are revealed: Norma is fifty; Betty is twenty-two. But we are never told Joe's age. Director Billy Wilder hesitated before casting William Holden in the part of Joe, for Holden was then in his mid-thirties and Wilder had visualized Joe as younger. Yet Holden's age, apparent in his appearance, underscores Joe's cynicism and makes his renunciation of Norma and Betty even more complex.

In many ways Joe is a westering Horatio Alger, a frontiersman who has traveled from the small city to the big city. But Joe as frontiersman is not a young man filled with hope in the conquest of a new land. He is not Huck Finn, rafting down the Mississippi with the black slave Jim.

Nor is he James Fenimore Cooper's Leatherstocking, the solitary scout retreating in a slow but inevitable path across the prairies to the West, before the onset of civilization. Joe is hardly akin to the cowboys who, like Shane, will overcome underlying despair to bring order out of chaos, to right a moral universe gone awry, to destroy the villains single-handedly because of superior righteousness risen to confront chaos and superior skill at the manly arts: fighting and shooting a gun. Joe bears scant resemblance to his literary precursor, the idealistic materialist Jay Gatsby of Fitzgerald's *The Great Gatsby*. Gatsby concealed indeterminate social roots to create, like Norma Desmond, his own lush Eden. But in the end he is killed, like Joe, in a swimming-pool setting. Unlike Jay Gatsby, Joe Gillis is a man without illusions, buffeted about by Hollywood, ready to quit.

Indeed, with Joe Gillis the frontier saga stops. He has moved from Dayton to Hollywood, seeking to make his fortune, and he has ended up a failure. Sunset Boulevard is the last road he can traverse. There is no place further to go; it ends at the ocean. Symbolically, we see the street first as police cars careen down it to investigate Joe's death. We then see it in flashback, as Joe races down it, fleeing from bill collectors attempting to repossess his car. The frontier mythology, a lodestone of American lore, reaches its apogee in 1950 in the vision of a young man racing his car along Sunset Boulevard, pursued by bill collectors trying to repossess the vehicle that is, in mythology, if not in actuality, every American male's most treasured possession. For it is supposed not only to get him where he wants to go, but also to demonstrate to all others his masculinity.

Like all Horatio Alger heroes, miraculously befriended by men of wealth, Joe encounters his patron in the form of Norma. But "Lady Luck," when she appears, can be both positive and negative, both "fair" and "foul." Betty articulates that possibility to Joe when (not yet knowing about Norma) she refers to that classic plot in which a boy helps an old lady across a street, and the old lady turns out to be a millionaire just waiting to meet someone kind to whom she can leave her fortune. But it is not the benevolent "Algeresque" tycoon nor the sexless "little old lady" who discovers Joe. It is Norma Desmond. And Norma demands Joe's body and his undivided attention in return for material possessions and a sometime knowledge of fame.

If a woman were offered such an arrangement, we might call her a Cinderella and envy her chance to move overnight from poverty into luxury. So it was for the young female protagonist in *Rebecca*. But Joe cannot be Cinderella; that role is nearly impossible for men of Joe's sort. Men in this country must make it on their own: through conquering the West, or Hollywood, or a career, or themselves. They do not know the real story of the patronage behind Horatio Alger's heroes' success; our success mythology conceals it. The gigolo is a European role, associated in the United States with the smooth sensuality of a Rudolph Valentino, or with those "lounge lizards" of flapper fame who danced at teatime with aging women and created something of a scandal in the early 1920s.

A standard theme of Western literature has been the young man's coming of age, often by moving from the country to the city, occasionally by becoming involved with an older, established woman who introduces him into society or initiates him into sophisticated pleasures. From the eighteenth century onward French authors, in particular, employed this theme in what has come to be called the "novel of initiation": one finds it in Benjamin Constant's *Adolphe,* in Stendhal's *The Red and the Black,* in Flaubert's *Sentimental Education.*

But with the exception of the novels of Henry James it is not really an American theme. What happens to young American men, in contrast to their French counterparts, is somewhat different. Either they proceed along their course in tandem with other men. Or in the Western novel, for example, by virtue of their compelling masculinity they prove irresistible to a young woman, often a schoolteacher, who may domesticate them but who cannot stop the inevitable gun battle between the hero and the villain, no matter how hard she tries. Or they ride off into the sunset, on to new adventures or other bouts with love and death.

Norma is located in the past, but Joe is situated in the present. He is wholly contemporary to the post–World War II period. He is tough and self-controlled. His speech is interlarded with the era's slang. Holden delivers his lines with a midwestern twang and a rapid-fire tempo redolent of the common people and of the rapid pace of urban modernity. He is a master of the fast quip, based on quick timing and brashness that grows out of the fatalism and sarcasm of city streets. This is not the prince of the fairy tale, nor the naive young man from the provinces come into the city, the picaresque hero of the eighteenth-century French Pierre Marivaux or the English Henry Fielding. This is not the delicate Cherubino mooning over his mistress in Beaumarchais's and then Mozart's *Marriage of Figaro.* Joe is not especially reminiscent of the Adonis figure who will appear prominently in this book. (The 1950s, however, transmogrified the soft, gentle Adonis of legend into the symbol of a weight-lifting, muscle-bound male persona.)

Joe is a man of the people, of indeterminate social origins and common demeanor. His type will contribute to the formation of the American hero still in vogue: the Rocky, the Rambo, the Ronald Reagan. Norma is a representative of Europe, the Old World whose aristocratic, class-bound societies have been defeated by the might of American democracy. Joe points to the future: to the man of the people as the hope of the world. Or he symbolizes its opposite: the common man as a petty, dishonest type.

The post–World War II era glorified this common man. He was cynical and tough. He was laconic, virile, self-possessed, street smart. His immediate antecedents lay in the "hard-boiled" men of the 1930s who populated detective stories and proletarian fiction, who posed as gangsters and G-men, who made their mark in many of the romantic movies and the "screwball" comedies of that era. They alone instinctively knew how to master women, the wealthy, an incomprehensible economic system gone to pieces, a moral universe no longer operating according to the old verities. Do you remember Clark Gable, the man of rough-hewn style, as a nosy journalist mastering Claudette Colbert in *It Happened One Night* and as the smooth, sarcastic Rhett Butler dominating Vivien Leigh in *Gone With the Wind*?

Emotional depression, we are told, during the 1930s became endemic among men out of work. Because masculine authority was undermined, superheroes like Dick Tracy and Superman arose, and Tarzan was refurbished to compensate, to give men back their sense of mastery. Dashiell Hammett's Continental Op and Raymond Chandler's Philip Marlowe—the most famous among the hard-boiled dicks—possessed no superhuman strength. But they were tough, ready to fight, and imbued with a special heroism ever the more modern because tempered with the cynicism of understanding. Two world wars, the Depression, the rise of Hitler—all had created confusion and disillusionment within the novelistic imagination. Writing in the later twentieth century is replete with the stories of little men, of average men, of men whose masculinity is flawed. These are the antiheroes of the modern age. Strains of this antihero and the hard-boiled combined in the figure of Joe Gillis.

The persona of this admired male of the 1950s was also forged in World War II. This epic event, in boot camp and barracks, in foxholes and cockpits, wiped away careers and class and created one man, the GI Joe, so-called because he wore an ordinary uniform, the government issue clothes of the ranks of soldiers. This war was, indeed, the triumph of democracy, fought by troops hand to hand. Or, in a major confrontation with technology on the battlefield, it was fought by men challenging tanks or flying airplanes daringly across channel or sea.

James Stewart or Alan Ladd or John Wayne (famed film cowboys) starred in the war films of this era, lending their former heroic personas as conquerors of evil in the American West to the valorization of war. But invariably, in almost all of these films, there was a moment when an ordinary soldier, emboldened by valor, stepped into the limelight to defy all odds of survival to save a buddy or to take a strategic hill. Class in particular was intermixed in the army and in the films: the heroic amalgam that emerged was no longer of the elites. By the 1950s the nation had a new dominant heroic type for men.

Joe Gillis is, if nothing else, an ordinary man. His very name, Joe, is the classic American moniker for commonality, immortalized as GI Joe in World War II. In order for Joe to fit into Norma's elite world, she must teach him how to dress and how to act. She buys him clothes. She teaches him, he tells us, "bridge, tango steps, what wine to drink with what fish." When Joe attempts to leave her on New Year's Eve after he discovers that he is the only guest invited to her party, he chastises her not for her age position but for her class position. "You need a Valentino, a big shot, someone with polo ponies," he tells her.

After World War II, American filmmakers for a time made many movies reflecting on the nature of evil. Partly this trend was in response to the rise of Fascism and the enormity of the war. During the war, Hollywood had had to gloss over these subjects with the patina of patriotism. The United States had to be portrayed as virtuous, evil as located in foreign places. With the end of the war, human inhumanity could be fully explored. The advent of the nuclear age, knowledge of Hitler's atrocities, the spread of Communism, postwar internal social dislocations—these factors created a situation in which moral degradation seemed everywhere. Joseph McCarthy would eventually place blame on the Communists. Filmmakers working in what came to be known as the film noir tradition equally saw evil everywhere. But they regarded the most common of men, even those fashioned in the heroic mold, potentially as villains. There was no conspiracy; evil was ubiquitous. And so was the possibility of heroism.

It is possible that, in the end, Joe casts off villainy and becomes heroic because he comes to the kind of self-knowledge that many analysts tell us is the true goal of the Western heroic tradition. He has met his dragon, Norma of wealth and fame, the representative of a false materialism he had wrongly coveted, and he has conquered her—and in the process himself. By this interpretation his self-knowledge involves the realization that he cannot succeed, that he has no real affection for Norma, and that, following a proper moral creed, he must tell Norma the truth about everything. He must tell her that he has lied to her, that Max has lied to her, that Cecil B. DeMille has lied to her. He has reached emotional maturity while she is still a child. That comparison between them is implied in his parting words to her: "There's nothing tragic about being fifty—not unless you try to be twenty-five."

He has finally decided to return to Dayton, the small city, to leave the sunset city for the town of day. He has determined to return to that home place now revisioned as nirvana and so often seen in films of this era as where the good life is to be found. Like Odysseus in the *Odyssey* (an originating text of the Western heroic tradition), Joe leaves his goddess temptress, his Calypso, with her promise of immortality, for the simpler pleasures of his native home.

But this interpretation of the meaning of Joe is based partly on our accepting that Norma has no possibility of succeeding, that she is simply an inappropriate, aging woman for whom both a renewed film career and a love affair with a younger man are impossible. In fact, this may not be the case. Much of our perception of the action of the film is guided by Joe's voice-over narrative, and he delivers this narrative after Norma has killed him. (The film, as I mentioned earlier, is an extended flashback.) In his first comment about Norma, Joe intimates that she is not inevitably doomed to fail. Looking at the untended grounds surrounding her house, he compares the place to the mansion of Miss Havisham in Charles Dickens's *Great Expectations*. The plot of this nineteenth-century novel involves the coming of age of a young man, Philip Pirrip (Pip), and the manipulations of Miss Havisham, a wealthy, eccentric old woman. Like Norma Desmond, Miss Havisham has barricaded herself away from the world in her decaying mansion, living out some fantasy version of a long-ended past.

But here the comparison falls apart. In Miss Havisham's case the events which launched her into a fantastic time warp involved her betrayal by a fiancé on their wedding day. A recluse, Miss Havisham lives among the tattered and never removed relics of that day, the clocks stopped at the exact hour the lover's rejection letter reached her. In the room in which Miss Havisham spends her time there are spiders and cobwebs and even the moldy remains of her ancient wedding cake.

The situation for Norma Desmond is different. If antique, the interior of her house is in repair. It is only the surrounding grounds which are run-down, the swimming pool in disrepair. Into these grounds, the area of leisure and play, Norma does not seem to venture before Joe's appearance. They belonged to a happier time, of youth and joy, when Rudolph Valentino danced in the ballroom, and the "waxworks" were vital and at the height of their careers. But that does not mean the exterior cannot be restored. Indeed, Norma has the grounds redone and the swimming pool repaired once Joe has moved into the house and into her bed.

There is more. When Joe initially moves into the garage apartment on her property and begins to rewrite the script that is to be the vehicle for her comeback, Norma is in control. As Max moves Joe out of his apartment without Joe's knowledge and settles with the bill collectors, one senses that this has happened before. This may not be the first man Norma has lured into her house through her fame and her money. She may not have been actively searching for a man like Joe, but she was waiting. And she was ready when he appeared.

Then there is the matter of her clothes and her makeup. Norma does not wear tattered, faded garb. Gloria Swanson was considered one of the best-dressed Hollywood stars of the 1920s, and Norma Desmond continues to dress in regal style. Norma often wears clothes made from a leopardskin-spotted fabric. These costumes seem an indication of her predatory nature. Or is it meant to be ermine, the fur which traditionally symbolized European royalty? (Swanson herself had been the first Hollywood star to marry royalty; for a time she could call herself the Marquise de la Falaise, although her noble husband was penniless.)

The heavy makeup Norma wears does give her both a witchlike and a Kewpie-doll appearance, as I have noted. But is it so different from that worn by other actresses of the day, by Bette Davis, for example, or Joan Crawford? Take a close look at the appearance of women in the illustrations in this era for the *Ladies' Home Journal,* or *Life,* or *The Saturday Evening Post.* These women do not all look young and virginal. Some look mature, competent, maternal. The standard interpretation of the history of women in the 1950s is that the postwar mystique dictated that women once again were to find their primary function in home and family. Is it surprising, then, that an important image for women was one of maturity, or that maturity might be blended in the same face with convoluted childishness or rapacious control? Women mirrored in their appearance their common stereotypes as men's dependents or their unfortunate masters.

We too easily conflate the American worship of youth into universal domination over the cultural models of women's appearance. During the 1920s and the 1960s, it is true, the look of youth strikingly predominated. In the intervening decades, however, when the Depression, war, and Cold War created vast insecurities, the look of maturity was part of a complex female typology reflected in women's faces. Norma has that look.

What does Joe have to offer Norma? In the beginning what he really has to offer her is sex. Having him rewrite the script she has previously written seems initially motivated partly by her desire simply to have him stay with her by offering him a salary so large that he cannot refuse. As the movie progresses, Norma does become dependent on Joe. But the dependence is relative, not absolute. It must be seen in the context of what becomes her attempt to make a comeback. There is a phone call from Cecil B. DeMille, a phone call that she interprets as indicating his interest in the script that Joe is rewriting. When she thinks that a comeback film may become a reality, she becomes self-possessed, calm. The phone message in addition to Norma's determination makes even skeptical Joe think that her dreams of a return may not be delusional.

Tennessee Williams handled a similar situation in his 1959 play, *Sweet Bird of Youth*. His resolution is instructive in analyzing *Sunset Boulevard*. Williams's play also is about a famous aging actress, down on her luck, offered only minor roles. Like Norma she is also involved with a younger man, whom she alternately clings to and then controls throughout the action of the play. During most of the play she is critical of her appearance. Then the phone rings with a Hollywood offer. She is invigorated. She no longer needs the younger man as her security. Now we realize that he, too, is an aging person—a former football player with few successes after his initial adolescent glory. As she leaves him, returning to Hollywood, she seems youthful and he seems old. So might it have been for Norma, if the phone message which energized her had been a summons from DeMille to return to the screen rather than a query from a DeMille assistant about renting her antique car for a film.

Was Norma's dream of a screen comeback so farfetched? Norma had visualized as her comeback film a screen version of the story of Salome and John the Baptist. The idea immediately seems as antique as her car, the huge out-of-date luxury auto which Max, playing the chauffeur, drives for her. It seems another throwback to the world of the past in which she is encased. For Salome was the most famed vamp role of the World War I period. The Dance of the Seven Veils, which all Salomes then performed, for decades early in the twentieth century had created a scandal around whoever performed it—whether the performer was a Metropolitan Opera diva or a vaudeville headliner.

Yet the film that Cecil B. DeMille is shooting when Norma visits him on the set is another biblical epic, *Samson and Delilah*. This was the first of such epics which DeMille made in the 1950s. They were films which seemed to satisfy an American craving for Christian certainty in the uncertain Cold War world. They also seemed to proclaim to anti-Communist crusaders, for whom Hollywood had become a central target, that Hollywood was a Christian, not a pagan, place.

A film version of Salome would actually be made several years after *Samson and Delilah*. The young Rita Hayworth would play the role of Salome. But this version of the story would have in it as a central character Herod's wife, Salome's stepmother, a middle-aged woman of beauty and evil sexuality. Shakespearean actress Judith Anderson would play the part, and her characterization would be charged with the kind of melodramatic intensity that Norma Desmond exuded. One could visualize Desmond playing such a role with panache.

To watch Norma Desmond closely in *Sunset Boulevard* is to see two versions of her. The first is a negative version, attuned to the negative attitudes toward aging women current in the postwar years, to the personifications of them as castrating mothers and as hysterical menopausal women. The second, albeit less evident, more subtextual, is a more positive rendering. Within this reading of her meaning lies the realization that there might be possibilities for Norma, that neither her personality nor the environing culture is entirely closed to her ambition, to her perhaps justifiable need for support and success.

As a person Norma Desmond locates herself in the 1920s, the heyday of her career and of that of Gloria Swanson. But as I roam the historical record, and as I view *Sunset Boulevard* again and again, which is my wont, another figure besides Judy Garland and the Wicked Witch of the West superimposes itself on Gloria Swanson qua Norma Desmond, and I see another meaning in this film about aging people. That figure and that meaning involve Sarah Bernhardt, the renowned actress of the late nineteenth century. To me Swanson qua Desmond looks like Bernhardt and acts like Bernhardt must have acted.

Bernhardt was an "emotional" actress par excellence, to borrow Garff Wilson's designation of nineteenth-century female thespians.[7] Her most popular roles were as Cleopatra and Phaedra—passionate women who haunted the imagination of playwrights over the ages. In the nineteenth-century dramas written about these women, love and death were the real plots. They served as vehicles for Bernhardt and other actresses to display flamboyant theatricality and emotionality, with dramatic physical movements and outbursts of fear and rage and other raw emotions compelling to nineteenth-century audiences.

Bernhardt carried this emotionality into her personal life. She kept her public entertained with reports of her luxuries and her amours and with extravagant stories of sleeping in a coffin and keeping around her a menagerie of animals, including a chimpanzee. She maintained her stardom until well into her seventies, attracting younger male companions along the way. Sarah Bernhardt was a prima donna, with all its overtones of regal emotionality. And so was Norma Desmond.

To us Bernhardt's acting, like the plays in which she starred, would probably seem naive and overdone. One gets this impression from the brief Bernhardt film footage extant. And a similar emotionality characterizes Gloria Swanson's acting, both in her 1920s films and in *Sunset Boulevard*. But this is not *Sunset Boulevard*'s only point of view. Desmond herself advances a different possibility, suggesting that our eyes are conditioned by the times in which we live. It is she who has remained big, Norma says. "It is the pictures that got small." Reflecting on her past, Desmond passionately defends actresses in silent film as the real craftspeople and attacks the advent of sound in movies as destructive of a revered theatrical tradition brought into film.

This argument of Desmond's rings with a fundamental truth: in it are the words of a woman of wisdom. The past should not be denigrated simply because it is the past, she seems to say; progress is not inevitably superior. Part of the intent of *Sunset Boulevard* (whether conscious or not on Wilder's part) may be to celebrate past eras when women like Norma denied domesticity to be historical actors throughout the stages and the span of their lives.

From this perspective *Sunset Boulevard* may relate to that early-twentieth-century era when the image of the "New Woman" reflected women's movement into education, the professions, the work force, and women's reform organizations. Sarah Bernhardt, as an independent, self-supporting woman, was an icon of that age, a representative of women's advance in the personal sphere brought into the public realm. Norma Desmond in *Sunset Boulevard* existed long after that time of achievement. Her post–World War II era was one of a new retreat into domesticity for women. Where she might have shone brightly during the 1890s, in the 1950s she was obsolete, a relic of a forgotten past.

The Meaning of Hedda Hopper

A MONG THE CAST of aging characters in *Sunset Boulevard*, there is one I have purposely overlooked. I have neglected her because, unlike the others, she had triumphed in her real life over adversity in interesting, if appalling, ways. The character is Hedda Hopper, the era's renowned Hollywood gossip columnist. She appears in the final frames of the film. Like Cecil B. DeMille, she plays herself and not a fictionalized version of herself. If you do not watch *Sunset Boulevard* closely, you may miss her. She appears briefly after the shooting has occurred and the police and press have arrived. In this scene, set in Norma's bedroom, Norma is at her dressing table, preparing herself for the descent down the stairs among the throng of newspaper cameramen and reporters. Hopper is seated on Norma's bed, phoning in her story of the shooting to her newspaper.

Even though Hopper's appearance is brief, it does not seem accidental. For Hopper, like Desmond, was an aging woman at the time of the filming of *Sunset Boulevard*. Yet her present success and her past struggles were different from those of Norma Desmond—and those of Gloria Swanson. Then in her mid-sixties, Hopper was at the pinnacle of her career. More importantly, it was a career that had reached success only a decade earlier. Throughout her life she had struggled to maintain herself in the entertainment industry. During those years, she had been only one of scores of not very successful actresses. Although she played in many films, mostly she landed small parts. As she aged she moved from ingenue roles to character parts.

Hopper's life was mostly a series of ups and downs. Governed by a driving will and energy, however, she never gave up. She took whatever work she could get: lectures, publicity work for studio heads, posing for fashion illustrations. Yet she was known in Hollywood for the parties she gave: she had a particular gift for friendship. Even during the days when she was a character actress hanging on to a career, her home was a social center. She knew everybody. Yet she suffered many career disappointments. As she grew older, they increased. She attempted to get work as a radio actor, but the station heads told her: "This is a business for youth. There is no room for has-beens."[8]

But Hopper did not give up. Then in 1937, when she was fifty-three, what can be seen as either a stroke of incredible luck or the result of a lifetime of hard work came her way. Studio heads decided to dethrone the imperious, contentious gossip columnist Louella Parsons by creating a rival to her. They chose Hedda Hopper. "Comebacks, as Hollywood knows them, are for the most part anticlimactic, often bordering on the pathetic." Thus began a biographical entry on her life in the 1940s. And this passage continued: "Hedda Hopper's re-emergence in the film limelight since 1940, however, may be cited as one of the few spectacular exceptions."[9]

There is another side to Hopper's life. Early in the 1920s she had married the famous comic actor DeWolf Hopper. When they divorced, she never remarried. It is probable that she never again had a deep relationship with a man. Her biographer regards this avoidance of men as a character deficiency: he traces her reluctance to a Quaker upbringing which instilled in her an aversion to sex. But the facts of her life easily support a different conclusion. Based on her experiences with a domineering father and a difficult husband, Hopper had early on come to the conclusion that men could not be trusted. Thus she determined to make it through life on her own—no matter how hard the struggle. However unclearly, she sensed how difficult patriarchy could be on women. She conducted a life in which romantic love was not the sine qua non of her existence.

One can dislike Hopper for the shallowness of her newspaper views, for her exploitation of people's lives, and for her involvement with McCarthyism. I make no brief for that side of her character. In fact, I suspect that Wilder's intent in bringing her into the film was partly to make the point that the Hollywood future belonged to the kind of crass conservatism that Hopper on one level represented. Her biographer asserts that Hopper's column soared in readership only after she became "bitchy," after she began to conflate rumor with truth in her column and to deliver subtle but pointed attacks on individuals. Thus women's words, Norma Desmond's theatrical talk, even the gossip that has always functioned among women as an informal communication network, to bind people together and to understand their realities, are here reduced to babble, to the spreading of innuendo, to spite. Joe Gillis's voice-over narrative, the patriarchal speech, is really important. That is what we listen to, and believe.

And Hopper's aloneness has problems. Because in Western culture we are accustomed to the individuation of women and to their bonding with men, we accept a world in which Betty and Norma compete for the same man and in which Hopper sensationalizes this kind of competition in her column. What if these two—Betty and Norma—were to come together? What if Norma were to ask Betty to rewrite the screenplay, and Hopper, instead of using Norma as a subject for journalism, were to come to her aid? But Wilder's fantasy is attuned to patriarchal reality, and his message only faintly has a feminist intent.

Throughout *Sunset Boulevard* Norma's bed is an important symbol. It is important that Hopper is sitting on the bed when she first appears. The actual bed Wilder used was a valuable antique: it had once belonged to Marie Antoinette. Ornate, it is in the form of a boat. It is baroque in design, with its foot a tall prow crowned with a cupid. One thinks of Cleopatra's barge, sailing down the Nile, in Plutarch's famous depiction borrowed by Shakespeare in *Antony and Cleopatra*. Shakespeare describes the Egyptian queen as "the serpent of Old Nile," with Phoebus's pinches wrinkled "deep in time." Yet Cleopatra also possesses an "infinite variety," that "age cannot wither."[10] But Norma's bed, unlike Cleopatra's barge, is fixed in space; it goes nowhere.

Norma is often filmed in the bed. She is filmed in it after her suicide attempt. She is filmed in it made up with face creams and skin tighteners in a futile attempt to reclaim her youth. The bed dominates the bedroom, which itself looks like the boudoir of a queen—huge, ornate, with brocade and satin and flounces everywhere. Now at the end of the film, Hedda Hopper casually sits on the bed. She is making a phone call, dictating her column to a subordinate. She is telling the world of Norma Desmond's crime. Now Hedda Hopper has claimed it—the bed, Norma's space, the immediate future.

Hedda Hopper may represent the future, but Norma is not unidimensional. With all her flaws, she is both realistic and yet fantastical. She is an aging woman attempting to come to terms with her aging at the same time that she is a symbol of the past who at times understands the grandeur of her symbolism. Yet in the end her failure lies in her rigidity, her inability to see that life might hold out other courses, equally fulfilling, to the one she had followed in her youth and during the years of her great screen triumphs. But she would have to find those paths herself. There were no press agents to define them for her. There was only Max, a person from her past who wanted, as badly as Norma, for the past to remain the present.

PART TWO

The Ancient World: From Prepatriarchal Times to the Early Medieval Era

M Y MEDITATION on the history of aging women and relationships redounds to ancient times: to the goddesses and younger male god-consorts contained in the earliest religious pantheons. It continues to ancient Greece and to that fifth-century Athenian city-state world of eminent philosophers like Plato and dramatists like Euripides in which male same-sex love was valorized and the position of women was problematic. I extend my story to the era of Roman republicanism, when women occupied a freer position, and to the Roman imperial era, when strong strains of misogyny emerged.

Throughout, I am concerned with issues of aging and authority, both real and symbolic, with the ways in which aging women were both denigrated and empowered. In Homer's *Odyssey,* a foundation text of Western literature and gender traditions, I find encoded in the story of Penelope traces of the goddess/young god typology. Remnants of this ancient tradition are also indicated in the biography of the seventh-century B.C.E. poet Sappho, especially in her presumed relationship with the young man Phaon. The heritage continues in figures of Hellenistic and early medieval hagiography who inform the arts: they include Philosophia, Fortuna, and the Sibyls. Many of these figures combine age and youth as part of their personas.

Within Western experience lies a long legacy of denigrating aging women, especially in their postmenopausal years. (To this generalization fifth-century B.C.E. Athens may be an exception.) Yet, even then, stereotypes of aging women drew from their presumed rampant sexuality. Despite presentations by Plato and others of aging women as wise, both spiritually and sexually, alternative exempla lay in the witch and the go-between, the aging female broker for paid heterosexual intercourse.

Western dualistic thought has characteristically bifurcated women as either sexual or spiritual. (Within Christianity, the opposing Eve and Virgin Mary figures represent the dualism.) These perceptions were applied to aging women, as well.

Thus the character of Norma Desmond resounds across the ages. It responds to that archetypal pattern of good and ill, of the personification of aging women as both "fair" and "foul," as figures of wisdom, of desire, or of danger.

CHAPTER TWO

The Possibilities for Penelope

LONG BEFORE the advent of written records, many ancient cultures paid homage to powerful goddesses. They were nature incarnate, Mistresses of Animals, Queens of Heaven, rulers of the underworld. In some regions state sovereignty passed through them. Isis, the name of a major Egyptian goddess, for example, translates as "throne." In Celtic legends, aging goddesses offered their bodies to several men, often brothers. The one who accepted the offer gained both the kingship and the old woman transformed into a youthful version of her former self.[1]

In Sumer the central goddess was Inanna. In Babylonia she was Ishtar. In Anatolia she was called Cybele.* In Canaan, she was Ashtoreth, or Anath. So the Bible variously identifies the goddess figure in its Old Testament tales of the conflict between the Canaanites, the original goddess-worshiping inhabitants of the land of Canaan, and the in-migrating tribes of Israel, pastoralists with a patriarchal, monotheistic religion devoted to the god Jahweh.

Primary goddesses in Egypt were Isis, Neith, and Nepthys. In Greece they included Gaia, Rhea, and Dione. In ancient Celtic tales the goddess Danu was sacred to the Tuatha de Danann, a tribe of wanderers who had come to the British Isles in some remote, legendary time. In India Kali was the Hindu triple goddess of creation, preservation, and destruction. According to the Roman historian Tacitus, writing in 98 C.E., the cult of Nrthus the earth mother existed in Germanic Europe at the time of the Roman Conquest. In Nordic tales Erda was the earth mother; Frieda was the goddess of spring; the Valkyries were the nine martial daughters of

---

*Anatolia is present-day Turkey; Sumer and Babylonia were located in today's Iraq.

Erda and Wotan, the fire god. In his *Ring of the Nibelungen* Richard Wagner immortalized these figures of German mythology.

Goddesses could have many identities; many individual figures could embody them. And they could take many forms. They were virginal and maternal, sexual and spiritual, young and old. In Scotland powerful old crones were supposed to inhabit many rural areas. The Caillagh Ny Groamagh lived on the Isle of Man, Black Annis in the Hills of Leicester, the Cailleach Bheur in the Highlands. They were aged female personifications of winter who with the advent of spring were transformed into young women. (Transformation tales of old women into young women are especially characteristic of Scottish and Celtic mythology.)

Like the Indian Kali, goddesses were often triune in form: they were goddesses of past, present, and future; or of heavens, earth, and underworld; or of the seasons: spring, winter, summer, or of the cycle of aging, as daughter, mother, and crone. They could embody birth, life, and death: they could be goddesses of regeneration, like the transformative Scottish crones. Some scholars see these meanings combined around the three figures in the seventh-century b.c.e. *Homeric Hymn to Demeter* of Persephone, the daughter, Demeter, the mother, and Hecate, the old woman, the crone.[2]

Tripartite goddesses also appear in the tripled female figures of Greek myth: the Moirae, or Fates, who through their weaving determined human fortune; the Horae, who presided over nature and the seasons; the Graces, or Charities, dispensers of compassion, mother love, sensual delight. The Erinyes, or Furies, represented the vengeful side of the goddess; they pursued those who committed crimes against families, especially mothers. The tripled trio, the nine Muses, inspired poetry, song, and chronicle. In Arthurian legend, nine goddesses were led by the sorceress Morgan le Fay, King Arthur's sister. She lived on the island of Avalon and wielded her magical power, for good and ill, throughout the Arthurian legends.[3]

Steeped in antiquity, Sigmund Freud expressed bafflement over the goddess religions which underlay the patriarchal stories he used for central concepts in his work, like the Oedipus complex. Yet in his "Theme of the Three Caskets," Freud interpreted the three stepsisters of the ancient Cinderella folktale as well as the three daughters of Shakespeare's King Lear and the three caskets in *The Merchant of Venice* as indications of the continued motif of the triune goddess in later European eras. He might also have included Shakespeare's three weird sisters of *Macbeth,* chanting over their caldron. They were the metaphorical descendants of the ancient triple goddess Wyrd, or Fate, who controlled human destiny in her book of life.[4]

In ancient legend, goddesses often had young male consorts. For Cybele of Anatolia there was Attis. For Inanna and Ishtar of Sumeria and Babylonia, there were Damuzi and Tammuz. For Isis of Egypt there was Osiris. The goddess–young god pair most familiar in modern times is perhaps Aphrodite and Adonis. Aphrodite, the goddess of love, abducted the young Adonis and then vied with Persephone, the goddess of the underworld, for his favor.

The meaning of these young gods is obscure. Most scholars think that their primary function was to represent the yearly cycle of the seasons enacting the impregnation of the earth by vegetative seed. But whether, as such, they represented the coming together of man and woman, of youth and age, in symbolic comity, or the destructive vengeance of the goddess as barren winter destroying both mature vegetation and the young consort to make way for a new one, remains at issue. Or were they transitional figures, indicating the incursion of a male prototype along the historical progression from matrifocal, goddess-centered societies to patriarchal, god-centered ones?

No less than for the young gods, the sources for understanding the goddesses are difficult to interpret. For their worship predated the appearance of written texts. Statues confirming the existence of predominating goddesses date from as early as 20,000 B.C.E. But written records for the Mediterranean region, for example, do not appear until about 3000 B.C.E., in Sumer. By this time patriarchal religions were becoming dominant. The earliest records from the Greek world date from about 1500 B.C.E., from the island of Crete, in what are called the Linear B tablets. These clay tablets are largely temple account books providing little more than the names of gods and goddesses.

Scholars who study the early goddesses often turn for evidence to archaeological materials: to statues and artifacts, to skeletal and architectural remains. With regard to Greece, the center of my inquiry, Emily Vermeule focuses on the many Neolithic figurines of women with swollen bellies and buttocks. On the basis of these small sculptures she concludes that "all Greece worshipped the same type of fertile earth mother." This goddess, however, had a different name in each locality. The Linear B tablets, Vermeule points out, designate each goddess as "potnia" or "lady" with local names following to distinguish each "lady" of a differing village.[5]

In addition to material remains, scholars interpret later mythologies and legends, extrapolating from them indications of earlier times. I will initially employ this latter technique, using as my focus Homer's *Odyssey,* written in the eighth century B.C.E. Along with its companion text, the *Iliad,* it is one of the earliest extant Greek writings. It examines the male heroic, and both critiques and glorifies male violence. Characterizations of gods and goddesses abound in its human world filled with divine intervention.

The events of the *Iliad* and the *Odyssey* take place during the Trojan War and its aftermath. The *Iliad* focuses on the war, when a coalition of forces from the Greek city-states fought for ten years to conquer the Anatolian citadel of Troy. The Greeks fought the war to reclaim Helen, the wife of the Spartan king Menelaus and presumably the world's most beautiful woman, whom the Trojan prince Paris had abducted. Paris had abducted Helen with the help of the goddess Aphrodite, in payment for his having awarded Aphrodite the prize in her contest with Hera and Athena over beauty.

The *Odyssey* narrates the ten-year wanderings of the Greek warrior Odysseus as he tries to return home from Troy and eventually does reach Ithaca, his island home. It also tells the story of Odysseus's wife, Penelope, as she awaits him in Ithaca. Throughout the twenty years of his absence she has refused to declare him dead, even though no one has known where he was and the presumption of many was that he had died. Nor has she been willing to marry any of the suitors who had come to Ithaca some four years before Odysseus's return, hoping to gain her as a wife, and who have remained, encamped on Odysseus's land, waiting for her decision.[6]

The *Odyssey* long existed in oral form. Wandering bards delivered it orally to local audiences, much as Odysseus tells the story of his adventures to the royal court in the Kingdom of Phaeacia, his last stop before his return to Ithaca. Along with the *Iliad,* it was transcribed in the eighth century B.C.E., presumably by an unknown storyteller named Homer. Initially a folk memory, the *Odyssey* as written text expresses cultural recollections beyond the voice of any individual author. Some scholars see variants of standard folktales in it, especially the one of the absent hero returning home. Given the power of women in the *Odyssey,* some analysts have speculated that a woman, not a man, transcribed it.[7]

On the surface, the *Odyssey* is a story of male heroism and wifely devotion. For Penelope resists the advice given her that, after twenty years of Odysseus's absence, she ought to remarry. The *Odyssey* seems a patriarchal creation, designed to show men how to be warriors and women how to be wives. Yet, as in *Sunset Boulevard,* there is a subtext in the *Odyssey.* Involving Penelope, the subtext is one of female power. For present in the work, in several guises, is the story of the goddess and the young god, the aging woman with the younger man, in its original, divine form.

To this interpretation of the *Odyssey,* two facts about its central characters are key: first, the men who fought the Trojan War and their wives who remained in Greece are in their thirties and forties; second, the suitors are young.

Twenty years have passed since the Greek warriors left their homeland to fight at Troy. Most have now returned home. In addition to their female partners, some of these warriors are major characters in the *Odyssey:* there are Helen and Menelaus of Sparta, and Agamemnon and Clytemnestra of Argos and Mycenae. These men and women have grown children, and some of these children appear in the narrative. Agamemnon and Clytemnestra of Argos are the parents of Orestes, Electra, and Iphigenia. Hermione is the grown daughter of Menelaus and Helen of Sparta. Telemachus, a major figure in the narrative, is the son of Penelope and Odysseus.[8]

The second important fact about the central characters of the *Odyssey* is that the men who have come to Ithaca to woo Penelope, presuming Odysseus dead, are all young. Throughout the narrative they are consistently described as "young." Indeed, they often seem hardly older than Telemachus, as several of them describe their recollections of the magnificence of Odysseus when they were still boys.[9]

Consider the matter for a moment. Here we have, as a central character in a revered text, an aging woman desired by younger men. And not just a few young men are involved. There are 108 of them. What does this mean? Why has Homer taken this theme as the centerpiece of the story, juxtaposing Penelope's drama with these young men in her home against Odysseus's drama in returning home from Troy? Why do these young men desire the aging Penelope, and why would she consider their suit?

Penelope and the Suitors:
The Issue of Heroism

IN THE FIRST INSTANCE, the *Odyssey* is a tale about heroism. The quest of the male characters is to become heroes, to gain a reputation during life and even after death for unsurpassed boldness and bravery, for athletic and battle prowess, to be better than other men in the conduct of life, to be generous, but to overcome. From this perspective, it is a didactic tale in which successful heroes are posed against failed heroes. And it is in this context of heroism that the suitors desire Penelope.

In Homer's heroic lexicon, Odysseus is the ideal hero, the man to emulate. For in his wanderings, in his unending quest to return home, Odysseus is continually beset by the perils to which Poseidon, god of the sea, exposes him. Yet in the midst of dangerous situations, faced by a variety of monsters, Odysseus never loses his self-control or his bravery. And he is clever, a skilled storyteller who tells the story of his wanderings before the King and Queen of Phaeacia. He is adept at creating stratagems and self-disguises. When he returns to Ithaca, he successfully disguises himself as an old man to determine the situation in his home. Only his old nurse recognizes him. But she is especially perceptive, as old women in Western literature occasionally are.

In contrast, the suitors are not heroic, and that is their problem. They defend neither honor nor property. They have encamped at Odysseus's home, demanding that Penelope declare Odysseus dead and choose one of them as her new husband. On the face of it, the demand is not outrageous. Now that Telemachus is grown, Penelope is no longer needed as regent. Her refusal to make a choice has become destructive of social harmony: to a certain extent she bears the blame for the suitors' rapacity. Even Telemachus advises her to choose one of the suitors to marry so that the issue of his inheritance will be resolved.

In the Homeric world, the coming together of a band of suitors in competition for the hand of a desired woman was not unusual. Odysseus had won Penelope in such a manner. She had been a princess of the Spartan royal house and a cousin of Helen and Clytemnestra, who were half sisters. Odysseus had won her in marriage by besting her other suitors in a footrace. Helen herself, by legend, was so desired at the point of her marriage decision that she, too, had a large number of suitors.[10]

The problem with Penelope's suitors, however, is that their actions violate all conventions of honor. Granted that they have waited nearly four years for Penelope to decide and that she has continually put them off, finally postponing her decision until after she finishes weaving a death shroud for Odysseus's father. But, again to avoid the decision, she unravels each night what she has woven during the day. Yet no matter Penelope's chicanery, the suitors do not act justly. They spend their days in riotous feasting, cohabiting with Odysseus's slave women, consuming the products of his land, wildly overindulging the Greek ethic of hospitality to strangers. The goddess Athena, who often intervenes in the action to aid Odysseus, calls their behavior "disgraceful." Telemachus, learning throughout the drama how to be a hero, goes to Sparta to seek advice from Menelaus, his father's companion in the Trojan War. Menelaus, whom the *Odyssey* calls "spear-famed" and "of the great war cry," is scornful of the suitors. He calls them timid and unmanly.[11]

When the suitors attempt to act decisively, they are unsuccessful. They fail in their scheme to kill Telemachus. When Penelope finally devises a contest to determine whom she will marry, they fail her test. None of them are able to string Odysseus's bow and shoot an arrow from it through twelve battle axes lined up on the wall.

Eurymachus, their leader, despairs at having failed the test. He calls his failure "a grief beyond all others." But, curiously, it is not the loss of Penelope that concerns him. Rather, he expostulates that there had always been other eligible women in Ithaca whom he and the other suitors could have pursued as wives. What seems to concern him is that the suitors have shown themselves inferior to Odysseus. Eurymachus concludes that calumny will color their reputations. Rather than becoming famous, they will become notorious, a "shame for men unborn to be told of."[12]

Penelope is the wife of an acclaimed hero. The suitors desire her, in the first instance, because of this connection. In this context her age does not seem to matter. Menelaus of Sparta adduces this motive when Telemachus visits him. Not only does Menelaus dismiss the suitors as timid and unmanly, but he also declares that they want to claim possession of Odysseus's greatness by possessing the body of the woman who was his sexual partner. The author of the *Odyssey* underlines this comment, for Telemachus repeats it on separate occasions both to Penelope and to Odysseus.[13]

Yet Penelope herself is a hero of sorts. What she has to offer the suitors in addition to her position as Odysseus's wife is also a reputation for valued female behavior. In many ways Penelope is a mirror image of Odysseus. In remaining faithful to him, she is bold and courageous. In devising the stratagem of weaving the shroud, she is intelligent and clever. They are similar to one another. Upon their reunion Odysseus acknowledges this similarity when he compares Penelope to a good and just king whose land and people prosper under him. As a woman, she could not restrain the suitors, but she was able to preserve his patrimony and to remain faithful to him for many years.[14]

Yet they are different. Both are wards of Athena; both share in her cleverness. But Penelope does not wander, she weaves. Athena is often associated with weaving; in Hesiod's *Works and Days* Athena teaches Pandora, the first woman, to weave; in her weaving Penelope tries to assemble and reassemble her fate. Yet whatever Penelope's actions, she operates in the private world of women. When she enters the public world of the suitors, she veils her face and takes servant women with her. When Telemachus asserts authority over her, she acquiesces. She is described throughout the narrative as "circumspect" and "prudent." Penelope, devoted to the men of her family, is a patriarchal model for women.[15]

Antinous, another leader of the suitors, describes her attraction. She is "dowered with the wisdom bestowed by Athene, to be expert in beautiful work, to have good character and cleverness, such as we are not told of, even of the ancient queens . . . Tyro and Alkmene . . . for none of these knew thoughts so wise as those Penelope knew. . . ." Before the *Odyssey* begins, Agamemnon, King of Argos and a Greek leader in the Trojan War, has been killed by his wife, Clytemnestra, and her lover, Aegisthus. Now a shade in the underworld, he comments on the perfidy of women. But he exempts Penelope: "How good was proved the heart that is in blameless Penelope . . . and how well she remembered Odysseus, her wedded husband. Thereby the fame of her virtue shall never die away, but the immortals will make for the people of earth a thing of grace in the song for prudent Penelope."[16]

Still, as Marylin Katz and others have pointed out, there is an indeterminancy in her character. Odysseus never swerves in his desire to return home. But after others have informed Penelope that Odysseus has returned, she hesitates. She decides to initiate the contest among the suitors to determine whom she should marry, perhaps indicating that within her may lie the perfidy that her relatives Helen and Clytemnestra displayed, that in the end she does not intend to be faithful to Odysseus.[17]

Throughout the Western heroic tradition, the hero is almost always, ultimately, associated with a woman. Thus the suitors look to Penelope for validation. Usually the woman is the hero's reward for the successful solving of a riddle or the slaying of a dragon or some other triumph in competition. Generally she is a princess of royal blood. Her elevated class position and her connection with the ruling family give an additional confirmation to the triumphant hero. For he who is the ablest of men ought to rule men, and he ought to mate with the most desirable female. The sexual coupling of the princess and the hero promises a new fruitfulness and a new beginning.

But in that later tradition of princesses awakened by a kiss or chosen because the shoe fits, or rescued from a dragon, never is the princess a middle-aged woman with a grown child. Rather she is young and virginal. She is often counterbalanced by aging women, vindictive stepmothers and witches, or wise women of the forest. (Only rarely in this tradition do works foreshadowing the later "novel of initiation" upend this convention.) But the only mortal women in the *Odyssey* older than Penelope are the mothers of heroes, mostly shades in Hades, and the aging servants in her household, especially the devoted former nurse of Odysseus.

Thus we return to the initial question: Why would the young men, Penelope's suitors, desire an older woman? I have argued that heroism is the key. I would, however, not deny the attraction of property. In a much later European era, in some areas noble families institute primogeniture (inheritance by eldest son), and younger sons are left with limited resources. In this later period, affluent older widows become attractive to these men. But this is not the case with Penelope. Her successful suitor can expect to receive rich gifts from her father, but this suitor will have to extend gifts in return. In fact, the *Odyssey* indicates that Penelope periodically has considered marrying whichever suitor displayed the greatest willingness to provide such gifts.

Whether or not the suitor who marries Penelope can claim the throne of Ithaca remains a moot point. Within the text, mention is made on several occasions that the "gods" will determine the issue, although there is some desultory discussion of Telemachus's becoming king. The suitors' unsuccessful plot to kill Telemachus may be based on the example of Aegisthus killing Agamemnon of Argos and, through marriage to Clytemnestra, claiming the throne of Argos. Oedipus established his right to the throne of Thebes through marrying Jocasta, and Menelaus became King of Sparta through Helen's position as the previous king's daughter. Perhaps Odysseus's successor as Penelope's husband might similarly claim the throne of Ithaca. Miriam Robbins Dexter thinks that ancient conventions of sovereignty passing through union with goddesses were apparent in the cases of Jocasta with Oedipus and Helen with Menelaus and that they might also apply to Penelope.[18]

Yet in the case of these women—of Helen, Jocasta, and Penelope—age does not seem to be a factor in what happens to them. Helen is still desirable. She is as potently attractive as when Aphrodite chose her for Paris as the most beautiful woman in the world, and his abduction of her precipitated the Trojan War. Despite all she has done, Menelaus cannot reject her: the exoneration is that she was bewitched into leaving him. Nor does Jocasta's age seem to be any consideration in Oedipus's loving her—or in his leaving her. In the *Odyssey,* Jocasta and Oedipus, like Agamemnon, are shades in Hades. But in Sophocles' moving description of their relationship, in his play *Oedipus the King,* they have been happily married for some time before they discover their unfortunate family bond. What breaks them apart is the horror of incest. In their own eyes, their age disparity is not an issue.

In investigating this question of age disparity, the riddle which the menacing Sphinx posed to Oedipus and which he had to solve as a condition of her leaving Thebes, provides an interesting perspective. The question posed by the Sphinx in her riddle was: what animal has four feet in the morning, two at noon, and three in the evening? The answer was man. As an infant, man crawls on hands and knees; as an adult, he walks upright. In old age, he walks with the help of a cane. This tripartite division of aging divided infancy from youth and youth from old age. It could be that Oedipus and Jocasta viewed each other as if in an age continuum and not at disparate levels. Neither was an infant; neither was aged. Both were young, standing firmly on two feet, even though technically a generation separated them.

To further decipher this issue of aging in women among the Greeks, it may be useful to go beyond the *Odyssey* and to place Penelope in the context of other female figures. And here the physiological state of menopause may play a role. Indeed, the seventh-century *Homeric Hymn to Demeter* contains a distinction between pre- and postmenopausal women. The poem tells of Demeter's search for her missing daughter, Persephone, whom Hades, god of the underworld, has abducted and taken to his realm. In her search for Persephone, Demeter disguises herself as an old woman. The description of her disguise is revealing. For by making herself look old, Demeter modified, more than anything else, her beauty. She looked "like an old woman who was past childbearing, past the gifts of Aphrodite."[19] In other words, Demeter as an old woman possessed neither the beauty nor the sensuality that Aphrodite, the goddess of love, bestowed on women in their childbearing years. In contrast,

Penelope, Jocasta, and Helen could still be appealing because they could still bear children.

More than that, however, few comments are made in the *Odyssey* about Penelope's age because her situation with the young suitors may have resembled that between the goddesses and young gods. In no sense am I attempting to argue that Penelope herself was part of a divine pantheon, although as the daughter of the nymph Periboea she possessed partial divine origins. (So did Helen of Sparta, who was the daughter of Zeus.)[20] Jenny Strauss Clay convincingly argues that both the *Odyssey* and the *Homeric Hymns* demonstrate the end of the Hesiodic "golden age," that legendary time described in Hesiod's *Works and Days,* when mortals could gain immortality through mating with gods and goddesses.[21] To prove this point, Clay notes that Odysseus returns home to Penelope, the mortal woman, rather than staying with either of the goddesses Circe and Calypso, with whom he spends time in the course of his travels and each of whom separately offers him immortality if he remains with her.

Many themes of desire and danger, of the power of aging women and of its overturning are present in the saga of the *Odyssey*. Moreover, there is a divine precedent for what happens to Penelope, and that precedent can be useful in deepening readings of this text.

The Odyssey:
A Subtext of Female Authority

GREEK MEN viewed women as governed by mental irrationality and destabilizing sexual drives. Eventually such beliefs would contribute to the creation of the strict patriarchy of classical Greece. They are also present in the *Odyssey*. The importance of Penelope's virtue, for example, is heightened by the contrast which is drawn between her and Clytemnestra. Throughout the work, Clytemnestra is depicted as an example of female infidelity: not only did she openly live with her lover, Aegisthus, while her husband, Agamemnon, was at Troy, but she also participated in killing him when he returned. "There is no trusting in women," Agamemnon tells Odysseus, when Odysseus encounters his shade in Hades.

The Greeks regarded female sexuality as so uncontrollable that women could not resist male seduction. The author of the *Odyssey* tells us that Clytemnestra briefly resisted Aegisthus. But when he took her "to his own home" he easily seduced her.[22] In his own territory she could not restrain herself. Some commentators argue that Penelope stayed in her quarters when the suitors were in the house because she feared that if she went among them her female sexual nature might overwhelm her and she might become another Clytemnestra. On the other hand, one might read her caution as proceeding out of fear of the suitors' lack of restraint. This lack of restraint extended throughout her husband's property; it might ultimately be directed against her.

Yet the Greeks did not always view even Penelope as unilaterally virtuous. There are other legends concerning her fate, legends which are not part of the official version of the *Odyssey*. These alternative legends present a Penelope who is different from the virtuous woman of Homeric legend. In one of these alternative myths, in fact, Penelope succumbs to the suitors. Whether she chooses this outcome or whether the suitors force her into it is not made clear. Nor is it entirely certain whether she marries one of them or, alternatively, has intercourse with a number of them.[23]

Yet one suspects that this legend is a later misogynistic rewriting of Penelope's story, designed to cast aspersions on her "circumspection" and to make her more like the standard lustful woman of the Greek male imagination. And what also seems interesting about these accounts is the purported result of this union between Penelope and the suitors, the child that is presumably conceived. That result is the god Pan, half human and half beast, a being with a human body and a ram's head and feet. Originally a nature spirit, Pan later becomes a symbol in the Greek pantheon of rampant sexuality.

Other legends regarding Penelope took the continuation of her saga in a different direction and made of it one curiously paralleling that of Jocasta and Oedipus. In these accounts, an oracle informed Odysseus that his son would kill him. In line with this prophecy, in this story Odysseus banishes Telemachus from Ithaca. But in the kind of mistaken identity situation which is often characteristic of myth, Telemachus is not the right son and thus banishing him does no good. For, according to this story, in Odysseus's wanderings he had fathered a son by Circe, one of the divine enchantresses he had encountered. It is this son, Telegonus, who inadvertently kills Odysseus. He then marries Penelope, and the two of them go to live with Circe on her island. Meanwhile, as if to complete some family circle, Telemachus reappears and marries Circe.[24]

Why was there this repetition of the Oedipus myth? Why do some commentators choose to couple Penelope with a younger man, and in the case of the second story, involving her marriage to Telegonus, a younger man with whom she had a curiously maternal relationship (since he was the son of her husband by another woman)? To encounter so similar a story of mother-son coupling in a second setting seems to indicate a certain ritualized meaning to both of them. They seem to draw from some deeper, hidden meaning, some stratum of reality that the myth both elucidates and obscures. Indeed, Homer's world is a patriarchal world, one in which men rule and women obey, hiding like Penelope their real intentions just as she veils her face in public. But masked beneath Homer's patriarchal world is another world, one in which women are freer, without such restraints.

The powerful female monsters that Odysseus encounters in his travels—Scylla, Charybdis, the Sirens—are representatives of this world. So is the goddess Athena, Odysseus's protector, who controls much of the action of the *Odyssey* (although much of the time she seems a surrogate male). Some scholars note that Nausicaa, the young princess of Phaeacia who discovers Odysseus on the island's beach after he has been shipwrecked, seems more like a goddess than a young mortal woman.[25] Her mother, Queen Arete, wields great authority in their island home. She possesses such good judgment that the people of Phaeacia regard her as akin to a "god" and bring disputes to her to adjudicate. Helen of Sparta, too, is a figure of authority. Her beauty, her status as a daughter of Zeus, her knowledge of magic and drugs, give her a special power.

Even Penelope cannot be contained entirely outside this world. When Telemachus explains why he feels constrained from sending her back to her parents and asserting his right to Odysseus's property, one of the main reasons he cites is his fear that Penelope will send the Erinyes to torment him. The Erinyes are those spirits who, originally associated with the matrifocal order, protect the rights of mothers under patriarchy. Fear of the Erinyes haunts the Greek patriarchal consciousness even in later ages, until Aeschylus in the *Oresteia* renders them harmless through the argument that men are ipso facto more important than women because their sperm creates life, while women contribute only inert matter. Once this principle, enunciated in the play by Athena, is acknowledged, Orestes is exonerated for having killed Clytemnestra, and the Erinyes are transformed into benign protectors of the patriarchal order.

The *Odyssey* contains more hints of female authority. When Odysseus journeys to the underworld to find his way home, it is the goddess Circe who directs him to go there and the "revered" goddess Persephone, Hades' consort, who seems the real ruler of the chthonic realm. Persephone sends the shades of wives and daughters of princes in the underworld to talk with Odysseus in what seems an attempt to state some important principles of gender relations. Indeed, the shade of Odysseus's mother, who has died during his absence and whom he meets in the underworld, tells him to "remember these things for your wife, so you may tell her hereafter."[26]

This encounter between Odysseus and the wives and daughters of princes is central to the *Odyssey*. Here we have a group of women connected with royal authority who are analogous to Helen, Clytemnestra, and Penelope. They come from an earlier age: among them are Alkmene and Tyro, whom the suitors compared unfavorably with Penelope. Here they are portrayed differently. They glory in patriarchy and its values. Their conversations with Odysseus concern their pride in their husbands and hero sons or in having been "seduced" by a god. They celebrate their sons for prowess in battle, for being boxers and breakers of horses.[27]

The final story is told by a queen named Iphimedeia. This queen, we learn, had intercourse with the god Poseidon and bore two extraordinary sons to him. It would be hard to visualize mortal men more powerful. They were fully "nine fathoms" in height (or fifty-four feet). But they possessed that human arrogance so often met in legend. This arrogance encouraged them to think that they could conquer the gods. They formulated plans to build a tower in the sky and to make war against the Olympians. The gods could not permit this, and so they deputized Apollo to kill the two brothers.

Such a cautionary tale of humans overreaching themselves is often told in world mythologies—as in the story of the Tower of Babel or of Icarus flying too close to the sun. But the story of Iphimedeia's sons might also be read as a tale of failed rebellion, of sons banding together to resist their mother's conquerors and, by implication, the divine conquerors of all those queens whom Odysseus met in the underworld. Most of these women had slept with—or been raped by—a god. The issue here is the coupling of Iphimedeia and Poseidon, which the *Odyssey* presents as a case of seduction, but which could also be viewed as a case of rape. Because Greek males believed that women could not resist seduction, by definition rape was hardly possible. Iphimedeia's sons in defying the gods might be seen not as taking the martial nature of heroism beyond realistic limits, but as defending a mother—or a matrifocal order—under attack.

The heroic ethic which is at the core of the *Odyssey* is intended to justify men's domination over women. But the *Odyssey* also contains the veiled story of an age in which women possessed authority. In this age, relation-

ships between aging women and younger men were not prohibited; indeed, they may have constituted a prototype. As well, indications of the
overturning of that order are also present in the *Odyssey*.

We see this order in that muted world of female power I have just
described. It is, moreover, explicit in two relationships which Odysseus
has during his journey homeward: his relationships with the sorceress
Circe and especially with the nymph Calypso. Odysseus remained with
Circe for only a year, but he stayed with Calypso for seven years.

Alone among the enchantresses whom Odysseus encounters, Calypso
attempts no violent action against him. She wants to make him her
permanent consort, to grant him eternal youth and divine status. But the
patriarchal Greek gods would not allow goddesses to share their privilege
of cohabiting with mortals. The goddess–younger male relationship had
to end. The Olympian gods send Hermes, their messenger, to tell Calypso
that she must give up Odysseus. Calypso explodes in anger. But she can
do nothing. Zeus is all-powerful, and she must obey him. She allows
Odysseus to resume his journey home. Yet her long speech to Hermes
contains a list of relationships between goddesses and younger men and
describes the ways in which the gods ended those relationships. What she
says may reveal much about patriarchal practices, even within a divine
community.

> You are hard-hearted, you gods, and jealous beyond all creatures
> beside, when you are resentful toward the goddesses for sleeping
> openly with such men as each has made her true husband. So when
> Dawn of the rosy fingers chose out Orion, all you gods who live at
> your ease were full of resentment, until chaste Artemis of the golden
> throne in Ortygia came with a visitation of painless arrows and
> killed him; and so it was when Demeter of the lovely hair, yielding
> to her desire, lay down with Iasion and loved him in a thrice-turned
> field, it was not long before this was made known to Zeus, who
> struck him down with a cast of the shining thunderbolt.[28]

Goddesses and Young Gods:
Comity and Contention

G REEK MYTHOLOGY—like most Mediterranean my-
thologies—is replete with stories of relationships between goddesses and
younger men. In the first instance, the younger males became the lovers
of the goddesses. In the second, they formed bands of followers or of
priests to the goddesses, like the Kouretes who served the many-named
goddess on the island of Crete. Finally, heroes of legend have special
relationships with goddesses, like Odysseus with Athena. Sometimes these
relationships are sexual; sometimes they are not. Most local heroes claimed
descent from a local earth nymph or mother goddess, like Heracles and
Hera or Achilles and Thetis.[29] In the end, however, the mission of the
hero might include killing a divine female figure, as in Perseus slaying
Medusa or Oedipus causing the death of the Sphinx. Within these legends
the patriarchal overturning of goddess-centered religions may be seen.

The stories which involve sexual or love relationships between goddesses and young men are legion. Aphrodite, for example, had a number
of other young lovers besides Adonis. There was Phaethon, son of Helios,
who drove the chariot of the sun too close to earth and was killed by
Zeus with a thunderbolt. Aphrodite was also involved with Anchises, a
shepherd. Aeneas, the son born to them, was the legendary founder of
Rome. The story of their association is told in detail in the *Homeric Hymn
to Aphrodite.*

In addition to Aphrodite, the moon goddess, Selene, and her sister,
Eos, goddess of the dawn, also had involvements with young men. It was
said, for example, that when the moon disappeared in the mornings,
Selene was visiting her young lover, Endymion, who slept in a cave.
Because of his perpetual sleep, he never grew old. The *Odyssey* mentions
several of Eos's relationships. "Dawn of the golden throne [Eos] carried
Kleitos away, because of his beauty, so that he might dwell among the
immortals."[30] In her list of relationships, Calypso speaks of Eos's lover,
Orion, eventually transformed into a constellation of stars. But Eos especially loved the young Tithonis, and she loved him so much that she asked
Zeus to grant him eternal life. Yet, like many supplicants in this kind of
mythological request, she made an error in her plea, and what she wanted
did not occur as she had envisioned. Eos forgot to ask for eternal youth

for Tithonis in addition to eternal life. Thus he aged, and she abandoned him.

The concluding passages of Hesiod's *Theogony* list many additional relationships. These include those between Kadmos and Harmonia, daughter of Aphrodite; Chrysaor and Kallirhoe, daughter of Okeanos; and numerous ones between the daughters of Nereus, the old man of the sea, and various mortal men.[31] Many of the major Olympian goddeses were also involved at one time or another in such relationships. Aphrodite had a number of them. Hera replicated the pattern in her relationship with Zeus, for she was his older sister. According to one legend she had determined to marry him when he was a child and she was grown. Demeter had intercourse with Iasion in the "thrice-turned field" of Crete, as Calypso tells the story in the *Odyssey*. Iasion is elsewhere identified as a Cretan Kourete. Even the virgin goddess Artemis became involved with young men. But sexuality was not a part of her association with Hippolyte, and the young hunter Actaeon was killed by wild boars when he spied on her nude body while she was bathing.

For the most part the goddesses are the initiators of these relationships. Many of the young men seem passive. They are often identified with flowers. Hesiod's *Theogony* tells the story of Phaethon and Aphrodite. "While he still had the soft flower of the splendor of youth upon him," Aphrodite "swooped down and caught him away and set him in her holy temple to be her nocturnal temple-keeper."[32] When Adonis died, according to one legend, anemones sprang from his blood. After the death of Attis, the young male lover of the Phrygian goddess Cybele, in Anatolia violets sprang from the ground on which his blood dripped.

In addition to Greek texts like the *Odyssey,* the Near Eastern texts which describe such relationships also depict their goddesses as powerful. Inanna of Sumer in the third millennium *Hymn to Inanna* is the "proud Queen of the Earth Gods, supreme Among the Heaven Gods," who makes "the heavens tremble and the earth quake."[33] When the Babylonian hero Gilgamesh rejects the goddess Ishtar in *The Epic of Gilgamesh,* her curse kills his companion, Enkidu, and her outcry helps bring on the great flood.[34] The power of the goddesses can bring eternal life to their young paramours. But that power can also bring death. Zeus's thunderbolts kill Iasion. Artemis shoots Orion with an arrow. Horses pulling his chariot trample Hippolyte. A boar gores Adonis.

Because of the gentleness of many of these dying young men and the flower imagery often accompanying them, some scholars have argued that they were meant to be dying and then reviving vegetation gods. As such (in an analogy with human procreation) they represented a masculine persona needed to germinate the goddess identified with the earth. Or, alternatively, they might symbolize the earth's growing cycle, with death in the winter and renewal in the spring. Thus, because they were yearly reborn, these men could never grow old. They had to be depicted as young.

Relationships between goddesses and young men could be both fulfilling and threatening. This threatening mode seemed to signify ancient deadly rites of renewal whereby the young consort may have been yearly killed to make way for a new representative of springtime revival. James Frazer's famed *Golden Bough* is focused around his interpretation of such a presumed incident in ancient Italy. The *Homeric Hymn to Aphrodite* involves a long discussion of the mating of Aphrodite with the shepherd Anchises on the slopes of the Cretan Mount Ida. When Anchises discovers that he has slept with a goddess rather than with a mortal woman, he becomes frightened. He implores Aphrodite: "Don't permit me to live impotent among men from now on. Pity me. For a man who sleeps with immortal goddesses loses his potency."[35]

Yet no such negativity is evidenced in the experience of Odysseus with Calypso or in the relationships discussed in Hesiod's *Theogony,* in which goddesses often offer immortality to their younger male lovers. In many myths goddesses protect young men as babies from the wrath of gods or other goddesses. Rhea provides such protection for Zeus, when she hides him from the wrath of his father, Kronos, in a cave on the Cretan Mount Ida and has the Kouretes make a loud noise so that his crying will not be heard. Nymphs hide Dionysus from Hera, and the three daughters of Cecrops care for Erichthonius, the originating King of Athens. In the central Egyptian myth involving Isis and Osiris, Osiris is dismembered by his brother, Set, and Isis, his sister, reconstitutes him.

In other instances, some of the young men involved with goddesses remain eternally alive. Their stories seem intended to convey a message about the inevitability of aging and the necessity of enjoying life for its own sake. Human beings, the message seems to be, cannot be gods. Who would want to be Endymion, eternally young, but spending all his days sleeping in a cave? Then there is Tithonis, abandoned by the goddess Eos because of a quirk in her request to Zeus, her failure to ask for eternal youth as well as eternal life. In the *Epic of Gilgamesh* (its earliest version from the first half of the second millennium B.C.E.), the hero Gilgamesh refuses to have anything to do with the goddess Ishtar. In consequence it seems that she will forever exclude him from her benefits. But at the end of the story, he accidentally discovers a plant that will restore his youth. As he picks a stalk, however, a serpent (an animal identified with goddesses) snatches the plant away from him. Gilgamesh is faced with his own mortality and with the fact that only life, with its potentially exciting adventures and the pleasure of telling those adventures to others, remains to him. Like Odysseus, Gilgamesh is a storyteller.

Of these youths of ancient legend, Attis, Adonis, Tammuz, and Damuzi became cult figures of importance, with ceremonial observances devoted to them. Most of the others appeared in a tale or two and then disappeared. Endymion and Tithonis, for example, were not worshipped; there were no shrines to them or rituals connected with their legends, unless in local situations. Varying rituals, both similar and different, characterized the worship of the four central young male figures I have cited, and the extant descriptions of many of these rituals contain no indication of violence.

Take, for example, the yearly Adonis festival, held in the Near East and Greece. This festival, limited in participation to women, paid tribute to women's sorrow over the removal of Adonis from the human community, but any actual death of the young god was not reenacted. Rather, the ritual seems related to that myth about Adonis in which Aphrodite and Persephone vie for the young man's love, and Zeus decides to divide Adonis's time between the two goddesses, decreeing that he spend part of the year with Persephone in the underworld and part with Aphrodite above ground. In a variant of all those myths relating to the seasonal dying and reviving of vegetation, Adonis does not really die, he simply disappears from the human world for a time.

In the Adonis ritual, women assembled so-called Adonis gardens, composed of moistened seeds of grain placed in small pots. The seeds would sprout and decay within a few days. Then the women would weep, beat their chests, and tear their clothes, simulating regular mourning behavior. In the seventh century B.C.E., the Greek poet Sappho described this behavior:

> *Delicate Adonis is dying, Cytherea; what are we to do?*
> *Beat your breasts, girls, and tear your clothes.*

A similar ceremony was performed in the Near East to mourn the death of Tammuz: a biblical passage in Ezekiel refers to women weeping and wailing at the gates of Jerusalem over Tammuz.[36]

The major ritual in these ancient religions was the *hieros gamos,* or "sacred marriage." It was a ritual celebrating not death but life. In the "sacred marriage," human representatives of the goddesses and the young gods retreated from the gathering of believers and simulated—or actually performed—a sacred act of sexual intercourse. The act symbolized the importance of sexuality to all life. The union of goddesses and gods through their human representatives symbolically ensured that crops would grow, that animals would reproduce, that procreative love would extend throughout the land.

The *hieros gamos* was performed throughout the Near East, where it probably originated. Some scholars think that the Old Testament Song of Solomon, an erotic love poem incongruous with the stern patriarchal god, Jahweh, derived from texts celebrating the sacred marriage ceremony. The ritual was less common in Greece than in the eastern Mediterranean. But it was celebrated, for example, as part of the Anthuseria, a yearly Athenian festival in honor of the god Dionysus. One of the most famed literary depictions of the sacred marriage ceremony occurs in the *Iliad.* Zeus and Hera sleep together on Mount Ida, where "underneath them the divine earth broke into young, fresh grass, and into dewy clover, crocus and hyacinth so thick and soft it held the hard ground deep away from them."[37]

In the *Odyssey,* Homer seems to burlesque the *hieros gamos* in the story of the god Hephaestus secretly arranging a public display before the gods of the adulterous lovemaking of Aphrodite, his wife, and Ares, the god of war. But the emphasis that Penelope and Odysseus place, after his return, on the bed that he built for them at the time of their marriage could indicate the importance of the sacred marriage to Homer.

In the third century B.C.E., the Greek poet Theokritos described a sacred marriage ceremony associated with the worship of Adonis in the city of Alexandria. In Theokritos's story, two women have come to hear a local female poet celebrate the rites in verse. By her description, these rites involved a private night of love between Aphrodite and Adonis. Then, at dawn, the women carry the Adonis figure to the shore, there to mourn his return to the underworld, with their hair loosened and breasts bare, and their song "high-pitched and clear."[38]

Of all the heroes, the woman poet intones, Adonis alone exists in both the underworld and the human world. Being both dead and alive seems to give him special potency. Throughout Theokritos's poem the two women spectators complain about their husbands' inattention; Adonis seems to represent to them a gentle eroticism absent in their lives. At the end of the story, their conversation echoes the final words of the female poet to whom they have been listening:

> *Farewell, beloved Adonis.*
> *Come make us happy again soon.*

By focusing on the erotic, life-enforcing side of these religions, I do not deny that violence could be a part of them. It is hard to avoid the evidence, especially from the Near East, that these goddesses could represent war, as well as peace. They could be stern or capricious judges of human failings, and they could seek retribution through human sacrifice. In many Mediterranean mythologies, goddesses ruled the underworld, as Persephone does in the *Odyssey*. The earth they so often embodied is, after all, a place of burial as well as of procreation.

Another look at the religious ceremonies for the four young gods under review (Adonis, Attis, Damuzi, and Tammuz) reveals that violence was part of the ceremonies held for the Anatolian goddess Cybele and her consort, Attis. The ritual focused on the legend of Cybele and Attis in which Attis castrated himself for having been unfaithful to Cybele. At the penultimate point of the ceremony of mourning for Attis, the new priests of Cybele (called galli) castrated themselves.

Once the galli had undergone castration, they wore female clothing. Many scholars think that this cross-dressing is the key to understanding these men who seemed to want to remake their bodies as female. They thereby became akin to the goddess; they participated in her power. Or, a drive toward androgyny, the desire to become a gender that is neither male nor female, may be the key. Cross-dressing as part of priestly practice can be found throughout history and across cultures. To break down the gulf between male and female may indicate the desire to reconcile the other awesome dualisms between heaven and earth, animal and human, life and death, to create a holistic universe.[39] In some personifications, the goddesses themselves took on the look of androgyny: both the Egyptian Isis and the Near Eastern Aphrodite were sometimes depicted with both breasts and phalluses, or with beards.

Women mourning for the death of the young god; the sacred marriage; castration and cross-dressing—these are the major elements in the rituals surrounding the worship of goddesses and young gods. Yet at what point in time these various practices became part of the religions of the Mediterranean region is not precisely known. Early evidence, dating from about 6000 B.C.E., comes from the work of archaeologists James Mellaart, at the Neolithic town of Çatal Hüyük, in Anatolia, and of Marija Gimbutas, in Central and Southeastern Europe. Both find goddess figures predominant in size and number, but the young god is also present. In Çatal Hüyük, he is sculpted as a hunter, standing outside goddess-dominated shrines. He is accompanied by bulls and leopards. Gimbutas's young god is most often depicted either in the form of a phallus or in an animal shape, especially as a bull, with a massive body suggesting virility.[40]

The date of 6000 B.C.E. is significant. For this early Neolithic period marks the beginnings of trading communities, of settled agriculture and animal husbandry, of the use of metals. At this time, scholars speculate, humans finally came to understand the male role in conception: they gained this knowledge especially through animal breeding. Before then the argument is that women were preeminent because the conception and gestation of humans was seen as entirely in their power. Matrifocal societies were agricultural societies centered around producing successful harvests. Male-centered societies based on herding (so-called animal "husbandry") or on metal technology had male gods. (The thunder god, Zeus, for example, initially headed the pantheon of northern Indo-European tribes that invaded Greece.) Either by conquest or infiltration, patriarchal herding societies took over agricultural matrifocal societies.

In opposition to this scenario of male takeover, Marija Gimbutas offers a different possibility. Based on the evidence of early Neolithic bird and snake statues with breasts and long, phallic necks which seem to combine male and female characteristics, she argues that there was a period of gender combination, of androgyny, before male conquest. Indo-European invasions in 4000 B.C.E. shattered this time of what she sees as peace and equality between humans and animals and males and females. The relationship between goddesses and young gods exemplified this unity. She writes: "The male divinity in the shape of a young man or a male animal appears to affirm and strengthen the forces of the creative and active female. Neither is subordinate to the other; by complementing one another, their power is doubled."[41]

The Kouretes, Dionysus,
The Eleusinian Mysteries

IN ADDITION TO their relationships with young men as lovers, goddesses also interact in myth with groups of younger men who serve as priests or as special followers in their ritual processions. Among these are the Kouretes, followers of the goddess on the island of Crete. The Kouretes are not present in the *Odyssey,* but they are nonetheless important in understanding the goddess/young god typology. Moreover, the goddesses also have special relationships with the heroes, men who come to represent a revered sort of virtue to the Greeks. Odysseus in the *Odyssey* is one such hero.

Initially these two types seem removed from one another. The Kouretes were priests in service to a goddess, and they were usually depicted in legend in groups. The heroes acted alone and were secular figures, although scholars think that local cults glorifying them arose after their deaths. Both were involved with the transition from matrifocal to patriarchal societies. The Kouretes began in service to a goddess and transferred their allegiance from her to a male god. The god Dionysus was central to this transition. With regard to the heroes, each claimed descent from a local earth goddess. But the stage of dependence did not last. Like Theseus with Ariadne or Jason with Medea, they abandoned the goddess. Or, like Perseus with Medusa and Oedipus with the Sphinx, they were responsible for her death. It was the heroes, like Theseus and Heracles, who interacted in legend with the Amazons and destroyed them.

The hero's diminution of the goddess, however, could involve nothing so dramatic as death or abandonment. Take, for example, the tale of Hippolytus and Phaedra. This is the story of a stepmother, Phaedra, who attempts to seduce Hippolytus, her stepson. Variations of this tale can be found in the folk traditions of many lands, as in the biblical story of Joseph and Potiphar's wife. Many scholars interpret the story as representing transhistorical and transregional sentiment against stepmothers in ages when mothers died young. But its resonances extend further, to include the reduction of women of power to spiteful harridans. For in the story Hippolytus rejects Phaedra's advances. She then falsely accuses him to his father of attempted rape. Thus the aging husband gains the fulcrum of power, and the aging woman's sexual desire becomes foolish, even dangerous.[42]

Phaedra originally was a Cretan princess, and the island of Crete is central to Greek mythology. The Kouretes, for example, were located on Crete. Strabo called them armed and orgiastic dancers; Hesiod said that they were lovers of sport and dancing. Euripides described them as carrying torches in nocturnal sacerdotal processions in the Cretan mountains.[43] The reference to arms and dancing calls to mind their role as protectors of Zeus when his mother, Rhea, hid him as an infant in a Cretan cave to save him from Kronos's murderous wrath. The Kouretes danced and created a din with weapons and musical instruments so that his father would not hear his crying. The reference to sport is reminiscent of the famed Cretan bull-leaping exercise in which young men (and women) somersaulted over the horns of bulls. The Kouretes' participation in religious rites in the Cretan mountains indicates that the Cretan goddess was a goddess of mountains, of peaks, of the highest places. She had a number of names, probably relating to Cretan regional variations: she was variously called, for example, Britomartis and Diktynna.

Occasionally in ancient texts the Kouretes are called Corybantes, a name also given to the band of males who followed the goddess Cybele. And, indeed, Crete was probably first settled from Anatolia, in about 3000 B.C.E.: many scholars see resemblances between Cybele and the Greek Artemis, as mistresses of animals and goddesses of the out-of-doors. Circe in the *Odyssey* also has these aspects, for all around her forest home are "lions, and wolves of the mountains...."[44] Yet despite the resemblances in these goddesses, the Kouretes seem different from the eunuch priests of Cybele, although there is some indication in remaining pictorial representations that they adopted female attire for ceremonial occasions. If anything, they seem closer in attributes to masculinized heroes like Heracles than to androgynous figures like Adonis. The word *kouros* means "youth." The kouros statues of the sixth century B.C.E., some of which still exist, possibly were intended to represent them. These sculpted young men have one leg placed forward; on their lips is a haunting smile.

As a group in Greek mythology the Kouretes play little role outside of the island of Crete. None of the Olympian goddesses have such a band of young men serving them. (Nor, it might be added, do any of the Olympian gods have such a band, with the exception of Dionysus.) Only occasionally are the Kouretes individuated. According to one legend, however, they were the originators of the Olympian games. In this tale the hero Heracles is counted among them, and he decides that they should compete in a footrace to determine the greatest Kouros, the leader of the group for the year. Out of this footrace the Olympian games presumably developed.

Two extant texts provide our major information about the Kouretes. The texts are Euripides' fifth-century play *The Bacchae* and the *Hymn to the Kouretes,* a brief second-century B.C.E. writing found in clay fragments on Crete. Both texts tell the same story. Sacred goddess objects used in ritual by the Kouretes are stolen and then transferred to the worship of a male god.

In the *Hymn to the Kouretes,* the Kouretes worship kouros. This god is identified as he whom Rhea gave to the "shield nurturers," and they "with noise of beating feet hid away." According to Euripides in *The Bacchae,* the Kouretes were the first of the "whirling dancers" who beat the drums and played the "whirling flute." "Then from them to Rhea's hands the holy drum was handed down." But it was "stolen by the raving Satyrs." This group of male acolytes then gave it to their leader, Dionysus.[45]

Within the Greek pantheon, Dionysus is an especially androgynous figure. By Euripides' description in *The Bacchae,* he is gentle and soft, beardless. Like Athena he was born from Zeus's body but then raised by nymphs who dressed him as a girl to conceal him from Hera. He is also passionate: a god of ecstasy and the bringer to Greece of the vine which produced the wine essential to Greek ritual and life. He is also a bull god—a representative of phallic sexuality. He is a "render of men . . . who delights in the sword and bloodshed." Dionysus's gentleness attracts women to him, and they join his followers, the Maenads. But Dionysus also brings madness to them and inspires them to violence, involving tearing apart animals and even human infants.[46] As a young god, given his nature both feminine and masculine, Dionysus seems to stand in a transitional position between matrifocal and patriarchal orders.

It is tempting to argue that the figure of the young god, especially when characterized by gentleness, was the creation of the matrifocal imagination, that women created him because with him they could experience reciprocity. This argument is too presentist to sustain for long, and it remains speculative. Yet it reads into the remote past what is present in the later European imagination. To the Greeks, Adonis was the seducer, attached to the world of women and pleasure and thereby excluded from the world of war and hunting. He was the antithesis of warrior heroes like Heracles.[47] Throughout the ages Adonis becomes the symbol of male beauty and, more than that, the symbol of a sensitive maturity. This sensitivity is a trait in men that many women in many ages seem to desire and rarely seem to find.

Freud argued that women invariably desire their sons. If this is so, it may be because they have watched their sons grow through the stages of life. They have watched them mature from infancy to youth, to adulthood, to the final appearance of the adult patriarchal male. Although women have always participated, through childrearing, in the production of this male, the final outcome, the fully adult male of the type whom they are supposed to desire, may be a figure from whom they really want to flee.[48]

All the young male gods were not the same god, nor were all the goddesses the same goddess. For many, their involvement with young men was only an incident, an episodic occurrence that might be central to their ritual but did not define their being. Often identified as "mother" goddesses, they were in fact not always the mothers of the young men with whom they united. Aphrodite and Cybele were not the mothers of their consorts: in originating legends, Attis was a shepherd Cybele chanced upon and Adonis was the son of the king of Cyprus and his daughter. Hera was Zeus's sister, as were the goddesses involved with brother gods in Egypt. Ever since Freud, scholars have made the error of seeing the goddess/young god association as reflecting only some sort of primal Oedipal relationship, some way in which it grew out of the psychological states of modern man written into the ancient past.

The "motherhood" of the great goddesses was a generalized fact: it was of the earth, the animals, of all people. Savina Teubal makes this point in her interpretation of the biblical Sarah as a priestess of the Babylonian Ishtar when she notes that sacred marriage ceremonies in myth so rarely produced children. The product of these sexual unions was not individual progeny but bountiful harvests and a fruitful people.[49]

The goddesses, too, were not bound to the men with whom they united. Many scholars agree that the virginity of goddesses like Athena and Artemis was intended as a sign not of sexual innocence but of independence. Thus Hera bathed in the spring near Argos each year not to regain that internal tissue, that virginal hymen which has been, over the ages, so important to patriarchal culture. Rather she meant to assert her freedom, her independence, from that culture.

Within Greek legend, women do not often bond with one another. Thus despite their close kin connection, Clytemnestra, Helen, and Penelope do not interact. Nor is the mother-daughter bond especially strong among them. Penelope has no daughter. As depicted by Greek dramatists, Helen's daughter, Hermione, is a narcissistic woman estranged from a mother who abandoned her when she left Sparta. Clytemnestra is close to Iphigenia, but her daughter Electra is obsessed with killing her.

In Greek mythology, goddesses are most often rivals to one another. This factor of female competition is strikingly evident in that story which more than any other represents the founding gender mythology of Western civilization. In what later came to be known as the Judgment of Paris, Hera, Athena, and Aphrodite dispute which of them is the most beautiful. Zeus deputizes Paris to adjudicate, and he chooses Aphrodite after she promises to reward him with the world's most beautiful woman. That woman is Helen of Troy, and Paris's abduction of Helen causes the Trojan War. Thus what is important to women is appearance, and what is important to men is possessing women. Women compete over beauty and men compete to retain the women they possess, even to the point of murderous war.

To these generalizations about female separation and competition there is one major exception. But it is so striking an exception that it deserves elaboration. In Greek legend, one story in particular brings women together rather than keeping them apart. Moreover, its elements cast doubt on the universality of the "mother-son" dyad as the originating divine couple of Mediterranean religion and suggest that, in fact, women bonding with women may have been the original coupling. The legend is that of Demeter and Persephone, of the mother bereft over the loss of her daughter abducted by Hades, the god of the underworld. A celebration of female solidarity lies at the heart of this story. And so does Demeter's anger at patriarchy's central violent acts against its daughters, the acts of rape and incest. For Hades, Persephone's abductor, is her uncle. Alternatively, in some versions of the story, Zeus is Persephone's father, and it is he who rapes her. In this variation, Dionysus is their son.

The importance of the legend of Demeter and Persephone is further indicated by the fact that out of it grew the most important mystery religion of the Greek world, the Eleusinian Mysteries.[50] The central rite of this worship was celebrated yearly in the town of Eleusis, close to Athens. The date of its origin is unknown, although excavations of the site suggest that it dated at least to Mycenaean times, to the period when warlords ruled Greece and the Trojan War may have been fought. Eventually patriarchal elements came to permeate the rites at Eleusis: the major ceremony there probably eventually involved the symbolic birth of a son, perhaps after the performance of a *hieros gamos*. Still, Demeter and Persephone retained prestige. The Eleusinian religion was always popularly called the religion of the "two goddesses." Even during the ages of strict Athenian patriarchy, women, but not men, addressed prayers to Demeter and Persephone.[51]

While searching for the young god figure, scholars have explored the possibility that Mediterranean religions began with the worship of "two goddesses." The *Homeric Hymn to Demeter,* with its lengthy account of Demeter's search for Persephone, perhaps indicates this possibility. Sculptural evidence of a male god figure dates only to 6000 B.C.E.; female figures date from 20,000 B.C.E. Both James Mellaart in Anatolia and Marija Gimbutas in Eastern Europe find evidence of female figures sculpted in pairs. But the infrequent occurrence of such couples leads both scholars to conclude that they are not especially significant.

Other scholars look to the close relationships between Inanna and Erishkegal in Sumerian legend or between Isis and Nepthys in Egypt as evidence that the Demeter and Persephone myth, the mother-daughter connection, preceded that between mother and son. But we do not know. In the *Odyssey,* Persephone is depicted as the powerful Queen of the Underworld. The goddess Demeter is depicted in terms of her sexuality, seen in heterosexual terms: Demeter has intercourse with Iasion, one of the Kouretes, on the island of Crete. That is all that Homer, in this text, reveals.

The Meaning of Telemachus

Before concluding this reconstruction of the goddess/young god relationship, I want to return to the *Odyssey* and especially to one character to whom I have not paid much attention. That character is Telemachus, the son of Odysseus and Penelope. In many ways the *Odyssey* is his story, and his story is one of learning how to be a hero. Indecisive at the story's outset, afraid to do much about his mother's predicament, by the end of the saga he has come to patriarchal maturity. When the suitors fail to thread the bow, Telemachus picks it up and is on the verge of threading it when Odysseus stops him, wanting to extract vengeance in his own way.

In reality, Telemachus does not want to kill the suitors. In fact, he counsels Odysseus to let them go. They apologize to Odysseus for what they have done; they offer to make full restitution of his property.[52] But Odysseus will not listen. The killing of the suitors was inevitable throughout the story. From the beginning of the epic, Athena alluded to the necessity of their death. Odysseus's honor must remain unbesmirched, no matter the violence required.

Odysseus, a gifted storyteller and master of disguises, earlier in the *Odyssey* actually criticized the heroic ideal of bodily competition and bloody struggle. Insulted by a young Phaeacian nobleman for his refusal to participate in an athletic competition, Odysseus drew from his repertoire of responses to praise the storyteller who has "comeliness in his words." "So it is," he continued, "that the gods do not bestow graces in all ways on men, neither in stature nor yet in brains or eloquence." There are, he implies, many ways to come to justice, to respond to what this athlete might consider an egregious slight.[53]

The conception of Odysseus as heroic is predominant in the *Odyssey*. And in this early heroic lexicon, his craftiness, his slyness, his ability at disguise are praiseworthy characteristics. In later tradition, however, he will come to be seen as too prudent and too tied to his home—as insufficiently bold and daring. In later tradition Achilles and Heracles will become the predominant representatives of appropriate masculinity.[54] But the ending of the *Odyssey* casts Odysseus in a martial mode. No modern hero of the Western cowboy or detective drama could outdo Odysseus, as he hacks to death 108 men, with only the help of Telemachus and a few servants (although with Athena's guidance). And the deed is done inside the house, in the room where his family would otherwise gather for food and for entertaining, in a place that is partly Penelope's, in interior domestic space. Odysseus does not teach Telemachus how to tell stories; he teaches him how to kill.

The *Odyssey* is a book whose culminating scene I would like to rewrite. And if I were to rewrite the bloody battle between Odysseus and the suitors, I might put in its place a scene of life and of love, a description of the *hieros gamos,* a scene of the coming together of the man and woman in equity and caring. I might end it with Odysseus's bed and with the carrying out of Telemachus's plea for forgiveness.

The Sumerian *Hymn to Inanna* contains a scene where the goddess, Inanna, and the young man, Damuzi, come together for the sacred marriage. What I like about this description is not only the blending of genders but also the blending of ages. Inanna is older than Damuzi. But age becomes irrelevant to their relationship in the midst of the joy engendered by their mutuality.

In the end neither seems older than the other, and each seems capable of playing for the other multiple support roles. They can be, alternatively, mother and father to each other; or, as the case may be, brother and sister. In their lush interaction:

> *Plants grow high by their side*
> *Grains grow high by their side*
> *Gardens flourish luxuriantly.*

When Inanna hesitates to take Damuzi as her consort, her mother, Ningal, counsels her:

> *My child, the young man will be your father.*
> *My daughter, the young man will be your mother.*
> *He will treat you like a father.*
> *He will care for you like a mother.*
> *Open the house, My Lady, open the House!*[55]

CHAPTER THREE

Goddesses Revealed and Obscured:
The Story of Sappho and Phaon

*T*RADITIONS OF powerful goddesses, of aging women as wise creators, continued in Greek and Roman times. Throughout the Greek and Roman periods, mystery religions remained popular. Many of them centered on the worship of goddesses: the cults of Cybele and Isis, for example, as well as that of Demeter and Persephone at Eleusis, had large followings. The city of Ephesus on the Anatolian coast was the center of the worship of Diana, popular throughout the Mediterranean region. According to the Bible's Book of Acts, when Saint Paul, proselytizing for Christianity, visited Ephesus in the fifth decade of the first century C.E. he encountered great resistance from Diana's followers.[1]

The triumph of Christianity by the fourth century C.E. brought the destruction of these religions. But during the Hellenistic era and during the centuries after, philosophers and theologians created a hagiographic universe out of Greek and Roman mythology with Eastern admixtures. (The Hellenistic era comprised the period from Alexander's fourth-century B.C.E. conquest of Greece to the Roman conquest of Egypt in 30 B.C.E.) Early Christianity tolerated and even included this cosmos in its theology. In this world of Neoplatonic, anthropomorphized beings, female figures—like Philosophia and Fortuna—were often the most powerful abstractions. This syncretism went to the heart of Christianity, which incorporated goddess traditions into the figure of Mary, the mother of Jesus, and transposed the ancient cults' central rituals of the sacred marriage and of death and rebirth into the saga of a virgin mother and a son crucified on a cross.[2]

Mary was a figure subordinate to the masculine godhead. But through her spirituality she afforded women authority. The sainthood of her own mother, Anne, who had by legend borne her daughter when she was forty, extended this dignity to older women. Yet a competing tradition denigrated aging women, representing them on the one hand as comic and on the other as dangerous—as "go-betweens" in a vast culture of prostitution, providing women for men, or as "witches," possessing magical, evil powers. Both stereotypes were related to that endemic belief in Western culture in the continued sexuality of aging women, even when no longer fertile.

Economic and political structures underlay the waxing and waning of these alternative positions in the ancient world—as in later times. In Greece, by the fifth century B.C.E. the Homeric tribal aristocracy with overtones of matriliny gave way to a more commercialized world. The Athenian city-state emphasized the individual family (the *oikos*) as the building block of the state. Correspondingly, women's position declined. Alternatively, Alexander's conquest of the known world in the fourth century B.C.E. and his establishment of a bureaucratic empire resulted in an enlargement of women's sphere and eventually in the appearance of powerful women consorts and rulers like Cleopatra. The early Roman state, established in the eighth century B.C.E., evolved an aristocratic order not without resemblance to that of the Homeric world, and it also took a more benign view of women. On the other hand, the Emperor Augustus's establishment of a dictatorship in the first century C.E. designed to shore up what appeared to be deficiencies in Roman society fostered misogyny. Christianity both extended this misogyny and, through traditions of female sainthood, undermined it.

The intertwinings of aging women's independence and the underminings of that independence can be seen in the mythologies constructed around the life of the seventh-century B.C.E. poet Sappho, who lived on the island of Lesbos off the coast of Anatolia. Her story, especially the legend of her relationship with the young man Phaon, reflects many of these motifs.

Sappho: The Background

THE MOST FAMOUS STORY from the ancient world concerning the partnering of an older woman with a younger man is that of Sappho and Phaon, presumably the pilot of the ferry between Lesbos and the Anatolian mainland. Because of Phaon's beauty, so the story goes,

Sappho fell passionately in love with him. Yet because she was middle-aged, he eventually rejected her. Disconsolate, she supposedly killed herself by jumping from cliffs on the island of Leukas into the ocean.

Due to the paucity of sources, the details of Sappho's life as well as of the presumed relationship with Phaon remain largely conjecture. Yet, although Phaon probably never existed, Sappho was a real historical figure. In her own day she was celebrated throughout the Greek world: she was called "the poetess," as Homer was called "the poet." By Plato's age she was acclaimed as part of a Greek triumvirate of past geniuses: there were Homer, Socrates, and Sappho. Her profile appears on coins from ancient Lesbos; she is one of the few historical figures to appear on early Greek vases.[3]

Because in later centuries Christian leaders periodically destroyed her work on account of its presumed eroticism, no complete poem by her exists today. The portions we possess were taken mostly from transcriptions in later Greek and Roman writings. In addition, during late nineteenth-century excavations in Egypt, archaeologists discovered fragments of her poems on pieces of the discarded paper used in the papier-mâché-like wrappings of mummies. Her readership extended throughout the Mediterranean world of her day. Even so, the remaining corpus of her work is small, hardly enough to fill the pages of a small book.

Sappho's work was lost during the Middle Ages. However, the fourteenth-century discovery of Ovid's *Heroides,* his fictionalized letters from famous women of mythology to their lovers, reintroduced knowledge of her. Among his pairs, Ovid included the real Sappho and the probably fictionalized Phaon. From the fourteenth century onward Sappho became a symbol of female artistic genius. Popular collections of brief biographies of eminent women of history, which Giovanni Boccaccio initiated with his fourteenth-century *Concerning Famous Women*, not infrequently included a laudatory section on Sappho. In later ages for a woman to be called "sappho" was to lay claim to artistic genius. Yet behind the paeans to her greatness always lurked the other supposed reality: that she had destroyed her genius because of an overpowering passion for a young man.[4]

From the point of view of the life of Sappho, additional interpretative possibilities regarding the *Odyssey,* the tradition of goddesses, and the nature of Greek culture can be explored. Among these are issues relating to friendships among women and to the sacred or profane association with men involved in the sacred marriage. As well, Sappho's life story and its later retelling in legend raises the issue of the position of women in the Athenian warrior culture, with its sophisticated politics and philosophizing, and with, by the fifth century B.C.E., a male homosocial base. In a sense, the eroticized young male of the heterosexual sacred marriage became the linchpin of a male system of desire, which incorporated, yet at the same time excluded, women.

The themes in Sappho's writing and in her life and the later fate of that writing and of her biography raise issues relating to traditions of aging women as wise or as foolish, as self-directed or as sexual. Appearance and objectification are also central subjects in the meaning of Sappho. In addition, investigating her meaning raises the issue of dualisms endemic in Western thought, particularly the one which has defined aging women as especially "the other"; as beings largely divorced from male desire yet threatening to patriarchially defined systems of desire.

Sappho and Phaon: A Story of Love and Beauty

WHO WAS Sappho? What the sources reveal is that she came from a wealthy family, that she was married for a time, presumably to a wealthy merchant, and that she had a daughter. She was educated; she probably traveled and competed in the poetry contests then held throughout the Greek world. Alcaeus, a renowned contemporary male poet from Lesbos, was her friend and perhaps her lover. She may have been involved in politics: some sources suggest that she was exiled from Lesbos for a time because of political involvements. But much about her life is not certain. The paucity of contemporary sources surrounds her with mystery. One scholar speculates that even the name Sappho may have been a pseudonym.[5]

Later Greek and Roman sources, as well as her extant poems, seem to indicate that at some point she began teaching young women and that they came from throughout the Greek world to study with her. Whether or not she opened a school for them is a matter of debate, as is the curriculum taught at the school. Some scholars think that her young women acolytes were in training to become poets, learning the craft from a great artist. Others think that Sappho taught her students only composition and rhetoric. Conversely, because she composed a number of odes for use at weddings, some scholars think that the training she provided was in the social skills needed for marriage. But there may have been subversion in her teaching. In Lesbos and the nearby mainland states of Lydia and Caria, laws and customs accorded women more freedom than in many Greek states. At the time Sappho lived, Lesbian women were known for their independence. (Lydia and Caria were the supposed home of the mythical Amazons.)

Finally, the argument was advanced early in this century that her school was connected with a temple to the goddess Aphrodite and that she was the high priestess of the temple, with her students as initiates.[6] Most recent scholars discount this interpretation, but some support for it might be found in her poems about Aphrodite. In one she implores Aphrodite to leave Crete and to come to the sacred grove on Lesbos, which is filled with apple trees. In another she speaks of girls dancing around an altar of love. The young god is also present in her poetry. Her poem about Adonis is one of the earliest extant descriptions of women's mourning ritual for him.

The major focus of Sappho's poems is on love and sensual desire, and her special sentiments are directed toward the young women around her. The emotions she enunciates about them seem more than statements of friendship. Scholars generally agree that her love for them and theirs for her probably included physical involvement. Thus she wrote of one of her young students:

> *I bid you, Abanthis, take [your lyre?] and sing of*
> *Gongyla, while desire once again flies around you,*
> *the lovely one—for her dress excited you when you*
> *saw it; and I rejoice.*
> *[for when] I look at you face to face, [not even]*
> *Hermione [seems to be like you], and to compare you*
> *to golden-haired Helen [is not unseemly] . . .[7]*

Not until a century or so after her death did the story of Sappho's unrequited longing for a young man appear. Some of the fifth-century vases which depict Sappho also depict Phaon. Sappho does not appear as a character in plays by Aeschylus, Sophocles, and Euripides. With his mordant comic pen Aristophanes often satirized aging women, but he did not choose to impugn Sappho. The misogynistic comedy writers of the fourth century, however, seem to have mocked her. Because only a few fragments of these fourth-century works about her have survived, we do not know their precise treatment. The Sappho-Phaon story was apparently featured, however, since one of these plays was entitled *Phaon* and another was called *Leukadia* (the name of the cliffs from which she presumably leaped).[8]

In her own age and for some centuries after, her reputation precluded any attempt to denigrate her work. What then seems to have occurred was the invention of a tale of heterosexual rejection on the basis of her age—or the embroidering of a relationship which may have occurred and the details of which became obscured over time. No modern scholar believes that Sappho was involved with a man named Phaon. But the story embedded her fame in the framework of a typical woman's life. She was not unique; her unrequited love for a man made her, in the end, only ordinary. For what really mattered to her was not the women who surrounded her but rather a beautiful young man whom her fame might fascinate for a time, but who would inevitably leave her, an aging woman.

Socrates drank the hemlock and took his life because he held to his own beliefs over acquiescence to state doctrine. Sappho killed herself not out of strength but out of weakness, because of ungovernable passion and the fear of aging. She became a menopausal woman for whom a sexual attachment to a young man became a way of escaping age, of fleeing the inescapable loss of desirability. Her love for a young man replicated that connection between older and younger men idealized in fifth-century Athens. But her failure only proved that women could not deal rationally with such relationships, that they would eventually be destroyed by their irrationality.

The most complete rendition of the Sappho-Phaon story from the Graeco-Roman world is contained in Ovid's first-century C.E. *Heroides*. Sappho is Ovid's letter writer, and she writes Phaon just after he has rejected her. She is the desperate lover, willing to do anything to regain her beloved. Her students no longer interest her: "The love that belonged to many maids you alone possess." She can no longer write poetry, for she was dependent on her young male lover for her inspiration. "My genius had its power from him; with him they were swept away." Ovid repeats the tradition that Phaon was tall and beautiful and that Sappho was small, dark, and ugly. Sappho has no control over the relationship; the power is Phaon's.[9]

Ovid rendered the Sappho-Phaon story as real, and, indeed, her poems indicate that she may have had some involvement with a younger man. "I am overcome with desire for a boy because of slender Aphrodite," writes Sappho. But her poems further indicate not that this younger lover abandoned her but that, if such a relationship existed, she was the one to end it. Here is the major passage: "But if you are my friend, take the bed of a younger woman, for I will not endure being the elder one in a partnership."

Given the fragmentary state of Sappho's work, interpreting such a brief statement is perilous. Yet it should be viewed in the context of Sappho's view of love, and that view is not unambiguously favorable. As often as Sappho implores Aphrodite for the gift of passion, her descriptions of it are not entirely laudatory. For it is a "loosener of limbs." It is an emotion that, as many Greek writers presented it, could produce madness. And there is also her tribute to the goddess Artemis, different in her depiction from Aphrodite. She portrays Artemis, the virgin hunter, as free because she is free of the tyranny of love.

> Artemis swore the [gods'] great oath: By your head, I shall always be a virgin [unwed], [hunting] on the peaks of the [lonely] mountains: come, grant this for my sake. So she spoke, and the father of the blessed gods nodded his consent; and gods [and men] call her [the virgin, shooter of deer], huntress, a great title. Love, [loosener of limbs], never approaches her. . . .

Thus Sappho rejects her lover in a willful, not a despondent, tone: "I will not endure being the elder one in a partnership . . ." An aging wise woman, she is no longer interested in experiencing the difficulties of love. She sees her future, and her aging, as solitary. But there is no reason to conclude from the lines she wrote about aging that she was in despair. "The moon has set and the Pleiades; it is midnight, and time goes by, and I lie alone." The lines as much indicate a triumphant acceptance of aging, a coming to terms with individual aloneness, as they do a sense of failure.[10]

The fantastical elements that permeate the Sappho-Phaon story also cast doubt on its validity. And the fantasy seems related to the goddess/ young god typology. In the first instance the name Phaon is a variant of Phaethon, and both of these names are Greek variations of the Semitic name Adonis, Aphrodite's primary lover. The name Adonis means "lord." Thus the story itself may have been derived from legends regarding Aphrodite and Adonis, important figures in Sappho's poetry. Indeed, old tales regarding Aphrodite assert that, disconsolate over having lost

Phaethon, she herself presumably leaped off those same Leukadian cliffs which, white and massive, were a landmark in the ancient world and remain so today. They were popularly known as "lover's leap."[11]

From them, in a rite devoted to Apollo, the Leukadian inhabitants had, in ancient times, thrown a criminal into the sea to expiate community sins. This scapegoat rite, however, was as much symbolic as sadistic. Despite the actual height of the cliffs, the story is that the culprit wore a mass of bird wings to break the fall, and rescue boats hovered at the bottom of the cliffs. The point is that to later imaginations these were safe cliffs: lovers leapt from them as an antidote to the "madness" of love, not intending suicide. Even Sappho, according to Ovid, leapt from the cliffs not to kill herself but to cure herself. Moreover, as Hesiod reveals in the *Theogony,* the ocean had originally been the realm of Hecate. From the womb of this generative goddess Aphrodite had been born when the seed of Kronos fell into the sea.[12] The ocean, then, was restorative, bringing peace, quenching the fires of love.

There is further fantasy within the Sappho-Phaon story. Enmeshed in it is an age transformation experience not unknown to goddess/young god relationships and which would later appear in European folk and fairy lore. In this case, the transformation involved Phaon and his position as the pilot of the ferry between Lesbos and the mainland. As the story went, Phaon had not always been a beautiful young man. Rather, he had previously been old and ugly. He became irresistible to women only as the result of the boon of beauty granted to him by the goddess Aphrodite, who happened one day to be his passenger. Beauty, however, was not the primary gift given him. Rather, the original Phaon was not young but old and what Aphrodite gave him was youth.

Sappho's identification with Aphrodite in her poems underscores the transposition in the Sappho-Phaon story from the divine woman to the human one. Moreover, Phaon's original identification as old seems related to his position as ferryman. The mythological figure Charon who piloted the boat between the earth and the underworld across the River Styx was supposed to have been a cranky old man, who demanded large sums of money to ferry dead souls across the river. In the Sappho-Phaon story, the supposed reason that Aphrodite gave the boon of youth to Phaon was because he had not charged her for the trip. Thus the older Charon, the messenger of death, may have been transposed into the younger Phaon, the bringer of Sappho's tragic fate.

The subverting of the older relationship between goddesses and young gods was hereby utilized to remodel Sappho's life story. The goddess of ancient myth became the great poet Sappho. The dying god of ancient ritual was transposed into an old man and then transformed into a young man. Thus in the Sappho-Phaon tale divine mythology becomes human. But the human story, filtered through the patriarchal imagination, involves a reversal. With divinity removed, the mortal woman becomes powerless, helpless in her desire for a young man, even though this mortal woman was a poet of renown.[13]

And Sappho is ugly, while Phaon is beautiful. This small detail of the story (which historically may or may not be true) is important in understanding the transformation sequence of age into youth. For transformation myths in which old individuals become young are not uncommon in later European folk and fairy tales. But in later Western tradition, they usually take a different form. Rather than old men being transformed into young men, more often old women are transformed into young women. Sometimes the transformation occurs so that they will be appropriate lovers for the young heroes of the tales (as in the story which the Wife of Bath tells in *The Canterbury Tales*). Or, as with Alcina in Ariosto's *Orlando Furioso,* or Duessa in Spenser's *Faerie Queene*, these "loathly ladies" (as they are often called) are really evil witches who take on the temporary appearance of youth so that they can lure unsuspecting men into their clutches.

When men are transformed in later tales, most often the transformation is not from age to youth but rather from an animal form to a human form, as in Beauty and the Beast or the Frog Prince. In these stories the love of a beautiful woman, expressed through a kiss, releases the beautiful prince imprisoned in an animal exterior. Such variations in an ancient folk motif undoubtedly have multiple meanings. But what interests me here is the extent to which aging men in this later tradition are hidden in an animal form and aging women remain exposed as aging women. Women are thus vulnerable to beastly descriptions of their personal appearance which focus on their presumed ugliness.

The impassioned grotesques in Greek mythology are mostly ugly aging women: the Furies, the Harpies, Lamia. Old men are more kindly souls. The Sileni, followers of Dionysus, are cheerful drunks; Tiraeus, the blind prophet who had been both a man and a woman (and who maintained that women enjoy sex more than men) seems wise and forgiving. In these descriptions of aged women as vengeful and ugly, the goddesses are transformed and their power defused, as conceptions of ugliness and beauty come to be major conceptual categories of Western dualistic modes of thought.[14]

Sappho is ugly, and Phaon is beautiful. Our Western rational and technological mode of thought, many feminists have argued, is based on drawing distinctions between bifurcated conceptual categories. Reason and emotion, nature and culture, good and evil, are some of the dualisms by which we order our world and which serve as the basis for dividing people. The cross-dressing of the Galli was perhaps based on the attempt to bridge these divisions. Marija Gimbutas's speculations about early Neolithic androgyny resonate with such holism. Two of the dichotomies characteristically drawn especially interest me: that between youth and age and between ugliness and beauty. For if sharp distinctions are drawn in these areas, any holistic pattern of aging allowing flexibility and individuality becomes difficult to achieve. And if the young are beautiful and the aging ugly, comity between them may be unattainable.

Moreover, within these categories lies a fundamental problem with objectification, that characteristic definition of women in terms of physical appearance which denies their individuality. Thus the aging Sappho was rendered doubly the other: she was not only an irrational aging woman, she was ugly: witchlike in physicality but, even then, impotent to attain her goals.

Yet beauty was not, then as later, an inevitably beneficent quality, even for the young. To individuals beauty could bring destruction, to society, chaos. Those conceptual categories of ugliness and beauty always had nuances which cast doubt on their universal validity. Thus the beauty of Helen of Troy, famed in her own day and ever since, plunged her world into warfare and brought her only an ambivalent happiness.[15]

Nor was beauty, in the ancient world as after, always equated with a precise physical appearance. Anticipating a theme common to centuries of writing on personal appearance, Sappho asserted that qualities of character and not the look of face or body were what counted in judging beauty. For "he that is beautiful is beautiful as far as appearances go, while he that is good will consequently also be beautiful."

There was also the long tradition, built on centuries of reasoning like that of Sappho's, that history's most beautiful women possessed positive qualities of spirit rather than of face or figure. Plutarch accessed the tradition in his biographical remarks about the Egyptian queen Cleopatra in his *Lives*. According to Plutarch, Cleopatra's features were pleasing, but she was not beautiful. Her attraction lay in the force of her personality, her wit and ability at conversation, what we might call charisma. "Her beauty was not altogether beyond compare," wrote Plutarch, "but her companionship was irresistible and spellbinding. Her appearance, added to the persuasiveness of her conversation and to her character … had something animating about it."[16]

This tradition of beauty as absent when one might think it essential will continue to distinguish later individuals featured in my story. These include Alice Perrers, the mistress of Edward III of England in the fourteenth century and the possible model for Chaucer's Wife of Bath. They extend to Diane de Poitiers, in the sixteenth century the famed lover of Henry II of France. In the seventeenth century they include Ninon de Lenclos, the famed courtesan and friend of philosophers. The *salonnières* of the eighteenth century also fit into this category, as does Sarah Bernhardt, the eminent nineteenth-century actress. With regard to all of these women it was often said that they were not really beautiful, that they captivated through qualities of spirit.

Yet whatever beauty has been, it has rarely been socially cohesive. Rather, its focus on narcissistic individualism, on a perfection only with difficulty attained, has engendered counterproductive envy and competition. Men strive in athletic contests, at least displaying attained skills. Women compete in beauty contests, like that of the Judgment of Paris. But the contests over physical beauty only extend objectification and further devalue difference, creating narrow standards that few women can really approximate. In the ancient world the women of Lesbos had a reputation for beauty; some sources report that beauty contests among women were held there. If Sappho was in fact ugly, how did she fare? Or were the reports of the beauty of Lesbian women and of the contests over it held on Lesbos fictions of a later patriarchal imagination?[17]

Beauty is a central subject in Sappho's poetry. But here rivalry is not intended. Rather, the enjoyment of each other's pleasing appearance unites women. "My lovely friends," writes Sappho, "how could I change towards you who are so beautiful?" Her students seem like her daughters, and she represents her love for them as akin to what she feels for her own child. For Sappho beauty is a generalized quality. Possessed by many, it becomes universalizing. Evident in individual situations, it yet transcends age or objectified cultural standards. It can be ubiquitous, possessed by many, not just a few. It can involve individual self-realization, or it can be generated in the context of fulfilling relationships.

Athenian Standards:
The Problematics of Pederasty

"THAT THE [MALE] YOUTH, the *kouros*, was raised to
its ideal gives Greek culture as a whole its peculiar character." Thus
concludes classicist Walter Burkert.[18] Athenian civilization of the fifth
century B.C.E. found in the idealization of the appearance of young men,
who had once been consorts of goddesses, a primary beauty standard. The
most praised relationship in ancient Athens was that between an older
man and a younger man. And these presumptions impinged on definitions
and situations for women.

In classical Athens women lived within authoritarian families. They
married at young ages, often as young as twelve. Men, on the other hand,
did not marry until the age of thirty, until after they had completed
military service. Aristotle contended that the ideal marriage was between
a woman of eighteen and a man of thirty-seven. This age difference,
according to many, produced the best physiological matings. "It is highly
wrong," wrote Euripides, "to join together two young persons of the same
age, for the strength of the man lasts far longer, while the beauty of the
female body passes away more rapidly." This age differentiation also
reinforced male domination in marriage.[19]

Throughout history and across cultures, for older men to marry
younger women has not been uncommon. Behind this practice anthropologists have found various motives. These have ranged from aging men's
psychological desire to re-create their youth through union with young
women to the economic drive in polygamous societies for aging men to
have additional wives as symbols of wealth or as supplementary laborers
within the family economy. (This last motive often operates to aid aging
wives who find hard labor too difficult.) Whatever the cause, such marital
arrangements grant power to aging men. They can create what some
anthropologists term a "gerontocracy."[20]

The practice of aging men marrying young women can also generate
the basis for its undermining. For younger wives may outlive aging
husbands, becoming widows outside of male control. Moreover, high rates
of female death in childbirth can generate a situation in which men,
marrying younger wives as they age, multiply the age gap between partners and make even more inevitable the creation of widows. And, in
societies with regular participation in warfare or other kinds of violence,

rates of death among adult males can approximate those of women in childbirth, thereby further contributing to the creation of widows. In later eras of European history a proportion of these widows will marry younger men.

In ancient Athens, however, such behavior was not common. The key factor here as later was property. When women controlled their property, they controlled their life disposition. In later European experience marital dowries which remained under women's authority after their husbands' death would afford autonomy. But Athenian law and custom gave men power over property. Husbands controlled dowries. If divorce occurred, the head of the woman's natal family assumed proprietorship. Sons, not widows, inherited family estates. If a couple had no sons, many fathers adopted a son-in-law or a male child from another family.[21]

Moreover, if a father's death resulted only in a female heir, the law required this woman to marry an older male relative of her father even if she had to divorce a husband to do so. This practice, intended to ensure family property intact, was so institutionalized that a name was given to the woman involved; she was called an *epiklaros*. Evidence suggests that the practice produced marriages between young women and their uncles.[22] Indeed, Athenian law decreed that men could not marry women older than they.

In Athens patriarchy for citizen women was rigid. They were not formally educated. They were sequestered in separate living quarters. They veiled themselves when they left their homes; older slaves accompanied them when out-of-doors. They were not present at men's entertainments. At these events either prostitutes or hetairai, educated noncitizen courtesans, provided any desired female companionship. Evidence suggests that selective female infanticide was practiced to ensure positive adult sex ratios. However, polygamy was not a part of marital arrangements, although a husband could have a concubine. Married couples established their own households; thus the mother-in-law role, which in many societies affords aging women authority, was muted.[23]

Yet many of the restrictions on women's freedom were lifted for aging women in their postmenopausal years. They could move around the city with impunity; they served as messengers and midwives. The age of forty marked the dividing line when both men and women were credited with greater rationality and authority. In all probability this age was, for many women, the time when menopause occurred. In the *Theaetetus,* Plato wrote that postmenopausal midwives knew chants and administered drugs that could "induce labour and relieve the pains" and could "bring a difficult birth to a successful conclusion." He also noted that these aging midwives were Athens's most skilled marriage matchmakers, although he cautioned that in pursuing this end there was some danger they might be confused with go-betweens procuring for prostitution.[24]

Priestesses were selected from among postmenopausal women: in Athens fourteen aging women, the *gerarai,* were the priestesses of Dionysus. In public cults some forty aging women served as priestesses, and many more held subpriestly positions. The woman chosen as the Pythia at Delphi, the priestess at the Greek world's major oracular site, had to be postmenopausal. Aging women also served as ritual mourners at funerals, although by law they could not perform this service outside their own family until they were over sixty years of age.[25] Athenian sons by law had to support their mothers in their old age, thereby honoring these women's revered contribution to the state through the production of sons.

Yet aging women occupied an ambiguous position in this Athenian culture which glorified young males. If they were mothers of aristocratic families, in drama the tendency was to idealize them and to display close family bonds, as Homer does in the *Odyssey* in the relationship between Odysseus and his mother. Aristocratic women like Euripides' Hecuba or former nurses in a number of plays often serve as wise commentators. On the other hand, like Clytemnestra aging women were portrayed as evil. Or they might be satirized as foolish. Aristophanes employs this mode of presentation in several plays highlighting involvements between older women and younger men. The most notable example is his *Ecclesiazusae,* or the *Congresswomen.*

In the *Ecclesiazusae* the social order has been overturned and women control the government. But female irrationality has brought the establishment of a communal state, in which even age and sexual hierarchies have been overturned. The new women rulers have decreed that men must have sexual intercourse with old women before young women and with ugly women before beautiful women. Aristophanes seems to consider this reversal ludicrous. Thus one young male character, realizing that the new order requires him to have sexual relations with three old women before he can approach the young woman he desires, invokes in desperation male gods and heroes. (He also makes a scathing reference to the heavy makeup the older women seem to be wearing.)

Oh Heracles! Oh Pan! Oh ye Corybantes! Oh ye Dioscuri! Why, she is still more awful! Oh! What a Monster! Are you an ape plastered with white lead, or the ghost of some old hag returned from the dark borderlands of death?[26]

Representations of the filial piety toward aging women characteristic of Greek drama found resonance in reality. Aging women were valued for their household skills; they knew the rituals of the ceremonies and festivals which were a constant part of Athenian life. In his plays Aristophanes often mocks older women. But in his *Lysistrata,* the chorus of aging women is contumacious, wise, and youthful in disposition. As in many societies which view women's sexuality as dangerous during their reproductive years and their biological functions as potentially polluting, once women became menopausal they were accorded more freedom. Representations of aging women as heavy drinkers can be found in the plays of ancient Athens, as well as portrayals of them as witches. But these stereotypes, which would become endemic in Roman culture, were muted in the Greek world.

Yet classical Athens was preeminently masculine. The Athenians of this age privileged male same-sex relationships, specifically those between older men and adolescent boys. From this kind of relationship comes our word pederasty: in Greek *pais* means "boy" and *erastes* means "lover." Young men were the primary love objects. It was not that women were not considered beautiful: goddesses and courtesans are described as beautiful; the Greek word for "beautiful" (*kalos*) applied to both women and men. Yet in artistic representations, ideal female beauty approximated the young male body, with breasts added and minus external genitals. The depilation of bodily hair practiced by women reflected the regard for young males as the ideal. The pillar which stood in front of every Athenian house had a head of Hermes on top of a phallus. Hermes, like Apollo, was a special patron of young men. Hermes' son, Eros, at first a figure without any particular plastic representation, by the fifth century had become a beautiful young man. Eros was especially the god of same-sex love.[27]

In fifth-century Athens, while young women remained at home, young men spent their days in athletic training and educational tutoring in special sections of the male gymnasium. The gymnasium contained baths and athletic equipment; men of all ages congregated there for exercise, leisure, and conversation. These buildings were adorned with statues of Hermes, Heracles, and especially Eros. Men exercised in the nude. That the naked bodies of young men might attract older men does not seem unreasonable.

Recent historians disagree over the nature of Greek homosexuality. They note that young men convicted of prostituting themselves could lose their citizenship. They further note that the older men did the pursuing and that young men inviting notice could be censured. Indeed, Plutarch's later description of the courting of the young Alcibiades by a number of older men and of Alcibiades' reluctance to yield to any of them underscores this point. The ideals of moderation and of self-control were central to the Greek ethos; these ideals could vitiate passionate attachments.[28]

Yet as David Halperin points out, it is difficult to gainsay the Greek tradition grounding same-sex relationships in a mentoring function.[29] Arguments tracing them to prestate male initiation ceremonies may falter because of the hazy proof of the existence of these ceremonies. Still it seems they functioned to bring young men into the community of Athenian free adult males. The expectation was that the older men would mentor their young partners toward proper citizenship. "For I cannot say what is a greater good for a man in his youth than a lover, and for a lover than a beloved," states the character Phaidros in the *Symposium*. Phaidros also contends that all great statesmen had been so partnered in their youths.[30]

Athenian male same-sex love, with its emphasis on guidance toward virtue, can be interpreted as paralleling the woman-centered love that Sappho may have practiced. She also may have taught students a richer style of living, a fuller use of mind and body. Mentoring relationships characteristically comprise nurturing, guidance, and a mental involvement that can become passionate and physical. Although Socrates was remembered as being ugly, the tradition was that Alcibiades accepted him as a lover because of his mental and moral excellence; his appeal lay in spiritual, not physical, qualities.[31]

Yet Athenian male-centered love was also of an exclusionary sort which valorized male desire and provided an intense bonding experience among men. The subordination of women in ancient Athens was due more than anything else to what was regarded as their voracious sexuality and their polluting biology in the context of the motivation to keep intact the family line, located in the *oikos,* the private basic building block of the public state. Citizenship was determined by the status of the mother, not the father.[32] Penelope may have been an ideal, but Clytemnestra was the feared model of behavior. In the xenophobic world of the militaristic Greek city-states, in which over the centuries Athens was consistently threatened by war, fears about the dilution of patriarchal inheritance through female adultery were institutionalized in laws and customs. Such fears remained constant in later European ages, but they were heightened in the relatively small Athenian territory.

Yet concerns also existed about young males and their willingness to conform to the competitive, militaristic requirements of the Athenian state. The Greeks considered children, both male and female, as wild and requiring taming.[33] Historical examples of young men putting self-importance before state service were only too apparent in the cases of Achilles in the *Iliad* initially refusing out of personal pique to come to the aid of the state and in the suitors violating Odysseus's honor in the *Odyssey*. The brilliant Alcibiades, often cited in contemporary texts, was an example both of a hero in the making and of heroic character used for self-service. Because of his outrageous behavior, he was eventually banished from Athens. The first part of Plato's *Republic* focuses on the issue of educating young men; so fearful is Socrates that the goal of dedication to heroic state service may not be realized that he suggests the past be rewritten to eliminate any moral failure on the part of heroes like Achilles.[34]

Crucial to understanding Athenian pederasty is the age at which young men were considered appropriate mates. In descriptions of ideal appearance it is the amount of hair on the face that matters: the greatest beauty in young men was presumed to be at that time in the teenage years just before they developed a beard, when cheeks would have only fuzz on them.[35] "Beardless" was the customary eroticized term, in ancient Athens as it would be in later centuries. In the *Symposium,* Plato describes Achilles as not only beautiful but also "beardless." Ovid characterized his fictionalized Phaon in the *Heroides* as still in the "age of first down" that "stirs men's love."[36]

Like women and children, these "beardless" boys, on the verge of entering their military service to the state, had to be brought into submission. But their submission also involved teaching them to be dominant, to be heroic warriors. Their real beauty lay in the promise of muscular bodies and full-bearded faces. The Greek ideal was neither the wily Odysseus nor the feminized Adonis; rather it was Heracles, the hero who performed Herculean labors to prove his position as the son of Zeus who could "protect both gods and man against destruction." Thus Plato describes the wrong kind of young male lover as "soft rather than tough ... accustomed to luxurious and effeminate living, supplying his natural deficiency of complexion by the use of cosmetics."[37]

These young men could not be trivialized. They were welcomed, if initially vicariously, into participation in the Greek state of free adult

males, built upon class and gender hierarchy, through the mechanism of
love. But it was partly the martial ideal of self-control they were being
taught; thus some scholars argue that they were supposed to display no
pleasure during the sexual act.

Yet under Athenian male same-sex love the male sense of self involved
a male continuum in which women were regarded, more than anything
else, as part of men. As keepers of the *oikos,* women were identified with
the political goals of the expansion of state population and the fears of
destruction by wanton military force. Metaphorically, one might posit that
the erotic Sappho, relating to women as well as to men, became the
masculinized Athena, born from the brain of Zeus. Athena, Athens's
founding deity, was the goddess of war as well as of wisdom. On her
shield she bore a representation of the head of Medusa, the woman with
hair of snakes as symbol of horror. But Medusa was also a woman who,
in ancient legend, had once rivaled Helen of Troy in beauty.

Still the Eleusinian Mysteries were always associated with women. Such
an association was even more the case with regard to the yearly ritual
celebration known as the Thesmophoria. In this Athenian ritual women
moved out of their homes to an area at the foot of the Acropolis. For
three days they celebrated both their childbearing role and their temporary
freedom from household responsibility. Within the *oikos* their skills at
spinning and weaving and other elements of homemaking were not
discounted. John Winkler and other recent revisionists of the scholarly
position that Athenian women were rigidly oppressed have argued that
Athenian women possessed a "double consciousness" of their identity,
realizing their importance in the household and their central position in
rites pertaining especially to Dionysus and to Demeter and Persephone.
Yet consistent fears of women and the attempt to contain them, Page
DuBois argues, permeated Athenian culture. Central to these fears was
the concern with the power of woman as mother, who was parthenogenic,
like the earth, and omnipotent, adequate in herself, not needing the male.[38]

The work of Plato is, in particular, contradictory on this issue of
women's position. Plato begins the *Republic* with an intimation of participating in goddess rites; in the *Phaedrus* he attributes to Sappho his belief
that mind as well as body had to be involved in fulfilling relationships as
well as his knowledge of Orphism, another mystery religion centered
around goddess worship that had surfaced in the seventh century B.C.E.
In the *Timaeus* he endows the world with a female soul, "in origin and
excellence prior to and older than the body."[39]

His most famous reference to an independent woman, however, is contained in the *Symposium,* where he refers to Diotima, a wise woman from Mantinea. The reference occurs in the passages analyzing various types of loves and their relationship to his conceptions of two versions of the goddess Aphrodite. One is the common Aphrodite, born of the union of Zeus with a woman. The second is the heavenly Aphrodite, born solely of the seed of the male god Kronos spilled into the ocean. The common Aphrodite, he argues, inspired only an inferior male love for women; the second, the heavenly one, inspired a superior love for men.

Yet a wise woman, Diotima, suggests an even richer kind of love. This love does not involve sexual possession but rather is based on an ascetic, spiritual contemplation that is "far above gold and raiment and beautiful boys and men." Plato associates Diotima with a real city, Mantinea, and reveals that through prayer and sacrifice to the gods she kept the plague away from Athens for ten years. Yet scholars disagree over whether Plato's Diotima was actually meant to be a real woman or simply a metaphor for male creativity viewed in a generative, and hence female, manner. Still, viewed in the context of Plato's references to wise women and goddesses elsewhere in his work, it is reasonable to speculate that Diotima reflects some understanding of the possibility of women's previously divine authority, of an archetype still existing in cultural consciousness. Page DuBois's work about Athenian recognition of the ancient and earthly powers of women underscores this possibility.[40]

In this regard an interesting source is the funeral oration in Plato's *Menexenus.* This oration is delivered by Aspasia, the famed hetaira whom Pericles, Athens's great fifth-century statesman, eventually married. Most scholars consider the speech to be a fiction. But what Aspasia has to say about women and the origins of Athens may be revealing of a male "double consciousness" about women, an understanding of their historical position as creators as well as the patriarchal subversion of that originating position. For Aspasia describes the original Athenians as autochthonous, as men who sprang by parthenogenesis from the land and who were nurtured by the earth who bore them. Then, when the earth had raised them, she introduced male gods as their rulers and teachers. It was these men, Aspasia concludes, "who taught us the primary arts, and the possession and use of weapons in the defense of our fatherland."[41]

Thus Plato in brief encompasses the original mythology of the primacy of the mother, of the passage of power to males, and of the creation of that combination of militarism and creative thought that underlay the culture of ancient Athens. In the end, however, in Aspasia's words, the motherland had become the "fatherland."

The Roman Scenario:
Women's Power and Sexuality and Their Obverse

In the first century c.e. the Greek philosopher
Plutarch wrote a dialogue entitled *On Love*. This dialogue differs from
Plato's writings on the subject. In this treatise Plutarch explores the
situation of Ismendora, a wealthy thirty-year-old woman, who loves Bacchon, a handsome youth of eighteen. The dialogue addresses two issues:
first, should Bacchon ignore convention and marry Ismendora, and, second, is the love of men for each other preferable to their love for women?

On the issue of heterosexual versus same-sex love, Plutarch's answer is
simple. Women's intelligence and physical attractiveness can equal men's;
thus they are capable of the highest love. "The noble lover of beauty,"
writes Plutarch, "engages in love wherever he sees excellence and splendid
natural endowment without regard for any difference in physiological
detail." Plutarch sees no problem in the marriage of Ismendora and
Bacchon. He dismisses the jokes that Bacchon's young hunting companions make about his prospective marriage to an older woman. To the
dialogue disputants who argue that Ismendora will control her younger
husband, Plutarch replies that the older male rivals for Bacchon's favor
are just as likely to become domineering. Like any male mentor, the
virtuous and intelligent Ismendora can lead Bacchon toward a productive
life. "What is so dreadful about a sensible older woman piloting the life
of a younger man?" queries Plutarch.[42]

Plutarch lived at a time when women had attained many freedoms,
despite Roman laws initially meant to constrain them. In Rome of the
first century c.e., the male realms of politics and the professions remained
closed to women. But Roman mores had not sequestered them nor denied
them an education. Although bisexuality was common among Roman
men, there seems to have been no ritualized attention to male same-sex
love. Wives presided equally with husbands in household religion; the
Vestal Virgins, six virgin women who tended the state's sacred fire and
symbolized its might through purity, served from the time they were
young girls until they were in their forties. In contrast to the Athenians,
the early Romans did not view women in terms of pollution or, before
the late republican era, their independent position as threatening. Rome's
founding goddess was Venus, the goddess of love. The Roman Venus,

unlike the capricious Greek goddess of love, Aphrodite, was a benign deity.[43]

Roman family law originally was structured around a male patriarch, the "paterfamilias," holding life-and-death power over his family. But over the centuries Roman women gained the right to apply to the courts to contravene the decisions of fathers or guardians. Eventually well-to-do women gained a certain amount of control over their dowries and over the right of divorce. Moreover, such forces as growing individualism and concepts of pleasure engendered by the material wealth of imperial Rome created social conditions conducive to moderating the constrictions of the patriarchal family.

Among the elites, women married at young ages, and age disparities of a decade or more were not uncommon between husbands and wives. These disparities, however, were never so large as among the Greeks. This pattern of age at marriage inevitably produced numbers of widows, but these women did not tend to remarry. The Roman elites held to the ideal of the *univora,* of the woman who expressed her marital loyalty by having only one husband during her lifetime.[44] Family inheritance not uncommonly passed through widows, who were trusted to pass family funds to the next generation. Later European inheritance practices which favored widows reflected these Roman precedents.

Within the family, according to Judith Hallett, fathers especially valued daughters; women were always called by a feminine form of their father's family name, no matter how many marriages they contracted. Hallett finds in elite society strong expressions of "matrilineal" sentiment even though Roman society was at base patriarchal.[45] In line with this woman-oriented sentiment, Roman mores also accorded respect and authority to aging women. Sons were expected to support aging widowed mothers. In Roman society, prestige accumulated with age: the Romans referred to the maternal and paternal ascendants as *magnus,* or "great." They thus established a precedent for the later European practice of calling these relatives "grand" parents. And, the respect accorded aging women could extend beyond the family: some Roman medical authors praised women knowledgeable about female physiology and suggested the existence of an oral healing tradition among women.[46]

Despite writings which celebrated the matrons of Rome's early years, late republican and imperial authors often criticized individual, powerful women. Plutarch presented Ismendora in a positive light as wealthy, socially respectable, and a powerful personality. In these traits, she resembled many legendary women of the late republican and imperial eras. The reputations of these women, however, have suffered in writings about them. Thus Clodia, known for her affair with the poet Catullus in the first century c.e., had a series of younger lovers after the death of her husband. Because of her behavior, considered licentious in a woman, Cicero called her a "Clytemnestra." The poet Martial wrote about the "chaste" Laevina who bathed in Lake Avernus and then "falls into flames, leaves her husband, and follows a youngster."[47]

In that same century Julia, the daughter of Caesar Augustus, engaged in such presumed libertine behavior that her father banished her from Rome. Messalina, whose name has become legendary for sexual depravity, was the wife of Emperor Claudius. Claudius's third wife, she was married to him when she was fourteen and he was forty-eight. (Such an age disparity makes one suspicious of her supposed sexual misdeeds.) The satirist Juvenal pilloried her in his sixth and tenth satires, accusing her of such depravity that she spent many nights as a brothel prostitute and that she had forced a young man into undergoing a public and humiliating mock marriage with her.

> *This blue-blooded sprig of the higher nobility—*
> *wonderfully handsome, too—is raped and doomed by one glance*
> *From Messalina's eyes. . . .*
> *You refuse her commands, you'll die before lighting-up time. . . .*[48]

To blame Rome's decay on women was not uncommon in late Roman times and ever since. Because women asserted a right to erotic freedom, because they seemed unwilling to bear children, because their actions served to overturn gender and family regularities, the argument concludes that they undermined state stability. Infidelity and divorce seem to have been common in late republican and early imperial Rome, and falling birthrates were a constant concern. Some male writers blamed women for the situation. The laws decreed by Emperor Augustus to reinstate the sanctity of marriage in 18 b.c.e. and 9 b.c.e. established that men between the ages of twenty-five and sixty and women between the ages of twenty-five and fifty were obliged to marry or to remarry. These laws enshrined a ten-year age distinction between men and women in their older years. And, further underscoring this age distinction, prospective wives were supposed to be fertile. Legally, postmenopausal women were thereby excluded from contracting marital relationships.

Roman beliefs about the perfidy of women are evident in Juvenal's

vituperative writings. Juvenal praised sexuality between men and boys:
"Isn't it better to sleep with a pretty boy? Boys don't quarrel all night, or
nag you with little presents while they're on the job, or complain that you
don't come up to their expectations, or demand more grasping passion."
Juvenal contended that married women, often outrageous in behavior,
like Messalina took young male lovers. Drawing from myth, Juvenal also
cited the case of Phaedra with Hippolyte, the stepmother who tried to
seduce her stepson and then, when he refused her, falsely accused him to
his father of attempted rape. Young men, Juvenal contended, acquiesced
to such relationships only out of material greed. In the process, lusting
older women corrupted them into becoming what we call gigolos:

> *Maybe the first time your dream-boy goes with a married*
> *Woman he'll really love her. But when she gets in the habit*
> *Of giving him little presents, it won't be long before*
> *He's become the perfect gigolo, taking them all for their eyeteeth—*
>
> *And remember, there's nothing these women won't do to satisfy*
> *Their ever-moist groins. . . .*[49]

This belief in aging women's sexuality was endemic in imperial Rome.
Thus Ovid depicted the aging Sappho's love for Phaon as an eroticized
impulse, as a desire for his body. And in his fictionalized letter from
Phaedra to Hippolyte in his *Heroides,* Ovid explained the reasons for
aging women's desire. "Love has come to me," writes Ovid's Phaedra,
"the deeper for its coming late." For "she who yields her heart when the
time for love is past, has a fiercer passion."[50]

Upon occasion, this view of aging women as sexual could redound
to their benefit. Both Plutarch, who praised women, and Ovid, often
misogynist, contended that as lovers older women were preferable to
younger women. In *The Art of Love,* a treatise which influenced all later
European writings on erotic relationships, Ovid defined love as an art
"learned late."

> *All the more, if she's past the bloom of her youth, in her thirties . . .*
> *That's a good age, young man, and even a little bit older.*
> *Don't forget, the mature have greater skill in the business:*
> *What experience brings, they are adept to employ. . . .*
> *They are proficient, adroit; they know how not to seem old.*

Drawing from legend, Ovid cited the example of Hermione, the daughter of Helen and Menelaus of Sparta. Hermione was obviously considerably younger than her mother. Her youth notwithstanding, Ovid contended that no one would prefer the daughter to the mother. In this comparison appearance was not precisely the issue to Ovid, despite Helen's reputation for beauty. Rather, what mattered was Helen's greater experience through aging at lovemaking and at making herself desirable.[51]

In contrast to these positive views about aging women expressed by Ovid, other Roman authors viewed sexualized aging women as foolish and dangerous, especially when past menopause. (And Ovid himself expressed such negativity in another writing which I will presently review.) Those aging women Aristophanes ridiculed in the *Ecclesiazusae* as repulsive to the young men they desired pointed the way to the evolution of two aging women characters often found in the writings of Roman poets and dramatists. These characters were not comic but rather were abhorrent and even dangerous. The first was the go-between, the aging whore who, no longer able to attract men, became a procurer of younger women for men. The second was the witch, the aging woman as demonic, with supernatural powers.

Witches and female go-betweens, the so-called lenas, abound in those two major novelistic satires of imperial Rome: Apuleius's *Golden Ass* and Petronius's *Satyricon*. In these books aging sexualized women are present: they prostitute themselves, and they act as go-betweens. They are lenas lurking on street corners or working as vendors, ready to provide women to suit men's tastes, soliciting business with innuendo. They often have access to magic and witchcraft. The narrator of the *Satyricon* meets an old, friendly woman selling vegetables. She soon turns out to be a procuress who takes him to a whore's house. In Apuleius's *Golden Ass*, the central character is turned into an ass partly because he refuses to become sexually involved with the aging woman/witch with whom he has been staying. "She is a witch of the first rank," an acquaintance informs him. "For as soon as she sees an attractive youth, she is on tenterhooks of admiration, and she rivets her eyes and her lustful mind upon him."[52]

The most important description in Roman literature of the go-between as witch is contained in Ovid's description of the old woman Dipsas in his *Amores*. Dipsas is an "aged hag," with "wispy white hair," cynical about love, contemptuous of men. In the *Amores*, Dipsas gives advice to a young woman about how to exploit men sexually for financial gain. In his presentation, Ovid seems to mock Dipsas and to suggest that her power exists more in rumor than in reality. "She's the local witch," writes Ovid, who chants "earth-splitting spiels," "whirls the magic wheel," "culls herbs," "brews aphrodisiacs." Yet he cannot entirely deny her potency. For she can reverse the flow of water and change the weather, "cloud or sunshine, blood red stars (believe it or not) or a bloody moon." At night she changes herself into a bird, "probably flits about in owlish feathers." At least, Ovid concludes, "that's what people say."[53]

The entwined association between the lena's power and Ovid's insinuated undermining of that power is most apparent in the charge that Dipsas is, in fact, a drunkard; so alcoholic that "rosy Dawn has never seen her sober." The charge of drunkenness seems to underscore the degradation of this woman, the depths of depravity into which she has sunk as a sexual purveyor. More than that, the drinking of wine in Roman society was connected to class and gender distinctions: the law forbade respectable married women from drinking wine.[54]

In Rome, as in Greece, wine was associated with the god Dionysus, the legendary provider of the grapes for wine and the only god to have a troupe of women followers. They were the Maenads, a band of women prone to frenzied spiritual possession. Thus Dipsas's drunkenness, with its similar implication of loss of self-control, also signified the mystical powers of the Maenads. Or, given the insulting portraits of drunken old women in Roman drama, the common connection drawn between aging women and what we would call alcoholism may have been meant to trivialize and contain those powers.

Mysticism, the vine, and spirit possession shade into sexuality. For Dipsas's drunkenness could also be interpreted as a metaphor for insatiable sexual desire and by extension the sexual desire of all women, acted out by the elderly outside the bonds of procreative community on the part of women who use their aging wisdom perversely to control not only men but also other women. Juvenal contended, as did others, that go-betweens raised their daughters to be prostitutes, to be certain of support when their own bodies were no longer appealing. "It's profitable," writes Juvenal in the *Sixth Satire*, "for an old whore to bring up her daughter to the trade."[55]

Insinuations of female sexual collusion extended beyond the immediate family, and in the presentations of other authors, speculations about motivation went beyond Juvenal's economic pragmatism. Dipsas in Ovid's depiction included in her band of scheming women not only herself and the young woman she attempted to persuade into prostitution but also the girl's maid, her mother, her sister, and her old nurse. All stood together in a sexual conspiracy designed to entrap men and to gain some sort of depraved power over them.[56] Such perverse fantasies, evident in important Roman texts, would reemerge in later centuries as a basis for identifying and persecuting aging women as witches.

These fantasies had a basis in beliefs about the body. Both Greeks and Romans accorded honor to postmenopausal women, released from the potentially polluting menstrual situation. But a countervailing tradition also existed. For these people believed, as would Europeans in later ages, that menstruation was therapeutically beneficial for women, since it withdrew potentially damaging humors from the body. With the end to menstruation, the body had no way of dispelling these humors; they remained in place, capable of wreaking havoc, both mental and physical.[57]

Plutarch's writing about the wise Ismendora in *On Love* constitutes an alternative construct to these beliefs about the dangerous sexuality of aging women. Yet a third symbolization existed, one drawn from notions of aging women as wise creators. Plutarch himself drew from this tradition in his treatise on Isis and Osiris. Plutarch was a Greek living in the Roman Empire. In his brief biographical remarks about Cleopatra, he showed an understanding of her person as well as her politics. He was also a priest of the Delphic oracle: he bore responsibility for interpreting the mystical pronouncements of the Pythia, the high priestess of Delphi. He daily encountered the matrifocal traditions which underlay Delphic ritual. He also was versed in Platonic thought.

Plutarch found unexceptionable the case of Ismendora and Bacchon. For did it not resemble the story of goddesses and young men, of desire universalized? In his treatise on Isis and Osiris, an important source on the worship of Isis during the Roman era, Plutarch implied such a connection. Human beings yearn for beauty, Plutarch wrote in this text, for the Platonic contemplation of the good. And Plutarch's beauty, as well as his ideal of virtue, overflowed with maternal generativity. "With this beauty Isis, as the ancient story declares, is forever enamoured and pursues it and consorts with it and fills our earth with all things good and fair that partake of generation."[58]

Neoplatonic Idealism:
Woman as Philosophical Symbol and Practitioner

PLUTARCH's egalitarian attitude toward aging women and toward their involvement with younger men reflects a long tradition celebrating women's wisdom. Both Diotima and Ismendora stand in a line of aging women who inspire and guide. One thinks of the mythological Athena, Odysseus's mentor. Or there is Sophia of the Hebrew tradition, the wise woman of the biblical Book of Proverbs, who existed "before the mountains had been shaped, before the hills." By her guidance "kings reign and rulers decree what is just."[59]

This Sophia is also a central figure in the Gnostic gospels, written during the several centuries after the death of Christ and associated with the Gnostic Christian sects of this period. These texts, alternative accounts of the life of Christ and of Christian doctrine, were excluded from the canonized books of the official Bible, compiled by councils of bishops in the fourth century C.E. Eventually they disappeared, to be discovered in Egypt in the 1950s.[60]

In the Gnostic gospels, Sophia is the mother of the god creator. As such, she has infused her son with her energy and wisdom. She stands aside God the Father and the Son to form a trinity alternative to the Christian one with the female divinity neutered into the Holy Spirit. In later Jewish cabalistic beliefs, Sophia becomes the Shekinah, the embodiment of God's power and intelligence, whose radiance permeates the universe.[61]

The centuries which comprised the Hellenistic era witnessed the creation of a rich symbolic pantheon. New abstract figures came into being to take precedence over the personages of Greek and Roman mythology. Roman syncretism and superstition brought the invention of figures like Fortuna, the goddess of luck, an abstract and anthropomorphic amalgam of a number of Greek and Roman goddesses.[62] Moreover, the philosophical system known as Neoplatonism, which originated in the city of Alexandria in Egypt in the third century C.E., combined Platonic idealism with Eastern mysticism to create an additional hagiographic universe. In this universe human virtues and vices were personified as abstracted beings, as in the "seven deadly sins." These several symbolic universes, both separately and in combination, continued to permeate Western expression until rendered more or less obsolete by eighteenth-century rationalism.[63]

In this tradition of women as wise, as progenitors of knowledge and insight, a number of late Roman and early Christian female figures are illustrative. Neoplatonists, for example, divided Plato's female soul of the *Timaeus* into a higher portion which fashioned individual souls from the divine source and a lower portion, natura, which generated the phenomenal world. (In later medieval thought, natura became the goddess Natura, the embodiment of nature.)[64]

Other wise women figures of these early centuries included the Sibyls, ten female prophets who, absent from Greek mythology, first appeared in early Roman times. Also important were Fortuna, whose origins dated from late Roman times, and Philosophia, a personification of the inspiration for the philosophical enterprise who appeared in later centuries. Real women, too, could be included in this Neoplatonic enterprise. The flesh-and-blood Saint Catherine of Alexandria was a learned woman who, martyred because of her Christian beliefs, became the patron saint of early Christian philosophers. She occupied a place in the tradition, dating to Hesiod, that male intellectual and artistic enterprise was inspired by the Muses, the nine representatives of the arts who were the daughters of Zeus and Memory.

Consider the Sibyls, ten female visionaries of venerable age who were presumed to have lived in various places throughout the Mediterranean world. Their supposed prophecies were collected into a volume called the *Sibylline Books*, the origin of which was lost in legend. Eventually the *Sibylline Books* became Rome's most sacred text. The Sibyls continued the ancient Greek oracular tradition into later times. Many of these prophets existed in mythological fantasy rather than reality. But in late Roman times they included the Pythia of Delphi, still a renowned female prophet. They also included the Cumaen Sibyl, a seer who lived in caves at Cuma on the Bay of Naples and whose oracular predictions in the Roman world rivaled in importance those of the Pythia.[65]

In addition to the Sibyls' prophetic insight, what is interesting about them is that each was supposed to have predicted the birth of Christ. This assumption incorporated them into Christianity. They became the precursors of abbesses and female saints; they provided a link between goddess religions and patriarchal Christianity. The Sibyls are often included in those later collections of brief biographies of women which Boccaccio, among others, wrote. In these they are celebrated for Christian piety, for being pagan women who reinforced a Christian message.

Attention to the Sibyls in later European tradition partly derives from the prominence of the Cumaen Sibyl in Virgil's famed first-century B.C.E.

Aeneid. In this text she is the guide of the hero Aeneas in his journey to the underworld. What is especially interesting about Virgil's depiction of this figure is that she is both young and old. She blends age diversity in a manner characteristic of ancient goddesses and of Neoplatonic figures like Philosophia. Virgil alternately calls his Sibyl young and old, a maiden and an ancient seer. She possesses the independence of virginity and the wisdom of aging, combining past and present.[66]

In this tradition of women as the inspirers of creativity, the generators of wisdom and invention, Diotima, Sophia, and the Sibyls were the forerunners of Philosophia in that central early medieval work, Boethius's sixth-century *Consolation of Philosophy.* The influence of this work can be found as late as Dante's fourteenth-century *Divine Comedy.* (Dante probably modeled Beatrice after Boethius's Philosophia.) Like Plato's Diotima, Philosophia is the guide to a spiritualized understanding of reality: she represents Boethius's reconciliation of Christian mysticism with Platonic idealism. In fact, Boethius describes Philosophia as Plato's mother. To Boethius, Philosophia was "a woman of majestic countenance whose flashing eye seemed wise beyond the ordinary wisdom of men. Her color was bright, suggesting boundless vigor, and yet she seemed so old that she could not be thought of as belonging to our age."[67] Like Virgil's Sibyl, Philosophia also combined youth and age in her persona.

Within this philosophical and sacerdotal tradition, the abstract Philosophia was joined by Saint Catherine of Alexandria, a fourth-century flesh-and-blood representative of this conception of wise women. Of pagan background, Catherine was supposed to have mastered the entire corpus of Greek philosophy. Despite this pagan erudition, she accepted Christianity, even to the extreme of being martyred on account of her Christian faith. So powerful was the admiration for her action that, once sainted, she became the patron saint of Christian philosophers. Many, we are told, prayed to her for guidance.[68]

This idea of woman as the source of wisdom, as the inspirer of philosophical reasoning, remained in existence through much of the medieval period. Its basis lay especially in the biblical passages about Sophia. According to Marina Warner, these passages were read from the pulpit on the feast days of the Virgin Mary as late as the tenth century. The visions of medieval female mystics, Warner finds, not uncommonly included a female figure of wisdom as well as the masculine Christ. Female Christian writers like the tenth-century Hrosvitha of Gandersheim identified wise women in their work. In her play *Sapienta* Hrosvitha dramatized through allegory a story of martyrdom reminiscent of Saint Catherine's saga. The name Sapienta is a version of Sophia, and Sapienta, the play's protagonist, is a scholar who has converted to Christianity. In Hrosvitha's version, Sapienta's daughters, Faith, Hope, and Charity, are executed because Sapienta will not renounce Christianity in favor of the goddess Diana.[69]

Yet as valuable as Philosophia was to medieval women writers, this figure of woman as wisdom also provided an unfortunate link between ancient traditions of female divinity and the newer Christian patriarchalism which was inimical to this overriding women's authority. To endure execution rather than recant one's faith may be honorable, but there is a subtext in all these stories about the execution of pious women. It is a subtext implying the execution of female learning. Within the late Roman Empire, Alexandria was a center of learning and also of renowned women scholars. Its famed library, the repository for ancient texts as well as current knowledge, was called the "museum," the place of the Muses. Saint Catherine was martyred there. But so was Hypatia, the eminent Neoplatonic scholar. Hypatia's fifth-century c.e. martyrdom, which occurred a century after that of Saint Catherine, was different. For a mob of fanatic Christians murdered Hypatia for her "pagan" beliefs; she was the last important opponent to the Christianization of Egypt.[70]

During these centuries the trivialization of Sappho also continued. Seen in the context of the fate of these other female thinkers, Sappho's story gains greater force and poignancy. The Sappho-Phaon story can be traced to the fifth century b.c.e.; the Roman poet Ovid codified it in the first century c.e. for the ages in his *Heroides*. At the time Ovid wrote, the corpus of Sappho's work was still extant. It was during the Christian eras that it was either lost or destroyed; the presumed reason was its eroticism. Sensual love between women could not be tolerated; nor could the wisdom of a female writer whose fame in ancient times had once rivaled that of Homer and Plato.

Patriarchal diminutions of traditions of women as the source of wisdom and their reduction into foolish erotic aging women can be seen in the story of Sappho and Phaon. This discounting of aging women is also present in traditions regarding the syncretized female figure Fortuna, probably the most influential and long-lived among these abstracted female images I have cited. Fortuna emerged in early Roman experience, combining in her persona characteristics of many major goddesses. She represented a variety of oppositions: she was order and disorder, wisdom and stupidity, strength and weakness. Yet she did not reconcile opposites (as Philosophia might be seen to do). Fortuna was the ancient forerunner of our "lady luck," an irrational force outside of human control. As such, she was depicted as blind, as incapable of seeing the implications of her action. In later Western iconography she had two faces: one was young and fair, the other aged and ugly. It was said that she lured men with her young beauty and rejected them with her aged maturity. She was both "fair" and "foul."[71] As the latter, she bore relationship to the figure of the witch.

Aging women may have remained over the centuries folk figures who provided for local communities healing, magic, and the accumulated wisdom of long-life experience. Even there, however, two conflicting traditions about menopause existed: the older tradition held that the ending of the menstrual flow brought the positive concentration of these fluids in the brain to produce wisdom; the second tradition posited that the failure, through menstruation, to purge the body of evil humors brought the concentration of these negative forces in the brain to produce aging shrewishness or even a disposition to witchcraft.

Moreover, the potency of women as the progenitors of wisdom within the high-culture tradition of literature, philosophy, and iconography perilously declined over the centuries. By the thirteenth century Thomas Aquinas's Aristotelianism reduced the female creative principle first enunciated by Plato to passive matter acted on by male vitalism.

Renaissance Neoplatonism, its interest in alchemical representations of male and female intertwinings and of ancient goddess religions, brought a reinvigoration in many writings of the concept of woman as creator. "Popular Renaissance literature," writes Carolyn Merchant, "was filled with hundreds of images associating nature, matter, and the earth with the female sex."[72] The figures with which Michelangelo covered the Sistine Chapel ceiling included not only Christian saints and prophets; five Sibyls were also part of his artistic panoply. As in much of his work, Michelangelo used male models for these female bodies intended to illustrate gender interconnections of power and knowledge.

Following tradition, his Cumaen Sibyl is both old and young. "We see her in left profile," writes Norma Goodrich, with "deeply wrinkled folds of aged flesh, leathery-textured skin, mouth slightly agape, raised eyebrows, but very alert eyes, scanning the pages [of her Sibylline book]. . . . All else about her, except her massive strength of swelling back and powerful shoulder, is aged. Overall she exudes great personal power." She could hold up the world, Michelangelo said of her.[73]

Renaissance secularization, however, also brought an eroticization of women, an objectification of their bodies which would become standard in succeeding Western art. By convention, the nude woman would be posed not for her own enjoyment but for that of the male viewer. In artifacts and statuary, women as personifications of abstract qualities like virtue and justice would continue to the present, as in the United States' Statue of Liberty, a representation of the goddess Athena constructed in the late nineteenth century. But these personifications are easily reduced into trivial versions of former grandeur or into sexualized objects of desire, into pornographic representations of women's power as the power to please men—or to threaten them.

So it was too that the nomenclature of the Muses, whose invocation became a standard opening for the works of male poets over the centuries, ultimately became the basis for words like "amusing" and "bemused." These are playful and charming words, hardly related to the grandeur of Hesiod's originating presentation of the Muses as giving poets their voices "and power to sing the story of things of the future, and things past."[74]

And there is Machiavelli's famed sixteenth-century discussion of Fortuna in *The Prince*, a discussion which paints a differing picture of the power of aging women. In his depiction of Fortuna, Machiavelli drew on the convention of women's uncontrollable sexuality to make Fortuna a persona easily manipulated by men, especially by young men. This manipulated Fortuna, in contrast to the independent ancient goddesses, carries forward the convention of Sappho, not independent, but manipulated by Phaon.

For, Machiavelli contended, no woman could resist a young man's wooing. When a man is confronted by an ambiguous life situation, Machiavelli wrote, he should act boldly. For "it is better to be impetuous than cautious." Bold action, Machiavelli continued, would always ensure a better fortune,

> for fortune is a woman, and it is necessary, if you wish to master her, to conquer her by force. . . .

More than this, young men were more likely to secure a better fortune than older men because of the audacity characteristic of their nature, a comely audacity irresistible to women:

> And, therefore, like a woman, she [Fortuna] is always a friend to the young, because they are less cautious, fiercer, and master her with greater audacity. . . .[75]

Machiavelli wrote in the sixteenth century. By that period traditions of eroticized younger men, as well as of aging women, were both similar to and different from what they had been in the many previous centuries of Western development. As time passed, the old themes and topoi both changed and remained the same.

PART THREE

Aging Women in Advance and Retreat: From the Medieval Period to the Eighteenth Century

MY HISTORICAL EXPLORATION of aging women and relationships proceeds through the medieval and early modern European centuries, eras of feudal localism and early state formation. I analyze twelfth-century institutions that allowed women the possibility of greater authority. These included the urban guild structures, which often permitted women ownership, in addition to family inheritance customs, especially in England and France, which favored widows. Courtly love, dating to the eleventh century, was located outside marriage and thus was by definition unconventional. Its tenets did not disparage cross-age associations in which women, because of their age and social rank, might take command.

I note incursions on these institutions and practices as, by the thirteenth century, Europe entered a lengthy era in which the position of women declined, reaching a low point with the seventeenth-century witchcraft persecutions. Over these centuries monarchs consolidating centralized state power employed men in their nascent bureaucracies. They thereby often undermined regional bodies in which women, by reason of inheritance, had participated. Expansive monarchs also valorized the patriarchial family as representing in miniature the centralized state, thereby positioning the father in the family as akin to the male monarch heading the state. The decline in the guild structure, especially with the rise of capitalism, brought male takeovers of formerly female occupations and ownership.

Demographic differences periodically produced—both locally and regionally—"high sex ratios." Under these ratios, with women in short supply, younger men were drawn to aging women. Before romantic love by the late eighteenth century became predominant in marital formation, financial motivation could produce such cross-age associations. Ancient conventions about the sexuality of aging women, even after menopause, also continued.

The English poet Geoffrey Chaucer's Wife of Bath in his fourteenth-century *The Canterbury Tales* elucidates many of these trends. As well, the story of her young fifth husband, Jenkin, illuminates the subject of young men and their ambiguous position in a European social system in which popular ideologies about life-cycle and gender irregularities as well as demographic imbalances could serve to contest the dominant commitment to hierarchy. Defined as the possessors of a domineering sexuality, young men generated both fear and desire on the part of others.

In the European past as the American present, aging women have exhibited more-powerful personalities as they have aged. This power has both given them authority and rendered them suspect. Alongside Chaucer's Alison of Bath existed both the shrew and the witch; these ancient stereotypes of aging women were still extant and were still easily applied to actual assertive aging women. My meditation on medieval and early modern European history ends with the seventeenth-century witchcraft persecutions and the eighteenth-century silencing of the French *salonnières*. The men these talented intellectual women championed reduced them into becoming more than anything else mentors of men. Along the way I will discuss the sixteenth-century case of Queen Elizabeth I of England. For her exploitation of young men to maintain her power affords a significant variation to the themes under review.

The figures of the wise woman and the witch have been two polarities in European systems of thought and action with regard to aging women. They are apparent in Chaucer's complex personification of the Wife of Bath. They can be seen in Billy Wilder's Norma Desmond, manipulative and scheming, bewitching Joe Gillis with her fame and money but, with wisdom about the nature of that fame, at least partially understanding the Hollywood moviemakers who had cast her aside. Yet in contrast to Alison of Bath, Norma Desmond was insufficiently calculating, or tough-minded, and without a viable career to give her identity. Norma could fight back only through murder; Alison of Bath found many ways to assert her identity.

CHAPTER FOUR

The Wife of Bath
as Historical Prototype

WITHIN MODERN MEMORY, the best-remembered aging woman from the early European past is probably the fictionalized Wife of Bath in Geoffrey Chaucer's *Canterbury Tales*. Created by Chaucer in the late fourteenth century, Alison of Bath provides another example no less striking than Penelope or Sappho of age involved with youth. In Chaucer's story this fourteenth-century widow is traveling to the city of Canterbury with a group of pilgrims to see the Christian relics there. Like Sappho and Penelope (and like Norma Desmond), Alison of Bath is not lower-class in status. Rather, wealthy and world-traveled, she is an entrepreneur in the cloth trade. Yet she has been what we would call "upwardly mobile." By clever marriages to men older and affluent, she gained her position through inheritance. Now in her forties (or perhaps even older), she conducts her life as she pleases. The survivor of five husbands, she remains undaunted.

By the late fourteenth century, Europe had passed through the ages of Roman imperial control and decay, of Charlemagne's eighth-century rebuilding of union and empire, and of the ninth-century retreat into a localism produced by invasions from north and east. By the tenth century that interlocking system of aristocratic and martial loyalties known as feudalism had developed as protection against invaders and for aggrandizement of nobles and their families. By the fourteenth century even feudalism was in decline. It was undermined in the first instance by the growing power of the centralized state, furthered by kings like England's Edward III. (Chaucer served Edward III directly as a diplomat and as what we would call an administrative assistant.) The growth of the entrepreneurship which Alison of Bath exhibited also undermined the feudal order.

Alison of Bath's fictionalized life, as well as the tale of courtly love set at the court of the mythical King Arthur she tells to her companion travelers, affords a vista for examining important themes in the story of age-disparate relationships. For courtly love, by spiritualizing women, countered conventions of their insatiable sexuality and recentered nonfamilial love around heterosexual attraction. Like many cultural reconceptualizations in their initial phases, it possessed a socially leveling quality, validating relationships which crossed class lines as well as age lines.

It also drew from a pattern of behavior whereby feudal noblewomen, often married at young ages to much older men, sometimes formed special relationships with the boys sent to their warrior husbands for training in knighthood. Over the centuries courtly love would spawn a system of gallantry which exploited women as much as empowering them, but that development awaits a later exposition in my narrative.

Historian Joan Kelly has argued that the position of women reached a high point during the Middle Ages and declined during the Renaissance.[1] I would extend her thesis to suggest that the twelfth century in particular was a favorable time for women. The cult of courtly love, which originated in the late eleventh century, both furthered and reflected this situation. The decline began in the thirteenth century. In that century in the realm of philosophical speculation, Aristotle's gender conservatism replaced the Neoplatonic celebration of women. The higher sex ratio of the twelfth century began to fall; this drop produced larger numbers of women vis-à-vis men and probably acted to worsen women's valuation. And, during the thirteenth century, monarchs extended state control, identified with male prerogative.

As a fictionalized, transhistorical character, Alison of Bath stands above these developments. Yet rooted in a certain reality, she provides access to visualizing the possibilities in the lives of real women of her status and experience. She symbolizes the polarities of authority aging women could command and the antagonism they could arouse. Contained in the biography Chaucer creates for her and in the tale which he puts in her mouth are important insights into the nature of aging women in European society. Her story explores the choices available to them in a Christian culture interlaced with pre-Christian, pagan elements drawn from Europe's Roman and pre-Roman past.

Natalie Davis has suggested that early modern European women in England and France turned every meeting into an occasion for swapping tales: at the mill, the washing stream, the fountain, the baker's shop. By her account, the European tale tradition was not simply literary but was also real—and it was associated with women. Through Davis's rendering, the garrulous Wife of Bath becomes representative of all women, of whatever class or status.[2]

From her story and from that of her young fifth husband, Jenkin, much can be learned about social control, personal independence, and gender relations. Jenkin attempts to batter Alison into submission and to silence her voice through lecturing her from misogynistic texts. His actions are emblematic of those various attempts over the centuries to silence aging women—through calling their wisdom foolish "old wives' tales"; through the witchcraft persecutions; through the reduction of the image of salon women to manipulative society ladies; through the portrayal of Norma Desmond, the aging film star, as mad. Throughout the next three chapters of this work the story of the Wife of Bath will provide a unifying thread for disparate economic, cultural, and literary matters.

The Canterbury Tales and The Wife of Bath: An Initial Interpretation

ALISON OF BATH in Chaucer's *Canterbury Tales* is hardly a subsidiary, "wifely" character. On the contrary, she is lusty and unrestrained. She is independent, bound by no visible ties of family or kinship. Between the ages of twelve and forty, she reveals in the narrative of her life, she married three aging men for their money, inheriting from each. Wealthy then in her own right, she married two younger men, the last one twenty years younger than she. Each tried to dominate her, but in each case she gained the upper hand. Now she is journeying to Canterbury and, she implies, looking for another young man to marry. Indeed, some analysts of *The Canterbury Tales* think that she has her eye on the young clerk who is one of her companion travelers.

The language of the Wife of Bath is ribald and earthy. Her sexuality is evident and she exults in it, just as she exults in her strength and authority. "For truly, I am all Venusian in feeling, and my brain is Martian. Venus gave me my lust, my lickerishness. And Mars gave me my sturdy hardiness." She laments that age has taken away her youthful beauty and poisoned her "prime." But her regret is brief. She expects to find a husband and enjoy sex once again. "In wifehood I will use my instrument. As freely as my Maker has it sent. If I be niggardly, God grant me sorrow! My husband he shall have it, eve and morrow."[3]

Alison of Bath's references to Venus and Mars and to her "instrument" are telling, for they indicate the masculine mold in which her character is cast. Early European physiological theory posited that male and female genitalia (the penis and the clitoris) were similar rather than different in form and purpose. It was also believed that women, like men, ejaculated in intercourse a type of semen, produced by orgasm and necessary for conception. Yet the female characters created by early writers rarely so openly discuss their sexual appetites as does the Wife of Bath: the topos of "woman on top" was troubling to the patriarchal imagination, as historian Natalie Davis reminded us some time ago.[4] The motif of the "patient Griselda," who obeyed her husband no matter his demands, was probably preferred: even Chaucer offered it as an alternative gender possibility in his clerk's tale.

Alison's references to Venus and Mars are taken from the stage-of-life theorization based on the seven signs of the astrological zodiac. This schema was popular in medieval and early modern Europe. In its depiction, Venus, the goddess of love, governed the postpuberty years, when sexuality was paramount, while Mars, the god of war, was ascendant in the stage immediately following. That Alison views herself in terms of these youthful categories underscores the intermixing of youth and age in her character.[5]

Moreover, in most life-cycle descriptions, these stages governed by Venus and Mars applied only to men. That Alison viewed herself as molded within a male model is also important in understanding her. She relates to that tradition, evident in Boccaccio's fourteenth-century *Lives of Eminent Women* and strong in Renaissance writers, of valorizing and critiquing the powerful women of myth and of history as "viragos." As such, they were exceptions to their gender, women whose force proceeded from both a glorious and a troubling masculinity in their dispositions.

Great literary characters are multifaceted in meaning. Thus it is not surprising that scholars disagree over Chaucer's intent in creating Alison of Bath. Their interpretations range the spectrum from feminist to antifeminist. Some scholars think that Chaucer meant to mock his creation, that he liked neither her independence nor her bossiness. From this point of view he portrayed her as the descendant of those aging former prostitutes in literature like Ovid's Dipsas and her descendant, the Old Woman in the thirteenth-century *Romance of the Rose,* a major text of that century. Such an interpretation raises interesting possibilities in understanding her, but it fails to deal not only with the general female tale tradition but also with her considerable economic success. For Alison of Bath is not a former entrepreneur now a failure as she ages. She belongs in the realm of imagination to that successful group of cloth entrepreneurs who in the real world had made Bath a central entrepôt for textiles. Alison is not a tawdry broker between men and women in matters of the flesh. She is a talkative spinner of tales who is much more than just a spinner of yarn. This is not an untutored woman telling a suspect "old wives' tale." Rather she is a woman of the world knowledgeable about life. "Teach us younger men of your technique," the pardoner says to her.[6]

Her name is important, too. Robert Haller has argued that the name Alison was typically, in medieval stories, a prostitute's name. But it was also, as other scholars have pointed out, a variation of Alice, and Alice was the name of Alice Perrers, the mistress of King Edward III, whom Chaucer served. By force of personality, Perrers had risen from humble beginnings to become a lady-in-waiting to the queen. With the queen's death, she became the king's mistress. Like many courts in early Europe, Edward's court was filled with powerful women, accomplished at intrigue. For a time while Edward was terminally ill, Alice Perrers governed the country behind the scenes.[7]

The interpretation of Alison of Bath as a prototypical shrew or evil go-between meant to warn women also rests on too obvious a reading of the tale she tells. Surprisingly, she does not draw her story from her own experiences of merchant shops and city streets. Rather, she turns to the feudal world of knights and ladies: her tale is drawn from the tradition of chivalric romance and is set at the court of King Arthur. Arthur was the mythical king of England whose sagas were first written down in the twelfth century from the oral stories of Celtic bards who migrated to Brittany in the sixth century and who fled to France after the 1066 Norman invasion. By the fourteenth century the exploits of Arthur and his knights had come to constitute a model world of romance and warfare, a literary tradition in historical guise. It was also a world where, as Chaucer describes it, "the fairies ruled."

Scholars think that Chaucer originally intended the story which the sailor tells for the Wife of Bath. And, indeed, the sailor's earthy tale of wifely deception seems more appropriate for a woman of the people than one drawn from the aristocratic tradition of courtly love. But by placing in Alison's mouth a story of chivalry, Chaucer not only brought her closer in characterization to the powerful court women he knew, but also gave

her a universal significance. She is not simply a woman of the people who
reflects in a bawdy manner on the world she knows best. Rather, she
presents a complex vision of good and evil, of youth and age, within the
allegorizing and high-culture world of the courtly tradition. She combined
the high-culture tradition of the troubadour with the popular-culture
tradition of the fabliaux, those ribald tales which, drawn from oral tradition, first appeared in urban centers in the twelfth century. As such, the
Wife of Bath stepped across class lines to become, it might be said, a
version of everywoman.

Here she is the wise woman: Athena to Odysseus, Diotima to Plato,
Philosophia to Boethius, a goddess as mentor. Accordingly, the central
female figure in the story she tells is both old and young, like those ancient
crones of Celtic mythology, like Alison herself. The line of descent may
be clouded but is nonetheless apparent: from the Caillagh Ny Groamagh
of the Scottish Isle of Man or Scathan, the warrior queen of the Tuatha
de Danann, both Alison and the old crone of her tale are drawn along
the lines of those transformative women of ancient lore. Chaucer was
versed in earlier traditions of the wise woman: he had translated both
The Consolation of Philosophy and *Romance of the Rose* into English.[8] He
knew firsthand both Philosophia and the go-between, both the wise
woman and the old bawd, Dipsas's descendant. These figures occupied
polarities of European attitudes toward aging women.

Alison's tale begins in that male world of violence which she had
already encountered through Jenkin, as he lectured her from misogynistic
clerical texts and then attempted to batter her into submission. In her
story a solitary knight is hunting in a field. Chancing on a woman
alone, this "lusty bachelor" rapes her. Yet the tale rapidly loses its male
orientation. The denouement to the crime is played out in a woman's
world. First, King Arthur decides that Queen Guinevere and her ladies
will decide the penalty for the crime. Next the punishment is that the
knight, having compromised his honor in women's eyes, must find out
what women want from men, how they would structure gender relations.

Like most knights of the chivalric stories this knight must embark on
a quest. But it is a quest with conventions upended. For it involves no
battles, only a question, and in the course of the knight's search masculine
and feminine will be reversed. For the knight himself and not the conventional lovely lady will become the desired prize.

An old crone, a typical "loathly lady" of medieval romance, provides
the answer to the question Guinevere had posed. The crone is Alison in
the garb of enchantment, transported back to fairyland. And the answer

the crone gives the knight is the same answer Alison, by implication, has given Jenkin: women want power in relationships. They want their own voice, their own authority. As payment for her response, the old woman, following the "loathly lady" literary convention, demands that the knight marry her. Once he does so, in accordance with the ancient plot, she turns into the beautiful woman of his desires. So did those aging women of the ancient Celtic tales.

Such transformation stories, I have argued, valorize beauty and leave aging women isolated, their ugliness exposed. In the prologue to *The Canterbury Tales,* Chaucer describes the Wife of Bath as "gap-toothed," with large buttocks and a red face. Yet if she is "foul" (a word Chaucer uses to describe the crone of the tale), he also calls Alison "fair." For she is fair of spirit and of self-presentation, qualities also apparent in the crone of the fairy tale. The latter is, as Priscilla Martin calls her, the "Wise Woman of the Forest." As Alison's ideal self she is calm, reasonable, and wise.[9]

The lesson that Alison's crone teaches is a broad lesson about the relativity of class, age, and gender. Honor is not class related, she argues. Gentility comes from God and is not the automatic gift of rank. The nobility are not ipso facto good because they are nobility. Rather, poverty stimulates beneficent enterprise and forces self-understanding. By extension age also is a leveling and ennobling force. It brings the wisdom that gives answers to life's riddles. It teaches the knight that there is a woman's world, the world of Guinevere, where power must be moderated and women heeded.

The message, however, is not completely clear. The punishment initially given the knight—that he go on a quest—seems hardly commensurate with the violent crime of rape he has committed. But Chaucer appears to employ the original rape primarily as a metaphor for male domination. He thereby downplays its reality as a crime. And at the end of the Wife of Bath's tale, Chaucer seems to accept his culture's attitudes about the sexual voracity of women. For the crone only gains the knight's assent to continue the marriage after she persuades him that aging women are less likely to be unfaithful to husbands than are younger women. Yet given the Wife of Bath's sexualized behavior, Chaucer may have intended this proposition as more ironic than accurate.

Still, the knight's honor, bound up with a wife's possible infidelities, is of preemptive importance. He may be able to divorce himself from his class assumption that nobility of character is confined to the aristocracy, but he cannot revise his conventional beliefs about gender. Here Chaucer may have meant to reveal courtly love's reverse side. Based on extramarital relationships, it contributed to male suspicion of women as much as it furthered the spiritual definition of women's nature and created comity between the genders. Like many broad cultural repositionings, its initial thrust may have been radicalizing, but it carried within its categories the seeds of its own ethical reversals.

My reading of the meaning of the Wife of Bath, however, ends on an ambiguous note. I have noted that Jenkin beat Alison, but I have not mentioned that his beating rendered her deaf. Although Alison gained the upper hand in their marital controversy, in the end she does not hear. Or perhaps she does not listen. To the end she remains unabashedly heterosexual and manipulative, and with a considerably masculine personality. Her tale exhibits a wisdom which resounds throughout the ages; her application of it to her personal life seems problematic. Despite five conflicted marriages, she seems intent on finding a sixth husband.

Alongside the wisdom of aging women stands the opposite: censoriousness, the power of an aging personality misapplied. This character is there in the evil stepmothers and aging women who guard princesses in towers in fairy stories, in aging women enforcers of nineteenth-century Victorianism, even in Hedda Hopper's malice.

Both positive and negative readings can be applied to the Wife of Bath: she is both "fair" and "foul." Whatever Chaucer intended in creating her, as for Homer in the *Odyssey* or for Billy Wilder in *Sunset Boulevard,* a variety of cultural signs regarding women filtered through his creative imagination. These various, opposing signals resonate in his narrative. They provide him the material to invent a figure of such complexity that even feminists cannot deny the force of this creation of a male author. Nor can she ever be completely deciphered. The possibilities of further illumination still remain many.

The Twelfth and Thirteenth Centuries: The Cult of Courtly Love and Its Undermining

WITHIN THE EUROPEAN EXPERIENCE crones and queens are perhaps not unlikely confederates, given traditions of magical female authority in folktales and fairy tales. Female authority is present, too, in that major medieval construction, the cult of courtly love, as in the

Wife of Bath's tale. Courtly love in the form of love poetry exalting women, composed by aristocratic troubadours and wandering minstrels, first appeared in the late eleventh century in the south of France, where powerful women overlords had existed for some time.[10] Courteosie shaped heterosexual relationships for centuries, at least among the upper classes. It ennobled extramarital love and, fusing passion and spirituality, in its purest form it allowed exalted desire to transcend class and age, permitting the formation of unconventional relationships.

Recent interpreters of courtly love (even in its twelfth-century heyday) view it cynically, as a phenomenon which actually benefited noble lords, rather than their ladies. By this interpretation it functioned as a means of keeping the loyalty to their lord of young men in training for knighthood. Throughout the medieval period, boys were sent to live in the households of kin of higher status to receive training in knightly skills; there they constituted a group whose youthful contentiousness needed containment. A high sex ratio characterized the twelfth century: often there were not enough women for the young men to marry. Courtly love diverted their attention to a matter of the spirit focused on their noble mistress and supervisable by the lady's husband (her legal overlord). It allowed those young men who might have to marry below their noble station the fantasy of high female preferment. Moreover, recent interpreters note that mostly men wrote the love poetry and that the women in it often seem remote, without character, possibly only mirrors to reflect the concerns of their male admirers.[11]

Such explanations reintroduce the power of patriarchy to provide a useful corrective to those who, presenting courtly love as a leveling, protofeminist force, forget the omnipresent rule of the fathers. But those explanations which deny women's influence overlook indications of female authority implicit in the training for knighthood as well as in chivalric romances and tales of knightly quests. In these stories, distinct from troubadour lyrics, women have access to what Joan Ferrante has called "subtle or hidden ways to power."[12] Whether textual or subtextual, there were ways that women could assert themselves in these eras.

The twelfth century was an expansive age. It was a time of population growth due to good harvests, of commercial enhancement due to trade with the Near East, and of urbanization, as towns grew to serve commercial and population increases. The guilds then came into being, as a way of organizing urban economic production. Universities grew in size and number. Kings expanded their territories and began to create state bureaucracies.[13]

To counter this last trend, the nobility in many areas instituted the practice of "primogeniture," or inheritance by firstborn sons. They thereby solidified knightly ranks against royal power by keeping family holdings together. In the process, however, they produced a distinct group of young men, the so-called second sons. Economically disenfranchised, these young men often had to make their own way in a society with new institutions and commercial possibilities both inviting and intimidating. Courteosie offered them participation in a new nobility of spirit, the adoration of a special woman, designed to inspire better self and social perception.

The expansiveness of the age can be interpreted in other ways as benefiting women. Freed from external menace, Christian knights fought two crusades in the Near East. They left many wives behind as chatelaines managing estates. Demographically, this was a period in transition from the high sex ratios (more men than women) of earlier centuries to the reverse situation by the thirteenth century.[14] Still the greater numbers of adult men than women in the population had the probable impact of enhancing the estimation of women. Moreover, despite the introduction of primogeniture, local variation still guaranteed that some women inherited property. And increased urbanization brought the development of the guild system, under which some women emerged as masters and merchants.

Within courtly love, indications of women's prestige were encoded. In spiritualized terms courtly love mirrored feudalism's vassal-serf relationship, turning women into rulers, sometimes called by their adulators "midons," or lord, a form of address normally reserved for their spouses. Behind courtly love also lay Christian beliefs about the sanctity of women saints; it foreshadowed the late-century beginnings of the cult of the Virgin Mary. It also drew from Christian and Platonic abjurations to self-mastery and the attainment of virtue through abnegation of self and the adoration of a perfect ideal.

Moreover, courteosie replicated, without copying, the cult of friendship among men who, for some centuries, had had their sworn companions, or *compainz*. In the monastic tradition male friendships were viewed as a way of engendering spirituality. On the battlefield friends fought together and cheered each other on. Thus did Roland and Olivier in that famed late-eleventh-century battle epic, *The Song of Roland*. In such closeness, recent scholars argue, many took up same-sex love.[15]

The cult of courtly love both reflected the humanism of the "Renaissance of the Twelfth Century" and encouraged this intellectual movement toward gender sensitivity. It paralleled the Neoplatonism of the School of Chartres (whose members celebrated the goddess "Natura" and traced their most direct precedent to Boethius). It added resonance to Peter Abelard's arguments about women's spirituality, his biblical exegesis which countered canonical readings to find in the Bible special virtue accorded women, from Hannah and Deborah of the Old Testament to the Marys of the Gospels. He honored the ancient Sibyls, proposing, as did others, that these female mystics had been the first prophets to predict the birth of Christ.[16] These cultural forces together created a cultural current, if not a precise social reality, in favor of women's authority.

Dress ratified women's prestige in this era. Largely overlooked by historians, what people wore is a telling indicator of broad cultural meanings. In the last decades of the eleventh century occurred a style shift. The change primarily involved upper-class men's dress. It centered around a change in the length of the male upper covering from short to long; in other words, male dress more than ever before came to resemble female dress, with the wearing of long robes, indicating women's enhanced position. Contemporary chroniclers traced the change in dress to what they saw as specific attempts to please women. In the early twelfth century, Orderic Vitalis wrote that "our wanton youth is sunk in effeminacy, and courtiers, fawning, seek the favours of women with every kind of lewdness."[17]

Because most of the troubadours came from the lesser nobility (and some from the peasantry), Meg Bogin has called the cult of courtly love a "coquetry of class."[18] More than that, it was also a "coquetry of age." For an additional impulse behind it was the authoritative input that noblewomen could have in shaping the character of the boys who were sent to their households to receive training in knightly skills. This system of the exchange of young people was initially designed to foster kin loyalty to overlords and to improve the prospects of related families of lesser status. It existed for centuries. As a young man in the mid-fourteenth century, Geoffrey Chaucer participated in it. The son of a London wine merchant, he vastly improved his prospects by entering at a young age the service of the Countess of Ulster, King Edward's daughter-in-law. His experience within this noble household opened up to Chaucer his eventual career as a diplomat and statesman. He also may have gained from it a particular sensitivity to gender relations.

With family goals predominant in marital arrangements, noblewomen were often married at young ages to men much older than they. Thus it is not surprising that these ladies of the manor might turn for affection to the younger men whom they may have mothered in earlier years. For young men entered the training for knighthood at very young ages, often as young as seven. During the early years of their apprenticeship, before they were considered old enough at twelve or fourteen to begin learning martial skills, they served as pages. In this capacity they were under the supervision of the lady of the manor, the manager of the household.

Most often pages served as messengers (a function still evident in our use of the term "paging" to mean attempting to deliver a message). But they could also serve in a variety of other ways. They waited on tables, answered doors, helped remove clothing, prepared baths, partnered chess games, assisted in falconry and hunting. Chivalric romances are filled with young male pages performing such services. Their female identification is evidenced by the fact that, in France, they were called *demoiseaux,* a term also applied to young women.[19] In later European literature, women often dressed as pages when they took a perilous voyage or in some other manner traversed gender boundaries.

In Marie of France's twelfth-century *Lay of Equitan,* the king has fallen in love with a woman of the lesser nobility, and his rank frightens her. To soothe her, he suggests that she think of him not as her king, her superior in rank, but as her page, her young servant in love. Marie of France's *Lay of Gugemar* is the story of the love between a "demoiseau" and a woman married to a much older man.[20] In the anonymous courtly romance *Parténopeus de Blois,* the fairy ruler Melior chooses Parténopeus as the most promising young knight she can find. She draws him to herself by magic and keeps him with her secretly until he is old enough to be presented to her people. Over the next centuries the special courtly relationship between the page and the lady, the feminized young man and his female cicerone, recurs in a number of texts which draw from courtly love conventions. It is to be found, for example, in Ulrich von Lichtenstein's *Frauendienst,* written in the early thirteenth century, and in Antoine de la Sale's mid-fifteenth-century *Le petit Jehan de Saintré.*[21]

These latter two works reflect a growing critique of courtly love by presenting their noblewomen protagonists as especially narcissistic and capricious. They nonetheless continue the literary examination of age-disparate relationships. Lichtenstein's work (the title of which translates as *Service of Ladies*) purports to be an autobiography. In it, as a boy of twelve, Lichtenstein obsesses about attaining spiritual excellence through entering the service of a high-born lady whom he can adore. After ten years of service in the household of a princess whom he worships in secret, he petitions for her favor once he has been knighted and has become a known minnesinger (or German troubadour). She grants his request only reluctantly and from a distance. In *Le petit Jehan de Saintré* the lady, cousin to the Queen, chooses the young man of twelve to be her special favorite. The relationship lasts for over a decade, until she deserts the short, slim John of Saintré for a stout, lusty Abbot.[22]

If women in troubadour lyrics retreat into the background as manipulated objects of male desire, they reemerge in other sources as both creators of courtly conventions and as personages with a power beyond objectification. Women in the courtly romances and the Arthurian sagas, for example, often possess the power of magic, the ability to cast spells and to heal. In the person of Morgan le Fay, they possess the ability to counter the power of kings. In *Tristram and Isolde* a magic love potion made by the Queen Mother to ensure Isolde's power over the King she has been required to marry causes many plot complications when the wrong individuals drink it. In Chrétien de Troyes's twelfth-century *Cligés,* the female protagonist is accompanied by a nurse named Thessala, "who was skilled in necromancy, having been born in Thessaly, where devilish charms are taught and wrought." In de Troyes's *Yvain,* women whom Yvain encounters give him magic rings that render him, at one point, invisible, and at another, invincible. In another episode, when Yvain is driven mad by misunderstandings, a lady and her two servants, finding him asleep in the forest, rub on his head a healing ointment, given them by "Morgan the Wise." And it was Morgan who, having raised the Arthurian knight Lancelot, gave him a magic ring with the power to free him from enchantment.[23]

Furthermore, modifications in the design of playing pieces in the game of chess, a popular social pastime from the ninth century on, provide additional illumination on the subject of women's twelfth-century authority. Chess was originally introduced from the Near East: in the original game a wise man, or vizier, accompanied the king. By the twelfth century, however, in Europe, the queen came to replace the Arabic male figure of wisdom. Two analysts of extant twelfth-century chess pieces assert that the new queen pieces have a visionary quality. This quality, they think, reflects a sense of wisdom lingering on from the Arabic wise men. Or, these scholars speculate that their sculptors may have modeled the new queen pieces after representations of ancient European goddesses.[24]

Such goddess figures, according to art historian Ilene Forsyth, were common in medieval Europe. They were graphic sculptural remains from pre-European, pre-Roman times. They formed the basis of what became, beginning in the Carolingian eighth century, the "throne of wisdom" sculptures, the Madonna as the so-called *sedes sapienta.* In these personifications Mary was the figure of wisdom. Her imperial majesty, her position as Queen of Heaven (as she was called in Carolingian Europe), overshadowed that of her son, who in these sculptures is shown seated on her lap as a grown man, but in miniature. According to Forsyth the "throne of wisdom" sculptures were the single most important religious objects during the medieval period. They were often considered to have the power to work miracles. As late as the late twelfth century they still dominated the tympanum of most of the major cathedrals. The type began to decline throughout Europe in the thirteenth century, as other visualizations of the Madonna emerged.[25]

The authority of women in this era extended beyond the literary and the magical to reappear in the lives of well-known historical actors. What do we make of the life of Eleanor of Aquitaine? She was the granddaughter of Duke William of Aquitaine, often identified as the first troubadour. She was also the heir and overlord of vast lands in the south of France. In 1152 she divorced one king, Louis VII of France, to marry another, Henry of Normandy, subsequently Henry II of England. Henry was twelve years her junior: she was thirty and he was eighteen when they married.

The ascetic Louis VII, devoted to religion, stifled Eleanor's aesthetic, romantic impulses. But they emerged in her furthering of courtly love as Queen of England both in her court in Aquitaine and in the one she established in England. At her English court, Thomas of Britain wrote *Tristram and Isolde;* Marie of France may have composed her lays; it is possible that the Arthurian legends in their written form may have been generated. Bernard de Ventadour, renowned as the age's foremost troubadour, played that part for her both in Aquitaine and in England. He dedicated to her songs of devotion: to Ventadour she was *Mos Aziman,* "my magnet." Finally, Henry II, disliking the relationship, banished the troubadour from England.[26]

Eleanor's influence is also apparent in the courtly love legacy she fostered among her descendants, especially her son Richard the Lionhearted, her daughter Marie of Champagne, and her granddaughter Blanche of Castile. Her son Richard the Lionhearted was renowned for his ability at vocal expression as well as at combat. A troubadour as well as a warrior, his popular title, "lionhearted," indicated both a warlike disposition and a feminine side: in medieval animal symbolism the lion indicated gender intermixing.[27]

Her daughter Marie of Champagne fostered a notable site for literary expression at her own court in one of France's most important central provinces. Despite the fact that Marie was Eleanor's daughter by Louis VII and that Eleanor had had to leave her with the French king when she married Henry of Normandy, Marie preserved her mother's heritage. In her court in Champagne, she was the patron of two of the century's most important writers, Chrétien de Troyes and Andreas Capellanus (Andrew the Chaplain). (Chrétien de Troyes was the author of several important Arthurian romances; Andreas Capellanus in *The Art of Courtly Love* produced what is considered the most important medieval exegesis on courteosie.) In Aquitaine and Champagne, Eleanor and Marie taught the arts of courtesy to numbers of young women and men of the ruling nobility.[28]

In 1200, Eleanor personally chose her granddaughter Blanche of Castile to marry the French king, Louis VIII. (This king was the grandson of her ex-husband, Louis VII, through his second wife, the woman he married after he and Eleanor were divorced.) Blanche was raised at a Spanish court steeped in the troubadour tradition. After she came to France, she was the worshipful love object of her noble cousin, the famed troubadour Thibaut of Champagne, ten years her junior. Their relationship, and Blanche's rejection of Thibaut, became legendary in the annals of courteosie.

Eleanor was thirty when she married Henry of Normandy, then eighteen; Blanche was ten years older than Thibaut. This pattern of age reversal was not untypical of courtly love which, in its earliest manifestation, had to it a leveling quality. Consider, for example, the argument in *The Art of Courtly Love,* written by Andreas Capellanus in the 1180s. In this text we have an early analogue to the Wife of Bath's story of Queen Guinevere and her ladies sitting in judgment on an issue pertaining to gender relationships. For Capellanus purports to transcribe the dialogues that took place at a court of courtly love, presumably of a session that might have occurred at Marie of Champagne's court. In this dialogue (which has a legalistic flavor probably derived from the analogous courts of law that male overlords held), men and women of various social classes debate the nature of love. Queen Eleanor makes the final disposition; Capellanus frames the exposition as though he were telling it to a young man named Walter.

In *The Art of Courtly Love,* love has a transcendent quality. It is an emotion related not to age or class but to personal nobility, to qualities like kindness and courage. What matters is not status, age, or appearance; what matters is the nature of individual character. Thus the case is made that true lovers can come from across age or class lines. What we have in this work is a case of the troubadour's lofty lyrics brought down to earth, of amor individualized and expanded to allow minstrels to love noble ladies and the latter their pages.

Capellanus's Queen contends that young men may prefer sexual relationships with older women. For she avers that with regard to "the natural instinct of passion . . . young men are usually more eager to gratify it with older women than with the young women of their own age." Capellanus's Queen further postulates that "a woman, whether young or somewhat older, likes the embraces and solaces of young men better than those of older ones." (These passages foreshadow modern conclusions that the height of women's sexual drive occurs at an older age than does men's. They also may indicate an understanding of the male decrease in sexual performance capability with age.)

In a dialogue between an aging noblewoman and a younger man of lesser rank, the noblewoman deprecates the possibility of any further romantic involvement on her part because of her age. But the man prevails with the argument that her appearance belies her negative self-appraisal. Love can occur at any age, because love is a matter of the spirit, not of fixed life-stage definitions. "There seems to be a youthful enough beauty in the appearance of your person," he asserts, "from which it is clear that a youthful beauty is strong in your heart, for the outward appearance shows clearly what is the disposition of the mind within."[29]

Within *The Art of Courtly Love*, one hastens to add, Capellanus sets limits to the universalizing power of love. He denounces homosexual love. He sets the outer age limits of desirability for women at fifty and for men at sixty. Beyond this point, he contends, neither gender has any desire for sex. Within his schema for relationships, he excludes the peasant class and includes only the bourgeoisie and the nobility. He argues that noblemen always have the right to rape peasant women: to him the peasantry are a breed apart, without rights against their superiors. Capellanus's queen does not dispute this assertion.

Surveying medieval civilization, the nineteenth-century American historian Henry Adams regarded Eleanor of Aquitaine, her daughter Marie of Champagne, and Eleanor's granddaughter Blanche of Castile as dominating the spirit of the twelfth and thirteenth centuries. Adams called them, simply and grandly, the "three Queens."[30] But if Eleanor and Marie were central to the origins and definitions of courtly love, Blanche of Castile, it might be said, presided over its demise.

The position of women, I have argued, declined during the thirteenth century. A resurgent, conformist Christianity dominated this age. During this century persecution of the Jews began and that of homosexuals escalated. Double monasteries, comprising both monks and nuns, were closed. These institutions had sustained female writers like the twelfth-century Hildegard of Bingen. Aristotelian thought, which drew strict gender differentiations, came to dominate religious and philosophical thought. It reached its height in the work of Thomas Aquinas. The brutal Albigensian Crusade was directed against heresy in the south of France, a center of the troubadour tradition. The Inquisition, directed toward ending heresy, found courtly love as subversive as religious disbelief. Some troubadours were silenced. Others renounced earthly for celestial love and the adoration of women for the love of the Virgin Mary.[31]

Blanche of Castile was regent for her son, Louis IX, for nearly fifteen years. In the capacity of interim ruler she displayed administrative capabilities no less striking than those of her grandmother, Eleanor of Aquitaine. She pacified the nobility and initiated administrative reforms. She continued the building of Paris and the construction of Notre Dame and Chartres cathedrals. Yet her achievements can be seen as furthering that long historical trend in nation-state building that would undermine women's autonomy. Moreover, her deep religiosity ratified the age's Aristotelian and Christian conservatism.[32]

In the late twelfth century the dominant architectural figure for Christianity's most important female representation continued to be the Virgin Mary. Yet most sculptures no longer exhibited the "throne of wisdom" motif. Rather, they showed Mary and the adult Christ seated next to each other in heaven in what is called the "Triumph of the Virgin" presentation. During Blanche's reign, this motif of equal authority was replaced by one in which Christ crowned Mary as the Queen of Heaven. This replacement theme might be seen as reflecting Blanche's deference to her son as well as Louis's great piety—in 1297 he was canonized as Saint Louis. But it also emphasized Mary's humility. By the end of the fourteenth century, this "Coronation of the Virgin" scene further emphasized Mary's humility by showing her on her knees before Christ.[33]

Blanche was the mother of Louis IX, but she was also involved in one of courteosie's most famed relationships: with her cousin, Thibaut of Champagne, himself a troubadour of renown. Despite their equality of rank and the romantic poetry he wrote to her, she consistently rejected him. In fact, he was a leader of the lordly faction that opposed her, and on one occasion at her request he lifted the siege of a castle where she and her son were staying.

The rejection of aspiring lovers by noble ladies was always characteristic of the cult of courtly love. But this rejection of Thibaut of Champagne by Blanche of Castile was more than an example of a typical pattern. It was symbolic of the ending of the troubadour tradition, a casualty partly of the rise of Christian fervor.

A misogyny which still remained strong also undermined this tradition. The ending pages of Andreas Capellanus's *Art of Courtly Love* contain a diatribe against women, listing the standard charges of vanity, irrationality, shrewishness, and uncontrolled sexuality. The fabliaux, popular tales often emerging in urban settings, mocked unfaithful wives and boorish husbands (as well as the courtly tradition itself) and influenced the later tale tradition present in Chaucer's *Canterbury Tales*. The greatest allegorical work of the thirteenth century, *Romance of the Rose*, explored issues of vice and virtue through the plot medium of a lover's search for his lady, imprisoned in a castle. Guillaume de Lorris began the work in the 1230s, and he composed his beginning sections according to the respectful gender conventions of courteosie. But when Jean de Meun concluded the work in the 1270s, his tone was more cynical, more contemptuous of women. His critique of women eventually sparked the beginnings of the so-called *querelle des femmes* (the argument over women's virtues and their vices) which would occupy French and English writers over many centuries.[34]

Courtly love ennobled women and afforded access to creativity in shaping social behavior. It offered, as well, an implicit critique of that martial, feudal world which encased it. Yet if it softened that world it negated neither its violence nor its code of honor which encouraged physical reprisal for presumed affronts. Throughout the chivalric romances women urge men on to maintain their warrior reputations. They most readily select men as lovers who are the victors at tournaments or in hand-to-hand combat. The onset of love only heightens the passion for battle.

Thus Cligés's love for Fenice in *Cligés* heightens his martial intent. "Boldness and love, which holds him enthralled, makes him eager for the fray." Cultural convention dictated that the courtly heroine encourage this warlike response. "Thus, doubly she shows the devotion of a sweetheart, fearing at once his death, and desiring that honour may be his." In Jean de Meun's ending passages of *Romance of the Rose,* the metaphor of the melee, love as war, concludes the young man's quest to possess his rose, his love. You shall know, relates the young man narrator, "how I carried on until I took the bud at my pleasure."[35]

Gender intermixing existed in these chivalric tales in men wearing attire resembling women's dress, or in the egalitarianism of a text like Andreas Capellanus's *Art of Courtly Love,* or in romances like Chrétien de Troyes's *Erec et Enide,* in which the hero and the heroine mirror each other. Yet male power and the quest for martial adventure still remain paramount, constituting the dominant narrative, the preeminent text.

Yet one striking scene in Arthurian legend intermixes gender and aging with generativity to create a profound critique of male violence. The episode is part of the Perceval/Parsifal legend, and Chrétien de Troyes's *Perceval* contains it in its earliest written form. The episode involves a mother-son relationship. Indeed, this scene poses the world of mothers to that of fathers, to suggest that age and maternality can bring a wisdom to counter erotic domination and the martial mode. Too often in Western culture the convention has been one of women willingly sacrificing sons for warfare, applauding violence in the name of state interest.[36]

In *Perceval,* Perceval's mother has come to fear martial conventions which have brought the death of her husband in battle. Thus she has raised Perceval away from society with no knowledge of knighthood. They have lived in that forest setting which in fairy tales seems magical, outside of normal arrangements. Yet in an encounter which seems inevitable, as Perceval reaches manhood he meets a group of knights riding in the forest. He is enchanted by "the jingling coats of mail and the bright, gleaming helmets and the lances and shields ... [and] the green and vermilion catching the light of the sun, and the gold, blue, and silver...."[37]

Despite his mother's pleas, Perceval leaves her to become a knight. This action seems to indicate the futility of hiding a young male from his warrior destiny. But Perceval is not an ordinary Arthurian hero. For he is the first of the Arthurian knights to encounter the Grail, that receptacle of plenty which promises eternal fulfillment. Traceable to a number of such vessels in Celtic legend, the Grail later came to be identified as the chalice at Christ's Last Supper. Perceval also is the first of many Arthurian heroes to fail to retain the Grail after his initial encounter with it.

Perceval's failure at first seems to involve his keeping silent when he should have spoken at a banquet at which the Grail is presented. The mistake is puzzling, for it hardly seems grave enough to carry the penalty of the Grail's disappearance. But then he learns that his punishment in actuality stems from his having abandoned his mother, and thereby, through her grief, caused her death.

Freudian scholars have interpreted the Grail as the female womb and the Arthurian search for it as a working out of Oedipal irresolutions;

scholars of ancient goddesses view it as symbolic of the generativity of these divine figures. One might also regard it as a doubling of the mother principle, as representing that place where Perceval's mother raised him, the forest which Perceval left, mistaking the gleaming knights for angels and not for the devils his mother took them to be. Thus the Grail becomes a symbol of peace, a horn of plenty to counter phallic horns summoning to war or goring victims. Perceval failed to realize that he should have followed not the martial pathways of knighthood but rather the pacific wisdom of his mother, "the widow lady of the lonely wild forest."[38]

The Wife of Bath as Topos: The Evidence from Demographic and Social History

To PLUMB THE historical reality of Chaucer's depiction of the Wife of Bath, one needs to place beside it statistical and narrative evidence. And in so doing it becomes apparent that throughout medieval and early modern Europe, marital and erotic relationships between aging women and younger men existed in all classes—from the royalty to the peasantry.

In the elaborate statecraft of medieval and early modern Europe, marriage was used to cement state alliances. In this intricate power game unmarried aging women, as well as young women, could be useful collateral. Or women who themselves held power might use their own persons as a means of gaining increased authority or personal pleasure. Historians have stressed royalty's propensity to betroth their children at very young ages. But they have overlooked the less common but nonetheless real phenomenon of age-disparate unions, evident, for example, in the case of Eleanor of Aquitaine and Henry II. Henry II's mother, Matilda of Normandy, herself had married his much younger father, Geoffrey, Count of Anjou, as a way of shoring up the connection between the two most powerful duchies in northern France (Anjou and Normandy). Isabella, the favorite daughter of Edward III, Chaucer's patron, at the age of thirty-three in 1365 married Enguerrand de Coucy, a Norman lord eight years younger than she.[39]

When power politics were at stake, the English Tudors in the sixteenth century particularly disregarded age differentials. Catherine of Aragon was six years older than Henry VIII; Mary Tudor was eleven years older than Philip of Spain. Elizabeth Tudor's most important marital negotiation, carried out over thirteen years, was with Catherine de Médicis's youngest son, the Duke of Alençon, who was twenty years younger than she.

Pleasure as well as power could motivate these noble relationships, and both qualities could further them or undermine them. Thus in sixteenth-century France Louise of Savoy, the mother of King Francis I, at the age of forty-six and after twenty-five years of widowhood became enamored of Charles of Bourbon-Montpensier, a young friend of the king. When Montpensier refused her advances and called her an "ugly, dried-up old harridan," she fabricated evidence of treason to have him brought to trial and stripped of all titles and land. In France in the late seventeenth century the Countess of Orléans, Louis XIV's niece, objected vigorously to the proposal that she marry Louis's homosexual brother, her uncle who was twelve years younger than she. But the retort to her objections was that "among people of your rank age has no importance." She had inherited large estates through her mother, and Louis wanted access to them.[40]

Similar behavior could be found in classes other than royalty. In France commentators as varied as the protofeminist court poet Christine de Pizan in the fifteenth century and the sophisticated courtier Pierre de Brantôme in the sixteenth century noted that wealthy widows were marrying younger men. So widespread was the practice among sixteenth-century Parisian upper-class women that in 1560 Francis I issued an edict placing limits on the amount of gifts that a widow with children could give to a second husband. In 1576 the French Estates General passed a law forbidding widows to marry persons "unworthy of their condition." In Germany in the sixteenth century and in England in the seventeenth century, pamphleteers condemned what they saw as the common practice of indigent male members of the aristocracy and bourgeoisie marrying wealthy older widows for their money.[41] Indeed, the existence of a large body of cautionary literature addressed to this issue from medieval times onward speaks to the fact of its occurrence.

Writing about laboring women under preindustrial capitalism, Richard Vann has noted that it was not unusual for women of this group to be older than their husbands. In the Scandinavian countries, widowed peasant women often remarried their young male farm workers. As late as 1790, in Salzburg, more than half of all carpenters' wives were considerably older than their husbands. Some time ago Peter Laslett noted that in many regions of England when women married they were on the average at least two to three years older than their husbands. More recently, Laslett has identified this age divergence as a distinctive feature of European marriage.[42]

In preliminary observations, Keith Thomas calculated the age disparities between marital partners listed in several censuses of the poor in English towns. His conclusions validate those of Laslett. Of 454 married couples whose ages were noted in the Norwich census of 1579, the wives were older in 127 cases. In 64 cases they were older by at least ten years. This second figure yields a statistical incidence of 14 percent, or more than 1 in 10. In his exhaustive history of the family in early modern Europe, Lawrence Stone concludes that in seventeenth- and eighteenth-century Europe, in about 20 percent of all first marriages wives were older than their husbands by five years or more. In 1977, when Stone's book was published, the figure stood at 7 percent.[43]

Economic considerations, in the first instance, lay behind such relationships. Among all classes family and financial imperatives were primary considerations in marital choice. In many eras and many areas older women possessed the monetary resources that could bring economic advancement or survival. In the first instance, daughters could inherit family property when there were no sons. In contrast to many non-Western lands, inheritance did not revert to males in collateral family branches, nor did fathers, as in ancient Greece or in non-European regions, adopt sons or sons-in-law with the result that family inheritance did not pass to daughters. Laws against bigamy prevented polygamy or concubinage, and complicated statutes against incest placed a brake on the kinds of in-family marriages involved in the ancient Athenian *epiklaros* situation.[44]

From the medieval period onward among people of means, especially in England and in Northern Europe, inheritance patterns favored widows. In England, France, and the Netherlands, after the death of their husbands, widows retained the dowries their families had contributed to the marriage. Moreover, in many regions of these countries they also were the beneficiaries of a financial settlement negotiated for them at the time of the marriage and payable in the case of their husband's death (the so-called dower, or jointure, which could include the dowry). In England legal precedent established dower at one-third of a husband's property, although the amount could be larger. If husbands desired, they could leave all their property to their wives. And throughout many regions of England and France, statused women who remarried kept their titles and other privileges of rank even when they married men of lesser rank.[45]

In addition to money and goods, women could also inherit family businesses. Under the precapitalist guild system, wives, not sons, often inherited businesses and guild memberships. Because wives often worked along with their husbands when homes and businesses occupied contiguous space, it was assumed that wives were both competent and entitled to carry on family businesses. Moreover, at least in England, wives could own their own businesses. Under the English common law, women could apply for *feme sole* (unmarried woman) status.[46] This dispensation allowed them to circumvent the legal restrictions on married women's right to own property.

The wealthy widows to whom I have referred were not homebound women suddenly enriched by a husband's demise. Many of them had responsibilities in family businesses and in managing country estates and other property. A rich source of English family history in this premodern era is the extensive papers of the Paston family, rural gentry whose archive spans the fourteenth to the seventeenth centuries. In these papers the women appear competent and independent. The husbands often lived for periods of time in cities, tending to business matters, while their wives stayed at home managing provincial properties. They oversaw agricultural operations, sold crops and bought provisions, arbitrated labor disputes, and collected rents.[47]

Writing about the English town of Brigstock in the fourteenth century, Judith M. Bennett found a pattern of similarly strong women. But in this case the pattern, which will periodically appear in this book, seems a function of aging. In this typical late-medieval village, widowhood brought a new gender equivalency. For as many aging men retired from public life, widows, inheriting property, began for the first time to participate in the market economy.[48]

Those Parisian widows cited in the sixteenth-century French legislation for marrying younger men similarly were not leisured ladies engaged in self-indulgent behavior, as suggested by the legislative discussion about them. Rather, many were managers of complex domestic enterprises. Parisian magistrates, for example, usually owned estates outside of the city in addition to city homes. The wives of these magistrates were often responsible for supervising the collection of the rents on these estates and for overseeing such activities as harvesting and winemaking.[49]

Before the seventeenth century, as capitalism's growing dominance eroded guild structures and more gender-balanced entrepreneurship, women actively engaged in managing more than a small number of businesses. They were especially active in those based on crafts like spinning and weaving which women had long carried on in their homes. For example, in the city of Bath, a center of the woolen trade, women were prominent entrepreneurs. Under the "putting out" system of production then used, entrepreneurs bought fleece from sheepgrowers and arranged for artisans to spin it into thread and then into cloth, for export abroad. Thus the Wife of Bath was drawn along the lines of one of these brokers of note: her products were so fine, according to Chaucer, that they rivaled the cloth of Ypres and even of Ghent, the day's centers of wool making.

To young men economically disadvantaged by primogeniture, these women could be attractive marital prospects. "I wish your good speade with the widow," was common encouragement by the seventeenth century in England given to men bent on enhancing their life positions. And the attraction could extend downward in the class structure, to journeymen within the guild structure. This was especially the case by the fifteenth century, as guilds in many areas became closed corporations, with restricted hereditary membership. By then sometimes the only way an apprentice could achieve master status was by marrying the widow of a master. In parish registers in Sweden as late as the nineteenth century the following notice was not uncommon: "He produced a document showing that, although a journeyman up to now, he gets full rights as a master, as soon as by the marriage to the widow he becomes owner of the workshop and tools."[50]

In his early-seventeenth-century novel, *The pleasant Historie of John Winchcombe, in his yonguer yeares called Jack of Newbery,* English writer Thomas Deloney tells the story of the courtship and marriage of young Jack, an apprentice, to his employer, a "comely ancient widow." Like the Wife of Bath, Deloney's widow is a clothmaker, although her entrepreneurship seems modest in comparison with that of Alison of Bath: she manages an artisanal shop with spinners and weavers producing wool to be sold to middlemen. Deloney describes her as "reasonable" in wealth. Financially successful and erotically aggressive, the widow of Newbery has many suitors. But she prefers Jack, young and good-humored, who has already singled himself out from his rowdy drinking companions by his desire to get ahead. On his part, she is simply too attractive a marital prospect for this ambitious man to refuse.[51]

Deloney's novel has the ring of verisimilitude to it. The novel's protagonist, Jack of Newbery, was an actual individual who lived during the reign of Henry VIII and who became a popular hero because of well-publicized aid to the king. Thomas Deloney was an itinerant peddler who on the side wrote picaresque tales drawn from the lives of his fellow working people. He is often cited as the first English novelist.

European marital patterns and family structure also contributed to a situation favorable to marriages between older women and younger men, especially among families of limited means. By the fifteenth century a distinctive Western European marital pattern among classes other than the nobility and the well-to-do had come into being. Under this pattern women and men did not marry at especially early ages. Rather, they waited until they were in their late twenties or early thirties. In all probability, economic events produced the caution. For the large population expansion of the twelfth and thirteenth centuries resulted in the overcrowding of available resources, producing periodic famine and a density of habitation which was fertile ground for epidemic viruses.

The bubonic plague epidemic (the Black Death) of the middle and late fourteenth century killed as many as one-half of the European population. These high mortality rates taught peasants and workers to be cautious. Calculating the odds, however unconsciously, they realized that having large numbers of children would upset the balance between available resources and the support of human life. Postponing marriage became a rudimentary form of birth control in line with what one historian has called "a realistic and ruthless family strategy."[52] As early as the 1370s, figures from England show that of all women over the age of fourteen, only 67 percent were married. By the seventeenth century, the figure was down to 55 percent.[53]

In contrast to the upper classes, parents with limited means did not necessarily provide dowries or marriage portions to their children. Still, couples were expected to have some capital accumulation before they married. Faced with these realities, men and women put off marriage until such time as their parents either signed retirement agreements with them, deeding them the property in return for guaranteed support, or died and willed them some inheritance. Or through their own employment they might by then have accumulated some savings.

Moreover, women as well as men were expected to contribute funds to the family marital capital; to provide their own dowry, if you will. This system was so widespread in Western Europe that it has come to be called the "dotal system of marriage exchanges."[54] It not only gave young people a certain freedom in marital choice but it also could place older women at an advantage. Indeed, in some ways it became difficult for young women to contemplate marriage unless their parents could provide them with a dowry or they could find an older man with money willing to marry them. Older women who had worked and saved some capital were attractive marital choices.

Or, other forms of valuable expertise might be theirs. They might, for example, possess the knowledge of a trade. In agrarian regions their expertise might lie in the knowledge of farming procedures: one analysis terms this sort of knowledge "cultural capital of expertise."[55] And, when survival was the issue, conventions about appearance and aging could be set aside. Thus the priest of the French village of Sennely, close to Orléans, in the seventeenth century noted that his parishioners did not care too much about physical attractiveness when it came to marriage. Only financial position concerned them.[56]

Moreover, once spouses died, European people remarried quickly. The economic situation was generally so difficult for families of limited means that the death of a spouse could mean disaster, for women as well as men shared the burden of family economic production. Historian Jean-Louis Flindrin thinks that the practice of the peasants of the French Cantal was typical throughout Europe. There, soon after the burial of the deceased marital partner, the surviving spouse would hold a communal celebration and choose a new husband or wife.[57]

Such speedy remarriage as Flindrin documents was particularly the case for men, for convention dictated that men should not perform women's work. In this situation a postmenopausal woman could be attractive. Steven Ozmont tells the story of a man from Cologne in the sixteenth century who chose to remarry a well-to-do woman partly because of her money and partly because she could no longer bear children. He had already had two children by his first wife, and he simply did not want any more.[58]

Yet men were not always the ones to exercise choice in these matters; aging women, too, had areas of control. For example, with regard to aging women, marriage to younger men might be a guarantee of being taken care of in old age: thus such associations could function as a rudimentary form of old-age relief. English Restoration playwright William Wycherley's *Plain Dealer* concerns the competition between an older and a younger man vying for the hand of a wealthy widow, twenty years older than the younger man. (Age-disparate relationships form a central subject of English Restoration drama.) With regard to the match, the younger man asserts: "Because I have nothing to keep me after her death, I am the likelier to take care of her in her life."[59]

Economic, Social, and Demographic Complexities

B Y STRESSING the extent to which cross-age relationships existed in medieval and early modern Europe, I do not mean to suggest that they were universal. Younger sons did not always marry older women, and journeymen did not always marry masters' widows. Sometimes the older women rejected younger suitors. In the concluding section of the thirteenth-century *Romance of the Rose,* Jean de Meun noted that both Ovid and Juvenal had advised young men seeking wealth to marry rich older women. But he also cautioned that such women were often shrewd and suspicious of the false flattery that would sway young women. Thus the suitor of an older woman should take care "not to do or say anything that might look like a ruse when he wants to steal her love or even to bring her honestly into the snares of love." Ralph Houlbrooke tells the story of a Suffolk widow who in the 1550s broke off a projected match with a young man because she had asked his father to contribute sixty pounds as a marriage portion, and he would only contribute forty.[60]

Considerable cultural prohibitions against such age-disparate unions existed. Catholic homilies as well as Protestant tracts on marriage advised that men should be older than their wives. Such an age differential ensured the maintenance of that patriarchal order as much a part of European hierarchy as social class and life-stage positionings. For some, cross-age relationships between aging women and younger men were a perverse overturning of the gender order which they viewed as fixed by nature. Thus one Scandinavian priest averred that marriage between old widows and young servants was so unnatural that it was akin to "sodomy."[61]

Europe was generally a pronatalist culture, and many parents undoubtedly regarded children as potential security in old age. Such beliefs made procreativity important in marital choice. Yet a rising capitalist mentality, especially in England, vitiated this impulse. When parents paid more attention to providing for their children's futures rather than envisioning their offspring as contributors to family support, they became more a "cost" than a "benefit."[62]

Generational conflict also existed. It was endemic in the male youth groups—the Burschenschaften in Germany, the Abbayes de la Jeunesse in France, and comparable groups in England—which existed not only for fellowship but also as enforcers of community morals. Through charivaris, the "rough music" of discordant drums and cymbals, they censored individual actions. In France and Italy, although not in England, marriages between older and younger individuals could provoke the noisy protests. Yet whether such marriages always provoked charivaris or whether the marital couple could buy off the protesters is not entirely certain from the sources. The possibility of such community disapproval, however, might easily serve as a deterrent to age-disparate relationships.[63]

Husbands who wished to prevent wives from remarriage after they died and relatives unhappy about widowed mothers' control of family property might attempt to introduce legal restrictions on widows' remarriage and property rights. The latter impulse, for example, seems to have motivated the restrictive legislation on widows' remarriages in sixteenth-century France. With regard to tradesmen, in some cities guild regulations permitted widows to continue in husbands' trades only so long as they did not marry. In other cities many trades were closed to women. Thus while women were important producers of woolen cloth in Bruges and Leiden, they did little similar work in Cologne, even though it was a center of woolen production. And while women controlled the making of clothes in Leiden, they were barred from these crafts in Paris. There were women merchants and retailers in London, Lübeck, and Cologne, but access to such work in Utrecht and Paris was denied them. In sixteenth-century Coventry, England, widows supervised the businesses they inherited only until their eldest sons had completed their apprenticeships. The sons then assumed control. And in this city widowed women had only a scant chance of finding new husbands. Nine times as many widows as widowers resided in the city.[64]

Demography, too, could both further and hinder these relationships between older women and younger men. The effect of gender ratios in populations on relationships we might prefer to identify as primarily emotive can be striking in any era or region. Thus some analysts argue that the freer position of women in the earlier Middle Ages had to do with their lesser numbers in the population. Once a "low sex ratio" appeared in the later Middle Ages, women's position declined.

But the workings of these numerical gender ratios could be complex. They could, for example, impact in different ways on age cohorts within the population. Take the example of the influence of female death in childbirth. This stark reality of early modern life regularly and substantially decreased the numbers of young and middle-aged women. But it also could have the demographic impact of leaving older women a significant numerical group available for marriage. Moreover, in many regions this demographic age imbalance was multiplied by the propensity of older men to marry increasingly younger women as they aged, as first and second wives died and these men acted according to cultural imperatives which identified beauty with youth or their desires for ensured generativity. But when older men appropriated younger women, then younger men might find only older women available as marriage partners. This principle, apparent in tribal and early agricultural societies, also operated in medieval and early modern Europe.

Yet we must not forget the male violence endemic in this period. This violence especially characterized the behavior of younger men. A study of mortality rates in England in the fourteenth and fifteenth centuries (the period of the Hundred Years' War between England and France) finds that 46 percent of all men died violently after their fifteenth year. This startling figure was the result of their participation in wars and tournaments or their execution due to capital offenses. Such a large decline in numbers of young men could offset that diminution in the numbers of women due to death in childbirth. Thus this same study finds that of a group of individuals, both male and female, alive in 1330, 18 percent of the men reached the age of fifty-four while 50 percent of the women reached the age of forty-nine.[65]

Once again the demographic fact emerges: if women could survive their childbearing years, their life expectancy could be greater than that of men. One factor furthering courtly love was probably the large number of men who died in the Crusades and left widows behind them. And many of the Parisian women in the sixteenth century who were marrying younger men were the widows of men who had died in that century's wars of religion.

Moreover, workings of illnesses like the plague impacted on all sex ratios and marital customs. In his history of old age in Europe, Georges Minois maintains that the epidemics of the fourteenth and fifteenth centuries, especially the plague, singled out children and young adults, thereby leaving a larger proportion of older people vis-à-vis the young than previously. What this situation produced in terms of family formation, according to Minois, was that more older men competed for younger women, leaving many younger men no option but to turn to older women. This demographic imbalance, Minois contends, lay especially behind the many fifteenth-century commentaries on the phenomenon of age-disparate relationships.[66]

Inheritance customs could combine with demographic positionings in significant ways to further age-disparate relationships. Writing about marriage patterns among the peasantry in medieval Europe, Michael Postan noted some time ago the existence of what he called a "marriage fugue," or a "point-counter-point" with regard to age and youth. In this situation, characteristic of regions of settled agriculture, younger sons with little expectation of inheriting parental property would marry older women (often considerably older women), who themselves had inherited property from deceased spouses. After the older women died, the men would marry women much younger than they. These women, in turn, upon the death of the older husbands would themselves marry two or three more times, often to men much younger than they.[67]

A fugue implies a repetitive pattern on a single theme. Indeed, this pattern of older men marrying younger women and then leaving them as widows at older ages had already occurred in fifth-century B.C.E. Athens as it would later occur in Renaissance Italy.[68] But it was not always the case that women automatically married downward in age cohort when demography raised the possibility. Sometimes family or economic imperatives, or their own inclinations, allowed widowed or unmarried women the possibility of remaining alone, outside the boundaries that relationships might create for positive or negative ends. In ancient Rome, I have noted, honor was accorded women who remained faithful to one husband throughout their lives and did not remarry when they were widowed.

For women with economic means, widowhood could bring authority and autonomy. Thus in Siena, Italy, in the thirteenth century, the many women left widows by older husbands took advantage of Siena's expanding economy to trade in real estate, to lend money, and to manage the production and distribution of the grain and other staples grown on the estates they owned outside of the city. Remarriage rates among them were not sizable. Investigating Genoa in the same period, Diane Hughes finds a situation both similar and different. She traces the numbers of widows who did not remarry to the fact that when upper-class women in Genoa remarried, they had to leave their children with their first husband's family and relinquish all claims to guardianship. Such restraints, however, were not required of artisan widows. Children from first marriages went with their mothers into second marriages: thus artisan widows remarried in large numbers. And, they were counted excellent marriage prospects. In addition to the income from their dowries, which they kept throughout their lives, they were often the chief beneficiaries of their husbands' estates.[69]

Peter Laslett examined the records for households in a hundred rural communities of sixteenth-century England. He found that 13 percent (or over one household in ten) were headed by widows. Some of these widows eventually remarried. Although Laslett did not investigate legal rights or personal attitudes concerning children, what seems predominant in his sources is the pleasure these widowed women attested to in setting up their own households and the vigor with which they resisted men who courted them.[70]

What about those sixteenth-century Parisian widows whom the government officially chastised for marrying younger men? How many were involved? Were the actions of just a few sufficient to raise a general fear? With regard to them, memorialist Brantôme contended that the majority did not remarry because they enjoyed being single. He wrote: "They want friends and lovers, but no husbands, out of love for the freedom that is so sweet. To be out from under the domination of a husband seems to them paradise. . . ."[71]

Indeed, was Chaucer's fourteenth-century Wife of Bath really free as she attempted to achieve autonomy in marriage at a time when law and custom decreed that husbands should have control? Would she not have been better off to have continued her life of independent travel and of conversation, not with misogynist men but with her neighbor, her friend also named Alison, her gossip, as Chaucer, adopting the day's common term for women friends, called her?

In certain regions of Europe the kind of freedom that unrestricted inheritance might bring was severely constrained by social and family customs which upheld masculine privilege. Thus in Mediterranean states, for example, among upper-class families family honor was so closely identified with female purity that extensive restrictions were placed on freedom of action for women. In later ages the thirteenth-century situation in Siena and Genoa was unusual for Italy as a whole.

Although dowries here as elsewhere reverted to wives after their husbands' deaths, the natal family head usually took control over the disposition of these dowries. There seems little evidence in Italy of older women marrying younger men, even though the initial age disparities between husbands and wives at marriage were sizable.[72] Indeed, the homosexuality that foreign travelers to Italy noted in the city-states there may have partly originated from the lack of older women available for young men as sexual and emotional partners.[73]

Moreover, throughout Europe by late medieval times women's freedom to control inherited family funds eroded. In Siena the erosion began as early as the late thirteenth century, when a series of restrictive laws were passed forbidding the use of property in a manner which would deprive the widow's children of its benefits. In France, as I have noted, the erosion began in the sixteenth century and seems to have been related to the growth of the patriarchal state, with its incursions into the earlier individualistic and regional arrangements that allowed women some autonomy. Writing about Europe in general, Anne Lise Head-König traces sixteenth-century restrictions on women to rapid population growth, which strained economic resources and, creating labor surpluses among men, fueled attempts to contain women. In England, a lessening of widows' rights seems to have occurred in the seventeenth century, the age of the witchcraft persecutions, of the increasing hegemony of a capitalist order, and of the misogyny apparent on the Restoration stage and in English Restoration court behavior.[74]

Throughout Europe during these centuries many provinces and cities began to demand that widows and unmarried women choose male guardians, to oversee their financial affairs and appear for them in court. The reasons for this legislation were varied and complex: in Strasbourg, for example, the city council passed such legislation to prevent women from going into convents and disinheriting their relatives in favor of the church. Yet it was not so much women's independent action that disturbed this governmental body: it was rather that the city would lose the taxation power over this money when it passed into religious hands. In addition, beginning in the mid-fifteenth century, many guilds began to impose limitations on women's rights of inheritance. For example, in many areas widows were permitted to operate family businesses for only a limited period after their husbands' deaths. They could not take on apprentices, hire new journeymen, or buy new raw materials. These restrictions seem to have been particularly designed to benefit journeymen who saw widows as a hindrance to their being able to open their own shops. They were especially characteristic of cities in which journeymen had their own organizations.[75]

For aging women at the bottom of the economic scale, these issues of remarriage I have been discussing were often irrelevant. All statistical studies of remarriage (whatever the region or the century) show a sizable drop in remarriage rates for women over the age of forty, unless a sizable oversupply of men existed. Moreover, throughout the European and American experience until recent times, the vast majority of widows were poor. They were the gleaners in the fields in rural areas and the street sweepers and ragpickers in urban areas. This majority had minimal economic resources. In London in the sixteenth century most of the one-

Sunset Boulevard: Norma Desmond (Gloria Swanson) and Joe Gillis (William Holden). (Courtesy of Paramount Pictures, Gloria Swanson, and the William Holden Trust)

The Goddess and the Young God.
(Soprintendenza Archeologica per le
Provincie Cagliari e Oristano)

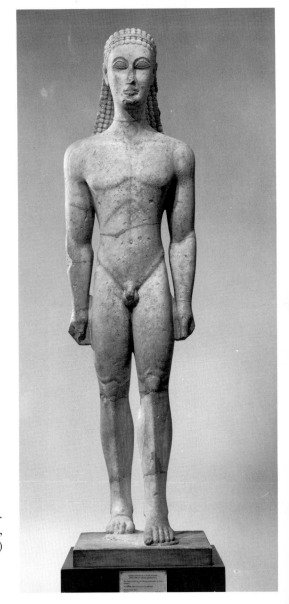

Kouros statue, Greek, c. 600 B.C.E.
(The Metropolitan Museum of Art,
Fletcher Fund, 1932)

Diana of Ephesus, probable forerunner of the Black Madonna.
(Soprintendenza Archeologica delle Province di Napoli e Casertu)

Old Market Woman, Greek. (The Metropolitan Museum of Art, Rogers Fund, 1909)

Madonna and Child, Auvergne, France, second half of twelfth century. (Courtesy of Duke University Museum of Art, Brummer Collection)

Cumaean Sibyl, a model for aging women. Michelangelo, Sistine Chapel. (Art Resource)

The Young Man with the Old Woman, Hans Sebald Beham. From Max Geisberg, *The German Single-Leaf Woodcut, 1500–1550.* (By permission of Hacker Art Books)

The Old Man with the Young Woman, Hans Sebald Beham, c. 1550. From Max Geisberg, *The German Single-Leaf Woodcut, 1500–1550.* (By permission of Hacker Art Books)

The Holy Family (Saint Anne, Mary, Jesus, Joseph, John the Baptist), Agnolo Bronzino, c. 1527–28. An early prototype for the grandmother. (National Gallery of Art, Washington, Samuel H. Kress Collection)

Witches Concocting an Ointment to Be Used on the Sabbath, Hans Baldung Grien, 1514. (Courtesy of Dover Books)

Two Women at a Window: The Duenna with Her Charge, Bartolomé Esteban Murillo, c. 1655–60. (National Gallery of Art, Washington, Widener Collection)

Jupiter Kissing Cupid: the eroticized young male. Raphael, sixteenth century.
(Art Resource)

Unicorn tapestry: male tights and short tunics. (The Metropolitan Museum of Art, Gift of John D. Rockefeller, Jr., 1937)

Sergeant Major with Lance, Hans Sebald Beham, c. *1550.* From Max Geisberg, *The German Single-Leaf Woodcut, 1500–1550.* (By permission of Hacker Art Books)

Portrait of Giovanni Emo, a condottiere. Giovanni Bellini, c. 1475–80. (National Gallery of Art, Washington, Samuel H. Kress Collection)

A Rake's Progress: The Rake Marries a Wealthy Older Woman, William Hogarth. (The Henry E. Huntington Library and Art Gallery)

ABOVE: *Queen Elizabeth Being Carried by Her Courtiers,* Robert Peake the Elder,
c. 1600. (Private collection, Sherborne Castle)

OPPOSITE TOP: *Margaret Fuller During the Siege of Rome,* Thomas Hicks.
(By permission of the Houghton Library, Harvard University)

OPPOSITE BOTTOM: Marchese Giovanni Angelo Ossoli. (By permission of
the Houghton Library, Harvard University)

Elizabeth Cady Stanton (left), a nineteenth-century model of appearance for aging women, and Susan B. Anthony (right), whose appearance was criticized. (Library of Congress)

Sarah Bernhardt.
(The Bettmann Archive)

Colette at eighty.
(The Bettmann Archive)

"The Garden Committee reports that Mrs. Bernard Thayer, Mrs. Harrison S. Quigley, and Mrs. Thompson Sperry have all seen pussy willows."

Cartoon of the clubwoman. (Drawing by Helen E. Hokinson; © 1940, 1968 The New Yorker Magazine, Inc.)

third to one-half of the urban population listed in the tax assessment rolls as having no goods were women. In Italy, according to David Herlihy, aging women without families were often so poor that they roamed from town to town, living as beggars. They were usually not listed on the tax rolls. Such a situation was replicated throughout Europe in this period.[76]

Yet Herlihy, writing about Italy, found the situation for these women not entirely bleak. For in carnival songs and folktales, in hints contained in official documents and private records, he found evidence of the existence of an oral culture among women. Herlihy thinks that these writings also indicate that women banded together to sustain one another. In the Italian Renaissance, Herlihy concludes, a supportive culture for older women in poverty existed. That culture consisted of other older women.

A Case Study of Difference: Montaillou, France, in the Fourteenth Century

IN HIS STUDY of fourteenth-century Montaillou, a Mediterranean province in the south of France, Emmanuel Le Roy Ladurie tells a story which differs from the one I have been sketching. In Montaillou there was no "dotal system of marital exchange." Instead, young men and women remained under the tight control of their natal families, and marriages were arranged for them at fairly young ages. Within marriage husbands were supposed to be dominant, and wife beating was not uncommon. On the surface, and particularly with regard to young wives, patriarchy seemed total.[77]

Yet other factors were also in operation in Montaillou to produce another social reality, an alternative text to the one I have just outlined. In this alternative text, aging women were both privileged and powerful dispensers of community advice and possessors of community honor. In the first instance, following the common pattern, in Montaillou older widowed men often married young women and these women in turn outlived their older husbands. Moreover, within most families sons were favored and, as is not uncommon in highly patriarchal societies, mothers bonded closely with sons. These connections produced both mutual dependency and favoritism in later life. In addition, throughout the fourteenth century in Montaillou more women than men over fifty were always alive.

For, as seems constant throughout European history, if women could survive their childbearing years, their life expectancy was often greater than that of men.

So strong was the matrilineal strain within this patriarchy that, with the death of a husband, a widow could become the head of her household, singled out by the title of "Madame." Sometimes the sons of these widowed female family heads would drop their father's surname as their last name and take up their mother's matronymic. Sometimes sons-in-law would take up residence with their wives within their wives' mothers' household; they might take their mother-in-law's surname as their own. Men in their fifties in Montaillou were considered old and past usefulness to the community. Women of similar age were respected and accorded special deference.

The history of aging women is filled with ironies and inconstancies. In most regions of Western Europe, I will presently argue, aging women were not accorded such privileges. Married sons and daughters did not live with their natal families, and privileges accorded aging parents were often offered grudgingly. Both the mother-in-law and the grandmother roles were attenuated. These life-cycle roles, notable in modern times, were undermined by late ages of first marriage, by residence patterns, and by cultural attitudes which stressed aging women's sexuality above their wisdom, their potential social danger above their potential social contribution.

Even in Montaillou, however, not all aging women followed the matrifocal pattern I have described. Some of the most interesting passages in Le Roy Ladurie's book concern the story of Beatrice de Planissoles, the widow of the chatelain (the feudal overlord) of the region. De Planissoles originally came from the lesser nobility, and she had married above her rank. But because she was of the aristocracy, the kinds of social patterns that Le Roy Ladurie finds among the peasantry did not apply. She had inherited money: she was able to keep her original dowry throughout her life. She lived a life of relative freedom. When married, she had affairs. Widowed and past menopause, she fell in love with a young priest. They began to live together.

But the independence that de Planissoles claimed eventually ended. Despite her status and her wealth, patriarchal attitudes were too strong for her to manage throughout her life to elude them. For, unfortunately for de Planissoles, Montaillou was a region in which in the fourteenth century the Church had embarked on a crusade to end the clergy's common practice of living with women in quasi-marital arrangements.

Clerical celibacy was now to be the norm, and the papal Inquisition was to enforce the dictate. Alarmed, Beatrice de Planissoles and her young lover moved to a remote town in the Pyrenees mountains. There they hoped that the church hierarchy might overlook them. Yet their relationship lasted only for another year. For the young priest began to fear that the Church would track him down even in their remote retreat. The problem was not only his relationship with de Planissoles but also his involvement with Catharism, a mystical form of Christianity widespread in southern France.

Thus the young priest abandoned Beatrice. Even that, however, was not enough. Brought before the Inquisition for questioning, he disassociated himself from her, denouncing her in the process. He called her "a wicked old woman" and suggested that she had enchanted him. His final charge was to insinuate that she was, in fact, a witch.

CHAPTER FIVE

Aging Women, Power, and Sexuality: From the Wife of Bath to the Witch

THUS FAR WITH REGARD TO early Europe I have primarily discussed the sociology of women's power, the ways in which, through the ownership of property, or the disposition of wills, or husbands' absences on business or at war, aging women might assert authority. But there are also physiological and personal dimensions to my story, and these alternative realms of experience need to be explored. These areas involve a complex of issues revolving around individual and cultural definitions and constructions of self. Attitudes toward menstruation and menopause, key experiences of women's lives, are central. Definitions of the life cycle, of opinions about the stages and seasons of life, also are involved. And matters concerning sexuality are crucial.

These psychological and physiological subjects are both separate and intertwined, and I will deal with them from both vantages. To provide a relevant framework, I will initially explore them from a cross-cultural perspective. For anthropologists' recent work on aging women in tribal and preindustrial agrarian societies sheds illumination on this issue of the authority of women as they age. Their findings are twofold: women as they age may gain power, but this power may provoke categorizations of them as witches, as persons with the ability to invoke a world of spirits for ends either beneficial or malevolent.

The Cross-Cultural Comparison

Wᴵᴛʜɪɴ ᴍᴀɴʏ ᴘʀᴇsᴛᴀᴛᴇ sᴏᴄɪᴇᴛɪᴇs, anthropologists find an improvement in the status of women as they age. Judith Brown thinks that this shift is so powerful "across a wide range of societies," that "post-parental women move toward a position of matriarchy." Concomitantly, a major personality shift takes place, whether the cause or the result of the change in status. Almost invariably, writes Brown, "the shy and submissive girl becomes an imperious and managing older woman."[1]

Such a change with regard to temperament can be discerned within the Western experience. For example, over the centuries didactic and literary writings about age-disparate relationships reiterate the claim that aging women will invariably gain dominance over their younger partners and challenge male authority. Textual renderings as disparate as Chaucer's fourteenth-century presentation of the relationship between Jenkin and Alison of Bath and Daniel Defoe's discussion of such couplings in his eighteenth-century *Conjugal Lewdness* depict aging women as too powerful for young male partners to control.

The late-fourteenth-century instructions about proper behavior from the elderly Goodman of Paris to his young wife caution her against asserting herself, especially as she ages. The most reprehensible women, he avers, are those of older age who "little by little . . . take upon themselves authority, command, and lordship." Or, there are "certain old hags, which be sly and play the wise woman. . . ." Chaucer's merchant expostulates in *The Canterbury Tales:* "These old widows . . . they know so much of spells." Thomas Deloney's seventeenth-century Jack of Newbery thinks long and hard before he decides to agree to his "comely ancient dame's" proposal of marriage. For he fears that she will dominate him, reversing intolerably accustomed gender roles.[2]

But aging women's power was never unqualified, and it is problematic that their status necessarily increased with age. They might occasionally manage businesses or serve as midwives or the heads of nunneries. But they were barred from the kinds of institutionalized positions aging men could hold as justices or magistrates, clerics or professors. The grandmother persona, which by the nineteenth century would become a locus for aging women's authority, awaited the domestication of sentimental love within the family and new demographic patterns which would allow more women greater longevity. Before the nineteenth century, late ages of marriage and childbearing among peasants and workers meant that most women of these classes died before their children had begun to procreate.[3]

Among the upper classes, a group which married and bore children at younger ages, traditions of deference and formal behavior militated against cross-age sentimental bonding between grandchildren and grandparents. Early on, the aging woman of high rank in England came to be called a dowager. This term, initially meaning a widowed woman living off her dower, came to imply a regal, emotionally distant, aristocratic woman.[4]

Anthropologists identify a number of variables which may produce powerful aging women. Important among these is the cumulative knowledge gained from life experience. Deference proffered in societies in which survival partly depends on the wisdom of the aging may contribute. Aging women may be revered because of their craft skills or their knowledge of herbs and plants. The experience of mothering children, of possessing power over them, may teach domination. The hormonal changes which accompany the aging process may trigger the change in temperament. In the many societies in which men marry younger women, these young wives may learn assertive behavior from their aging husbands.[5]

European experience replicated these factors, with the exception of two important variables often key to aging women's increased authority. The first is the high status accorded to mothers-in-law in patrilineal societies with strong mother-son bonding. The second is a positive valuation of menopause which liberates aging women from the perceived pollution of menstruation and enables them to engage in freer behavior in the postmenopausal years.

In Europe, strong mother-son bonding was not the rule, aside from certain areas, like Mediterranean regions. The widespread adoption of a nuclear family form under which husband and wife established their own home rather than taking up residence with parents vitiated the power of mothers-in-law. The later ages of first marriage further diminished their potential control. It is revealing that the stereotype of the mother-in-law as family harridan was muted in early European ages; in both folk and elite tradition the stepmother rather than the mother-in-law was the most common family villain.

In many prestate societies, equally important to aging women's social power is a positive valuation of menopause. With the end of menstruation and their reproductive potential, aging women's bodies are freed from the responsibilities and dangers of reproduction, or from negative associations with menstruation as polluting, or from a physiological cycle different from men. In egalitarian societies this life-course transition may be simply cumulative of female life development; in more patriarchal societies aging women may cross gender lines to become some variation of honorary men.[6]

In this regard the European situation was especially complex. The end to menstruation freed aging women from whatever menstrual taboos existed, but these were not major. Menstruating women were not sequestered (as they are in many prestate societies). Nor were they regarded as unclean. Indeed before the nineteenth century, as a physiological process, Europeans viewed menopause as more negative than positive. The blood loss associated with menstruation was viewed as beneficial for women's bodies, and its end was regarded as unhealthy. Moreover, the sexuality viewed as governing women's nature was regarded as still in operation when it came to aging women. But the existence of this drive in postreproductive women was often deemed especially perverse, heightening the potential for charges of witchcraft against them.

In her cross-cultural study of middle-aged women, Pauline Bart found only a few societies in which women's status did not improve as they aged. But in those societies, one striking characteristic emerged in her work. That characteristic was a similar cultural valuation with regard to women, a valuation which, in assessing cultural status, focused on sexual attractiveness rather than on women's craft abilities or technical knowledge. When such was the case, young women were invariably the cultural lodestars and aging women's status was downgraded.[7]

In exploring the ramifications of this argument for the Western tradition, the bifurcated personification of aging women as exemplars of either sexuality or spirituality is central. Conceived as moral beings, aging women stood outside objectification, their qualities of what we might call high character comprising an implicit critique of the normal idealization of youth and the standardization of beauty around youthful characteristics like unwrinkled skin and pigmented hair color. There was, indeed, always a contrapuntal strain in Western expression by which aging women, like Jack of Newbery's "comely ancient dame," could be considered attractive.

Yet the conception of aging women as sexual was never so clear-cut or positive as their spiritual personification. Being perceived as sexual gave them the possibility of both power and pleasure, but it also brought the probability of danger. There was always a way in which the patriarchal gaze, much in evidence with the onset of Renaissance secularism, could reduce any woman into a bawdy being. In her study of Petrarch's Laura, Nancy Vickers has asserted that many Renaissance authors particularized women, reducing the parts of their bodies to fetishized objects of desire.[8] With regard to aging women, however, the objectification was both particular and general, extending from a negative individuation of body features to an all-encompassing fantasy of evil.

Indeed, with regard to aging women, fantasies about witchcraft, the most perverse of imaginings which we today might call pornographic, often contained a vision of all women as part of a vast culture of inverted prostitution.[9] In this conspiratorial fantasy all women, possessed of an overriding sexuality, were potential witches intent on dominating men through their bodies. Moreover, aging women controlled this perverted witchcraft culture. They were, by all accounts, a majority group among those women accused of witchcraft. In European literature and in actual life aging women served as procurers in the premodern culture of prostitution. From regarding them as the "go-betweens" in sexual vice it was one step to seeing a diabolical purpose behind aging women's ordinary actions. Times of social insecurity and rapid change bring scapegoating. Thus these fantasies became invested with historical force as the strains produced by the religious and cultural upheavals of the Reformation and Counter Reformation brought massive witchcraft persecutions, with older women as primary targets.

With regard to this issue of sexuality and power, two strains existed simultaneously and, indeed, upon occasion intertwined. The first was positive for women, involving freedom and fulfillment; the second was negative, involving debasement and, finally, persecution. Each in various ways will form the subject of the current chapter and the one following, when the subject of Jenkin's gender (the gender of men) will be reintroduced.

And, in this exploration of text and countertext, I will investigate one crucial theme of this book thus far underplayed: the theme of life process, of the chronological situations of women as they pass through the process of aging. For aging in Western culture has never been defined as a continuum, all of a piece; rather, it has been regarded as a process, culturally defined, with stages and plateaus.

Aging Women and Sexuality in the European Tradition

*E*UROPEAN BELIEFS about the sexuality of aging women were based on physiological theories dating to Aristotle and Galen. According to their ideas four qualities (hot, cold, dry, and moist) and four humors (blood, red choler, black choler, and phlegm) determined body chemistry and behavior. The qualities and the humors could have both positive and negative effects; their production varied by gender and by age. But what was key to both gender distinctions and to aging were the humors and especially heat, the vital fire which provided body energy and played a large role in determining sexual drive.[10]

These physiological theories further posited that men were hotter than women and that aging people (whether male or female) were colder than younger people. In 1579 pamphleteer John Stubbs criticized Elizabeth I of England for proposing to marry the French Duke of Alençon, the son of Catherine de Médicis and Henry II. Stubbs was against the marriage because, among other reasons, he contended that the young duke would never remain faithful to the aging queen. "It is quite contrary to his young appetites. . . ."[11] In 1579 Elizabeth was forty-six and Alençon was twenty-three. It seems that in Stubbs's view Alençon was young and hot-blooded, with a strong sexual drive, while Elizabeth was old and cold-blooded, with fading sexual desires.

Yet other views about aging women's sexuality differed considerably from those of Stubbs. Europeans may have believed that men had hotter blood than women and thus a heightened sexual drive. But they also believed that women's sexual and reproductive organs governed their emotional functioning: thus their sexuality virtually determined their being. Galen had posited that the uterus was directly connected to the brain, and this belief was not challenged until the nineteenth century. The common belief also was that women required regular sexual intercourse not only to conceive but also for stable emotional functioning. The bathing of women's reproductive organs by male semen was supposed to be emotionally therapeutic, and female orgasm was considered important to smooth bodily functioning as well as to conception.

With regard to aging women, these theories supported the belief in their continued sexuality. Although coldness might govern their body energy, their sexual organs still existed, with direct influence over the brain, and with a continued need for heterosexual intercourse. Galen had argued that the limbs and backs of widows who had not had intercourse for some time would ache from the buildup of the semen inside them, and this belief remained current during later centuries. Advice writer William Gouge in the seventeenth century counseled that marital duty required intercourse for women past their childbearing years. Echoing this belief for France in a similar time period, the courtier Pierre de Bourdeille, the Abbé de Brantôme, in his major work on the women of his age, told the story of a woman of "pretty advanced age" who consulted a physician as to whether she should remarry. She complained to the doctor that she had experienced all sorts of "evil humours" since the death of her husband. Yet, she continued, she had never been troubled by such ailments when her husband was alive, since "because of the constant exercises they performed together, the humours were consumed."[12]

Moreover, sophisticated medical opinion was not unified in the belief that coldness governed the constitutions of aging women. Thus Brantôme wrote that he had consulted doctors on this issue and that they had told him that old women could be so "ardent and hot-blooded, that cohabiting with a young man, they do draw all ever they can from him...." Or, as this passage also implies, satisfying aging women's sexual ardor could be at the expense of the energy of young men. Aging women's sexuality could be dangerous, draining of the life force. It could involve a perilous attempt to regain youth through absorbing youth from a young sexual partner.

In the first scene of Shakespeare's *A Midsummer Night's Dream,* the fairy queen Titania loves the adolescent Puck. In this fairyland her ardor seems not much more than a fleeting fantasy, a bagatelle of desire. Yet the play's initial lines treat the passion between an aging woman and a young man as dangerous. (The reference to a "stepmother" draws on the story of Hippolytus and Phaedra, or Joseph and Potiphar's wife):

> *How slow*
> *This old moon wanes!*
> *She lingers my desires,*
> *Like to a step dame, or a dowager*
> *long withering out a young man's revenue.*[13]

There is also the physiological fact that many menopausal women experience flashes of heat, due to the decreasing glandular production of the hormone estrogen. These experiences of heat (as women undergoing menopause well know) can occur numerous times in a single day as well as for a period extending three or four years or even longer. European physiological theory connected heat with sexuality; thus the possible conclusion was to regard this experience of heat as an indication of a heightened sexuality. So in England the saying went that "he that would an old wife wed must eat an apple before he goes to bed."[14] The apple, the fruit connected with Eve's downfall in the Garden of Eden, was considered an aphrodisiac.

That aging women are sexual beings is a consistent theme in European literature in the premodern period. Chaucer's Alison of Bath, with her "lust and lickerishness," is one such woman. The Italian heroine of Boccaccio's fourteenth-century *Corbaccio,* a woman close to forty, spends her time attempting to seduce men. She wears fashionable clothing to give her a look of elegance appealing to young men. "I could not satisfy her lust," declares one of her lovers. In his 1509 *The Praise of Folly,* Erasmus wrote corrosively about relationships between aging women and younger men, tracing their occurrence to aging women's sexual desires:

> Now it is even more amusing to see these old women, so ancient that they might as well be dead. . . . They are as hot as bitches in heat, or (as the Greeks say) they rut like goats. They pay a good price for the services of some handsome young Adonis. They never cease smearing their faces with makeup. . . . They drink a lot. . . .[15]

Celestina, the famed aging go-between of Fernando de Rojas's sixteenth-century play, *La Celestina,* identifies herself as seventy and expostulates, "Old though I am, God knows I still have the yen." And, Cleopatra, the wanton woman of Shakespeare's play whose passionate attractiveness to men made her a transhistorical symbol of female seductiveness, was "the serpent of Old Nile." She was with Phoebus's pinches "wrinkled deep in time." And there is Shakespeare's famous judgment about Cleopatra: "Age cannot wither her, nor custom stale/Her infinite variety."[16]

In Shakespeare's *Hamlet,* both Hamlet and his father's ghost criticize Hamlet's mother Gertrude's aging sexuality. When Gertrude was married to Hamlet's father, virtue seemed to define her being; she seemed a "radiant angel." But she could not resist her brother-in-law Claudius's amorous advances. Like Clytemnestra with Aegisthus in Aeschylus' play, male physical ardor excited in Gertrude an erotic response she could not control. She gave in to a man, Hamlet bitterly charges, of great sexual "gifts . . . that have the power so to seduce." Just as the young Ophelia probably could not resist Hamlet, so Gertrude could not resist Claudius. "Frailty, thy name is woman," declares Hamlet. He refers to aging women as well as to young women.[17]

In his 1621 *Anatomy of Melancholy,* Briton Robert Burton put the case about aging women's sexuality contemptuously: "Of woman's unnatural, insatiable lust, what country, what village doth not complain? Mother and daughter sometimes dote on the same man...." And, he continued, "whilst she is so old, a crone, a beldam, ... she caterwauls, and must have a stallion, a champion, she must and will marry again, and betroth herself to some young man." In the contemporaneous *Insatiate Countess,* a play constructed around long-term European ideas of women's sexual insatiability, John Marston drew on an equally venerable convention about aging women's propensity to hire young men for sexual purposes when they could no longer attract men on their own. "They buy venery, bribing damnation, and hire brothel slaves."[18]

However, stories about these relationships contained in English seventeenth-century chapbooks—cheap, popular tracts—presented aging women's sexuality positively. These texts imply that aging women's eroticism, rather than their economic status, attracted young men. As Thomas Wythorne had asserted in his sixteenth-century autobiography, "He that wooeth a widow must not carry 'quick' eels in his codpiece, but show some proof that he is stiff before."[19]

The tradition beginning with Ovid that older women are better lovers than younger women continued. The twelfth-century queen in Andreas Capellanus's *Art of Courtly Love* stated as a physiological fact that "as regards that natural instinct of passion, young men are usually more eager to gratify it with older women than with young ones of their own age." Pierre de Brantôme made a similar comment in the sixteenth century with regard to men's preference for older courtesans rather than younger ones: "The truth is that while youth is most able to attract the love of some men, with others it is maturity, a sufficient age, a practiced wit, a long experience, good conversation, and a well-trained wit, that are the most seductive features." Further, Brantôme continued, the sexual desire of many aging women could be greater than that of younger women:

> So I have seen some that neither at the beginning nor the middle of life are ready to be excited, but only at the end. And rightly do men say that in these matters the end is more fierce than the other two ages.[20]

Aging women's social mentoring of young men could involve a sexual initiation. Thus from the fifteenth century on it was not uncommon for younger noblemen to turn to older courtesans for instruction in both sexual technique and fine manners. Such instruction could be part of the European tour that young English noblemen characteristically took; in fifteenth-century France fathers chose courtesan-mistresses for their sons.[21] In seventeenth-century Paris Ninon de Lenclos held a school in gallantry for young noblemen. Lenclos may have been what we would call "promiscuous," but she chose the men to whom she was available.

In addition to being viewed as sexually experienced, aging women were also often viewed as sexually aggressive. This convention is evident, for example, in the medieval story of the loathly lady—the story which Chaucer employs in the Wife of Bath's tale. The sexual aggressiveness of aging women is also a theme of the fabliaux, those bawdy thirteenth-century tales in which wives, both old and young, regularly deceive their husbands. It is there in the common folktale in which a stepmother tries to seduce her stepson and, when he rejects her, denounces him as the aggressor to his father. It is there in the painterly conception of the Devil Queen who tempted Saint Anthony in the Egyptian desert, beginning in the mid-fourteenth century, as a middle-aged voluptuary.[22]

Older women as sexualized beings are present in two important sixteenth- and seventeenth-century English texts on the subject of age-disparate affection: namely Thomas Wythorne's *Autobiography of Thomas Wythorne* (1597) and Thomas Deloney's *The pleasant Historie of John Winchcombe, in his yonguer yeares called Jack of Newbery* (1626). (Lawrence Stone identifies the Wythorne work as the first intimate and secular English autobiography; Deloney's work is often cited as the first English novel.)[23] Both tales are steeped in eroticism. Thomas Wythorne, an itinerant music teacher in well-to-do households, is pursued by almost every older woman he encounters, even by the aristocratic mothers of his pupils. Working-class and servant women with some property attempt to lure him into marriage; the housekeeper of the estate adjacent to the one where he is employed cooks him dinner and, while proposing marriage to him, offers him "a delicate dish." Jack of Newbery's "comely ancient dame" woos him with bawdy stories and hints of future sexual performance. When he warns her that so "lusty" a young man might never be able to love an older woman, she replies that "she would take him down in his wedding shoes."[24]

And there are the aging women of English seventeenth-century Restoration drama who eagerly pursue men and who, like their most famous exemplar, Lady Wishfort in Congreve's *Way of the World,* fool themselves into believing that younger men desire them for themselves and not for their money. William Wycherley in *Love in a Wood* declares: "These useful old Women are more exorbitant, and craving in their desires, than the young ones in theirs." Or, as Aphra Behn, the famed female seventeenth-century playwright, put it:

> *If there be inequality in Years, There is so too in*
> *Fortunes, that might add*
> *A Lustre to my Eyes, Charms to my Person, And make me*
> *fair as Venus, young as Hebe.*[25]

The eroticism of aging women could also be perceived as prurient. A lifetime of experience and the ability to engage in intercourse without the possibility of pregnancy could be viewed as perverse, as a depraved reversal of the accustomed ways. Even the presumed ugliness of aging had to it an erotic quality, the quality of being beyond the ordinary, of stretching the limits of the visible beyond the socially acceptable, of indicating new realms of vice. Among the most erotic scenes in early pornography are those between aging brothel madams and the young men they choose to satisfy their lust: "old bawds," the convention went, "prefer rampant youth." John Cleland's 1748 *Fanny Hill,* famed as the first "best-selling" English pornographic novel, contains such a scene. In *Fanny Hill* Cleland describes the erotic coupling of the matron of the house, "squab-fat; red-faced and at least fifty," with a "tall brawny young Horse-grenadier, moulded in the Hercules style: *in fine,* the choice of the most experienced dame, in those *affairs,* in all London."[26]

Underscoring these high and popular culture sources is the classic nursery rhyme of the old woman who lived in a shoe and who had so many children she didn't know what to do. The shoe has characteristically been a Western symbol for sexuality. Or there is the expression "old bag," to refer to an aging woman, bag being slang for the vagina.

"Old bag" is an insulting phrase, but more positive attitudes could apply. Thus Brantôme (who wrote extensively about aging women) was aware that sexuality could be heightened among aging women because they no longer had to worry about becoming pregnant (if they were postmenopausal). "And another and yet greater advantage for them is this," wrote Brantôme. "Being now aged and coming nigh on to their fifty years, they need feel no more fear of getting with child, and so have full, plenty, and most amply freedom ..." In *Conjugal Lewdness,* Daniel Defoe implied something similar when he wrote that aging women married young men because these women were driven by sexual urges. For, he concluded, he could conceive of no other reason.[27]

The Story Viewed
from Life-Cycle Literature

THUS FAR THIS WORK has paid scant attention to life-stage distinctions among aging women, to the place on the cycle of aging individual women occupy. This omission has been purposive, for the complexities of this issue necessitate a separate presentation. But to understand cultural attitudes toward aging as well as individual women's experiences, it is important to recognize that later Europeans, like their Greek and Roman predecessors, drew a distinction between a stage of midlife and one of old age, for women as well as for men.

From the Greeks onward, philosophical and popular speculation attempted to decipher how life proceeded and what individuals might expect at each stage of the life course. This theorization seems to have been a way of understanding the dimensions of life process in a world fraught with disease and violence. It was a means of providing expectational boundaries and models for life socialization in hierarchical societies. It drew from comforting classical concepts of the unity of the universe and the interdependence of everything within it: the cycle of the seasons, the movement of the planets, the course of human life. It made time more comprehensible in centuries when it was easily and capriciously shattered by death.

The most famous example of life-stage theorization from the European past occurs in Shakespeare's play *As You Like It,* in the act 2, scene 7, "All the world's a stage" speech. The courtier Jaques delivers this speech, and he suffers from the emotional malady of melancholy, an affliction which Renaissance thinkers judged to be either a sign of madness—or of genius. Here Shakespeare divides the ages of life into seven stages, in line with astrological reasoning based on the seven planets. Such reasoning was popular in the Renaissance, a time when a classical revival was accompanied by a renewed interest in magic and mystery, in alchemy and astrology.[28]

Like most life-cycle theorists, Shakespeare does not include women in his "seven ages of man." He makes this omission despite the fact that after the character Jaques announces that "all the world's a stage," he goes on to state that on this stage "all the men *and women* [are] merely players" (italics mine). Aside from infancy and old age, Shakespeare chooses only male types to illustrate his seven ages: women and their life experiences of domesticity, marriage, and childbearing are not included. The infant, "mewling and puking," is followed by the "whining school-boy." Next there is the lover, "sighing like a furnace," then the soldier, "full of strange oaths." The justice, "full of wise saws," is followed by the "pantaloon," the aging man. The seventh—and last—stage is desolate old age.

Recent writers on European life-cycle literature note the absence of women within the tradition while offering little explanation for the omission. Yet that women were usually overlooked resulted partly from the presumption that only male activities and roles were important. Moreover, physiological theory held that male and female had the same sexual endowments; thus on these grounds male might subsume female. So the male persona served for all humanity in a life drama where women most often symbolized abstract qualities (like Natura or Dame Fortune), removed from real life experience.

Yet the omission of women also may have resulted from a consternation about the exact cycle of their lives. For the dominant view was that women's aging differed physiologically from that of men. In this schema based on difference (which dated from Galen) women were viewed as coming to maturity sooner than men and as aging more quickly than they.[29]

The first part of this belief about women's aging—the idea of women's earlier maturation—is apparent in the Anglo-Saxon "age of consent" laws. These laws, dating from Roman times, defined the age at which young women and men were considered sufficiently mature to be judged capable of being consensual partners in sexual intercourse. In these laws the age for women was always younger than that for men, as it continued to be in the twentieth century. Roman precedent set the "age of consent" at twelve for females and fourteen for males.

That girls in general grow faster than boys and that they seem mature when boys still look like children is a reality of modern gender growth. It was a reality not unknown in early times. In *The Art of Courtly Love,* Andreas Capellanus asserted that women's cold temperament explained their earlier maturation. For "a cold object warms up more quickly with the addition of a little heat than a hot one does if you add a little more." Moreover, women's earlier maturation explained their earlier aging. "In everything in the world which has life or spirit the sooner nature brings it to perfection the sooner by the same law, it is wasted by age." The belief in boys' later maturation is also apparent in that perception (deriving both from observation and from classical belief) that a boy did not become fully sexually mature until his beard was full grown, until he might be as old as eighteen. The adolescent boys in Marguerite de Navarre's sixteenth-century *Heptaméron* are more interested in hunting than in women, as is Shakespeare's Adonis in *Venus and Adonis.* Like Hippolyte in Euripides' drama, Shakespeare's Adonis is not yet ready for a mature erotic relationship.[30]

The anonymous author of *Aristotle's compleat masterpiece,* first penned in the seventeenth century and for the next century or so Europe's most popular treatise on sex, expressed the belief that women matured at fourteen or fifteen, while males did not reach maturity until sixteen or seventeen. In his influential seventeenth-century life-cycle treatise, Henry Cuffe traced these ideas to Aristotle. (Cuffe was a professor of Greek at Oxford University.) "Women are sooner perfected than men," wrote Cuffe, "being sooner fit for generation, sooner in the prime of their age, and finally sooner older." Cuffe's belief also seems related to a variant European notion that young women were hotter than young men and that, their energy sooner consumed by this quality, women aged sooner than men.[31]

Yet such beliefs did not gainsay the fact that women, like men, could experience a time of satisfaction in the middle stage of life, in that decade or so for men exemplified by Shakespeare's judge. The idea of the *puer senex* (literally of the "youth of aging") resounded through much life-cycle theorization: many writers believed that men reached the height of their productive powers between the ages of thirty-five and fifty. Some writers extended this conception of a positive middle period to women: a *puella senex* concept could extend to women, even though occurring at younger ages. Moreover, drawn from the popular four-stage life-cycle division based on the cycle of the seasons, the idea also existed that the third, autumnal, period was a privileged time of life.

Ovid established this convention in his passages on life stages in the *Metamorphoses,* when he described the autumnal age as one "ripe and mellow, in temper midway between youth and age." In the *Art of Love* he called it "the year's most beautiful season." For aging women as well as for aging men, it could be a positive time. European writers over the centuries often describe aging women in terms of a pleasing "autumnal" period. Boethius's depiction of the aged beauty of Philosophia in *The Consolation of Philosophy* echoes through later depictions of her. Her descendant Reason in the *Romance of the Rose* is described as "neither young nor white with age, neither too tall nor too short, neither too thin nor too fat." The just mean, dating from Aristotelian and Ciceronian speculations about moderation and sobriety, resounds in these life-cycle orderings. In the sixteenth century François Rabelais delivered a paean to an aging woman beautiful of body and spirit in his "Two Epistles to Two Women of Different Humours." This woman was, by his description, as fair as she was virtuous; indeed, he averred that her "Autumn may with Spring Compare."[32]

Concepts of beauty in Western culture also illustrate the positive qualities of middle age for women. From the maidens of medieval courtly love poetry with their blond hair and light skin, to the elegant, etherealized women of Botticelli, young women were consistently presented as the preeminent models of beauty. This convention extended to Raphael's plump female figures and to the coy eighteenth-century Fragonard women and on to the small and thin nineteenth-century "steel-engraving lady" of the fashion plates. But an alternative tradition existed. In the first place, there was the belief that beauty was dangerous, "a snare and delusion," in the biblical phrase. Helen of Troy's physical beauty caused the Trojan War. Or, as Ovid described it in the *Metamorphoses,* physical beauty was "that which entraps gods."[33]

Whether spirituality or sexuality defined women and the relationship of these qualities to beauty were issues in the *querelle des femmes* which occupied European writers from the early fifteenth century onward. Christine de Pizan initiated the pro-woman side of the debate with a rebuttal to the misogyny of the *Romance of the Rose.*[34] In her 1404 *Book of the City of Ladies* (a volume of brief biographies) de Pizan addressed the issue of aging women and beauty. Analyzing the thirteenth-century courtly love relationship between Blanche of Castile and Thibaut of Champagne, de Pizan concluded that the younger Thibaut loved his older cousin because of her virtue. Thibaut was, according to de Pizan, "amazed by her [Blanche's] enormous goodness and virtue, and was so overwhelmed by love that he did not know what to do." Moreover, de Pizan also noted that she knew several other women who had been approached more frequently by young men when they were older than when "in their greatest flower." It was, de Pizan concluded, their "outstanding goodness" that caused them to be loved.[35]

Renaissance writers, in their revival of Platonic ideas, wrote extensively about the concept of beauty. Their Neoplatonism is known for the argument that women's physical beauty could lead men toward spiritual fulfillment. But there were variations in a position which initially seems to valorize youthful appearance. First, they realized that beauty is a relative quality, existing in "the eye of the beholder." As Castiglione wrote in *The Courtier:* "in love, as in everything else, our minds judge differently, and so it often happens that what is pleasing to one is most odious to another." Marsilio Ficino, in his influential *Commentary on Plato's Symposium*, echoed Castiglione's judgment: "But we one time think the appearance of a body is handsome and another time think it ugly, and, various people may think differently about it at the same moment."[36] Agnolo Firenzuola, in his important 1535 treatise on beauty in women, noted that true beauty is a "chimera," an expectation hard to find. Its perception is relative to the inclinations of the observer. "Nora," he wrote, "so ill-favoured as she is, appears most pleasing in the sight of her Tomaso."[37]

Renaissance writers also followed Plato in arguing that facial features were not necessarily key in producing beauty; rather qualities of character, of spiritual disposition, counted.[38] Firenzuola drew on the Platonic division between two Aphrodites, the one sensual and the other spiritual, in sorting out types of beauty and their appeal. Like Plato, he preferred the spiritual model. In fact, in Firenzuola's opinion, only virtuous women could maintain their beauty over time. "Those women whose conscience is spotted by some foulness," wrote Firenzuola, "fall into a certain fever of the soul." This process, he continued, "leads to a disposition of the humours, which by vapors spoil the face."[39]

Maintaining a high standard of virtuous, unselfish behavior could also continue beauty into a woman's later years. Rabelais's pious married woman had maintained such a high standard of virtuous behavior and benevolent action that her goodness was reflected in a beautiful face. "Your outward Beauties much, your inward Graces more," wrote Rabelais. This kind of woman, whose consistent goodness was proven over a number of years, could lead men on to better lives. "Matron, adorn'd so richly in your Mind,/That in your Looks the Treasures we may find."[40]

More than this, the French belief that physical beauty, no matter its connection with spirituality, increases with age was already apparent by the seventeenth century. It was enshrined in the legend of the beauty of the aging Diane de Poitiers, the mistress of Henry II, twenty years older than he, and in that of the seventeenth-century Ninon de Lenclos. Courtier Anthony Hamilton, Count Grammont, who spent time in the late seventeenth century at both the French and English courts, reported that the phrase "increasing in beauty as one increases in years" was current at that time.[41]

The beliefs I am charting about the superiority of spiritual beauty to physical beauty may not be apparent in the visual and plastic representations of painters and sculptors of these centuries. These artists seem most often to have focused on objectified young women as their subjects and to have avoided the alternative ethical imperative regarding women which was part of their cultural matrix. According to Elizabeth Cropper, however, how to portray connections between beauty and morality posed a significant dilemma to artists working in these representational fields. Allegorical settings or the inclusion of symbolic background objects like birds or flowers, representing virtue, might provide signals for moral meanings. But how the single moment of painting could capture the intrinsic beauty of character, upon which the virtuous identity which signified true beauty should be based, was a puzzle they never really solved.[42]

One of the most profound discussions of beauty and aging women in early European literature occurs in the ending scene of Shakespeare's *The Winter's Tale*. In this scene the perception of an aging woman's wrinkles becomes a metaphor for the general difficulty in ascertaining virtue, while those wrinkles themselves represent virtue. Leontes, King of Sicily, twenty years previously had falsely sentenced to death his wife, Hermione, on an incorrect charge of adultery. Although King Leontes thinks Hermione died in prison, during the intervening years she has been hiding in the home of her faithful servant, Paulina. Paulina now brings the repentant king to her home to effect a reconciliation. At the meeting Hermione poses as a statue. Paulina describes Hermione's appearance.

> *As she lived peerless*
> *So her dead likeness, I do well believe,*
> *Excels whatever yet you look'd upon*
> *Or hand of man hath done; . . .*

At first, however, Leontes is not certain he agrees with Paulina's praise of Hermione, for he sees signs of aging in the face of the statue. He replies: "But yet, Paulina, / Hermione was not so much wrinkled; nothing / So aged as this seems." Immediately, however, this evidence of the passage of time in her face reminds him of both his suffering in the years of separation and his own responsibility for that suffering in having doubted her honesty and sentenced her to death. "I am asham'd," he says. "Does not the stone rebuke me / For being more stone than it? O royal Piece, There's magic in thy majesty, which has / My evils conjured to remembrance." He begs her pardon doubly, "That e'er I put between your holy looks / My ill suspicion." He has come to understand that true beauty lies in the reality of her aging face.[43]

Women and Old Age

W OMEN IN MIDDLE AGE may have had access to the category of beauty. But that middle period for women was, by definition, sooner reached and shorter in extent than that of men. Physiologists based that appraisal on a variety of suppositions: on women's sooner reaching maturity, on their supposed earlier development of aging coldness, on their weaker bodies, on an estimation of women as wearing themselves out because they were supposedly emotionally the more changeable sex, even on a misconception of them as idle. The arguments were many, and they followed cultural misogyny extended into perceptions of gendered aging bodies at variance with other ideas about anatomical similarity between men and women.[44]

Women in their latter years were largely excluded from the category of beauty. Shakespeare described the last two stages of the male life cycle as characterized by the pantaloon and then by a retreat to infancy. Ovid's description was no less bleak: "Then aged winter comes shivering in, with tottering steps, its hair all gone, or what it has turned white." And, Ovid continued, extending his field of vision to women as well as to men: "Helen weeps too, when she sees herself in the glass, wrinkled with age."[45]

In understanding European attitudes toward women's life cycle and their process of aging, this disjunction between middle age and old age is key. The view of middle age as a time of wisdom and contentment, or alternatively as one of passionate sexuality, and of old age in sharp contrast as a time of despair, especially for women, breaks the cycle of life apart at its peak. Thus the old peasant woman is easily scorned as an impoverished widow. Or she becomes forgotten by community relief, reduced to her own devices by a society focused on youth. She gleans in the fields or goes door to door, begging, a threatening figure to those economically better situated. Her pleading later becomes homogenized into the Halloween children's chant of "trick or treat." Her effigy was the most common victim of bonfires lit throughout Europe on the old feast days—Halloween, Christmas, the solstices—which James Frazer observed still occurring in the late nineteenth century. "We are burning the witch," participants at the bonfires would say. And sometimes they would add "or the old woman."[46]

Few elderly women can claim, even today, that "autumnal majesty" that might be theirs during their middle-aged years. We today bemoan white hair and wrinkled faces. But in early ages when epidemic disease was rampant, faces were further pitted by smallpox scars and (from the sixteenth century on) by syphilitic lesions. Dietary diseases were endemic in populations with inadequate food supplies—or with food lacking in basic nutrients. Over the centuries thinness was generally in vogue among the upper classes. But this was not always the case for the peasantry and the bourgeoisie, who often associated thinness with starvation and weight with prosperity. Thus the classic stereotype of the witch was of a woman with a gaunt body. She was presumed to be thin, not fat, hungry, not prosperous.

In these early centuries, what we call the "diseases of aging" must have been widespread. For women these diseases especially must have included osteoporosis, a condition caused by the decrease in calcium production with aging. This decrease generates a loss of bone mass and a consequent shortening and distending of body height. In his 1584 *Discovery of Witchcraft,* Reginald Scot noted that the period of life after the age of sixty-three was popularly called "the Crooked Age."[47] The term "dowager's hump," coined to describe the bent-over body posture of sufferers from severe osteoporosis, indicates that the illness crossed over class lines to afflict the wealthy as well as the poor, the nobility as well as the peasantry.

Rich and poor could unite in this fear of the outcast position of aging, its very body type outside cultural valuations of wholeness. "Mirror, mirror on the wall, who is the fairest one of all," queries Snow White's stepmother. Her plaint is not only about beauty but also about aging. For she fears that her stepdaughter's reputation for beauty will supplant her own, undermined by the process of aging. Consider the sixteenth-century case of Queen Elizabeth of England, who for nearly a half century was courted by younger men. By the age of thirty-five she covered the mirrors in her palaces so that she would not have to watch the aging of her face. In her London palace she installed a laboratory for a chemist who promised to extract an elixir of youth for her, to find the fabled "fountain of youth" searched for by many adventurers.[48]

Yet exactly when old age occurred could be a conundrum. In the twelfth century Andreas Capellanus seemed to cap women's active sexual years at fifty, although Ovid had seemed to set forty as his limit. In his *Lives,* Plutarch mentions that Cleopatra was thirty-two at the time of her involvement with Mark Antony. Such an estimation of an age which in modern times is hardly considered old makes startling Shakespeare's statements about her as old, as "wrinkled deep in time." (Plutarch wrote that she was then at the height of her attractiveness.) Throughout the early modern era women are denoted "old" that we would probably categorize as young or middle-aged. Chaucer's merchant in *The Canterbury Tales,* for example, seems to include any woman over thirty in his category of "old widows." Yet one member of the Paston family, planning to marry a forty-year-old woman, characterized her as attractive. And Brantôme, ever appreciative of aging women, wrote consistently of the continued beauty of women in their fifties and sixties.

Analysts of the life-cycle literature of this period find that men were considered to reach the height of their abilities at the age of thirty-five and that these did not decline until the age of fifty. Physiological theory about women's earlier maturity and their earlier decline would seem to close off these later years of vigor to them. But historians note that people in these early centuries often did not know how old they were; that they counted their life cycle not in terms of birthdays but rather by important turning points, like their First Communion, or marriage, or the birth of a child.

There is also the indication that some women, especially aristocrats and courtesans, may have successfully concealed their age. Boccaccio's fourteenth-century Corbaccio, for example, wore heavy makeup and affected an air of elegance which attracted young men. She claimed to be twenty-eight, although her actual age was "closer to forty than thirty-six." From the sixteenth to the eighteenth centuries upper-class women painted their faces with a white concoction known as ceruse, especially designed to hide smallpox scars. If thickly applied, it provided a masklike covering. In the seventeenth century Robert Burton contended that especially through this use of heavy makeup many women successfully concealed their age.[49]

Even the impact of menopause in terms of age grading cannot be precisely determined. For over the centuries in medical and didactic sources there is confusion as to exactly when menopause occurs. And this confusion complicates the whole issue of when women can be said to enter the last stage of life. Present-day historians seem convinced that before the modern era women entered menopause at ages considerably lower than today. They assume that where women today seem to begin menopause in their late forties and to end the process in their early fifties, in times past these limits were reduced to the early and mid-forties. Yet contemporaries were not as certain as are modern researchers about these age estimates. In sources from the medieval period onward estimations ranging throughout the forties and sometimes extending into the mid-fifties can be found.[50]

This confusion may be related in the first instance to the fact that menopause is a body process which takes place over a number of years. And, given nutritionally unbalanced diets, it is probable that amenorrhea (failure to menstruate) was a common experience of women of all classes and that the final stopping of the menses was difficult to pinpoint. Moreover, since childbearing was spread throughout the life cycle and since babies were commonly nursed for several years, it is additionally probable that the stopping of the menstrual cycle produced by nursing also made diagnosing the onset—and the ending—of menopause difficult. The many concoctions suggested in medical treatises and household advice books from early times for starting the menstrual flow would suggest that such was the case.[51]

Moreover, in premodern cultures not far removed from pagan roots and still believing in magic, what intrigued observers was not always the regular occurrence of events which interests modern scientific minds but rather the extraordinary happening which seemed to prove the reality of divine intervention. Writers from this period remark on women who bore babies in their late forties and fifties. When she was forty-six, Elizabeth I's doctors told her that she would remain fertile for at least six more years.[52]

Elizabeth's doctors' overoptimistic prediction was doubtless related to her continuing intent to use her body as a negotiating pawn of her statecraft. Yet in pronatalist cultures, women probably did not want to admit the end of their childbearing years. The various terminologies employed in the past to designate what we call menopause give indication that such was the case. In seventeenth-century England, for example, menopause was called "the end of the flowers." ("Flowers" was a word referring to women's beauty.) By the eighteenth century menopause was called "the dodging time," as if women wanted to delay the ending of their generativity. In his popular eighteenth-century medical treatise on women, Jean Astruc wrote that "some women, unwilling to accept the inevitable, deny their periods have stopped. It should be made clear to them that they are now old women." Moreover, because before the nine-teenth century menstruation was viewed as a beneficial purging of body humors, menopause was regarded as problematic; indeed, as I shall presently argue, it was connected to witchcraft.[53]

The popular tradition extolling women of the Bible who had had children at advanced years bolstered this unwillingness of women to accept the end of their fertility. This tradition began with Sarah in the Old Testament and extended to the New Testament Elizabeth, the mother of John the Baptist, and Anne, the mother of Mary. These three biblical women had miraculously borne children at older ages, even, in the case of Sarah, long past menopause. In particular, Saint Anne was worshiped as the patron saint of childbirth. She supposedly was forty when Mary was born. In this regard the passage in Shakespeare's *Antony and Cleopatra* in which Charmian, Cleopatra's servant, tells a fortune-teller her greatest desire, is revealing. "Let me have a child at fifty," she requests. With reference to the position of Elizabeth and Anne in the biblical narrative, she fantasizes that this child may be one "to whom Herod of Jewry may do homage."[54]

On balance, the European tradition did not accord women high regard in their waning years, once they had became postmenopausal. But there was an alternative point of view, one under which they could be, like Alison's crone, people of wisdom, spirit, and, ultimately, desire. This point of view, for example, emerged in Arthurian legend; it can be found, as I will later point out, in folktales and fairy tales. The Arthurian version seems drawn from ancient personifications of goddesses as tripartite personages, as not only maidens and mothers but also as crones. In this Arthurian redaction, heroes in their wanderings meet three women of differing ages. The men learn much from the encounter.

The fable first occurs in the Gawain adventure, in which the knight Gawain meets three stately queens living in a luxurious, enchanted castle. They are a grandmother, a mother, and a daughter. Mysterious at first, they turn out to be King Arthur's mother, Gawain's own mother (whom he had presumed dead), and his sister, of whose existence he had not known. Like Perceval's mother in the Perceval stories, they are another pacific center in the world of knightly violence; their existence represents the generative female life cycle's condemnation of that violence.[55]

In his late-fifteenth-century retelling of the Arthurian stories, *Le Morte d'Arthur,* Thomas Malory individualizes the episode. He makes of it a parable of courtly love and of the power of aging within the life cycle, with no family relations involved. In *Le Morte d'Arthur,* three adventuring knights, Sir Gawain, Sir Ywain, and Sir Marhalt, meet three women of differing ages. (Ironically, Malory calls them all damosels.) Malory's first "damosel" is fifteen years of age: she wears a garland of flowers around her hair. The second damosel is thirty: she has a circlet of gold on her head. "The eldest damosel," Malory tells us, "had a garland of gold about her head, and she was three-score winters of age or more [sixty or more]; her hair was white under the garland." Each of the knights chooses one of the women to be his companion. Sir Ywain makes the first selection. Surprisingly, he chooses the eldest woman despite her white hair and her age. But it is on her wisdom and experience that he bases his choice. "For she has seen much," says Sir Ywain, "and can best help me when I have need."[56] On these grounds, the grounds of the value of wisdom and experience, in this interpretation, age has dignity and meaning.

The Go-Between and the Witch

In HIS INTERESTING ESSAY on the image of aging women in medieval literature, William Mathews locates their sexuality in a comic tradition. He posits that these women were partly figures of fun, their "randy" sexuality irresistible to writers like Chaucer who had a satiric bent. There is merit in Mathews's argument. With her wit and joie de vivre, the Wife of Bath resembles great male comic characters like Shakespeare's Falstaff. There is playfulness, too, in Alison's courtship of the young clerk, Jenkin, as they dally in the meadow and as she watches him, a pallbearer at her husband's funeral, with "legs and feet so clean-cut and so fair."[57]

There is a playfulness, too, in many medieval fabliaux and in tales of flirtation between mistresses and pages. This playfulness is apparent in the relationship between Titania and Puck in *A Midsummer Night's Dream*. It continues into Pierre de Beaumarchais's eighteenth-century rococo world of *The Marriage of Figaro,* where sexuality is partly a game and life partly a comic entertainment. Like pages throughout the ages Cherubino adores his mistress, and she returns his affection sweetly and secretly, by wearing his ribbon near her heart. The literary and folk treatment of even witches could be humorous, as in the comic English Mother Shipton, the daughter of the devil. Mother Shipton is a kindly domestic magician, although endowed with preternatural wisdom.[58]

Such playfulness, however, becomes satiric in English Restoration drama and eighteenth-century portraits of aging narcissistic women like Madame Wishfort in Congreve's 1700 *The Way of the World,* or Mrs. Malaprop in Sheridan's 1774 *The Rivals,* who believe they are actually attractive to the men they desire. The satire is present even in *The Marriage of Figaro,* in the housekeeper Suzanne's lust for Cherubino. Her appetite abates only when she discovers that he is her son.

Yet the comic tradition Mathews investigates has within it not only a satiric edge but also a mordant side, a presentation of aging women so vitriolic that it is indeed deadly. This mordant edge, this literary view of aging women's sexuality as unnatural and even dangerous, is apparent in the personification in Western literature of the older woman as the "go-between," as the person who arranges individual relationships between women and men.

As she emerges in European literature, the "go-between" is one of two types. Either she is a nurse, a governess, or a friend who facilitates a romantic relationship between her charge and a man, as Juliet's nurse does in *Romeo and Juliet.* Or she is a sexual procurer, an "old bawd," an older woman who for financial remuneration provides young women as sexual partners for men. Within this literary tradition, the go-between can be a middle-aged woman, like Marguerite's neighbor, Martha, in Goethe's *Faust,* who unwittingly serves the devil's purpose in arranging a meeting between Faust and Marguerite. More often, however, especially when her role is that of an "old bawd," she is a woman of advanced age, the descendant of the female procurers of Roman comedy and especially of the figure Dipsas, in Ovid's *Amores.*

Both of these types of aging go-betweens—the romantic intermediary or the sexual procurer—were not only fictional characters. They were also actual types of women who existed in Western society. Young women of the upper classes often had nurses who raised them; in many Western regions young women before marriage were chaperoned by older women who were supposed to oversee their interactions, especially those with men. This idea of oversight was based on a cultural convention at variance with the sexualized version of aging women. In this alternate convention older women were seen as beyond the bounds of sexuality and thus as capable of restraining the sexuality of younger women.[59]

In literature this type is often depicted as foolish, as a sentimental aging woman who does not exactly know what she is doing. In *Romeo and Juliet* the nurse is garrulous and loving, forgetful, bawdy, easily manipulated by Juliet because of her affection for the young woman she nursed as a baby and has served ever since. In *Faust,* the devil is easily able to entice the foolish, romantic Martha into arranging the meeting between Faust and Marguerite.

Yet there is an undercurrent of danger in the foolish sentimentality of even these presumably safe aging women. For it is young women's sexuality above all which they oversee and which they often cannot, in the end, control. Or, in an alternative version, the amorous young men who desire their charges play on their sentimentality and their sublimated sexuality to turn them from duennas to co-conspirators in an exciting game of conquest that they themselves can vicariously enjoy. Thus Cervantes in *Don Quixote* tells the story of the duenna of the Queen's eldest daughter who allows a young man without social position to court her royal charge because of the "trinkets" he gave the older woman and his singing which "turned all the senses to quicksilver." He enchanted her mind and body; she became a "go-between."[60]

The aging woman as sexual procurer was both similar to and different from the figure of the duenna. She was a woman steeped in sensuality, a latter-day version of Aphrodite, the goddess who herself served as procurer for Paris with Helen. So is all women's passion compromised by this literary convention, their loyalty to each other easily undermined by their narcissism, their competition over beauty, over men. Thus Aphrodite, wanting the prized apple for her beauty, plays the pimp for Paris. Similarly, Eve serves as the go-between between the serpent and Adam, her sexuality additionally compromised by her perversion of her partner.

Like the nurse and the duenna, the go-between was a real social type. For many centuries prostitution in the West was organized partly on an ad hoc basis. Older women, many of them former prostitutes, acted as brokers in the trade. These aging go-betweens were familiar figures in many cities, and procuring was not always their only livelihood. In both Spain and Italy, they also served as hairdressers and cosmeticians. Or, like Celestina in Fernando de Rojas's sixteenth-century *Celestina,* they told fortunes, prepared love potions, and sold magical talismans and amulets. They also could be midwives or dispensers of medical advice.[61]

The dominant literary convention with regard to the procurer, the "old bawd," depicts her as old, as a woman with white hair and a decrepit body. She does not have the peasant lustiness of Juliet's nurse nor the middle-class smugness of Goethe's Martha. She lives at the margins of society, providing a scorned service. Dipsas in Ovid's *Amores* is the prototype of this character in Western literature. Her outlines can be found in the most famous go-between procurers in early European literature: in the Old Woman in the thirteenth-century *Romance of the Rose,* and in Celestina of Rojas's *Celestina.* In Rojas's play, Celestina is a woman of seventy, known by everybody for being put in the stocks as a witch "that trafficked in young girls selling them to priests and one who broke up a thousand marriages."[62]

From definitions of aging women as sexualized creatures and as go-betweens dangerous to social harmony, it was only one step to accusing them of being witches, individuals who bound themselves diabolically to the devil through an infernal sexual pact. In the sixteenth century François Rabelais wrote about a virtuous aging woman of "autumnal beauty," never warmed "but by the Nuptial Fire." But he also railed against the danger of the potentially uncontrollable sexuality of aging women and of their connection to witchcraft:

> *Old Brimstone Bawd, with Brandy flaming Red,*
> *That mak'st a curs'd rank Brothel of thy Bed,* ...
> *Who scatt'rest Plagues with thy Contagious Breath*
> *Damn'd Witch, thou dost in magic far excel*
> *Medea, and the Blackest Fiends of Hell* ...
> *Damn'd Harridan, with Reeking Lust more drunk*
> *Than Messaline.* ... [63]

Through the witch's pact with the devil she gained the power to perform malevolent acts against fellow community members, especially males, and to serve as conduits to bring others, especially young women and men, into Mephistopheles's service. That most women persecuted as witches were old women is a demographic fact historians are currently noting. Recent compilations of statistics for a number of regions during the massive witchcraft persecutions of the sixteenth and seventeenth centuries—in the Jura region of Switzerland, in portions of France and England—show that the median age of suspected witches was between fifty-five and sixty-five years of age. Witches in New England during the seventeenth century were somewhat younger (between forty-five and fifty). Nonetheless, they were hardly young or even, by those centuries' definitions, middle-aged. Yet although the age-distinctive character of the witchcraft phenomenon has been indicated, the meaning of this correspondence between gender and aging for the Western experience has hardly been plumbed.[64]

Recent scholarship on witchcraft in Western Europe, dominated by historians' emphases on demography and on social, rather than literary, sources has focused on the startling fact that widespread persecutions did not really begin until the sixteenth and seventeenth centuries. This refocusing of the chronology of the subject has revealed the extent to which the Protestant Reformation and the Catholic Counter-Reformation both were destabilizing forces, stirring up, especially among theologians but also among the general public, a willingness to accept as reality a paranoid vision of a devil-worshiping religion. This paranoid vision involved crazed rides on broomsticks and midnight anti-masses with wild sexual orgies (the Walpurgisnacht of the German imagination). It also included magical animals (the witches' familiars) and a determined host of minor demons (the incubi and the succubi) who worked along with the aged witches to foster community disorder and the recruitment of new members to the Satanic faith.[65]

Concomitantly, there seems to have been a willingness to scapegoat European society's most vulnerable members—its aging women—as the cause of widespread social ills. This scapegoating may have been fueled by what seems to have been an increasingly negative attitude toward women in general during these centuries. Recent investigations of the gender composition of those brought to trial over the centuries reveal much higher percentages of men in the scattered trials that occurred before the sixteenth century than previously thought, while these percentages of men vastly declined in the sixteenth and seventeenth centuries. Moreover, this new emphasis on these later centuries as the height of organized witch-hunting and trials also reveals the extent to which the leaders of both the Protestant Reformation and the Catholic Counter-Reformation were intent on extinguishing folk beliefs about magic and sorcery still widespread throughout Europe after centuries of Christianity.

But such focus on the trials and on what was in reality a time of terror overlooks what is clear in literary sources: the designation of "witch" as specially applied to women was ever-present in Western culture.[66] This designation consistently could be used to categorize women as individuals outside of acceptable cultural boundaries, as beings destructive to individual and social comity. In Montaillou, Beatrice de Planissoles was accused by her young clerical lover of having bewitched him into loving her. Alice Perrers, the mistress of Edward III in the fourteenth century, was charged with having bewitched the aging king, although she was acquitted. Accusations of witchcraft played a major role in the conviction of Joan of Arc, and Henry VIII extracted himself from his marriage to Anne Boleyn, Elizabeth I's mother, by successfully charging her with adultery and witchcraft and forcing her execution.

In Thomas Wythorne's autobiography, when the housekeeper of the adjoining manor proposes marriage, his fellow servants are amazed that he would even consider a woman so much an old "witch," as they characterize her. And in Shakespeare's *The Winter's Tale,* when the servant Paulina brings King Leontes to her home to view the statue of Hermione, his wife, she avers that she employed no sorcery in the statue's metamorphosis into a human being. "You'll think," Paulina states, "Which I protest against, I am assisted / By wicked powers." When it came to aging women, even to so loyal a servant as Paulina, sorcery was a possibility. Among the peasants of Normandy, according to Martine Segalen, age-disparate unions between aging women and younger men were regarded as provoked by Satan. A traditional proverb there was: "Young lad, old hag, devil's union." And satiric writers during the Renaissance stressed the Roman image of the old woman "as always more or less a sorceress."[67]

In classical Athens, as in many non-Western cultures, postmenopausal women were released from the restrictions placed on them because of their supposed dangerous sexuality. But aging women in early Europe were granted little surcease from such restrictions. Their sexuality, which might have inspired them to express a universal eroticism unbounded by time, actually rendered them even more fully the pawns of patriarchy.

Thus with the available evidence before them that most witches were aging women, the Dominican friars and professors at the University of Cologne, Heinrich Krämer and Jacob Sprenger, in their major witchcraft manual, the 1458 *Malleus Maleficarum (Witches' Hammer)*, wrote the epochal statement that "all witchcraft comes from carnal lust, which in women is insatiable." In their interpretation older women became witches largely because of substantial economic loss; lust leading to diabolism occurred primarily among younger women.[68] Other interpreters, however, included the spectrum of age in charges of deviant lust.

In 1550 the Italians Arnoldo Albertini and Jerome Cardan called witches "mostly old women who can find no lovers." According to a sixteenth-century Spanish friar, the insatiable sexuality of aging women could lead them to take up with the devil. "Once they are old, and men pay no attention to them, the women have recourse to the devil to satisfy their appetites." Conversely, the devil's minions, the demons, took up with old women precisely because the latter were so grateful to have lovers that they could easily be controlled. According to Richard Burton, one of the reasons that the devil's penis was described as icy cold in the stories of his sexual interactions with his female followers was because of the assumption that aging women, being cold-blooded according to early physiological theory, would experience the satanic organ as cold.[69]

Old women witches in fairy tales are depicted as beings with crooked backs, red eyes, and long noses. Of the external organs of the body, the nose continues growing with age, and the nose, in European folk belief, was a phallic symbol connected with sexuality.[70] The red eyes, too, were a telling symbol of the fire of sexuality raging within the witch. Thus the type of physical appearance—bent, gaunt, and wrinkled—which would place women in a category outside of beauty, outside the normal world of desire, made her a menace to that world. As she grew more "ugly," she grew more sexual and demanding. The description of the witch in the Grimm brothers' story, "Jorinda and Zoringel," is telling. She was a crooked old woman, yellow and lean, with large red eyes. She also possessed "a hooked nose, the point of which reached to her chin."[71]

Even menopause was culpable in leading aging women on to witchcraft. To some people the infertility of aging women was an attractive means of birth control, while the wealth of some aging women rendered irrelevant their precise location in the life course. Yet there was an alternate medical viewpoint. In early European times, most doctors regarded menstruation as beneficial to women, as providing a monthly purging of those evil humors which might otherwise induce doubly reprehensible behavior on the part of the weaker, less rational sex. The relationship between menstruation and the production of the ovum remained undiscovered until the mid-nineteenth century. Before then menstruation was viewed as akin to bloodletting, the official medical remedy for most bodily disorders. Conversely, the ending of the menstrual cycle was viewed as negative, as a process whereby evil humors remained present in the body, capable of adding to that complex of female wickedness which could turn aging women into witches. According to one seventeenth-century French physician: "When seed and menstrual blood are retained in women besides [beyond] the intent of nature, they putrefie and are corrupted, and attain a malignant and venomous quality."[72]

In his seventeenth-century treatise on witchcraft, Reginald Scot traced its origin among aging women to the operation of melancholy in the blood. He reasoned that the end of women's monthly bleeding, which had regularly relieved them of this malevolent bodily humor, made it almost impossible for aging women not to be susceptible to witchcraft. "Why should an old witch be thought free from such fantasies, who (as the learned philosophers and physicians state) upon the stopping of their monthlie melancholic flux or issue of blood in their age must increase therein."[73]

As a condition melancholy was associated with the astrological sign of Saturn. And in the popular astrological system, both aging and witchcraft were also associated with this sign. The typical discussion of the symptomology of melancholy described it as characterized by cold extremities but with a great heat, a fire within the body. Again, the heat flashes of menopause furnished ample evidence of the melancholic symptomology. Moreover, the belief was that the failure to menstruate caused the uterus to travel around the body, eventually negatively influencing the brain. And, long-standing medical belief had it that an extended absence from heterosexual sexuality on the part of a woman could further her tendency toward mental disturbance.[74]

Many taboos regarding the activities of menstruating women existed throughout European societies. For example, butter churned by menstruating women was not supposed to thicken, and bread dough was not supposed to rise when menstruating women kneaded it. But there were also fears with regard to menopausal women. Thus Albertus Magnus's *Book of Secrets* warned that the eyes of a child in a cradle would be damaged if a postmenstruous woman looked at it, while there was a widespread German superstition that a hunter would find no game if an old woman crossed his path. John Lyly, Shakespeare's predecessor at the court of Elizabeth I, consistently wove folk beliefs into his allegorical court dramas. In his play *Sapho and Phao* (composed during the protracted courtship of Elizabeth I and the Duke of Alençon), a lady-in-waiting to Queen Sapho asserts: "I would not have a weasel cry, nor desire to see a glass, nor an old wife come into my chamber, for then though I lingered in my disease, I would never escape it." And there was the belief that intercourse on the part of a young man with an aging woman might substantially drain his energy.[75]

As sexualized beings, aging women were malevolent creatures, the devil's "go-betweens" to the human world. So an old German proverb expressed it: "Where the Devil cannot go, he sends an old woman." These women themselves were supposedly engaged in a vast conspiracy of secret prostitution, as they controlled those young female devils (the succubi) and the young male devils (the incubi) whom they sent to seduce others and to enlist them in their satanic worship. Reginald Scot contended that "old witches are shown to procure as many virgins for Incubus as they can, whereby in time they grow to be excellent bawds." It is not surprising, given the overlap in attitudes, that Fernando de Rojas in his literary treatment of the go-between envisioned part of Celestina's social containment as being confined in the stocks for being a witch.[76]

By official description witches were powerful women. Sprenger and Kramer advised that, during the interrogation preceding the beginning of a trial, the feet of the accused witch should not be allowed to touch the ground. Moreover, she should be brought into the courtroom backward, to moderate the force of her initial gaze on her interrogators. (Thus there seems acknowledgment of the power of ancient folk beliefs connecting women with the earth as well as beliefs about the so-called third eye, the magical eye which aging women especially were supposed to possess.)[77]

But if witches were powerful they were also powerless, the pawns of Satan. As women in this new system they were still prey to possession by the force of passion, as was Clytemnestra, in the Greek tale, or Gertrude, in Shakespeare's presentation. Thus Reginald Scot proclaimed that any woman, in truth, could be a witch. "And if it were true, honest women may be witches, in delight of all inquisitors: neither can any avoid being a witch, except she locke herselfe up in a chamber." Indeed, it seems telling that, as Shulamith Shahar argues, the two derogatory names most commonly used by women against women in the medieval period were "whore" and "witch." All women could be whores; all women could be witches.[78]

The completed figure of the witch, recent scholars conclude, was the product of the creators of high culture. Both lay and clerical writers by the sixteenth century had grafted stories about religious heretics as devil worshipers onto popular folk beliefs about demons and wise women. One of the ways to access those folk beliefs (even if attenuated by the Reformation's campaign of extermination) is through folktales and fairy tales, the remnants of older oral traditions written down from the seventeenth to the nineteenth century by cultural preservers like the Countess d'Aulnois in France and the Grimm brothers in Germany.

In the first instance these tales are filled with malevolent witches and evil enchantresses who work their wiles on young women and men. Thus an aged enchantress imprisons Rapunzel in a tower and another one tries to kill Hänsel and Gretel. Snow White's stepmother knows magic and creates the poisoned apple which Snow White bites, causing her to fall into the deep sleep from which the prince awakens her.[79]

But beside the aging evil woman in these tales stands her opposite: an aging good, or wise, woman. As mothers of kings, these aging good women refuse to follow evil instructions that will result in the deaths of

the good young women their sons have married. As women of indeterminate status living alone in the frightening, encircling forests of fairy tale
land, these aging good women offer havens of comfort and security. They
take in stray individuals who have run away from abusive families. They
help women in peril escape from evil forces pursuing them.

The most interesting among them is perhaps the devil's grandmother.
She is a kindly old dame who helps people escape from the devil's service.
Indeed, she is a figure much at variance with the aging woman/witch
defined by her involvement in malevolent devil worship. Rich in human
sympathy, the devil's grandmother overcomes her diabolical grandson by
domesticating him: she tricks him into revealing the sources of his power.
In one story, Satan reveals a secret out of gratitude for her service in
pulling lice out of his hair. Like Mother Shipton or Mother Goose, she is
the forerunner of the grandmother, the figure who will later emerge as
an ideal of appropriate life-styles for aging women.

In early modern Europe, aging women were silenced in many ways.
The witchcraft persecutions were only the most striking, the most visible.
If, in fact, their life experiences could foster wisdom and self-reliance,
their assertiveness could bring reprisals in the form of sentencing to stocks
or cucking stools. The latter method of punishment, the ducking in water,
seems related to notions of the tongue as the potential producer of fiery
persuasion. It also seems related to the idea of women who speak too
much and too long as in violation of the the physiological principle that
dry coldness was supposed to characterize aging women. So the water
was meant to put out their false fire.[80]

Elite writers like Shakespeare mocked oral traditions relating to medical remedies; they denigrated aging women's wisdom as no more than
"old wives' tales." Thus they made the female tradition of wisdom synony-
mous with mendacity or uninformed superstition. Even today we associate
"old wives' tales" with the foolish garrulity of aged women, senile, and,
as the use of the term "wife" implies, still subordinate and under spousal
domination. Yet those tales, according to feminist scholars, often constituted a body of popular medical knowledge, as well as relating to local
traditions and folk stories. Still, as early as Galen, the traditional herbal
medicine women practiced was dismissed as "old wives' tales."[81]

In a parallel manner the powerful strain of storytelling women had
long practiced was, by the eighteenth century, trivialized into tales for
children told by Mother Bunch or Mother Goose. (Scholars note the use
of the name of an animal reminiscent of Europe's ancient bird goddesses.)
And when trivialization was not sufficient, sexuality was employed. In

early European literary sources exists the figure of the "old trot," a close relative to the "old bawd," but one sufficiently distinct to require differentiation. In contrast to the "old bawd," the intermediary in the trade of the flesh, the old trot had only a secondary expertise in procuring. Moreover, this expertise was so attenuated that it sounds in the literary convention almost like an afterthought, a cover designed to denigrate whatever medical relief based on folk traditions women might provide.

The derivation of the name "old trot" remains obscure. Scholars waver between attributing it in the first instance to the term "trot," a crude nomenclature related to fast walking. Or alternatively it may have been derived from the name of an actual historical figure, Trotula of Salerno, a woman associated with Europe's first medical school at Salerno in the eleventh century and whose treatise on women and medicine is still extant. The word "midwife," derived from "medwyfe," means wise woman. But over the ages this wisdom increasingly came under assault. By the eighteenth century the term "Mother Midnight" in England was used interchangeably to refer to the aging sexual procurer, "the old bawd," as well as the woman healer, the midwife.[82]

The two major informants whose tales the Grimm brothers used as the sources for their epochal collections of European folktales and fairy tales were old women. One was the nurse of the woman who later became William Grimm's wife. The second informant was a fifty-five-year-old grandmother from Kassel, "whose memory kept a firm grip on all the sagas." Many of these tales originated (or were passed through) spinning rooms where women gathered in the evenings and told each other tales so that they could keep awake. (The European term "fairy" derives from fata, the Fates, who spun the thread of life, of birthing, dying, and tale spinning.)[83]

Or, on cold winter's evenings or hot summer's nights it was not uncommon for village storytellers to pass down the lore of the folk to their communities. These storytellers were not uncommonly women. They were the "old wives" who often told the tales. Thus, for example, John Lyly describes the tale-telling practice in his *Sapho and Phao*. "The winter nights are long," muses the Sibyl who is a major character in Lyly's play, "and children delight to hear old wives' tales." It was at evening parties, comments one historian of medieval France, that "the strange legends and vulgar superstitions were created." "It was there that the matrons, whose great age justified their experience, insisted on proving, by absurd tales, that they knew all the marvellous secrets for causing happiness or curing sickness."[84]

"By night, the village Matron, round the blazing Hearth, suspends the Infant Audience with her Tales."[85] So went one British recollection, posing the warmth and light of the evening fire as a counterweight to other kinds of fires associated with aging women: the fire of sexuality or of speech or the fire from the bonfire, the burning of the witches.

Within European belief, fire was associated with men. The earliest male gods were gods of the "fiery" sun; female gods were associated with the moon, with water, generativity, cleansing. It was fire that Prometheus stole from the sun and gave to the progenitor man he created. This ancient correspondence between fire and masculinity probably played a part in producing the humorial theorization about the gendered temperature of the human body and the relationship of heat to sexuality.

Moreover, within European folk tradition fire could be dangerous to women. In the fairy tales of the Grimm brothers, women are issued oblique warnings about even tending the domestic fire of the hearth. It was fire that burned the witches; in succeeding ages the burning of witches was re-created in those fires that, in their nineteenth-century form, James Frazer wrote about so eloquently in *The Golden Bough*.

In European physiological theory, among men, young men were considered the "hottest," the most dynamic (and dangerous) of all men. They were young "bloods," "sparks," "hotspurs." Some scholars of witchcraft draw interesting connections between young men and witches. They find, for example, that young men often were identified as being the primary subjects of the witches' sexual lust. Conversely, young men in certain areas were the primary accusers of these women.[86]

The silencing of women's voices, the putting out by fire of the perverse fire of their tongues, occurred not only in the persecution of the witches, mostly women of the popular classes. This silencing also occurred in the ending of the authority of the voices of the women of the Parisian salons. These latter were upper-class women far removed from the world of the witches, even though, at least during the seventeenth century, they were contemporaries. Thus two contradictory traditions here come together: the one of aging women as social mentors, as the creators of medieval *courteosie* and of seventeenth- and eighteenth-century intellectual milieus, and the other of aging women as malevolent intermediaries, as "go-betweens" in sexual dealings. In the worlds of either emotion or reason, aging women could become too dangerous, requiring special containment.

CHAPTER SIX

The Eroticized Young Male and Women's Response

THROUGHOUT EARLY EUROPEAN WRITINGS on gender runs a strain of censoriousness not only against younger man/older woman couplings but also against age-disparate relationships when the man is older. In literature, this condemnation can be found in the tales told by the miller and the merchant in *The Canterbury Tales,* in the fifteenth-century *Fifteen Joys of Marriage,* in Castiglione's sixteenth-century *Book of the Courtier*, and in continental farces in which foolish old men are married to young women.[1] Twelfth- and thirteenth-century caroles, Europe's first formal dances, often contained a mimetic interlude in which a young wife and a young man, impersonating a supposed paramour, pantomimed the deception of her older husband.[2] In the sixteenth-century commedia dell'arte, the comic old doctor lusts after young women: he is the "pantaloon" of Shakespeare's sixth stage of life, of "shrunk shrank" and "childish treble."

This negative attitude toward aging men was based in particular on the supposition that young wives would never remain faithful to aging husbands. Many are the stories in early European literature in which aging men are simply not able to keep up with their younger wives, who want to hunt and dance and who expect much sexual pleasure. Their older husbands, easily worn out, soon displease them. In the twelfth-century lays of Marie of France, the older husband locks up his young wife in a tower, but she escapes with her young lover. In literary fantasy youth outwits age: young wives regularly deceive aging husbands in the fabliaux, in Chaucer's *Canterbury Tales,* in Boccaccio's *Decameron,* and in Marguerite de Navarre's *Heptaméron.* The fixation over the centuries with the cuckold (the term for the husband of an adulterous wife) may have originated in this perceived inability of aging husbands to satisfy young wives.[3]

This theme is a major subtext in Shakespeare's *Othello*. It is an important reason for Iago's easily convincing Othello that his wife, Desdemona, has been unfaithful to him with his subaltern, Cassio. For Desdemona and Cassio are young, while Othello has "declined/into the Vale of years," as he describes himself. Othello desires Desdemona's companionship on his next military expedition, not for sexual fulfillment, but so that she can continue to profit from his wisdom.

> *I therefore beg it not,*
> *To please the palate of my appetite;*
> *Nor to comply with heat—the young affects*
> *In me defunct. . . .*
> *But to be free and bounteous to her*
> *mind. . . .*

Iago ratifies his master's self-portrait as an aging man with a waning sexual drive. He describes Othello, among other failings, as lacking "sympathy in years."[4]

These perceptions of divergent life-stage sexuality in men were based on the same physiological theories which underlay beliefs about women's sexuality. According to that calculus of heat and cold which determined human composition, men as they aged were presumed to become colder. Thus they had less ability to perform sexually (heat being a key to sexuality). Only with difficulty could they satisfy younger wives who, by physiological definition, were hotter and moister than they.

That aging men experience a diminution of the ability to achieve penile erection is a physiological reality known to early Europeans. Cicero's treatise on old age, a preeminent text for centuries after, contains such knowledge. It can be found in Castellanus's *Art of Courtly Love,* in Castiglione's *Courtier,* in Marguerite de Navarre's *Heptaméron,* in Brantôme's *Vies des dames galantes.*[5]

Othello's overreaction to charges of his wife's infidelity indicates the potential depth of aging men's sexual insecurities. On the other hand, his willingness to accept Iago's definition not only of Desdemona's inherently sexual nature but also that of the young man, Cassio, indicates the ambivalent position that young men occupied vis-à-vis older men. For if, as heirs of patriarchy, young men occupied a privileged gender position, still their vitality could endanger society.

European states, upheld by military might, needed the prowess and daring of young men as heroic soldiers. But these same qualities could become excessive, needing containment. Do not forget the young suitors of the *Odyssey,* despoiling Odysseus's possessions. The thirteenth-century *Romance of the Rose* presented the common perception: "Youth pushes men into folly, debauchery, ribaldry, lechery, excesses, and fickle changes of heart." Castiglione's sixteenth-century *Courtier* echoed this statement. "Young men are prone to quarrel," wrote Castiglione. They are "changeable, liking and disliking in the same instant...."[6] It was a common judgment over the ages.

Just as both separate and intertwined histories of aging women and men can be written, a history of young men can also be plumbed. The history of Alison of Bath remains incomplete without the story of Jenkin; that of the old crone, the loathly lady of Guinevere's land, remains partial without that of the unbridled knight needing domestication. And, adding young men to the mix involves a deeper penetration into what might be called the sexual "system of desire" of early Europe. This system of desire, socially constructed, molded individual sexual perceptions of self and others as well as behavior in gesture and dress, and in what we might call "body language." It involved not only the negative eroticization of aging women but also multivariate attitudes about the bodies and behavior of young men. For during these centuries, women were not the only subjects of desire. Women were not the only persons who were presented in art and literature as sexually alluring. Young men also were erotically depicted.

Laws in most European countries forbade homosexual acts, but much evidence suggests these laws were regularly violated: by noblemen with their pages; by soldiers and sailors in communities of men without women; by young men of the peasant and working classes putting off marriage until later in life. If anything, bisexuality may be the proper term to describe male sexual proclivities in early modern Europe. In the seventeenth century, according to Randolph Trumbach, the word "effeminate" had two meanings. In the first place, it referred to a "smooth-faced" Ganymede, the young male as a pederastic partner. It also referred to an adult male obsessed with women.[7] At a time when physiological belief connected women with men and women's bodily frame and genital construction were regarded as similar to those of men, eroticized male dress reflected the visualization of this connection, associated with young males.

The Judgment of Paris, the competition judged by Paris between Hera, Aphrodite, and Athena over beauty, I have maintained, was the founding gender myth of Western culture. But the myth also established that Paris himself was exceedingly beautiful. As a young man, he had previously been a consort of the nymph Oenone, before Zeus chose him to judge the contest.

As an entrée into this history of the eroticized young man, a subject virtually uninvestigated, I will begin by discussing male clothing. For the styles of dress young men wore reveal much about their erotic selves and others' varying perceptions of them. This subject of male eroticization is not simple. In Western art, for example, personifications of young male figures, in contrast to similar eroticized female figures, were not objectified. John Berger has described the artistic objectification of women as their presentation in terms of "submission" to the (male) viewer's "feelings" or "demands."[8] Such was not the case with young men. Or to use a terminology common to feminist film and art history criticism, the male "gaze" did not trivialize them, as it did women.

A long homoerotic tradition in art feminized boys and rendered them in terms of a sexual passivity considered inappropriate in adult males. (The androgynous putti of the Victorian era were their descendants.) But young men were active figures in European tradition. They were suffused by physiological "heat"; in dress they determined the male mode. In early European art Cupid, a young male, was the active god of love who shot the arrows that provoked desire; Aphrodite, often objectified, was a removed personage. To me these young men seem to be "subjects" rather than "objects," and so I designate them in the following exposition.[9]

The subjectification rather than objectification of young men allowed them an area of control: they had cultural power that women did not possess; they were only with difficulty contained. In fact, part of their mission was the control of women. Thus I will argue that resurgent attempts to increase male domination are evident in the exposure of male legs as a new style of male garb in the fourteenth century and in the bulky male costume and exposure of the shape of the genitals, beginning in the late fifteenth century and continuing through the sixteenth century. These changes relate to the theme I have been tracing of nation-state formation and the "masculinization" that accompanied it.

Male power and the attempts to contain it will become both more complex and clearer in my discussions of the transliteration of the medieval traditions of courteosie into the later conventions of gallantry and those of cuckoldry, or the seduction of one man's wife by another man. These conventions created contention among men, but they also were based on male homosocial identification, the power of all men upheld whether by violent or seductive behavior, whether by taking on the role of the rapist or the rake.

I conclude this exposition of male eroticism by a discussion of two situations in which women's control over young men was important. These two settings are the court of Queen Elizabeth I of England in the sixteenth century and the Parisian salons of the seventeenth-century *précieuses* and the eighteenth-century *salonnières*. In the latter, what emerges is an early protofeminist attempt to contain men, to moderate their aggressive demeanor through the infusion of the female values of spirituality and gentleness.

Yet with the eighteenth-century French salon women, it might be said, these attempts boomeranged. For important philosophers, especially Jean-Jacques Rousseau, turned against their patronesses on the grounds that these women's actions were producing a dangerous effeminancy among men. By the late eighteenth century, Rousseau added his voice to what had become a cultural chorus extolling motherhood, domesticity, and a new, strengthened masculinity.

Male Dress and Body Type: Class, Athleticism, Warfare, and Sexuality

*I*N LATE MEDIEVAL and early modern Europe young male bodies, not just female ones, were eroticized. In art and literature, in costume and behavior, young men's bodies were alluring. Is it any wonder that medieval nuns in their ecstatic visions, according to Caroline Bynum, often perceived their highest moment in marriage to Christ, depicted in those ages as a beautiful, desirable young man? Or that the Wife of Bath was first attracted to Jenkin by his "legs and feet so fine and fair"? Here is Chrétien de Troyes's description of Cligés, his knightly hero in his twelfth-century Arthurian romance, *Cligés*. "He was in his flower.... He was more comely and charming than Narcissus.... His locks seemed made of a fine gold, and his face was of a fresh rosy colour. He had a well-formed nose and a shapely mouth, and in stature he was built upon Nature's best pattern...."[10]

Or there is Chaucer's fourteenth-century description of a young squire in *The Canterbury Tales* as a "lover and lusty bachelor."

> *Prinked out he was, as if he were a mead,*
> *All full of fresh-cut flowers white and red.*

Singing he was, or fluting, all the day;
He was as fresh as is the month of May.
Short was his gown, with sleeves both long and wide. . . .
He could make songs and words thereto indite,
Joust, and dance too, as well as sketch and write.
So hot he loved that, while night told her tale,
He slept no more than does a nightingale. . . .[11]

In the sixteenth century there were Shakespeare's sonnets, our very models of love poetry. Shakespeare wrote them to a young man, probably the Earl of Southampton, his patron at the time. Southampton was renowned for his beauty; he was the most frequently painted young man of his age. Like many Elizabethan courtiers, he was vain about his appearance, and he wore his hair in long blond curls, which he often decorated with bows and ribbons. Here are the famous lines from the eighteenth sonnet: "Shall I compare thee to a summer's day? / Thou art more lovely and more temperate."[12]

If nothing else, the history of clothing tells us that the young male body was eroticized in late medieval and early modern Europe. The emphasis on parts of the body associated with sexuality began in the late eleventh century, with the adoption of elongated, pointed shoe styles. It spread to the fourteenth century, when short jackets, long legs, and the exposure of the shape of the genitals became the vogue. By the late fifteenth century the preferred body type for men became more massive, while broad and blunted shoes replaced the long pointed ones. The codpiece, a sheath which enclosed the penis, was also developed in this time period.

In the sixteenth and seventeenth centuries, dress for men once again became more feminized, with the periodic addition of decorative and softening features. At the same time the jacket became longer. In the hands of the English sports-minded squirearchy of the seventeenth and eighteenth centuries, this longer jacket, its decorative elements increasingly removed for country wear, began to take on the look of the modern tailored and plain sports coat. Yet throughout the history of these changes long, lean legs, covered with fitted tights or tight trousers, by and large continued in style. Their vogue would continue until the mid-nineteenth century, when long, unfitted trousers finally became predominant and remained so until the present.[13]

During nearly seven centuries—from the eleventh to the nineteenth—portions of men's bodies were on erotic display in attire often analogous to what women were wearing to delineate bosoms or show glimpses of legs. And the male display, with its open showing of the shape of the legs and the penis, was in many ways more bold than that of women.

It would be foolish to argue that eroticism alone lay behind the genesis of these fashions. Social class was also involved. It is a truism of fashion history that the elites display status through dress and that change in styles is most often produced by competition among these elites. (I will presently argue, however, that the popular classes can also influence the mode.) For example, the elongated shoes (called poulaines) were related to perceptions of aristocratic feet as long and slender and peasant feet as broad and clumsy: elongating the shoes made these distinctions more precise. The sectors of society vying for precedence expanded and reduced the length of the shoe as they competed for control of this mode, which remained in fashion for nearly four centuries (from the late eleventh to the late fifteenth).[14]

The military métier of aristocratic males also played a role in the genesis of these fashions. The long shoes, for example, were probably the invention of Norman knights to produce a better fit for their feet in stirrups: Norman soldiers depicted in the Bayeux tapestry celebrating the 1066 conquest of England have long, slender coverings on their feet.[15] The Normans were preeminent medieval warriors who, descended from eleventh-century Norse invaders who settled Normandy, conquered England and Sicily, and were heavily represented in the European forces that fought the Crusades. Given their reputation, it is reasonable to assume that others would be influenced by their dress.

The short coats of the fourteenth century also may have derived from a military source: from the new heavy metal-plate armor which was invented to withstand the projective force of the arrows of the longbow and the crossbow, new and deadly weapons of this era. In contrast to the old chain-metal armor, which fit loosely over the body, the new plate armor was cut and hinged to body contour. It had a joint between hip and leg at the point the new jackets ended.[16]

Furthermore, the more massive body type of the late fifteenth century appeared at the time that warfare itself became more ferocious, with the success of the Swiss infantry phalanx. This battle formation involved massing infantrymen into a compact group holding long pikes in front of themselves. This new phalanx formation proved invincible against mounted cavalry. Drawing on the common foot soldier, it spelled the doom of the aristocratic cavalryman on his horse.[17]

Too, the shift in the shape of the shoe from long and pointed to flat and blunt also was probably related to the success of the Swiss peasant troops, who wore this shape of shoe. Finally, the codpiece may have been invented to protect the penis during battle: in *Gargantua and Pantagruel* Rabelais contended that such was the case. Yet one recent scholar has argued that the codpiece was in fact devised as a protective device to prevent the staining of expensive fabrics by the oily, mercury-based cream applied to the penis and used as a treatment for syphilis, suddenly epidemic in Europe in the 1490s.[18]

The importance of the Swiss peasant soldiers to the creation of this new late fifteenth-century mode is further evidenced by another innovation they introduced. Serving as mercenaries among the army which defeated the forces of Charles the Bold of Burgundy in 1476, the Swiss seized a large cache of elegant Burgundian court clothing. To fit into the clothing, and also as a mark of their contempt, they slashed the garments and then wore the ripped clothes. They launched thereby a clothing vogue that remained for nearly a century, as fashionable men wore slashed shirts and breeches with complex designs and patterns sewn in the slashes both to cover up their bodies and to draw attention to them.[19]

Yet the fashion importance of these Swiss mercenaries can be overemphasized. More than anything their importance was symbolic: they symbolized the innovations in warfare and statecraft of the late fifteenth century, as infantry replaced cavalry and firepower began to be used. Their rough physiques and independent way of life mirrored that masculinity projected by an expansive group of "new" monarchs who were asserting claims to a conception of monarchical power as "heroic" or "divine." Among these new monarchs were Charles VIII of France and Henry VII of England. In Italy buccaneering military captains known as condottieri organized armies from among paid mercenaries like the Swiss to provide military forces for Italian rulers and, in a number of instances, to themselves become rulers of these states. Like their soldiers the condottieri were mostly upwardly mobile men from the lower classes.

Historian Lauro Martines describes the fifteenth century as an age of strident assurance. Verbs of domination, he asserts, controlled the language of its writers. Painters revived the classical Hercules, and they often depicted this figure as dominating women or as in a struggle with the goddess Fortuna. The objectification of women in art, as I have noted, escalated. Princes, courtiers, and condottieri were the most common male subjects of quattrocentro art. Machiavelli captured their rough-hewn spirit in *The Prince,* his paean to their ability. "Fortune," wrote Machiavelli, "especially when it wants to render a new prince great...raises up enemies and compels him to undertake wars against them."[20]

Finally, the athleticism which accompanied soldiering was also reflected in the fashionable male body type. Whether this ideal body type was smaller (as in the fourteenth century) or larger (as in the fifteenth), it was broad-shouldered and slim-hipped, with thin legs. Some show of muscle was important; indeed, the new short jackets of the fourteenth century were padded in the shoulders and drawn in at the waist to heighten the look of an exercised body. This tailoring remained standard over the centuries that this athletic look was predominant.

Moreover, the athletic look was precise and, as is often the case in the history of Western dress and body type, difficult to achieve. For example, under male garb, legs were to have a muscular bulge in the calf, a feature attainable only through vigorous exercise. In addition, the shape of the leg was to be lean, its muscles stretched by long hours of horseback riding. This was an activity almost exclusively available to aristocrats because of the cost of the horse. Chaucer makes these details of fashion explicit in describing the legs of his austere reeve (or estate manager) of *The Canterbury Tales* as thin, but nonetheless unattractive because they had no muscle bulge. "They were very lean, and like a staff," wrote Chaucer, "with no calf to be seen."[21]

The eroticism of these fashions, their sexual intent, was never far from their meaning. Take, for example, the case of the poulaines. Norman soldiers may have invented them. The common contemporary explanation of their origin, however, was that a Duke of Anjou, Fulk le Richin, designed them in the last decade of the eleventh century to hide a growth on his foot.[22] This derivation is plausible. Fulk was a hardy knight, known for a taste for fashionable garb. By the end of the eleventh century the houses of Anjou and Normandy had intermarried. (Fulk was the grandfather of Henry of Normandy.) Their representatives intermingled during the First Crusade (1095), in which Fulk participated. It is possible that he derived the idea of the shoe from his Norman compatriots.

Yet so rarely do contemporaries in this early period delineate the origin of any fashion that one becomes suspicious when a precise derivation is given. And in the case of the poulaines, the presumed growth on Fulk's foot is reminiscent of the cloven hoofs of the devil or the deformed feet of the sexually aggressive dwarves of European folktales. Indeed, there may have been more complex connections between the shoe and the Angevin ruler. In his own day Fulk was renowned for his marital involvements: he had married and divorced two wives to expand his territory. To do so, he used those churchly definitions of consanguinity that later enabled Louis VII and Eleanor of Aquitaine to divorce one another and that Henry VIII unsuccessfully tried to apply in his efforts to divorce Catherine of Aragon.

Yet Fulk's third wife, Bertrade, turned the tables on him and divorced him to marry none other than the King of France. Thus he had been, in the day's parlance, "cuckolded," his personal and sexual disfigurement more shocking than a growth on his foot. For the loss of his wife questioned his virile ability to satisfy and his economic power over women as property. In England the shoes were known as cornadu, the horned one. This usage seems a reference to the figurative animal "horns" the cuckold was supposed to grow on his head. It seems another indication of the sexualized nature of these shoes.[23]

European folk belief categorized feet, like noses, as related to the penis, the size of one reflective of the size of the other. Thus at one point the fashion was that the extensions of the poulaines should be filled with sawdust so that they would stand upright. And it was not unknown that some wearers of these shoes would shape and color the extension to resemble a penis. In 1367 the French king Charles V prohibited the wearing of poulaines shaped like penises.[24]

Whether the codpiece was initially designed for protection in battle or against illness, it also was a sexualized garment, for it riveted attention to the male sexual organ. The conservative parson in *The Canterbury Tales* thundered against the short jacket's exposure of the shape of the genitals. In fourteenth-century mystery and miracle plays, devils as characters often wore large false penises, indicating the sexuality that they had inherited from the god Pan, their classical mythological progenitor. In the commedia dell'arte the older male characters also often wore large false penises or masks with large noses. In *Much Ado About Nothing,* Shakespeare pointed both to fashion's construction of the codpiece and its connection to male virility and sexuality when he referred to Hercules, a Renaissance emblem of triumphant masculinity, "in the smirched worm-eaten tapestry, where his codpiece seems as massy as his club."[25]

The fashion for long shoes ended just about the time the codpiece came into vogue, in the last decades of the fifteenth century. In other words, one might argue that the sexualization of the foot was transferred to the more obvious sexual organ. The word "cod" itself originally meant scrotum; later it came to mean pouch, or bag. Finally, by the end of the seventeenth century it gained the connotation of "fool." This word indicates its out-of-date nature and the comic strain present in early European literature and life. In popular parlance by that date it also meant "pal," referencing men's sexual camaraderie, the brotherhood of the tavern, the battlefield, the monastery. Young men, entering this fraternity, by this date were denoted by another interesting word: "codling" was the term applied to them.[26]

Moreover, eroticism was implicit in battle garb itself, for a continuing convention connected love and war. Throughout the chivalric romances, as I have noted, women urge men on to maintain their warrior reputations; they prefer tournament victors as lovers. Cupid "shoots" love arrows to stimulate passion; the metaphor is attack. "All's fair in love and war," we say. Or we refer to the "battle between the sexes," using aphorisms common for centuries. The "arms" of battle become equated with the "arms" of love. Then there is the convention that men in uniform are irresistible.

In this heritage, the onset of love only heightens the passion for battle. In the sixteenth century Castiglione wrote that in war women "make men fearless and daring beyond measure." Thus love becomes an inspiration for ritualized, legitimized violence, the eroticisms of love and war intermixing. "If one could assemble an army of lovers that would fight in the presence of the ladies they love," writes Castiglione, "that army would conquer the whole world."[27]

The Meaning of Youth

To untangle the meaning of any clothing or body mode is not simple, for encoded in each are complex messages. But what interests me further about this eroticized male style is its connection to youth, what it tells us about young men's identity. For a constant in the commentary about this male dress was that young men were its initiators. From early times young men defined themselves by the dress they wore; they often determined the mode. Thus both Orderic Vitalis, who wrote about the twelfth-century Normans, and Geoffrey de Vigeois, chronicler of Marie of Champagne's court in that same century, wrote that young men wore the shoes with pointed toes: Vigeois called these young men "insolent." In the fourteenth century, chroniclers in both Florence and Milan identified young men as the initiators of the day's short fashions.[28]

Portraiture and painting validate this observation. Over the ages, in these media young men often look gaudy, with the shape of bodies exposed, while aging men wear longer styles, often in black. In Shakespeare's *Much Ado About Nothing*, the character Borachio fulminates against the power of fashion in young men's lives: "What a deformed thief this fashion is. . . . How giddily a' turns about all the hot bloods between fourteen and five-and-thirty." Indeed, many fashion analysts note that men's clothes were even more decorated than women's clothes and that, if anything, their changes in styles were more frequent.[29]

That young men functioned as fashion innovators in early European centuries should not seem surprising, given their ambiguous cultural position as both powerful and powerless. As heirs of patriarchy, they naturally assumed a power which was also lent them by prevailing physiological belief about the dynamism and energy of youth as a male life stage. But as classes and occupations, as well as population size, expanded and contracted over the centuries of European development, their economic position and consequent class assignment could become uncertain. This uncertainty underscored definitions of their dynamism as dangerous and further impelled them toward self-mastery and cultural contribution through dress.

In medieval and early modern Europe young men were not without authority. In villages and towns, bands of youths took an active part, through charivaris and other joyful and censorious celebrations, in enforcing both community mores and the concerns of their own age group. From the twelfth century onward, in the burgeoning cities the university students were fractious and unruly. They were preparing, as clerks, for positions in law or medicine, or in the Church, or in the growing bureaucracy of national governments and regional states. From the ranks of these clerks came the anonymous individuals who transcribed into written form the twelfth- and thirteenth-century fabliaux, those popular tales of erotic adventure, of wives deceiving husbands with clerks and clerics. In Germany from among the clerks (the so-called ministeriales) came the minnesingers, the troubadours of that region. And the ministeriales gave their name to the minstrels in France.[30]

The nobility produced another group of young men whose status, like that of the clerks, was not unrelated to their own endeavors, to what they could themselves make of themselves. I am here referring to the nobility's younger sons. Under systems of primogeniture, their position was anomalous, for they were often almost superfluous. Male heads of families over the ages desired above all to hold the patrimony together, especially as kings attempted to further national control. Before primogeniture began to be enforced on a widespread basis in the twelfth century, many examples existed of family landholdings being decimated through disputes over inheritance through collateral lines.[31]

Over the ages these younger sons could be difficult. In Wolfram von Eschenbach's twelfth-century *Parzifal,* the young hero parts amicably from his older brother who has inherited the family property. Parzifal asks only for a horse and a small retinue so that he can begin his adventuring. But in Shakespeare's *As You Like It,* the younger brother, similarly dependent on his older relative, the inheritor of the family property, accuses his brother of gross negligence in having failed to educate and support him as a gentleman. In 1609 the Earl of Northumberland in his *Advice to His Son* drew from humoral theory to posit a biological basis for such rivalry: "Brothers, young and inconsiderate in the former part of their years (if not some rare and extraordinary nature), whose humours, if not satisfied to the full, as they conclude is due to them out of the rights of birth, being born of one flesh and blood . . . presently they will be angry with laws that have made a difference, and with the elders, if they share not to the proportion of their desires."[32]

At best these younger sons might hope that their older brothers, the family heirs, might die or that their fathers would provide for them some sort of career in Church or state. In the twelfth and thirteenth centuries they provided most of the troops for the Crusades to the Holy Land; the Norman knights who conquered Sicily were mainly younger sons looking for land of their own. Or in those ages they spent their time competing in the tournaments held throughout Europe. Their hope was that they might unseat a mighty lord and thereby win his horse and armor. If they captured such a noble in battle, they could hold him for ransom. The Arthurian legends of wandering, questing knights were based on their situation.[33]

Even in England, where aristocratic entry into the professions or trade was not considered demeaning, there were problems with overcrowding in these employments and with these young men's perceptions of entitlement to aristocratic privilege. During Elizabeth I's reign, planting settlements in Northern Ireland was suggested as a means of employment for younger brothers no longer able to enter the abandoned Catholic monasteries. In 1623 government support for their colonization to the New World was suggested. English Restoration drama of the 1660s and 1670s is filled with humorous references to the "younger son" problem. In France they were given a name: they were called cadets. Regarding their situation, Norbert Elias has written that they appeared over the centuries in "the most disparate social masks." They were crusaders and robber leaders. They emerged "as mercenaries in the service of great lords; finally they form the basis of the first standing armies."[34]

To all these groups of young men, self-presentation was an important part of self-definition. It was important that these young men, essentially between classes, maintain some control over the look of their attire. It would be difficult to argue that students began the vogues for long shoes and short tunics: from early times the prefects who governed universities issued dress regulations for students. Still, although the students at the University of Paris were supposed to wear gray gowns which came down to their feet, the fact that regulations were promulgated indicates that many students were, in fact, wearing fashionable attire. In the thirteenth century they were forbidden to wear shoes which were long and pointed. By the fifteenth century they were forbidden to wear robes which were too short, too tight, which were open in front, and which left the neck bare. The *Carmina Burana,* a thirteenth-century collection of student songs, gives a sense of their boldness:

> *Our birds unfledged must now take wing,*
> *Our donkeys tune the lyre and sing,*
> *Bulls dance in hall, and heralds' calling*
> *Is mocked by knaves at the plow-tail bawling.*[35]

Evidence suggests that, in fact, the short fashion for men was derived from working-class models, especially from subgroups within the working class characterized by an aura of masculine prowess or an interesting occupation. Thus, for example, minstrels had long worn short tunics. The minstrel Taillefer was celebrated in legend for having led the Normans in their first charge at the 1066 Battle of Hastings. The Chevalier de la Tour Landry in his late fourteenth-century book of advice to his daughters tells the story of a noble who, when his son appeared wearing the short jacket, exclaimed that he looked like a minstrel. For over a century—from the mid-fourteenth to the early sixteenth—part of the mode involved wearing tights with a different color for each leg. This fanciful feature, which may seem garish to modern eyes, resembled traditional minstrel costume, as Castiglione noted in *The Courtier.*[36]

Falconers and archers, men of legendary hunting and battle skill, also wore short tunics. It may be that the padded-shoulders and nipped-in waist look, long a part of the body line of male dress, was derived from the body type archery in particular produces: the shoulder and arm power required to pull the bow produces large arm and shoulder muscles. I have already discussed the influence of the fifteenth-century common man's military style on the creation of fashion.

The point here is that young men were both part of emerging hierarchies of class and occupation and in opposition to them. Thus they both conformed to social norms and rebelled against them. They expressed their rebelliousness in clothing, a medium of expression so obvious that scholars like Mikhail Bakhtin and Natalie Davis, studying folk culture in carnivals and festivals, failed to notice it. By embracing in dress the virility of soldiers or the frivolity of minstrels, they expressed through their bodies the marginality of their transitional state, while providing a warning of their social power.[37]

In the world these young men inhabited dress for men as well as for women was still a costume. Thus it was fanciful and colorful and on one level meant to counteract the harsh realities of omnipresent death and disease in a life-cycle experience of youth which could be only too short. Or, conversely, it could be painfully long. For both men and women in these ages marriage was an important step toward achieving their culture's definition of maturity, and for those men with limited property, marriage could be a difficult proposition. Thus how men looked and how they presented themselves, what they wore, became important.[38]

The erotic clothing men wore was partly designed to appeal to women, to provoke an erotic awakening in them.[39] Europeans of these ages believed that love was a capricious passion, that it could strike at any moment. In this they believed that the eyes, and what the eyes saw, were crucial. What primarily provoked love was thought to be the quality of beauty, usually defined as the pleasing appearance of the person looked at. As I have argued, there was variation in the definition of what constituted "pleasing appearance"; in this instance what interests me is that body of literature which suggests the centrality of dress to the production of personal sexual appeal.

Thus as early as the mid-thirteenth century there is Guillaume de Lorris's advice in the *Romance of the Rose*. "Outfit yourself beautifully in both dress and footwear. Beautiful garments and adornments improve a man a great deal . . ." In his seventeenth-century *Anatomy of Melancholy*, Robert Burton was even more explicit. "Beauty is more beholden to art than nature, and stronger provocations proceed from outward ornaments than such as nature hath provided," he wrote. And he continued: "When you have all done, the greatest provocations of lust are from our apparel."[40] There is also Sir Walter Raleigh's grandiloquent (and possibly apocryphal) gesture in throwing his expensive cloak over a puddle so that Queen Elizabeth would not stain her shoes. More than anything else this gesture demonstrates both the importance—and the studied unimportance—of clothes in both of their lives. It also illustrates Raleigh's initial appeal to the queen as the most expensively dressed and fashionable man at the court.

The eroticized young male body appealed not only to women; it also had a homoerotic dimension. In a culture built around male bonding, with a homosexual tradition dating back to the Greeks, same-sex attraction was endemic. In his *Christianity, Social Tolerance, and Homosexuality,* John Boswell convincingly argues that same-sex love among men was widespread in the twelfth and thirteenth centuries. From his evidence young men seem to have been the primary objects of attraction. For in that era Ganymede was the term used to refer to men drawn to same-sex relationships. The name Ganymede refers to that beautiful young man whom Zeus took as a lover in that classical myth which for later centuries symbolized same-sex male love.[41]

However, Boswell contends that by the fourteenth century, in line with a growing enforcement of conformity, homosexuals became a persecuted minority. That young men then began to expose their legs may reflect the seeming triumph of heterosexuality. From the late eleventh century to the early fourteenth century men had worn long, loose-fitting gowns which had an androgynous look to them. Now men definitely took up wearing the bifurcated garments that would become for centuries the desiderata of gender difference in fashion. It was not that same-sex male love disappeared. It was that the widespread legal codes which were enacted against its existence and the condemnatory statements about sodomy consistently in prescriptive literature may have propelled men into exposing their bodies as a way of showing their difference from women's bodies.

I have argued that the new short male dress of the fourteenth century may have derived from military armor. Yet to our modern eyes the short jackets hardly look martial. If anything, this garb has the look of what little boys used to wear many decades ago, when they were kept in short pants before donning long trousers. Or, as some historians point out, it seems in keeping with the elegant late-thirteenth- and early-fourteenth-century international Gothic style, with its elongation, its sinuosities, its natural motifs, and with the gentle, smiling young women and men who abound on its architecture. From this perspective the costume seems decorative rather than dangerous, playful rather than ominous.

There is, indeed, still an androgynous look to this male garb, a way in which it seems more than ever to draw from Attic homoerotic precedent. In this light, the cleanshaven male face accompanying this mode seems important, for it seems a continuation of Greek preference. Thus the narrator of the thirteenth-century *Romance of the Rose* describes his young male protagonist as with only a little down on his face, "neither beard nor moustache."[42]

Yet these are modern meanings I read into the past, and precisely the opposite could be the case. It could be that the new exposure of male legs (a major change in style of dress) indicated a new resolve to dominate over women, to reassert control. This new assertion of authority would be in line with what many historians of women have identified as a worsening of women's position from the late medieval period onward. The fifteenth-century bulky male body could be seen as in line with this trend. Just as the short styles of the fourteenth century echoed the elegance of High Gothic art, the bulky styles of the fifteenth century may have echoed the straight, square lines of Renaissance art, creating powerful prototypes of masculine domination. In art, Michelangelo sculpted a powerful, muscular David, in contrast to Donatello's small, sleek version of a century previously.

Yet it is important to go backward in time and to realize that before the appearance of the shortened costume of the fourteenth century, men had worn long gowns (shortened, of course, for battle). These, in turn, had been an innovation of the late eleventh century. The chroniclers of that era trace the introduction of the long gowns to the attempts on the part of young men to please women by dressing like them.[43] It is further worthy of note that, at the time in the fourteenth century that the troubadour tradition was declining, the dress associated with it also disappeared. The reappearance of men's legs marked a reassertion of both power and eroticism neither simple nor (as is always the case in matters of dress) entirely conscious on the part of the wearers of the mode.

Within this style equally as important as the shortened jackets (which I have discussed at length) were the tights, which I have thus far treated glancingly. In fact, they were not an entirely new item of dress. For several centuries, under their long robes men had worn leg coverings known as braies. (Women, on the other hand, often wore no such coverings because of the fear that they might provoke, by friction, some sudden "heat" in the genitals of overly sexual women.) To expose the braies as tights was to bring to light a crucial, long-hidden body differentiation in the area of gender. It was also to put an end to the medieval jokes about domineering women constructed around word plays on who, in a marriage, was wearing the braies.[44] It was now evident, at least from costume, who were the men and who were the women.

Yet if the braies disappeared as undergarments, in France they reappeared in an interesting form. For the French term for the English "codpiece" was "braguette," a word derived from the term "braie," its precise meaning a "little braie." So once again what had been hidden became exposed, the sexualization of the codpiece underlined by terminology derived from what had been, for several centuries, the male undergarment.

Eroticism as Pleasure and as Danger

*T*H U S F A R I have purposefully not been precise in my use of the term "erotic." Yet it can take on a number of meanings—either in the person projecting a sexual image or in the eyes of the beholder responding in a sexual manner. On the one hand, it can be soft and gentle. Or it can be hard and demanding. The young man can be the feminized "page." But he can also be the Arthurian hero Perceval, seduced by the glitter of soldiers to take up his masculine, warrior destiny. Ominously, in defining that warrior destiny, the first action Perceval takes once he has left the forest, the peaceful place associated with his mother, is to attack an unarmed, undefended woman he accidentally encounters. At this point in the narrative, Perceval has much to learn about gender relations, and the later death of his mother and his search for the Grail will provide him significant instruction.

Let me return to two of the examples with which I began this exposition of the eroticized young man: to Chrétien de Troyes's Cligés and to Chaucer's squire of *The Canterbury Tales*. Here a subtle but nonetheless important distinction exists. Cligés seems an erotic male of a gentle sort. He is "comely and charming," "in his flower." Chaucer's young squire is also described in terms of freshness and flowers. But he is also possessed of a hearty sexual drive, of a heat that invests him with the ability to extend his lovemaking, his phallic resonance, throughout the night: "So hot he loved that, while night told her tale / He slept no more than does a nightingale." The implication is that no woman could resist such a performance.

The distinction I am drawing between eroticism as gentleness and eroticism as domination is present throughout early modern European literature. Take, for example, Shakespeare's presentation of young men's sexual selves in *Romeo and Juliet*. Romeo's love for Juliet is gentle. He muses at length about her desirability and her aloofness. Then he awakens her love in the sometime manner of fairy tale romance—with a kiss. There is reciprocity between them and mutual care.

Yet the play begins with a different depiction of male erotic behavior. Here two servants of Juliet's Capulet family discuss women in terms of phallic domination, even of violence. Gregory and Sampson are the names of the servants. As the play opens, they discuss their animosities against the House of Montague. Each expresses determination to excel in physical prowess, should the quarrel between the Montagues and the Capulets eventuate in armed confrontation. Their fantasies become sexual. They draw a comparison between their penises and their swords. Their discussion turns toward women and rape, which they fantasize women as enjoying. Here are the relevant passages, from act 1, scene 1:

GREGORY: The quarrel is between our masters and us their men.
SAMPSON: 'Tis all one, I will show myself a tyrant; when I have fought with the men, I will be cruel with the maids; I will cut off their heads.
GREGORY: The heads of the maids?
SAMPSON: Ay, the heads of the maids, or their maiden-heads; take it in what sense thou wilt.
GREGORY: They must take it in sense that feel it.
SAMPSON: Me they shall feel while I am able to stand; and 'tis known I am a pretty piece of flesh.[45]

Young men could be dangerous—and the danger existed across the centuries for women of any age. The culture of college students at the University of Paris in the thirteenth century, for example, was steeped in violence. These young men drank to excess; they brawled with one another; they were known to break into homes and rape women. In the feudal period women outside the protection of husbands or father were at risk. In the original version of the Sleeping Beauty tale (before later moralists sanitized it), the prince did not kiss the sleeping beauty; rather he took advantage of her defenselessness and raped her.[46]

In *The Canterbury Tales* the Wife of Bath's tale revolved around a fourteenth-century episode of rape. The Goodman of Paris advised his young wife to keep distant from men in public places "and most of all with overweening and idle young men, who spend more than their means, and be dancers, albeit they have neither land nor lineage." According to Jacques Roussiard, prostitution in the south of France in the fifteenth century was organized to keep young men under control. J. L. Flindrin contends that rape was common in cities in the same area in this period and that it was collective, perpetrated by groups of bachelors.[47]

Marguerite de Navarre's character Hircan in *The Heptaméron* argues that when a man desires a woman, he is ipso facto justified in taking her by force. There is Machiavelli's advice to young men in *The Prince* to seize fortune if she puts up any resistance.[48] The women in Shakespeare's comedies consistently fear male attack when they leave the protected space of their families: they don masculine garb and personalities when they venture unprotected into the broader world. From the Renaissance onward, the eroticized, glorified rape of women by gods was a major theme of artists. Both Christine de Pizan and Marguerite de Navarre protested the assumption of women's insatiable sexuality which under-lay it.[49]

In his study of Somerset, England, in the seventeenth century, G. R. Quaife concludes that tavern patrons regaled each other with fictitious stories of having seduced the town's married women. Yet fantasy could easily turn into reality. For these men viewed women of the same or lower status as legitimate sexual prey; even well-off widows were in danger of sexual assault by their male servants.[50]

In early modern Europe masculine youth was regarded as naturally flamboyant. Young males were by all descriptions "hot-blooded." European physiological belief generally held that men's blood was naturally hotter than women's and that young men's blood was the hottest, the most sexual, of all. In his seven-stage exposition of the life cycle, Shakespeare described the young male character symbolic of his stage of youth as "the lover, sighing like a furnace," the furnace indicating the raging heat of a young man's desire. Shakespeare's contemporary, the sometime doctor John Vaughan, more precisely described Shakespeare's third stage. He contended that it existed in young men from fourteen to twenty-two. He called it "the stripling years," and averred that it was characterized by "prodigious lechery." In his famed advice letters to his son, Lord Chester-field in the eighteenth century recommended that the young man should control his hot blood by having himself bled from time to time.[51]

In premodern Europe, the martial mode permeated men's lives. Exaggerated notions of valor and honor made noblemen quick to take offense. As the tournament and the joust declined in favor during the sixteenth century, the duel replaced them. Castiglione's *Book of the Courtier* was aimed at furthering civilized constraints in personal style, but the author emphasized that, notwithstanding, the "true profession" of the courtier was that of "arms." Even Castiglione's proper peacetime recreations, like horsemanship, fencing, wrestling, and tennis, should be chosen to enhance battle acumen. And the courtier's deepest fear should be that he would not display courage. "And, just as among women the name of purity, once stained, is never restored, so the reputation of a gentleman whose profession is arms, if ever in the least way he sullies himself through cowardice or other disgrace, alway remains defiled before the world . . ."[52]

Such exaggerated notions of self-pride and of the possibility of continual challenge to personal integrity fueled that male distrust of women and of other men contained in the idea of cuckoldry, of having one's masculinity publicly humiliated by the seduction of one's wife by another man. From the eleventh century on the fear of being cuckolded and of being called a "cuckold" was a constant in the male mentality. Many analysts have speculated that cuckoldry was really a bonding mechanism among men, that it grew out of male traditions of competitive humor, of harsh, although familiar raillery among men at the expense of women (as Shakespeare often treats it). It brought all men to the same level, while it upheld aggression as a part of male bonding because of the personal mirroring implicated in such intimate male associations. Yet what fueled its venom was the belief that women could not be trusted, that they could not control their sexual impulses to remain loyal to spouses. Thus it implied that men should keep tight control over women.[53]

The concern with cuckoldry was especially virulent in the sixteenth and seventeenth centuries, when it became a preoccupation in the work of writers like Shakespeare and Rabelais. During these centuries monarchs created new nobles to support them and the merchant classes gained new prominence, contesting the values and the authority of the old feudal nobility. Warfare became more deadly and intense, with the invention of guns and cannons and new battle formations based on the foot-soldier infantry rather than the aristocratic mounted cavalry. Historians have interpreted these eras as "anxious" and "unstable."[54] Indeed, one might speculate that as aging women were persecuted as witches during these centuries of instability, all women became prey to increased suspicions about their sexual loyalties.

In *The Book of the Courtier* Castiglione castigated the male fashion of wearing "sundry colors," of "laces and fringes." He criticized men for paying too much attention to hair and beards, for pampering themselves as women did. His work prefigured, if it did not already reflect, that decline in aristocratic authority attendant on the bureaucratization of national governments, which reduced their governing function, and the professionalization of armies, which undermined the nobility's very meaning as a masculinized warrior caste. The message of *The Courtier* seems directed both toward moderating any ensuing social violence aimed inward and toward making certain that masculinity remained paramount in any new codes. Castiglione called for all men to forgo variation in dress and to wear black. This was the fashion in conservative Spain, Europe's leading sixteenth-century military power.[55] But black was also the color traditionally worn by aging men.

Over the ages the number of words which came into being to describe the male of courting and sporting age vastly increased, giving the lie to Castiglione's hope that a masculinized conservatism might triumph. Let us take a look at the expanding lexicon, itself an indication of the growing importance of male eroticism as medieval courteosie developed into early modern gallantry, with its implied feminization of men. In the thirteenth century in England, nobles and those who aspired to that status were simply courtiers, those who frequented courts. By the fourteenth century, however, they could be gallants, dashing and bold, fitted for pleasure. By the fifteenth century they could be "ladies' men." In that century the word cavalier also came into being to describe them.[56] It was a term related to the French word *chevalier* and to the military word "cavalry." These three words all derived from the French *cheval,* the word for the horse, an animal indispensable to aristocratic self-definition.

By the sixteenth century libertine, beau, rogue, and spark appeared. The seventeenth and eighteenth centuries also witnessed another expansion, to include words like rake, blood, blade, and Lothario (originally a character in William Davenant's 1630 *Cruel Brother*). In these centuries in particular the aristocracy attempted to rationalize its increasingly vestigial existence through elaborate disguises seemingly difficult to emulate. At the same time the growth of complex urban cultures encouraged the intermingling of individuals looking toward the main chance through the assumption (or creation) of what seemed the mode.

Many of the words I have listed are expansive words, suited to cultures in which male eroticism was predominately virile and dominant. On the other hand, most can also have an additional meaning indicative of that erotic gentleness which also existed alongside the dominant martial demeanor. Courtiers and cavaliers could be powerful or foolish fellows, and the rakes, bloods, sparks, Romeos, and Lotharios (omnipresent on the

Elizabethan and Restoration stages) could woo women with honesty as well as with force. Then there were the additional descriptive words "fop" and "coxcomb," words with a pejorative edge and words which, like jade and spark, had originally been applied to women before changing their gender designation.

These words indicated that male gallantry, with its multivariant levels of meaning, could border on effeminacy, on a feminization of male behavior which might be appealing to women but which threatened prevailing virile masculinity. Sexuality defined for men as "bisexuality" may have been inviting, but in some manner it may have been confusing to definitions of self in the rapidly changing early modern European world. Indeed, the assumption often was that men who dressed in the height of fashion did so to attract women, that "fops" and "beaux" who made a profession of "gallantry" "preferred ladies' dressing rooms to men's in club or tavern."[57]

Yet a shift in intent could bring another meaning to these kaleidoscopically connected words. For eroticism could be steeped in deceit. As such it was linked to the male seducer, the predator for whom women were sexual conquests. By the seventeenth century the male bent on female conquest had assumed epic form in the figure of Don Juan. This was a new Faustian man whose goal was not knowledge but conquest and who did not require the devil as intermediary: he himself had demonic force. This personification would redound over two centuries in seventeenth-century libertines and eighteenth-century Lovelaces, Casanovas, and de Sades. For them the epic male quest became the conquest of women for cynical, power-driven ends.

They were the descendants of the male adventurers and conquistadores of the fifteenth- and sixteenth-century eras of discovery and conquest. They took Renaissance epicureanism and philosophical libertinism—the drive to stretch social limits to attain freedom—toward a narcissistic male sexuality emboldened at women's expense. As Anne Denys notes, the practice of libertinism as directed against women incorporated the strategies of the hunt and of warfare.[58]

Even fops and coxcombs, figures seemingly constructed in alignment with female sensitivity, could be rogues at heart. In his *Memoirs of a Coxcomb,* John Cleland describes the career of a young man "seeking to reduce women to my point for the sake of my pleasure as well as of my vanity," in line with a "libertine" taste for variety. This taste led him to seduce both young and old women through "the insolent parade with which I displayed my person and my dress. I was at that nice point . . .

when imminent manhood brings on essential maturity for action, without abating anything of the smooth of youth. . . . I declared war within myself against the whole sex."[59]

William Hogarth immortalized the young man manipulating an older woman for her money in his famed series of engravings, *A Rake's Progress.* The fifth drawing in the series shows the rake in a marriage ceremony with an older woman, as he progresses through a flawed chicanery toward his eventual incarceration in debtors' prison.[60]

How masculinity ought to be constructed or, alternatively, how domination might be mediated were central concerns of the European literary imagination and central issues of more than one social setting. Male Renaissance monarchs seemed to resolve these issues around aggressiveness and martial might. The later Don Juan tradition subverted the customs of courteosie to create new avenues of gender domination. But these were not the only resolutions. Centuries before Chrétien de Troyes had counterposed maternal pacifism to knightly militarism. The figure of the page, a female construct, I have argued, counterposed femaleness to the dominant male style. Renaissance individualism, the interest of its writers in ancient hagiography and alchemical gender intertwinings, produced a questioning of rigid gender conventions. This questioning was especially evident in Elizabethan England in the work of writers like Spenser and Shakespeare, who responded to the presence of a woman on the throne.[61]

Moreover, from the Renaissance onward writers created male antiheroes whose battle perspicacity was attenuated by personal naïveté or the ancient quest conducted amid comic misadventures. By the eighteenth century, picaro figures like Fielding's Tom Jones or Marivaux's Jacob of *Le paysan parvenu* combined these impulses to create a major literary prototype, the innocent feminized male coming to adulthood in a perilous, masculine world. In these so-called "novels of initiation," young male characters have liaisons with older women, who teach them the ways of the world. In France, according to Joan DeJean, seventeenth-century male authors began the genre by refurbishing the Sappho-Phaon tradition, especially Phaon's rejection of Sappho. They did so, according to DeJean, as a means of undermining the authority of the novels the salon women, the *précieuses,* wrote.[62]

Yet the young men of the "novels of initiation," often of dubious birth or from the peasant or working classes, have one foot in that camp of rogues and scalawags who, in England at least, formed the subject matter of some of the earliest popular novels.[63] They were descendants in their way of Thomas Deloney's Jack of Newbery, quite ready to improve his position when the opportunity presented itself in the person of an aging woman. Yet the innocence of these young male protagonists was also endemic. It is evident in Fielding's references to Tom Jones as "Adonis" or to Beaumarchais's adoption of the name "Cherubino" (or little cherub) for his similar young man. In Mozart's operatic adaptation of Beaumarchais's *Marriage of Figaro*, the character of Cherubino is often sung by a mezzo-soprano, by a female voice.

The innocent naïveté of these young men bears relationship to that gentleness which I have identified as part of young men's eroticism. Yet such innocence and its corollary, an incipient spirituality, could also be dangerous to women. From this vantage the life stage of youth for males functioned as an avenue in which young men were socialized into patriarchy, taking on in their costumes and characters a femaleness they could, ultimately, control. Like Shakespeare's boy actors playing female characters, they demonstrated a virtuoso gender intermixing until, in the end, they validated those patriarchial matrimonial arrangements which are the usual denouement of Shakespeare's comedies. And, along the way, using Shakespeare's boy players once again as metaphor, they had erotic appeal to both men and women.[64]

Alternatively, young men become soldiers, moving through Shakespeare's life-cycle stages of the lover, "sighing like a furnace," to that of the soldier, "full of strange oaths." Mark Kann has identified soldiering as a primary way, in the past and the present, through which young men have been disciplined to accept patriarchy, to give up unruly behavior in service to the state. In the *Marriage of Figaro* Beaumarchais underlines this argument when Figaro makes fun of Cherubino, the young page who is leaving his place in his mistress's boudoir to become a soldier. As author, Beaumarchais subtly critiques Figaro's stance. "Goodbye Cherubino," says Figaro. "You are going to lead a very different life, my child. No more hanging about the women's quarters the livelong day, no more sweet drinks and pastries. . . ." Now Cherubino, as a soldier, must become a man. "Just veteran soldiers, by God, weather-beaten and dressed in rags, a huge musket that weighs a ton. Right! Turn! Left! Forward March! To Glory. . . ."[65]

In her study of Renaissance women writers, Constance Jordan maintains that "pro-woman" writers like Christine de Pizan were as interested in reforming male behavior as in promoting greater possibilities for women. These women writers wanted to inspire virtue and sensitivity as expected male, as well as female, character traits.[66] Such an intent was also apparent among the seventeenth-century French *précieuses*, who also defined new conventions of comity between women and men to curb aggressive masculinity.

Yet the *honnête homme*, the masculine ideal of unalloyed virtue the *précieuses* attempted to further, was only partly realized. For, as personified by the eighteenth-century philosophes, these new-style men of virtue turned against their patrons, the eighteenth-century salon women, the descendants of the seventeenth-century *précieuses*. Forgetting former motives and rebelling against present milieus, the philosophes made domesticity the ideal for women, and Queen Marie Antoinette and her attendants played at being shepherdesses.

Yet it was not only that the philosophes portrayed the aristocratic salon women as frivolous, their life-style detrimental to their families and to their children. They also accused them of having created an effeminized, inappropriate masculinity, without the boldness and control these men of the mind wanted. Ultimately, by this argument, it was women who were responsible for having created the rake and the Don Juan, archetypal cultural figures replicated in reality who manipulated and abused them. As has not been uncommon, the victims were turned into the perpetrators, and women were accused of having created patriarchal figures who in actuality controlled them.

Elizabeth I of England:
The Conventions of Courteosie as Control

W OMEN, I HAVE ARGUED, were central to the creation of courteosie, those codes and conventions dating from the medieval period and intended to moderate male aggressive behavior, to soften warlike demeanors. Additionally, in that long debate over women's nature which began in the fifteenth century and which lasted at least until the eighteenth century, women writers not only counterposed a belief in women's spirituality to the popular view of women as insatiably sexual but they also critiqued male aggressiveness and their manipulation of women, the ways in which a false gallantry had overtaken the original chivalric sentiments, to make of women, seemingly men's midons, or lords, under the old conventions of courtly love, in actuality their pawns.

In literature and in memoirs, women enjoyed and laughed at fops and coxcombs, but they also realized the potential danger of these types of men. Marguerite de Navarre wrote in *The Heptaméron* that the basis of women's honor was gentleness, patience, and chastity. For men, on the other hand, "all your pleasure is derived from dishonoring women, and your honor is derived from killing other men in war."[67]

This critique of domineering masculinity was neither strident nor thoroughgoing. Nor did all women of authority participate in it. For example, Elizabeth I of England as the female ruler of a mighty state may have inspired a questioning of gender conventions, but her own life validated, as much as it critiqued, predominant notions of masculine aggressiveness. She used the conventions of chivalry to maintain control of the men around her, but she also upheld a domineering masculinity, one based on martial force.[68]

Elizabeth's court, for example, was particularly masculine. There were 175 men and about a dozen women in attendance on her as elite government officials or household employees. Sixty of these men served as "gentlemen pensioners," comprising a special guard rarely far from her side. Comparisoned in cloth of gold and silver, they were part of that spectacle of splendor in which Elizabeth embedded herself. They were popularly called "the spears" because of the magnificent lances they carried. Usually chosen from among the gentry, they became liaisons at court for important noble families. The guard was a way of utilizing young sons to represent the local polity being shaped into a Tudor nationality. They also signaled Elizabeth's authority over a masculine world.[69]

In addition to family connections, Elizabeth also chose these men for their virility and attractiveness. Thus men without rank could catch her eye. Christopher Hatton did so when dancing; Edward de Vere when jousting in her castle tiltyard. She singled others out of crowds lining the paths she traveled or from among her palace servants. And from among these men she chose a special favorite, to engage personally with her in the elaborate Renaissance conventions of courtship. For the most part these men were younger than she, like Christopher Hatton, or Walter Raleigh, or the Earl of Essex, who was the son of her first favorite, the Earl of Leicester. Indeed, her major marriage negotiation, beginning in 1579 and lasting for ten years, was with the Duke of Alençon, Catherine de Médicis's son, who was twenty years younger than Elizabeth.

By casting herself in the role of a medieval lady with a circle of young men to pay her court, Elizabeth upended the convention whereby male monarchs kept official mistresses, international symbols of male sexual power. She seized a male prerogative and made young men, some of them of aristocratic lineage and others dependent on her largesse, into her subalterns. Moreover, her ultimate control may have been that she created at her court a constant "beauty contest" among young men jockeying for positions near her.

In the work of Sidney, Spenser, and Shakespeare, Elizabeth's rule inspired a notable literary exploration of the meaning of gender. More than this, male dress became especially feminized during her reign. The heavy shoulder padding and the prominent codpiece characterizing previous male attire were considerably downplayed, if not entirely eliminated. Many fashionable men wore rigid corsets and high heels. A padded extension hanging over the stomach resembled either a refigured codpiece or a pregnant woman's belly. Fashionable men curled their hair and wore long locks tied with ribbons, as did Shakespeare's Duke of Southampton. "Their niceness in apparel transnatureth them, making them weak, tender, and infirm," wrote Puritan Philip Stubbes. "We may seem rather nice dames than manlie men."[70]

Yet Elizabeth did not intend to change male behavior, only to control it. The classical goddess imagery in which she clothed herself was drawn from figures—like Diana, or Cynthia, or Britomartis—associated in myth with young men. But warfare was her métier as much as any male ruler of her time. The Elizabethan explorers and "seadogs" were renowned warriors. Elizabeth was not a Marguerite de Navarre who advocated spirituality and pacifism. She was a female ruler who attempted to maintain her authority by often presenting herself in masculine guise. Her focus on control is apparent in her own body and clothing. Tightly corseted, with a tall, starched ruff around her neck, with skeletal thinness giving her an anorexic look, she projects self- as well as social domination.

If anyone influenced Elizabeth's self-creation, it was perhaps Diane de Poitiers, the noble mistress of French king Henry II who was twenty years older than her monarch-lover. Their relationship began in 1533. To keep her lover's interest, Diane cloaked the Valois court in the conventions of courteosie and identified her own image with that of the mythological virgin hunter Diana, who in myth had several involvements with younger men. Diane held tournaments and festivals; she introduced a court etiquette based on the conventions of *Amadis of Gaul,* the still-popular fourteenth-century chivalric romance which was revised and expanded in the sixteenth century. She encouraged the king in his beloved sport of hunting and, by participating with him, added a masculine element to her female persona.[71] Diane kept Henry's interest for twenty-six years, until his death in 1559 from wounds suffered when jousting in a tournament. (Elizabeth assumed the throne of England in 1557.) Henry II was married to Catherine de Médicis; the Duke of Alençon, Elizabeth's much younger suitor, was their son.

In Elizabeth's London palace, jousting and tournaments were continual activities; there was a castle tiltyard. By using the conventions of chivalry to surround her, she kept unruly young men under control. Because these young men were drawn from major aristocratic families, indirectly she extended authority through them throughout her realm. And the caprice by which she could add to her retinue men of no standing further increased her power over the influential men who surrounded her. When necessary she asserted her authority directly. Thus she exiled the Earl of Southampton from her court after his aggressive behavior at one of her tournaments.

In 1584, in the midst of the Duke of Alençon's protracted courtship of Elizabeth, playwright John Lyly wrote an Elizabethan version of the Sappho/Phaon legend, in his play *Sapho and Phao*. In this play, Lyly overturns the ancient convention of the young man spurning the older woman. Queen Sapho in the play not only conquers her love for Phao in order to rule her kingdom, but also takes over Venus's role as the goddess of love, with Cupid, Venus's son, as her minion. To Lyly, Sapho [Elizabeth] was a "princely Eagle," who "swayed the scepter in her brave court." It was appropriate that she rule not only over her kingdom but also over "the fansies of men." And, in Lyly's version, rejected by Sapho [Elizabeth], Phao indicates that he will spend the rest of his life "sighing and wishing, the one for my bad fortune, the other for Saphoes good."[72] In these words Elizabeth's sovereignty was acknowledged, not only over her kingdom but also over the men who served her and those who courted her.

The Salon Women:
Authority Established and Overturned

ELIZABETH OF ENGLAND adopted masculine conventions to validate her rule. In contrast, an initial impulse behind the founding of both the seventeenth- and the eighteenth-century salons was the negative reaction on the part of aristocratic women of literary bent to the domineering and manipulative nature of male behavior in the French royal court. In the seventeenth century the problematic ruler was Henry IV, and the female innovator was the Marquise de Rambouillet. In the eighteenth century the regency regime of the Duke of Orléans early in the century was at issue, and Madame de Lambert reinvigorated the salon as counterweight. The action of these women was bold: at one stroke they created the basis for female domination of the Parisian social and literary world. They provided elite women rich venues for the development of *courteosie* and new avenues for social expression at a time when urban growth and the middle-class desire to emulate the aristocracy provided a group from which imitators arose.[73]

During the seventeenth century writers like Molière seem to have critiqued them. But during the eighteenth century their authority expanded to the extent that they made and broke literary reputations. They controlled elections to the French Academy, even though women were excluded as members. In the seventeenth century the term *précieuse,* with overtones of ridicule, was used to describe them. By the eighteenth century they were simply the *salonnières,* the salon women, holding their "bureaux d'esprit," a contemporary term for their endeavors. With regard to the eighteenth century, wrote Jean-Jacques Rousseau, women had a "universal power." Glory and fortune, he continued, were "under their control."[74]

When they began their enterprises the salon women were typically not young. To launch a bid for social eminence took fortitude and skill, the courage and self-confidence of increasing years. In the eighteenth century many of the major salons were initiated by women who learned hostess techniques as protégées of older *salonnières.* Madame de Tencin "trained" Madame Geoffrin; Madame du Deffand, Julie de Lespinasse. In their famed study of the eighteenth-century salon women, Edmond and Jules de Goncourt identified the salon women as being in their forties—and often older.

Mentoring young men was part of the project of these aging women. Often in competition with each other, salon women vied for new faces and voices to provide freshness and diversity within their intellectual milieu. At their gatherings young, unknown authors could gain a hearing. Their reputation as mentors of young men, as gatekeepers to the elite social and literary world of France, was important to their authority. In the seventeenth century, when medieval conventions of courtly love found direct resonance in writings and in behavior, Madeleine de Scudéry was known for her association with the poet, Paul Pellison, eighteen years younger than she. In the eighteenth century, wrote Rousseau in his *Confessions,* with regard to the salons and referencing his own experience as a provincial young man coming to Paris, "a young man . . . with a passable face and who manifests some talent is always sure of being welcomed."[75]

Issues of gender comity concerned these women creators of a new social space. In particular, the *précieuses* emphasized spiritual above physical fulfillment. This emphasis was motivated by their negative reaction to male aggressiveness, as well as to men's control of women's bodies, and what they saw as the specious belief in women's sexual voraciousness. They developed the idea of the *refus d'amour,* or the rejection of physical seduction, and of the *tendre amitié,* the love which resembled only deep friendship. Both constructions indicated their uneasiness with unbridled male libertinism and their desire to curb domineering masculinity. They attacked the heroic ethic of masculinity and denigrated physical force as a mark of inferiority, identifying "physical sensitivity with superior humane virtues."[76]

Ninon de Lenclos, their seventeenth-century compatriot, differed from them in using her body for financial gain. She thereby turned male libertinism to her advantage. Yet even she extolled friendship as the true kind of fulfilling relationship. Her ideas resonated in the eighteenth-century *amitié amoreuse.* This notion of platonic friendship was evident, for example, in the friendship between the Marquise du Deffand and Horace Walpole, twenty-three years her junior. With regard to the close friendship between the seventy-year-old Benjamin Franklin and the younger Madame de Brillon, her husband wrote Franklin that his wife was "not content to please you by the kind of charms you can meet any day . . . but by a combination of all virtues which will make her your friend, in the true sense, were she old, were she ugly, were she a man."[77]

Yet there was a difference between the seventeenth- and eighteenth-century women of the salon. For the latter there was no make-believe "country of tender," the playland invented at Madeleine de Scudéry's salon, a make-believe world in which romantic longing and emotional interchange took the place of physical possession. They had no male role like that of the *soupirant,* the man who sighed in vain for the favor of his chosen lover. Their need for a safe space removed from masculine aggressiveness was never so great as that of their predecessors of the earlier century: they rarely received in bed. Nor did they continue the tradition of the *ruelle,* the private space around that bed to receive friends and platonic lovers.

Two striking developments occurred to change the situation, to make these women more accepting of heterosexual sexuality because they indeed gained more control of their bodies. First was the partial breakdown of the double standard and the aristocratic extending to women of their class the possibility of adultery. If they were discreet and their husbands were accommodating, aristocratic women, like their husbands, might indulge in extramarital relations. Second was the fact that by the eighteenth century the aristocracy began to practice birth control. The average number of children of France's high noble families dropped from 6.5 in the seventeenth century to 2 in the eighteenth century. Fears of death in childbirth and hostility against a domineering male sexuality were thereby mitigated.[78]

Yet as the *salonnières* gained greater renown, their woman-centered intent diminished. To a certain extent the success of the seventeenth-century *précieuses* in making a mark on manners, on speech, and on the contours of the literary world made the issue of gender realignments less pressing, less needful of change. The *précieuses* had had a hand in fashioning the *honnête homme*, the ethical male modeled along an ideal of moderation, of measured indulgence. As an ideal type he stood in opposition to the manipulative male cynicism of unmitigated gallantry: in him were strains of puritan control and of the aristocratic notion of courtesy, of "good breeding." In many ways the model *honnête homme* of the seventeenth century was realized by the philosophes, intellectuals who envisioned societies drawn by rational contract and who worried about inhumanity and deceit.

Moreover, the seventeenth-century Neoplatonism which had itself impelled the *précieuses* to challenge domineering masculinity on the basis of female spirituality was succeeded by an eighteenth-century rationalism which occasionally ratified gender equality but which also reinvigorated centuries-long traditions of defining women as nonrational and thus as domestic and inferior. The seventeenth-century *précieuses,* intent on reclaiming their bodies, made relationships the core of their program. Having gained a partial success, the eighteenth-century *salonnières* could become occupied by issues relating to humanity, not to gender.

Some scholars have argued that the power these women possessed was not real power, that it was secondary, and under male control. In the seventeenth century, Madeleine de Scudéry in *Clélie* and *Le Grand Cyrus* wrote novels of substance. In the eighteenth century, Madame de Tencin wrote sentimental tales and Madame de Lambert a few ethical treatises. But salon women as authors were the exceptions, not the rule. "They themselves posed as ignorant," writes one analyst, "and any compositions which have come down to us were written for private perusal."[79]

By this reasoning they facilitated authorship; they rarely produced written words on their own for public consumption. Their gift was fleeting conversation, their skill lay at intrigue. From this perspective they fulfilled, it might be argued, only that go-between role accorded aging women in Western civilization. Yet Diderot wrote that the the men they supported talked to them "incessantly." "They accustom us to discuss with charm and clarity the driest or thorniest subjects." Hence, he concluded, "we develop a particularly clear, facile way of explaining ourselves."[80] Whatever they said, the men absorbed. Unacknowledged publicly as collaborators, they remain only sounding boards.

The attack on the salon women, the silencing of their voices, was both direct and subtle. It was based both on a new dedication to women as most properly domestic beings and on continuing, if reconceptualized, concerns about definitions of masculinity. Like the female *précieuses* of the seventeenth century, the male philosophes of the eighteenth century worried about manipulative male gallantry. But they turned the analysis of the seventeenth-century women on its head. For as much as on male aggression, what they focused on was male effeminacy, on that softening of men which the conventions of gallantry seemed to produce, and which they viewed as unfortunate. They saw this tendency as the result not of male but rather of female manipulation, the manipulation of aristocratic women indulging in frivolity and excess. So Rousseau declaimed with contempt: "Every woman at Paris gathers in her apartment a harem of men more womanish than she."[81] The aging aristocratic woman roué, Madame de Merteuil of Choderlos de Laclos's *Les liaisons dangereuses,* using her body and her intelligence to seduce the young Danceny and to control her former lover, might be seen as a prototype of their discontents.

By the end of the eighteenth century the sentimentalized, domesticated nuclear family, centered around women as mothers, had become the ideal. The isolation of women in the home was offered as a way of saving individual women from worldly corruptions. For men, the separation offered a way of shoring up their masculinity. In many ways Rousseau returned to a celebration of the domineering masculinity of the old heroic prototype. In his writings, women are given some control: Rousseau acknowledges that their household power over sons and husbands will produce dependencies in men. But metaphors based on warfare are there in his thought. Ideas, he held, cannot be cultivated in sedentary salons, but only on the field of battle. Only through the combative process that men use when on their own, attacking and being attacked in return, can true ideas germinate.[82]

When they wrote about aging, eighteenth-century women often welcomed what they characterized as its tranquillity. By this statement they seem to have meant that age allowed them to be beyond the exploitative side of gallantry, in which sexual consummation was the major end. So there are the famous passages in *Les liaisons dangereuses* in which Madame de Merteuil discusses two kinds of aging women. The first sort, she contends, when they see their beauty fade, fall into depression and become either spiteful or apathetic. Then there are those who replace "seductive charms" by kindness and cheerfulness and whose wisdom and self-understanding make them the natural confidantes of the young.[83]

Madame de Merteuil's comments offer one model of positive aging in a century when white hair, interestingly, was the vogue.[84] But there is also the case of Julie de Lespinasse, the close friend of D'Alembert who came from impoverished roots to become a major salon hostess. She ended her life involved in a disastrous relationship with a young man of no particular promise who scorned her. Finally, there is Ninon de Lenclos, who in the seventeenth century flaunted all conventions by openly declaring her contempt for marriage and her intention to live her life on the model of a male libertine, supporting herself as a courtesan who chose her patrons. Her genius at garnering publicity for a privatized epicureanism popular among the day's philosophers brought her the support of many of Paris's leading intellectuals: for this reason her daringly unconventional life-style did not bring her greater opprobrium.

There is, however, the story, probably apocryphal but nonetheless significant, that she finally gave up her libertine life-style when a young lover turned out to be her son whom she had abandoned years before. When she revealed their true relationship to him, so the story goes, he shot himself. Horrified, she retired to a convent for the rest of her life. In the end, even Ninon de Lenclos was punished for violating conventions of age and gender behavior.

PART FOUR

From the Philosophes to Freud: Aging Women in More Modern Eras

EIGHTEENTH-CENTURY FRENCH PHILOSOPHES acclaiming domesticity added another voice to a chorus calling for a new companionate, patriarchal family, and for new behaviorial ideals. Women writers in the centuries-long *querelle des femmes* had counterposed spirituality to sexuality; the *précieuses* had continued the message. Seventeenth-century Puritans added a family dimension by demanding marital conjugality over against Catholic celibacy and courtly infidelity.

By the eighteenth century, writers like the English Samuel Richardson limned the economic and psychological benefits of marriage for women within the domesticated, patriarchal family. Early feminists like Mary Wollstonecraft critiqued both aristocratic fashionable women and libertine men as detrimental to their program of educating women for virtuous self-knowledge and effective mothering. The middle class found the domesticated family's emphasis on self-control in keeping with their capitalist goals, while the companionate ideal provided them with a welcome distinction. Fears of working-class sexuality, in addition to a new focus on the mother-child bond and on love as the cornerstone of marriage, accelerated the trends under review. And, reflecting the rest, physiologists now contended that male and female genitalia were different rather than similar, while medical writers rejected old ideas about the necessity of female orgasm for conception and contentment. Broad destabilizing social forces—the advent of industrialization, the many political revolutions—further advanced the new family and gender definitions. By the early nineteenth century, the domesticated, patriarchal family became a haven of security. The sentimentalized, domestic woman was its linchpin.

Along with this major shift in cultural mentality came new attitudes toward aging women. As sexuality became contained within marriage, the new female villain became not the older woman, as in past ages, but the unmarried woman, potentially outside of the boundaries of patriarchal family control. Aging women in this nineteenth-century world were no longer automatically denigrated. Rather, from one vantage they became a doubled version of younger women. Like their younger counterparts, from the conservative perspective they were the potential providers of a new family spirituality. Alternatively, to woman's rights advocates their greater morality implied an imperative toward reform participation. The key to this change in attitude with regard to aging women lies in the privileging of spirituality central to the new domesticated family. It also lies in new views about menopause under which many came to view the cessation of menstruation not as dangerous but as liberating.

These attitudes reached their apogee in the late-nineteenth-century era, as women entered the work force and the professions, advanced in level of education, and launched transatlantic movements of woman-centered reform. Between 1890 and 1920 occurred an era of signal advance for women, in keeping with the reform sentiment of this period. A shift, however, occured in the 1920s, as core cultural beliefs came to emphasize sexuality, rather than spirituality, as basic to the nature of women and identified it with young women. The "sexual revolution" of the 1920s, enshrined in new dances and new styles of dress, had ambiguous impacts on the prospects of women more generally. Once again, as in the past, defining women as sexual beings was problematic for them.

From the early nineteenth century on, cross-age relationships between aging women and younger men declined. They were undermined by many of the same forces that produced the sentimentalized, domesticated family. Indeed, the reverse situation, namely older men with younger women, increased. This trend reflected a new masculinization—a reassertion of masculinity as power—which would wax and wane throughout the nineteenth century, to emerge strongly by its end.

I begin my discussion of the nineteenth century with the American writer and social critic Margaret Fuller. I end it with the French novelist Colette. Both married men younger than they; both had much of value to say about aging and relationships. With regard to the twentieth century, I focus on menopause, partly because it has emerged in the recent era as a central process in women's lives, especially given the larger numbers of women living to older ages than ever before in the European and American past. I also emphasize menopause because its history demonstrates the open and subtle ways in which a new devaluation resembling an older one can impact on aging women's lot.

The Nineteenth Century: Margaret Fuller and Colette— Continental and Anglo-American Comparisons

IN THE SPRING of 1846 Margaret Fuller, famed American journalist and writer, began a European tour as the guest of friends. A year later, in the city of Rome, she accidentally met the Marquis Giovanni Angelo Ossoli while at a vespers service in Saint Peter's Basilica. From this encounter a romance developed. He soon wanted to marry her, despite a ten-year gap in their ages (she was thirty-six; he was twenty-six). At first she resisted, leaving Rome to travel north with her friends. After a brief period, however, she returned alone to be with Ossoli. In 1848 she bore a son, and a year later they married.[1]

The attraction between Margaret Fuller, the self-supporting daughter of New England Calvinists, and Giovanni Ossoli, the youngest son of an impoverished noble family, was initially one of opposites. She was an intellectual; he was largely uneducated in books. She was emotionally unrestrained; he was quiet and controlled, albeit supportive and loving. Having lost his mother when he was a child, Ossoli probably found Fuller's authority attractive. As for her, he reminded her of her mother and brother; he also bore resemblance to the young women she had mentored during her years teaching school and with many of whom she had become very close.

Above all, both were committed to the Italian revolutionary cause, and this shared enthusiasm cemented their relationship. From her landing in London, Fuller had progressed from an observer of leftist persuasion to an enthusiast for direct action; Ossoli was involved in the Italian liberation movement known as "young Italy." They carried out their romance in the midst of the excitement of the Italian revolution of 1848. While he served on the barricades, she worked for a time as a hospital nurse. In the months surrounding the birth of their child, she wrote a history of the revolution. They left Italy in 1850 to return to the United States. However, their lives and that of their child were tragically lost when their ship was wrecked approaching the New York shore. The manuscript of Fuller's history of the revolution also was lost in the shipwreck.

The story of Margaret Fuller's life and of her marriage elucidates the complexity of attitudes toward aging women. Often scorned as a spinster during her American years, Fuller found a greater acceptance among continental Europeans. And once she married and had a child, old derisions evolved into encomiums. With a conventional life trajectory, Fuller could be considered more a "true" woman than a deviant one.

How Fuller would have lived her later life we do not know. Her writings on the subject of aging, however, are reformist. In *Woman in the Nineteenth Century* she envisioned a positive role for aging unmarried women as social reformers and as exemplars of human self-realization. With regard to relationships, she called for a gender intermixing modeled on the older woman–younger man association. And, she looked for a more positive attitude toward aging women's natural appearance. In this exposition, she drew on the centuries-long valuation of inward qualities over external ones. This tradition continued in the nineteenth century.

Yet Fuller herself realized the strength of the status quo. The definition of aging women as perversely sexual may have ended, but it was replaced by a definition of aging unmarried women as perversely asexual. The grandmother persona emerged to offer aging women a new self-definition, but older views of aging women as inevitably ugly also continued. These definitions, both positive and negative, were designed to uphold the companionate family with the spiritualized mother and the domesticated father as its linchpins. So powerful was the cultural impulse behind this family form that it impacted even on standards of physical appearance, on the ways in which women of various ages were supposed to look. And this encoding of women's bodies, the inscription of convention on their persons, is apparent in various attitudes toward the aging Margaret Fuller as "beautiful" or "ugly."

With regard to these issues, differences existed between the Anglo-American articulation and that of France. When Fuller traveled to the continent, she encountered these differences. The disparities are also apparent in the writings of Colette, the turn-of-century French novelist who has been perhaps the preeminent literary analyst of relationships between older women and younger men.

Margaret Fuller and Giovanni Ossoli

*T*HAT FULLER MET the man she married in Italy should not seem surprising. In Victorian America she had been an anomaly. In an era when the womanly ideal was small and demure, Fuller was tall and commanding. A brilliant intellectual, educated in the day's learning by a father who treated her like a son, she did not fit the female model of propriety and domesticity. Many found her too masculine. She did not defer to men; she openly displayed her erudition and her conversational ability. Nineteenth-century America reprobated the Renaissance "virago," the woman of authority with masculine characteristics. But when Fuller wrote about Queen Elizabeth I of England in *Woman in the Nineteenth Century,* she praised the famed ruler for governmental skill but critiqued her for using stereotypical feminine wiles as a means of control.[2] Despite the potential personal pitfalls in the stance, Fuller preferred directness.

The Boston-area male Transcendentalists admitted her to their intellectual comradeship; she edited their magazine, *The Dial.* But they married much more conventional women. Ralph Waldo Emerson verged on deep emotional involvement with her, but he seemed to find what he called her "effulgent" nature too commanding. Nathaniel Hawthorne drew on her character to construct the figures of Zenobia in *The Blithedale Romance* and Miriam in *The Marble Faun.*[3] Both of these "dark ladies," as Nina Baym has noted, possess desirable qualities of interior strength and intensity lacking in their male counterparts. Yet in his notebooks, published after his death, Hawthorne left to posterity a scathing indictment of the Fuller/Ossoli relationship. He characterized Fuller as a woman driven by sexual desire and Ossoli as little more than a gigolo. "As for her toward him, I do not understand what feeling there could have been except it was purely sexual; as for him toward her, there could hardly have been even this, for she had not the charm of womanhood. . . ."[4]

The English essayist Thomas Carlyle, renowned for his call for a revitalization of the male heroic, met her at a gathering in London. Drawing on negative stereotypes of unmarried aging women, he called her a "lean, lilting old maid." Her close friend, the Unitarian minister James Freeman Clarke, repeatedly told her that he considered her far too "superior" to other women ever to consider a romantic involvement. In other words, he found her abilities personally threatening, her power too great for him to handle. When she married Ossoli, Emerson expressed surprise to one of her New England friends that any man would want to marry her.[5]

Fuller's meeting with Ossoli was a chance occurrence. Yet it drew on preexisting themes in her biography. Ann Douglas posits that in the 1830s and 1840s Fuller wanted to live her life like a literary heroine.[6] The relationship with Ossoli may have given her the chance to do so. Her friends often called her the American Corinne, likening her to the legendary poet-heroine of Germaine de Staël's 1808 novel, *Corinne.* Elements of Fuller's romance with Ossoli curiously replicated those of the fictionalized character. Ossoli's name sounded like Oswald, Corinne's sometime lover; Fuller and Ossoli met at Saint Peter's, a place where Corinne and Oswald furthered a growing attraction.[7]

Fuller's literary idols—Goethe, Germaine de Staël, George Sand— had all been involved in older woman/younger man relationships: Goethe as a younger man and de Staël and Sand as older women. In Italy Elizabeth Barrett Browning and Robert Browning became Fuller's close friends—Barrett Browning nearly a decade older than her husband. When Fuller was in Paris she met George Sand and Sand's former younger lover, Frédéric Chopin. In her journal Fuller called Chopin an "Ariel" to Sand, likening him to Prospero's servant in Shakespeare's *The Tempest.*[8]

In her writings, Fuller focused on the goddesses of antiquity as models of female independence and human comity. Like all highly educated people of her day in the United States, she was versed in the classics. But where male readers like Thomas Jefferson responded to general ethical and political themes in Cicero and Ovid, Fuller concentrated on discussions of women in classical sources and on the goddesses whose power lingered in those texts. Fuller died before the mid-nineteenth-century research of Johann Bachofen elucidated the existence of those female divinities: his work on the subject, *Mother Right,* was not published until 1861. She died before Sir Arthur Evans late in the century discovered the palaces of the ancient civilization on Crete and Egyptologists by accident found lost poems of Sappho in mummy wrappings.

Yet the ancient goddesses were important to her. They were her favorite topic of discussion in the famed conversations she held for women in Boston in 1839 and 1840. The ideal woman, she wrote in *Woman in the Nineteenth Century,* is embodied in goddesses like Diana and Minerva and especially in Demeter and Persephone, the "great goddesses," as she called them. She described George Sand as follows in her journal: "There may have been something of the bacchante in her life, and of the love of night and storm, and the free raptures amid which roamed over the mountaintops the followers of Cybele, the great goddess, the great mother."⁹

Fuller was versed in the tradition of the ancient goddesses and their younger consorts. Fuller's brother concluded his edition of *Woman in the Nineteenth Century* with a poem by her entitled "The Sacred Marriage." (One assumes this poem relates to the ancient ceremony.) In this poem she wrote:

> *Twin stars that mutual circle in the heaven*
> *Twin parts for spiritual concord given,*
> *Twin Sabbaths that inlock the Sacred Seven: . . .*
> *A world whose seasons bloom from pole to pole,*
> *A force which knows both starting-point and goal,*
> *A home in heaven—the Union is the Soul.*¹⁰

Fuller here explored the intertwinings of gender and independence, of autonomy and union, of the need for women to stand alone and of the fulfillment that could come through another. Women, she thought, were more gifted than men with intuitive powers, with a "mysterious fluid" which she thought partook of the divine. Women were Sibyls and Muses, she wrote, the seers of visions, those who understood the mysteries. But men could also possess this authority. "There is no wholly masculine man, nor feminine woman," she wrote. "Man partakes of the feminine in the Apollo, woman of the masculine in Minerva."¹¹

Yet Fuller had misgivings about her relationship with Ossoli. These concerns were revealed in her apprehensions about their decision to move to the United States. She wrote her mother that she was troubled about how Ossoli would respond to her as the years passed and her aging became more evident. She worried that her intellectual friends in the United States would not accept him. In Italian cities there were taverns where he could pass the time while she debated intellectual issues; this was not always the case in the United States. Behavior acceptable in Italy, she worried, would be unacceptable in her native land; even her educated friends might frown on their age difference.¹²

She may also have had other concerns. In an earlier story called "Aglauron and Laurie" she depicted the relationship between a character named Emily and a younger man, V-. In this story Fuller wrote about how some women need men not for protection but for tenderness. "Have you never heard tales of youthful minstrels and pages being preferred by princesses, in the land of chivalry, to stalwart knights, who were riding all over the land? . . ." Most people, she thought, would consider such young men effeminate, but she would not agree. Yet the relationship in her story failed. The problem was that the young man, V-, became too dependent on Emily. Fuller concluded that Emily "was infinitely blest, for a time, in his devotion, but presently her strong nature found him too much hers, and too little his own."[13]

In her 1845 *Woman in the Nineteenth Century,* written two years before she met Ossoli, Fuller attempted to come to terms with her then unmarried state and with the public descriptions of her as "ugly." Marriage to Ossoli may have been a life resolution for her, but this work indicates the possibility of other satisfactory endings. In *Woman in the Nineteenth Century* she admitted that aging spinsters could be difficult. Scorned by society, they could be "partial," "harsh," "officious," "impertinent." Yet because of their aloneness, they could reach a better self-understanding, a closer self-communication. "Such a use of it [aloneness]," wrote Fuller, "is made by saints and sibyls." Moreover, without family responsibilities, they could serve society. The modern, complex era needed their skill. They could employ their abilities "for the good of all men and not just a husband."[14]

Furthermore, Fuller commented on attitudes toward aging women's appearance. Her words encompass her own experience. In photographs and paintings of Fuller, to our eyes her appearance may seem pleasant, even beautiful. But considered unattractive by her peers, described by Carlyle as a "lean, lilting old maid," she must have suffered self-recrimination. In her writings she addressed personal discomfort by raising constraints visited on her to all aging women—and there overturning them. Indeed, Fuller called for a new standard of physical appearance for aging women. "Perhaps the next generation," wrote Fuller, "looking deeper into this matter, will find that contempt is put upon old maids, or old women, at all, merely because they do not use the elixir which would keep them young." (By elixir she probably meant cosmetics.)[15]

In Fuller's ideal the look of age, not of youth, is the model. Wrinkles and sagging skin, she indicated, ought to be celebrated, not denigrated. What mattered about youth and what she wanted to include in the aging female ideal was youthful vigor, youthful energy. She proposed a model in keeping with her call for women to become reformers, or nurturers, or to form gender-balanced relationships. "No one thinks of Michelangelo's Sibyl . . . as old," she wrote. Indeed, she chose the Sibyl of the Sistine Chapel as her model of beauty for aging women. She concluded her passages about aging women by extolling the Michelangelo painting:

Look at the Sibyl. She is withered; she is faded; the drapery that enfolds her has in its dignity an angularity, too, that tells of age. . . . But her eye, that torch of the soul, is untamed, and, in the intensity of her reading, we see a soul invincibly young in faith and hope. . . .[16]

Aging Women and Younger Men: The Victorian Context

NEGATIVE ATTITUDES toward aging unmarried women evident in the English and American reaction to Fuller's aging as well as in her own concerns about her relationship with Ossoli indicate broader cultural resonances in which such associations between age and youth became increasingly problematic. Many indices reveal a decrease in the occurrence of these kinds of relationships by the nineteenth century. Where earlier statistics demonstrate men's marrying upward in age range, by the late eighteenth century, among the elites in England and the general population in the American colonies, husbands were about five years older than wives at the time of marriage.

Rates of remarriage also indicate a change. Philippe Ariès finds significant the figures compiled by Edward A. Wrigley and Roger Shofield which show that in England before 1650 the remarriage rate stood at 25 to 30 percent, while by the nineteenth century it dropped to 10 percent. (In other words, fewer individuals left alone by the death of a spouse were choosing to remarry.) Ariès thinks that in explaining what he terms this "surprising" decrease, a decline in the rate of remarriage between older women and younger men was important.[17]

Moreover, the existence of large numbers of aging unmarried women during the same time period also indicates a lessening of these cross-age relationships. Such rates of unmarried women had long existed among peasants and workers; they now spread to the middle class and the elites. Among the English elites approximately 5 percent of daughters remained unmarried in the 1590s. By the early eighteenth century and throughout the nineteenth century the percentage among the elites was 25. Within the general English population for the nineteenth century the percentage stood at about 10 percent, although contemporaries at various points estimated that as many as one in four women were not marrying. In the United States, population discontinuities produced by migration to the cities and the frontier produced percentages of unmarried women in some areas as high as in England.[18]

Among the literati, relationships between older women and younger men still existed. Well-known women could still attract younger men: as real-life examples of these sorts of involvements one might mention writers George Eliot and Germaine de Staël; actresses Lillie Langtry and Sarah Bernhardt; feminists Lucy Stone and Charlotte Perkins Gilman. In aristocratic society older women were still mentors to younger men: in Paris, according to Stendhal, "a duchess is never more than forty for a bourgeois."[19] Among farmers and workers, too, such relationships did not disappear. As late as the 1790s in Salzburg, Germany, the majority of carpenters' wives were considerably older than their husbands. Studying French folk traditions in the nineteenth century, Arnold Van Gennep found that in parts of Ile-et-Vilaine about one-third of the wives were fifteen years older than their husbands.[20]

But these instances went against the general trend. More important was the obverse situation in which younger men married women of the same age—or these younger women married older men. Those aging widows who in earlier centuries had often been important marital prospects tended to remain unmarried (a situation not necessarily disadvantageous to them).

A number of developments produced this decrease in age-disparate relationships. In the first place, the new capitalist economic order brought with it the removal of the workplace from the home to business offices and factories and new status imperatives for middle-class women to display wealth through leisure and to end involvement in family businesses. These changes lessened the opportunities for contacts between wives and apprentices that might result in courtship and marriage if the women were widowed. More rigid class divisions between workers and employers lessened workers' attractiveness to older middle-class widows.[21]

The emergence of romantic love as a major factor in marital choice also played a part in the decline in cross-age relationships between aging women and younger men. For the advent of romantic love was accompanied by an increased emphasis on physical qualities of attraction, especially on the female youthful ideal. Parents and other social arbiters encouraged this model as another way of regulating courtship in terms of age when they no longer had direct control; in many ways the new definitions of appropriate spouses were as rigid as older ones, those based on family and financial considerations.[22]

Demography also played a part in the decline in these cross-age relationships. In England, for example, late-seventeenth- and early-eighteenth-century declines in infant mortality operated differentially on males and females. Probably because of stronger female constitutions, more girls than boys profited from the new conditions to survive infancy and childhood. This factor ultimately produced a "negative sex ratio," with more adult women than men available for marriage. Then, as often occurred in this demographic situation, men less readily married upward in age range. Concurrently, state officials in England and France interpreted newly gathered population statistics incorrectly. At a time when population in these nations was actually expanding, the official position was precisely the opposite. Concerns about state security generated by the presumed population declines brought pleas from state officials and popular commentators alike for increased birthrates. With this appeal, women no longer fertile became less attractive marital choices.[23]

Above all, new definitions of women's sexuality were key to new attitudes toward aging women which made them less desirable marriage partners (as much as these new definitions made marriage less necessary for them). Along with other changes in gender meanings, a reversal in definitions of women's sexuality occurred in the eighteenth century. Centuries-old beliefs about women's sexual voracity and the similarities between men's and women's genitalia and their sexual responses were transposed. Men's and women's sexual natures—and even their genital structures—were now considered different; women's spirituality was often stressed above their sexuality.

Negative reactions to aristocratic gallantry underlay this spiritualization, as well as the impulse that male sexuality needed containment. Middle-class fears of the working class and their presumed eroticism, especially with the growth of cities and of large working-class populations, also played a role. New humanitarian views of childhood produced by Enlightenment humanitarianism and Romantic sentimentality and a new emphasis on the mother-child bond were also involved. This emphasis, in turn, engendered a new accent on maternality, on women's childbearing function, seen as related to the purity of the child, now transferred to the mother as well.[24]

During the eighteenth century these new ideas and the behaviors proceeding from them were important, but not dominant. Roy Porter has documented the extensive sexualized society of eighteenth-century England.[25] Lusty aging women abound in the English literature of that age: one can find them in Daniel Defoe's famed female characters as they age: in Moll Flanders and Roxana. Additional compelling examples are found in Henry Fielding's Lady Bellaston of *Tom Jones* and Mrs. Slipslop of *Joseph Andrews.*[26] Then there are Richardson's evil aging women: Mrs. Jewkes, the menacing housekeeper in *Pamela* who guards Pamela for Mr. B——, and the aging brothel madam in *Clarissa.* Indeed, in eighteenth-century London midwives cum healers cum go-betweens still existed: in this century they were called "Mother Midnight."[27]

Yet for every seductive matron or menacing housekeeper in eighteenth-century fiction, there is a mother, or an aunt, or a grandmother whose only concern is marrying off a daughter, or a niece, or, because there seems nothing else for wealthy widows in England in particular to do, all the daughters in her social circle. Fanny Burney's *Evelina,* written in 1778, is an interesting novel in this regard. For it is transitional, showing both the old and the new attitudes toward aging women.

Evelina, the novel's heroine, comes to the city of Bath (a major social and courtship arena) as the protégée of a distant older female relative, deputized to find her a wealthy husband. As a woman, Evelina's cicerone is without sexual resonance. But Evelina also has a grandmother, a Madame Duval, who wanders through the plot with her "friend," M. Du Bois. Evelina is embarrassed by this mysterious and flirtatious grandmother, who does not act the way an older woman should. But Evelina is never certain of Madame Duval's age. "She must have been married very early in life; what her age is, I do not know, but she really looks to be less than fifty."[28]

Eighteenth-century imperatives toward the domesticated, spiritualized woman became especially strong by the nineteenth century. Heightened religious, economic, and political dictates even more than before called for individual and social purification through the medium of the mother in the home. Revolutionary and republican movements, especially in the United States, produced the ideal of a "republican" mother, of a domestic woman who would further civic virtue through instilling morality in husband and children. These political motivations, focused on the home, were joined by the directives of evangelical religion, especially strong in England and the United States. Presbyterian and Congregational reenergizing around piety, joined by the new Methodist sect, found major proponents among women. In turn, evangelical ministers directed these women to bring evangelicalism's moral message into their homes.[29]

This notion of the spirituality of women did not necessarily deny their sexuality: options in sexual expression existed. Recent research in nineteenth-century sex and behavior manuals has found a variety of stances on the issue of whether or not women enjoyed sexuality: historians now discount older views of Victorianism as entirely reprobating women's sexuality.[30] In fact, as Karen Lystra points out, in many ways sexuality and spirituality could intricately combine in spousal relationships, each impulse furthering the other. Sexual congress, in the nineteenth century as today, could become a natural expression of spiritual outpouring, of romantic and then marital love.

But by defining women's proper place in terms of marital heterosexual sexuality, the Victorian family ideal created divisions among women. These divisions existed especially between married women, enclosed in heterosexual space, and unmarried women, by definition outside of that space. Even though Margaret Fuller defended unmarried women on the grounds of their potential social usefulness, she also reflected dominant conventions when she proposed that marital sexuality had special benefits and a superior cultural meaning. She wrote: "Marriage is the natural means of forming a sphere, of taking root. . . . Those who have a more full experience of the instincts have a distrust as to whether the unmarried can be thoroughly human."[31]

Behind this extraordinary statement by a major critic of social conventionalism lies the yearning of a passionate woman for the heterosexual union which her culture held out as providing the highest personal satisfaction. Within it also lay a privileging of heterosexual sexuality, the "more full experience of the instincts," in Fuller's words. The passage also contains an indication of the extent to which the isolating of unmarried women could proceed: they could be considered as not only socially deviant but even as not "thoroughly human."

These cultural beliefs about women's sexuality are revealed in eighteenth- and nineteenth-century attitudes toward aging unmarried women in England and the United States. Margaret Fuller was not the only cultural commentator to describe in an unflattering manner both cultural beliefs regarding aging unmarried women and the actual behavior of this group. The earlier undefined nature of these women was now regularized in a negative manner by the terms "spinster" and "old maid" which were applied to them. Before the late seventeenth century the term "old maid" existed only episodically. In earlier ages the term "spinster" was either an occupational designation for women spinners or a generic title indicating gentility: it implied no opprobrium.[32]

By the eighteenth century these definitions changed. As "superfluous women" (a term used to describe them) spinsters and old maids were often scorned. In literature, features formerly pertaining to witches, including long noses and pointed chins, were often used to describe their appearance. But there was little satanic or mysterious about popular depictions of them. Typically they were described as querulous gossips, devoid of the dignity natural to married, childbearing women. Literary spinsters in the eighteenth century desperately desired husbands and affected foolish, youthful behavior. The most famous of them was Tabitha Bramble, in Tobias Smollett's 1771 *The Expedition of Humphry Clinker*. Described by Smollett as a "maiden of 45," Tabitha Bramble is a comic character who spends the novel chasing men who evade her. She is "tall, raw-boned, awkward, and flat-chested." Her nose is long and sharp. In "temper" (to us temperament) she is "proud, vain, imperious, prying, malicious, greedy and uncharitable."[33]

Indeed, the decline in witchcraft persecutions by the eighteenth century was not unrelated to the shift in the definition of aging, unmarried women's sexuality. (Reflexively, the decline also probably played a role in the definitional change.)[34] Words traditionally associated with witchcraft lost their ominous meanings. The word "crone," initially associated with the wisdom of aging women, was subsequently reversed to imply inappropriateness. By the nineteenth century it was transmogrified into "crony," a word referring to an aging man's close companions. Consider as well what happened to the name "Tabitha." In early times Tabitha (in Greek meaning "gazelle") was associated with witchcraft. By the eighteenth century, shortened to tabby, it was commonly applied to spinsters. (This transposition occurred after Smollett gave the name Tabitha to his spinster protagonist.) Next the word "tabby" was applied to aging cats, perceived as frequent companions to aging women living alone. As the frightening witch became the comic spinster, her "familiar," the demon in animal form who did her bidding, became the domesticated cat, the tabby.[35]

By the early nineteenth century the go-between as a real and a literary type was also beginning to disappear. The brothel madam remained in operation, her power legitimated by virtue of its being contained in a house, in domestic, private space. But in terms of street prostitution, slowly male pimps, not aging women bawds, took over controlling the trade. In England the advent of control by pimps was the result of governmental campaigns to end prostitution. These campaigns forced prostitutes to rely on men for protection against legal authorities.[36]

As maternal figures, women became the creators of hearth and home, not its destroyers. They soothed and supported men; they did not threaten them. The aging woman living alone, even if in contention with her community, was no longer dangerous. For her sexuality was under control by virtue of its being nonexistent. Rather, she became simply eccentric.

Witchcraft as a theme was not absent from the Gothic tales popular in this period. Witches are there in Gothic tales, but so are male ghosts and ghouls. In Gothic tales the real villains are often demonic males, descendants of the epic Faust and Don Juans of previous ages, and the forerunners of later male monsters: Dr. Frankenstein's monster, the vampire, Dr. Jekyll's split personality as Mr. Hyde.[37]

Even among writers influenced by Gothic prototypes, Enlightenment rationalism, its humanitarian drive to expose obscurantisms seen as dangerous, also applied.[38] In the writing of Nathaniel Hawthorne, the American writer who more than any other explored the meaning of seventeenth-century New England witchcraft, witches are primarily domesticated figures or carnival, Halloween-like characters, bogey-people of the mind. In *The House of the Seven Gables*, Hepzibah Pyncheon is a stereotypical eccentric spinster, probably the most famed American literary representative of the type. She is "gaunt," "rigid," "rusty." Although she is the descendant of a seventeenth-century witch, her association with anything approaching witchcraft is trivial. Her witchcraft is associated with brackish wells and cups of tea "productive of internal mischief." The young Phoebe in the novel practices the real "witchcraft," as Hawthorne describes it, through her ability at housekeeping and gardening.[39]

Negative characterizations of aging unmarried women, like those of Tabitha Bramble and Hepzibah Pyncheon, continued throughout the eighteenth and nineteenth centuries. The anonymous author of the 1785 *Essay on Old Maids* titled chapter headings according to the prevailing stereotypes: on the credulity, curiosity, affectation, envy, and ill-nature of old maids. In the opinion of this author "old maids," especially the "superannuated" beauties, were "worse than the witches of old." No longer could aging women bewitch others; now they simply annoyed those around them. Margaret Fuller wrote in *Woman in the Nineteenth Century* that spinsters in real life were "partial," "harsh," "officious," and "impertinent."[40]

Do you remember the game of "old maid"? In the 1950s it was widely played by American children; it can still be found on sale today. It developed from an early card game based on a regular deck from which all the queens but one were removed. This unpaired card became the one to avoid; the game's loser was the player who at the end still possessed the unmatched queen. In the nineteenth century, in special "old maid" decks, an ugly scowling woman fitting the common stereotype replaced the queen.[41]

Beneath the unflattering stereotype of spinsters lay their essential asexuality. They were "maids," virgins without the freshness of youth, unilaterally old. They waited on others; the name "maid" implied servanthood. In her novella *The Old Maid,* set in the 1870s, Edith Wharton describes the cultural perception of spinsters as "like withered babies." They had not developed full maturity, full sexual knowledge. In Wharton's story, family members warn even the children never to say anything in front of the family's unmarried women members that could shock them.[42] Indeed, some medical writers claimed that women possessed no sexual drive until they had experienced intercourse: thus in this basic biological feature married women differed from unmarried women.

Attitudes toward aging unmarried women (and the distinctions drawn between them and married women) are apparent in differing prescriptions (and descriptions) of the look of aging women's bodies, especially those of unmarried aging women. Early in the century the ideal for aging women became one of weight, not of thinness. In a complex passage in *Woman in the Nineteenth Century,* Margaret Fuller discussed this model while critiquing it. She noted that the common term of praise for the appearance of older women was "fair, fat, and forty." Yet when Fuller wrote this book, she herself at thirty-five was both thin and unmarried. Her dislike of this weighty standard for aging women, of what she called "matron beauty," is apparent in her further statement that this plump look was too often displayed by "common" women who resembled a "coarse, full-blown dahlia flower."[43]

In the 1870s and 1880s, Elizabeth Cady Stanton toured the country as a lecturer on the lyceum circuit. Press reports praised her appearance as a model for aging women. Then in her fifties and sixties, Stanton's body was rotund, even fat, by the standards of today. Nonetheless, that was the way aging women were supposed to look. "Plump as a partridge," went one description in 1870, "with a well-formed head . . . she would be taken for the mother of a governor or president."[44] Married to reformer and politician Henry Stanton, Cady Stanton was the mother of five children.

The reference to the "plump" Cady Stanton in the context of motherhood taken together with the unmarried Margaret Fuller's critique of weight in aging women provides an entrance into understanding the meaning of this appearance standard of weight for aging women. The standard was related, in fact, to women's marital sexual fulfillment and the valorization of motherhood, perceived, as with pregnancy, in an idealized bodily inscription associated with weight gain. Married women, contained within heterosexual sexuality and presumed to be procreative, would naturally gain weight: in their bodies they would display their position.

Women often pregnant, especially in an era which denigrated exercise for women and which recommended hearty eating for pregnant and nursing mothers, would naturally gain weight only with difficulty removed.

Those standards of thinness so apparent in the emaciated "steel-engraving" lady look of early century applied primarily to young, unmarried women: women older in years were supposed to gain weight. Thus an interesting cultural anomaly existed. The Victorian convention was that pregnant women were not to show themselves in public; the proof of the actual sexual deed was to be hidden, kept within family confines. Yet the domesticity and maternalness which surrounded it were publicly celebrated in the idealization of plumpness for married women.

These attitudes can also be seen in the common perception that aging unmarried women inevitably maintained the thin bodies, which, attractive in young women before they married, were not attractive in aging women. This attitude explains Carlyle's curious use of the term "lean" with regard to Fuller. "Lean" was a term in those centuries most commonly applied to pieces of meat, to objects not robust: it was not exactly a synonym for thin. In previous centuries the descriptions of witches as lean or gaunt had been related to their lower-class position, their lack of sufficient food. Now a class stereotype was translated into a gendered stereotype: the perception of aging women unmarried and without children as unnatural, so unnatural that their deficiencies were supposed to be apparent even in their bodies.

Susan B. Anthony, Elizabeth Cady Stanton's reform associate, never married. She had, throughout her later years, a body unmarked by major weight gain. Press reports about her often described her as gaunt, as looking like a witch. This association of the state of singlehood with leanness persisted in depictions of spinsters and old maids, whether prescriptive or descriptive, fantasized or actual.

It is in this context that we can further understand Fuller's description of Michelangelo's Cumaen Sibyl, her model of aging beauty, as having an "angularity that tells of age." While standing above her age's stereotypical, confining attitudes with regard to aging and to unmarried women, on one level Fuller internalized them. Assuredly there were contented spinsters and even plump unmarried women in nineteenth-century America. But Fuller's eyes, like those of many, were blinded by stereotypes which she applied not only to other individuals but also reflexively, and in some ways tragically, to herself.

In his analysis of physiologists' views of gender in these eras, Thomas Laquer has written that "the bodies of women became the battleground

for redefining relations of men and women."[45] I would amend his trenchant observation to read that contention was inscribed on the bodies of
varieties of women in differing ways and that unmarried aging women
bore the brunt of what was, in effect, a reallocated misogyny.

Yet even women within marriage were not free from negative valuations. For negative stereotyping could also extend to aging women—even
if married—thereby reducing what was otherwise a privileged group to
the marginality imposed on spinsters. For one strain of thought found
unattractive all aging women, especially as they reached middle age. A
popular joke among men was that "any man would gladly change his
wife of forty for two twenties." By age thirty-five in England and the
United States rural and conservative women donned white caps under
which they tucked their hair, symbolically containing their sexuality.[46]

Aging women were major creators and enforcers of Victorian conventionalism. Enacting this role brought them both respect and a reduction
to caricature. Mrs. Grundy (a character in playwright Thomas Morton's
1798 *Speed the Plough*) became a symbol of Victorian conventionalism.
Thomas Beer's vitriolic portrait of the aging woman as a "Titaness" in
"hot black silk" enforcing a sterile conformity throughout the Midwest
in the post–Civil War period bears the ring of some truth.[47] Queen
Victoria's name eventually was borrowed to denote the era's prudery; her
dour, unsmiling appearance after the death of her husband symbolized
conventionalism among women for over a half century.

Modes of belief in the Victorian era reprobated a variety of women's
bodies—married and unmarried, middle-aged and old. These conceptions
contributed to discontent and divisions among women, operating to extend patriarchy's control in an era when women's superior spirituality
seemed to offer them a special stance. Old valuations of aging women as
witches ended in an era of rationality, but new estimations encompassed
new restrictions. One set of restrictions was connected with the privileging
of women within marriage over women who remained unmarried; the
second was the categorization of even aging married women as outside
the bounds of male desire.

Within the eighteenth and nineteenth centuries, as Thomas Laquer
asserts, relations between men and women may have been redefined. This
redefinition was apparent in new physiological views about women's
bodies, the rise of a new sentimentalized family based on love between
husband and wife, and a new spiritualization of women. All on one level
operated to improve women's position and to increase their authority. Yet
patriarchy had not ended; it had been remodeled around new categoriza-

tions. Women's new spiritualization, for example, when divorced from sexuality, provided a justification for reform activity. But insofar as its connection to marital sexuality was dominant, it divided women from one another, as did other categorizations of women extant.

How women themselves responded to these contradictory messages is difficult to say. But it is revealing that even Margaret Fuller, who contested the negative stereotyping, was at the same time influenced by new definitions of sexuality and asexuality to express yearnings for heterosexual love and to critique spinster behavior. Thus this major nineteenth-century proponent of women's independence revealed that she herself had internalized prevailing standards. She offers a forceful example of the power of conventionalism and of that patriarchal order which is often its corollary.

Victorianism: Spirituality, Aging, and Appearance

DOMESTIC IDEOLOGY, I have argued, depicted aging unmarried women as outside the cultural category of beauty, as removed from women within the charmed circle of domesticity. And even married women could be defined negatively. But throughout the Victorian era, another series of attitudes and personifications with regard to aging women discounted neither married nor unmarried women.

In the first place, the grandmother emerged as a positive persona, her emphasis on spirituality offering a justification for celibacy, domesticity, or social involvement. In the second place, predominating reform sentiment brought to the fore centuries of reasoning relating appearance to attributes of character rather than to physical look. Both of these developments gave women impetus to remain unmarried or to bond with other women.[48]

The grandmother figure made her strongest appearance in the United States. In the eighteenth-century colonies, earlier European demographic patterns under which grandmothers had been few in number were reversed. A lack of urbanization produced an increased life expectancy as well as a greater number of individuals surviving to older ages. A young age of first marriage and parenthood among all classes meant that larger numbers of women were still alive when their daughters bore children and these children moved through the life span. Later ages of first marriage in the antebellum era probably reduced the numbers of grandmothers, although older conceptions of this role still applied.[49]

At base, three types of grandmothers appeared in fiction, advice books, and memoirs. Each grew out of prevailing general stereotypes of women; each reinforced varying cultural signals of proper behavior for women, strengthening the message given women generally. First was the grandmother as cipher, the woman who doted on her grandchildren and existed in a haze of handiwork and sentimentality, sitting in her rocking chair, a piece of furniture designed, like a baby's cradle, to soothe. This grandmother was associated with innocence, with a lack of sexuality. Her image was suffused with calmness, reinforcing the serenity that the mother was supposed to provide for the family.[50]

A second grandmother figure was enmeshed in domesticity. She was the bustling homemaker, often caring for grandchildren. In her person she showed the strength of aging; she expended her considerable energy on the personal needs of others. A third grandmother figure was socially active, even involved in reform. The "republican" grandmother joined the "republican" mother. She was a forthright woman who had supported her family during the Revolution to emerge as a heroine in her own right. In the antebellum United States, George Washington's mother, Mary, in addition to his wife, Martha, emerged as a revered model for aging women. "Let our daughters but return to the active and industrious habits of their great grandmothers," asserted a writer of behavior advice, "and we should soon see a generation who might safely compare with the noble matrons of '76—the Mary and Martha Washingtons. . . ." Assuredly asexual, this grandmother figure was a potent actor behind that ideology of reform domesticity, launched by evangelicalism, which recent literary analysts have ennobled into a major nineteenth-century reform trajectory.[51]

In her recollections of her childhood in early nineteenth-century New England, Eliza Cabot remembered one of her grandmothers absorbed by housekeeping, her identification with domesticity symbolized by the cookies she baked every time her grandchildren visited. But Cabot also remembered her grandmother Perkins, a widow who raised eight children, ran a grocery store, and was one of the founders of the Boston Female Asylum. Cabot's grandmother Perkins bears resemblance to the indomitable aging female character found in women's fiction of this era, as in Harriet Beecher Stowe's portrayal of the grandmother in *Oldtown Folks*. Stowe's grandmother was "as soft-hearted to children as any of the meekest of the tribe who bear that revered name [the name of grandmother]." But she was also "a tower of strength and deliverance, a valiant old soul, who fearlessly took any bull in life by the horns, and was ready to shake him into decorum."[52] This was a woman capable of coping with any possibility, of making herself into what was required of her.

The grandmother as social and family guide furthered women's ability to overcome negative stereotypes of singlehood and aging. Alternative positive attitudes about appearance also aided them in self-determination. In *Woman in the Nineteenth Century* Margaret Fuller drew on this tradition when she cataloged her idealized aging woman with wrinkled face and white hair. Aging as an ethical experience which could enrich women and through this authorization render them beautiful was a common motif in nineteenth-century writings proceeding both from high and low culture; from both woman's rights advocates and more conservative commentators. Thus one writer in 1850 contended that "the face in which health, intelligence, virtue and cheerfulness are shining must always please, and it will retain its attractions long after mere external loveliness has faded and passed away." Variety actress Lola Montez in her popular beauty manual wrote that a woman could be as beautiful at fifty as at thirty, for she had the added advantage of wisdom in her face. She was then a "Juno" or a "Minerva."[53]

The impulse to purify ethical values as well as social institutions characterized nineteenth-century reform. This regenerative impulse was apparent in the celebration of women's spirituality within the family. By the latter half of the nineteenth century it overflowed these boundaries to emerge in varieties of reform imperatives, some of them personal. By late century the contours of a "culture of beauty" emerged, composed of both amateurs and self-styled professionals who promoted various techniques and products as a way of attaining "beauty." This culture was both commercial and noncommercial, and before the 1920s predominance of commercialism, its reformist thrust was especially authoritative. The reformist advice posited that to improve appearance, women should utilize natural means, not artificial ones. Rather than dieting or using cosmetics to change the look of faces and bodies, women should exercise and eat healthy foods.

The argument was further advanced that mental attitude was central to physical appearance. More than this, beauty writers by late century contended that women could alter the way they looked by mental effort. On the one hand, this argument took the conservative form of asserting that women could prevent wrinkles from appearing in their faces by never moving their facial muscles. On the other hand, the advice was more authentic: personal beauty could be produced by adopting an ethical concern for the well-being of others or for society in general. Spiritual beauty, in this version, would inevitably produce physical beauty. This ethical impulse drew from older arguments, dating to Sappho and Neoplatonic imperatives, that spirituality, not physicality, was what counted in a pleasing appearance. Now beauty manuals as well as woman's rights writings put forth the opinion that young women could not be beautiful because they had not lived long enough to reflect in their faces any real character, any real experience of life.[54]

The opinion was also expressed that the beauty of young women was only a *beauté du diable*—a limited seductiveness given them by the devil. They could quickly lose this beauty if they did not enhance interior qualities of mind and spirit. From the influential eighteenth-century writings of William Hogarth on beauty, true beauty had been viewed as related to a curved line (corresponding to the curves of women's bodies). In terms of age, many writers referred to this curve as capricious, as peaking early in some women and as taking different, unfortunate, forms in others. Following one line of this analysis, the beauty of prostitutes could only be ephemeral, for anything controlled by Satan could not last. Yet without the regenerating power of an ethical attitude this dangerous diabolical beauty could extend even to respectable women.[55]

Elizabeth Lynn Linton, a popular British advice writer of midcentury, forcefully expressed these ideas, while applying them to a specific case. Linton wrote scornfully of the aging woman who tried to make herself look twenty years younger in order to have the "reputation of a love affair with a younger man." Against this person Linton juxtaposed the woman who accepted her aging appearance while, as Margaret Fuller had prescribed, maintaining youthful energy. Linton described her ideal aging woman as different from her peer who lusted after younger men. Linton's woman was one "with her happy face and softened manner, who unites the charms of both epochs, retaining the ready responsiveness of youth while adding the wider sympathies of experience. . . . Consequently she remains beautiful to the last. . . ."[56]

Reformist writers on aging beauty, like Linton, only occasionally refer to the size or shape of the body in their generalized paeans to spirituality. But by late century weight in women was increasingly part of the ideal standard for all women, not only aging women. The connection between maternity and marriage produced it. It was also the outcome of the increasing public popularity of variety and burlesque actresses. Their round, corseted bodies were meant to exude sexuality: these women were considered voluptuous, not fat. Thus sexuality reentered as a category which, by late century, was becoming more available to aging women.

This factor further explains Fuller's reference in *Woman in the Nineteenth Century* to "matron beauty" as in many instances displayed by a "common" woman who resembled a "coarse, full-blown dahlia flower." Fuller may have herself yearned for beauty, but she did not like the overtones of the variety stage in ideal standards of appearance.

In her pathbreaking analysis of inadequate representations of gender history, Joan Scott especially cites what she calls the "standard treatment" of the Victorian ideology of domesticity. This standard treatment, according to Scott, involves presenting Victorian domesticity "as if it were created whole and only afterwards reacted to instead of being the constant subject of great differences of opinion."[57] Scott's observation can be extended to include the failure to incorporate the multifaceted and conflicting prototypes of women which existed in this era: the aging woman as invariably ugly; the spinster as unnatural; the grandmother as the multiplied, admirable version of idealized domesticity, individual self-realization, and valued reform activity; the aging woman as ethical beauty. These models molded women; women both accepted and rejected them in defining themselves.

Thus some women were emboldened to reject marriage and the family to remain spinsters and unmarried widows. In antebellum Petersburg, Virginia, according to Suzanne Lebsock, widows remained unremarried by choice, not by lack of suitors. Writing about widows in Philadelphia and Chester counties from 1750 to 1850, Lisa Waciega finds that the majority of widows of all social classes did not remarry. Susan B. Anthony remained unmarried by choice throughout her life to pursue her career as a reformer. She was well aware of how marital responsibilities seriously hampered the outside involvement of her married compatriots. So attractive was independence to many nineteenth-century women that, according to Lee Chambers-Schiller, a "cult of single blessedness" existed among them.[58]

Rejecting the divisions which pejorative definitions of the female body generated, other women were enabled to bond together, whether mothers with daughters, aging women with kin, or women left alone, without male support. In her study of Oneida County, New York, Mary Ryan concludes that local literature celebrated mother-daughter bonds and that this perception of female solidarity was upheld by statistics showing that half of all native-born females over sixty were widowed and that more than 90 percent lived with children. Writing about women in Michigan during the century from 1820 to 1920, Marilyn Ferris Motz finds the existence of female-linked kin networks available for support to individu-

als in difficult times: for example, elderly widows counted on their daughters and daughters-in-law to nurse them in return for earlier service they
had given to these kin.[59]

Writing about New York City in the period from 1789 to 1860, Christine Stansell uncovered a similar pattern. Within tenement neighborhoods,
women coping with poverty in their daily lives formed extensive networks
of association with each other. They constantly visited each other in their
homes; they interacted on the streets and stoops which functioned as an
extension of the crowded, decrepit rooms they inhabited. Men often
deserted them; they helped each other financially. In addition, according
to Stansell, the sheer vitality of these women, who lived in "shifting
communities of cooperation and contention," impelled them to create
their friendship networks "out of a sometimes boundless energy, a voracity
for involvement in the lives of others."[60]

In addition to the positive and negative symbolizations and attitudes
toward aging I have described, one further arena of self-definition was
significant. This realm involved menopause, a central experience for all
aging women. Surprisingly, by the mid-nineteenth century menopause
was redefined in terms more positive than negative, reversing centuries
of belief in the evil effects of the change of life. Medical and behavior
writers now thought that menopausal and postmenopausal women often
experienced a heightened vitality, a special zest. But because of the complexity of the subject of menopause as well as its late-century intertwining
with many of the themes regarding aging and appearance I have just
reviewed, I leave its full exposition for my succeeding chapter on the
twentieth century. Menopause as subject and experience adds yet another
complexity to that series of forces contesting for the definition of Victorian
domesticity and of aging women in these eras.

The Masculine Perspective:
Older Men and Younger Women

THE DENIGRATION of aging, unmarried women, as well
as the positive attitudes toward women's self-creation without men, were
factors relating to women which underlay the decrease in relationships
between aging women and younger men. But considerations relating to
men also were involved, and these components require analysis. An analy-

sis of these elements also sheds light on the negative stereotyping of aging women in an era which celebrated women's spirituality and presumably accorded them a special role in shaping, through the home, a more virtuous culture.

The first consideration which indicates a change in male disposition was the trend toward marriages of older men to younger women. Peter Gay notes this phenomenon in France and England; David Leverenz makes reference to its occurrence in the United States. Lenore Davidoff and Catherine Hall think that business and professional men, putting off marriage until they were financially secure, then operated according to an ideal of youth in women in choosing marital partners.[61]

The issue of marriage between older men and young women is an identifiable theme in English and American literature of this era. In both Nathaniel Hawthorne's *Scarlet Letter* and his *Marble Faun,* the problem for his "dark ladies," for Hester Prynne and Miriam who have an evil secret in their pasts, stems from an initial marriage to an older man. In Charlotte Brontë's *Jane Eyre* as in Oliver Wendell Holmes's *Elsie Venner,* younger women bring life to older men broken in spirit. In Louisa May Alcott's *Little Women,* however, the reverse is the case. The gentle and moral, older Professor Bhaer is a more suitable match for Jo than the young Laurie, who as a young man indulged in libertine behavior. The professor will be able to domesticate the rebellious Jo, and thus to fulfill her real aspirations in ways that Laurie perhaps never could.[62]

Novelists utilized many variations on the theme of aging men with young women. But at the heart of this theme as a lived reality lay the issue of control. Many historians argue that the advent of capitalism, with its intensely competitive dynamic, in addition to the advent of a dynamic woman's rights movement, created such insecurities for men that new male prototypes and behaviors emerged.[63] Given these insecurities, self-control and control of others was imperative.

By the nineteenth century, men's earlier aristocratic flamboyance was contained. As aristocratic gallantry turned into middle-class courtesy, older male types oriented toward celebrating (or victimizing) women (for example, the fop and the coxcomb) took on countercultural colorations to emerge as parts of artistic bohemias or of the sporting and courtesan cultures associated with the theater, especially in Europe. That remasculinization of men for which Rousseau had called as a counterweight to the aristocratic salon culture he despised now came into being (as did the dominance of the domestic ideal of which he had also been the prophet).

All men, following businessmen, began to wear black, long symbolic of male power—and of its corollary, the kind of sensible control that Castiglione had called for as early as the sixteenth century. The *honnête homme* of the seventeenth-century *précieuses* had now become the "Christian gentleman." Even in public this man showed his respect for women by deferring to them. This model doubtless contained sensitivity: "etiquette" applied to men as well as to women. Novelists created gentle heroes throughout the century: one can discern such types, for example, in the male protagonists of authors who, like Stendhal or Henry James, worked within the "novel of initiation" tradition. It is there in Charles Brockden Brown's Arthur Mervyn and Herman Melville's Pierre.[64]

But control was there, too, and the reassertion of patriarchy: the gentleman of early century was the forerunner of the imperalist and pugilist of late century. Increasingly in the nineteenth century the look for men was older, more solid, with the stockiness of the football player or of the well-fed businessman. Throughout the nineteenth century, from Thomas Carlyle onward, periodic appeals were issued for the recrudescence of the dynamism often identified with Napoleon as a male cultural hero. Walter Houghton notes that John Bull was a symbol of England in its imperial era and that this male figure was huge, animal-like, with a cudgel in his hand.[65]

In the mid-nineteenth century, in her story "Aglauron and Laurie," Margaret Fuller had praised the appeal of a young man's gentleness while conceding that most individuals would find him effeminate. "Manliness" was the masculine ideal of late century: it meant "a neo-spartan virility as exemplified by stoicism, hardness, and endurance."[66] By late century novelists were fascinated with soldiers, adventurers, and hunters. The rise of a new masculinized heroic was also evident in the development of sports like football and organizations like the Boy Scouts. It was there, too, in the imperialist who conquered native peoples and the cowboy who defended virtue in the American West. It would culminate in the figures of the urban detective, Superman, and Tarzan; finally, in the common soldier as heroic in World War II and in the new 1950s redefinition of the Adonis figure as a muscle-bound athlete rather than a gentle young man.

In marrying younger women, older men followed a practice standard for centuries but one which took on new meaning in the nineteenth-century world. In this period Enlightenment humanitarianism, Romantic sentimentality, and evangelical morality through the ideology of domesticity dictated that women were to infuse new moral standards through their influence on family members within the home. But having much older husbands must have made any such infusion on the part of wives doubly difficult. As some women married men old enough to be their fathers, patriarchal control in the fullest generational sense was reinstated.

Yet, of course, the inevitability that numbers of these older men would predecease their wives re-created that historical situation so often occurring in the form of moneyed older women with powerful personalities. In this nineteenth-century era, however, they seem not to have readily remarried. Here that obverse side of the Victorian domestic ideology which frowned on female sexuality applied. Within marriage, sexuality may have been full and free. But outside marriage widows were not viewed as deficient without sexuality. That age-old belief that widows were dominated by sexual desire was now overturned. And, in this case, a significant group of women were enabled to draw on positive nomenclatures of the unmarried state.

The ideology of domesticity afforded a certain security to women. When combined with notions of female moral superiority and the crusade to moralize men within the home, it also afforded a certain authority. Some historians have contended that women were the primary creators of domesticity, for they realized its advantages.[67] But women's new authority brought the recrudescence of symbolizations of predominating man. The nexus of cause and effect here is virtually seamless and difficult to penetrate. But, as had happened in the past and would happen in the future, at a significant turning point in gender experience, patriarchy did not disappear but rather was redefined, and the redefinitions tended to divide women and to bring men together around definitions of powerful masculinity.

Anglo-American and Continental Comparisons

THUS FAR my discussion of conceptions of nineteenth-century sexuality and spirituality has been confined primarily to England and the United States. But a difference existed between these two countries and continental ones. Popular writers often remark on this difference, but scholars have rarely addressed it. The difference is evident in the story of Margaret Fuller and her relationship with Giovanni Ossoli. In the United States and England, Fuller, the unmarried intellectual, met critical scorn, her appearance often an issue. In France and Italy she was accepted. Her appearance was considered unremarkable, even attractive. This divergence, I think, can be seen initially in dominant motifs in the literature of the two regions.

In France, for example, writers continued to use the older woman/ younger man motif. It is prominent in many nineteenth-century French novels, like Benjamin Constant's *Adolphe,* Stendhal's *The Red and the Black,* and Gustave Flaubert's *Sentimental Education.* Balzac, de Maupassant, and Zola all wrote novels in which young men's desire for social preferment, economic advance, intellectual and emotional wisdom, and physical possession of sexually experienced women draws them toward older women. These older women can provide their younger lovers with an *éducation du sentiment,* that sentimental education which is an initiation into the ways of the world.

Sometimes these aging women are, as in Balzac's *Lost Illusions,* aristocrats who hold entrée to high social circles. Sometimes, as in Flaubert's *Sentimental Education* or de Maupassant's *Bel Ami,* they are married to journalists or other creative men, and they possess the reflected charisma of creative spouses as well as access to their husband's professional world. For the most part the older women are of a higher social class than their younger paramours. Rarely, however, are they involved with salon culture, itself largely a casualty of the Revolution.

Yet no formula is involved: the aging women could vary by class and personal disposition. Thus Madame Rênal in *The Red and the Black* is a simple woman, happiest in her garden and with her children. In Emile Zola's *Nana* and in Alphonse Daudet's *Sapho,* the older women are stars of the Parisian demimonde. They possess a powerful sexuality which is in some ways liberating but is also perverse. Their sexuality draws on conventions about aging brothel madams and their taste for virile young men. The young Gaussin in Daudet's *Sapho* associates his family in the provinces with nature and health and his passion for Sapho as evil and uncontrollable, as "some dangerous fever such as one contracts from the exhaltations of marshy ground."[68]

This initiation motif in which an aging woman molds a young man did not especially interest nineteenth-century American and British authors. In England the theme occasionally appears in the so-called society novels of Benjamin Disraeli. But Disraeli was a recorder of English upper-class society which preserved some of the older, aristocratic conventions. He himself was married to an older woman. In the United States, Henry James employed its possibilities in a number of novels, notably in *The Ambassadors.* But James was probably the most European of nineteenth-century American writers.

At the opening of the nineteenth century in the United States, Charles Brockden Brown used the theme with interesting effect in *Arthur Mervyn,* as did Herman Melville at mid-century in *Pierre, or the Ambiguities.* In Brown's exploration of a young man's coming to the city, his hero Arthur Mervyn rejects the virginal romantic heroine to marry an older, sophisticated woman who is not only not attractive but who is also Jewish. In Melville's *Pierre* all of the older women characters turn out to be flawed. Pierre is betrayed by all of them, from the stereotypical town spinsters who too easily spread gossip, to his adored mother who cannot tolerate ethical imperfections, to Isabel, his presumed older sister. Pierre's life in New York City, an urban place which is often the location for education in these novels, becomes a nightmare. The beauty of both his mother and Isabel (in many ways mirror images of each other) produces only a destructive narcissism.

Melville describes their attractiveness in a passage which I interpret as intentionally ironic. Age, Melville seems to say, can be as seductive as youth, its interior beauty as deceptive as the exterior beauty of youth:

> Beautiful women—those of them at least who are beautiful in soul as well as in body—do, notwithstanding the relentless law of earthly fleetingness, still seem, for a long interval, mysteriously exempt from the incantations of decay; for as the outward loveliness touch by touch departs, the interior beauty touch by touch replaces that departing bloom, with charms, which, underivable from earth, possess the ineffaceableness of stars. Else, why at the age of sixty, have some women held in the strongest bonds of love and fealty, men young enough to be their grandsons? And why did all-seducing Ninon unintendingly break scores of hearts at seventy?[69]

Anglo-American writers evidence a notable difficulty in writing about aging women as sexual beings. Some years ago Leslie Fiedler observed with regard to gender conventions in American fiction that in the classic tales of adventure by Cooper, Twain, or Melville, men really desire to embrace nature and to flee cities and organized society, identified with women. Indeed, sexualized women in American and English novels often have French names or backgrounds. Pierre's Isabel, for example, is presumed to have had a French mother and to have spent much of her childhood in France. Henry James's powerful aging women, like the devious Madame Merle of *Portrait of a Lady* or her honorable compatriot Madame de Vionnet of *The Ambassadors*, are often French.

Consider what Briton Arnold Bennett wrote in his journal about writing *The Old Wives' Tale,* a novel about aging women published in 1908. Bennett was interested in investigating the greater sensuality and freedom permitted aging women in Paris. He constructed a story about two sisters, one living in provincial England and one in Paris. He had no problem portraying as erotic the relationships the Parisian sister had while she was still young. But as she aged, he could not cast her character in a French mold. He made her the typical English widow woman, controlled, clever at shepherding her resources and then buying a hotel to manage until she retired, back to England to be with her sister.[70]

His original conception for *The Old Wives' Tale,* he once wrote, had come from seeing "an old whore" in Paris. But he could not portray his heroine, Sophia, in such a manner. He simply couldn't visualize an Englishwoman acting like that. So he created a Frenchwoman, Madame Foucault, as a prostitute frequented by young men. And here is what the proper, controlled Englishwoman, Sophia, says about Madame Foucault, her protector in a time of troubles, when Sophia discovers her occupation:

> As a woman of between forty and fifty the obese sepulchre of a dead vulgar beauty, she had no right to passions and tears and hope, or even the means of life; she had no right to expose herself picturesquely beneath a crimson glow in all the panoply of ribboned garters and lacy seductiveness. It was silly; it was disgraceful.[71]

Past practice and present reality combined to create these differentials between the French and the Anglo-American experience. The cult of courtly love had its genesis in France: its strongest roots lay in that land. Cherubino, the page infatuated with his mistress who was an eighteenth-century apogee of that tradition, was very much a French creation. The story of Sappho and Phaon, too, had special resonances in France. So did the tale of Phaedra and Hippolytus, especially through Racine's play about the pair of lovers which was a classic of the French theater throughout the nineteenth century.

One could argue that while the French writers using the "initiation" theme regarded aging women seriously, English writers like Fielding employed it mainly to satirize these relationships and especially the older women partners. Susan Gubar has argued that the misogyny of eighteenth-century English Augustan satire was rarely equaled in the Western imagination.[72] Although French eighteenth-century literature was hardly exempt from contempt for women, the gross exaggerations present in the writings of Pope and Swift by and large were not part of the French literary treatment of women.

The acceptance of women as learned ladies or as social cicerones was also stronger on continental than on Anglo-American soil: the seventeenth- and eighteenth-century French salons were replicated only in pale versions in England and the United States. In these countries pejorative terms like "bluestocking" came into being to mock women of intellect. Only with difficulty did Hester Chapone and Mary Montagu in London attract Walpole and Johnson to their gatherings. What Anne Hollingsworth Wharton depicts as "salons" in the United States seem to have been little more than social gatherings with a few literary types present.[73]

For upper-class Englishmen, all-male clubs were major eighteenth- and nineteenth-century recreational and social institutions. But when Lord Bolingbroke in the eighteenth century attempted to establish one in Paris, it was a failure. Such exclusively male places appeared in Paris only later in the nineteenth century. In France men and women preferred to socialize together. Conversely, French travelers touring England found absurd the practice there of separating men and women for after-dinner conversation.[74]

In the eighteenth-century French salons, both Briton Horace Walpole and American Benjamin Franklin participated in sentimental and erotic relationships. But they concealed these relationships when they returned to their own lands. Walpole practiced this deception despite the fact that his correspondence with Madame du Deffand, a leading *salonnière* twenty-three years older than he, remains to this day a model of literary exposition. Nineteenth-century women writers like Germaine de Staël or George Sand, who maintained both literary reputations and individualized lifestyles, were rare in both England and the United States. In these countries the literary counterculture was, before the end of the century, simply neither sufficiently large nor self-confident to sustain women of this sort. And, according to Alexis de Tocqueville, writing in 1840, French married women were allowed much more freedom than their counterparts in the United States.[75]

The French tradition of age-disparate relationships between older women and younger men and of the continuing eroticism of aging women was enshrined in many ways. Not the least of these ways was its identification with certain famed historical personages. Diane de Poitiers in the sixteenth century was the mistress of Henry II throughout his reign. The seventeenth-century Ninon de Lenclos became over the ages a symbol of enlightened pleasure and dignified aging. Rousseau's Madame de Warens, the free-spirited older woman with whom he lived in the country before he came to Paris and whom he immortalized in his *Confessions*, was estranged from her husband and took younger men as lovers.[76]

But these distinctions between France, England, and the United States can be carried too far. Indeed, location may be the key. The more liberated French attitudes may have been Parisian and thus urban in location. In her study of nineteenth-century industrialists in the North of France, Bonnie Smith depicts a group of women as sexually repressed and as socially domineering as any in Puritan lands. Writing about nineteenth-century French middle- and upper-class women, both Margaret Darrow and Barbara Corrado Pope find a cult of domesticity among them. Despite the widespread presumption that older women are celebrated within French tradition, the nineteenth-century French had a term for aging women as pejorative as any in the English vocabulary. *La crise de la quarantaine,* "the crisis of forty" was the term, as though aging (and in this case the onset of menopause) produced inevitable emotional difficulties.[77]

On the other hand, statistics cited by Claire Moses suggest that the numbers of unmarried women in France in the nineteenth century were comparable to those in the United States and England. That no comparable "spinster" stereotype arose in France probably had to do with the Catholic tradition of the preferability of celibacy to marriage. The lack of the spinster stereotype may also indicate a difference in the nature of transcontinental "Victorianism," weaker in France than in England and the United States.[78]

However, in nineteenth-century French novels of initiation by Balzac, Stendhal, and the rest, women's experience of aging is not depicted completely positively. For the most part the older women partnered with younger men in these works are below the age of forty and are portrayed as still beautiful. Yet even though they have not yet reached "the crisis of forty," in every case their experience of aging is troubling. Madame de Bargeton in Balzac's *Lost Illusions* is thirty-six and "could have passed as a young girl." Still, she has reached "that terrible age when a woman begins to regret the years of her beauty that have slipped by without her having had any joy in them." In *Adolphe,* Ellénore's aging and not her indeterminate social status eventually becomes the major reason Adolphe's family opposes her. As Adolphe's father states: "She is ten years older than you; you are twenty-six; you will look after her for another ten years; she will then be old. . . . Boredom will overtake you."[79]

Madame de Rênal in *The Red and the Black* is only thirty to Julien

Sorel's twenty. But when he seems to reject her, she immediately traces the problem to their age difference, even though Stendhal as narrator as well as other characters in the novel call her beautiful. But, as Stendhal tells us, her suspicions are fueled by the fact that "when the subject is love, a difference in age is, next to that in wealth, one of the most common themes of provincial humor."[80]

Colette: The Theme of Age and Youth

WITHIN FRENCH LITERATURE, the novel of initiation reached its high point in the works of Colette. Usually identified with the Chéri novels (*Chéri; The Last of Chéri*), the theme of love between age and youth permeates all of Colette's work. It is a central motif, for example, in *The Retreat from Love* (the last of the Claudine novels), as well as in *The Ripening Seed, The Awakening Dawn,* and *Julie de Carneilhan.* The inverse relationship, that between an older man and a younger woman, also appears in several of Colette's works, notably in the Claudine novels and in *Gigi,* the last short novel she wrote.

The use of this theme, in the first instance, reflected her own biography. When young she married a much older man; when she was older she married a much younger man. Her first husband, Henri Gauthier-Villars (known as "Willy") was fifteen years older than she: she married him in 1893 when she was sixteen and he was thirty-two. Her last husband, Maurice Goudeket, was seventeen years younger than she. She met him in 1925 and married him in 1935.[81] Yet as much as her own biography infuses all her work, it is only partially the source of this focus on age-disparate love. In employing this theme she drew from long-standing French literary conventions, namely from the "initiation" motif that appeared in the seventeenth century with the retelling of the Sappho-Phaon legend.

The Pure and the Impure was the title she gave to that work which she once called her best book. The phrase can be employed to characterize the central meaning of much of her work. For what interested Colette was examining women's experience of aging in the context of their rich ongoing sexuality and elucidating how accepting or rejecting either sexuality and age or both of them might bring women freedom—or bondage. Shifting meanings of domination and liberation, of truth and falsity, of age and youth, of masculine and feminine, of the pure and the impure (of the "foul" and the "fair") ricochet throughout her work. They underline her equally strong intent to upend conventionalities, to present ethical problems and possibilities as they emerge within shunned relationships and subcultures. What better theme for these purposes than the "deviant" relationship between young and old examined in its full, human depth?

The aging women protagonists in Colette's novels are women of privilege, with independent incomes. This is not a working-class group. With the exception of Renée Nere and Mitsou, both music hall performers whose stories are drawn from Colette's own experiences on the stage, the necessities of life do not concern them. Julie de Carneilhan may be down on her luck, but she still has a servant and a stylish flat in Paris. Colette's mother, Sido, is increasingly the most important figure in Colette's work, and her poverty is an important manifestation of the character Colette creates for her. Still Sido is an educated woman, with a love of reading. Broad issues of women's work-force entry or questions of social injustice do not concern Colette. Her novels are rooted in social reality, but psychological states of being are what concern her.

Colette's women protagonists are multifaceted individuals. They are both powerful and powerless, both strong and weak, and often these characteristics are combined in the same individual. Their power initially lies in an implicit masculinity which many of them possess. *The Break of Day* is a partial roman à clef in which Colette uses her own name for the central character. In this book the character Colette is described as with "a kind of mannishness, a hail-fellow-well-met manner. . . ." In *The Ripening Seed,* Camille, the mysterious woman in white, is described as her young male lover's master. The young man notes that the name Camille could be used for either a man or a woman. Colette's own name was her father's last name, not her surname. She was actually named Sidonie-Gabrielle Colette.[82]

In the first instance, the power of these older women protagonists (themselves older in each of her novels as Colette herself ages), resides in their powerful sensuality. Because they are experienced in the techniques of love and because they exude this knowledge in voice, movement, and gesture, young, sexually unsophisticated men cannot resist them. This irresistibility is expressed most clearly in *The Ripening Seed.* In this novel, the sixteen-year-old Philippe is seduced away from his childhood sweetheart by Camille, the woman in white. Wealthy and sophisticated, she lives in an eroticized paradise, with a parrot indicating its tropical resonance and an emphasis on fleshy food, on exotic spices, on soft, luxurious couches having an oriental cast.

In contrast to the young, "angular" Vinca, Camille has "a too fat chin, lips artificially reddened."[83] But this initial negative description foreshadows the "impure" which will shortly become "pure," the "foul" which will become "fair," the sensuality which will shortly become irresistible to Philippe. Resonating to her age's cultural models of attractiveness in aging women, Colette describes her heroine Camille's rounded, curved body as voluptuous, not overweight.

Vinca, the young woman in *The Ripening Seed*, tries to retain her hold on Philippe by seducing him. With bravado, she contends she is as sexually knowledgeable as his older paramour. But her boast is not true; she does not satisfy him in their sexual encounter. That very fleshiness, that eroticism which Arnold Bennett presented through the eyes of an Englishwoman as obscene in his *The Old Wives' Tale,* in Colette's novels is alluring, enticing, thrilling. *"Ces plaisirs qu'on nomme, à la légère, physique"* (those pleasures which we lightly call physical), wrote Colette in the renowned ironic phrase. Through the irony she inverted the standard perception that physical pleasure in relationships is secondary to some deeper, more spiritual bond.

Physical pleasure, too, could have special resonance, especially for young men first experiencing it. Love was much more than the bonding between the young. The intermixing of ages could bring variety to long relationships between equals. Thus she wrote in *The Break of Day* that "married life becomes a career, and sometimes a bureaucratic system in which the only circumstance that takes us out of ourselves is that balancing trick which, at the appointed time, impels the greybeard towards the flapper, and Chéri towards Lea."[84]

With her first husband, Willy, Colette lived in the sophisticated Parisian world of journalists and novelists, poets and playwrights. It was into this world that the eighteenth-century culture of gallantry, of sensuality unconfined by social boundaries or the family setting, had migrated. The vitality of this milieu contributed to that positive title "La Belle Epoque" employed to characterize this era and also to the more negative "fin-de-siècle," a term referencing its decadence. Colette herself knew well the world of the theater, in which she eventually became a performer, and that of the demimonde, the place of Zola's Nana and the other great cocottes of her age. For her first husband, Willy, was a habitué of the demimonde, a gossip columnist, and an early master at manipulating public opinion. Colette "ghosted" the early Claudine novels under his name; Willy engineered her early public notoriety after she cut her hair in defiance of current styles and did some acting on the popular stage.

When he brought her to Paris Willy perceived that the innocence of his seventeen-year-old wife would fascinate his older, sophisticated companions. She used herself as the model for the adolescent character Claudine in the books she wrote during this period. Could it also be that those adolescent males she later created—Philippe of *The Ripening Seed* and Chéri of *Chéri*—were also based on her own experiences as young in the sensual, exotic world they later encountered? Could it be that Philippe and Chéri were versions of Colette herself?

As her first marriage broke apart, for a time she participated in Parisian lesbian circles: the Marquise de Belbeuf was her lover. In *The Pure and the Impure* she wrote about this world both critically and lovingly. "Where could I find messmates like those . . . Baronesses of the Empire, lady cousins of Czars . . . exquisites of the Parisian bourgeoisie." Cross-age relationships were not unknown in these circles, and Colette recorded their existence. "Some of these ladies fondly kept in their protective and jealous shadow women younger than they, clever young actresses, the next to the last authentic demimondaines of the epoch, a music hall star. . . ."[85]

Before her marriage to her second husband, Henry de Jouvenel, she had supported herself as a music hall performer, often touring the provinces. Jouvenel was a wealthy, aristocratic journalist who eventually became a member of the French parliament. By the time she married him she was a well-known author. Colette's novelistic worlds, those of aristocratic self-indulgence and of bourgeois smugness, of the Parisian demimonde and the provincial music halls, were based on her own experience. As in her own life and those of her novelistic characters, they swirl around each other and intertwine, sometimes liberating and sometimes confining. Thus what entraps Annie in *Retreat From Love*—her penchant for young men—liberates Lea in *Chéri*.

The beauty of adolescent young men, their sensual charm, is a central theme in Colette's work. Philippe in *The Ripening Seed* is described as "cast in the mould of a young roman god's, gilded by the sun, set off by a crown of black hair, its grace impaired only by the faintest shadow— of a nascent moustache."[86] The name Chéri, which Colette bestowed on her most important adolescent male figure, translates as "beloved." This term resonates to the classic Greek epithet for the young male lover, also called the beloved, and to Beaumarchais's Cherubino, the literary prototype of the gentle, eroticized young male. Colette's mother, Sido, called each of her children, with loving familiarity, Chéri.

This appreciation of the young male body, based on a tradition of male eroticization extending back to the Greeks, was still strong in that theatrical subculture in which Colette for a time found her métier. Renée Nere explains in *The Shackle:* "I came from a métier where masculine and feminine ranked equal, where you used the same appreciative words for the marvelous legs and narrow hips of a handsome gymnast as for the shapeliness of a female acrobat or dancer."[87]

The fear of aging itself is a central issue for all of Colette's characters, even for her beautiful female protagonists in their early thirties. They consistently note weight gain, the appearance of wrinkles, the slackening of jawlines, the toughening of the skin. At forty-five the character Colette in *The Awakening Dawn* experiences the onset of menopause. This change of life impels her into the decision to transform her own experience of what she presents as culturally reprobated into strength. If, in fact, this event marked the beginning of the final descent into decrepitude, when beauty and desirability would decidedly no longer be hers, then she would herself renounce love. She would control her disengagement to make it an act of courage, not of degradation.

The decision excites Colette, as she realizes that love has never liberated her but has always created a false dependence, a loss of sense of self, and, with male infidelity, great personal hurt. "Autumn is the only vintage time," writes Colette. "It is the time for truce in the monotonous struggle for succession between equals." And she continues: "Then, in obedience to the law of the climacteric we can at last triumph over what I will call the ordinary run of lovers." The prospect excites Colette. "This is the first time since I was sixteen that I'm going to have to live—or ever did— without my life or death depending on love. It's extraordinary!"[88]

Behind Colette's call for disengagement lay her unhappy experiences with her two first marriages as well as her increasing reverence for her mother, Sido, a provincial woman whose spirit was intertwined with the fruits and flowers, the animals and children, she had raised and loved. This woman, rooted in the provinces and in nature, was as much a part of Colette's own persona as the sophisticated Parisians with whom she lived during much of her adult life. Lyrical, lush descriptions of nature abound in Colette's work, and they become even more abundant in her later biographical writings about her mother.

Lea of *The Last of Chéri,* who is the oldest of her major female protagonists, accepts aging by giving up her sensuality, by becoming "a healthy old woman, in short, with sagging cheeks and a double chin, well able to carry her burden of flesh and freed from restraining stays." Appalled by her, Chéri must face his own mortality, the fact that, at thirty, he is no longer a child. She will no longer love him or mother him. Their relationship has ended. His own wife, the younger woman for whom he left Lea, has proven to be professional and cold. Censorious of his refusal to accept adult masculinity, she will not take on Lea's role. Disconsolate, Chéri takes his own life. Perhaps his conclusion about his relationship with Lea is the final conclusion: "But we've been punished, haven't we, both of us—you for being born so long before me, me for having loved you above all the women in this world."[89]

Women to Colette are indomitable: Colette in renouncing love, Lea in allowing her body to go its natural way. Above all, Sido, her mother, is unconquerable. A matriarchal deity, her knowledge of plants and animals was comprehensive. According to a biographer of Colette, she was "the goddess Gaea, residing at the center of things." She lived in the provinces, where "what was pagan here remains so and is breathed with the air."[90]

But she was also a real woman, Chéri to her children. "Where a stranger's glance would have seen only a small elderly woman dressed like a peasant, . . . we, all of us, gained an impression of spontaneity, spryness, vivacity . . . the gaiety of those who having nothing more to lose—excel in giving and the pet names of a love which perhaps has made us resistant to other loves."[91] Yet Colette did find love at the end of her life. Her biographers agree that her relationship with Maurice Goudeket, after two unhappy marriages, was fulfilling. His support helped her to continue her writing through the difficult years when she developed a painful arthritic condition. Colette lived in Paris throughout World War II and the German occupation of France. As an older woman, France's most celebrated living writer, she became a symbol of the nation indomitable.

With regard to their relationship, Goudeket wrote in his memoirs that "for Colette and me, our disparity of age, such as it was, always worked in favor of our understanding and not against it." "For thirty years of unclouded happiness," he continued, "she had enabled me to live in an enchanted world, and offered me a picture of such greatness that I despair of being able to bear witness to it. . . ."[92] For Goudeket, cherishing Colette was an honor; their love was based on reverence as well as desire. What she had to offer him was substantial. Like Germaine de Staël with John Rocca or George Sand with Chopin or Margaret Fuller with Giovanni Ossoli, her wisdom and strength of character, forged through her decades of living, became the basis for a compelling relationship.

CHAPTER EIGHT

The Twentieth Century:
Menopause and Its Meaning

IN 1911 *The Dangerous Age,* a novel by Danish author Karin Michaelis, was published. It quickly became an international best-seller. A work of popular fiction (although of debatable aesthetic merit), its widespread readership nonetheless indicated Michaelis's sensitivity to public interests. The novel tells the story of Elsie Lindtner, a woman in her mid-forties, who has divorced her wealthy husband, taken a younger lover, and then alone gone to live on a remote island. What seems initially to be a story of middle-aged liberation, however, quickly turns into an indictment of her divorce, of her involvement with a younger man, and of her supposed mental irrationality produced by menopause. In Michaelis's exposition, Lindtner is undergoing "the dangerous age." "The dangerous age," according to Michaelis, is that period in women's lives between the ages of forty and fifty when most women's menstrual cycle stops and their reproductive years end. During this decade, Lindtner declares, "we are all more or less mad."[1]

As the novel progresses, most of Lindtner's middle-aged women friends suffer emotional breakdowns. Some alternate between mania and depression; some leave their husbands. Some become obsessive; one woman cleans her house over and over again. Another is institutional-ized and treated surgically. (The nature of the treatment is obscure, although it sounds as though it involves a hysterectomy, a surgical proce-dure sometimes used in this era for female mental imbalance.) Lindtner rejects her younger lover on the grounds that he will eventually leave her anyway because of her age. Lindtner's husband remarries a much younger woman, but in the sequel to *The Dangerous Age* she also ad-vances to the menopausal years and begins to act irrationally. "What is the use of all these discussions and articles about the equality of the sexes, so long as we women are at times the slaves of an inevitable necessity?" queries Lindtner.[2]

In 1912 appeared *Woman's Share in Social Culture,* by American writer Anna Garlin Spencer. Published one year after *The Dangerous Age,* this work of popular sociology contains what reads like a rebuttal to Michaelis. Spencer drew from contemporary evidence that women lived longer than men and were more vital in older years to assert that menopause afforded women a "second youth." In her view the menstrual cycle caused mood swings, and its end improved mental health. "When the climacteric of middle life is reached, nature gives a fresh start and a fresh balance of power." Further, relieved from childbearing, women could turn toward personal or social goals. And their experience as homemakers and mothers could translate into effectiveness in other activities. "All that has gone into the sacrificial service to family life," wrote Spencer, "may add a peculiar flavor and a special wisdom to personal achievement or to enlarged social service."[3]

The differing opinions of Michaelis and Spencer in the 1910s reflect two divergent opinions about menopause which have continued throughout the twentieth century. The first opinion has been that menopause is an illness, bringing a breakdown of body and mind. The second has been that menopause initiates a time of strength for women, a regrouping before entry into what Margaret Mead in the 1950s called a period of "post-menopausal zest."[4]

The interaction between these two points of view over the course of the twentieth century has been complex, especially since individual texts in all eras often contain both positive and negative positions. (In *The Awakening Dawn*, for example, Colette portrays menopause both as problematic and as potentially empowering.) For the most part, however, the interweaving of attitudes has corresponded to the cyclical nature of women's twentieth-century history, that movement from reform and activism in the early twentieth century to partial retrenchment from the 1920s to the 1960s. Again, however, there are also competing cultural discourses, operating within a dominant historical narrative.

In the late-nineteenth- and early-twentieth-century Progressive era, advice books and magazine articles as well as technical and popular medical writings foregrounded Spencer's liberatory point of view. After World War I, however, although the optimistic sentiments were still to be found, they were overwhelmed by a cacophony of voices asserting that menopause equaled illness. The negative views reached a nadir in the 1950s with the ubiquity of the Freudian interpretation, especially articulated by the American psychoanalyst, Helene Deutsch. They continue to the present in medical views that all menopausal women need to take the hormone estrogen.

Before the full meaning of Karin Michaelis's and Anna Garlin Spencer's texts can be assessed, however, they must be placed within other historical contexts besides the medical one. To understand menopause, one must also understand the history of aging in which it is embedded. In addition, further understandings of the history of menopause are to be found, for example, within the histories of sexuality, of professionalism, of commercialism and consumerism, of standards of beauty—as they have remained the same and changed over time.

The topic of menopause further connects with the ongoing feminist debate over the relative importance of biology and of culture in producing behavior. For like sexuality or gender, other primary areas of human self-identification, menopause is a physical experience conditioned by cultural constructions of its meaning. Triggered by hormonal changes, menopause produces a physical symptomology: most women experience some of the symptoms, which seem to have remained fairly standard over time. (Heat flashes, weight gain, a growth in facial hair, a decrease in the size of the uterus, and a drying of vaginal tissue are the most common experiences.) The issue becomes the extent of symptoms experienced by individual women and in the general population of women as well as the extent to which cultural signals can operate to magnify the symptoms—or to ameliorate them.

Survey data suggest that cultural signals are key to both the perception and the experience of menopause. From rudimentary nineteenth-century surveys to sophisticated recent ones, the data show that although almost all women experience some menopausal symptoms, only a small minority suffer severe symptoms. Yet doctors, drawing their illustrations from a patient population, identify the severe symptoms they encounter with the entire population of menopausal women and define all women undergoing menopause as requiring medical attention. The "medicalization" of menopause has been a consistent theme throughout the twentieth century; in the final analysis it may be more for the benefit of doctors than for the women they treat.[5]

Throughout the twentieth century, a major debate regarding aging women has focused on menopause. The debate has been international, carried on especially in medical journals but also, to a lesser extent, in popular periodicals. The central issues in this debate have been two. The first issue has been the extent to which menopause is an illness, producing physiological distress and mental disorder. The second, evident through the 1950s, was whether menopausal women invariably fell in love with young men. Once again sexuality became key to definitions of women's aging.

The former issue had a long history, dating to ideas about the connections between the uterus and the brain and about the tendency of aging women, with cold constitutions, to become melancholic. The second, a muted theme over the ages, became foregrounded with increasing Freudian influence, especially in the 1950s. Above all, however, this second theme of relationships between aging women and younger men reflected issues revolving around sexuality, in terms both of aging women's desire for intercourse and their need for it. Once again sexuality became key to definitions of women's aging.

Menopause and Aging: Positive Culture Valuations, 1890–1920

B ETWEEN 1 8 9 0 AND 1 9 2 0 a vigorous woman's rights movement spearheaded progressive changes for women. Women entered the work force and the professions; many legal discriminations were removed; formerly forbidden areas of sports and leisure opened up to them. Colette's success on the music hall stage and as a self-supporting writer reflected these important turn-of-century themes in the history of women. Newspapers and novels celebrated "the New Woman." This widely used phrase came to represent the new opportunities for women.[6]

But the "New Woman" was not only a young woman: older women also were included. What one observer called "the renaissance of the middle aged" was widely chronicled by the day's press, especially in the United States. New opportunities for aging women to leave the confines of home and family stimulated a new cultural imagery regarding them. For example, aging unmarried women, previously denigrated as unwanted spinsters, now were joined by "bachelor women," who lived in glamorous cities. Indeed, the powerful nineteenth-century negative stereotyping of the unmarried aging woman was now considerably muted.

"Old maids no longer exist!" declaimed one author. "Unmarried women, until they reach the age of thirty, shall be known as bachelor 'girls,' and after that age they shall be known as 'bachelor women.'" "The woman of fifty who only a few years ago would have been sent to the ranks of dowagers and grandmothers, today is celebrated for distinctive charm and beauty, ripe views, disciplined intellect, cultivated and manifold gifts." Thus wrote a 1903 observer in *Cosmopolitan* magazine.[7]

The liberatory sentiments regarding aging women in this era extended to the medical community. In these years medical researchers produced a large literature concluding that most women experienced little discomfort during menopause. In 1880 Dr. A. Arnold, a Baltimore medical school professor, contended that all recent medical studies of menopause reported no pathology associated with it. In 1897 Andrew Currier, in his oft-cited work on menopause, called the negative view a "hoary" tradition with no basis in fact. In 1900 Dr. Mary Dixon Jones, writing in the *Medical Record,* angrily called categorizing menopause as a "dangerous period" a "libel on the natural formation of one half of the human race." In 1902, in the *Medical Society of Tennessee Proceedings,* M. C. McGannon wrote that menopause was "in no sense a critical period."[8]

A new conceptualization of menstruation initiated the new views about menopause. By the late nineteenth century doctors discovered that menstruation was not simply a purging of the blood (the accepted viewpoint for centuries). Rather, experimentation showed that it was connected to the cyclical production of the ovum and thus directly to conception. Older ideas about menstruation's purgative benefit were now revised, and many physicians came to view the menstrual flow as an unfortunate failure in bodily processes designed to build up a fetus. With this new negative attitude toward menstruation, menopause could be viewed positively, as a regrouping of body forces away from childbirth toward other kinds of maternal, generative ends.[9]

The rejection of humoral theorization in this era bolstered the positive attitude toward menopause. With the repudiation of the ancient ideas about humors in the blood producing disposition and physiological conditions, those venerable beliefs about the dangers of the buildup of evil humors in the body with the onset of menopause ended. Moreover, ideas spawned by the new scientific principle that all energy was limited were positively applied to menopause. Because menopausal women did not menstruate and thus presumably did not lose energy through the menstrual flow, the argument was made that they were, in fact, retaining energy and increasing their vitality. One medical observer wrote in 1893 that it "is now generally recognized that the absence of menstruation may be beneficial as an important aid to the preservation and increase of the vital forces."[10]

The advent of the nineteenth-century birth control consciousness which resulted by the end of the century in a greatly reduced birthrate, especially in France and the United States, also encouraged a positive evaluation of menopause. With the impetus to limit births a popular reality (even though in opposition to state policy), menopause could be viewed positively for its birth control potential. The negative term "dangerous age" was one turn-of-century term for menopause. But there was also the neutral "turn-of-life," or "change of life."

For some time the French had denoted menopause negatively as *la crise de la quarantaine,* or "the crisis of age forty." But from France by mid-century came the more neutral term "menopause." The word was derived from the Greek *meno,* meaning "month," and *pausis,* meaning "ending." But rather than indicating an ending, it carries the connotation of a hiatus, a pause in the life course, rather than its finish. (On the other hand, coined by doctors, the term "menopause" and its widespread popular adoption also signified the placing of the condition under medical management.)

Then, too, throughout this literature on menopause runs a leitmotif that aging men, as well as women, experience a climacteric. In 1865 Dr. Francis Skae published his analysis of the records of two hundred patients treated for "climacteric insanity" over a period of eighteen years at the Royal Edinburgh Asylum. He noted that men as well as women suffered from this ailment.[11] This medical literature noted aging men's problems with enlarged prostates and with impotence. Ideas of limited sexual energy and of a closed "spermatic economy" which men could easily overuse and thereby drain themselves of needed vitality were current and were especially applied to aging men. In his popular 1888 medical advice book, J. H. Kellogg castigated older men for marrying younger women as severely as he criticized older women for marrying younger men because intercourse requires "the *most* exhausting expenditure of nervous energy."[12] Neither aging women nor men had, in his view, sufficient vitality for younger partners.

In his history of life-cycle thought, Thomas Cole asserts that by the nineteenth century elderly men came to be viewed as almost more feminine than masculine in character. In this high capitalist era, swiftly changing technology seemed attuned to the vigor of youth, and aging men seemed out-of-date. Cole does not investigate views regarding aging women, but my research indicates that the opposite opinion was held: they were often seen as becoming more powerful as they aged, as developing increased vitality and authority. To resolve the controversy over the effects of menopause, in 1857 Dr. Edward Tilt of London interviewed fifty-three women who had not menstruated for five years. All, he contended, "spoke of their great additional strength of constitution, and this result may be taken to harmonize with the popular belief."[13]

Views of menopause as beneficial to women continued. Many doctors cautioned that improperly attributing specific ailments to the change of life could result in diagnostic errors. Some, validating Anna Garlin Spencer's position in her 1912 *Woman's Share in Social Culture,* agreed that menopause ended the mood swings of the menstrual years. "They are less subject," wrote Edward Tilt, "to be led astray by too ardent an imagination." Many commentators suggested that women who suffered severe menopausal symptoms had not taken good care of themselves in their earlier life. Their diet had been deficient, and they had not exercised. As Pye Henry Chavasse explained, a woman who had "lived simply and plainly and who has exercised, will improve in constitution [during menopause] and have better health."[14]

Even those doctors who defined menopause as an illness often conceded that once menopause ended many women experienced new vigor and improved health. Writers in turn-of-century medical literature routinely commented on what Margaret Mead later called "post-menopausal zest." In 1882 novelist and advice writer Marion Harland painted a dismal picture of the symptomology of menopause. Yet she anticipated a disappearance of the symptoms once menopause ended. She quoted an anonymous physician: "When I want *good* work done, I look about me for a woman over forty-five." Moreover, despite Karin Michaelis's negativity toward menopause, she thought that the postmenopausal years should be a time of well-being, once the menopausal disequilibrium had ended.[15]

These views about the positive qualities of menopause for women pose a challenge to historians of aging, who heretofore have presented this turn-of-century period as a time of difficulty for aging people, in the face of a growing professionalism which denigrated their wisdom and an advancing technology which seemed to render them obsolete. Like Thomas Cole in his otherwise admirable study of life-cycle thought, in reaching this negative conclusion these historians have paid insufficient attention to women's experience. Changes in life-cycle definitions in addition to improved childbearing and gynecological treatment, among other factors, placed aging for women in a more positive light.[16]

By the late nineteenth century, decreasing rates of death at early ages plus declines in physical disfigurement in the aging population due to medical and dietary advances created some sense of expanding life among aging people, especially among women. Individuals at age twenty-five did not have notably longer life expectancies than previously. (Most of the gains in life expectancy were due to improvements in the rates of *infant* mortality, not to any substantial increase in the age span.) But better diet and medical advances such as successful gynecological surgery for women to correct debilitating conditions like prolapsed uterus, previously a common condition resulting from childbirth, put aging in a more positive light.[17] The prospect for women of having to live many years with chronic illness, even in middle age, was fading.

Moreover, statistics in census data and in such indices as life insurance actuarial tables were demonstrating the strength of women's life span.[18] What had often been the case now became apparent: if women could survive childbirth, they would live longer than men. Additionally, with the rejection of humoral theorization, the supposed coldness of women's constitutions was no longer a perceived factor condemning them to an earlier cycle of aging than men. Women's life cycle was seen as more in tune with men's. Thus, for women thirty or thirty-five was no longer the beginning of entry into midlife; rather, forty or forty-five became the entry into middle age.

Declining rates of childbirth plus the lessened risk of death in childbirth also enhanced women's perception of the entire life cycle. And, by the late nineteenth century middle-class women began to bear children at earlier ages and to cluster their childbearing in the early years of their marriages rather than throughout their procreative years. With the last child in school as early as their mid-thirties, they had the expectation of spending some years without domestic and child-care responsibilities. Thus they could develop a stronger sense of self or embark on philanthropic activities in this age of reform attention.[19]

As early as 1870 popular writer Fanny Fern noted the changes in the perception of women's life cycle. She traced the origins of these changes to the impact of the woman's rights movement and to the sense of vigor generated in women through leaving home for work. In 1895 *Vogue* magazine traced the changing perception to the challenge women had issued to men in the male public sphere by entering education, the professions, and reform work. "In the area of achievement the harem idea goes to the wall, and the sexes are young, middle-aged and old together—not the woman 15 to 20 years in advance of the man." The *Ladies' Home Journal* noted old age disappearing as older women marched in parades, joined organizations, and founded literary clubs.[20]

In this late-nineteenth-century era, some doctors claimed that with menopause many women became more beautiful. According to Dr. Charles Meigs, writing about the effects of menopause on the look of the body: "The complexion recovers its former tint, and new deposits of fat give roundness to the limbs. She begins to acquire a certain embonpoint." Meigs thought this weightiness attractive. Here is how Dr. Edward Tilt put it, his words reminiscent of what Ovid had written centuries before about the virtues of the "autumnal" time of life. "In many women, there is at the change of life and long after, an autumnal majesty so blended with amiability, that it fascinates all who approach them." In his popular work on the sexual life of women, German commentator Enoch Kisch wrote that the "over-ripe" sexual appearance of menopausal women was quite erotic and that certain men—especially young men—could not resist them.[21]

Appropriate to this turn-of-century era when women's possibilities seemed limitless, the model of beauty for all women, not just aging women, was not entirely youthful. As exemplified, for example, by English actress Lillie Langtry and American performer Lillian Russell, large hips and bosoms and weightiness of form were preferred. Throughout the nineteenth century, even in earlier eras in which thinness had been the beauty ideal for young women, a plump look had been favored in older women. This model had been in keeping with the valorization of maternity and the containment of sexuality within marriage. Through weight, older women signified their contented participation in the community of married, maternal women. The weighty beauty ideal also proceeded out of the popularity of actresses like Langtry and Russell whose figures reflected the voluptuous look of courtesan society and its milieu. (In the 1930s Mae West both glorified the look and caricatured it in her Diamond Lil film persona.) That age contributed to the turn-of-century beauty model is indicated by a style related to the body type of aging women. By 1890 fashion dictated a curved line from chin to waist. This line, under clothing, resembled the unsupported, sagging breasts of aging women.

This positive valuation of the body type of aging women drew from a number of sources. It was based, in the first instance, on the positive attitude toward aging I have delineated. It was also in line with the utopianism of the Progressive era, its commitment to sweeping social change, and with the positive response to the grandmother and the "New Woman" as social types. Progressive women justified women's reform involvement by extending the nineteenth-century belief in women's superior morality to a principle of transcendent cultural force. The "moral superiority of women" was the primary argument they used to justify both their participation in reform outside the home and the reform objectives they pursued. This belief in women's superior morality reinforced those ongoing ideas that superior ethical standards and not inherited appearance produced beauty and that the look of spiritual beauty could only be attained with age.

The turn-of-century positive attitude toward aging was also a product of a positive public response to the participation of aging women as members and leaders of voluntary and reform organizations. These women displayed a vigor which both reflected the idea about superior postmenopausal performance and contributed to its genesis. In both numbers and energy, older women dominated women's Progressive reform organizations. Although recent historians only occasionally have noted the phenomenon of age-linked volunteerism, contemporaries often remarked on it. Thus Anna Garlin Spencer commented: "The audiences composed of professional workers and members of reformatory organizations and leaders in philanthropy are often a striking testimony to the as yet half-conscious response of women to this call of their second youth."[22]

As older women left the home to participate in voluntary activities or to take up careers, their forcefulness brought a different perception of all older women. In the 1890s and 1900s feminist leaders like Elizabeth Cady Stanton, Susan B. Anthony, and Frances Willard remained active campaigners until well into their sixties. Mary Baker Eddy, a founder of the Christian Science Church, entered her vocation as teacher and healer in 1866 at the age of forty-five; she led the organized church until into her seventies. With regard to her experience of menopause, Elizabeth Cady Stanton, drawing on the contemporary liberatory view, described it as an empowering force. Her "vital forces," formerly contained in her reproductive organs, wrote Stanton, were now "flowing" to her brain, prompting her to leave her family for many months a year to pursue a career as a lecturer.[23]

Jane Addams was fifty-two and still active at Hull House when she seconded Theodore Roosevelt's nomination as the Progressive Party presidential candidate in 1912. Julia Lathrop became head of the Children's Bureau that same year, when she was fifty-four. In 1914, at the age of forty-seven, Lillian Wald became president of the American Union Against Militarism. She had never worked harder, states a biographer, and, as she wrote to a friend, she had never felt better.[24] Frances Perkins became FDR's Secretary of Labor in 1933 when she was fifty-two, and Eleanor Roosevelt's reform activities throughout her middle and later years are well known. One presumes that these women were menopausal or post-menopausal when they undertook these activities.

The career and reform involvements of older women in this era furthered women's positive definition of menopause and aging. But a group of actresses especially advanced the claims of older women to beauty. A number of prominent nineteenth-century entertainers, like Lillie Langtry and Lillian Russell, not only lived long lives but also remained active on the stage until into their sixties and seventies. They built their later reputations partly around their ability to retain beautiful appearances until late in life.

Perhaps the most famed female performer of international reputation was the French actress Sarah Bernhardt. Bernhardt continued her popular tours of the United States even when in her sixties. She played characters much younger than her numerical age and attracted younger male companions. Lou Tellegen, Bernhardt's young partner in one of her late nineteenth-century American tours, drew from the tradition that spirituality and vitality were the primary elements in attractiveness when he described Bernhardt as not physically beautiful. It was her vitality, her spirit, that was alluring. She was so magnetic, he reported, that he found her more appealing at sixty-nine than most women of twenty. On meeting Bernhardt for the first time when the actress was in her eighties, Colette wrote that "Sarah's youth and octogenarian coquetry almost left me speechless."[25]

"Thousands of women," wrote Mary Roberts Coolidge, "have seen Madame Sara [*sic*] Bernhardt, when long past middle age, play *L'Aiglon,* the part of a youth of nineteen; and many more thousands have read the interviews in which she explained how she kept her youthful figure by muscular activity and hygienic living." Bernhardt, Coolidge asserted, was a major model for women's positive aging.[26]

Aging women's access to more positive definitions of their later life-cycle development was also related to the rise of a more sophisticated business culture, motivated toward creating and exploiting consumption needs. Victorian codes about appropriate public behavior for women and older prohibitions on women's use of cosmetics were breaking down at the same time that cosmetic companies were expanding their markets and beauty parlors were increasing in numbers. Given the financial resources of aging women, they constituted a prime market for commercial beauty promoters. As early as 1888 Elizabeth Lynn Linton noted that the "kohl for the eyelids," the "eaux noire, brun, et chatain, which dyes the hair any shade," as well as the "rouge of eight shades" were being used mainly by the "femme passé" trying to make herself look young. (According to Linton, this woman was especially motivated by the desire to attract a young male companion.) It was no accident that *Vogue* magazine in the 1890s and 1900s published many articles about the new possibilities for aging women and praised their new access to youthful standards of appearance.[27]

Yet the commercialization of aging women's appearance, with commercialism's focus on youth and sexuality, fed into strains of negativity about aging—and about menopause. The 1920s would witness a signal expansion of American business and of its major emissary, advertising. In the 1920s, sexuality became the desiderata of desirable self-construction and youth the preferred time of life. Advertising broadcast these messages worldwide. The Progressive notion of women's superior morality which had underlain views of vital aging and the positive attitude toward menopause would be overturned.[28] With this change in the dominant cultural discourse, the positive valuation of aging women and of menopause would encounter serious difficulties. The stage was set, as I indicated in the first chapter of this book, for the emergence of Norma Desmond, not as Bernhardt's triumphant descendant, but as a middle-aged, menopausal failure.

The Negative Side, 1890–1920

OTHER ORIENTATIONS during the Progressive era countered the positive trends for aging women. Many doctors, for example, contested the optimistic view of menopause to assert that it was a serious illness requiring medical attention. Historian Carroll Smith-Rosenberg has delineated this negative medical appraisal of menopause.[29] Many doctors regarded menopausal symptoms as indications of a body in disorder. Many posited that menopause caused diseases of aging like cancer often occurring in women's later years. Many posited a similarity between menarche and menopause, suggesting that a similar physical and mental disequilibrium characterized both. With proof of the connection between menstruation and procreation, gynecologists as new medical specialists refurbished older ideas about the power of women's reproductive organs to present them as a unified, albeit delicate, system determining female character.

Michaelis's presentation of menopause as producing insanity resonated in the views of many gynecologists. Drawing on misperceptions standard for centuries, many gynecologists posited a direct linkage between the uterus and the brain. (Such a belief would result in the term "hysterectomy" for the removal of the uterus and ovaries, referencing the mental condition of hysteria and its presumed connection to female reproductive organs.) And such beliefs were extended to aging women. "Involutional melancholia" and "climacteric insanity" were terms used as early as 1865 in diagnoses of disturbed menopausal patients. By late century special diagnostic categories were reserved for menopausal spinsters: "old maid's insanity" was the term occasionally used. And, as doctors realized that menopause was a process occurring over a number of years, its potential to tyrannize over women expanded, extending as long as a decade, as it does in Michaelis's exposition.

Medical arguments may have a scientific basis, but they are influenced by cultural valuations and individual biases. In the first instance, developments in medicine as a profession probably played a role in the genesis and spread of these negative appraisals of menopause. In this era the medical profession was growing both in numbers of practitioners and in organizational structure. (The same process was also occurring in other professions like business and law.) The expanding medical profession focused on increasing the patient population: given their financial resources and vague symptoms, menopausal women were a potentially large client group. At the same time that doctors took over childbirth from midwives, they expanded the newly established field of gynecology to include menopausal women. The "medicalization of menopause" was entirely to their benefit.[30]

Moreover, women's movement into the professions during the Progressive era threatened both male control of those professions and of the larger male public sphere of which the professions were a part. Historians have often interpreted the medical arguments advanced during these decades in opposition to women's entry into college as in actuality a response to this development's implied challenge to the male public sphere.[31] Similarly, one might argue that negative medical definitions of menopause constituted another set of quasi-scientific explanations given to prevent another (and even potentially more powerful) group of women from leaving the home to challenge male public authority.

Beneath professionalization, however, lay that masculinization I have charted as underlying the nineteenth-century trend whereby older men married younger women. Doctors, like other men, drew from models of conservative male authority to assert control over women. They, too, had to deal with the vicissitudes of a rapidly changing world. And, for them, it was one in which the medical profession was attempting to reestablish a unified authority after a century of division between competing, contentious schools of medical therapeutics. In his analysis of the character of doctors in the nineteenth and twentieth centuries, G. J. Barker-Benfield finds them, like most American males, ambitious and competitive. Torn between work and family, they easily vented their frustrations on women patients.[32]

Liberatory movements for women in the Progressive era underlay medical notions of menopause as invigorating; but new cultural definitions of masculinity, which upheld gender differentiation, bolstered the alternative view of menopause as illness. Both men and women celebrated the implied gender equality of the "New Woman," and certain scientific discoveries overturned centuries' worth of reasonings about female physiological inferiority (as in the ending of humoral theorization). Yet other arguments indicated the appearance of a new misogyny. For example, Darwinian evolutionism (probably the age's most important scientific theory) held women to be inferior to men in strength, intelligence, and skill.

By the last decades of the nineteenth century, notions that aging women possessed an inappropriate sexuality also began to appear. By 1900 sexologists like Briton Havelock Ellis issued charges of lesbianism against unmarried career women and reformers. They declared heterosexuality to be the proper human orientation and hinted that women's friendships easily became sexual, thereby challenging the claims of women's superior morality and undermining the legitimacy of their separate bonding networks.[33] They went further. They posited that aging women were driven by a prurient sexual drive which could propel them into deviant, destructive behavior.

In his important 1905 chapters on women in *Studies in the Psychology of Sex*, a work repeatedly reprinted over the next decades, Havelock Ellis included fulsome references to pre-nineteenth-century writers' estimations of women as highly sexed. He drew from the French tradition of valorizing older women to contend that the sexual drive in women is especially strong at older ages. Indeed, he averred, strong sexual passion sometimes does not appear in women until after the menopause.[34]

Yet he viewed the appearance of this drive as problematic. In the first instance he saw it as the major cause of "old maid's insanity." In this case a heightened desire for heterosexual intercourse drove women without sexual experience to desire any men who were kind to them, even though these men had no interest in them. (Usually, Ellis asserted, the unfortunate men were clergymen.) In his estimation, aging women's prurient sexual desire could take additional forms. He cited numerous cases of older women, especially servant women, who he contended had seduced younger men, sometimes the boys who were their charges. And he continued by asserting that girls' interest in boys was mere curiosity, "but it is pathology when expressed by older women." To him these instances of seduction proved that women were more sexually aggressive than men and that their sexual aggression was dangerous. He concluded his discussion of aging women's sexuality with the assertion that the incidences of male rape were vastly overstated. A real problem, in his opinion, lay in the uncontrollable sexuality of older women and their desire for young men.[35]

Such ideas culminated in contradictory 1920s beliefs. The first was that regular heterosexual intercourse was necessary for effective human functioning. The second was that menopausal women were, on the one hand, devoid of sexuality and, on the other, possessed by a rampant, unstable sex drive only with difficulty contained. The belief in the value of intercourse, when extended to aging women, might seem to provide new possibilities for fulfillment. But so long as demographic imbalances resulted in more aging women than men, the sexual directive could only be frustrating.

Nonetheless, aging women's dangerous sexuality, in the schema of many sexologists and others, had to be controlled. Centuries before, such a conception had contributed to the persecution of aging women as witches. In the modern era, the perceptions of evil were more attenuated and the attempts at containment were nowhere as severe. They primarily produced a good deal of rhetoric against women's participation in social reform and woman's rights activities. Yet parallels can be drawn. The rhetoric was successful in casting doubt on feminist involvement and women's individual independence. In extreme cases, the identification of menopause with madness could bring hospitalization. When repackaged by Freud in a new "scientific" formulation, these ideas indicated that menopause was not a time of increasing vitality but rather a time for retrenchment, for dealing with an inevitable illness in women's lives.

The 1920s and 1930s:
Aging Women, Youth, and Sexuality

BOTH POSITIVE and negative views of menopause and of women's aging continued throughout the twentieth century. Self-help manuals on aging, like Walter Pitkin's 1932 best-selling *Life Begins at Forty,* began to appear in abundance in the 1920s and 1930s, as the increasing longevity of aging people became more and more apparent. These books were attuned to the American ethic of success through self-overcoming, and they pitched a message of assured self-empowerment— for women as well as for men.

Authors of self-help manuals and writers of other works drew from their own experience and from the results of scientific experimentation to repeat the turn-of-century message that menopause brought strength, not decline. In 1924, writing in the *Ladies' Home Journal,* Alice Ames Walker called middle age "gorgeous," with the "spurt of energy" it brought to women. In 1929 Spanish writer Gregorio Marañón wrote that many women in middle age acquired a newfound energy. This literature often highlighted historical figures who exemplified successful women's aging—like Sarah Bernhardt or the seventeenth-century Ninon de Lenclos. One observer concluded that Bernhardt must have been meno-pausal when she gave her most memorable performances "and looked most youthful and vital as Hamlet and the Duke of Reichstadt."[36]

This last author's identification of the menopausal Sarah Bernhardt with youth indicates a central theme that permeates post–World War I writing on aging and menopause. That theme revolves, ironically, around youth. Self-help manuals view aging people as being able to create a youthful demeanor for themselves. Aging actresses explaining the secret of their "beautiful" appearances refer to their ability to look "young." Even Anna Garlin Spencer in 1912 referred to aging women's involvement in social reform as generated by their entering a "second youth," thereby indicating the power of youthfulness even in the Progressive era, which held positive attitudes toward aging.

The beauty culture presented youth as the paragon and purveyed its products as being able to make aging women look young. The 1890s (a time of liberation for women) developed a model of beauty based on maturity. Still, even in that age, commercialism, associated with the devel-oping cosmetics business, celebrated youth and mostly offered aging women the option of restructuring themselves as young. In the 1900s Dr. Dys's dermatological products for women were widely advertised with the slogan, "Dys laughs at time." In the 1930s Jergens hand lotion advertisements were captioned: "The cruel signs of age can mock a woman's hands while her face is still young and fresh." In 1928 a commentator wrote that "age is not only extremely unfashionable today, but it is completely discounted commercially."[37]

An emphasis on youth was a groundswell in the 1890s, and its imperatives molded the dominant design for gender behavior in the 1920s. A new emphasis on heterosexuality was conceived in a youthful guise. In this decade the boyish flapper as female model enshrined this stage of life, and the flapper, with a thin and angular body resembling that of a young boy, bore scant resemblance to an aging woman—or to the beauty model of the 1890s. Thinness became the vogue; the natural weight gain of menopausal women was depreciated. Thus one commentator complained in 1919 that twenty years before women could "roll in fat and grow old in peace. No one thought of saying to you 'why don't you reduce?'" Times, however, had changed, and dieting to look young had become a craze. In France, Colette wrote of the "flowering" of the "disturbed" adolescent style. Another commentator hinted that the thinness had to it a prurient erotic dimension, based as it was on the look of a boy.[38]

Aging women were given access to the new youthful behavior at the same time that they were criticized for their participation. Both impulses are in view early in the 1920s when the period's popular journalism created something of a scandal around aging women, old enough to be grandmothers, dancing with young male partners at afternoon dances. The young men were called "lounge lizards" and the aging women "flapperdames." By participating in the day's fascination with public dancing (an important early symbol of twenties cultural rebellion), aging women publicly indicated their sexual interest and their ongoing youthfulness. But journalists' satirical reporting made the behavior seem comic and inappropriate.[39]

Several popular American women novelists in this era focused on the predicament of aging women in a culture which had developed a pride in youth into an obsession. Shades of Lindtner's *Dangerous Age* hover over both Gertrude Atherton's *Black Oxen* (a best-seller of 1923) and Edith Wharton's *A Mother's Recompense,* published in 1925. In both books middle-aged women protagonists struggle with the emotional damage caused by what both authors portray as the inevitable failure of their affairs with younger men. Such is the case even for Atherton's female heroine, Mary Zattiany, despite the fact that at the age of sixty she looks thirty, the supposed result of having undergone at a European clinic X-ray treatments designed to reverse the process of aging. Yet both heroines are stigmatized by young people who cannot understand them and by age peers who feel threatened by them. In the end, the only solution for both is to flee to Europe, where in the American imagination older women could lead freer lives.

With wealth and the appearance of youth, Atherton's protagonist in *Black Oxen* anticipates involvement in the European postwar social reconstruction. But with little money and few contacts, Wharton's heroine in Europe drifts from hotel to hotel, with little to do. She spends her time reflecting on her lost youth and on her estrangement from her daughter and son-in-law, a man who actually had been her lover before her daughter married him. An easy prey for gigolos offering temporary solace to lonely old women, she is another in a long line of such literary protagonists who originated in Colette's aging, indomitable cocottes of the French 1900s. Such a character type continued into the 1930s through the heroine of Fannie Hurst's maudlin and much-reprinted *Back Street* and in the 1950s in Tennessee Williams's mordant portrait of an aging American actress believing the lies of her young, expensive lover in *The Roman Spring of Mrs. Stone*.

Mary Zattiany deals with aging by becoming young, while Wharton's heroine suffers because of a failure to accept her aging. Indeed, Atherton makes clear that she does not think aging women can be attractive. Mindful to chronicle in detail how each character in her novel has "lost her looks" as she has aged, Atherton paints a portrait of aging as ugliness.[40]

By spotlighting her protagonist's X-ray treatments, Atherton emphasized the possibility of prolonging youth through chemical means. This focus reflected significant developments during these interwar decades. In the first instance, by the 1920s scientists had discovered the relationship between body hormones and women's menstrual cycle, and they had begun to isolate the hormone estrogen in laboratory settings. (By the 1930s many doctors were recommending estrogen for menopausal symptoms.) These discoveries seemed medical marvels in keeping with the messianic nature of the 1920s, its position as a postwar world luxuriating in new consumption items which trumpeted technology's triumphs and seemed to signal a utopian future attained through scientific achievement in partnership with capitalist production. The discovery of hormones portended not only new therapeutic avenues toward improved health but even the attainment of human perfectibility through the overcoming of the aging process.

Biological utopianism was the underlying theme of Atherton's *Black Oxen*. Although Atherton was seemingly unaware of the hormonal experimentation, her novel in many ways was a biological roman à clef which presented some of the day's more outlandish experiments to reverse the process of aging as though they were proven successes. European clinics catering to a wealthy clientele's obsession with remaining youthful purveyed most of these techniques. Atherton's favorite was the Steinach clinic in Switzerland, where patients underwent daily bombardments of X rays directed to the genitalia. Before writing *Black Oxen,* Atherton herself had undergone the X-ray treatment and had been convinced of its efficacy.[41]

Replacing human glands with animal glands and injections of animal hormones also gained some medical popularity (and notoriety). For a time doctors experimented with giving menopausal women thyroid extracts. By the 1930s doctors were prescribing the hormone estrogen as a panacea for menopausal ailments. In his work on menopause, Abner Weisman described how he established one of the first endocrine clinics in New York City and how, almost immediately, it attracted for treatment fifty to one hundred menopausal women every day.[42]

Hormonal therapy on the one hand held out the positive prospect of alleviating menopausal discomfort. On the other hand, its use implied a more pessimistic dimension, one which indicated that menopause was not a natural process but rather an illness, requiring medical intervention. By the 1920s doctors no longer believed that the uterus and ovaries directly determined a woman's character; rather control came from hormones and glands (which, of course, include the ovaries). Endocrinology, or the study of these glands and hormones, joined gynecology in positing that a woman's physiology ruled her functioning. And, once again, a woman's system was delicate and capricious. It could easily fall into disorder if proper hormonal balances were not maintained. Physicians' widespread prescription of what came to be called "estrogen replacement therapy" did not occur until the 1940s, after the 1938 distillation of an inexpensive form of estrogen which could be taken orally and did not require an injection. Subsequently, in medical literature menopause came to be termed a "deficiency disease."[43]

In addition to these ideas about the physiology of menopause, an equally pessimistic (and contradictory) set of opinions centered around menopausal women's sexuality. The belief that aging women were without sexual interest was common throughout this era. Yet many doctors expressed an opposing point of view; they contended that most aging women experienced a heightened sexuality. This opinion was in keeping with the twenties' emphasis on sexuality as central to human functioning; it also drew on survey data from the 1890s on indicating that menopausal women experienced an increased sex drive. (And studies of menopausal women in more recent years have continued to identify such a heightened drive.) Analysts of this phenomenon in the 1920s and 1930s often advanced explanations for it similar to ones currently given. Women's relief at no longer having to worry about birth control may cause the increased sexual disposition. Or it may result from the later-life peaking of a woman's sex drive or from the self-assurance produced by the process of aging. Hormonal rearrangements may also play a part.[44]

In keeping with the 1920s celebration of sexuality and with the realization that aging women might experience a heightened sexual drive, many doctors counseled that moderate sexual intercourse was beneficial for menopausal women, as long as it was contained within marriage. In his 1926 sex manual, *Ideal Marriage: Its Physiology and Technique*, Theodoor Van de Velde proffered such advice. (This work dominated the sex-advice market for decades; the thirty-seventh edition was published in 1961.) In this book Van de Velde noted the increased sex drive of menopausal women and counseled that with an "attentive husband" a wife's sexuality could be continued into old age. Yet to him proper sexuality was vaginal and phallic, and men should be in control. "What both man and woman, driven by obscure primitive urges, wish to feel in the sexual act," he wrote, "is the essential force of maleness."[45]

Other explanations given in this earlier period for menopausal women's heightened sexual drive, however, were not so positive. Following Havelock Ellis, many physicians viewed aging women's desire as pathological. Many of them located the increased sexuality in physiological genital changes accompanying menopause, in particular, in the shrinking of the uterus and changes in the vaginal tract. They often depicted these changes as repulsive, for in their analysis these alterations were key to an increased and perverse sexuality.

Even Theodoor Van de Velde (who did not subscribe to the argument about perverse sexuality) pejoratively described menopausal genital changes as the "obliteration of the vaginal pads and folds." Enoch Kisch went further. He referred to the "congestive conditions" of sensitive menopausal sexual organs. These changes presumably made sexual desire in aging women unbearable for them and drove them to unfortunate sexual experiences. He attributed the "unnatural marriages" which occasionally occurred between aging women and younger men to this female "pathology."[46]

In 1923 William Robinson underscored Enoch Kisch's admonition about the dangerous sensitivity of menopausal sexual organs when he cautioned that menopausal women should not engage in frequent sex. But the issue was not one of physiological discomfort or damage; rather, by increasing the "congestion of the generative parts," menopausal women might increase their sexual drive to the point of "nymphomania." (Nymphomania, or an obsessive preoccupation with and indulgence in intercourse on the part of women, was itself a new sexual and psychiatric category invented in this era to contain women through their sexuality.)[47]

Indeed, the idea that such increased sexuality might drive women insane was not without its advocates. According to some analysts, unmarried women were especially at risk, for they could incur "old maid's insanity" due to increased desire rendered even more desperate because they had never experienced intercourse. In *Black Oxen* Gertrude Atherton translated a medical stereotype into a literary personification as she told the story of a frantic aging unmarried woman, fearful she would go mad because of the lack of sex in her life. This woman intended to try Steinach's X-ray treatments to regain her youth and to attract a man. She now mourned her youthful decision to forgo marriage for a reform career. Most of all she feared developing old maid's insanity. "Some of us old maids do go mad," she told a confidante. "When Hannah de Lacey lost her mind three years ago I heard one of the doctors telling Peter Vane that her talk was the most libidinous he had ever heard."[48]

Writings on menopause in these eras depicted aging women's increased sexuality as so powerful that it took over the entire emotional system and came to control all actions, producing all kinds of deviant behavior. And when conservatives cataloged this deviant behavior, they fulsomely included almost any kind of unconventional action. They linked self-realizing and socially useful endeavors with self-destructive impulses like alcoholism. As early as 1920 Dr. Walter Gallichan articulated this conservative position:

> When a woman at age forty-eight shows signs of alcoholic intemperance, a craving for drugs, or becomes "converted" to a new religious creed, begins to exhibit an indifference to her husband and children, neglects the home, develops a passionate zeal for the emancipation of her sex, or falls ardently in love with a youth ... these ... are ascribed "the change of life."

Indeed, this literature often cited the pursuit of young men as a prime example of perverse menopausal sexuality. "Such explorations in the bypath of sexual immorality," wrote Sarah Trent, "usually begin during the unstable period of menopause."[49]

Charges of the effects of perverse sexuality ran the gamut of possibilities. They included lesbianism, repugnant to these authors set on heterosexuality as the proper behavior. English paleobotanist Marie Stopes was a birth control reformer who in her work often critiqued negative attitudes toward aging and menopause. But Stopes also contended that menopausal weight gain and increased facial hair not only made women look like men but also could turn women partly into men, desiring women. Focused on heterosexuality, she recommended that menopausal women take estrogen as the means of overcoming any changes in appearance or any lesbian urges. Alternatively she recommended increased heterosexual intercourse because, she claimed, male semen contained a hormone which stimulated the ovaries to increased estrogen production. In this way aging women could "keep feminine through intercourse."[50]

By the 1920s, according to Carroll Smith-Rosenberg, charges of lesbianism became a common way to discredit women professionals and reformers. This era saw the creation of an imagined "lady in lavender," an aging lesbian who sought revenge against men through feminist rhetoric and who, often a schoolteacher, taught her female students to dislike heterosexuality. More than this, charges of lesbianism were leveled even against aging women who sought friendship with other women. For, given their increased sexual desire, aging women might turn to one another for sexual relief. In her major 1945 work on menopause, Helene Deutsch diagnosed a condition she called "homosexual panic," when aging women ended lifelong female friendships because of the fear that they might become sexual.[51]

In the nineteenth century aging unmarried women had been stigmatized as removed from sexuality; in the 1920s they were stigmatized both for being asexual and, at the same time, for possessing a perverse sexuality. In this era old stereotypes were redrawn and new ones invented to contain women's public aspirations. Sheila Jeffries has written about this age's invention of female "frigidity" (the pathological inability to attain orgasm through heterosexual intercourse) as a way of both controlling women in marriage to regard intercourse as the key to contentment and of stigmatizing unmarried women without normal heterosexual outlets. Frigidity was the obvious opposite of "nymphomania," another presumed female sexual problem discovered in this age. Both, in combination with conservative constructions of lesbianism, formed expressional boundaries and expectations by which women of all ages and statuses (whether married or unmarried) were contained in eras when "all unrest among women was attributed to their unfulfilled needs for [heterosexual] sexual experience."[52]

This era also witnessed the creation of a prudish, out-of-date Victorian matriarch, in keeping with the twenties' focus on Victorianism as especially repressive. This figure, common in fiction and advice literature, was the forerunner of the 1950s controlling, unpleasant "mom." She possessed the intrusiveness of her Victorian forerunner without the countervailing balance of that age's ambiguity about sexuality to soften the stereotype and to lend it greater authority.[53]

By the 1930s, according to advice writer A. Béran Wolfe, many large hospitals had sections for mentally disturbed menopausal women. This development should not seem surprising, given the variety of supposed motives that could drive them to such mental imbalance that they required hospitalization. For in the conflicting imagery of the period, both the sexually deranged menopausal woman and her opposite, the asexual menopausal woman, could develop severe problems. Drawing from both characters, Walter Gallichan went so far as to differentiate between types of psychiatric ailments that could occur in menopausal women. Heightened sexuality could produce hysteria or nymphomania. But even women without desire could fall into menopausal madness. Their particular pathology could be "erotomania," or "a psychic sentimental state arising from a deep longing to be loved in the spiritual sense."[54]

More than that, according to other analysts, the end to the possibility of procreation could drive a menopausal woman mad, as she faced the loss of what was in reality her true female function. In his 1934 guide to the categories of mental illness for purposes of diagnosis, Edwin Hopewell-Ash revived the identification between menopause and "involutional melancholia." But in his view neither sexuality nor its lack produced the pathology; rather the end of reproduction caused it. "Consciously and unconsciously," he charged, "the whole female organization rebels at the abrupt ending of reproduction."[55]

In the 1930s, during economic depression, ideal women were personified as older, as more mature. In dress styles, skirts became longer, and shoulder pads, indicating more authority, were introduced. The boyish flapper gained height and a more mature look. In a time of economic troubles, the mother became a symbol of comfort and strength. Self-sacrificing mothers—like Ma Perkins or Molly Goldberg—dominated radio soap operas. In film, older women served as repositories of wisdom, teaching others humility in the face of adversity.[56] Ma Joad in John Steinbeck's *The Grapes of Wrath*, attempting to hold her Oklahoma migrant family together despite poverty and oppression, exemplified the mother as regenerator.

Nonetheless in this era aging women were still regarded as problematic. This stance can be seen in their ongoing representation as comic figures. In the 1920s "flapperdames" had danced with young male "lounge lizards." In 1930s films, scatterbrained wealthy matrons were standard characters in screwball comedies, reaching epic representation in Margaret Dumont as an aging socialite playing comic foil to the Marx Brothers. Cartoons caricatured middle-aged women: the foolish and infantile *New Yorker* clubwoman was a regular character in cartoons in the magazine beginning in the 1920s and for the next several decades. She had an overweight and shapeless menopausal body and a look reminiscent of the out-of-date, turn-of-century beauty ideal. This ideal had been based partly on a positive attitude toward aging.

By the 1940s cartoonist Helen Hokinson became the major creator of the *New Yorker* clubwoman cartoons. She depicted her subjects as naive and elitist, as the "girls" they were often called in the wider world. In her drawings the clubwomen have only a childish understanding of the world, of sexuality, of men, of themselves. At a time when aging women were the mainstays of a myriad of woman's rights and reform organizations, Hokinson's aging women are ineffective as leaders, and their clubs seem to exist so that wealthy, bored women can have something to do. Hokinson's women are narcissistic and uncomprehending of the world around them. They are assuredly matrons, the epitome of the asexualized word "matron," with its implications of an unpleasant, overweight body and of women who both serve and control, like police matrons or hotel matrons. Humorist Robert Benchley provided what must have been this era's most insulting description of aging women, as "aunt calling to aunt like mastodons bellowing across the primeval swamps."[57]

Moreover, the identification of aging women's wisdom as only "old wives' tales"—foolish and incorrect stories—was current in this era, as it had been for centuries. The association was present in the standard judgment that aging women passed on only incorrect information about menopause to younger women. And there was also the contention that unhappy menopausal mothers told their daughters that when they in turn reached menopause if they were not careful they would go insane and their husbands would leave them for younger women. Decades previously Karin Michaelis in *The Dangerous Age* had issued a warning about this eventuality. And whether women or the doctors they consulted reissued such a caution, it was current during the 1930s, and it would remain so for decades more.[58]

The Freudian View of Menopause

B Y   T H E   1 9 2 0 S, Darwinian arguments about the evolutionary inferiority of women had been largely discredited, just as fifty years earlier humoral theorization connecting menopause and dangerous humors in the blood had been discarded. But the old Darwinian confusion between what was biological (and thus inevitable) and what was cultural (and thus mutable) persisted. The confusion was continued in medical models of human behavior and in the Freudian schema of inevitable stages of psychic functioning. With regard to menopause, Freudian theories cemented the view that it was biological and pathological and that culture played little role in its construction.

Freud himself initiated the psychoanalytic view of menopause with his analysis of a fifty-year-old woman who suffered from debilitating jealousy due to her suspicion that her husband was having an affair with a young woman. Freud talked with her for several hours and, on the basis of this brief conversation, concluded that her fears about her husband's behavior were groundless. Instead, he decided that she was suffering from a reexperience of the "castration complex" of early childhood, from a reawakened sense of how maimed and inferior she was because she possessed, in her clitoris, only a castrated penis. Her jealousy, Freud concluded, was in reality a displacement for what she really wanted and that was a sexual liaison with her daughter's husband, her son-in-law, whose youth could counter her sense of waning attractiveness because of her age.[59]

Moreover, after many years of latency, the Oedipus complex also reappeared. But the complex now was in a new guise, for Freud's focus in this case was on the female participant rather than on the male. The aging woman was now the instigator of the attachment, and her desire was directed toward her son-in-law rather than her son. Like other medical researchers of his age, Freud thought that menopause produced an increased sexual desire, a heightened libido. He also thought that it involved a second youth, a reappearance of the characteristics of adolescence, which Freud also identified as a difficult period for women.

Aside from notes on the above case and references elsewhere in his writings to the similarities between puberty and menopause, Freud directed little attention to aging women. Indeed, his brief 1913 discussion in *Totem and Taboo* of relations between mothers-in-law and sons-in-law had focused more on what he then saw as a tendency for sons-in-law to feel an attraction to mothers-in-law rather than the reverse. And, although in this work about civilizations' origins he discussed the goddesses of antiquity, his focus was on their young male consorts. What emerges from this writing as important about these religions is not women's authority but rather the rebellion of sons against fathers and the sons' overturning of goddess worship—acts which Freud contended had produced civilization.[60]

Commentators have noted the absence of any significant theorization about women in Freud's psychoanalytic formulations, even though many of his early clients were women and women played a powerful role in his own personality development. By his admission, three aging women left lasting impressions on him. His childhood nurse, Nannie, probably initiated him into sexuality. His infatuation at age sixteen with a classmate extended to her mother.[61] This involvement probably prompted his remarks in *Totem and Taboo* about sons-in-law desiring mothers-in-law.

Finally, there was his mother. Amalia Nathanson was a young woman of twenty when she married the forty-year-old Jacob Freud, who already had two grown sons. Given this age disparity and Freud's position as her eldest son, it is not surprising that a close relationship developed between them on which he could build later notions of mother-son love. He was her favorite child, her "golden boy." It was she who nurtured in him dreams of success and of fame.

The aging Amalia Freud was temperamental and self-willed. By dint of her powerful personality, she controlled others. She lived to be an octogenerian, dying when Freud himself was near seventy. During his adulthood, he visited her every Sunday. It is no wonder that Freud had difficulty dealing with women in general in his writings and with aging women in particular. The death of his father in 1896 plunged him into that self-analysis through which he came to his major psychoanalytic formulations. But his mother's long life prevented him from ever coming to terms with her.

Freud's analysis of the industrialist's wife as suffering from a castration complex and an overactive libido suggests his ambivalence toward his mother. In his 1933 *New Introductory Lectures on Psychoanalysis* he delivered a personally telling attack on aging women. He contended that women as young as thirty were characteristically frightening because of their "psychical rigidity and unchangeability." Yet men of the same age, he claimed, were youthful and pliable. Women spent a lifetime dealing with penis envy and castration complexes, and they were exhausted by their process of personality formation, what Freud called "the difficult development to femininity." It was understandable, if regrettable, that women by the third decade of their lives became rigid and unreasonable. But, according to Freud, even this stability was only temporary. For in their forties, with the onset of menopause, women would once again experience great psychic insecurity.[62]

In her 1945 *Psychology of Women*, Helene Deutsch contributed the most important Freudian analysis of menopause. A member of Freud's original psychoanalytic circle who came to the United States in the 1930s, Deutsch had undergone analysis with Freud, and her work drew heavily from his ideas. Like Freud, her mentor, Deutsch identified a heightened sexuality as a major symptom of menopause. She, too, posited that menopause triggered a reappearance of the Oedipus complex and a return to the behavior patterns of adolescence, especially of its juvenile, even neurotic manifestations. Even in women previously well-adjusted to life, according to Deutsch, this adolescent syndrome would reappear. For it could never be ended within the psyche; it could only be repressed. "After the woman's many years of good and even very good adjustments to reality, of mature femininity and motherhood," wrote Deutsch, "the old gods of the [adolescent] nether world emerge."[63]

Deutsch was critical of aging women who used cosmetics or in some other artificial manner tried to regain a youthful look. Yet although she admitted that the contemporary glamorization of youth might provoke such behavior, she located its primary motivation in what she called "narcissistic self-delusion." This condition was another one of her adolescent neuroses which emerged with menopause. Deutsch also disparaged professional and activist women who rejected their femininity and became "pseudo-masculine." "Feminine" women, according to Deutsch, those who were gentle and demure, would retain greater youth and beauty throughout their lives than women who paid no heed to conventional gender divisions. And "feminine" women, who more easily attracted men, experienced a much less severe menopause, presumably because they had an active sex life. Drawing from misogynistic stereotypes of aging women which had been repeated for decades, Deutsch wrote that "feminine-erotic women, experienced in love, accept the inevitable [menopause] with greater dignity and calm than the spinsterish, frigid, even frustrated ones."[64]

Yet in Deutsch's view, menopause was so difficult an experience that all menopausal women faced the possibility of developing sexual neuroses. In the first instance, the "sublimated homosexuality of puberty" might once again reappear. This drive could produce that "homosexual panic" which impelled aging women to sever lifelong friendships with other women because of the fear these might become sexual. Moreover, menopausal women characteristically came to desire their sons-in-law. Or they took young lovers. They might engage in bizarre sexual behavior, as, according to Deutsch, "rape" and "prostitution" fantasies characteristic of adolescence also reappeared. Deutsch reported the case of a grandmother who, she maintained, had been arrested in a park for soliciting men. She also described a menopausal fifty-year-old woman who fantasized about a woman friend who "tenderly initiated adolescent boys into the mysteries of sensual love."[65]

Deutsch was sixty when she wrote *The Psychology of Women*. Her biographer reveals that although she had disliked her rigid abusive mother, her distant relations with her own grown children suggest that she had replicated some of her mother's behavior.[66] These experiences also suggest that her vitriolic portrait of menopausal women may have been personally inspired—by a negative attitude toward her mother and toward herself. Still, at the time she wrote the book, Deutsch had a thriving career as an analyst, an author, a lecturer, and a teacher: she seems to have qualified as one of her own "pseudo-masculine," inevitably discontented, women. How she reconciled these discontinuities between her personal life and her theories is difficult to comprehend. Yet in *The Psychology of Women* Deutsch also described (although briefly) a small minority of women who were able to cope successfully with menopause through careers or reform causes. By creating this group exempt from the normal menopausal problems, Deutsch may have exonerated her own career involvement.

By Deutsch's prescription, however, most women could escape the difficulties of menopause only by becoming doting, asexualized grand-mothers. In this manner they could repress once again the adolescent eroticized impulses which were the basis of so much of the menopausal predicament. And, by sublimating their sexual desires through affectionate relationships with grandchildren, especially grandsons, they might once again gain the phallus all women wanted and which sons, and now their sons' male offspring, could provide. Thus Deutsch recreated for aging women that Freudian scenario by which childbirth was the highest goal of women's lives. She discounted the possibility that aging women, without the responsibilities of childrearing, might consider a life-style more devoted to self and society. With Deutsch's writings, the nineteenth-century grandmother as master moralist or reform activist was lost in the twentieth-century rush to sexuality and in the definition of the sexuality of aging women as out of control and needing containment.

Throughout the 1920s and 1930s Freudian terms like "physiological castration" or "species death" to refer to menopause were present. The concept that women are ruled by their sexuality was ubiquitous. By the 1940s and 1950s war and postwar eras Freudian views seemed dominant. They provided a simple, presumably scientific explanation for the immense irrationality of war, locating it in individual neuroses which could be cured by medical expertise. Freudian gender conservatism continued to be comforting to a postwar world experiencing the dislocations of military demobilization, of McCarthyism and the Cold War, of the fear of destruction unleashed by the advent of the atomic bomb. In their 1952 liberatory work on menopause, Beka Doherty and Lena Levine worried that Freudian ideas were omnipresent in American culture. "There is hardly an area of life in which they are not felt.... It affects the life of everyday people by infiltrating through newspapers, magazines, popular books...."[67]

The psychiatric profession in the United States during World War II had focused on treating shell-shocked and battle-scarred soldiers. When military demobilization brought a reduction in military mental hospital positions, the large and growing number of psychiatrists and psychologists turned to women as clients. For their part, women seemed willing to define themselves as ill. In the 1950s most patient admissions to mental hospitals were women. "Climacteric insanity" as a definitional category confined almost exclusively to menopausal women was not dropped until the 1960s.

In this postwar era, variations on the Freudian ideas about menopause were manifold. In her popular book on aging, Mary Bard portrayed the romance between the forty-plus Candy and a younger man at a ski resort as motivated on his part by her resemblance to his mother and on her part by a "compulsion neurosis" to remain young. Building on the ideas of Helene Deutsch, psychoanalyst Laci Fessler argued that menstruation for women was akin to possessing a penis. Thus, she concluded, the end of menstruation was like losing that penis, and the loss produced a menopausal "castration anxiety."[68]

In her *Feminine Psychology,* Karen Horney posited the notion of a male "womb envy" of women in contradistinction to the Freudian female "penis envy" of men. In this work, however, she analyzed in Freudian terms the case of an older woman involved with a man twenty years her junior. In her analysis, Horney maintained that the older woman was suffering from a "father fixation." What the woman desired was not her younger lover, but rather her own son. But, according to Horney, this sublimated desire was not the end of the matter. The woman's son was in turn a stand-in for her father, her original forbidden object of desire. This original desire had produced all the rest, prompting her involvement with the young man.[69]

In his popular *Love Against Hate,* Karl Menninger took Horney's emphasis in a somewhat different direction. In this work, he worried about men with "mother fixations." Such men, he argued, could not handle normal relationships. In consequence, they usually engaged in cross-age associations, either with much older or much younger women. (Either variation seemed to him neurotic.) And, combining a number of relationships then considered deviant, Menninger added homosexuality to his list of dangers for "mother fixated" young men. Drawing on current theory that overprotective mothers often produced homosexual sons, Menninger asserted that the neurosis of cross-age connections was akin to that of homosexual relationships, since both were the product of unhealthy associations between parents and children. In his view none of these sorts of relationships were normal.[70]

In his 1947 book on aging, George Lawton offered a variation on Menninger's argument. To him young men involved with older women (or even younger women involved with older men) were seeking a parent and avoiding the responsibility of choosing partners their own age. Lawton viewed cross-age relationships as violating the American ethic of hard work, as encouraging young people to depend on others, rather than on themselves, for financial support. To him these relationships seemed a manifestation of the sybaritism of decaying ancient civilizations. As such, they indicated a dangerous weakness in modern times, a possible national decline into impotence. Like Deutsch, Horney, and Menninger, Lawton concluded that cross-age relationships between aging women and younger men were pathological.[71]

As early as the 1920s, there was concern about mothers being overly involved with their sons. In that era the phrase "tied to your mother's apron strings" was coined to refer to mother-son closeness. What was then a modicum of criticism, however, became a barrage by the 1950s. In that decade overprotective mothers presumably hampering the normal development of sons became viewed as a serious problem. Child care experts, led by Briton John Bowlby, contended that the mother-child bond was central to human development and that full-time involvement in childrearing should be required of all mothers. Yet psychologists like Erik Erikson maintained that many mothers were neurotic individuals who only with difficulty raised healthy children. In his 1956 *Childhood and Society* Erikson wrote that in the life cycle of many women "remnants of infantility join advanced senility to crowd out the middle range of mature womanhood, which thus becomes self-absorbed and stagnant."[72]

In the 1950s decade of renewed domesticity, women became special targets for complaints. Philip Wylie's *Generation of Vipers* (the famed wartime attack on "momism") singled out menopausal women for special vituperation. "Never before has a great nation of brave and dreaming men absentmindedly created a huge class of idle, middle-aged women." Wylie accused them all of malingering. "These caprices are of menopausal nature at best: hot flashes, infantilism, weeping, sentimentality, peculiar appetite, and all the ragged reticule of tricks, wooings, wiles, subordined fornications."[73]

In the 1890s, women's movement from the domestic sphere into the public arena of male-identified activities had produced both positive and negative attitudes toward menopause. In the 1950s negative views were vehement and widespread. In that era, according to Elaine Tyler May, the connection between containing the fears engendered by the atomic age and taming women as scapegoats for these fears was "pervasive and lasting."[74] With men away during the war years, many women had been on their own; after the war they had to be brought back under control. This perceived need to master women extended to aging women as much as to their younger counterparts. Monogamous marriages and childbearing could contain younger women. For older women, no longer capable of bearing children, defining menopause in terms of mental disturbance served as a brake on their independence.

The sentiments of Deutsch and Wylie and the other writers who regarded menopause as pathological were not unusual. When Simone de Beauvoir in her germinal 1949 work, *The Second Sex*, took up the subject of menopause, she followed Freudian views to characterize menopause as "the eventual mutilation" and "the dangerous age." Despite the classic French tradition of celebrating aging women, she drew from Helene Deutsch's writings to depreciate menopausal sexuality. "And since love is at this time more than ever before her main concern, it is normal for her to embrace the illusion that she is loved. Nine out of ten erotomaniacs are women, and these are almost all forty to fifty years old."[75]

But sexuality was not the only problem for menopausal women, according to de Beauvoir. As they realized the life deficiencies that aging and menopause caused, especially the end of beauty and love, their minds became unbalanced. With bleak futures to anticipate, they turned into shrewish, paranoid versions of their former selves:

> The moments of exaltation are succeeded by sad hours of depression. The organism manifests this rhythm because the decline of the female sex hormones is compensated for by an overactivity of the pituitary glands: but above all it is the psychological state that governs this alternation of mood. For the woman's restlessness, her illusions, her fervor, are only a defense reaction against the overruling fatality of what has been. She harps endlessly on her wrongs, her regrets, her reproaches: she imagines her relatives and neighbors guilty of dark machinations against her.

That de Beauvoir wrote venemously about aging women partly resulted from her cynical approach to gender in general. This cynicism is evident throughout *The Second Sex* and in her germinal book on aging, *The Coming of Age*. But her attitude toward aging, like that of Freud and Deutsch, also was the product of her own biography. Throughout her life she was troubled by the reality of aging. Like the women in the writings of Colette, the female protagonists in de Beauvoir's novels worry about signs of bodily decay, and she exhibited a similar concern about herself in her autobiographical writings. Even when in her forties and still vigorous, de Beauvoir thought of herself as an old woman, incapable of sexual response. Yet her lifetime companion, Jean-Paul Sartre, at the same age had an adolescent disposition and a series of much younger lovers.

Deirdre Bair, de Beauvoir's most recent biographer, traces these attitudes to de Beauvoir's upbringing among the conservative Parisian *haute bourgeoisie*, an upper-middle-class group whose members adhered to strict Catholic moral codes. De Beauvoir was raised to believe that women over forty became ciphers, devoted to church and family. Bonnie Smith has elucidated the nineteenth-century rigidity of this upper-class group; Simone de Beauvoir offers an example of the continuation of its attitudes into the twentieth century.[76]

When she was in her mid-forties, de Beauvoir formed a relationship with a journalist of twenty-seven, a man seventeen years her junior. The relationship lasted seven years. During its existence she wrote about the feeling of youth she gained through being loved by a younger man. But she had qualms about the validity of the association, about whether it had arisen from true human affection or from Freudian family pathology. She and her younger lover were happy, she wrote, in a kind of "incestuous mother-son relationship."[77]

De Beauvoir was forty when she wrote *The Second Sex* and sixty when she published *The Coming of Age* in 1970. During the next decade of her life, when she was in her sixties, she came to terms with the process of aging. To her surprise, she found her later years not a time of despair but rather of contentment.[78] During this decade she formed a relationship with Sylvie le Bon, a woman over thirty years younger than she. De Beauvoir denied that the relationship was sexual, but her biographers are not certain that she was telling the truth. She described this relationship in terms different from those she had used to depict her earlier relationship with a younger man. In this case Freudian terminology was absent. She refused to limit her younger partner to a daughter role or herself to that of a mother. They played the parental roles for each other, she averred, even as they alternated occupying life-cycle positions.

One might maintain, in fact, that de Beauvoir only came to full maturity during this last period of her life when she discovered that her fears about aging were groundless, and when she, in fact, took up a companionate relationship with another woman. Shortly before her death, de Beauvoir expressed her belief that, while love affairs between men and women do not last, in contrast great friendships among women often endure indefinitely.

A Return to Sunset Boulevard *and 1950s Films: Menopause as Confining and Freeing*

*I*N ANALYZING the film *Sunset Boulevard*, a movie embedded in the post–World War II era, I maintained that there were two versions of Norma Desmond. The first is a negative version, attuned to the negative attitudes toward menopause of that era. It is in keeping with the personifications of women as castrating mothers and as hysterical menopausal women evident in Freudian belief and in best-selling works like Philip Wylie's *Generation of Vipers*. The second, albeit less evident, more subtextual, is a more positive rendering, a realization that there might be possibilities for Desmond, that her environing culture was not entirely closed to her ambition and her need for support and success.

This second version of Desmond, I suggested, is apparent in the look of women in the 1950s, in a maternal presentation sometimes blended in the same face with convoluted childishness or rapacious control. In their appearance women mirrored their common sterotypes as men's dependents or their mothers or as sexually voracious beings.

Not all movies of the 1950s trivialized aging women. In *Tea and Sympathy* the wife of the domineering boy's school teacher who sleeps with a young student to prove to him his masculinity is a sympathetic character (although she is punished by banishment at the end of the film). In *All That Heaven Allows* surburban conformity is identified with the children of an aging woman. In the film the woman becomes a symbol of youthful rebellion by marrying her younger, nature-identified, gardener in violation of her children's conventions. In this film youth is conformist, repelled by an aging woman's sexuality, desirous of enforcing conventional standards for gender and age.

In 1938 Daphne du Maurier wrote *Rebecca*, the basis of the Hitchcock film, in which a young woman provides salvation for an aging man. But in 1952 she wrote *My Cousin Rachel*, a novel also made into a film which features the enduring appeal of an older, sophisticated woman. Similarly, in his plays and other writings Tennessee Williams often painted vitriolic portraits of aging, frustrated women without men. But in *Sweet Bird of Youth*, the aging actress who is the play's central character in the end is rejuvenated. And in *The Night of the Iguana*, a trio of aging unmarried women span the possibilities of women's aging, each character representing a differing life resolution. One of the characters is a neurotic spinster, censorious of everyone around her. The second is an independent woman, traveling the world. The third is an eroticized earth-mother type, who provides comfort and pleasure for the men in her life.

In the 1950s Joan Crawford especially played parts in which, as an aging woman, whether a sophisticated actress or a shopworn secretary, she was involved with younger men. In *Mildred Pierce* she loses her younger lover to her daughter. But in *Autumn Leaves* and *Female on the Beach* the relationships survive numerous threats to seem strong and enduring at the end of the films. And in *Humoresque* a comparison is implied between the sophisticated Crawford and the housewife mother of the young concert violinist she loves, and the comparison is not unilaterally in the mother's favor.

Throughout the 1950s medical authorities and popular writers critiqued Freudian views about menopause. Margaret Mead's famous formulation of the existence of "post-menopausal zest" was echoed by other, less well known commentators. Writing about the difficulties of being a widow during the "perilous years" of menopause, Zelda Popkin noted with alarm that menopausal women constituted a majority of psychiatric hospital admissions. Two-thirds of such admissions, she wrote, were people past thirty-five, and three out of every four of these individuals were women. The diagnosis of these female patients was invariably "involutional psychosis." This ailment, she explained, was popularly called "change of life melancholia."[79]

Yet in Popkin's view, it was women's fear of aging and of menopause, especially of the probable loss of desirability to men, that made the transition difficult. For the majority of women, she asserted, the physiological systems of menopause should not be severe. All the hospital admissions, she implied, were unnecessary, and the connection of menopause to a specific mental illness was alarming. And A. Béran Wolfe, whose 1935 *A Woman's Best Years* was still popular in the 1950s, adopted a surprisingly feminist explanation for women's difficulties with aging and with menopause. "In our patriarchal civilization," he wrote, "built as it is on masculine ideals and masculine morals, a woman even at best has no easy time of it."[80]

Even Helene Deutsch could not deny that some women seemed to become more self-reliant during menopause and that these women achieved professional advancement or took up worthwhile programs for self- or social improvement. Some even continued a rich, erotic life until the end of their days. In this regard, like a number of twentieth-century writers on aging women, Deutsch was drawn to the example of Ninon de Lenclos, the seventeenth-century Parisian noblewoman-courtesan whose erotic appeal still evident in her sixties seemed a model toward which aging women might aspire—or which they ought to avoid. "For three generations of climacteric women with youthful hearts," wrote Deutsch, "Ninon de Lenclos has been the ego ideal."[81]

But Deutsch also repeated the story that Lenclos's last romantic involvement, at the age of sixty-three and with a man of twenty-five, had turned to aversion when she discovered that he was her son, whom she had not seen since his birth. Repelled by the revelation, she retreated into a nunnery. With regard to this involvement, Deutsch concluded that "whether this modern Oedipus myth is true is questionable." Yet its truth or falsity was not the issue; what mattered to Deutsch was its symbolic value in underscoring her views about menopausal women. "Psychologically it is correct; the love object of the aging woman is the son."[82]

Thus Lenclos's life of love ended on a cautionary note. Her presumed violation of a social taboo underscored Deutsch's stated advice to menopausal women elsewhere in this work that they could best meet their need for love from young men by becoming the doting, asexual grandmothers of the male sons their children produced.

The Possibilities for Menopause in More Recent Eras

MENOPAUSE WAS DEFINED as both confining and freeing in the late nineteenth century. It was connected with a deviant sexuality from the 1920s onward. And, menopause was also "medicalized." Defining it as an illness, not an experience, doctors counseled all menopausal women to seek medical attention. In so doing, they continued to extend the venerable identification of a menopausal medical clientele suffering from severe symptoms to the entire population of menopausal women. They thereby avoided the reality that many women did not consult physicians because menopause did not trouble them.

The identification of menopause with illness continues to the present. In our own era have appeared ever new ailments, like osteoporosis, to make menopause an illness and not an experience. And estrogen is routinely prescribed for all the symptoms of menopause, while many doctors maintain that all women, no matter their symptomology, should take estrogen as they age.[83]

According to Emily Martin, the medicalization of menopause has been advanced not only by negative cultural attitudes toward aging and by the medical establishment's characteristic drive to control women but also by recent identifications in medical rhetoric between the female body and capitalist modalities. Martin finds that medical sources typically use phrases which subtly classify women's bodies as akin to manufacturing plants designed to produce babies and as hierarchical bureaucracies controlled by the cerebral cortex. In this rhetoric these structures, like many human inventions, are prone with age to breakdown or obsolescence.[84]

Thus the capitalist consumption culture may have created yet a new series of quasi-scientific metaphors, perhaps even more sophisticated than those of Darwin and Freud, designed to control women's bodies—and their aging.

Moreover, it is curious that limited attention today seems to be paid to the idea of a "male menopause" noted in turn-of-century medical writings. In the 1920s and 1930s, it is true, for a time men utilized hormonal and other rejuvenative therapies probably more frequently than did women. Steinach's clinic, for example, had as many male as female patients. I suspect that what troubled men then was not so much aging per se but a perceived lack of virility centering around impotence. Yet despite a continuing reference to a "male menopause" throughout twentieth-century medical writings, the subject remains largely unexplored.[85]

Much recent literature on menopause suggests that, like the experience of pregnancy and birth, that of menopause is highly individualistic and that each woman experiences it differently. Much depends on self-image and on life-style, as well as on biological tendencies. Women with a positive self-image and with an affirmative attitude toward aging experience less severe menopausal symptoms. Exercise and healthy diet can also be important; in the management of specific symptoms like heat flashes positive results have been registered with vitamin therapy and acupuncture.[86]

How then ought we approach menopause? Should we continue to hide any acknowledgment of its occurrence, silently passing through what we still call, in words freighted with life-cycle significance, "the change of life?" Should women, by their silence, allow the medical profession to assert, by default, the predominating voice in the definition of menopause?

Many feminists have called for the creation of new rituals celebrating women's life-cycle transitions: menarche and menopause are the two most often accorded recognition. We celebrate, through birthdays, the entry into life. Through funerals we commemorate its leaving. We honor, through weddings, family formation. But we pass through in silence the most important transitions of women's lives, their movement into procreation and their exit from it. Some of us, on our fiftieth birthdays, however, hold "crone" ceremonies, to celebrate our passage to the time of special wisdom and authority in our lives which we want our aging to provide.

In her *Journey Through Menopause*, Christine Downing provides another possible mode of celebration. In this book she tells the story of how she declared a moratorium from her regular life and took a trip around the world. Through this hiatus and this journey she hoped to access the spiritual significance of menopause. The lessons she learned on this voyage, however, were not what she expected. Her young male friend and companion on the trip, who was twenty-three years her junior, disappointed her. During the journey he became like an aggressive male hero on a quest, fighting obstacles along the way. More tranquil than he, Downing came to think of her journey as a rebirth, as a transformative returning to where she had originally been.[87]

To her surprise, she found spiritual mentors on this journey in several aging wise men she encountered. Their personas suggested to her that, in fact, old age may be a phase of life in which previous stereotypical gender behavior is modified, in which gender means "less and less." They were gentle and giving, in contrast to the warrior type her young male companion had become. Coming home, Downing sensed herself as transformed, as having passed through menopause able to see the miraculous in the familiar, as having transcended the ordinary.

As a life-cycle experience, menopause can be viewed in terms of its own definition. But it is also encased, as Downing's experience indicates, by the broader situation of aging. And, in contemporary times, aging has become of substantial interest. For demographic dispensations have created the possibility of a longer life span for more individuals, especially for more women, than ever before in history. Complex in individualized experience, menopause has had many meanings over the course of the twentieth century. The new developments in aging may once again shift the definitional boundaries of menopause, as it becomes even more a midlife experience in what is a long life.

PART FIVE

The Contemporary Period

MY STUDY of the history of aging women and relationships ends where it began, in the present. Dealing with contemporary
times raises issues concerning life enrichment for aging women. Contemporary medical discourse, I have argued, has problematized menopause.
But this negativity does not extend to other areas of study involving
women's aging.

As I read the literature on aging written by gerontologists and sociolo-
gists, by anthropologists and novelists, one primary thread in the contemporary cultural tapestry stands out. That is a thread indicating a substantial
change in life-cycle experience. In the first instance, present generations
of aging people are beginning to experience the life process in a way
different from the generations that preceded them. In addition, new
definitions are being devised for the life-cycle categories of youth, middle
age, and old age. Indeed, some analysts argue for the elimination of such
age groupings.

The greater longevity of aging women is an important issue in all of
this work. And, the possibility for women of life spans longer than those
of men raises the issue of relationships, of how women will fulfill the
need for significant others in their lives at older ages when sufficient
older men may simply not exist to form relationships with them. In the
Introduction I raised the possibility that the contemporary rise in the
incidence of age-disparate relationships between older women and
younger men might address this problem. I also proposed that this phenomenon of cross-age relationships might operate as an avenue toward
gender equality and as an indication of the overturning of patriarchy.

Given statistics I will cite which suggest that the recent increase in age-
disparate associations is confined to the well-to-do, I will in the end argue

that in fact they may be nothing more than a continuation of class privilege in a period of increasing distinctions between wealthy and poor. Coupling with younger men, affluent women may be doubly confirming their heterosexuality and avoiding opportunities for bonding with other women. Thus age-disparate relationships between older women and younger men may operate, by dividing women of various social groups, to support patriarchy rather than to overturn it.

Increasing disparities between the numbers of men and women at later ages in the life cycle, with more women than men at each stage, indicate that many women, whatever their inclinations, may inevitably have to live the later years of their life alone. Yet I do not regard this aloneness, as I have implied throughout this book, as a life deficiency. Rather, singlehood can be empowering. As Margaret Fuller suggested in the nineteenth century, it can be a way of reaching an increased self- and social transcendence. It may in fact be that neither heterosexuality nor even sexuality should be considered the summum bonum of life. Other means of self-definition may also provide rich life experience, and these other ways may afford increased access to a more just and egalitarian society in terms of age, gender, and class.

CHAPTER NINE

Aging and Ethnicity: Goddesses Reconsidered

THE INCREASING PROPORTION of older people in the population and their newer, more positive experience of the process of aging may prove to be revolutionary developments. One analyst contends that, because of these changes, a new era in human evolution is beginning. Another judges that the changes will have as great an impact on human history as social movements like immigration and urbanization which have substantially reshaped modern society.[1] To understand the present situation and future prospects of age-disparate relationships between older women and younger men, it is important to explore these developments in the history of aging.

And they need to be explored in terms of issues relating to definitions of aging. For the ongoing valorization of youth, of heterosexual sexuality, and of middle-class standards may, in fact, constrain any significant definitional modifications. Indeed, recent advances in cosmetic surgery (and the popularity of that surgery) have primarily had the effect of more than ever before extending the look of youth to aging people—as long as they have sufficient wealth to afford expensive cosmetics and medical procedures. In the area of appearance, to cite a key aspect of the definition of aging, a new conservatizing hierarchy based on youthful appearance and on class distinctions looms larger than ever before.

To explore this central ethical issue, I will ultimately return to another subject I raised in the Introduction without, at that point, investigating its ramifications. That subject is the perspective on aging offered by women who are neither white nor middle class. Black women, in particular, have experienced patriarchal victimization to attain what may be an admirable self-realization. And this self-realization is often evidenced especially during their aging years.

To illuminate this point, I will turn, as I often have in this book, to novelistic exploration. Aging women and their life definitions are important in the writings of three central twentieth-century novelists: the contemporary black writers Toni Morrison and Alice Walker and their acknowledged 1930s forerunner, Zora Neale Hurston. Here my initial emphasis on ancient goddesses as combining in their personas the stages and cycle of life returns in a new guise. For these authors turn to traditions of black goddesses in their own culture as a mode of analysis and of empowerment.

It is perhaps appropriate that I take this direction. For California, the name of the state in which I live and where the *Sunset Boulevard* story of Norma Desmond and Joe Gillis is located, derives from the name of a fantasized black Amazonian ruler, Califia. A literary figure, Califia appears at the end of the chivalric romance *Amadis of Gaul*, which dated from the fourteenth century and was expanded in the sixteenth century. Califia rules over a mythical land far over the oceans from the European continent. Early modern European explorers, themselves sailing across unknown seas, read such chivalric romances in leisure hours. Among these adventurers, discoverers of that land on the western coast of the American continent found it a place appropriate for the black Califia and her kingdom. Thus they named this realm California.

New Conceptions of Aging

WITHIN THE NEW and positive possibilities for aging, several cultural processes are paramount. The first is medical: advances in medical therapeutics and the containment of epidemic diseases have substantially increased life expectancy and contributed to larger numbers of aging people within the population: the "graying of America" is a common observation. Where only about 10 percent of most people in the European and American past could expect to live past the age of sixty-five, today nearly 80 percent of individuals can expect to reach that age. At the start of the century most deaths still occurred in infancy and early adulthood, but today two-thirds of all deaths occur after age sixty-five and 30 percent after age eighty. At present the median age of the United States population stands at thirty-two. Projections are that by the year 2050 the median age will rest in the mid-forties.[2]

Declining birth rates have also contributed to a larger number of aging people within the population. In 1982 individuals under twenty years of age stood at 31 percent of the population. Those between twenty and forty-four represented 39 percent of Americans. Nineteen percent were between forty-five and sixty-five and 12 percent were over sixty-five. If the current low levels of fertility and mortality are maintained, it is estimated that in the year 2050 individuals under twenty will comprise 18 percent of the population. Individuals between twenty and forty-four will constitute 28 percent of the population, and those between forty-five and sixty-four 25 percent. In this latter year a half century ahead, 29 percent of the population will be composed of individuals over sixty-five.[3]

The recent movement of the baby boom generation into the position of an aging cohort has produced some of this change. Born in that post–World War II era of intense family preoccupation, members of this huge age group are now in their forties. The baby boom generation has consistently impacted on all age ratios in the population. As I will presently argue, its special characteristics have been important in attitudes toward aging. Still, increased numbers of aging people in the population vis-à-vis the young would have existed without its various inputs, since this increase is partly based on the greater longevity of generations which preceded it.

Moreover, in the last decade or so, researchers focusing on aging have begun to revise earlier valuations of the process of aging as one of decline. Earlier generations of gerontologists, building on late nineteenth-century models of the aging body as one of decay, focused on the process of what was at one point called "senescence." Even today, according to developmental psychologist David Gutmann, a "depletion perspective" dominates conventional thinking in gerontology.[4] Yet many middle-aged and elderly people, following nutritional and exercise advice, have maintained vigorous bodies and minds into their seventies and eighties. Their success has undermined notions of elderly individuals as universally decrepit. New terminologies have been devised to take into account this new possibility of vigorous aging. Gerontologists commonly refer to the "new" old, and they draw divisions between the "young old" and the "old old."

As for menopause in an earlier era, diseases formerly linked to aging are now seen as the products of an ill-used body or of environmental factors. Experts agree that with proper diet and exercise many individuals can anticipate retaining vigor and health into their seventies and even later. Even wrinkled skin, it is now believed, is as much the product of exposure to the sun or of smoking or of a lack of moisturizing as of a natural biological process.

One of the major recent trends in the study of aging has been a focus on individuation. In reaction to previous decades of gerontological research based on the assumption of aging as decline, the new focus is on the perception that, as a process, aging takes a different form in each individual. (This new perception with regard to aging parallels a similar new focus in research on menopause.) The differing individual form will especially depend on heredity, attention to health, and life satisfaction. In their recent review of sociological literature on aging, Patricia Passuth and Vern Bengston stress that many studies show that "individuals of the same age often experience age in a wide variety of ways." Others have argued that research on aging ought to focus on this difference through the writing of biography and historical narrative, rather than on the statistical study which previously predominated.[5]

In their study of three hundred women ranging in age from thirty-five to fifty-five, Grace Baruch, Rosalind Barnett, and Caryl Rivers found a variety of what they call "lifeprints," or life experiences, among their subjects. In this work they propose that all life-stage theorization ought to be abandoned as inadequate to explain the individual lives of contemporary women.[6]

Many analysts of aging now assert that an older pattern of common cohort behavior no longer exists. Under this pattern, individuals spent their early years gaining an education before marrying in their late teens or early twenties and then working and raising their children until retiring in their early sixties. This pattern of common movement of age cohorts through the life cycle was in place by the 1900s; it existed through the 1950s and into the 1960s. Today, however, both men and women marry later. They move in and out of the work force and educational institutions. A trend toward bearing children at later ages also has created discontinuities in the older cohort pattern.

Moreover, divorce at any point during the life span can propel individuals into unexpected behavior. In an autobiographical statement written in 1987, when she was fifty-five, actress Elizabeth Taylor has probably articulated the feeling of many women of her generation about middle-aged dating: "I feel strange to be dating at my age. When I grew up women in their fifties were generally grandmothers who stayed at home with their husbands and were visited by their children and grandchildren."[7] Taylor's experience is common in the contemporary era in which people move in and out of behavior patterns which were more often age-graded throughout much of the preceding century.

The differences—and the new variations—are apparent in the differing life-span experiences of the women in Lillian Rubin's *Women of a Certain Age*, published in 1979, and in Baruch, Barnett, and Rivers's *Lifeprints*, published in 1983. Both studies conclude that their subjects experience midlife as positive. Yet Rubin, reflecting the older reality, contended that most people go through the various stages of life at roughly the same chronological ages. In contrast, writing some four years later, Baruch and her colleagues found much more variation.[8]

Reflecting on the new experience of variation, the *Ladies' Home Journal* in 1987 disseminated the scholarly findings to a popular audience. In the 1970s, the *Journal* asserted, books like Gail Sheehy's *Passages* popularized the idea of a common chronological life experience. These works drew from the findings of developmental psychologists like Erik Erikson, who looked on life development as a progress through fixed stages, with predictable emotional development at each stage. But in the 1980s these standard stages no longer existed, according to the *Journal*. "Chronological conformity," the magazine stated, "is no longer the case, especially for women. They now marry at any age, have children early or late, combine motherhood and career or forgo motherhood altogether." We now have, according to one analyst, a "fluid life cycle."[9]

The coming into existence of this fluidity may be breaking down prevailing ageism. As women in their fifties attend college with their children, as they divorce husbands and engage in dating behavior, as they raise young children born to them in their late thirties and forties, they move outside of older cohort generational patterns. They create a bond with others at different stages of the life cycle.

In 1983 Elissa Melamed sensed that the concept of "midlife" was changing so rapidly, even during the several years that she spent writing her book on the subject of aging, that it had moved from forty to fifty. There is in addition Gloria Steinem's oft-quoted retort on her fiftieth birthday to a reporter who asked her what it felt like to be fifty: "It feels a lot like what forty used to feel like." In 1986 *Newsweek* noted that sixty-year-olds looked on themselves as fifty-year-olds had two decades before.[10] The implication was that general ageism might soon disappear. For some time *Vogue* magazine each year has devoted a section of at least one issue to beautiful women in their forties. As women like Jane Fonda or Joan Collins, who have been popular beauty symbols, move into their fifties, it will be interesting to see if the magazine follows suit, to celebrate "beauty" in women's fifth and sixth decades of life.

Concurrently, advertisers' fixation on youth as the standard for sales promotion may also be breaking down. Recent market research has disproven old assumptions that aging people are frugal spenders loyal to long-used brands. What is often assumed to be the natural frugality of old people may actually reflect the orientation toward money of the generation which came to maturity during the economically troubled 1930s and that generation during the war and the postwar period which was composed of their children. Older people today seem to be increasingly consumption oriented, as they internalize the new attitudes about productive aging. Because of their numbers and their collective wealth, they are becoming a major market for products like aspirin, appropriate for the special needs of aging bodies. And, analysts have pointed to the predominately young age of Madison Avenue promoters as a major factor behind their insensitivity to the needs and potentials of aging people.[11]

Many analysts speculate that as the baby boom generation moves through the life span, its members will further these trends toward indulgence, since indulgence has always characterized the behavior of this group. Members of the boom generation ingested the narcissism of the 1960s and 1970s and the imperatives then broadcast by banks and other monetary agencies to utilize credit and spend above one's means. Habits developed in earlier years, according to this investigation, persist into older years.[12]

Recent analysts of aging often use movie and television portrayals of aging people as an indication of popular attitudes, since these broadcast media have played a powerful role in shaping and reflecting public perceptions over the last decades. In this area negative conclusions have been drawn: in both television and the movies youthful characters are models of positive living and aging individuals are stereotypically passive or eccentric. In her exploration of movie and television imagery regarding aging in the 1970s and 1980s, Andrea Walsh partly modifies these conclusions. She contends that the feminism of the 1960s and 1970s motivated the entertainment industry toward greater realism and sympathy in depicting aging women. But she finds many portrayals problematic.[13]

Walsh notes ambivalences about aging in two popular television shows which feature aging women. "Murder, She Wrote," centering on the crime-solving adventures of an older female mystery writer, rarely addresses the issue of aging. "The Golden Girls" explicitly focuses on aging in the lives of its three older characters, but it exploits stereotypes of menopausal women and treats serious issues of aging in a comic vein. According to Walsh, problems exist even in the 1971 *Harold and Maude,* a movie celebrated for its portrayal of the romance (both comradely and sexual) between a seventy-nine-year-old woman and a twenty-one-year-old man. Despite what seems a positive portrayal of the relationship, Walsh maintains that Maude is a maternal figure who dies once she has cured the young man of debilitating depression.

On the other hand, one could argue that, with her energy and joie de vivre, Maude represents youthfulness taken into aging. She may embody the romantic ideal of death as best experienced at the height of life, the "candle burning bright" mentality of countercultural groups throughout the modern era. From this perspective, the message of the movie may be that any period of aging can be the best time, that it is all a matter of perspective.

To revise stereotypes about aging which have persisted over the centuries of Western development is no easy matter. Nor is it easy for individuals to abandon old, inappropriate beliefs equating age with disability. Despite changes in attitude we still say "act your age," indicating the common assumption that there are age-appropriate behaviors. Newspapers always distinguish people by their age, as though location on a time continuum is a necessary means of human identification. We all know what Joe Gillis meant in *Sunset Boulevard* when he admonished Norma Desmond by telling her that "there's nothing tragic about being fifty—not unless you try to be twenty-five." Yet her behavior may have had nothing to do with youth or age; it may simply have been her way of behaving.

In China, as among Native Americans, people regularly inflate their age upward because of the veneration accorded aging wisdom in these societies. The adoption of such a practice seems almost inconceivable in the United States—so strong is our orientation toward youth. The greatest possible compliment one can give to an aging woman in this country is to tell her that she doesn't look her age.

In her popular advice column Judith Martin (Miss Manners) recently printed a letter from a seventy-one-year-old woman asking if she should reveal her age to the fifty-five-year-old man she was considering dating. Manners validated the potential relationship and replied that her correspondent did not need to disclose her age immediately, but eventually she should do so. What is important about the exchange, however, is the way in which the letter writer described herself. She portrayed herself as energetic and attractive and easily able to "pass" as decades younger than she actually was.[14] This woman justified her relationship with a younger man by depreciating her aging self.

This matter of looks may be key to the issue of ageism, for appearance is central to the perception of aging people. Much of the present attempt to neutralize the negative definition of aging involves giving aging people permission not only to act young but also to look young. A huge industry is being spawned around cosmetic products and surgical techniques designed to hide the look of age. A plethora of creams and lotions are being marketed which supposedly retard wrinkling. Face-lifts and liposuction are widely available and advertised by clinics specializing in these procedures. (Liposuction involves a suction technique designed to remove fatty deposits from the body.)

Recently, a technique to plump up the lips and make them look fuller has been devised and is gaining popularity. In this procedure substances like liquid fat or collagen removed from thighs, stomach, or buttocks by lipsocution are injected into the lips. As people age, one plastic surgeon points out, their lips lose fullness. The procedure to regain that fullness, which lasts only about two months, is perceived as making people look younger and sexier.[15]

In Los Angeles, often in the vanguard in techniques to achieve "beauty," billboards feature a picture of a small water-massage brush to firm up skin through water friction. The picture is captioned: "Regard cellulite as dirt." (Cellulite is a term for fatty deposits on the body; they are a normal feature of aging.) "Dermablend" leg and body makeup in various shades of ivory and brown is guaranteed to hide varicose veins, stretch marks, scars, bruises, and age spots. Dermacentre Clinics have opened to deal with wrinkles, hyperpigmentation, scars, and stretch marks. (The last is a normal result both of extensive weight loss from a large body and of the stomach extension and consequent skin stretching produced by pregnancy.) Yet techniques like liposuction may, in fact, destroy fat cells designed to be beneficial to aging bodies, especially the bodies of women, since recent research indicates that such cells may naturally generate the hormone estrogen.[16]

Our Western views about aging may be even more anomalous in light of anthropologists' studies of the status of aging women in a variety of societies. Pauline Bart's cross-cultural study with regard to middle-aged women is again instructive. In those few societies she studied in which women's status improved only minimally as they aged, the key variable was a cultural valuation based on sexual attractiveness rather than on craft ability, technical knowledge, or wisdom. When women were valued for appearance rather than ability, young women were the cynosures and aging women were downplayed.[17]

Distinctive appearance, I would submit, is the most common characteristic of aging. Despite individual differences in aging, all aging people eventually develop white hair, a wrinkled skin, increased fatty deposits, aging spots. One of the reasons that relationships between aging women and younger men have been so denigrated is the look of difference between the partners; thus the greater the age disparity the more censored is the behavior. But ought women attempt to "pass" as younger? Are there not benefits to being outside of the category of "beauty," outside of the male-defined realm of female worth?

In her autobiography, Joan Collins contended that her role of the middle-aged, powerful Alexis Colby on the popular evening soap opera "Dynasty" represented an important statement for the liberation of aging women. She made the same claim with regard to posing for a *Playboy* centerfold. "I felt I was breaking the ageism taboo that so many women feared and dreaded," wrote Collins. Although there is some truth to her contention, one might question what this liberation meant. Both Alexis's beauty and her power were the product of money: "Dynasty" was a world of the superrich. One might admire Alexis's drive and her intelligence, but her aging wisdom was the wisdom to manipulate and control. Alexis schemed and bullied her way out of every situation, using every associate as her pawn. Alexis's independence in "Dynasty" placed her beyond objectification, but Collins's spread in *Playboy*, her exposure of her body for the visual and sexual gratification of individual male readers, was an exercise in objectification.[18]

During the time that she starred in "Dynasty," in both the character of Alexis and in her private life, Collins married younger men. Yet neither the fictionalized nor the real relationship succeeded; in the latter case Collins, like many men of wealth married to younger women, eventually found herself in the divorce courts, with a huge alimony settlement demanded of her.

The issue of appearance becomes even more compelling with the recent announcement of discoveries involving the genetic and biological basis of aging. New drugs are being tested which seem to reduce skin wrinkling. Retin-A is a derivative of vitamin A; liposomes are microscopic molecules which can be loaded with material and targeted to reach "sluggish" cells. Geneticists at Baylor University are working on finding the body agent which causes cellular decay and thus the aging process itself. One of these researchers has recently reported: "Our results tend to support the hypothesis that cellular senescence in human cells is the result of programmed internal changes, not the accumulation of damage." If medical intervention can modify these internal changes, in time aging as a body experience may no longer exist.[19]

Growth hormone supplements, used to prevent dwarfism in children deficient in the growth hormone, have proved capable of slowing some effects of aging. Administered to twenty-one older men, the hormone built muscle mass, decreased fat, and thickened skin tissue. At present the hormone is extremely expensive, and it may have deleterious side effects.[20] But the discovery sparks fantasies of the reappearance of Steinach-like clinics, where wealthy people once went for X-ray treatments and injections of substances from animal glands to retard aging. Will even further distinctions come into being between the wealthy and the poor in the matter of appearance? Beyond that, as life span increases and scientists may discover the body agent that causes aging, vast ethical issues are raised. These issues include the meaning of aging for all of us and the nature of the relationships we all form.

The identification of aging with appearance raises another ethical issue, the matter of class. Given class differentials in diet and in access to health aids like regular exercise programs, entry to a more positive aging may be restricted primarily to people of means. Indeed, the media fascination with age-disparate relationships between aging women and younger men may mask the real issue of poverty among aging women, especially among single aging women. Throughout this book I have paid attention to this class issue, which exists in the present as in the past. A number of recent researchers have argued that there has been a "feminization of poverty" among the elderly over the last twenty years. Although poverty rates among the elderly have declined over the last decade, today women constitute 72.4 percent of the elderly poor, although they account for only 58.7 percent of all the elderly. Approximately 2.5 million or 15.2 percent of noninstitutionalized women aged sixty-five or over live below the poverty threshold, compared with only 8.5 percent of elderly men.[21]

Robyn Stone finds the reasons for these differentials in the higher rates of women living alone (due to greater rates of widowhood among them) in addition to men's greater earning potential at all points across the life span. Inequalities affecting women within the Social Security system and the lack of value assigned to women's unpaid labor as housewives also are factors in producing greater rates of poverty among aging women than aging men. Additionally, there is women's greater responsibility for caring for elderly parents, a factor which may limit their ability to participate in the work force on a regular basis. According to one analyst, many elderly women are "only one man away from poverty."[22]

The Marriage Crunch: Recent Actual and Ethical Meaning of Age-Disparate Relationships Between Older Women and Younger Men

O VER THE PAST five years or so, writers of letters consulting advice columnists like Ann Landers and Joyce Brothers have occasionally asked these columnists their opinion of age-disparate relationships between aging women and younger men. In 1990 Joyce Brothers advised a mother who had written because of concern about her twenty-seven-year-old son, who was dating women in their mid-thirties. B.K., the mother, in her letter asked Brothers: "Is this practice unhealthy and unusual?" Brothers answered with an unqualified no. She offered advice that echoed themes articulated over the centuries—from Plutarch to Andreas Castellanus to Daniel Defoe. There is, she contended, no difference between older men dating younger women and older women dating younger men. Young women frequently prefer older men because of their greater maturity and financial security. Why shouldn't young men find the same qualities attractive in older women? Besides, Brothers continued, women mature emotionally sooner than men and reach their sexual peak later; thus for a number of reasons the coupling of older women with younger men makes sense.[23]

Brothers also turned to demography for her answer. Citing Census Bureau statistics, she pointed out that in the United States single men in their twenties outnumbered single women of the same age by more than a 6-to-5 ratio, comprising about 2.3 million more unmarried men in their twenties than women of similar age. Moreover, these young men must compete for partners with older, more affluent men. Given these factors, dating upward in age range for heterosexual young men should be not only acceptable but even imperative.

Thus demography dictates what emotional and sexual response ratify. Yet Brothers's positive reply to the question of the acceptability of couplings between men in their mid-twenties and women in their mid-thirties is hardly surprising, given contemporary age definitions which still permit women in their thirties to be considered young. What about women in their forties and fifties? What about the *Harold and Maude* situation, in which a woman of seventy-nine becomes the sexual initiator of a man of twenty-one? In the film, the priest whom Harold visits finds disgusting the physical coupling of a young, virile body with an old, decaying one. Would most people respond in such a manner? Or is the contemporary permissive culture ready to accord respectability to a variety of formerly censored behaviors?

Over the past several decades, one can see changing attitudes. The rise in popularity of the feminist critique of Freudianism, as well as that of humanistic psychology, has been important in revising negative attitudes toward aging and age-disparate relationships. Feminists like Kate Millet have contended that Freud's behavioral categories like penis envy and Oedipal love are not biological, as he asserted, but rather result from patriarchal power relationships between males and females. (Indeed, given the numbers of mothers in the work force whose children spend significant time in child care, mothers and sons hardly have sufficient time together any longer to develop symbiotic Oedipal bonds.) Feminist neo-Freudians like Nancy Chodorow have shifted the Freudian blame placed on mothers for deficient personality development to fathers' lack of participation in childrearing.[24]

Books like Gail Sheehy's *Passages* have popularized a focus in concepts of personality formation on life-stage development rather than just the childhood years. As much as these works of humanistic psychology may be faulted for downplaying individual variations in life-cycle development, they have brought to the forefront the possibility of change throughout the life cycle. This personality development literature focusing on the life span often presents the middle years in terms of difficulty (the so-called mid-life crisis). But these writers also identify these years as a milestone period marking the transition to an older age which can be a pinnacle of life experience. Many now judge the middle period of life as a time which can culminate in what Abraham Maslow as early as 1939 called "self-actualization" and what Erik Erikson later categorized under the term "generativity."[25]

Much recent literature on this question of later life process finds that women more easily than men deal with both the transition to older age as well as the later years. Some analysts assert that women do not experience the mid-life crisis typical of men; others contend that even the "empty nest" syndrome, a period of depression into which women presumably fall when their children leave home, has ceased to exist. The acceptance of women within the work force, in particular, has provided mid-life women with new options and a sense of empowerment, while their own relief at the ending of the burden of child care counters any depression over familial and personal loss. Analysts identified with feminism as well as others within gerontology assert that women are more empathetic, open, and connected to others than men. Thus women more easily engage in the process of positive life review and of caring for others which many psychologists posit as the proper path to achieving "self-actualization."[26]

Once such academic and expert viewpoints become accepted within popular thought, we may see a heightened appreciation of aging women and a heightened occurrence of relationships between older women and younger men. Times of crisis generate conformity: the denigration of such age-disparate unions from the 1920s on had much to do with the crisis mentality of Depression and war. During these decades of insecurity, families had to be stable; hierarchies like the one based on separation between youth and age had to be preserved. Defining people as different and as strange in their difference provides a kind of self-satisfaction, a way in which negative categorization brings comfort.

Our own era of narcissistic individualism has had varied impacts on conforming trends. On the one hand it has produced self-indulgence, a definition of the good life in terms of material display and self-aggrandizing individual achievement. On the other hand, it has brought a willingness to allow others their own realms of successful performance. In combination with the widespread influences of feminism, it has produced a generation of young men raised by working mothers who do not hold to the old stereotypes of disparate gender behavior. It is a truism of the modern age that the older "male breadwinner" mentality, which viewed working wives as threats to their husbands' self-pride, has been seriously eroded. Concurrently, certain younger men pay scant heed to older imperatives about proper masculine behavior. *Ebony* magazine traces the genesis of the recent upsurge in age-disparate relationships between aging women and younger men among blacks to the freer motivations of a new generation of men raised according to the new, less bifurcated, gender definitions.[27]

Moreover, new scientific data regarding male procreation may erode venerable beliefs about women's attractiveness ending when their procreative ability ceases. These new data suggest a decline in male procreative ability with age. They also suggest a correlation between male procreative ability and their sexual performance ability. A decline in male procreative ability occurs after the age of thirty-five, with a marked change between the ages of forty-one and forty-five. This change can include low sperm count, blocked sperm ducts, and defective sperm. Defective sperm are a primary cause of miscarriage, and paternal age is more important than maternal age in at least one form of Down's syndrome.[28] These data suggest that although men can father children throughout their life span, doing so at later ages may be perilous.

Aging men's procreative ability has been questioned, and new medical technologies may break down the barrier between pre- and postmenopausal women, thereby positioning the latter as more attractive marital partners. Recently, physicians using sophisticated reproductive technologies have successfully induced childbearing in menopausal women. The procedure involves gathering eggs from younger, still fertile women (since menopause involves the end of a woman's egg supply). Fertilization is carried out in a test tube, a fertilized egg is implanted in the older woman's uterus, and gestation then takes place in that woman's womb. Hormonal supplements are given so that the fertilized egg will attach to the uterus. According to Marcia Angeli, suggesting that this procedure could have widespread application, "the limits on the childbearing years are anyone's guess."[29]

Yet whatever procreative possibilities exist for menopausal women, these possibilities cannot counterbalance the demographic fact that aging women outnumber aging men in the population in sizeable proportions. This fact, already apparent in the 1930s, became strikingly evident several years ago, when what came to be called the "marriage crunch" gained widespread media attention. A statistical study of recent marriage patterns by several Harvard and Yale professors generated the furor in 1986 and 1987. In this study, based on statistical projections from 1980 census figures, the authors contended that if a woman college graduate was not married by twenty-five she had only a 50 percent chance of ever marrying. If not married by thirty-five, her chances were 5 percent. By forty she had almost no chance of marriage. The implication was, by extension, that older women in general had no chance of remarriage.

Given rising rates of age of first marriage, especially among college graduates, the specter was raised of the recurrence of a large body of aging spinsters. The charge was insinuated that these women, like their nineteenth-century forerunners, would be incapable of finding husbands and true life satisfaction in marriage. They would once again become a presumed national problem. For months newspapers and magazines included stories on the issue; it generated headlines on evening television newscasts and became a regular part of comedians' patter. Interest reached a height when *Newsweek* devoted a cover to a graph showing that as women grow older their chances of marrying drop precipitously. *People* magazine showed pictures of Linda Ronstadt, Diane Sawyer, and other prominent unmarried women with a caption asking if these women were "old maids."[30]

Commentators pointed out the many flaws in the Harvard-Yale study: only individuals officially married were included; no attempt was made to investigate motives; male marriage prospects were overlooked; the data could be interpreted to yield differing statistical results. Even elite magazines like *Mademoiselle* pointed out that the "marriage crunch" might well disappear if the Harvard-Yale study's subjects had included census-designated "posslqs" (persons of the opposite sex sharing living quarters), in addition to lesbian women and women who preferred to be single. Writing in the *Los Angeles Times*, Ben Wattenberg cited a study by Jeanne Moorman, a demographer employed by the Census Bureau. Moorman contended, using the same statistics as the Harvard-Yale authors, that marriage rates for college women were actually on the rise and that all the projections of the celebrated study needed significant revision upward.[31]

Behind the mania over the "marriage crunch" lay fears of the impacts of feminism and of its possibility for revolutionizing traditional arrangements. Women working in remunerative employment outside of the home increase national productivity and swell family income for consumption as well as enhancing their personal life satisfaction. If they are married the threat they may pose to traditional arrangements is vitiated. Yet women not involved in stable marital heterosexual relationships are outside of male control; their very being threatens traditional definitions of the patriarchal family. Once again the specter of the "old maid" was used to contain women.

Some analysts of marital prospects for aging women have focused on demographic differentials at various points along the life span. And here they find striking disparities between women and men in later ages, apart from any projections as to their future marital prospects. Thus one observer noted that in 1985 for every hundred women between the ages of thirty-eight and forty-two, there were only seventy-seven men. For later ages, the demographic disparity is even more striking. By the year 2000, according to sociologist Matilda Riley, there will be sixty-five men for every hundred women sixty-five years of age and older, and thirty-seven men for every hundred women eighty-five years of age and older.[32] The fact that women on the average lived longer than men over the centuries consistently produced small numbers of women living to older ages. Under modern conditions of more effective health care this phenomenon has begun to have major population impacts.

Forming relationships downward in the age structure may be a solution for some of these women to the problem of the "negative sex ratio" among the aging. Indeed, available statistics seem to show that this behavior is on the increase. In 1985, of 255,000 women aged thirty-five to forty-four polled by the Census Bureau, 32 percent were living with younger men, while of 200,000 women aged forty-five to sixty-four, 23 percent were living with younger men. According to 1987 figures from the National Center for Health Statistics, in 1970, 16 percent of marriages were between older women and younger men, while in 1980 these figure stood at 22 percent.[33]

Yet if age ranges are taken into consideration, these differentials become much less substantial. In 1970, 3.7 percent of wives were five years or more older than their husbands; in 1980 the figure stood at 6.2 percent. And, as one analyst points out, this was an elite phenomenon. Most of these relationships were to be found among middle-class professionals.[34] Thus without a significant reversal in attitudes toward older people, it is difficult to see how couplings which overturn age categories can be anything more than a partial solution to this problem of aging women without men.

But is it a problem? Do we not privilege heterosexuality and overlook aspects of its nature as socially constructed by denigrating women living alone—or with other women? Is heterosexual intercourse the only key to personal fulfillment? In stressing that aging people maintain sexual responsiveness throughout their lives, have experts not created a new tyranny for aging people, one of obligatory sexual performance for personal fulfillment? Centuries-long definitions of aging women as sexual beings fed into the prevailing misogynistic ageism. Contemporary popular writings which valorize heterosexual intercourse run the risk of creating two opposing groups of aging women, those with men and those without. Once again, as so often in the past, women may be placed in the position of competing for men, now privileged by demography.

Statistics may elucidate reality, but they do not address issues of social ethics or private morality. Throughout this book I have addressed questions concerning relationships. I have suggested that Margaret Fuller and Colette found happiness with younger men, and I have praised the "sacred marriage" ceremony as a generative alternative to Odysseus's killing of the suitors. I have noted the evidence that younger men were major accusers of seventeenth-century witches and that in the eighteenth century Julie de Lespinasse's life was destroyed by her involvement with a younger man.

I have wished that Billy Wilder had scripted *Sunset Boulevard* differently, to make Hedda Hopper, Norma Desmond, and Betty Schaefer confederates and not opponents, and I have wondered if the Wife of Bath would not have been happier had she given up her obsessive search for a man and spent her time traveling and laughing with her friend, her "gossip," the other Alison. I have attempted to expose the myth of Sappho and Phaon; I have argued that in many eras widowhood was preferable to marriage; and I have suggested that Simone de Beauvoir found her greatest happiness in later life with a woman thirty years her junior.

At the end of the long journey I have taken in writing this book, I find myself more interested in personhood than in relationships. What interests me now is working out how one comes to understand the meaning of aging in one's own life, rather than in finding meaning through another, however satisfying that association may be. In 1975 therapists Jean Sanville and Joel Schor published their findings regarding their older women patients who had been involved with younger men. In every instance the relationship had succeeded for a time but had broken apart in the end. They concluded that for these women younger men had been a way station on the road to maturity. The relationships had represented an acting out of needs for dependence and power, a way of healing old wounds before moving on to greater independence.[35]

In *Journey Through Menopause*, Christine Downing found her younger male companion deficient, while she discovered several mentors in aging men. From this perspective, for women relationships with younger men may simply be a point on the life process, an event and not an ending.

Many women novelists in the twentieth century have turned their attention to this issue of aging contentment. Many have found life's truest joy in later years in solitude or in an elemental communion with nature. In her study of women's fiction in the twentieth century, Annis Pratt notes that many women authors develop in their later work the central figure of a wise old woman. These women are at home with themselves. They are often surrounded by plants and animals, while they share their wisdom with others. In works by Sarah Orne Jewett, Ellen Glasgow, Doris Lessing, and Mary Ellen Chase, according to Pratt, there is not so much a turning away from sensuality and relationships as an acceptance of a dialectic between these relationships and a wider world to explore. Still, what concerns these authors is moving beyond sexuality to self-fulfillment, to an enriched creativity and human understanding.[36]

This project of understanding aging may be a key task for feminists who in the 1960s launched that movement which has reshaped gender relations over the last three decades. These women, like Betty Friedan and Gloria Steinem, are now in their fifties and sixties. The task is especially important because the following generation, the so-called baby boom generation, has for the most part accepted the feminist goal of individual self-fulfillment while rejecting the goal of social justice. And, the generation following the baby boom cohort, the generation of young people now in their twenties and early thirties, seems even more self-centered. These young people were nurtured on the Vietnam War and on governmental scandals like Watergate. With declines in economic abundance in the United States, if they are middle-class they face for the first time since World War II the possibility of "downward social mobility." According to one analyst of this generation, middle-class young people have thrown themselves into their careers, finding in work the real modus vivendi.[37]

Just as gender justice means more than material gratification, so the wisdom of aging means more than simply extending the definition of youth into age, of allowing older people to think of themselves as young. And it means more than simply securing individual contentment, of finding a way to exist without taking others into account.

The task is rendered even more imperative in light of the fact that previous generations of feminists have not focused on aging as a central part of their agendas. During the 1890s, I have argued, many aging women became actively involved as members and leaders of woman's rights and reform associations: they were the mainstays of many Progressive-era organizations. This phenomenon holds true throughout the 1920s and 1930s and until the 1960s, when young women were the primary instigators of the era's feminism. From the 1890s to the 1960s, older women remained a major constituency of members and leaders in the women's clubs, the League of Women Voters, the Woman's Party, and other such organizations.[38]

Yet despite their aging, these activist women paid scant public attention to it; the matter of their life-stage position remained private. In contrast to women novelists exploring matters of life and death, of generativity and aging self-fulfillment, activists' attention was drawn to social issues or to matters like birth control and abortion which were issues for younger women. From Elizabeth Cady Stanton to Betty Friedan, from Charlotte Perkins Gilman to Andrea Dworkin, despite the depth and variety of feminist writings over the course of this century, the writings on aging women are few and far between. General books on women occasionally contain a chapter on aging; periodicals like the *Woman's Journal* or the

Woman Citizen, major activist sheets, from time to time include an article on the subject.

Margaret Mead in the 1950s wrote about "postmenopausal zest." But despite the popularity of *The Second Sex,* Simone de Beauvoir's negative comments about menopause and aging went unnoticed; Helene Deutsch and the Freudians seemingly carried the day. (On the other hand, Betty Friedan's forthcoming work on aging may reverse this trend. And, if Friedan's book has the same impact as her 1963 *Feminine Mystique*, aging may, indeed, become a major women's issue.)[39]

I do not deny that since the 1960s vigorous organizations advocating the rights of the elderly have appeared. The American Association of Retired People, for example, numbers its members in the hundreds of thousands. Its *Modern Maturity* depicts vigorous, attractive aging people. The decline in poverty among the elderly over the last decade is undoubtedly due to the political efforts of these organizations. The National Organization for Women has always included a task force on aging among its national task forces. Yet, among other commentators, Barbara MacDonald has castigated feminist scholars and activists for rendering as invisible the lives of older women. Her contention is that:

> From the beginning of this wave of the women's movement, from the beginning of women's studies, the message has gone out to those of us over sixty that your "Sisterhood" does not include us, that those of you who are younger see us as men see us—that is, as women who used to be women but aren't any more. You do not see us in our present lives, you do not identify with our issues, you exploit us, you patronize us, you stereotype us. Mainly you ignore us.[40]

The reason for this inattention is partly ironic: most American women of achievement have experienced their menopausal and postmenopausal years as sufficiently personally empowering and invigorating that they did not feel the need to comment on them. Other issues seemed more important: for Elizabeth Cady Stanton the compelling issues became birth control and religious obscurantism; for Susan B. Anthony, suffrage. Jane Addams's primary interest became peace; for Julia Lathrop, Florence Kelley, and Lillian Wald, interest in the social justice and social service issues they had pursued in their earlier years continued to be preeminent in their later lives. As was the case for Margaret Mead, postmenopausal zest was of real meaning to them.

Yet like the broader age cohorts to which they belong, feminists over the course of the twentieth century have often experienced significant generational discontinuity, as younger women coming to maturity have avoided or misinterpreted their message. This discontinuity was as much a part of the generation which came to maturity in the 1920s as it has been of recent "postfeminist" generations, searching for a "new traditionalism." In the 1920s the flapper era privileged sexuality and the family as primary sources of satisfaction for women and pictured their activist predecessors as mannish and unfulfilled. In the 1980s a new romanticization of the nuclear family went along with a similar demonization—this time not only of activist women but also of working women as unfulfilled if they have not married and had children.

In recent times the baby boom generation overlaps with the "postfeminist" generation. The latter involves those women who, now in their thirties and forties, believe that the gains in women's position over the last decades were easily achieved and that the "women's libbers" were man-hating, "bra-burning" radicals. Such a distortion of a movement whose politics extended throughout the political spectrum and without whose agitation the gains for women of the past twenty years could not have been possible borders on the laughable, if it were not so dangerous. There is healing to be accomplished and a generation of aging people, as well as younger ones, to address.

I have no specific agenda to put forward, no platform to propose. I have suggested my concern that aging women find ways of celebrating their aging and of redefining menopause as a positive experience. What interests me here are models for aging, symbols of empowerment that might span the generations to bring comity and to engender personal self-fulfillment as well as social change. How we construct ourselves as human beings, what kinds of social trajectories we decide to pursue, become even more compelling as we enter the last years of our lives. It may not be enough to claim the designation "wise" because we sense an increased personal authority with aging. "Crone" ceremonies held at the age of fifty may not be sufficient to address these issues. Indeed, we need to decide what the social as well as the personal category of "wisdom" implies.

At this point I want to return to those major figures with which I began this exposition of the story of aging women and to which I have upon occasion turned throughout this book: the figures of the ancient goddesses. I do not, at this point, intend further to pursue their relationships with younger men. Rather I want to explore the triune nature of those early figures: their existence as maidens, mothers, and crones, the ways in which their personas might be seen to encompass the cycles of aging to make the last stages of life more profound and empowering.

And I intend to do so in a context which I have not yet addressed in this book. In the Introduction I raised the issue of traditions of strength among black women and the meaning of that strength for all women. One might extend that speculation further to include Hispanic women and Native American women. Traditions of goddesses as symbols of female strength in Western European culture over the ages have become attenuated, often reappearing only with glimmerings of their former meanings. That is not the case among black women and Native American women, for whom a matrilineal past and a tradition of goddesses is reflected in the strength of aging women and the veneration accorded them. The denigration of aging women characteristic of the general American culture, for example, does not extend to black culture. Among blacks, aging women are valued.[41]

I have traveled a long distance, through many centuries of European development, to draw my last illustrations from people who have long been here. But I have recently realized that I myself am the child of European immigrants and that I was raised in an ethnically centered home. Yet once in the United States, my parents and grandparents accepted the mythology of modernization. They accepted what the culture of their new land held; they came to believe that virtue belongs to the young and that the aging are not wise, only obsolete. So my mother and grandmother became shapeless figures as they aged. What seemed to me then to be stupidity or senility in them I now realize was only emotional depression, the sense that life had passed them by. They had lost their European traditions in the rush to Americanize and modernize; they accepted the American valorization of youth, and they did not know how to be wise.

To re-create that sense, I find I must turn to other cultures. To provide clarity to my exposition, I have chosen black culture as a source of illumination. Alternatively, I could have surveyed Native American culture or Hispanic culture for such lessons. All have suffered minority status; it might be said of each in varying ways, that they have the potential of encompassing both the marginalized status within the dominant American civilization they inhabit and that dominant American culture center that encompasses them. The question I raised in the introduction to this work about black women's experience as paradigmatic of the experience of all women is here answered; their special season in suffering has created the potential for a special personality among them. As bell hooks has written of blacks:

> Living as we did—on the edge—we developed a particular way of seeing reality. We looked both from the outside in and from the inside out. We focused our attention on the center as well as on the margin. We understood both. This mode of seeing reminded us of the existence of a whole universe, a main body made up of both margin and center. Our survival depended on an ongoing public awareness of the separation between margin and center and an ongoing private acknowledgement that we were a necessary, vital part of that whole.[42]

In her study of mental health data collected on a national scale and broken down by race and class, Rose Gibson provides insight into the existence of this personality. She points out that up to the age of seventy-five, whites can expect to live longer than blacks. After that age, however, blacks live longer than whites. This greater life longevity is especially true for black women. According to Gibson, many factors contribute to what she calls a "racial mortality crossover." Biology may lie behind the differential: because blacks survive inadequate care earlier in life, they may be a more biologically select group at advanced ages. Psychological factors also may apply. There is, for example, less suicide among aging black females than among white females—or among black or white men.[43]

Gibson's data also show that aging black women have a more positive attitude toward life than any other group within American society. She traces this positive attitude to more effective help-seeking patterns in times of need. When seeking help, aging white women characteristically turn to spouses. When spouses are not available, they turn to other single family members, thus relying on limited numbers of individuals for aid. Aging black women, on the other hand, will depend on a variety of interactions and various kinds of informal kin and community support networks.

As I often have in this book, I will turn to novels for illumination. In this case my guides will be black writers Toni Morrison and Alice Walker and beyond them, Zora Neale Hurston, who profoundly influenced both Morrison and Walker. In the writings of Morrison and Walker, folk traditions of aging wise women with indomitable personalities forged through lives of suffering are preeminent. In Walker's works, in particular, traditions of the ancient goddesses become metaphors for the strength of aging women. Zora Neale Hurston's major work, her 1937 *Their Eyes Were Watching God*, is about the relationship between an aging woman and a younger man.

A Model for Empowerment:
Aging Women in Black Literature and Life

WITHIN WHITE CULTURE, the stereotype of the aging black woman has mirrored that of the white grandmother, as a person devoted to the service of others. The "Mammy" figure has long predominated in characterizations of aging black women. This persona was derived from southern plantation mythology of loyal women slaves who raised their mistress's children, supposedly loving these white children more than their own offspring. This stereotype of self-involvement in the service of others, of having no real race consciousness, has extended through post–Civil War imagery of black domestics and cooks happily working as servants in white households. The Mammy is apparent in the fictionalized "Aunt Jemima," devised early in the century as the brand figure of a popular line of pancake-making products. In Aunt Jemima advertisements the fictionalized black figure has a round, bulbous body and a contented smile on her face.

The Mammy stereotype is also there in the "Mammy" that white singer Al Jolson, in blackface, celebrated in the famous song in the first sound movie, *The Jazz Singer*. Her fame as a standard character of thirties films is exemplified by Hattie McDaniel's character in the movie version of *Gone With the Wind*, a saga of slavery and the Civil War. This Mammy, characterized according to the standard mythology, remains loyal to her white family throughout the war and after emancipation. Until 1991, McDaniel was the only black woman to have won an Academy Award for acting.

Yet, in opposition to this image of contentment, recent studies of plantation slavery conclude precisely the opposite. White mistresses overworked their slaves. The latter disliked their position and concealed discontent because constrained by their subordinate position. During the era of plantation slavery, comity between black and white women was difficult, if not impossible. Women of differing races were divided by the chasms of race and hierarchy and by a sexual system under which white women's husbands, the ultimate masters of both black and white women, often demanded sex of female slaves. Historian Catherine Clinton finds that black slaves had little contact with white households except in subordinate positions: the Mammy figure, she concludes, was a "figment" of the southern imagination constructed to romanticize slavery and to conceal its brutality. Elizabeth Fox-Genovese concurs. She writes: "Slaveholding women and slave women shared a world of mutual antagonism and frayed tempers that frequently erupted in violence, cruelty, and even murder."[44]

After Emancipation, such antagonisms also characterized relationships between white housewives and their black domestic slaves, both South and North. Because of racist and sexist attitudes endemic to industrial and clerical labor, domestic service was the major area of employment for black women until after World War II. If overt oppression and violent reaction on the part of servants was muted in this wage labor system, nonetheless investigators agree that old racist and class-bound attitudes permeated it. Servants were poorly paid; they were overworked; they were expected to subsume loyalties to their families to loyalty to the family of employment. The Mammy stereotype of black women's contentment in service continued to conceal discrimination and discontent, as according to historian Jacqueline Jones, "the white mistress–black maid relationship preserved the inequalities of the slave system."[45]

The Mammy figure has concealed many aspects of the realities of black women's lives. Her asexuality, for example, has covered over the sexuality of black women's aging and has perhaps served to reinforce similar attitudes about aging white women. Black women, however, have challenged this stereotyping of their sexuality. Black women vocalists of the blues tradition of the 1920s and 1930s especially expressed a subversive sexuality. The often large and voluptuous bodies of these women provided an alternative to the thin body of the white beauty ideal, while providing another, richer dimension to the "Aunt Jemima" look. They ratified what contemporary singer Bernice Reagon has written about alternative black beauty standards: "I came out of a black community where it was all right to have hips and to be heavy."[46]

The blues women reclaimed women's bodies from objectification, demonstrating the respect and power of aging women within the black population. They dressed and lived in high style, and the black community called them "goddesses" and "high priestesses." They also called themselves "Ma" (as in Ma Rainey, their originator); the term "red-hot mama" derived from the sexuality of their lyrics and style. This presentation posed a contretemps to folk traditions of sadness and sorrow, of the plaintive blues beat of their musical rhythms.

The physical presence of these women was an aspect of their authority; the throaty pathos or raucous country sound of their voices and the critical content of their lyrics implicitly protested poverty and racism, as well as male violence against women. They used the theme of relationships with younger men to assert authority: in her performances Ma Rainey would joke about craving young men, calling them "pig meat" and "bird liver." Their black audiences knew their songs and their life stories: these women vocalists instilled through their performances "a shared communal feeling half as entertainment and half as public ritual and celebration."[47] In this regard, their style was related to the "call and response pattern" typical of slave songs. This venerable pattern of song involved vocalized interaction between leader and follower, singer and audience. Many analysts view the method as characteristic of much black vocal and written expression.

The 1930s Depression precipitated a decline in sales in the black record industry that had supported and promoted the blues women. With fewer of their records being produced, their popularity decreased. Many of them, like Ethel Waters and Hattie McDaniel, survived financially by playing roles as film "mammies," the subordinated aging black women servants of 1930s films.

In addition to camouflaging black women's sexuality, the domesticated Mammy figure has also served to conceal black women's activism, their involvement in movements to effect social change. Since slavery and throughout this century, black women's participation in black reform and social service organizations has been as important as the participation of white women in similar white organizations. Black women have organized in church sodalities, in leagues for education and in women's clubs, in rural movements to stop lynching, and in urban movements for economic and social justice, especially during the 1960s. During the civil rights and antipoverty movements of that era local black women were crucial to organizing the black community in southern rural hamlets as well as northern urban ghettoes; often they were older and experienced and thus assumed leadership. "In every southwest Georgia county," wrote a student organizer, "there is always a 'mama.' She is usually a militant woman in the community, out-spoken, understanding, and willing to catch hell, having already caught her share."[48]

The domesticated Mammy figure has also been used to denigrate black women as destroyers of community harmony through the charge of having constituted a debilitating matriarchy as a major family organization. Such accusations lodged against white women in the post–World War II era became muted after the 1950s. But, directed against black women, they became of signal importance in the 1960s, especially through the famed Moynihan report on the black family. And the charges that black women created a destructive black matriarchy have continued to the present. The charge has been that the "matriarchal" family with father absent destroys the masculinity of black males, who become either apathetic or socially destructive without a male presence in the home in the form of the biological father. Thus by implication black women have been responsible for the socioeconomic ills of the black community.[49]

Yet Nancy Tanner has argued that matrifocality within the black community is not the same as the "momism" of white culture. "Momism," Tanner argues, proceeds from "gender-role dichotomization" (the drawing of precise differences between expected behavior of males and females). "It is affectively based, and it is of dubious legitimacy." But black matrifocality, according to Tanner, is based on drawing minimal differences between the genders. It is central to black culture, and it is normal and expected.[50] In contrast to whites, blacks expect that powerful women will exert authority in the family; their directing presence is not viewed as abnormal.

The "matriarchal" black Mammy overwhelming her children has further concealed the extensive support systems within black rural and urban communities. Many analysts have written about the black kin and friendship networks which provide child care and financial and emotional support to those within their communities who need these services. The Mammy figure and the charge of matriarchy have also obscured the varieties of domestic strategies black women employ to cope with home situations rendered even harsher by continuing extensive unemployment, decreasing government aid, and the difficulty of finding reputable day care.[51]

The underlying motif of the black Mammy figure as preeminently loyal to whites undercuts the real strength of black women within black communities. Maya Angelou's depiction in *I Know Why the Caged Bird Sings* of her strong-minded southern grandmother who raised her after her parents' divorce resonates in the powerful Lena Younger of Lorraine Hansberry's *Raisin in the Sun*. The wisdom and power of aging is also part of the characters of the many powerful, wise aging women in the works of Alice Walker and Toni Morrison. Within kin networks in black communities grandmothers or older "aunties" take in the children of divorce and death; they may raise the children of young women relatives considered too immature to parent children effectively.[52]

The importance of the grandmother in black communities, according to some scholars, can be traced to African roots. The West African societies from which most slaves were taken were matrilineal, if polygamous. In them, women lived in their own houses and raised their own children. Strong bonding among women was the norm: individual women called all women their own age "sister" and all women of their mother's age "mother." In these societies women were the farmers and traders. Some of them had women chiefs who looked after women's interests. Special deference was accorded to the elderly because of older people's perceived closeness to revered ancestors. These West African societies possessed an oral tradition, and within this tradition grandparents characteristically preserved and passed on family and tribal history, the lore and the wisdom of the folk.[53] Alice Walker acknowledges that she has often included older characters in her writings because so many of the stories she tells were stories that her mother first told her:

> Through years of listening to my mother's stories of her life, I have absorbed not only the stories themselves, but something of the manner in which she spoke, something of the urgency that involves the knowledge that her stories—like her life—must be recorded.[54]

Within the religion of these West African societies, divine pantheons often contained goddesses as either predominating figures or as coequal with male gods. Among the Yoruba, for example, the goddess Onile ("owner of the earth") or Oduduwa, as she was alternatively named, was recognized as the creator of the earth, as well as the progenitor of all human beings. Among the Ibo, temples that honored Ale (or Ala), the earth goddess, contained large sculptures of her with her children. In myth, she controlled all cosmic and chthonic forces.[55]

The black color of African goddess sculptures was related not only to the skin color of African women but also to the darkness of earth, to the soil as generative and maternal. Black is the color of fertile soil; more barren soils are lighter. Anthropologist Daniel McCall asserts that these African goddesses originated in Southwest Asia and that migrating peoples in the Neolithic period brought them to West Africa. The Egyptian goddess, Isis, often depicted as black, may have been a descendant of these black goddesses. And the famed black statue of the goddess Artemis (or

Diana) at Ephesus, the figure with multiple breasts covering her body, may have been modeled after these black African goddesses.[56]

Anthropologists Leonard Moss and Stephen Cappannari assert that the originating Near Eastern black goddess (filtered through the worship of Diana or Isis or Demeter brought to Europe) was also the source of European Black Madonnas. Black statues of the Madonna, many of them renowned for their ability to effect miracles, are to be found in churches and cathedrals in France, Germany, Italy, Poland, Spain, and Switzerland. Moss and Cappannari assert that chemical investigation has determined that the black color of many of these statues is not a product of aging over time; rather, the original artists intended them to be black. Roman settlers who worshipped Diana or Isis or Demeter, according to these anthropologists, brought the tradition of the black goddess as well as the black figures to Europe. With the triumph of Christianity, the earlier temples Roman settlers built to predominating goddesses were reconstructed as Christian churches. Concurrently, the original statues of ancient goddesses were reshaped into Madonnas, even as goddesses generally were reconstructed into the Virgin Mary of Christian belief. But the original statues still retained the blackness which indicated their heritage and celebrated the richness of the earth.[57]

If the oppression of black women is both similar to and different from that of white women, how do we differentiate between the two? In distinguishing between these differing oppressions, Aida Hurtado draws a compelling distinction between "seduction" and "rejection." White women, Hurtado argues, are seduced into a subservient role in a patriarchy controlled by white men. Black women, on the other hand, are from the outset rejected by that patriarchy.[58] Because patriarchial arrangements are often fashioned to give comfort and luxury to white women, many white women, she argues, experience no personal sense of oppression. Financial stability and woman-centered power within individual families may give them a false sense of equality. On the other hand, black women every day must face difficult encounters with racism, with government bureaucracy, with the deterioration of their communities. Even middle-class black women are not shielded from the indignities of being black and female. Thus poet Audre Lorde has written that:

> Women of color in America have grown up within a symphony of anger, at being silenced, at being unchosen. . . . And I say symphony rather than cacophony because we had to orchestrate those furies so that they do not tear us apart. . . .[59]

As a "new traditionalism" makes its way among white, middle-class women, and a "postfeminist" generation reinvents the myth of the sanctified domestic woman, the anger of black women at their trivialization may be the voice to which we should listen.

It is no accident, I propose, that among contemporary writers, black women have risen to the forefront. Their anger at the position of black women in white society, the powerful stories they have to tell about their people, the rich, lyrical cadences of the vocal and musical traditions from which they draw—all these features create a compelling novelistic dimension. These writers are the product of that black matrifocal tradition I have been tracing. Like Alice Walker, they tell their mothers' tales. Like the female blues singers, they articulate the sorrows and celebrations of their people. They glorify community by explicating its methods of survival and of transcendence. They draw on literary traditions like the slave narratives which powerfully represent human self-realization in the context of insupportable suffering. The tales they tell draw on that black oral tale-telling tradition which encourages retelling and expansion of basic themes and celebrates the storytelling skills of black people.[60]

Their themes, the cadences of their writing, relate to the rhythms of black music and speech on which so much of mainstream American popular culture in this century has been built. Like glossolaliac black fundamentalists, they speak in tongues, ecstatic and rapturous, common and encompassing, drawing through their polyphonic comprehensiveness both black and white women and men as their audiences. They want to reclaim matrilineal traditions and notions of black goddesses as symbols of holism and spiritual empowerment.[61]

Critic Barbara Christian has written: "This exploration of new forms based on the black woman's culture and her story has revitalized the American novel and has . . . opened up new avenues of expression, indelibly altering our sense of novelistic process."[62] Similarly, attending to black women's experience might open up new areas of sensibility, of understanding, and of authority for aging women within American culture as a whole.

Toni Morrison and Alice Walker*

THE NOVELS of Toni Morrison often include a group of women who have come to live together, whether bound by bloodlines or by a shared past. From her first novel, *The Bluest Eye*, in which three prostitutes inhabit the same apartment, to her most recent book, *Beloved*, in which three women of three generations live on the outskirts of town, these women usually exist on the fringes of their communities. They take in other outcasts and care for people abandoned by their friends, families, lovers. Thus Baby Suggs of *Beloved* runs a household "where not one but two pots simmered on the stove; where the lamp burned all night long. Strangers rooted there while children tried on their shoes. Messages were left there, for whoever needed them was sure to stop in one day soon."[63] Morrison's older women open their houses to those who need comfort and solace, as well as to those engaged in inner struggles who need to be near the vitality and strength of these women.

These older women also open their hearts to the people around them. Morrison's characters are never static, never fully defined in one state of being. As they grow, they develop. They face conflicts within both themselves and their community. Women such as Pilate and Baby Suggs, however, also represent a stability in the midst of flux. For it is they who possess a wisdom of the past and a knowledge of the workings of their communities. Both Sula, in *Sula*, and Sethe, in *Beloved*, retire, at the ends of the novels, to the bedrooms where their grandmother and mothers-in-law respectively lay before their deaths. They withdraw to the very spaces where they can feel the presences of their elderly relatives, where they can find peace in the memories of their mothers' and grandmothers' strengths and struggles. Both mothers' and daughters' retreats represent, finally, the failures of their communities, failures both to protect their members and to grow toward a deeper understanding of what these women have undergone.

If Eva and Baby Suggs have been broken by the hardship of their lives, then their daughters show how women grow into a fuller self as they age. What remains important about these older women is that, although often condemned by their communities for acts deemed reprehensible, they ex-

*This analysis of aging women in the novels of Morrison and Walker was written by Olivia Banner.

hibit, in their older age, a sense of strength and wholeness that provides them with their own sense of vision and of purpose. All of Morrison's characters must, at some point, come to terms with a self in solitude, independent of outside forces. It is especially her older women who are able to do so. Lena and Corinthian, Milkman's older sisters in *Song of Solomon*, live their lives in deference to Milkman. Yet when they reach middle age, the sisters free themselves from domination, finally able to tell Milkman the hurt he has caused them. They order him to leave their lives.

In three of Morrison's novels the tripartite organization of the matrifocal family replicates itself. In *Sula*, there is Eva, Hannah, and Sula; in *Song of Solomon*, Pilate, Reba, and Hagar; in *Beloved*, Baby Suggs, Sethe, and Denver. They do, in one sense, comprise three clans, in which the eldest symbolically or literally carries on the history of the family and beyond that the history of the black community, to deliver to the children what has come before. Baby Suggs makes sure that her daughter does not forget what white people have done to her; in *Song of Solomon*, Pilate will not allow Milkman, her nephew, to make the same mistake of incorporating himself unthinkingly into white society as Milkman's father has.

Karla Holloway and Stephanie Demetrakopoulos have written that "the older black woman in Morrison's work is the contemporary embodiment of the ancient goddesses, ancestral spirits and earth-mothers." In *Tar Baby* there are aging women who live in trees (a goddess symbol) and who inhabit dreams that are filled with symbols of fertility and life. It is Baby Suggs in *Beloved* who, through her appearance as a priestess, personifies the matrifocal role of the older woman. "Accepting no title of honor before her name, but allowing a small caress after it, she became an unchurched preacher, one who visited pulpits and opened her great heart to those who could use it."[64]

In warm weather, Baby Suggs takes her congregation into the woods, to the Clearing. There "she did not tell them to clean up their lives or to go and sin no more. She did not tell them that they were the blessed of the earth, its inheriting meek or its glorybound pure." These were messages passed on to oppressed peoples by their Christian leaders. Instead, she preaches a nature-bound religion, one which celebrates the life force in everyone. " 'Here,' she said, 'in this here place, we flesh; flesh that weeps, laughs; flesh that dances on bare feet in grass. Love it. Love it hard.' "[65] She keeps the community together, acting as both spiritual and emotional healer, adviser on all matters.

After all, it is the larger community that interests Morrison. Her greatest concern is the struggles of the black woman within a black community within a larger white world. As one commentator states: "Morrison's clan is a complex of values and mythologies. The presence of the ancestor is critical to its legacy and its promise and therefore blends the traditions of Africa with the contemporary realities of America. . . . A political view of age transmutes in Morrison to a view that encompasses the community, the culture, and especially the Black woman as she spiritually and physically carries the survival of the clan."[66] Baby Suggs is the one able to bring the black community together and teach them a new ethos of survival after emancipation; Baby Suggs is the force that heals Sethe, her daughter-in-law, after Sethe kills her own child trying to free her from impending slavery and death.

And it is Mother Earth, with the help of the old Creole woman Marie Therese, who accepts Son back into her arms at the end of *Tar Baby*. These women, then, carry the fate of the black community in their hands, as they provide the ability to understand the complexities faced by youth and to bring values of caring and nurturance back to their communities. They are the source of steadfastness and reliability in a community torn and changed throughout history.

Like Morrison, Alice Walker is concerned with the black community, but her writing is especially infused with a sense of women's spirituality. *The Color Purple* takes the form of letters written from Celie, a young black girl, to God. She addresses them in such a manner because, after her father has raped her, he tells her not to tell anyone but God about his act. Thus from the start of the novel male abuse is identified. Celie marries a man whose lover, Shug, returns. Shug is a singer, well-versed in the nightlife of big cities. She personifies the urban sophistication Celie lacks. As Celie nurses Shug back to life from sickness, the two develop a love for each other which becomes physical.

Celie discovers, when she and Shug are living together in Memphis, that Shug, now in her fifties, "got the hots for a boy of nineteen." As she explains it to Celie, she understands the difference in their ages but wants "just six months to have my last fling." Shug's love for the nineteen-year-old is pure lust: "He little. He cute. Got nice buns." In justification, she says, "I'm getting old. I'm fat. Nobody think I'm good-looking no more. . . . He's nineteen. A baby. How long can it last?"[67] Celie, left without Shug, develops a real relationship with her husband, teaching him to sew and sharing the secrets of her heart with him.

Celie's aging is a growth into understanding and freedom from the systems of patriarchy that have kept her in bondage. More importantly, as she grows she learns the value of loving everything around her, of writing to the "dear stars, dear trees, dear sky, dear peoples, dear Everything." She is now able to speak with the world around her, suppressing none of her knowledge and love. Through Shug and the worldview she teaches Celie inherent in their love, Celie grows from a hurt, abused child into a loving, robust, powerful woman. In fact, although Celie in old age feels "a little peculiar around the children," fearing that the children think that she and her peers are obsolete and out of step with the times, Celie herself has a different reaction. "I don't think us feel old at all," she asserts. "And us so happy. Matter of fact, I think this the youngest us ever felt."[68]

In *The Temple of My Familiar*, Walker takes this feeling to its extreme. Lissie, an old black woman, has lived for five thousand centuries, experiencing everything from evolution to the Civil War. She is always ready to impart her knowledge to those around her. Through Lissie, Walker reveals an ecofeminist philosophy. She uses the mouth of a great, wise older woman to impart this knowledge. Lissie recounts one of her lives: she lived in a tribal community of a few hundred people, her mother the queen of the tribe. "But she was not 'queen' in the way people think of queens today. No, that way would have been incomprehensible to her, and horrid. I suppose she was what queens were originally, though; a wise woman, a healer, a woman of experience and vision, a woman superbly trained by her mother. A really good person, whose words were always heard by the clan."[69] Thus Lissie puts forth the strength of older women as both leaders and teachers.

In addition, Lissie's mother has a familiar. "In these days of which I am speaking, people met other animals in much the same way people today meet each other."[70] Respect for animals and an understanding of their ways as equal to those of humans goes hand in hand with the tribe's way of life. Yet the story ends with Lissie incarnated as a boy, discovering he has white skin, and feeling his difference from the rest of the tribe, running to live forever alone, wearing dark skins which reassure him, yet which scare all the animals away. What the white tradition has done, Miss Lissie explains, is to destroy the African way of life, and in doing so, to desecrate a natural way of living through respect and love for the world around.

The problem Lissie faces is one faced by many of Morrison's characters: finding an African tradition in the attempts of white culture to erase black culture and, more importantly, struggling to find the black woman's tradition lost in a racist, male-dominated America. Part of Lissie's story takes her into the Inquisition and its slaughter of " 'pagan' heretics." In Lissie's mythology the daughters of the Moors were the first to be killed, for they wanted Christianity to allow the religion of the Great Mother, the religion of Africa, to exist in Europe as the Black Madonna. For Miss Lissie, this slaughter occurred because

> they said the mother of their white Christ (blond, blue-eyed, even in black-headed Spain) could never have been a black woman, because both the color black and the female sex were of the devil. We were evil witches to claim otherwise. We *were* witches; our word for healers.[71]

Moreover, the destruction of the followers of the black goddess obliterated the connection between black women and white women. "The blood sisterhood that African women shared with European women was gone as if it had never been."[72] Thus not only did patriarchal Christianity and Islam extinguish the worship of the goddess and tear apart African society but also through so doing it rent apart the ties that bound women to each other, helping to reinforce the structures of racism and sexism that keep women from helping each other.

Shug of *The Color Purple* reappears in *The Temple of My Familiar*. Her doctrines here are put forth in a pamphlet entitled *The Gospel According to Shug*. She states: "Helped are those who love the Earth, their mother, and who willingly suffer that she may not die. . . ."[73] Walker's use of an older woman, of a woman who has symbolically endured the pain of black women through all centuries and thus can serve as a spokeswoman for their sufferings, makes use of just that wisdom of mother earth. Walker brings back an African tradition which her characters are bereft of in America. She brings to them legends and stories which persecution has taken from them. And it is the older woman, the mother of the tribe, the goddess, who can speak for those who cannot speak, that brings forth wisdom.

Zora Neale Hurston: Their Eyes Were Watching God

BORN IN RURAL FLORIDA in 1901, Zora Neale Hurston was the progenitor of writers like Morrison and Walker, whose work reflects Hurston's focus on folk culture and the cadences of rural speech and mores. Famed in her own day, Hurston died in obscurity and poverty; it was Alice Walker who found her grave in an overgrown Florida cemetery and provided a headstone for her. Only recently has she been accorded a place in the canon of preeminent American writers.

In the 1920s and 1930s, Hurston was acclaimed a major talent. A graduate of Barnard College, trained in observation techniques by her teacher, anthropologist Franz Boas, she was among the first folklorists to collect the tales and traditions of the black folk of the South. As a novelist, she participated in the Harlem Renaissance and was a friend of Langston Hughes and Countee Cullen and the other members of that literary revival. Moreover, she counted herself among the 1920s movement of activists working toward the attainment of a "New Negro." Among artists this movement sought to repudiate racial stereotypes. According to her biographer, more than any black writer of her time, her work embodied an association with racial roots. "She was," according to this analyst, "the folk."[74]

Her 1937 novel, *Their Eyes Were Watching God*, reflects these themes in her own life. As well, the novel investigates issues relating to age and youth, to gender interactions and definitions and to the meaning of class identity. The work details the life story of Janie, a black southern woman living in the early twentieth century, as she attempts to reconcile her grandmother's class aspirations of upward mobility for her with her own desires for personal independence and for a romantic love that will have transcendent meaning. Janie is the daughter of a mother who was raped by her schoolteacher. She is raised by her grandmother, a former slave who was raped by her plantation master. Possessing light skin and a compelling beauty, Janie easily attracts men. She marries first a prosperous farmer and then a city man whose store becomes the center of the black community in which they live. Yet neither of these marriages brings her love or even contentment.

Both these husbands are older than she; both expect her to assume a subordinate role. Even her second husband, who initially attracts her with his stylish ways and his "hat set at an angle that didn't belong in these parts," eventually becomes surly and overbearing, employing physical beatings to ensure her submission. He denies her the right to speak in public or even to tell stories on her porch. For even though the porch is part of her house, in her community porches function as male-dominated public spaces for courting, joking, and storytelling.[75]

Left in her early forties a well-to-do widow, Janie attracts many men, drawn to her by her beauty and her money. Like many of the women of middle years whose stories I have chronicled in this book, Janie is faced in her midlife with choices both momentous and frightening. Up to this point her life has been conventional. She could continue it that way by marrying the respectable undertaker who is the most appealing possibility among the men of her own age who have come to court her.

When she meets and becomes involved with Tea Cake, a man twelve years her junior, her community is censorious. All the common epithets and arguments against such age-disparate relationships which have existed over the centuries are hurled against her. Her friends warn her that such a young man could only want her money. When he has taken possession of her bank account, he will speedily abandon her. The story of her townswoman Annie Tyler resounds in her ears, for it is a story often told in her community. At fifty-two Annie Tyler had been left a widow "with a good home and insurance money." But she lost it all to young men who took advantage of her. Finally, completely humiliated in the eyes of her community, she was taken away by her daughter to die in peace in a distant location.

> Mrs. Tyler with her dyed hair, newly straightened and her uncomfortable new false teeth, her leathery skin, blotchy with powder and her giggle. Her love of affairs, affairs with boys in their teens or early twenties for all of whom she spent her money on suits of clothes, shoes, watches and things like that and how they all left her as soon as their wants were satisfied.[76]

Yet for Janie with Tea Cake it is different. The odyssey they take together is one of shedding age barriers, class distinctions, gender rigidities, even cultural conventionalities. Tea Cake, as his name implies, has a gift for laughter and play. Under his tutelage Janie finds within herself the same life-enhancing abilities. Their love flourishes as together they take jobs as bean pickers in the Florida swamps. They abandon without regret her money and her social position to live among the kind of people Tea Cake has always claimed as his own. Among them Janie now finds true joy and nobility of spirit. What matters about their life here is not the work. Rather, what matters are the hours spent laughing, loving, joking, telling stories, singing, dancing. And, in contrast to her previous position as a woman of money and status who in reality lives in a nightmare of patriarchal subordination, Janie finds equality in this community of poverty. Her equality is symbolized by the men's acknowledgement of her abilities as a storyteller.

The men had big arguments here like they used to do on the store porch. Only here, she could listen and laugh and even talk some herself if she wanted to. She got so she could tell big stories herself from listening to the rest.[77]

Thus Janie acquires the power to speak; she finds her voice.

In the end of the novel, Tea Cake dies, after having been bitten by a rabid dog. In actuality Janie kills him with a shot from their gun as he, in a fit of insanity produced by the rabies he has contracted, attempts to kill her. The shooting itself is symbolic: it results from her basic human drive toward self-defense, but it also proceeds from her understanding that fate, or God, or whatever, has destroyed the person who brought her life's greatest joy. This love at its best had fulfilled what she had dreamed of at the beginning, when her grandmother persuaded her to marry for money and security. For her love for Tea Cake had been molded according to the organic unity exemplified throughout the novel by nature and especially by imagery connected with flowering trees.

Yet the murder in self-defense is also symbolic of the fact that even Tea Cake could and had participated in patriarchal domination. To assert his masculine mastery, he had occasionally beaten Janie. Although during the novel's progression she had seemed to forget these incidents, in the end her memory of them formed part of her reaction to Tea Cake's final episode of extreme violence.

What will happen to Janie we do not know. Assuredly as she ages she will not become like her grandmother, an older woman whose "head and face looked like the standing roots of some old tree that had been torn away by storm." A "foundation of ancient power that no longer mattered": that was Janie's grandmother before her death. Before Tea Cake died, he told Janie one possible truth about her aging. The truth was that she had found, in her middle years and with him, youth. "You'se uh lil girl baby all de time," he tells Janie. "God made it so you spent yo' old age first wid somebody else, and saved up yo' young girl days to spend wid me."[78]

But Tea Cake's truth is only one truth. After Tea Cake has died, Janie returns to the town where she had lived with her second husband, the place where she still possesses a house and is still a part of a community. Indeed, she returns to the women of that town, who are sitting on a porch, in space deemed male. She tells the story of her adventures with Tea Cake to them. It is day, and with the men at work the women draw strength from shared femaleness. They feel empowered, strong. With the men who "ruled" them absent, "their skins felt powerful and human."

Released for the day from heterosexual desire, male rationality becomes their province. Hurston, drawing from Biblical imagery, compares them to judges. "They became lords of sounds and lesser things. They passed nations through their mouths. They sat in judgment."[79]

Yet they are wise only for a moment. With the return of the men comes male objectification of women and the creation of divisions among women, anxious to please their men and jealous of each other. As they watch their menfolk admiring Janie's still-attractive face and body, the men inevitably objectifying her, they quickly return to conventionality and their normal censoring of Janie's behavior for having gone off with a young man and then not marrying him. The community of powerful women is broken, and Janie leaves them, to go to her own home.

Alone in her own house, Janie finds peace through romanticizing heterosexual love with her memory of Tea Cake. Here she seems to accept his judgment that, with him, she had become young and had realized her dream of oneness with nature, with herself, with another. Having achieved this wholeness in herself, she could never lose it. "Of course he wasn't dead. He could never be dead until she herself had finished feeling and thinking. The kiss of his memory made pictures of love and light against the wall."[80]

Yet, when Janie earlier had told the story of her adventures with Tea Cake to the women, Hurston had indicated a darker reality. For, Hurston indicates, as time goes by and the darkness of night comes, what has been beautiful in the dawn, in the youth of life, can become banal, oppressive, barren—as had Janie's first two marriages and her grandmother's life in its ending stages. In her bedroom, by herself in private space, the "kiss" of Tea Cake's memory "made pictures of love and light against the wall." In town, with the women in a public locale, as the day progressed during which she told her story the "kiss" took on a different meaning. For, as time went by, "time makes everything old so the kissing, young darkness became a monstropolous old thing while Janie talked."[81]

But this sense of the destruction of time passing might itself only be partial. For long before, when she was young, she had already learned that "God tore up the old world every evening and built a new one by sun-up." Even without Tea Cake, whether alone or with the women, the future held out hope.[82] The final truth of Janie's aging we can only wonder about and imagine. For Zora Neale Hurston, with all her wisdom, does not tell us. Life and its ending, in the end, remains mysterious.

Epilogue

THE THEMES I have charted and the stories I have told have been many and complex. Even then, there is more I could have investigated. I could have explored, for example, age-disparate relationships in recent works of literature like Brian Moore's 1956 *The Lonely Passion of Judith Hearne,* or John Braine's 1957 *Room at the Top,* or Larry McMurtry's 1966 *The Last Picture Show,* or Erica Jong's 1990 *Any Woman's Blues.* So often have recent novelists utilized this theme that such works are beginning to constitute almost a literary subgenre. (Love between aging women and younger men has emerged, too, as a subject in recent movies, like *Mrs. Soffel,* or *Bull Durham,* or *White Palace.*)

I have paid little attention to the topic of mother-son relationships, either in terms of eroticization or as analogues to my focus on a more adult typology. Nor have I especially examined conflict between generations. My reading of the social histories of individual regions and groups could have been endlessly extended, producing a tapestry so complex it might have been incomprehensible.

I have done minimal cross-cultural exploration, preferring instead to concentrate on the Euro-American experience in depth. Nor have I ventured into the subject of animal or primate behavior, despite recent work suggesting that aging females (among lions and elephants, for example) are the leaders among kin groupings who preserve memory and wisdom for the herd. A matrilineal organization also characterizes many chimpanzee groups (among primates closest to humans in genetic composition). Chimpanzees usually organize themselves with adult males kept separate from the band and with status passing through females in birth order proceeding from the mother. In her famed work on the chimpanzees of Gombe, Jane Goodall focuses on Flo, the aging dominant female still attractive to males of a variety of ages.¹ Such work suggests that the increased power of aging women, which I located as a constant in the European and American experience, may exist as a comprehensive natural strategy for survival and as a means of generational continuity.

My reading of the past has been intended to elucidate a number of themes. I have been concerned to illuminate the ways in which aging women have lived their lives, coping with empowering or disempowering stereotypes of them as dowagers, as grandmothers, as shrews, as Saint Annes, as wise women, as Sirens, or as witches. I have proceeded in line with my stated goal of providing a history that aging women can claim. I have read history as drama, both in individual lives and in the complex interweavings of society, politics, and economics. I have attempted to analyze cultural symbols and mythologies with regard both to general gender construction and how these have impacted on real societies and lives. I have noted important cultural and chronological breaks in aging women's experience. I have tried to show how, above all, these breaks can be grouped according to a cyclical progression in which ages of greater freedom seem to be followed by regressions into periods of greater repression.

Informing all else has been my focus on the primacy of patriarchy and the ability of this seminal institution to maintain masculine hegemony and gender hierarchy, despite variations in its effects over the centuries. Those cycles of women's experience I have identified correspond, I now think, to patriarchal regroupings, to the attempts to retain masculine dominance, especially when women contest it. These regroupings can be evidenced by a "remasculinization" of prevailing cultural modes, as in the Renaissance, or in the eighteenth-century response to the salon women, or in the late nineteenth-century reaction to the woman's rights movement of that era. Or they can take the form of negativizing redefinitions of images, idealizations, and stereotypes regarding women, as in the conflicting redefinitions of aging women's sexuality and of menopause over the centuries.

Behind regroupings and "remasculinizations," however, lies a consistent structure contained in the patriarchal valorization of violence and the continued objectification of women. This objectification is as apparent in today's billboard and magazine advertising as it was in the Renaissance eroticization of rape and the seventeenth-century pornographic fantasy that underlay the witchcraft persecutions.

When I began this book in the early 1980s, the theme of patriarchal redefinition and regroupings was not immediately apparent. At that point the successes of the women's liberation movement seemed assured, and the overturning of objectification and violence seemed only a matter of time. Such indices as women's entry into the work force and the supposed end to the double standard and new laws guaranteeing gender equality seemed to signal the end to patriarchy as a controlling institution. At the present point in time, nearly ten years later, I am not so certain. Signs of a new "feminine mystique" are all around us. Feminism has increasingly come under attack as outmoded and narcissistic; many individuals—even of liberal persuasion—reject even the use of the word "feminism."

And, a new remasculinization of our culture may be occurring. Thus we await the cultural impacts of a war in the Near East with almost no Western casualties and with technology triumphant, a celebration of masculine force triumphant. We listen to the commentary of men's leaders like Robert Bly. In his recent best-seller *Iron John,* Bly accuses the feminist movement of having "feminized" men, while he calls for the individual assertion of the "wild man" within all men and the reinstitution of male rites of passage, which he identifies as "still very much alive in our genetic structure."[2] To him the Adonis figure, the gentle male of classical belief I have praised, is regressive, and Zeus, the patriarchal god who overpowered women to gain hegemony, should become the symbol of a renewed masculine self-realization.

What all this means in terms of relationships and aging is hard to say. Will a new remasculinization produce a new generation of young men and women of conventional, gender-stereotyped disposition? Will aging women retreat to a stance of complacency? Will we discover the kinds of generational bonding and of wisdom that I find in the aging women portrayed by black women writers? Will new negative stereotypes based on old models of the spinster, of lesbians, of women activists, of aging women emerge (as they have in the past) to hamper the realizations of new agendas? Let us hope in the end we will be able to follow Carolyn Heilbrun's advice "to make use of our security, our seniority, to take risks, to make noise, to be courageous, to become unpopular."[3]

Throughout the writing of this book, in my own life I have lived the history I have written. In a sense, what I have learned through my reading and my own experience I knew at the beginning: that cultural conditioning is intensely powerful and that we all fear aging, even though we live in an era which, perhaps for the first time in history, offers us the possibility of overcoming traditional psychological and sociological barriers to accepting aging. Still we all contemplate coloring our hair or even undergoing face-lifts to maintain some appearance of youth. With regard to relationships, whether we are old or young and whether we form them with individuals of own own ages or of ages older or younger, they are never easy to continue or to perfect. They are always capable of producing complacency and betrayal, as well as contentment and joy.

Most of the individual tales I have told of aging women with younger men have been positive, in line with my stated purpose of celebrating not only aging but also unconventionality. Margaret Fuller found happiness with Giovanni Ossoli, as did Colette with Maurice Godeket. But I might also have told the story of Peggy Eaton, famed in the 1830s American Jacksonian era for her affair with (and marriage to) Senator and then Secretary of War John Henry Eaton. Left a widow many years later, at sixty-one she married her grandchildren's nineteen-year-old Italian dancing teacher who defrauded her of her fortune and then eloped with one of her granddaughters. Or there is Frenchwoman Gabrielle Russier, a 1950s French schoolteacher whose affair with one of her students caused a national scandal as well as her prosecution for corrupting the morals of a minor.[4] There are many such negative stories I could have told.

Passion and power are often at the heart of these stories, and they seem to show the depths of individual desire and contention, as well as the capriciousness of individual experience and of the narrative of history impacting on individual lives. Patriarchal power and hierarchy are also involved. In ancient myth Aphrodite and Persephone vied for the love of Adonis, as did Hera, Aphrodite, and Athena over the prize of beauty. Norma Desmond, hardly happy alone, yet incapable of friendship with women, found only despair in her affair with Joe Gillis. Even Margaret Fuller, a nineteenth-century forerunner of twentieth-century feminists, internalized cultural conventionalisms in her work as well as her life, as did Marie Stopes in the 1930s or even Simone de Beauvoir in the 1950s. All these examples show the power of patriarchy in dividing women and in influencing the self-construction of women of all persuasions.

Perhaps as I end this long historical meditation on relationships it is best to remember that we began this twentieth century in a time of hope, in an era when the "New Woman" was given many options for empowerment, none the least of which was friendship with other women and participation in social reform. Centuries-old denigrations of aging women and of menopause seemed to be overturned. Possibilities were there that barriers of age, race, and class might be ended. But this first wave of modern feminism was followed by an era when youth and sexuality became the measure of fulfillment and the position of aging women, like that of all women, became problematic.

Yet Clio, the Muse of history, is ever of ironic disposition: the past never repeats itself in exactly the same way. Thus it may be presumptuous of me to conclude on a troubled note. I prefer to offer hope. I prefer to assert that the new experience of aging and the new thinking about the later stages of life may, in fact, end aging women's position as doubly "the other." And this transition to a more promising future may afford us ways to overcome those dualisms of race, class, and gender that have troubled our civilization from its beginnings, and to return to what may have existed, whether in mythological construction or in reality: a prepatriarchal age of gender comity. Or perhaps rather than a return to an earlier age, this transition will be a maturing into a state of wisdom permeating all the ages and stages of life.

INTRODUCTION

1. Victoria Huston, *Loving a Younger Man* (Chicago: Contemporary Books, 1987), p. 2.

2. My argument here has been influenced by two sources. First, I respond to Terry Eagleton's concept that there are subtexts within texts that vary and enrich textual meaning. See Terry Eagleton, *Literary Theory: An Introduction* (Minneapolis: University of Minnesota Press, 1983), p. 178: "What seems absent, marginal or ambivalent about it [the literary work] may provide a central clue to its meanings." Second, although I respect Michel Foucault's concept of the ubiquity of power and its control, I am interested in what he has termed a "reverse" discourse: one that competes with the hegemonic power, even though it may occupy a secondary position. See Irene Diamond and Lee Quimby, eds., *Feminism & Foucault: Reflections on Resistance* (Boston: Northeastern University Press, 1988), esp. p. xi.

3. The marriage between Mohammed and Khadija lasted for twenty-seven years, until her death in 620.

4. Feminist literature on incest points out that, contrary to the implication of the mother-son taboo, most incest is father-daughter directed. Claude Lévi-Strauss, in *The Raw and the Cooked*, finds mother-son incest the subject of myth most often in gender-segregated cultures, in which mothers live in separate dwellings with other females and children. The myths relate to the boys' desire to remain among the women and not to undergo ritual initiation into manhood and segregated living. See Marilyn French, *Beyond Power: On Women, Men, and Morals* (New York: Summit, 1985), pp. 88–89.

5. Cf. James P. Henry, "The Archetypes of Power and Intimacy," in James E. Birren and Vern L. Bengston, eds., *Emergent Theories of Aging* (New York: Springer, 1988), p. 289.

6. See *Letters Written by the Earl of Chesterfield to His Son* (New York: Derby & Jackson, 1857), pp. 300–301.

7. *Don Juan*, V, 130–31. Quoted by John D. Yohannan, *Joseph and Potiphar's Wife in World Literature* (New York: New Directions, 1968), p. 3.

8. Benjamin Franklin to "My dear Friend," June 25, 1745, reprinted in Leonard W. Labaree, ed., *The Papers of Benjamin Franklin* (New Haven, Conn.: Yale University Press, 1961), vol. 3, pp. 30–31.

9. See Huston, *Loving a Younger Man*; Joyce Sunila, *The New Lovers: Younger Men/*

Older Women (New York: Fawcett, 1980); Arlene Derenski and Sally B. Landsburg, *The Age Taboo: Older Women–Younger Men Relationships* (Boston: Little, Brown, 1981).

10. The gigolette was a prostitute, usually young, who worked especially in dance halls. Along with her male *soutenir*, or accomplice, she was known for robbing her patrons. One observer noted that the older the gigolette, the younger the *soutenir*, with gigolettes of forty and accomplices of sixteen. Octave Uzanne, *The Modern Parisienne* (London: William Heinemann, 1912), p. 179.

The indispensable computer-located Wordperfect thesaurus lists synonyms for the word "prostitute" which are much more demeaning than those for the word "gigolo." Synonyms for prostitute include harlot, streetwalker, hooker. For gigolo the synonyms are companion, escort, lover. I am grateful to Jill Fields, a Ph.D. candidate in history at USC, for pointing out this difference to me.

11. Cf. Janet Zollinger Giele, *Women in the Middle Years: Current Knowledge and Directions for Research and Policy* (New York: John Wiley & Sons, 1982), p. 6; and Carol D. Ryff, "The Subjective Experience of Life-Span Transitions," in Alice S. Rossi, ed., *Gender and the Life Course* (New York: Aldine, 1985), pp. 97–113.

12. On the new men's studies, cf. Harry Brod, *The Making of Masculinities: The New Men's Studies* (Boston: Allen & Unwin, 1987). See also Lois W. Banner, "Men's Studies: A New Feminist Approach," *Signs: Journal of Women in Culture and Society* 14 (Spring 1989), 703–8; and Banner, "A Reply to 'Culture et Pouvoir' from the Perspective of United States Women's History," *Journal of Women's History* 1 (May 1989), 104–7.

13. David Leverenz, *Manhood and the American Renaissance* (Ithaca, N.Y.: Cornell University Press, 1989), p. 73.

14. Adrienne Rich, *Of Woman Born: Motherhood as Experience and Institution* (New York: Bantam, 1976), xv.

15. Cf. Gerda Lerner, *The Creation of Patriarchy* (New York: Oxford University Press, 1986), p. 10.

16. Susan Jeffords, *The Remasculinization of America: Gender and the Vietnam War* (Bloomington: Indiana University Press, 1989).

17. My argument here has been influenced by Jessica Benjamin, "The Bonds of Love: Rational Violence and Erotic Domination," *Feminist Studies* 6 (Spring 1980), 144–74.

18. Jeffords, *Remasculinization of America*, pp. 10–11.

19. Judith Bennett, "Feminism and History," *Gender & History* 1 (Autumn 1989), 267.

20. For a feminist deconstructionist sympathetic to the "essentialist" position, see Theresa de Lauretis, "The Essence of the Triangle or, Taking the Rise of Essentialism Seriously: Feminist Theory in Italy, the U.S., and Britain," *Differences: A Journal of Feminist Cultural Studies* 1 (Summer 1989), 3–37.

21. See Dominick La Capra, *History, Politics, and the Novel* (Ithaca, N.Y.: Cornell University Press, 1987), pp. 1–14.

22. See H. Aram Veeser, ed., *The New Historicism* (New York: Routledge, 1989), esp. Judith Lowder Newton, "History as Usual? Feminism and the 'New Historicism,' " pp. 152–67 (Newton traces the new critical field to feminist roots); Lynn Hunt, ed., *The New Cultural History* (Berkeley: University of California Press, 1990), p. 34. Philippe Ariès's most influential work is *Centuries of Childhood: A Social History of Family Life*, trans. Robert Baldick (New York: Alfred A. Knopf, 1962). Norbert Elias is best known for *The Civilizing Process*, trans. Edward Jophcott, 2 vols. (New York: Urizen Books, 1978).

23. Marina Warner, *Alone of All Her Sex: The Myth and Cult of the Virgin Mary* (New York: Alfred A. Knopf, 1976); *Monuments & Maidens: The Allegory of the Human Form* (New York: Atheneum, 1985).

24. Nancy C. M. Hartsock, *Money, Sex, and Power: Toward a Feminist Historical Materialism* (New York: Longman, 1983); Dorothy Dinnerstein, *The Mermaid and the*

Minotaur: Sexual Arrangements and Human Malaise (New York: Harper & Row, 1976); Rich, *Of Woman Born.*

25. *The Complete Works of William Shakespeare*, ed. William Aldis Wright (Garden City, N.Y.: Garden City Books), p. 710; Colette, *La naissance du jour*, *Oeuvres de Colette* (Paris: Flammarion, 1960), vol. 2, p. 326; Ovid, *The Metamorphoses of Ovid*, trans. Mary Innes (London: Penguin, 1935), pp. 369–70; Ovid, *The Art of Love*, trans. J. H. Mozley (Cambridge, Mass.: Harvard University Press, 1978), p. 139.

PART ONE
Sunset Boulevard: *The Movie, The People*

1. On Wilder, see Tom Wood, *The Bright Side of Billy Wilder, Primarily* (Garden City, N.Y.: Doubleday, 1970); and Maurice Zolotow, *Billy Wilder in Hollywood* (New York: Putnam, 1977).

2. According to several feminist critics writing about Shakespeare, great artists do not necessarily duplicate in their art the orthodoxies of their culture. "They may struggle, with, criticize, or transcend them." Carolyn Ruth Swift Lenz, Gayle Greene, and Carol Thomas Neely, eds., *The Woman's Part: Feminist Criticism of Shakespeare* (Urbana: University of Illinois Press, 1980), p. 4.

CHAPTER ONE   Sunset Boulevard

1. My quotes from the movie are based on my viewing of the film and my reading of the screenplay, located in the Cinema-TV Library of the University of California, Los Angeles.

In my interpretation, I have utilized Brandon French, *On the Verge of Revolt: Women in American Films of the Fifties* (New York: Frederick Ungar, 1978); Otto Friedrich, *City of Nets: A Portrait of Hollywood in the 1940s* (New York: Harper & Row, 1986); Anne Kaplan, *Women in Film Noir* (London: British Film Institute, 1980); Karen Linville, "The Films of Billy Wilder," Ph.D. diss., UCLA, 1980; Marjorie Rosen, *Popcorn Venus: Women, Movies, and the American Dream* (New York: Coward, McCann, & Geoghegan, 1973); Karen Stoddard, *Saints and Shrews: Women and Aging in American Popular Film* (Westport, Conn.: Greenwood Press, 1983); Andrea S. Walsh, *Women's Film and Female Experience, 1940–1950* (New York: Praeger, 1984).

2. Cf. Patrick Donald Anderson, *In Its Own Image: The Cinematic Vision of Hollywood* (New York: Arno, 1976).

3. Cf. George Eells and Stanley Musgrove, *Mae West: A Biography* (New York: William Morrow, 1982).

4. Gloria Swanson, *Swanson on Swanson* (New York: Random House, 1980).

5. Richard Koszarski, *The Man You Loved to Hate: Erich von Stroheim and Hollywood* (New York: Oxford University Press, 1983), p. 321.

6. Quoted in Victoria Secunda, *By Youth Possessed: The Denial of Age in America* (Indianapolis: Bobbs-Merrill, 1984), p. 66.

7. Garff B. Wilson, *A History of American Acting* (Bloomington: Indiana University Press, 1966), pp. 110–39.

8. George Eells, *Hedda and Louella* (New York: G. P. Putnam's, 1972).

9. Ibid., p. 201.

10. William Shakespeare, *The Works of William Shakespeare*, ed. William Aldis Wright (Garden City, N.Y.: Garden City Books, 1936), p. 1070.

CHAPTER TWO   *The Possibilities for Penelope*

1. To understand the ancient goddesses, I have used, in particular, Miriam Robbins Dexter, *Whence the Goddesses: A Source Book* (New York: Pergamon, 1990); Marija Gimbutas, *The Language of the Goddess* (New York: Harper & Row, 1989); Gerda Lerner, *The Creation of Patriarchy* (New York: Oxford University Press, 1986); Carl Olson, ed., *The Book of the Goddess* (New York: Crossroad, 1983); Monica Sjöö and Barbara Mor, *The Great Cosmic Mother: Rediscovering the Religion of the Earth* (New York: Harper & Row, 1987); Merlin Stone, *When God Was a Woman* (New York: Dial, 1976).

For particular regions, I have also used Katharine Briggs, *An Encyclopedia of Fairies: Hobgoblins, Brownies, Bogies, and Other Supernatural Creatures* (New York: Pantheon, 1976); Walter Burkert, *Greek Religion,* trans. John Raffan (Cambridge, Mass.: Harvard University Press, 1985); W. K. C. Guthrie, *The Greeks and Their Gods* (London: Methuen, 1950); C. Kerényi, *The Gods of the Greeks,* trans. Norman Cameron (London: Thames and Hudson, 1951); Roger Sherman Loomis, "Morgain la Fee and the Celtic Goddesses," *Speculum* 20 (April 1945), 183–203; Jean Markale, *Women of the Celts,* trans. A. Mygind, C. Hauch, and P. Henry (Rochester, Vt.: Inner Traditions, 1986); Raphael Patai, *The Hebrew Goddess* (New York: Avon, 1978).

2. See Dexter, *Whence the Goddesses,* p. 108.

3. Joanna Hubbs argues that in Russia, the Matrioshka doll, with a number of identical dolls inside her, each smaller in size, reflected the female deity. In the embroidery of Russian peasant women this goddess was triune: the virgin, mother, and wisewoman; or the seasons: spring, summer, winter. As the old and wise, although wicked, Baba Yaga she was both a creator and an evil witch. Joanna Hubbs, *Mother Russia: The Feminine Myth in Russian Culture* (Bloomington: Indiana University Press, 1988).

4. Sigmund Freud, "The Theme of the Three Caskets," in *On Creativity and the Unconscious: Papers on the Psychology of Art, Literature, Love, Religion* (New York: Harper & Row, 1958); Barbara Walker, *The Crone: Woman of Age, Wisdom, and Power* (New York: Harper & Row, 1985), p. 99.

5. Emily Vermeule, *Greece in the Bronze Age* (Chicago: University of Chicago Press, 1964), p. 21.

6. To aid in my understanding of the *Odyssey* I have used, in particular, M. I. Finley, *The World of Odysseus* (New York: Viking, 1954), and Charles H. Taylor, Jr., ed., *Essays on the Odyssey: Selected Modern Criticism* (Bloomington: Indiana University Press, 1969). I have also found helpful the essays in John Peradotto and J. P. Sullivan, eds., *Women in the Ancient World: The Arethusa Papers* (Albany: State University of New York Press, 1984), especially Marylin B. Arthur, "Early Greece: The Origins of the Western Attitude Toward Women," pp. 7–58, and Helene P. Foley, " 'Reverse Similes' and Sex Roles in the *Odyssey,*" pp. 59–78.

7. On the function of the *Odyssey* as folktale, see Denys Page, *The Homeric Odyssey* (Westport, Conn.: Greenwood Press, 1955). Samuel Butler in the nineteenth century first advanced the speculation of female authorship, which Robert Graves, in particular, has asserted more recently.

8. *The Odyssey of Homer,* trans. Richmond Lattimore (New York: Harper & Row, 1965), p. 340.

9. Ibid., pp. 338, 357. See Thomas Falkner, "Age Grading and Arete in Early Greek Poetry." Paper, Conference on Aging and the Life Cycle in the Renaissance, University of Maryland, College Park, April 1988. I have profited from conversation with Professor Falkner, who has validated my conclusions about the ages of the characters in the *Odyssey.*

10. See Joël Schmidt, *Larousse Greek and Roman Mythology* (New York: McGraw-Hill, 1980), pp. 121, 212. The story of Helen's suitors is told by Hesiod, in the fragmentary *Catalogue of Women.*

11. *Odyssey,* pp. 33, 73, 124, 256.

12. Ibid., p. 315.

13. Ibid., pp. 73, 124, 256.

14. See Foley, " 'Reverse Similes' and Sex Roles in the *Odyssey,*" p. 59.

15. For a reading of Penelope noting the inconstancies in her character but stressing her resourcefulness, her "heroism," constrained by social and gender conventions, see Sheila Murnaghan, "Penelope's *agnoia:* Knowledge, Power, and Gender in the *Odyssey,*" *Helios* 13 (Fall 1986), 103–13.

16. *Odyssey,* pp. 41–42, 350.

17. Marylin A. Katz, *Penelope's Renown: Meaning and Indeterminacy in the Odyssey* (Princeton, N.J.: Princeton University Press, 1991).

18. Finley, *World of Odysseus,* pp. 88–91, offers the most convincing argument for Penelope's sovereignty, based on the absence of Penelope's father in the story as well as her refusal to return to his home. Katz, "Penelope's Renown," p. 61, is not so certain. Dexter, *Whence the Goddesses,* p. 147, makes the case about the continuation of ancient goddess sovereignty.

19. *The Homeric Hymns,* trans. Charles Boer (Chicago: Swallow, 1970), p. 100.

20. See Schmidt, *Larousse Greek and Roman Mythology,* pp. 121, 212.

21. Jenny Strauss Clay, *The Politics of Olympus: Form and Meaning in the Major Homeric Hymns* (Princeton, N.J.: Princeton University Press, 1989), pp. 168–69.

22. *Odyssey,* p. 58.

23. Cf. Murnaghan, "Penelope's *Agnoia,*" p. 112.

24. Cf. Schmidt, *Larousse Greek and Roman Mythology,* pp. 259–60.

25. Cf. Pierre Vidal-Naquet, "Land and Sacrifice in the *Odyssey,*" in R. L. Gordon, ed., *Myth, Religion, and Society: Structuralist Essays* (Cambridge: Cambridge University Press, 1982), p. 92.

26. *Odyssey,* p. 174.

27. Ibid., pp. 174–76.

28. Ibid., p. 91.

29. Jane Ellen Harrison, *Prolegomena to the Study of Greek Religion* (Cambridge: Cambridge University Press, 1922), p. 264.

30. *Odyssey,* p. 231.

31. Hesiod, *The Works and Days; Theogony; The Shield of Achilles,* trans. Richmond Lattimore (Ann Arbor: University of Michigan Press, 1962), pp. 180–86.

32. *Theogony,* p. 184.

33. Diane Wolkstein and Samuel Noah Kramer, eds., *Inanna: Queen of Heaven and Earth: Her Stories and Hymns from Sumer* (New York: Harper & Row, 1983), p. 95.

34. *The Epic of Gilgamesh,* trans. R. Campbell Thomas (Oxford: Clarendon, 1930).

35. *Homeric Hymns,* p. 79.

36. *Greek Lyric,* trans. David Campbell, 4 vols. (Cambridge, Mass.: Harvard University Press, 1982), vol. 1, p. 155. The biblical passage about Tammuz is Ezekiel 8:14.

Henri Frankfort, *Kingship and the Gods: A Study of Near Eastern Religion as the Integration of Society & Nature* (Chicago: University of Chicago Press, 1948), p. 288, argues that the young men were not killed in the Near Eastern rituals. Anne Barstow, "The Uses of Archeology for Women's History: James Mellaart's Work on the Neolithic Goddess at Çatal Hüyük," *Feminist Studies* 4 (October 1978), 7–18, contends that this early Neolithic site on Anatolia (dating from c. 6000 B.C.E.), shows no evidences of sacrifice. If such sacrifice did occur, Bristow contends that its origin dated from later (and presumably patriarchal) civilizations. Such evidence has also been adduced for the civilization on the island of Crete. See Marymay Downing, "Prehistoric Goddesses: The Cretan Challenge," *Journal of Feminist Studies in Religion* 1 (Spring 1985), 7–22.

37. *The Iliad of Homer,* trans. Richmond Lattimore (Chicago: University of Chicago Press, 1962), p. 303.

38. Theokritos, "Fifteenth Idyll," in *The Idylls of Theokritos,* trans. Barriss Mills (West Lafayette, Ind.: Purdue University Studies, 1963), pp. 54–60. Judith Ochschorn, *The Female Experience and the Nature of the Divine* (Bloomington: Indiana University Press, 1981), pp. 125–26, speculates that women's worship of the young god, Adonis, may have dated from the end of the second millennium, when Mesopotamian laywomen were increasingly barred from participation in official religion.

39. Cf. Peter Ackroyd, *Dressing Up: Transvestism and Drag: The History of an Obsession* (New York: Simon and Schuster, 1979).

40. See James Mellaart, *Çatal Hüyük: A Neolithic Town in Anatolia* (New York: McGraw-Hill, 1967); Mellaart, *The Neolithic of the Near East* (London: Thames & Hudson, 1975). See also Barstow, "The Uses of Archeology."

41. Marija Gimbutas, *The Goddesses and Gods of Old Europe (6500–3500 B.C.): Myths and Cult Images* (Berkeley: University of California Press, 1982), p. 237. Based on her cross-cultural analysis of 150 tribal societies, Peggy Sanday finds, in her important work on this issue of goddess religions, that female creation symbolism tended to be present in gathering and agrarian societies with predictable environments. Hunting societies and those more technologically advanced have had masculine religious orientations. And, she concludes, p. 4, that "male dominance is a response to pressures most likely present relatively late in human history." Peggy Reeves Sanday, *Female Power and Male Dominance: On the Origins of Sexual Inequality* (Cambridge: Cambridge University Press, 1981).

42. For an examination of this theme in major stories and plays, see John D. Yohannan, ed., *Joseph and Potiphar's Wife in World Literature: An Anthology of the Story of the Chaste Youth and the Lustful Stepmother* (New York: New Directions, 1968). The name Phaedra means "bringer of light."

43. Jane Ellen Harrison, *Themis: A Study of the Social Origins of Greek Religion* (Cambridge: Cambridge University Press, 1912), pp. 23–25.

44. *Odyssey,* p. 157. See also Gregory Crane, *Calypso: Backgrounds and Conventions of the Odyssey* (Frankfurt am Main: Athenäum, 1988), p. 64.

45. Harrison, *Themis,* pp. 23–25; David Grene and Richmond Lattimore, *Complete Greek Tragedies,* 3 vols. (Chicago: University of Chicago Press, 1960), vol. 3: Euripides, *The Bacchae,* p. 547.

46. On Dionysus, cf. K. Kerényi, *Dionysos: Archetypal Image of the Indestructible Life,* trans. Ralph Manheim (Princeton, N.J.: Princeton University Press, 1976), and Walter F. Otto, *Dionysus: Myth and Cult,* trans. Robert B. Palmer (Bloomington: Indiana University Press, 1965).

47. Marcel Detienne, *The Gardens of Adonis: Spices in Greek Mythology,* trans. Janet Lloyd (Atlantic Highlands, N.J.: Humanities Press, 1977), p. 67.

48. In a variation on this argument, Lori Lefkovitz contends that the beauty and gentleness of Joseph within the Hebrew tradition became for later rabbinical commentators a negative, effeminate masculinity as they strove to create a more masculinized image for Jewish men, often stereotyped as unmasculine. See Lori Lefkovitz, "The Story of Joseph: Myths of Jewish Masculinity," *Changing Men* 18 (Summer/Fall 1987), 3–5, 44.

49. Savina Teubal, *Sarah the Priestess: The First Matriarch of Genesis* (Athens, Ohio: Swallow Press, 1984).

50. The "mystery" religions were designated by this term because their rites were

supposed to be kept secret. Only initiates were permitted to attend. And because this rule was only occasionally violated over the centuries of their existence, we have limited knowledge of their practices. It seems, however, that their attraction lay in elements similar to Christianity: they promised life after death and some element of mystical union with the godhead.

51. Eva C. Keuls, *The Reign of the Phallus: Sexual Politics in Ancient Athens* (New York: Harper & Row, 1985), p. 112. On the Eleusinian mysteries, the literature is large. Cf. K. Kerényi, *Eleusis: Archetypal Image of Mother and Daughter,* trans. Ralph Manheim (Princeton, N.J.: Princeton University Press, 1967); and Mara Lynn Keller, "The Eleusinian Mysteries: Ancient Nature Religion of Demeter and Persephone," in Irene Diamond and Gloria Feman Orenstein, eds., *Reweaving the World: The Emergence of Ecofeminism* (San Francisco: Sierra Club Books, 1990), pp. 41–51.

52. *Odyssey,* p. 322.

53. Ibid., pp. 125–26.

54. See W. B. Stanford, *The Ulysses Theme: A Study in the Adaptability of a Traditional Hero* (Ann Arbor: University of Michigan Press, 1968).

55. *Inanna: Queen of Heaven,* pp. 35, 37.

CHAPTER THREE *Goddesses Revealed and Obscured: The Story of Sappho and Phaon*

1. Cf. Acts 19:21–41. Diana was the Roman name of the Greek Artemis.

2. The Emperor Theodosius ordered the closing of all pagan temples in 398 C.E. In 432 a council of bishops proclaimed the divinity of Mary on the site of the temple at Ephesus in defiance of a crowd calling for the restoration of the worship of Diana. See John Holland Smith, *The Death of Classical Paganism* (New York: Charles Scribner's Sons, 1976). For a detailed account of the transposition of goddess traditions into the figure of Mary, see Pamela Berger, *The Goddess Obscured: Transposition of the Grain Protectress from Goddess to Saint* (Boston: Beacon, 1985).

3. A source on Sappho's life from ancient texts remains David M. Robinson, *Sappho and Her Influence* (Boston: Marshall Jones, 1924). See also Jane McIntosh Snyder, *The Woman and the Lyre: Women Writers in Classical Greece and Rome* (Carbondale: Southern Illinois University Press, 1989).

4. See Joan DeJean, *Fictions of Sappho, 1546–1937* (Chicago: University of Chicago Press, 1989), on the liberties taken over the ages in constructing Sappho's life and her meaning. Especially interesting is her argument that the French novel, dating from the seventeenth century, had its origins in male authors' discovery of Ovid's redaction of Sappho's life story into that of an aging woman consumed by the love of a young man. In this way they undermined the authority of contemporary women writers. On Sappho's later influence see also Judith Ellen Stein, "The Iconography of Sappho," Ph.D. diss., University of Pennsylvania, 1981.

5. Robinson, *Sappho,* p. 21.

6. Mary Mills Patrick, *Sapho and the Island of Lesbos* (London: Methuen, 1914), p. 106.

7. Quotations from Sappho's poems come from the translation by David Campbell, in *Greek Lyric,* 4 vols. (Cambridge, Mass.: Harvard University Press, 1982), vol. 1, pp. 2–205.

8. Margaret Goldsmith, *Sappho of Lesbos: A Psychological Reconstruction of Her Life* (London: Rich & Cowan, 1938), p. 276.

9. Ovid, *Heroides and Amores,* trans. Grant Showerman (London: William Heinemann, 1914), pp. 183, 195.

10. The statement about the setting of the moon may be a reference to the third personification of the goddess as the wise aging woman. The Pleiades were seven sisters, daughters of Atlas and followers of Artemis, whom Zeus had transformed into stars.

11. Paul Friedrich, *The Meaning of Aphrodite* (Chicago: University of Chicago Press, 1978), p. 125.

12. Hesiod, *The Works and Days; Theogony; The Shield of Herakles,* trans. Richmond Lattimore (Ann Arbor: University of Michigan Press, 1959), p. 147. In legend many goddesses leapt over cliffs into the ocean to escape pursuit. The Cretan goddess Britomartis had done so to escape Minos, the king of Crete; she had supposedly fallen into fishermen's nets. Diktynna, another name for the Cretan goddess, derives from the Greek word *diktys,* or "nets." After Oedipus solved the riddle of the Sphinx, this half-animal woman, according to one legend, also leapt from cliffs into the sea.

13. Eva Stehle has argued that the goddess/young god typology replicated cultural hierarchy because of the sexual subordination of young men; however, one could also assert that it validated the authority of women. See Eva Stehle, "Sappho's Gaze: Fantasies of a Goddess and a Young Man," *Differences: A Journal of Feminist Cultural Studies* 2 (Spring 1990), 88–125.

14. Within the later Greek imagination the goddess Hecate became, first, the aging form of the triune goddess, as implied in the *Homeric Hymn to Demeter.* Eventually she was transmogrified into a terrifying old witch, requiring expiation through offerings left at roadside shrines on nights of the full moon. To Hesiod writing centuries before, however, she had encompassed the entire persona of a great goddess. Her domain extended over "land, and sea, and sky." Hesiod, *Theogony,* p. 23.

15. With regard to Helen there was also the legend that there had been two Helens. The first, an evil Helen, had gone with Paris to Troy. The second, a good Helen, had lived in Egypt during the years of the war. This doubling was also replicated with regard to Sappho. Early legends had it that a prostitute named Sappho had had the erotic attachments and that Sappho, the poet, had only written about what the other Sappho had done.

16. Campbell, *Greek Lyric,* vol. 1, p. 97; Plutarch quote translated by Sarah B. Pomeroy, *Women in Hellenistic Egypt* (New York: Schocken, 1984), p. 8–9.

17. Judith P. Hallett, "Sappho and Her Social Context: Sense and Sensuality," *Signs: Journal of Women in Culture and Society* 4 (Spring 1979), 447–65, suggests that the beauty contests were holdovers from rites sacred to Hera and that they were meant to enhance individual self-image, not to undermine it.

18. Walter Burkert, *Greek Religion,* trans. John Raffan (Cambridge, Mass.: Harvard University Press, 1985), p. 143.

19. Walter Licht, *Sexual Life in Ancient Greece* (London: Routledge & Kegan Paul, 1932), p. 40.

20. Leo Simmons, *The Role of the Aged in Primitive Society* (New Haven, Conn.: Yale University Press, 1945), p. 178; Philip Silverman and Robert J. Maxwell, "Cross-Cultural Variation in the Status of Old People," in Peter N. Stearns, ed., *Old Age in Preindustrial Society* (New York: Holmes & Meier, 1982), pp. 46–69.

21. On these property matters see A. R. W. Harrison, *The Law of Athens: The Family and Property* (Oxford: Clarendon, 1968); W. E. Thompson, "Athenian Marriage Patterns: Remarriage," *California Studies in Classical Antiquity* 5 (1972), 211–25; David M. Schaps, *Economic Rights of Women in Ancient Greece* (Edinburgh: University of Edinburgh Press, 1979); Raphael Sealey, *Women and Law in Classical Greece* (Chapel Hill: University of North Carolina Press, 1990). I am aware that these economic arrangements, as well as the matter of homosexuality I will presently discuss, differed in other parts of Greece, notably in Sparta and Crete.

I am also aware that variations existed even under strict Athenian laws. Male relatives could refuse the *epiklaros* exchange, and female heiresses might then retain some control of property. Moreover, there were changes over time. For example, Pomeroy, *Women in Hellenistic Egypt,* p. 4, points out that during the latter years of the fourth-century Peloponnesian War, the absence of men at war year round resulted in women assuming male responsibilities. Until the men returned, upper-class women entered the public agora, gave testimony in court, and even lived with men to whom they were not married. And throughout these years there were wealthy hetairai.

22. Eva C. Keuls, *The Reign of the Phallus* (New York: Harper & Row, 1985), pp. 101–4. The marital exchange required of the *epiklaros* resembled, without replicating, the Hebrew practice of the levirate, under which widows were required to marry their deceased husbands' brothers, generally as second wives. Again, the motivation seems to have been to keep the family patrimony intact.

23. Cf. Helene P. Foley, "Women in Greece," in Michael Grant and Rachael Kitzinger, eds., *Civilization of the Ancient Mediterranean*, 3 vols. (New York: Charles Scribner's Sons, 1988), vol. 3, pp. 1306–50; Keuls, *Reign of the Phallus*; Sarah Pomeroy, *Goddesses, Whores, Wives, and Slaves: Women in Classical Antiquity* (New York: Schocken, 1975). Recent revisionists on this issue posit that within their homes women possessed flexibility of action; Raphael Sealey suggests describing them as living not in "oriental seclusion" but in "genteel withdrawal." *Women and Law in Classical Greece*, p. 154.

24. Plato, *Theaetetus*, trans. Robin A. H. Waterfield (New York: Penguin Books, 1987), p. 26. On the freedom accorded older women, see W. K. Lacey, *The Family in Classical Greece* (Ithaca, N.Y.: Cornell University Press, 1968), p. 175. Indeed, aging midwives seem to have been both celebrated and critiqued in Athens. The reduction of aging women's wisdom to "old wives' tales" already existed in this society: the Greek word for the phrase was *hythlos graun*.

25. Walter F. Otto, *Dionysus: Myth and Cult,* trans. Robert B. Palmer (Bloomington: Indiana University Press, 1965), p. 290; Jeffrey Henderson, "Older Women in Attic Old Comedy," *Transactions of the American Philological Association* 117 (1987), 105–29; Keuls, *Reign of the Phallus*, p. 150. My discussion of aging women in Athens has been informed by Henderson and by Bessie Ellen Richardson, *Old Age Among the Ancient Greeks* (Baltimore: Johns Hopkins University Press, 1933).

26. Aristophanes, *The Eleven Comedies,* trans. anon. (New York: Liveright, 1943), p. 398.

27. Licht, *Sexual Life in Ancient Greece*, p. 427; K. J. Dover, "Classical Greek Attitudes to Sexual Behavior," in John Peradotto and J. P. Sullivan, eds., *Women in the Ancient World: The Arethusa Papers*, p. 150; K. J. Dover, *Greek Homosexuality* (London: Duckworth, 1978), p. 70; Robert Graves, *The Greek Myths*, 2 vols. (New York: Penguin Books, 1955), vol. 1, p. 58. See also Jeffrey Henderson, "Greek Attitudes Towards Sex," in Grant and Kitzinger, *Civilization of the Ancient Mediterranean*, vol. 3, pp. 1249–63.

28. Cf. Plutarch, *Lives of the Noble Greeks*, ed. Edmund Fuller (New York: Dell, 1959), pp. 187–88. The argument about moderation is most forcefully stated by Michel Foucault, *The History of Sexuality*, vol. 2: *The Use of Pleasure*, trans. Robert Hurley (New York: Vintage, 1986).

29. Cf. David M. Halperin, *One Hundred Years of Homosexuality and Other Essays on Greek Love* (New York: Routledge, 1990).

30. Plato, *Symposium,* in *Great Dialogues of Plato,* trans. W. H. D. Rouse (New York: Mentor, 1956), pp. 76–77. See also David F. Greenberg, *The Construction of Homosexuality* (Chicago: University of Chicago Press, 1988), pp. 141–52.

31. According to Pausanius in Plato's *Symposium:* "it is called better . . . especially to love the highest and noblest born, even if they are uglier than others. . . ." p. 80.

32. Cf. Marylin B. Arthur, "Early Greece: The Origins of the Western Attitude Toward Women," in Peradotto and Sullivan, *Women in the Ancient World,* pp. 7–58; Keuls, *Reign of the Phallus,* pp. 116–17. On women's biology as polluting, see Ruth Padel, "Women: Model for Possession by Greek Daemons," in Averil Cameron and Amélie Kuhrt, eds., *Images of Women in Antiquity* (Detroit: Wayne State University Press, 1983), pp. 3–19.

33. Cf. Mark Golden, *Children and Childhood in Classical Athens* (Baltimore: Johns Hopkins University Press, 1990), p. 9.

34. Cf. Paul A. Rahe, "The Primacy of Politics in Classical Greece," *American Historical Review* 89 (April 1984), 265–93; Helen King, "Bound to Bleed: Artemis and Greek Women," in Cameron and Kuhrt, *Images of Women,* p. 111; Plato, *The Republic,* in Rouse, *Great Dialogues,* p. 188.

35. According to Pausanius in Plato's *Symposium,* p. 79: "They do not fall in love with those who are little boys, but with those who have mind, and that is nearly when they show the down on their chins."

36. Plato, *Symposium,* pp. 76–77; Ovid, *Heroides and Amores,* p. 187. Amy Richlin, *The Garden of Priapus: Sexuality and Aggression in Roman Humor* (New Haven, Conn.: Yale University Press, 1983), p. 37, notes that the pederastic ideal included a clear complexion and "sparkling" eyes and that the common depiction was like an adult but without bodily hair.

These were ancient conventions. In the *Odyssey,* a text without examples of same-sex love, when Odysseus encounters Hermes on Circe's island, Homer describes the god as "in the likeness of a young man with beard new grown, which is the most graceful time of young manhood." *Odyssey,* p. 159.

37. G. Karl Galinsky, *The Herakles Theme: The Adaptations of the Hero in Literature from Homer to the Twentieth Century* (Oxford: Basil Blackwell, 1972), p. 3; Graves, *Greek Myths,* vol. 2, p. 86; Plato, *Phaedrus and the Seventh and Eighth Letters,* trans. Walter Hamilton (Hammondsworth, England: Penguin Books, 1973), pp. 32, 39.

38. John J. Winkler, *The Constraints of Desire: The Anthropology of Sex and Gender in Ancient Greece* (New York: Routledge, 1990), esp. pp. 188–209; Page DuBois, *Sowing the Body: Psychoanalysis and Ancient Representations of the Body* (Chicago: University of Chicago Press, 1988), p. 91.

39. Plato, *Phaedrus,* pp. 32, 39. Plato, *Timaeus,* in *The Dialogues of Plato,* trans. Benjamin Jowatt. 2 vols. (New York: Random House, 1937), vol. 2, pp. 14–21.

40. Plato, *Symposium,* pp. 97–106. See also Halperin, *One Hundred Years of Homosexuality,* pp. 113–51: "Why Is Diotima a Woman?" and DuBois, *Sowing the Body.*

41. Plato, *Menexenus,* in *The Dialogues of Plato,* trans. R. E. Allen (New Haven, Conn.: Yale University Press, 1984), vol. 1, pp. 332–33.

42. Plutarch, *Moralia,* trans. Frank Cole Babbett, 14 vols. Vol. 9: *The Dialogue on Love* (Cambridge, Mass.: Harvard University Press, 1936), p. 415.

43. On Roman gender mores, see Marylin Arthur, "From Medusa to Cleopatra: Women in the Ancient World," in Renate Bridenthal, Claudia Koonz, and Susan Stuard, eds., *Becoming Visible: Women in European History,* 2d ed. (Boston: Houghton Mifflin, 1987), pp. 79–105; J. P. V. D. Balsdon, *Roman Women: Their History and Habits* (Westport, Conn.: Greenwood Press, 1962); Eva Canterella, *Pandora's Daughters: The Role & Status of Women in Greek & Roman Antiquity,* trans. Maureen B. Fant (Baltimore: Johns Hopkins University Press, 1981).

44. Suzanne Dixon, *The Roman Mother* (London: Croom Helm, 1988), p. 22. Jane F. Gardner cautions against overemphasizing the freedom of Roman women in any period. She points to continued power of fathers over daughters and moral attitudes promoting wifely fidelity. She attributes overblown conclusions about women's independence to a

group of misogynistic Roman writers and to late Victorian scholars of Rome who were reacting against the woman's rights movement of their day. *Women in Roman Law and Society* (Bloomington: Indiana University Press, 1991), pp. 257–65.

45. Judith P. Hallett, *Fathers and Daughters in Roman Society: Women and the Elite Family* (Princeton, N.J.: Princeton University Press, 1984), p. 329.

46. Ann Ellis Hanson, "The Medical Writers' Woman," in David M. Halperin, John J. Winkler, and Froma Zeitlin, eds., *Before Sexuality: The Construction of Erotic Experience in the Ancient Greek World* (Princeton, N.J.: Princeton University Press, 1990).

47. Canterella, *Pandora's Daughters*, pp. 131–32; J. P. V. D. Balsdon, "Women in Republican Rome," *History Today* 9 (July 1959), 455–62.

48. Juvenal, *The Sixteen Satires*, trans. Peter Green (New York: Penguin Books, 1967), p. 216.

49. Juvenal, *Sixteen Satires*, pp. 128, 215. See also Carol Clemeau Esler, "Horace's Old Girls: Evolution of a Topos," in Thomas M. Falkner and Judith de Luce, *Old Age in Greek and Latin Literature* (Albany: State University of New York Press, 1989), pp. 172–82.

50. Ovid, *Heroides and Amores*, p. 45.

51. Ovid, *The Art of Love*, trans. J. H. Mozley (Cambridge, Mass.: Harvard University Press, 1978), p. 150.

52. Petronius, *The Satyricon*, trans. William Arrowsmith (New York: American Library, 1959), p. 177; Apuleius, *The Golden Ass*, trans. Jack Lindsay (Bloomington: Indiana University Press, 1962), p. 53. While still a student Apuleius married the mother of a fellow student.

53. Ovid, *Amores*, trans. Guy Lee (New York: Viking, 1968), p. 27.

54. The reason for this regulation remains obscure, although it may have been related to the belief that wine was a natural abortifacient and thus could taint the purity of the family line by destruction of a fetus. Cf. Pierre Grimal, *Love in Ancient Rome*, trans. Arthur Train (New York: Crown, 1967). In addition, evidence suggests that by late Roman times men came to fear being poisoned by their wives and thus denied them access to a substance they associated with poisoning. Amy Richlin, "Roman Witches and Women Poisoners," paper, 1985.

55. Petronius, *Satyricon*; Apuleius, *Golden Ass*, p. 53. Juvenal, *Sixth Satire*, p. 136.

56. This sexuality can be seen in a possible interconnection between mysticism and physicality. Christian sources report that the Pythia of the Oracle of Delphi received her inspiration in a sexual manner. After eating hallucinatory laurel leaves, she sat on a three-legged stool over a cavern in the ground from which vapors escaped. She then went into a trance and delivered incantations. It was through her vagina that the spirit entered her; her divine revelations were connected to her sexuality. (The Pythia had to be postmenopausal.) William Woods, *A History of the Devil* (New York: G. P. Putnam's Sons, 1974), p. 83. Amy Richlin, *Garden of Priapus*, posits that the portrayal of old women as drunk or randy may have expressed an aversion to intercourse with them.

57. Hanson, "Medical Writers' Woman," p. 318.

58. Plutarch, *Moralia*, trans. Frank Cole Babbett, 14 vols. Vol. 5: *Isis and Osiris* (Cambridge, Mass.: Harvard University Press, 1936), p. 185.

59. Proverbs, 8:1–37. *The New Oxford Annotated Bible with the Apocrypha*, ed. Herbert G. May and Bruce M. Metzger (New York: Oxford University Press, 1977), pp. 777–78.

60. On the Gnostic gospels, see Elaine Pagels, *The Gnostic Gospels* (New York: Random House, 1979).

61. Willis Barnstone, ed., *The Other Bible* (New York: Harper & Row, 1984), pp. 29–30.

62. Morton Bloomfield, *The Seven Deadly Sins* (East Lansing: Michigan State College

Press, 1952), p. 33, points out that the gender of most Latin abstract nouns is feminine. Thus language and celestial personification here interact.

63. See Londa Schiebinger, *The Mind Has No Sex? Women in the Origins of Modern Science* (Cambridge, Mass.: Harvard University Press, 1989).

64. George D. Economou, *The Goddess Natura in Medieval Literature* (Cambridge, Mass.: Harvard University Press, 1972), pp. 54, 63.

65. See Norma Lorre Goodrich, *Priestesses* (New York: Franklin Watts, 1989), pp. 288–323, on the actual existence of the Cumaen Sibyl, which some scholars dispute. Legend had it that an old woman had brought the original *Sibylline Books* to an early Roman ruler.

66. Virgil, *The Aeneid. Ecologues. Gorgiacs.* trans. J. W. Mackay (New York: Modern Library, 1950), pp. 100–120.

67. Boethius, *The Consolation of Philosophy,* ed. James J. Buchanan (New York: Frederick Ungar, 1957), pp. 1–10.

68. See Prudence Allen, *The Concept of Woman: The Aristotelian Revolution, 750 B.C.–A.D. 1250* (Montreal: Eden, 1985), pp. 217–18.

69. Marina Warner, *Monuments & Maidens: The Allegory of the Female Form* (New York: Atheneum, 1985), pp. 180–85.

70. Edward Gibbon, *The Decline and Fall of the Roman Empire,* 2 vols. (Chicago: Encyclopaedia Britannica, 1952), vol. 2, p. 139.

71. Cf. Howard R. Patch, *The Goddess Fortuna in Medieval Literature* [1927] (New York: Octagon, 1978), pp. 15–50. Berger, *Goddess Obscured,* traces the evolution of the Roman figure of Terra Mater, the symbol of fruitful prosperity, into the twelfth-century figures of Luxuria and the mermaid, symbols of female sexual insatiability.

72. Carolyn Merchant, *The Death of Nature: Women, Ecology, and the Scientific Revolution* (New York: Harper & Row, 1980), p. 28.

73. Goodrich, *Priestesses,* pp. 297–98.

74. Hesiod, *Theogony,* p. 124.

75. Niccolò Machiavelli, *The Prince,* trans. Luigi Ricci (New York: New American Library, 1952), p. 123.

CHAPTER FOUR   *The Wife of Bath as Historical Prototype*

1. Joan Kelly, "Did Women Have a Renaissance?" in Joan Kelly, ed., *Women, History, and Theory: The Essays of Joan Kelly* (Chicago: University of Chicago Press, 1984), pp. 19–50.

2. Natalie Zemon Davis, *Fiction in the Archives: Pardon Tales and Their Tellers in Sixteenth-Century France* (Stanford, Calif.: Stanford University Press, 1987), p. 88.

3. Quotations from *The Canterbury Tales* come from Geoffrey Chaucer, *The Canterbury Tales,* rendered into modern English by J. U. Nicolson (Garden City, N.Y.: Garden City Publishing, 1934).

4. Natalie Davis, "Women on Top," in Natalie Zemon Davis, ed., *Society and Culture in Early Modern France* (Stanford: Stanford University Press, 1975), pp. 124–51. On early physiological reasoning concerning gender and sexuality see Thomas Laquer, *Making Sex: Body & Gender from the Greeks to Freud* (Cambridge, Mass.: Harvard University Press, 1990).

5. On life-cycle theorization, see chapter 6, below.

6. *Canterbury Tales,* p. 316. Feminist interpretations of the Wife of Bath include Mary Carruthers, "The Wife of Bath and the Painting of Lions," *Publications of the Modern Language Association* 94 (March 1979), 209–22, and Ann S. Haskell, "The Portrayal of

Women by Chaucer and His Age," in Marlene Springer, ed., *What Manner of Women: Essays on English and American Literature* (New York: New York University Press, 1977), pp. 1–14. For a view of Chaucer as unsympathetic to Alison of Bath, see Arlyn Diamond, "Chaucer's Women and Women's Chaucer," in Arlyn Diamond and Lee R. Edwards, eds., *The Authority of Experience: Essays in Feminist Criticism* (Amherst: University of Massachusetts Press, 1977), pp. 60–83, and Robert S. Haller, "The Old Whore and Medieval Thought: Variations on a Convention," Ph.D. diss., Princeton University, 1960.

For a reading of the Wife of Bath as powerless and self-destructive, see Elaine Tuttle Hansen, "The Wife of Bath and the Mark of Adam," *Women's Studies* 15 (1988), 399–416. Jon Cook, "Carnival and *The Canterbury Tales*," in David Aers, ed., *Medieval Literature: Criticism, Ideology, & History* (Sussex: Harvester Press, 1986), p. 179, offers a reading of her as a figure from the European carnival tradition who defuses gender discontinuities.

7. See F. George Kay, *Lady of the Sun: The Life and Times of Alice Perrers* (New York: Barnes & Noble, 1966). On Chaucer's life, cf. John Gardner, *The Life & Times of Chaucer* (New York: Alfred A. Knopf, 1977); Derek Brewer, *Chaucer and His World* (London: Methuen, 1978); Donald Roy Howard, *Chaucer: His Life, His Works, His World* (New York: Dutton, 1987).

8. Priscilla Martin, *Chaucer's Women: Nuns, Wives, and Amazons* (Iowa City: University of Iowa Press, 1990), p. 23.

9. Ibid., p. 62.

10. Reto R. Bezzola, *Les origines et la formation de la littérature courtoise en occident (500–1200)* (Paris: Champion, 1968), pp. 253–54. C. Stephen Jaeger, *The Origins of Courtliness: Civilizing Trends and the Formation of Courtly Ideals, 939–1210* (Philadelphia: University of Pennsylvania Press, 1985), pp. 178–79, notes a "softening" in masculinized behavior in the courts of Provence as early as the first part of the eleventh century. He cites especially chroniclers' reports of frivolous behavior and dress at the marriages of Constance of Arles and Robert the Pious of France in 1003 and Agnes of Poitou and the German Henry III in 1043.

11. The cynical interpretation of the cult of courtly love stems especially from the work of Georges Duby. Cf. *Le chévalier, la femme et le prêtre: Le mariage dans la France féodale* (Paris: Hachette, 1981). Duby's influence can be seen in Penny Schine Gold, *The Lady & the Virgin: Images, Attitude, and Experience in Twelfth-Century France* (Chicago: University of Chicago Press, 1985), and in Diane Bornstein, *The Lady in the Tower: Medieval Courtesy Literature for Women* (Hamden, Conn.: Archon Books, 1983).

Susan Mosher Stuard critiques Duby for presenting women as pawns when his own research suggests a more complex situation. See Susan Mosher Stuard, "Fashion's Captives: Medieval Women in French Historiography," in Susan Mosher Stuard, ed., *Women in Medieval History & Historiography* (Philadelphia: University of Pennsylvania Press, 1987), pp. 73–74.

12. Joan Ferrante, "Public Postures and Private Maneuvers: Roles Medieval Women Play," in Mary Erler and Maryanne Kowaleski, eds., *Women and Power in the Middle Ages* (Athens: University of Georgia Press, 1988), p. 213.

13. On the twelfth and thirteenth centuries, I have used, in particular, Roger Boase, *The Origin and Meaning of Courtly Love: A Critical Study of European Scholarship* (Totowa, N.J.: Rowman and Littlefield, 1977); Christopher Brooke, *The Twelfth Century Renaissance* (New York: Harcourt, Brace, & World, 1969); Friedrich Herr, *The Medieval World: Europe, 1100–1350* (London: Weidenfeld and Nicolson, 1961); Angela M. Lucas, *Women in the Middle Ages: Religion, Marriage, and Letters* (New York: St. Martin's Press, 1983); Herbert Moller, "The Social Causation of the Courtly Love Complex," *Comparative Studies in Society and History* 1 (1958–59), 137–63; M. M. Postan and Edward Miller, *The Cambridge Economic History of Europe*: vol. 2: *Trade and Industry in the Middle Ages*

(Cambridge: Cambridge University Press, 1987); Eileen Power, *Medieval Women,* ed. M. M. Postan (London: Cambridge University Press, 1973); Shulamith Shahar, *The Fourth Estate: A History of Women in the Middle Ages* (London: Methuen, 1983).

14. See Marcia Guttentag and Paul F. Secord, *Too Many Women? The Sex Ratio Question* (Beverly Hills, Calif.: Sage, 1983), pp. 53–77. The increased population of women, creating a low sex ratio, was probably due to dietary improvements, especially enriched sources of iron. See Vern Bulloch and Cameron Campbell, "Female Longevity and Diet in the Middle Ages," *Speculum* 55 (1980), 317–25, revising David Herlihy's conclusions based on urbanization and decreased violence, in "Life Expectancies for Women in Medieval Society," in Rosemarie Thee Morewedge, *The Role of Woman in the Middle Ages* (Albany: State University of New York Press, 1975), pp. 4–15.

15. Colin Morris, *The Discovery of the Individual* (New York: Harper & Row, 1972), p. 98; *The Song of Roland,* trans. C. K. Scott Moncrieff (Ann Arbor: University of Michigan Press, 1972), p. 66.

16. *The Letters of Abelard and Heloise,* trans. C. K. Scott Moncrieff (New York: Cooper Square, 1974), pp. 132–60. See J. L. Topsfield, *Chrétien de Troyes: A Study of the Arthurian Romances* (Cambridge: Cambridge University Press, 1981), pp. 1–10. Topsfield finds a connection between the Dukes of Aquitaine, the Counts of Poitou, and the School of Chartres. This connection dated to William, the father of Agnes of Poitou, in the early eleventh century. Topsfield suggests that both traditions can be traced back to Boethius.

17. *The Ecclesiastical History of Orderic Vitalis,* trans. Marjorie Chibnall, 5 vols. (Oxford: Clarendon, 1973), vol. 4, p. 189. See also Joan Evans, *Medieval Dress* (London: Oxford University Press, 1952), and below, chapter 6.

18. Meg Bogin, *The Women Troubadours* (New York: Paddington Press, 1976), p. 56.

19. Hobart C. Chatfield-Taylor, *Charmed Circles: A Pageant of the Ages from Aspasia's Day to our Own* (Boston: Houghton-Mifflin, 1935), p. 91.

20. Marie of France, *French Medieval Romances From the Lays of Marie de France,* trans. Eugene Mason (London: J. M. Dent & Sons, 1924), pp. 108, 15.

21. For background, see Joan M. Ferrante, *Woman as Image in Medieval Literature: From the Twelfth Century to Dante* (New York: Columbia University Press, 1975).

22. See Ulrich von Lichtenstein, *Service of Ladies,* trans. J. W. Thomas (Chapel Hill: University of North Carolina Press, 1969); Antoine de la Sale, *Little John of Saintré (Le petit Jehan de Saintré)* (London: George Routledge & Sons, 1931).

23. Chrétien de Troyes, *Arthurian Romances,* trans W. W. Comfort (New York: Dutton, 1975), pp. 193–220. In *Vita Merlini (The Life of Merlin),* of 1150, Geoffrey of Monmouth is precise about Morgan's power. She lived on the magical Island of Apples, according to this author, and she was the chief among nine ruling sisters. She was versed in healing and also possessed the power to change her shape and fly through the air. The *Vita Merlini* was one of the earliest texts establishing Arthurian themes. Geoffrey of Monmouth, *Vita Merlini,* trans. Basil Clarke (Cardiff: University of Wales Press, 1973), p. 101.

24. Hans and Siegfried Wichmann, *Chess: The Story of Chesspieces from Antiquity to Modern Times* (New York: Crown, 1960), p. 28.

25. Ilene H. Forsyth, *The Throne of Wisdom: Wood Sculptures of the Madonna in Romanesque France* (Princeton, N.J.: Princeton University Press, 1972), passim.

26. Roger Loomis Sherman, in *Celtic Myth and Arthurian Romance* (New York: Columbia University Press, 1927), p. 29, notes evidence of a Breton storyteller at Eleanor's court in the south of France in the years before she married Louis VII.

27. See Donald Furber and Anne Callahan, *Erotic Love in Literature: From Medieval Legend to Romantic Illusion* (Troy, N.Y.: Whitson, 1982), p. 32. In 1170, when Eleanor

took up residence in Aquitaine, to establish her son Richard as overlord she held a symbolic ceremony in which he was married to St. Valéry, the legendary martyr and patroness of the region. Herr, *Medieval World*, pp. 130–35.

28. June Hall Martin McCash has overturned John F. Benton's conclusion that Eleanor and Marie did not again meet after Eleanor left Louis's court. See June Hall Martin McCash, "Marie de Champagne and Eleanor of Aquitaine: A Relationship Reexamined," *Speculum* 54 (July 1979), 698–711; and John F. Benton, "The Court of Champagne as a Literary Center," *Speculum* 36 (October 1961), 551–91.

29. Andreas Capellanus, *The Art of Courtly Love*, trans. John Jay Parry (New York: Frederick Ungar, 1941), pp. 117, 176.

30. Henry Adams, *Mont-Saint-Michel and Chartres* [1905] (New York: Heritage Press, 1957), pp. 182–210.

31. Bogin, *Women Troubadours*, pp. 58–59.

32. Cf. Regine Pernoud, *Blanche of Castile*, trans. Henry Noel (New York: Coward, McCann, & Geoghegan, 1975).

33. Gold, *Lady and the Virgin*, pp. 43–68. Marina Warner, *Alone of All Her Sex: The Myth and the Cult of the Virgin Mary* (New York: Alfred A. Knopf, 1976), p. 183, quotes Simone de Beauvoir in noting that "for the first time in human history the mother kneels before her son; she freely accepts her inferiority."

34. John V. Fleming, *The Roman de la Rose: A Study in Allegory and Iconography* (Princeton, N.J.: Princeton University Press, 1969), p. 109, calls the second half of the work "a kind of intellectual rake's progress." The most comprehensive survey of the *querelle des femmes* remains Joan Kelly, "Early Feminist Theory and the Querelle des Femmes," in Joan Kelly, ed., *Women, History, and Theory: The Essays of Joan Kelly*, pp. 65–109.

35. Chrétien de Troyes, *Cligés*, in *Arthurian Romances*, trans. W. W. Comfort (London: Dent, 1975), p. 140; Guillaume de Lorris and Jean de Meun, *Romance of the Rose*, trans. Charles Dahlberg (Princeton, N.J.: Princeton University Press, 1971), pp. 352–53.

36. Jean Bethke Elshtain, *Women and War* (New York: Basic Books, 1987), pp. 191–93.

37. Chrétien de Troyes, *Perceval, or the Story of the Grail*, in Roger Sherman Loomis and Laura Hibbard Loomis, *Medieval Romances*, trans. R. S. Loomis (New York: Modern Library, 1957), p. 10.

38. Ibid., p 9. For goddess scholarship on the Grail legend, see, in particular, Barbara Walker, *The Crone: Woman of Age, Wisdom, and Power* (New York: Harper & Row, 1985), pp. 101–22. Topsfield, *Chrétien de Troyes*, pp. 207–12, persuasively argues that de Troyes here blended Christian and Celtic traditions.

39. Enguerrand de Coucy is the biographical center of Barbara Tuchman's *Distant Mirror*, a perceptive, popular rendering of the disastrous fourteenth century, the age of the Black Death and the Hundred Years' War. See Tuchman, *A Distant Mirror: The Calamitous Fourteenth Century* (New York: Alfred A. Knopf, 1978).

Robert the Pious, who married Agnes of Poitou in 1043, had previously been married to Rozala of Flanders, who was much older than he. He married her to acquire Flanders, which she had inherited, and then divorced her by reason of consanguinity.

40. Mark Strage, *Women of Power: The Life and Times of Catherine de' Medici* (New York: Harcourt Brace Jovanovich, 1976), p. 33; Francis Steegmuller, *The Grande Mademoiselle* (New York: Farrar, Straus, and Cudahy, 1956), p. 151.

41. See Christine de Pizan, *Book of the City of Ladies*, trans. Earl Jeffrey Richards (New York: Persea Books, 1982), p. 208; Pierre de Bordeille Brantôme, *Vies des dames galantes* (Paris: H. Beziat, 1936); Barbara Diefendorf, "Widowhood and Remarriage in Sixteenth-Century Paris," *Journal of Family History* 7 (Winter 1982), 379–95; Steven

Ozmont, *When Fathers Ruled: Family Life in Reformation Europe* (Cambridge, Mass.: Harvard University Press, 1983); Roger Thompson, *Women in Stuart England and America: A Comparative Study* (London: Routledge & Kegan Paul, 1974).

42. Richard T. Vann, "Women in Preindustrial Capitalism," in Renate Bridenthal and Claudia Koontz, eds., *Becoming Visible: Women in European History* (Boston: Houghton Mifflin, 1977), p. 197; D. Gaunt and O. Lofgren, "Remarriage in the Nordic Countries: The Cultural and Socio-Economic Background," in J. Dupâquier et al., eds., *Marriage and Remarriage in Populations of the Past* (London: Academic Press, 1981), p. 56; Michael Mitterauer and Reinhard Sieder, *The European Family: Patriarchy to Partnership from the Middle Ages to the Present*, trans. Karla Oosterveen and Manfred Hörzinger (Chicago: University of Chicago Press, 1984), p. 127; Peter Laslett, *Family Life and Illicit Love in Earlier Generations: Essays in Historical Sociology* (Cambridge: Cambridge University Press, 1977), p. 13.

43. Keith Thomas, "Age and Authority in Early Modern England," *Proceedings of the British Academy* 62 (1976), 244; Lawrence Stone, *The Family, Sex, and Marriage in England, 1500–1800* (New York: Harper & Row, 1977), p. 193.

44. These revolutionary changes in family policy resulted from the control over marriage of Catholic ecclesiastical courts rather than civil courts. Ecclesiastical dedication to celibacy made all marriages suspect, while the Church's vast wealth came largely from legacies from widowers and especially widows. Thus the Church discouraged remarriage among aging people. The anti-incest laws, which came to include not only distant blood relatives but also spousal relatives, stepparents, and godparents, were motivated by the policy of celibacy as well as by the fear that the natural affection among family and kin might produce a dangerous libidinousness. See Jack Goody, *The Development of the Family and Marriage in Europe, 1200–1800* (Cambridge: Cambridge University Press, 1983), pp. 48–102. The nobility used the laws on "consanguinity" to secure divorce, as did Eleanor of Aquitaine against Louis VIII and Henry VIII against Catherine of Aragon.

45. In his work on inheritance, Jack Goody posits that in most populations in the premodern era, 20 percent of families would have only daughters surviving to adulthood. This figure suggests that female inheritance may have been substantial in early eras. Jack Goody, "Inheritance, Property and Women: Some Comparative Considerations," in Jack Goody, Joan Thirsk, and E. P. Thompson, eds., *Family and Inheritance: Rural Society in Western Europe* (Cambridge: Cambridge University Press, 1976), p. 10.

46. Cf. Pearl Hogrefe, *Women of Action in Tudor England: Nine Biographical Sketches* (Ames: Iowa State University Press, 1977).

47. Ralph A. Houlbrooke, *The English Family, 1450–1700* (London: Longman, 1984), pp. 106–7.

48. Judith M. Bennett, "Public Power and Authority in the Medieval English Countryside," in Erler and Kowaleski, *Women and Power in the Middle Ages*, p. 23.

49. See Diefendorf, "Widowhood and Remarriage," passim.

50. Lawrence Stone, *The Crisis of the Aristocracy, 1558–1641* (Oxford: Oxford University Press, 1965), p. 622; Gaunt and Lofgren, "Remarriage in the Nordic Countries," p. 56.

51. Thomas Deloney, *The Pleasant Historie of John Winchcomb, in his yonguer yeares called Jack of Newbery* (London: H. Lownes, 1626).

52. Robert Wheaton, "Recent Trends in the Historical Study of the French Family," in Tamara K. Hareven and Robert Wheaton, eds., *Family and Sexuality in French History* (Philadelphia: University of Pennsylvania Press, 1980), p. 12–14.

53. George Huppert, *After the Black Death: A Social History of Early Modern Europe* (Bloomington: Indiana University Press, 1986), pp. 10–80. In the sixteenth century, according to Steven Ozmont, perhaps 40 percent of all women were single: 20 percent

were spinsters, and 10 percent to 20 percent were widows. *When Fathers Ruled: Family Life in Reformation Europe* (Cambridge, Mass.: Harvard University Press, 1983), p. 1. As late as 1700, according to Patricia Branca, 50 percent of women in France and 30 percent in England were unmarried. *Women in Europe Since 1750* (New York: St. Martin's Press, 1978), p. 73. Under what has come to be called the "European marriage pattern," with late ages of first marriage and many unmarried women, Edward Wrigley asserts that between two-fifths and three-fifths of women of childbearing ages were unmarried over these centuries. *Population and History* (New York: McGraw-Hill, 1969), p. 90.

54. Wheaton, "Recent Trends," pp. 12–14. See also John Gillis, *For Better, For Worse: British Marriages, 1600 to the Present* (New York: Oxford University Press, 1985).

55. Gaunt and Lofgren, "Remarriage in the Nordic Countries," p. 52.

56. Huppert, *After the Black Death*, pp. 5–6.

57. Jean-Louis Flindrin, *Familles: Parenté, maison, sexualité dans l'ancienne société* (Paris: Editions du Seuil, 1976), p. 114.

58. Ozmont, *When Fathers Ruled*, pp. 75–77. When in the mid-seventeenth century Briton Thomas Wright's first wife died, having borne seven children, "some people advised me to marry an old woman that would have no more children." Alan Macfarlane, *Marriage and Love in England, 1300–1840* (Oxford: Basil Blackwell, 1986), p. 62.

59. Flindrin, *Familles*, p. 115; William Wycherley, *The Plain Dealer* (London: Ernest Benn, 1979), p. 71.

60. *Romance of the Rose*, p. 349; Houlbrooke, *English Family*, p. 214.

61. Gaunt and Lofgren, "Remarriage in the Nordic Countries," p. 53. Historians of homosexuality point out that in early modern Europe, "sodomy" was a general term used to refer to any sexual coupling considered unnatural.

62. Macfarlane, *Marriage and Love*, passim. Macfarlane asserts that this transition occurred in England as early as the sixteenth century.

63. See Christiane Klapisch-Zuber, "The 'Mattinata' in Medieval Italy," in Klapisch-Zuber, *Women, Family, and Ritual in Renaissance Italy*, trans. Lydia Cochrane (Chicago: University of Chicago Press, 1985); Natalie Davis, "The Reasons for Misrule," in *Society and Culture in Early Modern France*, pp. 97–123; André Burguière, "The Charivari and Religious Repression in France During the Ancien Régime," in Hareven and Wheaton, *Family and Sexuality in French History*, pp. 84–110. Henri Rey-Flaud, *Le charivari: Les rituels fondamentaux de la sexualité* (Paris: Payot, 1985), finds the disciplining action more often took the form of attempted or actual rape and was primarily directed against unprotected women rather than age-disparate relationships.

64. Kathryn L. Ryerson, "Women in Business in Medieval Montpelier," in Barbara A. Hanawalt, ed., *Women and Work in Preindustrial Europe* (Bloomington: Indiana University Press, 1986), p. 137; Martha C. Howell, "Women, the Family Economy, and the Structures of Market Production in Cities of Northern Europe during the Late Middle Ages," in Ibid., p. 201; Charles Pythian-Adams, *The Desolation of a City: Coventry and the Urban Crisis of the Late Middle Ages* (Cambridge: Cambridge University Press, 1979), pp. 91–92.

65. T. H. Hollingworth, "A Demographic Study of the British Ducal Families, 1330–1475," *Population Studies* 27 (1973), 287–93.

66. Georges Minois, *Histoire de la vieillesse de l'antiquité à la renaissance* (Paris: Fayard, 1987), pp. 300–333.

67. See J. Z. Titow, "Some Differences Between Manors and Their Effects on the Condition of the Peasant in the Thirteenth Century," *Agricultural History Review* 10 (1962), 1–13. (Titow cites Postan.)

68. Alain Bideau, "A Demographic and Social Analysis of Widowhood and Remarriage: The Example of the Castellany of Thoissey-en-Dombes, 1670–1840," *Journal of Family History* 5 (Spring 1980), 28–43, offers a regional example in which the standard

pattern of older men marrying younger women in the mid-seventeenth century produced a group of older women who married younger men by the end of the century.

69. On Siena, see Eleanor S. Riemer, "Women, Dowries, and Capital Investment in Thirteenth-Century Siena," in Marion A. Kaplan, ed., *The Marriage Bargain: Women and Dowries in European History* (New York: Haworth Press, 1985), pp. 59–80. On Genoa, see Diane Hughes, "Domestic Ideals and Social Behavior: Evidence from Medieval Genoa," in Charles E. Rosenberg, ed., *The Family in History* (Philadelphia: University of Pennsylvania Press, 1975), pp. 115–43.

70. Elise Boulding, *The Underside of History: A View of Women Through Time* (Boulder, Colo.: Westview Press, 1976), p. 554.

71. Quoted by Nancy Lyman Roelker, ed., "Introduction," in "Papers From the 1981 Berkshire Conference: Widowhood and Rational Domesticity: Modes of Independence for Women in Early Modern Europe," *Journal of Family History* 7 (Winter 1982), 377.

72. In fifteenth-century Florence, husbands were on the average thirteen years older than their wives. Moralists recommended such a large age differential. See David Herlihy, "Veillir à Florence au Quattrocentro," *Annales* 27 (1969), 1341–42.

73. On homosexuality in Italy, see Guido Ruggiero, *The Boundaries of Eros: Sex Crime and Sexuality in Renaissance Venice* (New York: Oxford University Press, 1985).

74. See Riemer, "Women, Dowries, and Capital Investment," and Diefendorf, "Widowhood and Remarriage." See also Sarah Hanley, "Family and State in Early Modern France: The Marriage Pact," in Marilyn J. Boxer and Jean H. Quataert, eds., *Connecting Spheres: Women in the Western World, 1500 to the Present* (New York: Oxford University Press, 1987), pp. 54–58; Adrienne Rogers, "Women and the Law," in Samia I. Spencer, ed., *French Women and the Age of Enlightenment* (Bloomington: Indiana University Press, 1984), pp. 33–40; Anne Lise Head-König, "Demographic History and Its Perception of Women from the Seventeenth to the Nineteenth Century," in Karen Offen, Ruth Roach Pierson, and Jane Rendall, eds., *Writing Women's History: International Perspectives* (Bloomington: Indiana University Press, 1991), p. 27; Barbara J. Todd, "The Remarrying Widow: A Stereotype Reconsidered," in Mary Prior, ed., *Women in English Society, 1500–1800* (London: Methuen, 1985), pp. 65–73; Davis, "Women on Top," in *Society and Culture in Early Modern France*, p. 126.

Diane Owen Hughes notes that the rise of male-dominated communes as early as the thirteenth century in Italy brought the removal of women from public authority and increased control over such matters as private contracts and even women's rituals. See Hughes, "Invisible Madonnas? The Italian Historiographical Tradition and the Women of Medieval Italy," in Stuard, ed., *Women in Medieval History*, pp. 25–57.

75. Merry E. Wisner, "Women's Defense of Their Public Role," in Mary Beth Rose, ed., *Women in the Middle Ages and the Renaissance* (Syracuse, N.Y.: Syracuse University Press, 1986), pp. 4–6.

76. Charles Carlton, "The Widow's Tale: Male Myths and Female Reality in 16th and 17th Century England," *Albion* 10 (Summer 1978), 123; Louise A. Tilly and Joan W. Scott, *Women, Work and Family* (New York: Holt, Rinehart, and Winston, 1978), pp. 51–52; David Herlihy, "Old Women in the Italian Renaissance," paper, Conference on Aging and the Life Cycle in the Renaissance, University of Maryland, College Park, April 1988.

77. See Emmanuel Le Roy Ladurie, *Montaillou, village occitan de 1294 à 1324* (Paris: Gallimard, 1975).

CHAPTER FIVE   *Aging Women, Power, and Sexuality: From the Wife of Bath to the Witch*

1. Judith K. Brown, "Cross-cultural Perspectives on Middle-aged Women," *Current Anthropology* 23 (April 1982), 143–56; Judith K. Brown and Virginia Kerns, eds., *In Her Prime: A New View of Middle-Aged Women* (South Hadley, Mass.: Bergin & Garvey, 1985), especially the article by David Gutmann, "Beyond Nurture: Developmental Perspectives on the Vital Older Woman," pp. 198–211.

2. The *Goodman of Paris: A Treatise on Moral and Domestic Economy by a Citizen of Paris* [c. 1393], trans. Eileen Power (London: George Routledge, 1928), p. 177; Geoffrey Chaucer, *The Canterbury Tales*, rendered into modern English by J. U. Nicolson (Garden City, N.Y.: Garden City Publishing, 1934), p. 415; Antoine de la Sale [?], *Fifteen Joys of Marriage*, trans. Elizabeth Abbott (New York: Orion, 1959), p. 191. Inevitably "she seizes authority [over her younger husband] and would rule him and make him suffer many pains and torments."

3. According to George Huppert, no more than 5 percent of married couples in Western Europe during the early modern era lived with their parents. Marriage contracts often included clauses to safeguard the rights of parents who retired. There were regional variations. In fifteenth-century Florence, perhaps as many as one-half of married Florentine males continued to live under the authority of their fathers. Cf. George Huppert, *After the Black Death: A Social History of Early Modern Europe* (Bloomington: Indiana University Press, 1986), pp. 126–28.

4. Emotional closeness, however, could occur. Natalie Davis relates the recollection of the Countess D'Aulnois, the seventeenth-century collector of fairy tales: "My Grandmother had that fond love for me which women advanced in years have many times for Children by whom they expect the continuation of their Name and Family." Natalie Zemon Davis, "Ghosts, Kin, and Progeny: Some Features of Family Life in Early Modern France," *Daedalus* 106 (1977), 91. In preindustrial England, Peter Laslett finds significant "hints" of exception to the general rule that old people lived alone. He thinks that widows sometimes joined households to raise grandchildren. See Peter Laslett, *Family Life and Illicit Love in Earlier Generations: Essays in Historical Sociology* (Cambridge: Cambridge University Press, 1977), p. 208.

5. Cf. Gutmann, "Beyond Nurture," in Brown, *In Her Prime*, pp. 198–213.

6. Cf. Alma Gottlieb, ed., *Blood Magic: The Anthropology of Menstruation* (Berkeley: University of California Press, 1988).

7. Pauline Bart, "Why Women's Status Changes in Middle Age: The Turns of the Social Ferris Wheel," *Sociological Symposium* 3 (Fall 1969), 1–18.

8. Nancy J. Vickers, "Diana Described: Scattered Woman and Scattered Rhyme," in Elizabeth Abel, ed., *Writing and Sexual Difference* (Chicago: University of Chicago Press, 1982), pp. 95–109.

9. In this interpretation I have extended Gabriele Schwab's argument in "Seduced by Witches: Nathaniel Hawthorne's *The Scarlet Letter* in the Context of New England Witchcraft Fictions," in Dianne Hunter, ed., *Seduction and Theory: Readings of Gender, Representation, and Rhetoric* (Urbana: University of Illinois Press, 1989), pp. 170–91. Schwab writes of a "witchcraft pattern" which, originating in the Middle Ages, was an "epistemological framework" which interpreted the "relationship of historical subjects to society and external nature."

10. On these physiological theories, cf. Thomas Laquer, "Orgasm, Generation, and the Politics of Reproductive Biology," in Catherine Gallagher and Thomas Laquer,

eds., *The Making of the Modern Body: Sexuality and Society in the Nineteenth Century* (Berkeley: University of California Press, 1987), pp. 1–41; Ian MacClean, *The Renaissance Notion of Woman* (Cambridge: Cambridge University Press, 1980); Angus McLaren, *Reproductive Rituals: The Perception of Fertility in England From the Sixteenth to the Nineteenth Century* (London: Methuen, 1984); Hilda Smith, "Gynecology and Ideology in Seventeenth-Century England," in Berenice Carroll, ed., *Liberating Women's History: Theoretical and Critical Essays* (Urbana: University of Illinois Press, 1976), pp. 97–114; Thomas R. Cole, *The Journey of Life: A Cultural History of Aging in America* (Cambridge: Cambridge University Press, 1992).

11. *John Stubbs's Gaping Gulf with Letters and other Documents,* ed. Lloyd E. Berry (Charlottesville: University of Virginia Press, 1968).

12. William Gouge, *The workes of William Govge: in Tvvo volumes: the first domesticall duties. The second, the whole armovr of God* (London: John Beale, 1627), p. 131; Pierre de Bourdeille, Abbé de Brantôme, *Les vies des dames galantes* (Paris: Garnier Frères, 1963), p. 207.

13. *The Complete Works of William Shakespeare,* ed. William Aldis Wright (Garden City, N.Y.: Garden City Books, 1936), p. 387.

14. John Ray, *A collection of English proverbs digested into a convenient method for finding any one upon occasion* (Cambridge: J. Haynes, 1678), n.p.

15. Giovanni Boccaccio, *The Corbaccio,* trans. Anthony K. Cassell (Urbana: University of Illinois Press, 1975), p. 46; Desiderius Erasmus, *The Praise of Folly,* trans. Clarence H. Miller (New Haven, Conn.: Yale University Press, 1979), pp. 48–49. With regard to older men, Erasmus also wrote: "It is my doing [Dame Folly] that you see everywhere men as old as Nestor . . . fall[ing] head over heels in love with some young girl and outdo[ing] any beardless youth in amorous idiocy" (p. 48).

16. Fernando de Rojas, *La Celestina: The Spanish Bawd,* trans. Wallace Woolsey (New York: Las Americas, 1969), p. 61; Shakespeare, *Complete Works,* pp. 1065–70.

According to Christiane Klapisch-Zuber, in Florence in the fourteenth and fifteenth centuries, old women's sexuality was suspect. Because these women had probably experienced sexual intercourse, "they were considered prone, like the widow in Boccaccio's *Corbaccio,* to fall into debauchery." See Klapisch-Zuber, "The 'Cruel Mother': Maternity, Widowhood, and Dowry in Florence in the Fourteenth and Fifteenth Centuries," in Klapisch-Zuber, *Women, Family, and Ritual in Renaissance Italy,* trans. Lydia Cochrane (Chicago: University of Chicago Press, 1985), p. 123.

17. Shakespeare, *Complete Works,* p. 737.

18. Robert Burton, *The Anatomy of Melancholy* (Philadelphia: J. W. Moore, 1854), p. 452; John Marston, *The Insatiate Countess,* ed. Giorgio Melchiori (Manchester: Manchester University Press, 1984), p. 138.

19. Margaret Spufford, *Small Books and Pleasant Histories: Popular Fiction and Its Readership in Seventeenth-Century England* (London: Methuen, 1981), p. 160; Thomas Wythorne, *The Autobiography of Thomas Wythorne,* ed. James M. Osborn (Oxford: Oxford University Press, 1961), p. 26.

20. Brantôme, *Dames galantes,* pp. 105, 108.

21. Nina Epton, *Love and the French* (Cleveland: World, 1959), p. 84.

22. See Dale Hoak, "Witch-Hunting and Women in the Art of the Renaissance," *History Today* 31 (February 1981), 22–26.

23. See Lawrence Stone, *The Family, Sex and Marriage in England, 1500–1800* (New York: Harper & Row, 1977), p. 104.

24. Cf. Thomas Wythorne, *The Autobiography of Thomas Wythorne,* ed. J. Osborn (Oxford: Oxford University Press, 1961); Thomas Deloney, *The pleasant Historie of John Winchcomb, in his yonguer yeares called Jack of Newbery* (London: H. Lownes, 1626), p. 20.

25. William Wycherley, *Love in a Wood,* in *The Complete Plays of William Wycherley,* ed. Gerald Weales (New York: New York University Press, 1967), pp. 63–64; Aphra Behn, *Sir Patient Fancy,* in *The Works of Aphra Behn,* ed. Montague Summers, 6 vols. (New York: Benjamin Blom, 1967), vol. 4, p. 47.

26. Roger Thompson, *Unfit for Modest Ears: A Study of Pornographic, Obscene, and Bawdy Works Written or Published in England in the Second Half of the Seventeenth Century* (Totowa, N.J.: Roman and Littlefield, 1979), pp. 26–76. John Cleland, *Fanny Hill: Memoirs of a Woman of Pleasure* (New York: Penguin Books, 1985), p. 61. According to John J. Richetti, *Popular Fiction Before Richardson: Narrative Patterns, 1700–1739* (London: Oxford University Press, 1969), pp. 39–41, a standard theme of the English scandal novels of the early eighteenth century was the seduction of innocent male youths by older, lascivious courtesans.

27. Brantôme, *Dames galantes,* p. 211; Daniel Defoe, *Conjugal Lewdness, or Matrimonial Whoredom: A Treatise Concerning the Use and Abuse of the Marriage Bed* [1727] (Gainesville, Fla.: Scholars' Facsimiles and Reproductions, 1967), pp. 238–39.

28. On early life-cycle reasoning, cf. J. A. Burrows, *The Ages of Man: A Study in Medieval Writing and Thought* (Oxford: Clarendon Press, 1986); Samuel C. Chew, *The Pilgrimage of Life* (New Haven, Conn.: Yale University Press, 1962); Cole, *Journey of Life;* Mary Dove, *The Perfect Age of Man's Life* (Cambridge: Cambridge University Press, 1986); Creighton Gilbert, "When Did Renaissance Man Grow Old?" *Studies in the Renaissance* 14 (1967), 7–32; Elizabeth Sears, *The Ages of Man: Medieval Interpretations of the Life Cycle* (Princeton, N.J.: Princeton University Press, 1986); Steven R. Smith, "Growing Old in Early Stuart England," *Albion* 8 (Summer 1976), 125–41; Philippa Tristram, *Figures of Life and Death in Medieval English Literature* (London: Paul Elek, 1976).

29. Cf. David Herlihy, "Life Expectancies for Women in Medieval Society," in Rosemarie Thee Morewedge, *The Role of Woman in the Middle Ages* (Albany: State University of New York Press, 1975), pp. 1–4. See also John Gillis, *Youth and History: Tradition and Change in European Age Relations, 1770–Present* (New York: Academic Press, 1974), p. 7; Keith Thomas, "Age and Authority in Early Modern England," *Proceedings of the British Academy* 62 (1976), 235.

30. Andreas Capellanus, *The Art of Courtly Love,* trans. John Jay Parry (New York: Frederick Ungar, 1941), pp. 118–19.

31. *Aristotle's compleat masterpiece,* 22d ed. (London: Booksellers, 1741), pp. 2–4; Henry Cuffe, *The Differences of the Ages of Man's Life* (London: Lawrence Chapman, 1633), p. 106. Paul Gabriel Boucé, "Some Sexual Beliefs and Myths in Eighteenth-Century Britain," in Paul Gabriel Boucé, *Sexuality in Eighteenth-Century Britain* (Totowa, N.J.: Barnes & Noble, 1982), pp. 41–42, notes the belief about women's earlier aging due to heat in a number of eighteenth-century medical manuals, especially in the 1742 *Ladies' Medical Directory,* which calls it an "ancient vulgar error." Mary Wollstonecraft, *Vindication of the Rights of Woman* [1792] (New York: W. W. Norton, 1975), p. 150, notes the continuation of beliefs about women's earlier maturation by "some naturalists" as late as the late eighteenth century.

32. Ovid, *The Metamorphoses of Ovid,* trans. Mary Innes (London: Penguin Books, 1935), pp. 369–70; Ovid, *The Art of Love,* trans. J. H. Mozley (Cambridge, Mass.: Harvard University Press, 1978), p. 139; Guillaume de Lorris and Jean de Meun, *Romance of the Rose,* trans. Charles Dahlberg (Princeton, N.J.: Princeton University Press, 1971), p. 73; François Rabelais, *Gargantua and Pantagruel; The Five Books,* trans. Jacques LeClercq (New York: Heritage, 1936), pp. 440–44.

33. Cf. William Vaughan, *Directions for Health* (5th ed., 1617), p. 49; Capellanus, *Art of Courtly Love,* p. 38: "Love makes even an ugly woman seem very beautiful to her

lover." "The cause of love among fools is beauty, but among good men virtues of the mind." Both Sir Walter Raleigh in 1632 and Francis Osborne in 1656 cautioned their sons against the "dangers" inherent in marrying beautiful women. Louis B. Wright, ed., *Advice to a Son: Precepts of Lord Burghley, Sir Walter Raleigh, and Francis Osborne* (Ithaca, N.Y.: Cornell University Press, 1962), pp. 20–65.

34. Christine de Pizan was the widow of a nobleman at the court of King Charles VI of France; she supported herself by her writing. She is now considered the most important woman writer of this early period who utilized protofeminist themes in her work.

35. Christine de Pizan, *The Book of the City of Ladies,* trans. Earl Jeffrey Richards (New York: Persea Books, 1982), p. 208. Commenting on this same relationship between Blanche and Thibaut a century after Pizan's analysis, Brantôme wrote that "it is the nature of all merit and high perfection to provoke love." *Dames galantes,* p. 143. This idea about the superiority of spiritual beauty is also a central theme of Marguerite de Navarre's 1558 *Heptaméron.* Marguerite de Navarre, the sister of Francis I of France, was a major proto-feminist writer of the sixteenth century. See also Constance Jordan, *Renaissance Feminism: Literary Texts and Political Models* (Ithaca, N.Y.: Cornell University Press, 1990).

36. Baldesar Castiglione, *The Book of the Courtier,* trans. Charles S. Singleton (Garden City, N.Y.: Doubleday, 1959), p. 19; *Ficino's Commentary on Plato's Symposium,* chapter 18. Sixteenth-century Englishman Francis Bacon wrote that "there is no excellent beauty that has not some strangeness in the proportion." Quoted by Lori Hope Lefkovitz, *The Character of Beauty in the Victorian Novel* (Ann Arbor, Mich.: UMI Research Press, 1984), pp. 10–11.

37. Agnolo Firenzuola, *Of The Beauty of Women* [1535], trans. Clara Bell (London: James R. Osgood, 1892), pp. 21, 97. According to Jacob Burckhardt, Firenzuola's was the major sixteenth-century work on the subject of beauty. Burckhardt, *The Civilization of the Renaissance in Italy: An Essay* (Oxford: Phaidon, 1945), p. 211.

38. Although Arthur Marwick in his work on the history of beauty focuses on dominant, youthful standards, he also notes the cultural valuations regarding beauty and morality I am charting. See Arthur Marwick, *Beauty in History: Society, Politics, and Personal Appearance c. 1500 to the Present* (London: Thames and Hudson, 1988), pp. 60–61.

39. Firenzuola, *Beauty,* p. 92.

40. Rabelais, *Gargantua and Pantagruel,* pp. 441–42.

41. Anthony Hamilton, *Memoirs of the Count Grammont,* trans. Horace Walpole (Philadelphia, Gebbie & Co., 1888), p. 79.

42. Elizabeth Cropper, "The Beauty of Women: Problems in the Rhetoric of Renaissance Portraiture," in Margaret W. Ferguson, Maureen Quilligan, and Nancy J. Vickers, eds., *Rewriting the Renaissance: The Discourses of Sexual Difference in Early Modern Europe* (Chicago: University of Chicago Press, 1986), pp. 175–190.

43. Shakespeare, *Complete Works,* pp. 1295–96.

44. Cf. Andreas Laurentius, *A Discourse of the Preservation of the Sight; of Melancholike Diseases; of Rheumes, and of Old Age* [1597], trans. R. Surphlet (Oxford: Oxford University Press, 1938), p. 173. Cited by Alison Klairmont Lingo, "A Medical and Literary Perspective of the Older Woman in Early Modern France: A Preliminary View," paper, Conference on Aging and the Life Cycle in the Renaissance, University of Maryland, College Park, April 1988, p. 6. Lingo identifies this work as the only French treatise on this subject from the learned medical tradition during the early modern period.

45. Ovid, *Metamorphoses,* pp. 369–70.

46. Sir James George Frazer, *The Golden Bough: A Study in Magic and Religion,* abridged ed. (New York: Macmillan, 1925), pp. 607–58.

47. Antonia Fraser, *The Weaker Vessel* (New York: Alfred A. Knopf, 1984), p. 102. In

the thirteenth-century *Romance of the Rose*, p. 35, old age, included among the seven deadly sins, is a female figure "shrunken by a good foot from her former stature."

48. Violet A. Wilson, *Queen Elizabeth's Maids of Honour and Ladies of the Privy Chamber* (London: John Lane, 1922), pp. 95, 277.

49. Boccaccio, *Corbaccio*, pp. 43, 54–55; Burton, *Anatomy of Melancholy*, pp. 470–80.

50. For present-day estimates, cf. McClaren, *Reproductive Rituals*, p. 65. For the confusion of contemporaries, cf. Bonnie S. Anderson and Judith P. Zinsser, *A History of Their Own: Women in Europe from Prehistory to the Present*, 2 vols. (New York: Harper & Row, 1988), vol. 1, p. 105. Anderson and Zinsser note that seventh-century Visigothic law assumed that a woman over forty was infertile but that the twelfth-century abbess Hildegard of Bingen estimated that a woman's childbearing years extended into her fifties. Trotula of Salerno, writing in the eleventh century, advised that menstruation lasted until the age of fifty and that some women experienced it even later, if they had been well-nourished and lived an easy life. Beryl Rowland, *Medieval Women's Guide to Health: The First English Gynecological Handbook* (Kent: Ohio State University Press, 1981), p. 59. According to Vern Bulloch and Cameron Campbell, "Female Longevity and Diet in the Middle Ages," *Speculum* 55 (1980): 317–25, most authorities dated its onset at fifty, although earlier and later dates were given. *Aristotle's compleat masterpiece*, p. 3, identifies the end of menstruation as occurring at forty-five, although the "temperate go to 55 and have children."

51. Cf. E. Le Roy Ladurie, "Famine Amenorrhoea," in R. Forster and O. Ranum, eds., *Biology of Man in History: Selections from the Annales Économies, Sociétés, Civilisations*, trans. Elberg Forster and Patricia M. Ranum (Baltimore: Johns Hopkins University Press, 1975), pp. 163–78; Patricia Crawford, "Attitudes to Menstruation in Seventeenth-Century England," *Past and Present* 29 (May 1978), 47–73.

In her study of fertility in Renaissance Florentine women, Christiane Klapisch-Zuber finds that women ended giving birth at about thirty-five. She speculates either that they experienced an early menopause or that this was the point at which they were seen as entering old age and thus were required to end their procreative experience. Christiane Klapisch-Zuber, "The Last Child: Fertility and Aging in Florentine Women," paper, Conference on Aging and the Life Cycle in the Renaissance, University of Maryland, College Park, April 1988.

52. Neville Williams, *All the Queen's Men: Elizabeth I and Her Courtiers* (New York: Macmillan, 1972), p. 175.

53. Crawford, "Menstruation in Seventeenth-Century England," p. 55; David G. Troyansky, *Old Age in the Old Regime: Image and Experience in Eighteenth-Century France* (Ithaca, N.Y.: Cornell University Press, 1989), p. 117, quoting Jean Astruc, *Traité des maladies des femmes*.

54. Frances Parkinson Keyes, *St. Anne: Grandmother of Our Saviour* (London: Allan Wingate, 1956); Shakespeare, *Complete Works*, p. 1060. As late as 1857, in his popular *Change of Life*, Edward Tilt listed examples of women who had had babies in their fifties. This issue of birth at later ages was, according to Tilt, a matter of great importance "when expectancies depend on the possibility of the woman being fruitful." Edward Tilt, *The Change of Life in Health and Disease* (London: Churchill, 1857), p. 17.

55. Cf. L. T. Topsfield, *Chrétien de Troyes: A Study of the Arthurian Romances* (Cambridge: Cambridge University Press, 1981), pp. 282–93.

56. Sir Thomas Malory, *Le Morte Darthur*, ed. R. M. Lumiansky (New York: Charles Scribner's Sons, 1982), p. 105. Robert Lumiansky, *Malory's Originality: A Critical Study of the Morte d'Arthur* (Baltimore: Johns Hopkins University Press, 1964), p. 1, calls Malory's work "the most outstanding English book of the fifteenth century."

57. William Mathews, "The Wife of Bath and All Her Sect," *Viator* 5 (1974), 413–43.

58. K. M. Briggs, *Pale Hecate's Team: An Examination of the Beliefs on Witchcraft and Magic Among Shakespeare's Contemporaries and His Immediate Circle* (London: Routledge and Kegan Paul, 1962), p. 92. See also John Ashton, *Chap-books of the Eighteenth Century* (London: Chatto and Windus, 1882), p. 89.

59. *Goodman of Paris,* p. 52: "When you go to town or to church, you should be suitably accompanied . . . especially by worthy women . . . and never go near any suspected woman."

60. Miguel de Cervantes, *Don Quixote,* trans. John Ormsby, rev. and ed., Joseph R. Jones and Kenneth Douglas (New York: W. W. Norton, 1981), pp. 637–38.

61. Cf. Julio Caro Baroja, *The World of the Witches,* trans. O. N. V. Glendinning (Chicago: University of Chicago Press, 1961), pp. 101–2, and Lynne Lawner, *Lives of the Courtesans: Portraits of the Renaissance* (New York: Rizzoli, 1987), pp. 73, 151–59.

The Elizabethan doctor, Simon Forman, wrote of a gentlewoman, the wife of a church rector, who was "never without one bawd, or a cunning woman or other, to keep her company . . . to paint her, etc." A. L. Rowse, *Simon Forman: Sex and Society in Shakespeare's Age* (London: Weidenfeld and Nicolson, 1974), pp. 120–21. The first known play in the English language concerns a go-between persuading a young woman to service one of her clients. See Richard Axton, "Popular Modes in the Earliest Plays," in Neville Denny, ed., *Medieval Drama* (London: Edward Arnold, 1973), p. 16.

62. Rojas, *Celestina,* p. 67.

63. Rabelais, *Gargantua and Pantagruel,* pp. 441–42.

64. On witchcraft, I have used, in particular, Jeffrey Russell Burton, *Witchcraft in the Middle Ages* (Ithaca, N.Y.: Cornell University Press, 1972); Norman Cohn, *Europe's Inner Demons: An Enquiry Inspired by the Great Witch-Hunt* (New York: Basic Books, 1975); John Demos, *Entertaining Satan: Witchcraft and the Culture of Early New England* (New York: Oxford University Press, 1982); Carol F. Karlsen, *The Devil in the Shape of a Woman: Witchcraft in Colonial New England* (New York: W. W. Norton, 1987); Joseph Klaits, *Servants of Satan: The Age of the Witch Hunts* (Bloomington: Indiana University Press, 1985); Christina Larner, *Enemies of God: The Witch-Hunt in Scotland* (Baltimore: Johns Hopkins University Press, 1981); Alan Macfarlane, *Witchcraft in Tudor and Stuart England* (London: Routledge & Kegan Paul, 1970); G. R. Quaife, *Godly Zeal and Furious Rage: The Witch in Early Modern Europe* (New York: St. Martin's Press, 1987); Keith Thomas, *Religion and the Decline of Magic* (New York: Charles Scribner's Sons, 1971).

65. D. E. Underdown, "The Taming of the Scold: The Enforcement of Patriarchal Authority in Early Modern Europe," in Anthony Fletcher and John Stevenson, eds., *Order and Disorder in Early Modern England* (London: Cambridge University Press, 1985), p. 116, notes that in England between 1560 and 1640, local court records show a preoccupation with vocal public displays on the part of women. He traces this fixation to the fears of social breakdown in the sixty years before the Civil War, due to excessive population growth, inflation, and land shortage. He points out that both Keith Thomas and Alan Macfarlane came to a similar conclusion.

66. In making this argument about the omnipresence of the possibility of persecution, I have been influenced by Cohn, *Europe's Inner Demons,* especially by his tracing over time the construction of the details of the witchcraft fantasy and its origins in perversions of beliefs about the ancient goddesses (pp. 212–24).

67. *Autobiography of Thomas Wythorne,* p. 88; Shakespeare, *Complete Works,* p. 1296; Martine Segalen, *Love and Power in the Peasant Family: Rural France in the Nineteenth Century,* trans. Sarah Matthews (Oxford: Basil Blackwell, 1983), p. 58; Jacques Bailbe, "La thème de la vieille femme dans la poésie satirique du seizième et du début du dix-septième siècles," *Bibliothèque de humanisme et renaissance* 26 (1964), 110.

68. Heinrich Krämer and Jacob Sprenger, *The Malleus Maleficarum,* trans. Montague Summers (New York: Dover, 1971), p. 47.

69. Edward Bever, "Old Age and Witchcraft in Early Modern Europe," in Peter N. Stearns, ed., *Old Age in Preindustrial Society* (New York: Holmes & Meier, 1983), p. 154; Karlsen, *Devil in the Shape of a Woman,* pp. 156–57; R. E. L. Masters, *Eros and Evil: The Sexual Psychopathology of Witchcraft* (New York: Julian Press, 1962), p. 53; Burton, *Anatomy of Melancholy,* pp. 132–35. Bever finds the inclusion of older women as primary perpetrators in the charges of sexuality the result of the increasing immoderation of the witchcraft persecutions.

70. Cf. Mikhail Bakhtin, *Rabelais and His World,* trans. Helene Iswolsky (Cambridge, Mass.: MIT Press, 1965), p. 87.

71. *The Complete Grimm's Fairy Tales* (New York: Pantheon, 1972), p. 339. See John Widdowson, "The Witch as a Frightening and Threatening Figure," in Venetia Newall, ed., *The Witch Figure* (London: Routledge & Kegan Paul, 1973), pp. 200–220.

72. Crawford, "Menstruation in Seventeenth-Century England," pp. 53–5.

73. Reginald Scot, *The Discouerie of Witchcraft* (New York: Da Capo Press, 1971), p. 54.

74. Cf. Burton, *Anatomy of Melancholy,* p. 132; Hoak, "Witch-Hunting and Women in the Art of the Renaissance," p. 22; Longo, "A Medical and Literary Perspective," pp. 8–9. In 1611 Antonio of Cartagena conjectured that it was the existence of the mysterious menstrual blood in their bodies which provided old witches with the power to attract young men. Edward S. Gifford, Jr., *The Evil Eye: Studies in the Folklore of Vision* (New York: Macmillan, 1958), p. 26.

75. Vida Skultans, "The Symbolic Significance of Menopause and Menstruation," *Man* 5 (1970), 650; G. Stanley Hall, *Senescence: The Last Half of Life* (New York: D. Appleton, 1922), p. 45; John Lyly, *Sapho and Phao,* in R. Warwick Bond, ed., *The Complete Works of John Lyly,* 2 vols. (Oxford: Clarendon, 1932), vol. 2, p. 397.

In sixteenth- and seventeenth-century Spain, doctors warned new mothers against associating with old women, who could destroy both mother and child through the "vapors" they emitted, especially from the eyes, nose, and mouth. See Mary Elizabeth Perry, "Wrinkles and Rancour: Older Women in Counter-Reformation Spain," Paper, Berkshire Conference on the History of Women, Douglass College, Rutgers University, June 9, 1990.

76. Elborg Forster, ed., *A Woman's Life at the Court of the Sun King: Letters of Liselotte von der Pfalz, Elisabeth d'Orleans, 1652–1722* (Baltimore: Johns Hopkins University Press, 1984), p. 49; Scot, *Discouerie of Witchcraft,* p. 75.

77. *Malleus Maleficarum,* pp. 215–28. According to the *Malleus,* if the witch's feet touched the ground, she would be liberated. See also Cohn, *Europe's Inner Demons,* p. 252.

78. Scot, *Discouerie of Witchcraft,* p. 278; Shulamith Shahar, *The Fourth Estate: A History of Women in the Middle Ages* (London: Methuen, 1983), p. 275. (The epithet of disdain that men used against each other in Renaissance England was "whoreson.")

79. On Grimm's fairy tales I have used, in particular, *The Complete Grimm's Fairy Tales.*

80. John Webster Spargo, *Juridical Folklore in England, Illustrated by the Cucking-Stool* (Durham: University of North Carolina Press, 1944).

The association between the domineering woman and the witch can be seen in Noah's wife, a shrewish figure popular in medieval drama, who presumably obtained a potion from the devil to ferret out Noah's activities. M. D. Anderson, *Drama and Imagery in English Medieval Churches* (Cambridge: Cambridge University Press, 1963), p. 108.

81. Cf. Mary Chamberlain, *Old Wives' Tales: Their History, Remedies, and Spells* (London: Virago, 1981), p. 28.

82. On the "old trot" see Rowland, *Medieval Women's Guide to Health*. See also Robert A. Erickson, *Mother Midnight: Birth, Sex, and Fate in Eighteenth-Century Fiction* (*Defoe, Richardson, and Sterne*) (New York: AMS Press, 1986).

83. Karen E. Rowe, "To Spin a Yarn: The Female Voice in Folklore and Fairy Tale," in Ruth B. Bottigheimer, ed., *Fairy Tales and Society: Illusion, Allusion, and Paradigm* (Philadelphia: University of Pennsylvania Press, 1986), pp. 59–68. Rowe notes that Scheherazade's power to instruct in *The Tales of the Arabian Nights* derives from three kinds of women's knowledge: the knowledge of sexual passion, the knowledge of healing, and the wisdom to spin tales. See also Edward Shorter, "The Vieilée and the Great Transformation," in *The Wolf and the Lamb: Popular Culture in France From the Old Regime to the Twentieth Century,* ed. Jacques Beauroy, Marc Bertrand, and Edward T. Gargan (Saratoga, Calif.: Anma Libri, 1977), pp. 127–40.

84. *Complete Grimm's Fairy Tales,* p. 9; Ruth B. Bottigheimer, *Grimm's Bad Girls & Bold Boys: The Moral & Social Vision of the Tales* (New Haven, Conn.: Yale University Press, 1987), p. 115; Lyly, *Sapho and Phao,* in *Complete Works,* vol. 2, pp. 380–81; Paul Lacroix, *France in the Middle Ages* (New York: Frederick Ungar, 1963), p. 100. In Shakespeare's *Macbeth,* Lady Macbeth refers to "a woman's story at a winter's fire / Authorized by her grandam." *Complete Works,* p. 1041.

85. Spufford, *Small Books and Pleasant Histories,* p. 6. See also Robert Muchembled, *Culture populaire et culture des élites dans la France moderne: xvᵉ–xviiiᵉ siècles: Essai* (Paris: Flammarion, 1978), p. 66.

86. Quaife, *Witches,* p. 184; Demos, *Witchcraft,* pp. 156–7; Karlsen, *Devil in the Shape of a Woman,* p. 140.

CHAPTER SIX   *The Eroticized Young Male and Women's Response*

1. Baldesar Castiglione, *The Book of the Courtier,* trans. Charles S. Singleton (Garden City, N.Y.: Doubleday, 1959), p. 106. Antoine de la Sale [?], *Fifteen Joys of Marriage,* trans. Elizabeth Abbott (New York: Orion, 1959), p. 193, asserts that an old man who marries a young woman is even more foolish than an old woman who marries a young man.

2. Richard Axton, "Popular Modes in the Earliest Plays," in Neville Denny, ed., *Medieval Drama* (London: Edward Arnold, 1973), p. 29. Jack Lindsay, *The Troubadours and Their World of the Twelfth and Thirteenth Centuries* (London: Frederick Muller, 1976), p. 140, traces these dance interludes to earlier liturgical dances and beyond these to ancient ceremonies surrounding the rebirth of the young god.

3. Marie of France, *French Medieval Romances from the Lays of Marie of France,* trans. Eugene Mason (London: J. M. Dent & Sons, 1924), Lay of Gugemar, Lay of Yonec. Mikhail Bakhtin suggests that this venerable convention about gender behavior may have originated in ancient ceremonies of springtime renewal with the death or disappearance of the old god and the union of the goddess with a new, young god. Bakhtin's argument also suggests that the union between old and young which he theorizes underlay European folk festivals also may have originated in these ancient rites of religions centering on goddesses. See Bakhtin, *Rabelais and His World,* esp. pp. 239–43.

4. William Aldis Wright, ed., *The Complete Works of William Shakespeare* (Garden City, N.Y.: Garden City Books, 1936), pp. 957, 934, 948.

5. Cf. Maria S. Haynes, "The Concept of Old Age in the Late Middle Ages with Special Reference to Chaucer," Ph.D. diss., UCLA, 1956, p. 98.

6. Guillaume de Lorris and Jean de Meun, *The Romance of the Rose*, trans. Charles Dahlberg (Princeton, N.J.: Princeton University Press, 1971), p. 97; Castiglione, *Courtier,* p. 107. Drawing from political theorists, Mark E. Kann also notes the importance to patriarchal arrangements of the containment of young men. *On the Man Question: Gender and Civic Virtue in America* (Philadelphia: Temple University Press, 1991).

7. Randolph Trumbach, "The Birth of the Queen: Sodomy and the Emergence of Gender Equality in Modern Culture, 1660–1750," in Martin Bauml Duberman, Martha Vicinus, and George Chauncey, Jr., eds., *Hidden from History: Reclaiming the Gay and Lesbian Past* (New York: New American Library, 1989), p. 134. See also, in particular, James M. Saslow, "Homosexuality in the Renaissance: Behavior, Identity, and Artistic Expression," in Duberman et al., *Hidden from History*, pp. 90–105.

8. See John Berger, *Ways of Seeing* (Hammondsworth, England: Penguin Books, 1972).

9. Renaissance paintings of the Rape of Ganymede depict Zeus's conquest of the beautiful young male, Ganymede. Even in these paintings of nude young men, however, as reproduced in James Saslow's book on the topic, the subjects seem to struggle; they have some control over their situation. And when these Ganymede figures, according to Saslow, are painted as androgynes, as intermixings of male and female in accord with alchemical ideals of human achievement, the androgynous, perfected male triumphs over the earthbound, imperfect female. See James M. Saslow, *Ganymede in the Renaissance: Homosexuality in Art and Society* (New Haven, Conn.: Yale University Press, 1986).

10. Caroline Walker Bynum, *Holy Feast and Holy Fast: The Religious Significance of Food to Medieval Women* (Berkeley: University of California Press, 1987), passim; Chrétien de Troyes, *Cligés,* in *Arthurian Romances,* trans. W. W. Comfort (New York: Dutton, 1975), p. 127.

11. Geoffrey Chaucer, *The Canterbury Tales,* ed. J. U. Nicolson (Garden City, N.Y.: Garden City Publishing, 1934), pp. 3–4.

12. Shakespeare, *Complete Works,* p. 1405.

13. My perceptions of the general history of male fashion are derived, in the first instance, from my reading of fashion histories. Cf. Michael Batterbery and Ariane Batterbery, *Mirror, Mirror: A Social History of Fashion* (New York: Holt, Rinehart, and Winston, 1977); J. Anderson Black and Madge Garland, *A History of Fashion* (New York: William Morrow, 1980); François Boucher, *20,000 Years of Fashion: The History of Costume and Personal Adornment* (New York: Harry N. Abrams, 1987); Mila Davenport, *The Book of Costume,* 2 vols. (New York: Crown, 1948); Ludmilla Kybalova, Olga Herbenova, and Milena Lamarova, *The Pictorial Encyclopedia of Fashion* (New York: Crown, 1966); Diana de Marly, *Fashion for Men: An Illustrated History* (New York: Holmes & Meier, 1985).

14. Cf. Andreas Capellanus, *The Art of Courtly Love,* trans. John Jay Parry (New York: Frederick Ungar, 1941), p. 57.

At one point the toe extension reached such a length that, to permit walking, the floppy points of the shoes had to be held to the knees by chains. Some of the first sumptuary laws promulgated by the French monarchy in the thirteenth century related to the length of shoes: these laws limited even princes of the realm to wearing toe extensions no longer than twenty-five inches. (From the medieval period to the eighteenth century, European monarchs utilized sumptuary laws regulating dress to preserve class privilege. Most evidence suggests, however, that these laws were regularly violated with impunity.) Cf. Batterbery, *Mirror, Mirror,* p. 88.

15. Cf. Simone Bertrand, *La tapisserie de Bayeux* (Saint-Lèger-Vauban: Zodiaque, 1966). See also F. W. Fairholt, *Costume in England: A History of Dress to the End of the Eighteenth Century* (London: George Bell and Sons, 1885), p. 84.

16. On the fourteenth-century short fashions, see in particular François Boucher, "Les conditions de l'apparition du costume court en France vers le milieu du xive siècle," in

Recueil de travaux offert à M. Clovis Brunel (Paris: Société de l'école des Chartes, 1955), pp. 183–92; Joan Evans, *Medieval Dress* (London: Oxford University Press, 1952); Stella Mary Newton, *Fashion in the Age of the Black Prince: A Study of the Years 1340–1365* (Totowa, N.J.: Rowman & Littlefield, 1980); H. Platelle, "Le problème du scandale: les nouvelles modes masculine aux xiᵉ et xiiᵉ siècles," *Revue belge de philologie et d'histoire* 53 (1975), 1071–96.

17. On the history of warfare I have used Felix Gilbert, "Machiavelli: The Renaissance of the Art of War," in Edward Mead Earle, ed., *Makers of Modern Strategy: Military Thought from Machiavelli to Hitler* (New York: Atheneum, 1966), pp. 3–25; J. R. Hale, *War and Society in Renaissance Europe, 1450–1620* (Leicester: Leicester University Press, 1985); Michael Howard, *War in European History* (London and New York: Oxford University Press, 1976); William H. McNeill, *The Pursuit of Power: Technology, Armed Force, and Society Since A.D. 1000* (Chicago: University of Chicago Press, 1982); Ewart Oakeshott, *European Weapons and Armour: From the Renaissance to the Industrial Revolution* (London: Lutterworth Press, 1980).

18. François Rabelais, *Gargantua and Pantagruel,* trans. Jacques LeClerq (New York: Heritage, 1936), p. 459; Grace Q. Vicary, "Visual Art as Social Data: The Renaissance Codpiece," *Cultural Anthropology* 4 (February 1989), 3–25.

19. The contemporary Vatican Swiss Guards are ceremonial descendants of the Swiss mercenaries, who often served in the armies of the Italian city-states. Their present-day uniforms resemble fifteenth-century prototypes.

20. Lauro Martines, *Power and Imagination: City-States in Renaissance Italy* (New York: Alfred A. Knopf, 1979), pp. 217, 229; Peter Burke, *Culture and Society in Renaissance Italy* (New York: Charles Scribner's Sons, 1972), p. 198; Hanna Fenichel Pitkin, *Fortune Is a Woman: Gender and Politics in the Thought of Niccolò Machiavelli* (Berkeley: University of California Press, 1984); Ernst Cassirer, *The Individual and the Cosmos in Renaissance Philosophy,* trans. Mario Domandi (New York: Barnes & Noble, 1963), p. 73; Niccolò Machiavelli, *The Prince,* trans. Luigi Ricci (New York: New American Library, 1952), p. 107.

21. Chaucer, *Canterbury Tales,* p. 19.

"What a marvelous pair of legs," declaims the heroine of Wolfram von Eschenbach's *Parzival,* with regard to the hero. Von Eschenbach, *Parzival* (New York: Penguin, 1980), p. 14. "His leg is just but so so," notes Phebe in Shakespeare's *As You Like It,* referring to Rosalind disguised as a young man. Shakespeare, *Complete Works,* p. 686.

22. *The Ecclesiastical History of Orderic Vitalis,* trans. Marjorie Chibnall, 5 vols. (Oxford: Clarendon, 1973), vol. 4, pp. 187–89; C. Stephen Jaeger, *The Origins of Courtliness: Civilizing Trends and the Formation of Courtly Ideals, 939–1210* (Philadelphia: University of Pennsylvania Press, 1985), p. 179.

23. Vitalis, *Ecclesiastical History,* 4, 187–88.

24. P. L. Jacob, *Histoire de la prostitution chez tous les peuple du monde,* 6 vols. (Paris: Seré, 1851), vol. 6, p. 11. William A. Rossi, *The Sex Life of the Foot and Shoe* (New York: Dutton, 1976), p. 62: "In virtually all societies, the foot is believed to have magical fertility powers." Rossi contends that this power was due to the foot's connection with mother earth.

On the connection between the nose and the phallus, cf. Bakhtin, *Rabelais and His World,* p. 87.

25. James Cleugh, *Love Locked Out: An Examination of the Irrepressible Sexuality of the Middle Ages* (New York: Crown, 1964), p. 49; Shakespeare, *Complete Works,* p. 614.

26. Eric Partridge, *A Dictionary of Slang and Unconventional English,* 8th ed. (London: Routledge & Kegan Paul, 1984), pp. 235–36.

27. Castiglione, *Courtier,* p. 256. See also Denis de Rougement, *Love in the Western*

World, trans. Montgomery Belgion [1956] (Princeton, N.J.: Princeton University Press, 1983), p. 244.

28. Michael Foss, *Chivalry* (Norwich: Jarrold and Sons, 1975), p. 108; Newton, *Fashion in the Age of the Black Prince,* p. 6.

29. Shakespeare, *Complete Works,* p. 614; cf. J. R. Hale, *Renaissance* (New York: Time Books, 1965), pp. 112–13.

30. Cf. Friedrich Herr, *The Medieval World: Europe, 1100–1350* (London: Weidenfeld and Nicholson, 1961), pp. 81–90; Colin Morris, *The Discovery of the Individual, 1050–1200* (New York: Harper & Row, 1972). In his comprehensive social history of youth, *Youth and History: Tradition and Change in European Age Relations, 1770–Present* (New York: Academic Press, 1974), John R. Gillis does not discuss these issues of dress and behavior that concern me.

31. On younger sons, the literature is voluminous. Cf. Georges Duby, *Le chevalier, la femme et la prêtre: Le mariage dans la France féodale* (Paris: Hachette, 1981); Lawrence Stone and Jeanne C. Fawtier Stone, *An Open Elite* (Oxford: Clarendon, 1984); Joan Thirsk, "Younger Sons in the Seventeenth Century," *History* 54 (1969), 358–77.

32. Eschenbach, *Parzifal,* pp. 1–40; Shakespeare, *Complete Works,* pp. 665–69; Henry Percy (ninth Earl of Northumberland), *Advice to His Son* [1609], ed. G. B. Harrison (London: Ernest Benn, 1930), p. 75.

33. Pertinent to this point is the story with regard to Eleanor of Aquitaine and the desperation of younger sons which all biographers of her relate without comment. Having divorced Louis of France in Poitiers, Eleanor traveled to the north of France to marry Henry of Normandy. While en route from south to north, her retinue was attacked on two occasions by men aiming for control of her vast inheritance by forcing her into marriage. One of her attempted abductors was, in fact, Henry of Normandy's younger brother. The other, Thibaut of Champagne, eventually married her daughter, Marie, who kept Eleanor's courtly legacy alive in Champagne. Cf. Amy Kelly, *Eleanor of Aquitaine and the Four Kings* (Cambridge, Mass.: Harvard University Press, 1950), p. 80.

34. By the eighteenth century, according to Vera Lee, *The Reign of Women in Eighteenth-Century France* (Cambridge, Mass.: Schenkman, 1975), p. 3, they were called *les chevaliers.* "Perpetually short of cash, he tries to compensate at the gaming table or at the feet of some wealthy widow." See also Norbert Elias, *Power and Civility: The Civilizing Process,* trans. Edmund Jephcott (New York: Pantheon, 1982), vol. 2, p. 41.

35. Docteur Cabanes, *Moeurs intimes du passé,* vol. 4: *La vie d'étudiant au môyen age* (Paris: Librairie Albin Michel, 1920), pp. 22–60; "Carmina Burana," in *The Goliard Poets: Medieval Latin Songs and Satires,* trans. George F. Whicher (New York: New Directions, 1949), p. 143.

36. *The Book of the Knight of La Tour Landry* [1371], ed. G. S. Taylor (London: Verona, 1930), p. 129; Newton, *Fashion in the Age of the Black Prince,* pp. 9, 15; Castiglione, *The Courtier,* p. 122.

37. Cf. Bakhtin, *Rabelais and His World;* Natalie Davis, "Women on Top," in Davis, ed., *Society and Culture in Early Modern France* (Stanford, Calif.: Stanford University Press, 1975), pp. 124–51.

38. On marriage as a privileged and not an inevitable state, see John R. Gillis, *For Better, for Worse: British Marriages, 1600 to the Present* (New York: Oxford University Press, 1985).

39. In the anonymous Venetian sixteenth-century play, *La Venexiana,* two women desire a young man. He is described as without a beard, as "pink-cheeked." One of the women exclaims with regard to him: "That's manna which isn't found everywhere, these lads who look like angels." *La Venexiana: A Sixteenth-Century Venetian Comedy,* trans. Matilde Valenti Pfeiffer (San Francisco: Vanni, 1950), pp. 49, 75.

40. *Romance of the Rose,* p. 60; Robert Burton, *The Anatomy of Melancholy* [1621] (Philadelphia: J. W. Moore, 1854), pp. 470–73.

41. John Boswell, *Christianity, Social Tolerance, and Homosexuality: Gay People in Western Europe From the Beginning of the Christian Era to the 14th Century* (Chicago: University of Chicago Press, 1980).

42. *Romance of the Rose,* p. 41. In Shakespeare's *Much Ado About Nothing,* Shakespeare's character Beatrice exclaims: "He that hath a beard is more than a youth; and he that hath no beard is less than a man. . . ." *Complete Works,* p. 602.

43. Vitalis, *Ecclesiastical History,* vol. 4, p. 189.

44. Paul Lacroix, ed., *Le moyen âge et la renaissance* (Paris: Administration, 1848), p. 511; Walter Map, *De Nugis Curialium: Courtiers' Trifles,* ed. and trans. M. R. James (Oxford: Clarendon, 1983), p. 101; Urban Tigner Holmes, Jr., *Daily Living in the Twelfth Century: Based on the Observations of Alexander Neckam in London and Paris* (Madison: University of Wisconsin Press, 1952), p. 163.

45. Shakespeare, *Complete Works,* pp. 315–16.

46. *La vie d'étudiant au moyen âge,* pp. 22–35; Iona and Peter Opie, *The Classic Fairy Tales* (New York: Oxford University Press, 1974), p. 16. According to Chrétien de Troyes in *Lancelot,* the twelfth-century custom was that a woman alone would not be harmed. But if she was traveling under the protection of a knight who was challenged and defeated by another knight, then this second male could treat her as he chose.

47. *Goodman of Paris,* p. 107; Jacques Roussiaud, "Prostitution, Sex, and Society in French Towns in the Fifteenth Century," in Philippe Ariès and André Béjin, eds., *Western Sexuality: Practice and Precept in Past and Present Times,* trans. Anthony Forster (Oxford: Basil Blackwell, 1985), pp. 82–85; J. L. Flindrin, "Repression and Change in the Sexual Life of Young People in Medieval and Early Modern Times," in Robert Wheaton and Tamara K. Hareven, eds., *Family and Sexuality in French History* (Philadelphia: University of Pennsylvania Press, 1980), pp. 28–32.

48. Marguerite de Navarre, *L'heptaméron,* (Paris: Librairie Garnier Frères, 1942), p. 34; Machiavelli, *The Prince,* p. 123.

49. On rape in Western art, see Edwin Mullins, *The Painted Witch: How Western Artists Have Viewed the Sexuality of Women* (New York: Carroll & Graf, 1985).

50. G. R. Quaife, *Wanton Wenches and Wayward Wives: Peasants and Illicit Sex in Early Seventeenth-Century England* (New Brunswick, N. J.: Rutgers University Press, 1979).

51. John Vaughan, *Directions for Health: Letters Written by the Earl of Chesterfield to His Son* (New York: Derby & Jackson, 1857), pp. 427–28.

Contra Vaughan, many other life-cycle writers, in line with physiological belief that a young man's maturity did not occur until an age beyond fourteen, advanced the time of male youth's strident sexuality until their late teens or early twenties.

52. Castiglione, *The Courtier,* p. 32.

53. Peter Erickson views cuckoldry as part of a perverted masculine aspiration toward purity convoluted by a fear of women, while Eve Kosofsky Sedgwick views it as shaped not by brotherhood, but by an "extreme, compulsory and intensely volatile mastery and subordination, designed to more efficiently manipulate women's objectified status." Peter Erickson, *Patriarchal Structures in Shakespeare's Drama* (Berkeley: University of California Press, 1985), pp. 2–11; Eve Kosofsky Sedgwick, *Between Men: English Literature and Male Homosocial Desire* (New York: Columbia University Press, 1985), pp. 5–10.

54. See William Bouwsma, "Anxiety and the Formation of Early Modern Culture," in Barbara C. Malament, ed., *After the Reformation: Essays in Honor of J. H. Hexter* (Philadelphia: University of Pennsylvania Press, 1980), pp. 219–38; Theodore Rabb, *The Struggle for Stability in Early Modern Europe* (New York: Oxford University Press, 1975).

David Hunt, *Parents and Children in History: The Psychology of Family Life in Early Modern France* (New York: Harper & Row, 1972), pp. 73–5, finds men haunted by fear of wives' sexual unfaithfulness.

55. Castiglione, *The Courtier,* p. 120.

56. Johan Huizinga, *The Waning of the Middle Ages* (Garden City, N.Y.: Doubleday, 1956), p. 129: "The knight is transformed into the cavalier who, though still keeping up a severe code of honour and of glory, will no longer claim to be a defender of the faith or a protector of the oppressed." My derivation of these male words is derived from the *Oxford English Dictionary* and from the *Grand Larousse de la langue française*.

57. George Paston, *Lady Mary Wortley Montagu and Her Times* [1710] (London: Methuen, 1907), p. 32.

58. "The Political Economy of the Body in the *Liaisons dangereuses* of Choderlos de Laclos," in Lynn Hunt, ed., *Eroticism and the Body Politic* (Baltimore: Johns Hopkins University Press, 1991), p. 51.

My analysis of these male types draws from Robert Alter, *Rogue's Progress: Studies in the Picaresque Novel* (Cambridge, Mass.: Harvard University Press, 1964); Davis Bitton, *The French Nobility in Crisis, 1560–1640* (Stanford, Calif.: Stanford University Press, 1969); Jenni Calder, *Heroes: From Byron to Guevara* (London: Hamish Hamilton, 1977); Nora Epton, *Love and the French* (Cleveland: World, 1959); Robert Folkenflik, ed., *The English Hero, 1600–1800* (Newark: University of Delaware Press, 1982), especially Peter Hughes, "Wars Within Doors: Erotic Heroism in Eighteenth-Century Literature," and J. Paul Hunter, "Fielding and the Disappearance of Heroes"; Donald Furber and Anne Callahan, *Erotic Love in Literature: From Medieval Legend to Romantic Illusion* (Troy, N.Y.: Whitston Publishing, 1982).

I have also used Morton Hunt, *The Natural History of Love* (New York: Alfred A. Knopf, 1959); Philip Mason, *The English Gentleman: The Rise and Fall of an Ideal* (London: Andre Deutsch, 1982); Warren Roberts, *Morality and Social Class in Eighteenth-Century French Literature and Painting* (Toronto: University of Toronto Press, 1974); Ellery Schalk, *From Valor to Pedigree: Ideas of Nobility in France in the Sixteenth and Seventeenth Centuries* (Princeton, N.J.: Princeton University Press, 1986); Domna C. Stanton, *The Aristocrat as Art: A Study of the Honnête Homme and the Dandy in Seventeenth- and Nineteenth-Century French Literature* (New York: Columbia University Press, 1980); Dale Underwood, *Etheredge and the Seventeenth-Century Comedy of Manners* (New Haven, Conn.: Yale University Press, 1957); Harold Weber, *The Restoration Rake-Hero: Transformations in Sexual Understanding in Seventeenth-Century England* (Madison: University of Wisconsin Press, 1986).

59. John Cleland, *Memoirs of a Coxcomb* [1751] (London: Fortune Press, 1926), pp. 125, 230.

60. See David Bindman, *Hogarth* (New York: Oxford University Press, 1981).

61. Cf. Stevie Davies, *The Feminine Reclaimed: The Idea of Woman in Spenser, Shakespeare and Milton* (Lexington: University Press of Kentucky, 1986); Jean H. Hagstrum, *Sex and Sensibility: Ideal and Erotic Love from Milton to Mozart* (Chicago: University of Chicago Press, 1980).

62. On the French "novel of initiation" see in particular Veronica Jean Massey, "Older Women and Younger Men: The Initiation Narrative of the French Eighteenth Century," Ph.D. diss., Columbia University, 1983. See also Joan DeJean, *Fictions of Sappho, 1546–1937* (Chicago: University of Chicago Press, 1989).

63. John J. Richetti, *Popular Fiction Before Richardson: Narrative Patterns, 1700–1739* (London: Oxford University Press, 1969).

64. Cf. Lisa Jardine, *Still Harping on Daughters: Women and Drama in the Age of Shakespeare* (Totowa, N.J.: Barnes & Noble Books, 1983).

65. Kann, *On the Man Question,* p. 4; *Phaedra and Figaro: Racine's* Phèdre *translated by Robert Lowell and Beaumarchais's* Figaro's Marriage *translated by Jacques Barzun* (New York: Farrar, Straus and Cudahy, 1961), p. 121.

66. Constance Jordan, *Renaissance Feminism: Literary Texts and Political Models* (Ithaca, N.Y.: Cornell University Press, 1990), esp. p. 9.

67. Marguerite de Navarre, *L'heptaméron,* p. 307.

68. On Elizabeth I, I have used, in particular, Anthony Esler, *The Aspiring Mind of the Elizabethan Younger Generation* (Durham, N.C.: Duke University Press, 1966); Carolly Erickson, *The First Elizabeth* (New York: Summit Books, 1983); Stephen J. Greenblatt, *Sir Walter Ralegh: The Renaissance Man and His Roles* (New Haven, Conn.: Yale University Press, 1973); Elizabeth Jenkins, *Elizabeth the Great* (New York: Coward-McCann, 1959); Louis A. Montrose, "A Midsummer Night's Dream and the Shaping Fantasies of Elizabethan Culture: Gender, Power, Form," in Margaret W. Ferguson, Maureen Quilligan, and Nancy J. Vickers, eds., *Rewriting the Renaissance: The Discourses of Sexual Difference in Early Modern Europe* (Chicago: University of Chicago Press, 1986), pp. 65–87; Leah S. Marcus, "Shakespeare's Comic Heroines, Elizabeth I, and the Political Uses of Androgyny," in Mary Beth Rose, ed., *Women in the Middle Ages and the Renaissance: Literary and Historical Perspectives* (Syracuse: Syracuse University Press, 1986), pp. 135–53; Neville Williams, *All the Queen's Men: Elizabeth I and Her Courtiers* (New York: Macmillan, 1972); Violet A. Wilson, *Queen Elizabeth's Maids of Honour and Ladies of the Privy Chamber* (London: John Lane, 1920).

69. See W. T. MacCaffrey, "Place and Patronage in Elizabethan Politics," in S. T. Bindoff, J. Hurstfield, and C. H. Williams, eds., *Elizabethan Government and Society: Essays Presented to Sir John Neale* (London: University of London, 1961), pp. 95–126.

70. Philip Stubbes, *The Anatomie of Abuses* [1583] (New York: Da Capo, 1972), n.p.

71. On Diane de Poitiers, see Françoise Bardon, *Diane de Poitiers et le mythe de Diane* (Paris: Presses universitaires de France, 1963), and Édouard Bourciez, *Les moeurs polies et la littérature de cour sous Henry II* (Geneva: Slatkine, 1967).

72. John Lyly, *Sapho and Phao,* in *The Complete Works of John Lyly,* ed. R. Warwick Bond, 3 vols. (Oxford: Clarendon, 1942), vol. 2, pp. 371, 372, 413, 415.

73. On the *précieuses* I have used, in particular, Dorothy Anne Liot Backer, *Precious Women* (New York: Basic Books, 1974); Carolyn C. Lougee, *Le Paradis des Femmes: Women, Salons, and Social Stratification in Seventeenth-Century France* (Princeton, N.J.: Princeton University Press, 1976); Ian Maclean, *Woman Triumphant: Feminism in French Literature, 1610–1652* (London: Oxford University Press, 1977); and Roger Picard, *Les salons littéraires* (New York: Brentano's, 1943).

On the eighteenth-century salon women, I have used Helen Clergue, *The Salon: A Study of French Society and Personalities in the Eighteenth Century* (New York: G. P. Putnam's Sons, 1907); Elizabeth Fox-Genovese, "Women of the Enlightenment," in Renate Bridenthal, Claudia Koontz, and Susan Stuard, eds., *Becoming Visible: Women in European History,* 2d ed. (Boston: Houghton Mifflin, 1987), pp. 251–77; Edmond and Jules de Goncourt, *La femme au dix-huitième siècle* (Paris: Firmin-Didot, 1887); Eva Jacobs et al., eds., *Women and Society in Eighteenth-Century France: Essays in Honour of John Stephenson Spink* (London: Athlone, 1979); Abby Kleinbaum, "Women in the Age of Light," in Renate Bridenthal and Claudia Koontz, eds., *Becoming Visible: Women in European History* (Boston: Houghton Mifflin, 1977), pp. 217–35; Joan B. Landes, *Women and the Public Sphere in the Age of the French Revolution* (Ithaca, N.Y.: Cornell University Press, 1988); Samia I. Spencer, ed., *French Women and the Age of Enlightenment* (Bloomington: Indiana University Press, 1984).

74. Jean-Jacques Rousseau, *Julie, ou la nouvelle Héloïse* (Paris: Garniers Frères), p. 221.

75. Matthew Josephson, *Jean-Jacques Rousseau* (New York: Harcourt, Brace, 1931), p. 120.

76. Lougee, *Paradis des Femmes,* p. 32.

77. Claude-Anne Lopez, *Mon Cher Papa: Franklin and the Ladies of Paris* (New Haven, Conn.: Yale University Press, 1966), p. 57.

78. See Cissie Fairchilds, "Women and Family," in Spencer, *French Women and the Age of Enlightenment,* p. 101.

79. Clergue, *The Salon,* pp. 36–48.

80. Josephson, *Rousseau,* p. 147.

81. Joan B. Landes, *Women and the Public Sphere in the Age of the French Revolution* (Ithaca, N.Y.: Cornell University Press, 1988), p. 87; Rousseau, *Nouvelle Héloïse,* pp. 214–21.

82. Joel Schwartz, *The Sexual Politics of Jean-Jacques Rousseau* (Chicago: University of Chicago Press, 1984), p. 66; Londa Schiebinger, *The Mind Has No Sex? Women in the Origins of Modern Science* (Cambridge, Mass.: Harvard University Press, 1989), p. 157.

83. Choderlos de Laclos, *Les liaisons dangereuses* (Paris: Garnier Frères, 1961), pp. 266–67.

84. Connections between age and the vogue for white hair have not been explored. Most analysts think that the primary motivation proceeded from the impulse to extend class distinctions: both the powder used to whiten hair and the wigs that went along with it were expensive. The hairdressers employed by aristocrats and the wealthy were powerful advocates, for both the wigs and the whitening required constant attention. See Richard Corson, *Fashions in Hair: The First Five Thousand Years* (London: Peter Owen, 1965), pp. 215–24; 261–79.

Writing in the 1880s, Alfred Franklin traced the light hair to Queen Margaret, wife of Henry IV of France, in the early seventeenth century. Margaret's pages wore blond wigs in reaction to her husband's probable homosexuality and his penchant for cross-dressing and heavy makeup. Its continuation, Franklin suggests, had to do with women asserting control over men and the elderly control over young people. *La vie privée d'autrefois* (Paris: E. Plon, Nourrit, 1887), pp. 56–158. David Troyansky provides some support for Franklin. He finds a new respect for old people emerging in art and literature by the mid-eighteenth century, perhaps corresponding to his finding of declining mortality rates among the elderly. *Old Age in the Old Regime: Image and Experience in Eighteenth-Century France* (Ithaca, N.Y.: Cornell University Press, 1989), pp. 12–13, 27–76.

CHAPTER SEVEN   *The Nineteenth Century: Margaret Fuller and Colette—Continental and Anglo-American Comparisons*

1. On Fuller's life, I have used, in particular, Margaret Vanderhaar Allen, *The Achievement of Margaret Fuller* (University Park, Pa.: Pennsylvania State University Press, 1979); Paula Blanchard, *Margaret Fuller: From Transcendentalism to Revolution* (New York: Delacorte Press, 1978); Bell Gale Chevigny, *Margaret Fuller, The Woman and the Myth: Margaret Fuller's Life and Writings* (Old Westbury, N.Y.: Feminist Press, 1976); Marie Mitchell Olesen Urbanski, *Margaret Fuller's Woman in the Nineteenth Century: A Literary Study of Form and Content, of Sources and Influence* (Westport, Conn.: Greenwood Press, 1980).

2. Margaret Fuller Ossoli, *Woman in the Nineteenth Century, and Kindred Papers, Relating to the Sphere, Condition and Duties, of Woman*, ed. Arthur B. Fuller (Boston: John P. Jewett, 1855), pp. 64–65.

3. *Memoirs of Margaret Fuller Ossoli,* 2 vols. (Boston: Phillips, Sampson, 1852), vol. 2, p. 113. Many scholars think that the Fuller/Ossoli relationship inspired Hawthorne's conception of that between Miriam and Donatello in *The Marble Faun.* Like Ossoli, Donatello comes from an impoverished Italian noble family and is ten years younger than Miriam.

4. Nina Baym, "Thwarted Nature: Nathaniel Hawthorne as Feminist," in Fritz Fleischmann, ed., *American Novelists Revisited: Essays in Feminist Criticism* (Boston: G. K. Hall, 1982), pp. 58–77; Nathaniel Hawthorne, *The French and Italian Notebooks,* ed. Thomas Woodson (Columbus: Ohio State University Press, 1980), p. 115.

5. Joseph Jay Deiss, *The Roman Years of Margaret Fuller: A Biography* (New York: Thomas Y. Crowell, 1969), p. 32; Ann Douglas, *The Feminization of American Culture* (New York: Alfred A. Knopf, 1977), p. 266; Chevigny, *Margaret Fuller,* p. 93.

6. Douglas, *Feminization,* p. 271.

7. On de Staël's Corinne as a female icon, see Ellen Moers, "Performing Heroinism: The Myth of Corinne," in Jerome H. Buckley, ed., *The Worlds of Victorian Fiction* (Cambridge, Mass.: Harvard University Press, 1975), pp. 319–40. Moreover, Corinne in de Staël's novel bore traces of Attic precedent; Corinna, contemporary to Sappho, was another woman poet who played a lyre and recited her poems to music. Thus behind de Staël's Corinne lurked the Sappho/Phaon legend. Fuller was also often called "Corinna."

8. Fuller, *Memoirs,* vol. 2, p. 198.

9. Fuller, *Woman in the Nineteenth Century,* p. 51; Fuller, *Memoirs,* vol. 2, p. 197.

10. Fuller, *Woman in the Nineteenth Century,* p. 427.

11. Ibid., p. 116.

12. Fuller, *Memoirs,* vol. 2, pp. 274–75.

13. Fuller, *Woman in the Nineteenth Century,* pp. 191–216.

14. Ibid., pp. 96–98.

15. Ibid., p. 98.

16. Ibid., p. 99.

17. Lawrence Stone, *The Family, Sex and Marriage in England, 1500–1800* (New York: Harper & Row, 1977), p. 318; Robert V. Wells, *Revolutions in Americans' Lives: A Demographic Perspective on the History of Americans, Their Families, and Their Society* (Westport, Conn.: Greenwood Press, 1982), p. 54; Philippe Ariès, "Introduction," in J. Dupâquier et al., eds., *Marriage and Remarriage in Populations of the Past* (London: Academic, 1981), pp. 32–35. Lenore Davidoff and Catherine Hall, *Family Fortunes: Men and Women of the English Middle Class, 1780–1850* (Chicago: University of Chicago Press, 1987), p. 323, assert that by the end of the eighteenth century the idea that men would do well to marry an older, skilled woman was increasingly distasteful. Davidoff and Hall cite statistics from local records to substantiate the decrease in marriages between older women and younger men.

18. Stone, *Family, Sex and Marriage,* pp. 44–48; Michael Anderson, "The Social Position of Spinsters in Mid-Victorian Britain," *Journal of Family History* 9 (Winter 1984), 377–81; Ruth Freeman and Patricia Klaus, "Blessed or Not? The New Spinster in England and the United States in the Late Nineteenth and Early Twentieth Centuries," *Journal of Family History* 9 (Winter 1984), 394. For the United States, see Lee Chambers-Schiller, *Liberty, A Better Husband: Single Women in America: The Generation of 1780–1840* (New Haven, Conn.: Yale University Press, 1984).

19. Marie-Henri Beyle [Stendhal], *De l'amour* (Paris: Le Divan, 1927), p. 29.

20. Michael Mitterauer and Reinhard Sieder, *The European Family: Patriarchy to Partnership from the Middle Ages to the Present,* trans. Karla Oosterveen and Manfred Hörzinger (Chicago: University of Chicago Press, 1984), p. 127; Nora Epton, *Love and the French* (Cleveland: World, 1959), p. 318.

21. In the early eighteenth century Daniel Defoe, who chronicled these developments, wrote that in previous eras tradesmen's widows proudly assumed direct oversight of the businesses they inherited. "But now the ladies are above it," wrote Defoe. They "disdain it so much, that they choose rather to go without the prospect of a second marriage, in virtue of the trade, than stoop to the mechanic low step of carrying on the business." Quoted by Robert Palfrey Utter and Gwendolyn Needham, *Pamela's Daughters* (New York: Macmillan, 1937), p. 26. See also Margaret George, "From 'Goodwife' to 'Mistress': The Transformation of the Female in Bourgeois Culture," *Science and Society* 37 (Summer 1973), 152–77.

22. In the United States, a new emphasis on the physical attractiveness of women accompanied the introduction of sexual language into courtship. See John D'Emilio and Estelle B. Freedman, *Intimate Matters: A History of Sexuality in America* (New York: Harper & Row, 1988), p. 43.

23. On the gendered nature of the decline in infant mortality, see Stone, *Family, Sex and Marriage*, pp. 380–81. On fears of underpopulation, cf. Paul Gabriel Boucé, "Some Sexual Beliefs and Myths," in Paul Gabriel Boucé, ed., *Sexuality in Eighteenth-Century Britain* (Totowa, N.J.: Barnes & Noble, 1982), p. 37. Both Montesquieu and Rousseau viewed population increase as an index of civic and social virtue. Joan B. Landes, *Women and the Public Sphere in the French Revolution* (Ithaca, N.Y.: Cornell University Press), p. 86.

24. The literature on these changes is becoming vast. On changes in physiological point of view, see Thomas Laquer, "Orgasm, Generation, and the Politics of Reproductive Biology," in Catherine Gallagher and Thomas Laquer, *The Making of the Modern Body: Sexuality and Society in the Nineteenth Century* (Berkeley: University of California Press, 1987), pp. 1–35, and Laquer, *Making Sex: Body & Gender From the Greeks to Freud* (Cambridge, Mass.: Harvard University Press, 1990). On new family forms and women's spirituality, cf. Stone, *Family, Sex and Marriage,* and Ruth H. Bloch, "American Feminine Ideals in Transition: The Rise of the Moral Mother, 1785–1815," *Feminist Studies* 4 (June 1978), 101–26. On the rise of bourgeois sentimentality as a reaction to working-class sexuality, see Marlene Legates, "The Cult of Womanhood in Eighteenth-Century Thought," *Eighteenth-Century Studies* 10 (Fall 1976), 21–39.

25. Roy Porter, "Mixed Feelings: The Enlightenment and Sexuality," in Boucé, ed., *Sexuality in Eighteenth-Century Britain,* pp. 1–27.

26. Lady Bellaston is a "lady of fashion" who has had a series of young male lovers before Tom; Mrs. Slipslop is a forty-five-year-old housekeeper who has arrived at an age when she thinks she might indulge "in any liberties with a man, without the danger of bringing a third person into the world to betray them." Henry Fielding, *The History of the Adventures of Joseph Andrews* (New York: Modern Library, 1950), p. 21.

27. See Robert A. Erickson, *Mother Midnight: Birth, Sex, and Fate in Eighteenth-Century Fiction (Defoe, Richardson, and Sterne)* (New York: AMS Press, 1986).

28. Frances [Fanny] Burney, *Evelina, or the History of a Young Lady's Entrance Into the World* (Oxford: Clarendon, 1930), pp. 66–68.

29. On "republican motherhood," see Linda K. Kerber, *Women of the Republic: Intellect and Ideology in Revolutionary America* (Chapel Hill: University of North Carolina Press, 1980); on women and evangelicalism, cf. Douglas, *Feminization of American Culture,* and Nancy F. Cott, "Passionlessness: An Interpretation of Victorian Sexual Ideology, 1790–1850," in Nancy F. Cott and Elizabeth H. Pleck, eds., *A Heritage of Her Own* (New York: Simon and Schuster, 1979), pp. 169ff.

30. Peter Gay, *The Bourgeois Experience: Victoria to Freud,* vol. 1: *Education of the Senses* (New York: Oxford University Press, 1984); Carl Degler, *At Odds: Women and the Family in America from the Revolution to the Present* (New York: Oxford University Press,

1980), pp. 249–78; Karen Lystra, *Searching the Heart: Men, Women, and Romantic Love in Nineteenth-Century America* (New York: Oxford University Press, 1989).

31. Fuller, *Woman in the Nineteenth Century,* pp. 96–98.

32. Gwendolyn Bridges Needham, "The 'Old Maid' in the Life and Fiction of Eighteenth-Century England," Ph.D. diss., University of California, Berkeley, 1938, p. 19.

33. Tobias Smollett, *The Expedition of Humphry Clinker* (London: Oxford University Press, 1966), pp. 60–64.

34. Cf. John Demos, *Entertaining Satan: Witchcraft and the Culture of Early New England* (New York: Oxford University Press, 1982), pp. 390–95.

35. Needham, " 'Old Maid,' " p. 189.

36. Judith R. Walkowitz, *Prostitution and Victorian Society: Women, Class, and the State* (Cambridge: Cambridge University Press, 1980), pp. 211–12.

37. Cf. Montague Summers, *The Gothic Quest: A History of the Gothic Novel* (London: Fortune, 1938).

38. The many novels of Sir Walter Scott, the most popular novelist of the early nineteenth century, drew from the Scottish folklore of his native land. But in his work the figures of witches and magicians are peripheral to the main action, while skepticism of the supernatural dominates. Cf. Coleman Parsons, *Witchcraft and Demonology in Scott's Fiction* (Edinburgh: Oliver & Boyd, 1964), pp. 14–15, 85–90; John Lauber, *Sir Walter Scott* (Boston: Twayne, 1966), p. 124.

39. Nathaniel Hawthorne, *The House of the Seven Gables,* in *The Complete Novels and Selected Tales of Nathaniel Hawthorne,* ed. Norman Holmes Pearson (New York: Modern Library, 1937), pp. 1–10.

40. *A Philosophical, Historical, and Moral Essay on Old Maids,* by a friend to the sisterhood, 3 vols. (London: T. Cadell, 1785), vol. 1, pp. 88–91, vol. 3, passim.

41. See Rosalind Urbach Moss, "Reinventing Spinsterhood: Competing Images of 'Womanhood' in American Culture, 1880–1960," Ph.D. diss., University of Minnesota, 1989.

42. Fuller, *Woman in the Nineteenth Century,* pp. 96–98; Edith Wharton, *The Old Maid* (New York: D. Appleton, 1924), p. 154; Martha Vicinus, *Independent Women: Work and Community for Single Women, 1850–1920* (Chicago: University of Chicago Press, 1985), p. 17.

43. Fuller, *Woman in the Nineteenth Century,* p. 99.

44. Lois W. Banner, *Elizabeth Cady Stanton: A Radical for Woman's Rights* (Boston: Little, Brown, 1979), p. 123.

45. Laqueur, "Orgasm, Generation," p. 18.

46. Lois W. Banner, *American Beauty* (New York: Alfred A. Knopf, 1983), pp. 220–21.

47. Thomas Beer, *The Mauve Decade: American Life at the End of the Nineteenth Century* (New York: Scribner's, 1935), pp. 36, 59, continues into grotesquerie: "The Titaness in the garments of Cybele must be placated as the priests of the Great Mother were wont to do."

48. On female bonding, see Carroll Smith-Rosenberg, "The Female World of Love and Ritual: Relations Between Women in Nineteenth-Century America," *Signs: Journal of Women in Culture and Society* 1 (Autumn 1975), 1–29.

49. See John Demos, "Old Age in Early New England," in John Demos and Sarane Spence Boocock, eds., *Turning Points: Historical and Sociological Essays on the Family* (Chicago: University of Chicago Press, 1978), pp. 248–87, and Laurel Thacher Ulrich, *Goodwives: Image and Reality in the Lives of Women in Northern New England, 1650–1750* (New York: Alfred A. Knopf, 1980). Davidoff and Hall, *Family Fortunes,* p. 329, make the point about the smaller numbers of grandmothers with the upturn in age of first marriages. But these authors note, as does Lee Chambers-Schiller, the large numbers of

middle-aged aunts who served a grandmother function in these years. See Lee Chambers-Schiller, "'Woman Is Born to Love': The Maiden Aunt as Maternal Figure in Ante-Bellum Literature," *Frontiers: A Journal of Women's Studies* 10 (1988), 34–43.

50. See Barbara Welter, "The Cult of True Womanhood, 1820–1860," *American Quarterly* 18 (Summer 1966), 151–74.

51. *The Ladies' Wreath* (1850), p. 150. See Jane P. Tompkins, "Sentimental Power: Uncle Tom's Cabin and the Politics of Literary History," in Elaine Showalter, ed., *The New Feminist Criticism: Essays on Women, Literature, and Theory* (New York: Pantheon, 1985), pp. 81–104. On the cult of Washington's mother, see Nina Baym, "Women and the Republic: Emma Willard's Rhetoric of History," *American Quarterly* 43 (March 1991), 12–13.

52. Terri L. Premo, *Winter Friends: Women Growing Old in the New Republic, 1785–1835* (Urbana: University of Illinois Press, 1990), pp. 95–96; Harriet Beecher Stowe, *Oldtown Folks* (Boston: Houghton Mifflin, 1897), pp. 20–21.

53. Lola Montez, *The Arts of Beauty; or secrets of a lady's toilet,* 1858, quoted by Erna Olafson Hellerstein, Leslie Parker Hume, and Karen M. Offen, eds., *Victorian Women: A Documentary Account of Women's Lives in Nineteenth-Century England, France, and the United States* (Stanford, Calif.: Stanford University Press, 1981), pp. 468–69.

54. Cf. Banner, *American Beauty,* pp. 202ff.

55. Cf. Hermann Heinrich Ploss, Max Bartels, and Paul Bartels, *Woman: An Historical, Gynecological, and Anthropological Treatise,* 3 vols. (London: W. Heinemann, 1935), vol. 3, p. 348; Elizabeth Lynn Linton, *Modern Woman* (New York: Worthington, 1988), p. 349.

56. Elizabeth Lynn Linton, "La femme passée," *The Saturday Review,* July 11, 1868, in Hellerstein, Hume, and Offen, *Victorian Women,* pp. 470–71.

57. Joan Wallach Scott, "Gender: A Useful Category of Historical Analysis," in Scott, ed., *Gender and the Politics of History* (New York: Columbia University Press, 1988), p. 43.

58. Suzanne Lebsock, *The Free Women of Petersburg: Status and Culture in a Southern Town, 1784–1860* (New York: W. W. Norton, 1984); Lisa Wilson Waciega, "Widowhood and Womanhood in Early America: The Experience of Women in Philadelphia and Chester Countries, 1750–1850," Ph.D. diss., Temple University, 1986; Chambers-Schiller, *Liberty: A Better Husband,* pp. 10–46. See also Vicinus, *Independent Women,* p. 5.

59. Mary Ryan, *Cradle of the Middle Class: The Family in Oneida County, New York, 1780–1865* (Cambridge: Cambridge University Press, 1981), pp. 192–95; Marilyn Ferris Motz, *True Sisterhood: Michigan Women and Their Kin* (Albany: State University of New York Press, 1983), esp. pp. 33–35, 121–25, 155–68. For the entire United States, see Premo, *Winter Friends.*

60. Christine Stansell, *City of Women: Sex and Class in New York, 1789–1860* (New York: Alfred A. Knopf, 1986), pp. 45, 62.

61. Gay, *Education of the Senses,* p. 103; David Leverenz, *Manhood and the American Renaissance* (Ithaca, N.Y.: Cornell University Press, 1989), p. 141; Davidoff and Hall, *Family Fortunes,* p. 323.

See also Peter N. Stearns, *Be A Man! Males in Modern Society* (New York: Holmes & Meier, 1979), p. 56; Theodore Zeldin, *France, 1848–1945,* 2 vols. (Oxford: Clarendon, 1973), vol. 1, p. 302.

Analyzing the German family in this era, Heidi Rosenbaum offers an argument similar to that of Davidoff and Hall. She contends that in Germany these age-disparate relationships between aging men and younger women were common. Germans called them "reasonable" arrangements, to differentiate them from those between couples of the same age that were presumed to be based on "romantic" love. See Heidi Rosenbaum,

Formen der Familie: Untersuchungen zum Zusammenhang von Familien verhältnissen, Sozial-struktur und sozialem Wandel in der deutschen Gesellschaft des 19. Jahrhunderts (Frankfurt: Surhkamp, 1982), pp. 285–90.

62. Alcott's *Little Women* seems to draw from the precedent of Jean-Jacques Rousseau's *La nouvelle Héloïse*. In this novel the heroine, Julie, finds greater happiness in her daughterly relationship with a much older scholar than in her previous sexualized relationship with a young man. Yet in *Middlemarch,* George Eliot portrays a young woman's attraction to a seemingly wise old man as foolish romanticism when her older scholar husband turns out to be a pedantic fool.

63. For the classic exposition of this thesis, see Peter G. Filene, *Him/Her/Self: Sex Roles in Modern America,* 2d ed. (Baltimore: Johns Hopkins University Press, 1984). Its influence is especially apparent in Harry Brod, *The Making of Masculinities: The New Men's Studies* (Boston: Allen & Unwin, 1987). For Europe, see, in particular, Stearns, *Be A Man!* especially pp. 59–78, for working-class variations.

64. Sir Walter Scott established the tradition, continued in later women's Gothic fiction, even of today, of a "light" and a "dark" hero, one gentle and the other fierce and violent. See Alexander Welsh, *The Hero of the Waverley Novels* (New Haven, Conn.: Yale University Press, 1963). On the nineteenth-century romantic hero, see Raymond Giraud, *The Unheroic Hero in the Novels of Stendhal, Balzac, and Flaubert* (New Brunswick, N.J.: Rutgers University Press, 1957).

65. Walter Houghton, *Victorian Frame of Mind* (New Haven, Conn.: Yale University Press, 1957), p. 198.

66. J. A. Mangan and James Walrin, *Manliness and Morality: Middle-class Masculinity in Britain and America, 1800–1940* (Manchester: Manchester University Press, 1987), p. xi.

67. Nancy Armstrong, *Desire and Domestic Fiction: A Political History of the Novel* (New York: Oxford University Press, 1987).

68. Alphonse Daudet, *Sapho* (Paris: Flammarion, n.d.), p. 142.

69. Herman Melville, *Pierre, or The Ambiguities* (New York: Library of America, 1984), p. 167.

70. For Bennett's motivation in writing the novel, see Margaret Drabble, *Arnold Bennett: A Biography* (London: Wiedenfeld and Nicolson, 1974), p. 106.

71. Arnold Bennett, *The Old Wives' Tale* (New York: Modern Library, 1908), p. 394.

72. Susan Gubar, "The Female Monster in Augustan Satire," *Signs: Journal of Women in Culture and Society* 3 (Winter 1977), 380–94.

73. On the English bluestockings, see Emily Putnam, *The Lady: Studies of Certain Significant Phases of Her History* (Chicago: University of Chicago Press, 1969), pp. 247–81. On the American salons, see Anne Hollingsworth Wharton, *Salons Colonial and Republi-can* (Philadelphia: J. B. Lippincott, 1900). On the other hand, as Evelyn Gordon Bodek argues, the eighteenth-century *salonnières* may have been undone by including men. Without men present, the English women gained independence and the ability to publish their ideas with impunity, as did Fanny Burney and Hester Chapone, forerunners to Mary Wollstonecraft. See Bodek, "Salonières and Bluestockings: Educated Obsolescence and Germinating Feminism, *Feminist Studies* 3 (Spring–Summer 1976), 185–99.

74. Helen Clergue, *The Salon: A Study of French Society and Personalities in the Eigh-teenth Century* (New York: G. P. Putnam's Sons, 1907), pp. 33–34; Katharine M. Rogers, "The View from England," in Samia I. Spencer, ed., *French Women and the Age of Enlightenment* (Bloomington: Indiana University Press, 1984), pp. 357–59.

75. Alexis de Tocqueville, *Democracy in America* (New York: Modern Library, 1981), p. 488. According to R. F. Brissenden, *Virtue in Distress: Studies in the Novel of Sentiment from Richardson to Sade* (London: Macmillan, 1974), pp. 86–87 (writing about the eigh-

teenth-century origins of nineteenth-century conventions), sexual freedom was encouraged by the French aristocracy to a degree unknown in England. This difference allowed French literary convention to acknowledge eroticism but hampered such acknowledgment in England.

76. Henri Peyre suggests the power of the French literary "initiation" tradition in positing the power of Racine's play, *Phèdre,* over French men. (*Phèdre* retells the ancient legend of the relationship between the stepmother, Phaedra, and her stepson Hippolyte.) "French males of every generation, like Proust's enraptured hero watching La Berma in the part, have dreamed for years of the great actress . . . who had impersonated Phèdre in their youth. It would be no exaggeration to say that . . . the play and its burning picture of jealousy have done much to frame the French conception of love." Peyre, "The Tragedy of Passion in Racine's Phèdre," in Cleanth Brooks, ed., *Tragic Themes in Western Literature* (New Haven, Conn.: Yale University Press, 1955), p. 80.

77. Bonnie G. Smith, *Ladies of the Leisure Class: The Bourgeoises of Northern France in the Nineteenth Century* (Princeton, N.J.: Princeton University Press, 1981); Margaret Darrow, "French Noblewomen and the New Domesticity, 1750–1850," *Feminist Studies* 5 (Spring 1979), 41–65; Barbara Corrado Pope, "Angels in the Devil's Workshop: Leisured and Charitable Women in Nineteenth-Century England and France," in Renate Bridenthal and Claudia Koontz, *Becoming Visible: Women in European History* (Boston: Houghton Mifflin, 1977), pp. 296–324.

78. Claire Goldberg Moses, *French Feminism in the Nineteenth Century* (Albany: State University of New York Press, 1984), pp. 23–35. James F. McMillan, *Housewife or Harlot: The Place of Women in French Society, 1870–1940* (New York: St. Martin's, 1981), pp. 11–20, finds a spinster image emerging in France by the early twentieth century.

79. Honoré de Balzac, *Lost Illusions,* trans. Kathleen Raine (New York: Modern Library, 1985), pp. 50, 54; Benjamin Constant, *Adolphe* (Manchester: Imprimerie de L'Université, 1919), p. 63.

80. Stendhal, *Le rouge et le noir* (Paris: Garnier Frères, 1939), p. 90.

81. For biographical information, cf. Robert D. Cottrell, *Colette* (New York: Frederick Ungar, 1974); and Michelle Sardre, *Colette libre et entravée* (Paris: Stock, 1978).

82. Colette, *La naissance du jour, Oeuvres de Colette* (Paris: Flammarion, 1960), vol. 2, p. 369; *Le blé en herbe, Oeuvres de Colette,* vol. 2, p. 109.

83. *Le blé en herbe, Oeuvres de Colette,* vol. 2, p. 258.

84. Ibid., p. 326.

85. Colette, *Le pur et l'impur, Oeuvres complètes* (Paris: Flammarion, 1949), vol. 9, p. 58.

86. *Le blé en herbe, Oeuvres de Colette,* vol. 2, p. 264.

87. Colette, *L'entrave, Oeuvres complètes,* vol. 4, p. 309.

88. *La naissance du jour, Oeuvres de Colette,* vol. 2, pp. 326, 367.

89. Colette, *La fin de Chéri, Oeuvres de Colette,* vol. 2, pp. 186–89.

90. Cottrell, *Colette,* pp. 4–8.

91. *Journal à rebours, Oeuvres complètes,* vol. 12, p. 138.

92. Maurice Goudeket, *Close to Colette,* trans. Enid McLeod (London: Secker and Warburg, 1957), pp. 211, 216.

CHAPTER EIGHT   *The Twentieth Century: Menopause and Its Meaning*

1. Karin Michaelis, *The Dangerous Age* (New York: John Lane, 1911), pp. 49–89. On the novel's popularity, see G. Stanley Hall, *Senescence: The Last Half of Life* (New York:

D. Appleton, 1922), pp. 27, 388, and Karin Michaelis Strangeland, *Elsie Lindtner* (New York: John Lane, 1912), preface. (*Elsie Lindtner* is a sequel to *The Dangerous Age*.) French author Marcel Prévost called *The Dangerous Age* "the most widely read novel at the present moment." *Dangerous Age*, p. 10. References to *The Dangerous Age* recur in the works on menopause I have consulted. Cf. Olga Knopf, *The Art of Being a Woman* (New York: Alfred A. Knopf, 1934), p. 222.

Contemporaries traced the origins of the literary representation of menopause as "the dangerous age" to French author Octave Feuillet's 1860 play, *La crise*. See Octave Feuillet, *Scènes et proverbes* (Paris: Michel Levy Frères, 1860), vol. 3, pp. 33–96.

2. *Dangerous Age*, pp. 49, 58.

In researching this chapter, I have read historical medical literature on menopause in the nineteenth and twentieth centuries, relying on the extensive bibliography in Ellen Perlmutter and Pauline B. Bart, "Changing Views of 'The Change': A Critical Review and Suggestions for an Attributional Approach," in Ann M. Voda, Myra Dinnerstein, and Sheryl R. O'Donnell, eds., *Changing Perspectives on Menopause* (Austin: University of Texas Press, 1982), pp. 196–99. I have also used the bibliographies in the Surgeon General's Report and materials in the Library of Congress, the National Medical Library (Bethesda, Md.), and the medical libraries of the University of Southern California and the University of California at Los Angeles.

See also Lois W. Banner, "The Meaning of Menopause: Aging and Its Historical Contexts in the Twentieth Century," Working Paper Series, Center for Twentieth-Century Studies, University of Wisconsin–Milwaukee.

3. Anna Garlin Spencer, *Woman's Share in Social Culture* (New York: Mitchell Kennerley, 1912), p. 231.

4. Cf. Margaret Mead, typescript, "Woman in a Post-Industrial Society," Margaret Mead Papers, Library of Congress.

5. For a nineteenth-century survey, see Edward Tilt, *The Change of Life in Health and Disease* (London: Churchill, 1857). See also the lengthy discussion of this issue by Mary Dixon Jones, "Insanity, Its Causes: Is There a Correlation of the Sexual Function with Insanity and Crime?" *Medical Record* (1900), pp. 925–37. Jones criticizes doctors for confusing the entire population of women with their patient population.

More recent surveys include: Bernice L. Neugarten, "Women and Menopause," *Vita Humana* 6 (1963), 140–49; Boston Women's Health Collective, *Our Bodies, Ourselves* (New York: Simon and Schuster, 1976), pp. 265–80. The most thorough recent longitudinal study (of 2,500 Massachusetts women between the ages of forty-five and fifty-five) has reached similar conclusions about the lack of severity of menopausal symptoms for most women. For results of this survey and doctors' negative reactions to it, see *Los Angeles Times*, June 14, 1988. The percentages generally reported in such studies are that 10 percent of women experience severe symptoms and 10 percent experience no symptoms.

6. For surveys of these developments, for the United States, see Lois W. Banner, *Women in Modern America: A Brief History*, 2d ed. (New York: Harcourt Brace Jovanovich, 1984). For Europe, see Patricia Branca, *Women in Europe Since 1750* (New York: St. Martin's Press, 1978).

7. Anne H. Wharton, "The Prolongation of Youthfulness in Modern Women," *Chautauqua Collection*, Elizabeth Bancroft Schlesinger Library, Radcliffe College, p. 85; Ruth Freeman and Patricia Klaus, "Blessed or Not? The New Spinster in England and the United States in the Late Nineteenth and Early Twentieth Centuries," *Journal of Family History* 9 (Winter 1984), 394–413; Grace M. Johnston, "The New Old Maid," *Woman Beautiful* 2 (May 1909), 68; Mrs. Wilson Woodrow, "The Woman of Fifty," *Cosmopolitan* 34 (March 1903), 505. See also Lois W. Banner, *American Beauty* (New York: Alfred A.

Knopf, 1983), pp. 219–25. For France, especially Paris, see Octave Uzanne, *The Modern Parisienne* (London: William Heinemann, 1912).

8. A. B. Arnold, "The Menopause," *Medical and Surgical Reporter* 42 (June 5, 1880), 486–88; Andrew Currier, *The Menopause* (New York: D. Appleton, 1897), p. 5; Jones, "Insanity," pp. 85–107; M. C. McGannon, "The Menopause," *Medical Society of Tennessee Proceedings* (1902), p. 199.

See also Samuel K. Jennings, *The Married Lady's Companion, or Poor Man's Friend* (New York: Lorenzo Dow, 1808), p. 57; Samuel Ashwell, *Practical Treatise on the Diseases Peculiar to Women* (London: Samuel Highley, 1840), p. 196; M. A. Raciborski, *De la puberté et de l'âge critique chez la femme* (Paris: J. B. Baillière, 1844), p. 345; W. H. Byford, *The Practice of Medicine and Surgery, Applied to the Diseases and Accidents Incident to Women*, 3d ed. (Philadelphia: Lindsay & Blakiston, 1881), p. 185; Gustavus Eliot, "The Disorders of the Nervous System Associated with the Change of Life," *American Journal of the Medical Sciences* 106 (1893), 292; Alexander J. C. Skene, *Medical Gynecology* (New York: D. Appleton, 1895), p. 469; Mary R. Melendy, *Perfect Womanhood for Maidens-Wives-Mothers* (New York: K. T. Boland, 1901), p. 201; Palmer Findlay, *A Treatise on the Diseases of Women* (Philadephia: Lea and Febiger, 1913), p. 73.

9. See, in particular, Sarah J. Stage, *Female Complaints: Lydia Pinkham and the Business of Women's Medicine* (New York: W. W. Norton, 1979).

10. Eliot, "Disorders of the Nervous System," p. 212.

11. Francis Skae, "Climacteric Insanity," *Edinburgh Medical Journal* 10 (1865), 703–16.

12. J. H. Kellogg, *Plain Facts for Old and Young: Embracing Natural History and Hygiene of the Organic Life* (Burlington, Iowa: I. F. Seyner, 1888), pp. 384–85.

13. Thomas R. Cole, *The Journey of Life: A Cultural History of Aging in America* (Cambridge: Cambridge University Press, 1992), pp. 161–90. Tilt, *Change of Life*, pp. 3–5.

14. William Sisson Gardner, *A Text-book of Gynecology* (New York: D. Appleton, 1912), p. 13; Tilt, *Change of Life*, passim; Byford, *Practice of Medicine and Surgery*, p. 185; Pye Henry Chavasse, *Woman as Wife and Mother* (Philadelphia: W. B. Evans, 1871), p. 115.

15. Marion Harland, *Eve's Daughters* (New York: J. R. Anderson & H. S. Allen, 1882), p. 318.

16. Cf. W. Andrew Achenbaum, *Old Age in the New Land: The American Experience Since 1790* (Baltimore: John Hopkins University Press, 1978).

17. A prolapsed uterus involves the breakdown of the muscles holding the uterus in place. The condition produces the potential for the uterus to "fall" into the vagina, in extreme cases extending outside of the genital region and the body cavity.

18. Cf. John Stockton Hough, *Longevity; Or, the Relative Variability of the Sexes, Particularly with Regard to the Relative Liability of the Inheritance of Certain Transmitted Diseases. Considered in Relation to the Selection of Life Insurance Risks, with a View of Exhibiting the Unjustice of the Practice of Charging Higher Rates for Women* (New York, 1873).

19. Peter G. Filene, *Him/Her/Self: Sex Roles in Modern America*, 2d ed. (Baltimore: Johns Hopkins University Press, 1984), p. 11.

20. Fanny Fern, "The Old Maid of the Period," *Revolution* 5 (September 29, 1870), 196; *Vogue* (March 7, 1895), 146; *Ladies' Home Journal* 17 (July 1907), 6.

21. Charles Meigs, *Diseases of Women* (1847), p. 445; Tilt, *Change of Life*, p. 129; Enoch Heinrich Kisch, *The Sexual Life of Women in Its Physiological and Hygienic Aspect*, trans. M. Eden Paul (New York: Allied Book Company, 1925), p. 572.

22. Spencer, *Woman's Share in Social Culture*, p. 234. See also Mary Roberts Coolidge, *Why Women Are So* (New York: Henry Holt, 1912), and Mary Jo Buhle, "Politics and

Culture in Women's History," *Feminist Studies* 6 (Spring 1980), 37–42. Richard Jensen, "Family, Career and Reform: Women Leaders of the Progressive Era," in Michael Gordon, ed., *The American Family in Social Historical-Perspective* (New York: St. Martin's Press, 1978), pp. 267–80, finds older women more strongly prosuffrage than younger women. In Ann Firor Scott's reading of the 1,359 brief biographies of women whose lives ended no later than 1950 contained in *Notable American Women,* Scott notes that while men made their mark in the world early in life, these women were often innovative in middle age. Ann Firor Scott, "Making the Invisible Woman Visible: A Review Essay," *Journal of Southern History* 38 (November 1972), 635, review of Janet Wilson James, Edward T. James, and Paul S. Boyer, *Notable American Women, 1607–1950: A Biographical Dictionary,* 3 vols. (Cambridge, Mass.: Harvard University Press, 1971).

23. Lois W. Banner, *Elizabeth Cady Stanton: A Radical for Woman's Rights* (Boston: Little, Brown, 1979), pp. 109–10.

24. Robert H. Bremner, "Lillian Wald," in James, Wilson James, and Boyer, eds., *Notable American Women*, vol. 3, p. 528.

25. Lou Tellegen, *Women Have Been Kind: The Memoirs of Lou Tellegen* (New York: Vanguard Press, 1931), p. 211; Colette, *Journey for Myself: Selfish Memories,* trans. David Le Vay (Indianapolis: Bobbs-Merrill, 1972), p. 104.

26. Coolidge, *Why Women Are So,* p. 127.

27. Elizabeth Lynn Linton, *Modern Woman* (New York: Worthington, 1888), pp. 351–53. See also Kathy Peiss, "Making Faces: The Cosmetics Industry and the Cultural Construction of Gender, 1890–1930," *Genders* 7 (Spring 1990), 143–69. Peiss's interesting analysis overlooks issues of age.

28. See Sheila Jeffries, *The Spinster and Her Enemies: Feminism and Sexuality, 1880–1930* (London: Pandora, 1985).

29. Carroll Smith-Rosenberg, "Puberty to Menopause: The Cycle of Femininity in Nineteenth-Century America," in Smith-Rosenberg, *Disorderly Conduct: Visions of Gender in Victorian America* (New York: Alfred A. Knopf, 1985), pp. 182–96. For a similar argument with regard to France, see Peter N. Stearns, "Old Women: Some Historical Observations," *Journal of Family History* 5 (Spring 1980), 44–57.

30. Cf. Regina Markell Morantz-Sanchez, *Sympathy and Science: Women Physicians in American Medicine* (New York: Oxford University Press, 1985).

31. Cf. Miriam Lewin, "The Victorians, the Psychologists, and Psychic Birth Control," in Miriam Lewin, ed., *In the Shadow of the Past: Psychology Portrays the Sexes: A Social and Intellectual History* (New York: Columbia University Press, 1984), pp. 50–51.

32. G. J. Barker-Benfield, *The Horrors of the Half-Known Life: Male Attitudes Toward Women and Sexuality in Nineteenth-Century America* (New York: Harper & Row, 1976). The literature on turn-of-century misogyny is rapidly expanding. Cf. Elaine Showalter, *Sexual Anarchy: Gender and Culture at the Fin de Siècle* (New York: Viking, 1990).

33. Carroll Smith-Rosenberg, "The New Woman as Androgyne: Social Disorder and Gender Crisis, 1870–1936," in Smith-Rosenberg, *Disorderly Conduct,* p. 265. See also Lillian Faderman, *Odd Girls and Twilight Lovers: A History of Lesbian Life in Twentieth-Century America* (New York: Columbia University Press, 1991), pp. 37–61.

34. Havelock Ellis, *Studies in the Psychology of Sex,* vol. 1: *The Sexual Impulse in Women* [1905] (New York: Random House, 1942), p. 243.

35. Ibid., pp. 242–45; Havelock Ellis, *Man and Woman: A Study of Human Secondary Characteristics* (New York: Charles Scribner's Sons, 1908), pp. 224–25.

36. Alice Ames Walker, "Gorgeous Middle Age," *Ladies' Home Journal* 41 (September 1924), 27; Gregorio Marañón, *The Climacteric (The Critical Age),* trans. K. S. Stevens (St. Louis: C. V. Mosby, 1929), pp. 212–16; Joseph Rety, *Transition Years: The Modern Approach to "the Change" in Womanhood* (New York: Greenberg, 1940), p. 24.

37. Banner, *American Beauty*, pp. 223–25; *Good Housekeeping* 92 (March 1931), 163; Charlotte West, *Ageless Youth* (New York: Thomas Y. Crowell, 1929), pp. 413–14.

38. Edith Lowry, *The Woman of Forty* (Chicago: Forbes & Co., 1919), p. 33; Colette, *Journey for Myself*, p. 105; West, *Ageless Youth*, p. 64. (Some observers think that Colette herself had begun the look with her short hair and gamine appearance as a music hall performer in the 1890s.)

39. Cf. Freeman Tilden, "Flapperdames and Flapperoosters," *Ladies' Home Journal* 37 (May 1920), 17. In a revealing 1920 memoir, Rhoda Boughton, age ninety, regretted that the "new woman," who signaled the ending of the "drab dyspeptic years" of middle age to bring "vigorous pleasure" and "hard study," had evolved into the frivolous flapper. See Rhoda Boughton, "Girls Past and Present," *Ladies' Home Journal* 37 (September 1920), 18ff.

40. Gertrude Atherton, *Black Oxen* (New York: Boni and Liveright, 1923), pp. 172–73.

41. Gertrude Atherton, *Adventures of a Novelist* (New York: Liveright, 1932), p. 558.

42. Abner I. Weisman, *Women's Change of Life* (New York: Renbayle House, 1951), p. 55. Weisman, who wrote positively about menopause, judged that most of his patients came for the clinic's conviviality and that in reality nothing was wrong with most of them beyond a "mild neurosis."

43. Susan Bell, "The Medicalization of Menopause," in Ruth Formanek, ed., *The Meanings of Menopause: Historical, Medical, and Clinical Perspectives* (Hillsdale, N.J.: Analytic Press, 1990), p. 74.

44. See Skene, *Medical Gynecology*, p. 484; C. C. Norris, "The Menopause: An Analysis of 200 Cases," *American Journal of Obstetrics* 79 (June 1919), 774; Charles Upshur, "Menopause and Climacteric," *Virginia Medical Monthly* 51 (January 1925), 623–24; George Naphys, *The Physical Life of Woman: Advice to the Maiden, Wife and Mother* (New York: M. A. Donahue, 1927), p. 264; Grace Elliott, *Women After Forty: The Meaning of the Last Half of Life* (New York: Holt, 1936), p. 115; Edward Podolsky, *Sex Practice in the Later Years* (New York: Cadillac, 1950), p. 41.

Some recent analysts trace the increased sex drive to the increase in androgen concomitant with the decline in estrogen among menopausal women. See Rita M. Ransohoff, *Venus after Forty* (New York: Macmillan, 1987), p. 106.

45. Th. H. Van de Velde, *Ideal Marriage: Its Physiology and Technique* (New York: Random House, 1965), pp. 96–105.

46. Ibid., pp. 98–99; Currier, *Menopause*, pp. 206–7, citing Kisch.

47. William Robinson, *The Menopause or Change of Life. Women's Critical Age. Its Dangers and Disorders. Their Prevention and Treatment* (New York: Critic and Guide, 1923), p. 73.

48. Atherton, *Black Oxen*, p. 263.

49. Walter Gallichan, *The Critical Age in Women* (London: T. Werner Laurie, 1920), p. 90; Sarah Trent, *Women Over Forty* (New York: Macauley, 1934), p. 70.

50. Marie Carmichael Stopes, *The Change of Life in Men and Women* (New York: Putnam, 1936), pp. 183–200.

51. Smith-Rosenberg, "The New Woman as Social Androgyne," in Smith-Rosenberg, *Disorderly Conduct*; pp. 281–82; Helene Deutsch, *The Psychology of Women: A Psychoanalytic Interpretation* (New York: Grune & Stratton, 1945), vol. 2, p. 465.

Positive attitudes about lesbianism were occasionally expressed, especially when demographic realities dictated that many aging women had no possibility of finding heterosexual partners. Advice writer Grace Elliott recommended that lesbianism be considered as a solution. Elliott, *Women After Forty*, p. 114.

52. Jeffries, *Spinster and Her Enemies*; Ellen Dorothy Abb, *What Fools We Women Be!* (London: Cassell, 1937), p. 114.

53. Christina Simmons, "Modern Sexuality and the Myth of Victorian Repression," in Kathy Peiss and Christina Simmons, eds., *Passion and Power: Sexuality in History* (Philadelphia: Temple University Press, 1989), pp. 165–66.

54. A. Béran Wolfe, *A Woman's Best Years* (New York: Emerson Books, 1935), p. 48; Gallichan, *Critical Age*, p. 105.

55. Edwin L. Hopewell-Ash, *Melancholia in Every-Day Practice* (London: John Bale, 1934), pp. 41–42. On the misuse of "involutional melancholia" as a special diagnostic category of mental illness in menopausal women, see Myrna Weissman, "The Myth of Involutional Melancholia," *Journal of the American Medical Association* 242 (August 1979), 24–31.

56. Cf. Karen L. Stoddard, *Saints and Shrews: Women and Aging in American Popular Culture* (Westport, Conn.: Greenwood Press, 1983).

57. Cf. Helen E. Hokinson, *My Best Girls* (New York: World, 1941). For the Benchley quote, see Miriam Lewin, "The Victorians, the Psychologists, and Psychic Birth Control," in Lewin, ed., *In the Shadow of the Past*, p. 68.

58. Cf. Edward Strecker, *Fundamentals of Psychiatry* (Philadelphia: J. B. Lippincott, 1945), p. 107. In her survey of attitudes toward menopause in "Women's Attitudes Toward the Menopause," in Bernice L. Neugarten et al., eds., *Middle Age and Aging: A Reader in Social Psychology* (Chicago: University of Chicago Press, 1968), p. 196, Bernice L. Neugarten found women in the 1950s referring to menopausal problems as "old wives' tales."

59. For a discussion of Freud's analysis, see Ernest Becker, "Social Science and Psychiatry," *Antioch Review* 23 (1963), 53–65. See also Karen Horney, *Feminine Psychology* (New York: W. W. Norton, 1967), pp. 176–77.

60. Cf. Freud, "Types of Onset of Neurosis," in *The Standard Edition of the Complete Psychological Works of Sigmund Freud,* trans. James Strachey (London: Hogarth, 1953), vol. 12, pp. 231–38. *Totem and Taboo* is contained in *Standard Edition*, vol. 13, pp. 1–162. In this work Freud also argued that the real reason for mother-in-law jokes was to cover embarrassment over the attraction between mothers-in-law and sons-in-law.

61. For Freud's biography, I have used Peter Gay, *Freud: A Life for Our Time* (New York: W. W. Norton, 1988), and J. N. Isbister, *Freud: An Introduction to His Life & Work* (Cambridge: Polity Press, 1985).

62. Rosemary Agonito, *History of Ideas on Women: A Source Book* (New York: Putnam, 1977), p. 321.

63. Deutsch, *Psychology of Women*, vol. 2, pp. 462, 467.

64. Ibid., vol. 2, p. 474.

65. Ibid., vol. 2, p. 468.

66. For Deutsch's biography, see Paul Roazen, *Helene Deutsch: A Psychoanalyst's Life* (Garden City, N.Y.: Anchor, 1985).

67. Beka Doherty and Lena Levine, *The Menopause* (New York: Random House, 1952), p. 101. See also John C. Burnham, "The Influence of Psychoanalysis Upon American Culture," in Burnham, ed., *Paths into American Culture: Psychology, Medicine, and Morals* (Philadelphia: Temple University Press, 1988), pp. 96–110.

68. Mary Bard, *Forty Odd* (Philadelphia: J. B. Lippincott, 1952), p. 115; Laci Fessler, "The Psychopathology of Climacteric Depression," *Journal of the American Psychoanalytic Association* 19 (1950), 29.

69. Horney, *Feminine Psychology,* pp. 176–77.

70. Karl A. Menninger, *Love Against Hate* (New York: Harcourt, Brace, 1943), pp. 56–57.

71. George Lawton, *Aging Successfully* (New York: Columbia University Press, 1946), p. 124.

72. Quoted by Susan Contratto, "Mother: Social Sculptor and Trustee of the Faith," in Lewin, ed., *In the Shadow of the Past,* p. 243.

73. Philip Wylie, *Generation of Vipers* (New York: Rinehart, 1942), pp. 186–87.

74. Elaine Tyler May, *Homeward Bound: American Families in the Cold War Era* (New York: Basic Books, 1988), p. 109.

75. Simone de Beauvoir, *The Second Sex,* trans. H. M. Parshley (New York: Alfred A. Knopf, 1957), pp. 575–96. With regard to women's organizations, de Beauvoir wrote contemptuously that the older women members wasted most of their time in organizing their organizations: "They elect officers, frame a constitution, carry on disputes among themselves, and struggle with their rival association for prestige" (p. 592).

76. Deirdre Bair, *Simone de Beauvoir: A Biography* (New York: Summit Books, 1990), pp. 302, 440; Bonnie G. Smith, *Ladies of the Leisure Class: The Bourgeoises of Northern France in the Nineteenth Century* (Princeton, N.J.: Princeton University Press, 1981).

77. Bair, *de Beauvoir,* pp. 442, 448.

78. See Kathleen Woodward, "Simone de Beauvoir: Aging and Its Discontents," in Shari Benstock, ed., *The Private Self: Theory and Practice of Women's Autobiographical Writings* (Chapel Hill: University of North Carolina Press, 1988), pp. 90–113.

79. Zelda Popkin, "Widows and the Perilous Years," in Elizabeth Bragdon, ed., *Women Today: Their Conflicts, Their Frustrations, and Their Fulfillments* (Indianapolis: Bobbs-Merrill, 1953), pp. 181–92.

80. Wolfe, *A Woman's Best Years,* p. 18.

81. Deutsch, *Psychology of Women*, vol. 2, p. 474.

82. Ibid.

83. Judith Posner, "It's All in Your Head: Feminist and Medical Models of Menopause (Strange Bedfellows)," *Sex Roles* 5 (1979), 179–94, argues that in the 1960s, medical textbooks downplayed the severity of menopausal symptoms and, by suggesting discomfort was imaginary, did serious disservice to those women with severe symptomology. Yet the 1960s witnessed the continuation of the impulse toward universal hormonal therapy, especially with Robert Wilson's popular *Forever Feminine* (New York: M. Evans, 1966).

For a discussion of the problems and possibilities of estrogen therapy, cf. Andrea Boroff Eagen, "The Estrogen 'Fix,' " *Ms.* 17 (April 1988), 38–44.

84. Emily Martin, *The Woman in the Body: A Cultural Analysis of Reproduction* (Boston: Beacon, 1987), pp. 172–73.

85. Cf. Eugene Whitmore, *Keeping Fit After Forty* (New York: D. Appleton, 1928), p. 151. Recent research has discovered that men as well as women suffer from osteoporosis, losing roughly 2 percent of their bone mass per year. (*Los Angeles Times*, January 3, 1990.) But given the danger of prostate cancer among aging men, doctors are reluctant to prescribe hormones. They have shown little similar reluctance with regard to women. (*Utne Reader*, May/June 1990.)

86. Helena Harris, "A Critical View of Three Psychoanalytic Positions on Menopause," in Formanek, ed., *The Meanings of Menopause*, p. 75.

87. Christine Downing, *Journey Through Menopause: A Personal Rite of Passage* (New York: Crossroad, 1989).

CHAPTER NINE *Aging and Ethnicity: Goddesses Reconsidered*

1. Ken Dychtwald, *Age Wave: The Challenges and Opportunities of an Aging America* (New York: St. Martin's Press, 1989), p. 347; Alan Pifer and Lydia Bronte, "Introduction:

Squaring the Pyramid," in Alan Pifer and Lydia Bronte, eds., *Our Aging Society: Paradox and Promise* (New York: W. W. Norton, 1986), p. 3.

2. Cf. "The Senior Boom: How Will It Affect America?" *Fortune,* March 27, 1989, 62ff.

3. Jacob S. Siegel and Cynthia M. Taeuber, "Demographic Dimensions of an Aging Population," in Pifer and Bronte, *Aging Society*, pp. 102–3.

4. David Gutmann, *Reclaimed Powers: Toward a New Psychology of Men and Women in Later Life* (New York: Basic Books, 1987), p. 7.

5. Patricia M. Passuth and Vern L. Bengston, "Sociological Theories of Aging: Current Perspectives and Future Directions," in James E. Birren and Vern L. Bengston, eds., *Emergent Theories of Aging* (New York: Springer, 1988), p. 339; Gary T. Reker and Paul T. P. Wong, "Aging as an Individual Process: Toward a Theory of Personal Meaning," in Birren and Bengston, *Emergent Theories of Aging*, pp. 214–46.

6. Grace Baruch, Rosalind Barnett, and Caryl Rivers, *Lifeprints: New Patterns of Love & Work for Today's Women* (New York: McGraw-Hill, 1983), pp. 1–10.

7. Elizabeth Taylor, *Elizabeth Takes Off* (New York: Putnam, 1987), p. 104.

8. Lillian B. Rubin, *Women of a Certain Age: The Midlife Search for Self* (New York: Harper & Row, 1979), p. 8; Baruch, Barnett, and Rivers, *Lifeprints,* passim.

9. *Ladies' Home Journal* 89 (August 1987), 153–55; Bernice L. Neugarten and Dail A. Neugarten, "Changing Meanings of Age in the Aging Society," in Pifer and Bronte, *Our Aging Society,* pp. 33–41.

10. Elissa Melamed, *Mirror, Mirror: The Terror of Not Being Young* (New York: Simon and Schuster, 1983), p. 27; Dychtwald, *Age Wave*, p. 33.

11. Cf. Eva Pernice, "Madison Avenue's Blind Spot," *U.S. News & World Report,* October 3, 1988, 49.

12. See Landon Y. Jones, *Great Expectations: America and the Baby Boom Generation* (New York: Coward, McCann & Geoghegan, 1980).

13. Andrea Walsh, " 'Life Isn't Over Yet': Older Heroines in American Popular Cinema of the 1930s and 1970s/80s," *Qualitative Sociology* 12 (Spring 1989), 72–95.

14. *Los Angeles Times,* July 12, 1990.

15. *Los Angeles Times,* September 21, 1990.

16. See David F. Archer, "Biochemical Findings and the Medical Management of Menopause," in Ann M. Voda, Myra Dinnerstein, and Sheryl R. O'Donnell, eds., *Changing Perspectives on Menopause* (Austin: University of Texas Press, 1982), pp. 196–99.

17. Pauline Bart, "Why Women's Status Changes in Middle Age: The Turns of the Social Ferris Wheel," *Sociological Symposium* 3 (Fall 1969), 1–18. See above, chapter 5.

18. Joan Collins, *Past Imperfect: An Autobiography* (New York: Simon and Schuster, 1984), pp. 334–38.

19. "Are Aging and Death Programmed in Our Genes?" *Science,* October 7, 1988, 43.

20. *Los Angeles Times,* July 5, 1990.

21. Robyn I. Stone, "The Feminization of Poverty among the Elderly," *Women's Studies Quarterly* 17 (Spring–Summer 1989), 20–34. (Courtesy of Emily Abel, issue special editor.)

22. Ibid.

23. *Los Angeles Times*, March 9, 1990. In 1986 "Disgusted in Indiana" (who identified herself as forty-three years old) wrote to Ann Landers of her "shocking" discovery that her nineteen-year-old son was having a sexual relationship with the woman in her sixties with whom he lived and who paid for his college education. Landers advised this correspondent that she should tell her son about her feelings but should not be surprised if nothing changed. *Los Angeles Times,* September 3, 1986.

24. Kate Millet, *Sexual Politics* (Garden City, N.Y.: Doubleday, 1970), pp. 190–203; Nancy Chodorow, *The Reproduction of Mothering: Psychoanalysis and the Sociology of Gender* (Berkeley: University of California Press, 1978.)

25. Gail Sheehy, *Passages: Predictable Crises of Adult Life* (New York: Dutton, 1976); Abraham Maslow, "Dominance, Personality and Social Behavior," *Journal of Psychology* 10 (1939): 3–39.

26. Cf. Alice S. Rossi, "Sex and Gender in the Aging Society," in Pifer and Bronte, *Our Aging Society*, pp. 111–39.

27. *Ebony,* May 1988, 156–60.

28. Rossi, "Sex and Gender," in Pifer and Bronte, *Our Aging Society*, p. 119.

29. *Los Angeles Times*, October 25, 1990.

30. Cf. Jane Seskin, "When Older Women Marry Younger Men," *Woman's Day*, April 30, 1985, 85ff; Wade Carlson, "Why Younger Men are Marrying Older Women," *National Examiner*, October 8, 1985, 27; Katha Pollitt, "Being Wedded Is Not Always Bliss," *The Nation,* September 20, 1986, 239–40; Carol Tavris, "The Man Shortage: Is It Real? What Does It Really Mean? *Cosmopolitan*, October 1986, 264ff; Victoria Secunda, "Loving a [Much Younger] Man," *New Woman,* January 1987, 82; Bernard Gavzner, "Why More Older Women Are Marrying Younger Men," *Parade*, May 14, 1987, 12–13; Harry Brod and Harriet Bernstein, " 'That' Study: Another Look at the Marriage Crunch," *Men & Women Today*, January 1987, 1–2.

31. Ben Wattenberg, "Women and Marriage: A Different Look," *Los Angeles Times*, August 29, 1986.

32. Matilda White Riley, "Women, Men, and Lengthening the Life Course," in Alice S. Rossi, ed., *Gender and the Life Course* (New York: Aldine, 1985), p. 335.

33. Gavzner, "Why More Older Women," 12.

34. Ibid.

35. Joyce Sunila, *The New Lovers: Younger Men/Older Women* (New York: Fawcett, 1980), pp. 55–57.

36. Annis Pratt, *Archetypal Patterns in Women's Fiction* (Bloomington: Indiana University Press, 1981); Kathleen Woodward, "May Sarton and Fictions of Old Age," in Janet Todd, ed., *Gender and Literary Voice: Women and Literature* (New York: Holmes & Meier, 1980), pp. 108–27.

37. Cf. Wanda Urbanska, *The Singular Generation: Young Americans in the 1980s* (Garden City, N.Y.: Doubleday, 1986).

38. On the 1950s, Leila Rupp has concluded, in *Survival in the Doldrums: The American Women's Rights Movement, 1945 to the 1960s* (New York: Oxford University Press, 1987), p. 51: "The most striking characteristic of women's rights activists was their age. Eighty-eight percent were over 50 in 1950." With regard to the 1920s, Nancy Cott infers that the majority of activists were younger women. See Cott's *The Grounding of Modern Feminism* (New Haven, Conn.: Yale University Press, 1987), p. 97. Journalistic accounts, however, give a different impression. See Alice Ames Walker, "Gorgeous Middle Age," *Ladies' Home Journal,* September 1924, 27; and "What No One Told Me About Middle Age," *Woman's Home Companion*, October 1923, p. 133: "We, 'middle-aged women,' we order the household, run the committees, dominate the boards of directors." As with many issues concerning the history of aging, in-depth research is needed.

39. See Friedan's preliminary articles: "The Mystique of Age" and "Changing Sex Roles: Vital Aging," in Robert N. Butler and Herbert P. Gleason, eds., *Productive Aging: Enhancing Vitality in Later Life* (New York: Springer, 1985), pp. 37–45, 93–104.

40. Barbara MacDonald, "Outside the Sisterhood: Ageism in Women's Studies," *Women's Studies Quarterly* 17 (Spring–Summer 1989), 6.

41. Karla F. C. Holloway and Stephanie Demetrakopoulos, "Remembering Our Foremothers: Older Black Women, Politics of Age, Politics of Survival as Embodied in the Novels of Toni Morrison," *Women & Politics* 6 (Spring 1986), 15.

42. bell hooks, *From Margin to Center* (Boston: South End Press, 1984), preface. See also Patricia Hill Collins, *Black Feminist Thought: Knowledge, Consciousness, and the Politics of Empowerment* (Boston: Unwin Hyman, 1990).

43. Rose Gibson, "Outlook for the Black Family," in Bronte and Pifer, *Our Aging Society,* pp. 181–97. See also Pauline Bart, "Depression in Middle-Aged Women: Some Sociocultural Factors," Ph.D. diss., UCLA, 1967.

44. Catherine Clinton, *The Plantation Mistress: Woman's World in the Old South* (New York: Pantheon, 1982), pp. 201–2; Elizabeth Fox-Genovese, *Within the Plantation Household: Black and White Women of the Old South* (Chapel Hill: University of North Carolina Press, 1988), p. 35.

45. Jacqueline Jones, *Labor of Love, Labor of Sorrow: Black Women, Work and The Family, from Slavery to the Present* (New York: Vintage, 1986), p. 182. See also Phyllis Palmer, *Domesticity and Dirt: Housewives and Domestic Servants in the United States, 1920–1945* (Philadelphia: Temple University Press, 1989), pp. 65–87.

46. Quoted by Alice Walker, *In Search of Our Mothers' Gardens: Womanist Prose* (New York: Harcourt Brace Jovanovich, 1983), p. 2. On the "blues women" I have used Hazel B. Carby, " 'It Jus' Be's Dat Way Sometime': The Sexual Politics of Women's Blues," in Ellen Carol DuBois and Vicki L. Ruiz, eds., *Unequal Sisters: A Multi-Cultural Reader in U.S. Women's History* (New York: Routledge, 1990), pp. 238–49; Daphne Duval Harrison, *Black Pearls: Blues Queens of the 1920s* (New Brunswick, N.J.: Rutgers University Press, 1988).

47. Sandra Lieb, *Mother of the Blues: Ma Rainey* (Amherst: University of Massachusetts Press, 1981), p. 13; Harrison, *Black Pearls,* p. 57. My thanks to Lillian Schlissel for the Ma Rainey quote.

48. Sara Evans, *Personal Politics: The Roots of Women's Liberation in the Civil Rights Movement & The New Left* (New York: Vintage, 1980), p. 51.

49. Ironically, in the report Moynihan issued a disclaimer against the charge that "matriarchy" per se was the problem. His point was that blacks were disadvantaged because they were not in step with the majority of American families, which were father-headed. This latter contention is no longer correct, and the change makes even more imperative the investigation of alternative models of individual, gender, and family construction. See Daniel P. Moynihan, "The Negro Family: The Case for National Action," in John H. Bracey, August Meier, and Elliot Rudwick, eds., *Black Matriarchy* (Belmont, Calif.: Wadsworth, 1971), p. 140.

Recent evidences of the continuation of the stereotyping of "matriarchy" as a problem among blacks are noted by Maxine Baca Zinn, "Family, Race, and Poverty in the Eighties," *Signs: Journal of Women in Culture and Society* 14 (Summer 1989), 856–74.

50. Nancy Tanner, "Matrifocality in Indonesia and Africa and Among Black Americans," in Michelle Zimbalist Rosaldo and Louise Lamphere, eds., *Women, Culture & Society* (Stanford, Calif.: Stanford University Press, 1974), pp. 129–56.

51. Cf. Carol B. Stack, *All Our Kin: Strategies for Survival in a Black Community* (New York: Harper & Row, 1974).

52. Harriet Pipes McAdoo, "Black Mothers and the Extended Family Support Network," in La Frances Rodgers-Rose, ed., *The Black Woman* (Beverly Hills, Calif.: Sage, 1980).

53. Cf. Andrew Billingsley, *Black Families in White America* (Englewood Cliffs, N.J.: Prentice-Hall, 1968), p. 47; Rodgers-Rose, *Black Woman,* pp. 15–18.

54. Walker, *In Search of Our Mothers' Gardens,* p. 240.

55. Daniel F. McCall, "Mother Earth: The Great Goddess of West Africa," in James J. Preston, ed., *Mother Worship: Theme and Variations* (Chapel Hill: University of North Carolina Press, 1982), pp. 305–6.

56. Ibid.

57. Leonard W. Moss and Stephen C. Cappannari, "In Quest of the Black Virgin," in Preston, *Mother Worship,* pp. 53–74.

58. Aida Hurtado, "Relating to Privilege: Seduction and Rejection in the Subordination of White Women and Women of Color," *Signs: Journal of Women in Culture and Society* 14 (Summer 1989), 833–55.

59. Audre Lorde, *Sister Outsider* (Trumansburg, N.Y.: Crossing Press, 1984), p. 119.

60. Cf. Dianne F. Sadoff, "Black Matrilineage: The Case of Alice Walker and Zora Neale Hurston," *Signs: Journal of Women in Culture and Society* 2 (Autumn 1985), 4–26.

61. Mae Gwendolyn Henderson, "Speaking in Tongues: Dialogics, Dialectics, and the Black Woman Writer's Literary Tradition," in Cheryl A. Wall, ed., *Changing Our Own Words: Essays on Criticism, Theory and Writing by Black Women* (New Brunswick, N.J.: Rutgers University Press, 1987), pp. 16–37.

62. Barbara Christian, "Trajectories of Self-Definition: Placing Contemporary Afro-American Women's Fiction," in Marjorie Pryse and Hortense J. Spillers, eds., *Conjuring: Black Women, Fiction, and Literary Tradition* (Bloomington: Indiana University Press, 1985), p. 247.

63. Toni Morrison, *Beloved* (New York: Alfred A. Knopf, 1987), p. 87.

64. Karla Holloway and Stephanie Demetrakopoulos, *New Dimensions in Spirituality: A Biracial and Bicultural Reading of the Novels of Toni Morrison* (Westport, Conn.: Greenwood Press, 1987), pp. 159–60; Morrison, *Beloved,* p. 87. Dorothy H. Lee sees evidences of the use of imagery relating to goddesses throughout *Tar Baby* and *Song of Solomon.* "The woman in yellow [in *Tar Baby*] is reminiscent of the navelless Pilate in *Song of Solomon* who also suggests a primal mother goddess. In both novels the eggs suggest origins and a return to the past. Pilate's apples [which suggest the fertilizing knowledge of the folk] reappear in *Tar Baby....*" Dorothy H. Lee, "The Quest for Self: Triumph and Failure in the Works of Toni Morrison," in Mari Evans, ed., *Black Women Writers: A Critical Evaluation* (New York: Anchor, 1984), pp. 357–59.

65. Morrison, *Beloved,* p. 88.

66. Holloway and Demetrakopoulos, "Remembering Our Foremothers," pp. 20–21.

67. Alice Walker, *The Color Purple* (New York: Pocket Books, 1982), pp. 255, 257.

68. Ibid., p. 295.

69. Alice Walker, *The Temple of My Familiar* (San Diego: Harcourt Brace Jovanovich, 1989), p. 355.

70. Ibid., p. 356.

71. Ibid., p. 196.

72. Ibid., p. 197.

73. Ibid., p. 288.

74. Robert E. Hemenway, *Zora Neale Hurston: A Literary Biography* (London: Camden, 1986), p. 62.

75. Zora Neale Hurston, *Their Eyes Were Watching God* (Urbana: University of Illinois Press, 1978), p. 47.

76. Ibid., pp. 177–78.

77. Ibid., p. 200.

78. Ibid., pp. 26, 268.

79. Ibid., p. 10.

80. Ibid., p. 286.
81. Ibid., pp. 19, 44.
82. Ibid., p. 32.

EPILOGUE

1. Cf. Betty Ann Kevles, "Crucial Roles of Older Female Animals," *Los Angeles Times*, April 22, 1987; Jane B. Lancaster, "Sex Differences in Higher Primates," in Alice S. Rossi, ed., *Gender and the Life Course* (New York: Aldine, 1985), pp. 6–10; Jane Goodall, *In the Shadow of Man* (Boston: Houghton Mifflin, 1971).

2. Robert Bly, *Iron John: A Book About Men* (Reading, Mass.: Addison-Wesley, 1990).

3. Carolyn Heilbrun, *Writing a Woman's Life* (New York: W. W. Norton, 1988), p. 131.

4. Cf. Leon Phillips, *That Eaton Woman: In Defense of Peggy O'Neale Eaton* (Barre, Mass.: Barre Publishing, 1974); Mavis Gallant, *The Affair of Gabrielle Russier* (New York: Popular Library, 1971).

Index

Abbayes de la Jeunesse, 155
Abelard, Peter, 139
Actaeon, 77; *see also* Artemis
Addams, Jane, 282, 333
Adolphe (Constant), 262, 266
Adonis
  as model for young men, 11, 45, 85,
    107, 222, 260, 355
  with Aphrodite, 63, 76, 77, 79, 86
Adonis festival, 79–81
Adventures of Humphry Clinker
  (Smollett), 248
Aeneid (Virgil), 119
Afro-American women, aging
  African roots, 341
  Aunt Jemima figure, 337, 338
  blues singers, 6, 338–9
  family and community organizers,
    339–401
  life expectancy differential, compared
    with whites, 336
  and "Mammy" figure, 337–40
  positive life attitude, 336
  "red-hot mamas," 6
  under slavery, 338–9
  see also Black Madonna
age-disparate relationships; *see* aging
  men and younger women; aging
  women and younger men
ageism, contemporary
  in advertising, 319–20
  double discrimination, toward
    women, 6
  in movies and television, 320–1

age of consent laws, 176–7
aging
  attitudes toward, in China, 321
  among female animals, 353
  as individuation, in gerontological
    analysis, 318
aging men, 198–200
  and declining procreative ability,
    327–8
  and male menopause, 278, 309–10
aging men and younger women, 4–5,
  102–3, 196, 259–61, 302
aging women
  and biblical tradition, 185
  and class distinctions, 8, 160–1, 314,
    315
  in classical Athens, 102–5
  as comic figures, early modern
    Europe, 186
  as comic figures, twentieth century,
    296
  as enforcers of convention, 18, 136,
    252
  in film, 295–6, 320
  and Freudianism, 297–304
  limited roles of, early modern Europe,
    165–6
  and "marriage crunch," 328–9
  oral tradition among, 194–7
  Progressive era and, 276–84
  in Rome, 110–17
  salonnières, attitudes toward aging,
    230–1
  as sexualized, 171–5, 288–93

aging women (*cont.*)
  in soap opera (radio), 295
  Victorian era and, 243–58
  and witches, 168, 189–93
  and woman-to-woman bonds, 257–8
  see also Afro-American women, aging;
    aging women and younger men;
    duenna; France, aging women,
    presumption of more positive
    attitudes toward; go-between;
    grandmother; menopause; poverty,
    among aging women; wise woman
    as role for aging women; witchcraft
aging women and younger men
  in contemporary period, 1–13, 325–37
  in cult of courtly love, 136–48
  and demography, 155–61, 243–4
  and economic advancement, 149–61
  Elizabeth I (England) and, 223–6
  and European family structure, 150–1,
    245–8
  in Freudian psychology, 297–305
  nineteenth-century decline of, 243–6
  peasantry and, 153–7, 244–8
  recent analysis of older woman/
    younger man couples, 11–12, 331
  among salon women, 226–31
  among well-to-do widows, early
    modern Europe, 149–54
  see also aging men and younger
    women; aging women; youth, for
    males
Alcott, Louisa May, *Little Women*, 259
Alençon, Duke of, and Elizabeth I
    (England), 149, 169, 226
All About Eve, 40
All That Heaven Allows, 306
Amadis of Gaul, 225, 316
Ambassadors, The (James), 262, 263
amenorrhea, relation to menopause, 184
Amores (Ovid), 114–16, 187, 188
Anatomy of Melancholy (Burton), 172, 212
Anchises, 76; *see also* Aphrodite
Anne, Saint (mother of Mary)
  patron saint of childbirth, 185
  representative of aging women, 91–2
Anthony, Susan B., 7, 251, 257, 282, 333
Antony and Cleopatra (Shakespeare), 185
Aphrodite (Venus), 20, 63, 76, 81, 86, 87,
    95, 96, 97, 98, 109, 111, 201; *see also*
    Adonis, Anchises, Phaethon

Apuleius, *The Golden Ass*, 114
Ariès, Philippe, 243
Aristophanes, 95, 104–5, 114
  Ecclesiazusae, 104–5, 114
  Lysistrata, 105
Aristotelian gender conservatism,
    thirteenth century, 121, 131, 145
Artemis (Diana), 77, 86, 97; *see also*
    Actaeon; Black Madonna;
    Hippolytus and Phaedra; mystery
    religions
Arthurian legend, 62, 134, 141, 147
Arthur Mervyn (Brown), 260, 263
Art of Courtly Love, The (Capellanus),
    143–5, 146, 172, 176–7, 199
Art of Love (Ovid), 113, 177
As You Like It (Shakespeare), 175–6, 210
Athena, 20, 67, 68, 73, 77, 85, 86, 108,
    117, 122, 356
Athens (classical period)
  and pederasty, 102–9
  and women, 103–5: as keepers of the
    oikos, 108; as midwives, 103–4;
    postmenopausal, 103; as priestesses,
    104
Atherton, Gertrude, *Black Oxen*, 289–91,
    293
Attis, 63, 79, 81, 86; *see also* Cybele
Aunt Jemima figure, 337, 338; *see also*
    Afro-American women, aging
Autobiography of Thomas Wythorne, 173,
    191
Awakening Dawn, The (Colette), 267, 271

"baby boom" generation, 317, 320
Bacchae (Euripides), 95
Bakhtin, Mikhail, 212
Bart, Pauline, 167, 322
Balzac, Honoré de, 264, 265
  Lost Illusions, 262, 266
Beaumarchais, Pierre de, *The Marriage
    of Figaro*, 186, 187, 222
beauty, 15
  commercialization of, 283–4, 288–9
  contemporary, 321–4
  and flower and seasonal imagery, 23,
    173, 178, 184, 189
  influence of aging actresses, late
    nineteenth century, 283
  and maturity, post–World War II, 49

and old women, early modern
    Europe, 182
    relation to menopause, 281
beauty, concepts of, 15, 139
    and *Art of Courtly Love*, 144
    in classical Athens, 105
    dress, relation to, 212–13
    Fuller, Margaret, on aging, 242, 251
    in nineteenth century, 250–3, 255–7
    in 1920s and 1930s, 288–90, 295–6
    in Plutarch, 116
    in prestate societies, 165–7, 322
    in *querelle des femmes*, 178
    as relative, 99, 100, 178
    in Renaissance, 179–81
    Sappho, views of, 100–1
    and Wife of Bath, 135
beauty, in young men
    connection with "beardless"
        appearance, 107, 214
    in novels of Colette, 270
Beauvoir, Simone de, 303–5, 333
    Coming of Age, The, 6, 304, 305
    and Jean-Paul Sartre, 304
    Second Sex, The, 303, 304, 305, 333
    and Sylvie le Bon, 305
Behn, Aphra, 174
Bel Ami (Maupassant), 262
Beloved (Morrison), 344, 345
Bennett, Arnold, *The Old Wives' Tale*,
    264, 269
Bennett, Judith, 20
Berger, John, 201
Bernhardt, Sarah, 7, 51–2, 244, 283, 284,
    288
Bible, 61, 79, 80, 91, 117
birth control
    identified with younger feminists,
        contemporary era, 332
    impact on salon women, 229
    nineteenth century, 278
Black Madonna, 342; *see also* Afro-
    American women, aging;
    goddesses, ancient
Black Oxen (Atherton), 289–91, 293
black women, *see* Afro-American
    women
Blanche of Castile, 142–3, 144, 145–6
    relationship analyzed by Christine de
        Pizan, 178
    and Thibaut of Champagne, 145–6

Bluest Eye, The (Morrison), 344
Boccaccio, Giovanni
    Concerning Famous Women, 93, 132
    Corbaccio, 171, 183
    Decameron, 198
Boethius
    Consolation of Philosophy, 119, 178
    and Philosophia, 119, 178
Bogin, Meg, 139
Book of the City of Ladies (Pizan), 178
Book of the Courtier, The (Castiglione),
    179, 198, 199, 200, 208, 211, 216,
    217, 218–19
Book of Secrets (Magnus), 193
Born Yesterday, 40
Boswell, John, 213
braies, as undergarments, 214–15
Brantôme, Pierre de Bourdeille de, 149,
    159, 170, 172, 174–5, 199
Break of Day, The (Colette), 268–9
Brown, Charles Brockden, *Arthur
    Mervyn*, 260, 263
Brown, Judith, 165
Burney, Fanny, *Evelina*, 246
Burschenschaften, 155
Burton, Robert, *Anatomy of Melancholy*,
    172, 212
Byron, Lord, 10
    Don Juan, 10

Calypso, 75
Canterbury Tales, The, 8, 129–36, 146,
    165, 183, 198, 206, 207, 215; *see also*
    Chaucer, Geoffrey; Wife of Bath
Capellanus, Andreas, *The Art of Courtly
    Love*, 143–5, 146, 172, 176–7, 183
Carlyle, Thomas, 239, 242, 260
Carmina Burana, 209
caroles, aging man/younger woman
    motif in, 198
Castiglione, Baldesar, *The Book of the
    Courtier*, 179, 198, 199, 200, 208,
    211, 216, 217, 218–19
Catherine of Alexandria, Saint, 119
Chambers-Schiller, Lee, 257
chapbooks, sixteenth century,
    presentation of aging women's
    sexuality in, 172
charivaris, 155, 209

Chaucer, Geoffrey, 8, 21, 129–36, 139;
     see also Canterbury Tales, The; cult
     of courtly love; Wife of Bath
Chéri (Colette), 267, 270
chess, twelfth century, 139
Childhood and Society (Erikson), 303
chivalric romances, 134, 140–1, 146–7,
     208; *see also: Amadis of Gaul*; cult
     of courtly love; Chrétien de Troyes
Chrétien de Troyes, 221
     Cligès, 141, 146, 202, 215
     Erec et Enide, 147
     Perceval, 147–8
     Yvain, 141
Christine de Pizan, 19, 149, 217, 222
     Book of the City of Ladies, 178
Circe, 73, 75, 84
Cleland, John
     Fanny Hill, 174
     Memoirs of a Coxcomb, 220–1
Clélie (Scudéry), 229
Cleopatra, 9, 55, 92, 183, 190–1
Cligès (Chrétien de Troyes), 146, 202,
     213, 215
climacteric insanity, 285, 301; *see also*
     involutional melancholia; old
     maid's insanity
Clytemnestra, as symbol of sexualized
     woman, 71, 72, 73, 74, 86, 106,
     194
codpiece, 203, 205–6, 212–13
Cole, Thomas, 278
Colette, Sidonie-Gabrielle, 236, 238,
     267–72, 276, 289, 303, 330
     attitude toward aging, 271
     Awakening Dawn, The, 267, 271
     Break of Day, The, 268, 269
     Chéri, 267, 270
     and Gauthier-Villars, Henri, 267,
          269–70
     and Goudeket, Maurice, 267, 272
     and Jouvenel, Henry de, 270
     Julie de Carneilhan, 267
     Last of Chéri, The, 267, 271–2
     lesbianism, 270
     as music hall performer, 270
     and novel of initiation, 267
     participation in "Belle Epoque"
          culture, 269
     Pure and the Impure, The, 267, 270
     Retreat from Love, The, 267, 270

Ripening Seed, The, 267, 268, 269, 270
     sexuality of aging protagonists, 268
     as symbol of French nation, 272
     Shackle, The, 271
     and Sido, 268, 271
Collins, Joan, 323
Color Purple, The (Walker), 346–7
Coming of Age, The (de Beauvoir), 6,
     304–5
"coming of age" novel, 45, 221–2, 266–7
commedia dell'arte, aging male
     characters in, 198, 207
Commentary on Plato's Symposium
     (Ficino), 179
Concerning Famous Women (Boccaccio),
     93, 132
condottieri, 205
Conjugal Lewdness (Defoe), 165, 175
Consolation of Philosophy (Boethius), 119,
     178
Constant, Benjamin, 8
     Adolphe, 262, 266
Corbaccio (Boccaccio), 171, 183
Corinne (de Staël), 240
cosmetic surgery, contemporary, 321
courteosie, 130, 136–48; *see also* cult of
     courtly love
Crawford, Joan, 306–7
Crete, island of, as central in
     goddess–young god mythology, 63,
     76, 83, 84, 88, 95
crone
     and *Canterbury Tales*, 134–5
     ceremonies, contemporary period, 309,
          334
     relationship to "crony," 248
     as wise woman, 248
     see also wise woman, as role for aging
          women
Cross, John, 8
cross-age relationships, *see* age-disparate
     relationships; aging women and
     younger men
cuckoldry, 198–9, 207
Cuffe, Henry, 177
cult of courtly love, 130, 136–48, 224–5;
     see also Arthurian legends; chivalric
     romances; courteosie; love poetry,
     troubadours
Cumaen Sibyl, 121, 242–3; *see also* Sibyls
Cybele, 61, 63, 81, 84, 96; *see also* Attis

Damuzi, 63, 79, 89; *see also* Inanna
Dangerous Age, The (Michaelis), 273–4,
    275, 279, 296–7
Daudet, Alphonse, *Sapho*, 262
Davis, Natalie Zemon, 130–2, 212
Decameron, The (Boccaccio), 198
Deffand, Madame du, 227, 265
    and Horace Walpole, 228, 265
Defoe, Daniel, 245
    Conjugal Lewdness, 165, 175
Deloney, Thomas, *The pleasant Historie
    of John Winchcombe, in his younguer
    yeares Called Jack of Newbery*, 152,
    165, 221
Demeter, 70, 77, 87, 88; *see also*
    Persephone; Eleusinian Mysteries
DeMille, Cecil B., 28, 35–7
Desmond, Norma, 27, 30–55, 60, 128,
    284, 305–6, 321; *see also Sunset
    Boulevard*
Deutsch, Helene, 275, 294, 301, 302, 303,
    307, 333
    Psychology of Women, The, 299–300
Diana, *see* Artemis
Diane de Poitiers, 7, 179, 225–6, 265
Dionysus, 83–4, 85, 87, 104, 115
Diotima, 109, 117, 119
Dipsas, 114–15
Disraeli, Benjamin, 262
Don Juan (Byron), 10
dowager, 166
dowager's hump, 182; *see also*
    osteoporosis
dower (dowry)
    in classical Athens, 103
    as family contribution, 153
    as inheritance for widows, 150
    in Italy, 158–9
Downing, Christine, *Journey Through
    Menopause*, 309–10, 331
dress, male
    during reign of Queen Elizabeth I
        (England), 225
    in early modern Europe: athleticism,
        206; battle garb, 204–5; sexuality,
        203–4, 206–8; social class, 204–5;
        young men as style innovators,
        208–9
    in medieval era, 139
    seventeenth to nineteenth centuries, 203
duenna, 187–8; *see also* go-between

early modern Europe
    aging women, declining position in,
        159–60
    attitudes toward menopause in, 183–5
    beauty, concepts in, 178–81
    cross-age relationships in, 148–63
    guilds, 151–2, 160
    and life-cycle theory, 175–8
    and physiological theory, 169–70
    witchcraft in, 186–97
Ecclesiazusae (Aristophanes), 104–5,
    114
Eddy, Mary Baker, 7, 282
Eleanor of Aquitaine, 142–4, 148, 206
Eleusinian Mysteries, 87–8, 108; *see also*
    mystery religions
Elias, Norbert, 210
Eliot, George, 8, 244
    and Henry Lewes, 8
    and John Cross, 8
Elizabeth I of England, 7, 8, 169, 182,
    184, 202, 210, 213, 223–6
Ellis, Havelock, 286
    Studies in the Psychology of Sex, 286–7
Emerson, Ralph Waldo, 239
empty nest syndrome, 326
endocrinology, and definitions of female
    physiology, 291
Epic of Gilgamesh, 77, 78–9
Epiklaros, 103, 150; *see also* Athens,
    classical period
Erasmus, Desiderius, *The Praise of Folly*,
    171
Erec et Enide (Chrétien de Troyes), 147
Erikson, Erik, 303, 319, 326
    Childhood and Society, 303
Erinyes (Furies), 62, 73, 99
essentialism, in feminism, 20
Euripides, 95, 102, 104
    Bacchae, 85
Evelina (Burney), 246

fabliaux, 134, 173, 186, 198
Fanny Hill (Cleland), 174
feminine mystique, contemporary, 355
Feminine Psychology (Horney), 302
feminism, contemporary, attitudes
    toward aging, 331–4
Ficino, Marsilio, *Commentary on Plato's
    Symposium*, 179

Fielding, Henry, 8, 264
  Joseph Andrews, 246
  Tom Jones, 221, 246
Firenzuolo, Agnolo, 179
Flaubert, Gustave, *Sentimental Education*, 262
Flindrin, Jean-Louis, 152, 215
folk and fairy tales, 185, 194–7
  age transformation in, 99, 135
fop, as male role, 220; *see also* gallantry
Fortuna, 59, 120–1
  and Machiavelli, 122
France, presumption of more positive
    attitudes toward aging women in, 179, 231, 261–7
Franklin, Benjamin, 10–11, 265
  and Madame de Brillon, 228
Frauendienst (Lichtenstein), 140
Frazer, Sir James, *The Golden Bough*, 78, 197
Freud, Sigmund, 9, 287, 297–9, 326
  and Amalia Freud, 298
  *New Introductory Lectures on
    Psychoanalysis*, 298
  "Theme of the Three Caskets," 62
  Totem and Taboo, 298
Freudian interpretations, 8–9, 274–5, 276, 297–9, 326
  feminist critique of, 326
Friedan, Betty, 332, 333
frontier mythology, American, 43–5
Fuller, Margaret, 8, 16, 236, 237–43, 247, 249, 253, 260, 314, 330
  on aging women's appearance, 242–3
  American men's opinion of, 239
  attitude toward gender, 238
  attitude toward spinsters, 242
  and Cumaen Sibyl, 242, 251
  influence of ancient goddesses on, 16, 240
  journey to Europe, 237–8
  relationship with Giovanni Angelo
    Ossoli, 237–42
  Woman in the Nineteenth Century, 16, 238, 240, 249, 257
Furies, *see* Erinyes

gallantry, male, 131, 219–221
galli, 81, 100

Gargantua and Pantagruel (Rabelais), 205
generational conflict
  in early modern Europe, 155–6
  among modern feminists, 334
Generation of Vipers (Wylie), 303, 306
Geoffrin, Madame de, 227
gerontology, definitions of aging, 317–18
gigolo, 12–13, 16, 31, 45
Gilgamesh, 77, 78, 79; *see also* Ishtar
Gillis, Joe, 27, 30–55; *see also: Sunset
    Boulevard*
Gimbutas, Marija, 82, 88, 100
Gnostic Gospels, 117
go-between, 114–15, 168, 193, 197, 248;
    see also Dipsas; duenna; lena;
    Mother Midnight; old bawd; old
    trot; procurer
Goddesses, ancient
  Freud on, 62, 298
  relationships with daughters (Demeter
    and Persephone), 87–8
  relationships with other goddesses, 86–7
  relationships with young men, 76–86
  transformations from age to youth
    (Celtic and Scottish), 62
  as tripartite, 62–3
  see also Black Madonna
Golden Ass, The (Apuleius), 114
Golden Bough, The (Frazer), 78, 197
Goncourt, Edmond and Jules de, 227
Goodman of Paris, *Treatise on Moral and
    Domestic Economy*, 165, 216–17
gothic fiction, 33, 248–9
Graduate, The, 3
Grail, in Arthurian legend, 147–8, 215
Grand Cyrus, Le (Scudéry), 229
grandmother, 17
  as demographic reality, 253
  Freudian views of, 300–1, 308
  as ideal type, 253–5
  Roman roots, 111
"graying of America," 316
Great Expectations (Dickens), 48
Grimm brothers, 192, 194, 196, 197
Griselda motif, early modern Europe,
    132; *see also* Chaucer, Geoffrey
guild system, 9, 151, 160
Guttman, David, 317

Hallett, Judith, 111
Halperin, David, 106
Hamlet (Shakespeare), 161–2
Harold and Maude, 320–1, 325–6
Hawthorne, Nathaniel, 239, 249, 259
   House of the Seven Gables, The,
   249
Hecate, 98
Heilbrun, Carolyn, 355
Helen of Sparta, 71, 73, 86; *see also*
   Helen of Troy
Helen of Troy, 65, 66, 69, 70, 74, 87,
   178, 181; *see also* Helen of Sparta
Hellenistic era, and new hagiographic
   systems, 117–21
Henry of Normandy (Henry II of
   England), 148
   and Eleanor of Aquitaine, 143
Heptaméron (de Navarre), 177, 198, 199,
   217, 224
Hera, 20, 77, 87, 356; *see also* Zeus
Heracles, 76, 83, 84, 105; *see also*
   Hercules
Hercules, 204, 207; *see also* Heracles
Herlihy, David, 161
Heroides (Ovid), 96, 107, 113, 120
heroism, masculine
   associated with Adonis, 85, 107
   associated with Heracles, 85, 107
   Christian gentleman, 260
   and film noir, 47
   hard-boiled, 1930s, 46
   Horatio Alger, 44–5
   manliness, nineteenth century, 260
   Odyssey, 48, 66–71, 74, 88–90
   picaresque, 45, 221
   in Western novel, 45, 89, 260
   and women, 68–9
   and World War II, 46–7, 260
Hesiod, 68, 77, 78, 98
   Theogony, 78, 98
   Works and Days, 68
hieros gamos, 79–80, 330
Hildegard of Bingen, 7, 145
Hippolytus and Phaedra, 83, 170, 264;
   see also stepmother: seduction of
   stepson motif
Hogarth, William, 256
   Rake's Progress, A, 221
Hokinson, Helen, 296

Holden, William, 40, 42; *see also: Sunset
   Boulevard*
Hollywood films, as genre, 36
Homeric hymns
   Hymn to Aphrodite, 78
   Hymn to Demeter, 62, 70
homosexuality, *see* same-sex love, male
honnête homme, 229, 260; *see also:
   précieuses*
hooks, bell, 336
Hopper, Hedda, 53–5; *see also: Sunset
   Boulevard*
hormones, as related to menopause, 15,
   170, 275, 290–1, 308
   estrogen replacement therapy, 291
Horney, Karen, 302
   Feminine Psychology, 302
House of the Seven Gables, The
   (Hawthorne), 249
Hrosvitha of Gandersheim, 119–20
Hurston, Zora Neale, 316, 336, 337, 348
   Their Eyes Were Watching God,
   349–52
Hymn to Inanna, 77, 89–90
hysterectomy, late nineteenth century,
   273, 285

Iliad, The (Homer), 64
Inanna, 61, 63, 88, 89; *see also* Damuzi
involutional melancholia, 285, 295, 307;
   see also climacteric insanity; old
   maid's insanity
I Remember Mama, 33
Ishtar, 61, 63, 77, 78, 86; *see also*
   Tammuz, Gilgamesh
Isis, 61, 63, 81, 88; *see also* Osiris

James, Henry, 45, 262, 263
   Ambassadors, The, 262, 263
   Portrait of a Lady, 263
Jeffords, Susan, 19, 20
Jenkin, 128–36; *see also: Canterbury
   Tales, The*
Jordan, Constance, 222
Joseph and Potiphar's wife, 83, 170; *see
   also* stepmother: seduction of
   stepson motif
Joseph Andrews (Fielding), 246

Journey Through Menopause (Downing), 309–10, 331
Judgment of Paris, 20, 101, 200–1
Julie de Carneilhan (Colette), 267
Juvenal, 112–13, 115

Kann, Mark, 222
Katz, Marylin Arthur, 68
Kelly, Joan, 130
Kisch, Enoch, 292–3
Kouretes, 83–5
kouros, youth in classical Greece, 102
    as statue, 84

Laclos, Choderlos de, *Les Liaisons Dangereuses*, 230, 231
"lady luck," 121; *see also* Fortuna
Lambert, Madame du, 227, 229
Langtry, Lillie, 7, 244, 281, 283
Laquer, Thomas, 251–2
Laslett, Peter, 147–8, 156–7
Last of Chéri (Colette), 267, 271–2
Lawton, George, 302
Lays (Marie of France), 140, 142, 198
le Bon, Sylvie, 305
lena, 114; *see also* go-between
Lenclos, Ninon de, 7, 173, 179, 228, 231, 265, 288, 307–8
Le Richin, Fulk, 206–7
Le Roy Ladurie, Emmanuel, 161–3
lesbianism
    charges used to scapegoat women, 286, 294–5
    and Colette, 270
    and Sappho, 95–6
Lespinasse, Julie de, 227, 231, 330
Lewes, Henry, 8
Liaisons Dangereuses, Les (Laclos), 230, 231
life-cycle literature, 14–15, 19, 70, 132, 175–81, 318–19, 325–37
life expectancy
    blacks compared with whites, 336
    women compared with men, 102–3, 153, 156–7, 162, 279–80, 310
Linton, Elizabeth Lynn, 256, 283–4
Little Women (Alcott), 259
Lives (Plutarch), 100
Lorde, Audre, 342

Lost Illusions (Balzac), 262, 266
"lounge lizards," 45
love poetry, troubadours, 137, 139, 141
Lyly, John, *Sapho and Phao*, 193, 196, 226
Lysistrata (Aristophanes), 105

Macbeth (Shakespeare), 62
Machiavelli, Niccolò, 205, 217
    and Fortuna, 122
    Prince, The, 122, 205, 217
Madeleine de Scudéry, 227, 228
    Clélie, 229
    Grand Cyrus, Le, 229
    and Paul Pellison, 227
Madonna sculptures
    Black Madonna, 342
    Coronation of the Virgin, 145
    derived from goddess statues, 141
    as "throne of wisdom," 141–2
    Triumph of the Virgin, 145
Magnus, Albertus, *Book of Secrets*, 193
Malleus Malificarum (Krämer and Sprenger), 191, 194
Malory, Thomas, *Le Morte d'Arthur*, 185–6
"Mammy" figure, 337–8
Marguerite de Navarre, *Heptaméron*, 177, 198, 217, 224
Marie of Champagne, 142–3, 144
Marie of France, *Lays*, 140, 142, 198
Marquise de Rambouillet, 227
"marriage crunch," 328–30
Marriage of Figaro, The (Beaumarchais), 186–7, 222
marriage pattern, European, 152–3
Martin, Emily, 308
Martin, Priscilla, 135
Mary, Saint, mother of Christ, 118
    relation to traditions of goddesses, 91
    see also Madonna sculptures; Saint Anne
masculinization, 18–9
    in the contemporary period, 354–5
    early modern European dress, 214
    among eighteenth-century philosophes, 230
    and nation-state formation, 201
    late nineteenth century, 259–61

and professionalization, late
nineteenth century, 285–6
Renaissance, 214
Maslow, Abraham, 326
Maupassant, Guy de, *Bel Ami*, 262
Mead, Margaret, 273, 305
"post-menopausal zest," 274, 307
melancholy
as premodern mental ailment, 175
related to witchcraft, 193
in Shakespeare's *As You Like It*, 175
Mellaart, James, 82, 88
Melville, Herman, 264
Pierre, or the Ambiguities, 263
Memoirs of a Coxcomb (Cleland), 220–1
Menexenus (Plato), 109
Menninger, Karl, 302
menopause, 15, 20, 181–5, 192, 193, 258,
273–310
debate over, 273–6, 279
as empowering for women leaders,
nineteenth and twentieth centuries,
333
Freudian view of, 297–305
in *Homeric Hymn to Demeter*, 70
as individualistic, 309
male, 278, 309
medicalization of, 275, 284–8, 308–9
negative views toward, 192–3, 283–7
possibilities for procreation,
contemporary era, 328–9
sexuality and, 288–97
symptoms, 170–1, 275
taboos, premodern, 193
terminology for, 184, 266, 273, 278
and witchcraft, 192–3
menstruation, 117, 121, 166, 184–5, 193,
277, 290
Merchant of Venice (Shakespeare), 62
Metamorphoses (Ovid), 177–8
Michaelis, Karin, 285
Dangerous Age, The, 273–4, 275, 279,
296–7
Michelangelo, 121, 214
middle age, for women
early modern Europe, attitudes
toward, 177–81
modern period, attitudes toward, 280
mid-life crisis concept, 326
Midsummer Night's Dream, A
(Shakespeare), 170, 186

Minois, Georges, 157
misogyny
in eighteenth-century England, 264
in Helene Deutsch, *Psychology of
Women*, 299
medieval, 146
and Penelope's story, 72
Roman, 111–16
"momism"
and black women, 340
as charge against aging women, 295,
302–3
Montaillou (France), fourteenth century,
161–3
moral superiority of women argument,
nineteenth century, 281–2
Morrison, Toni, 316, 336, 340, 344–8
Beloved, 344, 345
Bluest Eye, The, 344
Song of Solomon, 345
Sula, 344, 345
Tar Baby, 345, 346
Morte d'Arthur, Le (Malory), 185–6
Mother Goose, and goddess traditions,
195
mother-in-law, 103, 162, 166, 297–8
Mother Midnight, 196, 246; *see also*
go-between; old bawd; old trot
Mother Shipton, 186
Mother's Recompense, A (Wharton), 289,
290
Moynihan Report (*The Negro Family:
The Case for National Action*), 340
Mrs. Grundy, as symbol of Victorianism,
252; *see also* Victorianism
Much Ado About Nothing (Shakespeare),
207, 209
Muses, 62, 120, 122
mystery religions
cults of Cybele, Isis, Diana, 91
Eleusinian Mysteries, 87–8
mystics, medieval female
visions of Christ figure, 119, 202
visions of female wisdom figure, 119

Nana (Zola), 262
National Organization for Women, 333
Neolithic period, 63, 82, 88, 100
Neoplatonic idealism, 117–23
new historicism, as methodology, 21

*New Introductory Lectures on
    Psychoanalysis* (Freud), 298
"New Woman," 52, 281, 286, 356
    applied to aging women, 276–7
New Yorker clubwoman cartoons, 296
Night of the Iguana, The (Williams), 306
nineteenth century
    Anglo-American and continental
        comparisons, 261–7
    decline in cross-age relationships, 243
    demography in, 244–5
    division among women, 247
    masculinization in, late century, 258–61
    mother-daughter bonds in, 257–8
    "republican" motherhood, concept of,
        246
    rise of beauty culture, 255–7
    sexuality in, 246–7
    standards of appearance in, 242–58
Northumberland, Earl, *Advice to His
    Son*, 210
novel of initiation, 69, 221–2, 261–7

objectification, in art
    of aging women, 18, 167–8
    of women, 18, 121–2; *see also*
        subjectification, in art, of young
        men
Odysseus, 64–75
Odyssey (Homer), 7, 18, 19, 59, 64–75,
    76, 77, 80, 88–90
    and male heroism, 61, 64–5
    see also Odysseus; Penelope;
        Telemachus
old age (women)
    in Arthurian legend, 185
    definition of entry into, 183
    as life-cycle stage, 181–6
    poverty among women in, 160–1,
        181–2, 324, 328
    remarriage among women in, 161–2
    see also old bawd; wise woman, as
        role for aging women
"old bag," 174
old bawd, 187; *see also* Dipsas; lena;
    go-between; old trot; procurer
"old maid"
    as card game, 249
    as term of contempt, 247–50, 329
    see also spinsters

Old Maid, The (Wharton), 250
old maid's insanity, 285–6, 293; *see also*
    climacteric insanity; involutional
    melancholia
old trot, 196; *see also* go-between
"old wives' tales," 131, 195–6, 296
Old Wives' Tale, The (Bennett), 264
On Love (Plutarch), 110
Osiris, 63; *see also* Isis
Ossoli, Count Giovanni Angelo, 8,
    237–43, 261; *see also* Fuller,
    Margaret
osteoporosis, 182, 308; *see also* dowager's
    hump
Othello (Shakespeare), 199
Ovid, 96, 113–16, 120, 181
    Amores, 114–16, 187, 188
    Art of Love, 113, 177
    Heroides, 96, 107, 113, 120
    Metamorphoses, 177, 178

page
    as standard female disguise, 264
    as young male type, 264
Parzifal (von Eschenbach), 210
Passages (Sheehy), 319, 326
Paston family, 151, 183
patriarchy
    continuation, in nineteenth century,
        252
    as feminist concept, 17–18
    among Greek gods, 75
    in Hollywood, 36
    and violence, 20
    and women as source of wisdom, 120
    and young men, as heirs of, 209
pederasty, 105; *see also* same-sex love,
    male
Penelope, 59, 64–75
Perceval (Chrétien de Troyes), 147–8
Perrers, Alice, 133, 190
Persephone, 63, 70, 73, 74, 87, 88; *see
    also* Demeter; Eleusinian Mysteries
Petit Jehan de Saintré, Le (La Sale),
    140–1
Petrarch, 168
Petronius, *Satyricon*, 114
Phaedra, *see* Hippolytus and Phaedra
Phaedrus (Plato), 108
Phaethon, 76, 77, 97; *see also* Aphrodite

Phaon, 59, 92–101, 221; *see also* Sappho
Philosophia, 59, 119
physiological theories, 132, 183, 245
    on aging men's sexuality, 198–9
    on aging women's sexuality, 169–71
    on differential aging between men
        and women, 102
    eighteenth-century modifications, 245,
        261
    of Galen, 169–70
    on genital construction, 132
    humoral, 169–70, 277–80
Pierre, or the Ambiguities (Melville), 263
Plain Dealer (Wycherley), 154
plagues, impact on sex and age ratios,
    fourteenth and fifteenth centuries,
    153, 157
Plato, 9, 11, 103, 107, 108–9
    Menexenus, 109
    Phaedrus, 108
    Republic, 108
    Symposium, 106, 107, 109
    Timaeus, 108, 118
pleasant Historie of John Winchcombe, in
    his younguer yeares called Jack of
    Newbery, The (Delony), 152, 165,
    167, 173
Plutarch, 113, 116, 117, 183
    Lives, 100
    On Love, 110, 116; treatise on Isis and
        Osiris, 116
pornography, aging women in early
    European, 174
Portrait of a Lady (James), 263
poulaines, 204–6
poverty, among aging women
    contemporary era, 324, 328
    early modern Europe, 160–1, 181–2
    "feminization of poverty," 324
Praise of Folly, The (Erasmus), 171
Pratt, Annis, 331
précieuses, 202, 221, 222–3, 226–31, 235
prestate societies, status of aging
    women in, 165–7, 322
primogeniture, 69, 138, 209
Prince, The (Machiavelli), 122, 205, 217
procurers, 184–97, 248; *see also*
    go-between
Psychology of Women, The (Deutsch),
    299–300
puella senex, 177

puer senex, 177
Pure and the Impure, The (Colette), 267,
    270
Pythia of Delphi, 104, 116, 118

Queen Kelly, 37, 40
querelle des femmes, 146, 178, 223

Rabelais, François, 178, 179, 189
    Gargantua and Pantagruel, 205
    Two Epistles to Two Women of
        Different Humours, 177, 178
rake, as male role, 201, 219
Rake's Progress, A (Hogarth), 221
Raleigh, Sir Walter, 212–13
rape, 18–19
    in *The Canterbury Tales*, 134–5
    in early modern Europe, 216–17
    in original Sleeping Beauty tale, 216
Rebecca (du Maurier), 34, 306
Rebecca (film), 34, 306
Red and the Black, The (Stendhal), 262,
    266–7
Renaissance
    and concepts of beauty in women, 179
    and life-cycle reasoning, 175–6
    and male dress, 205
    neoplatonism in, 121, 179
    objectification, in art, 167–8
"Renaissance of the Twelfth Century,"
    138
Republic (Plato), 108
"republican" mother, ideal type in
    nineteenth-century United States,
    246
Restoration drama, England, 154, 173–4,
    187
Retreat from Love, The (Colette), 267–70
Rich, Adrienne, 19, 22
Richardson, Samuel, 235, 246
Ripening Seed, The (Colette), 267–70
Rocca, John, 8, 272
Rojas, Fernando de, 188, 189,
    Celestina, 194
Romance of the Rose (Lorris and Meun),
    132, 146, 155, 178, 189, 200, 212,
    214
Roman Spring of Mrs. Stone, The
    (Williams), 290

romantic love, rise of, 127, 235, 244
Rome
    creation of old bawd and Dipsas,
        114–16
    family relations, 110–11
    female healers, 111
    misogyny of major writers, 113
    position of widows, 111
    prestige of aging, 111
    same-sex male relationships, 110
Romeo and Juliet (Shakespeare), 187–8,
    216
Rousseau, Jean-Jacques, 19, 202, 227,
    230
    and Madame de Warens, 266
Rubin, Lillian, 319
Russell, Lillian, 281, 283

sacred marriage, *see: hieros gamos*
salonnières, 197, 202, 226–31
salons, British, 265
salons, eighteenth century, French, 11,
    197, 202, 226–31
same-sex love, female, *see* lesbianism
same-sex love, male
    in classical Athens, 105–6; related to
        male socialization, 107
    in early modern Europe, 200, 213
    in Renaissance Italy, 159
    in twelfth and thirteenth centuries,
        138, 144–5
Sand, George, 240, 265
Sapho (Daudet), 262
Sapho and Phao (Lyly), 193, 196, 226
Sappho (Sapho), 59, 79, 92–101, 120
    biography, 94
    destruction of writings, 93, 120
    in later literature, 93, 221, 226
    and Phaon, 59, 92–101, 221
    relationships with students, 95, 96
    reputation, 93, 95
    view of beauty, 100–1
    view of love, 97
Sartre, Jean-Paul, 304
Satyricon (Petronius), 114
School of Chartres, 138–9
Scot, Reginald, 182, 192, 193, 194
Scott, Joan, 257
Second Sex, The (de Beauvoir), 303–5,
    333

senescence, as concept of gerontology,
    317
Sentimental Education (Flaubert), 262
sex ratios, 8, 127
    in early modern Europe, 156–7
    and male violence, 157
    in nineteenth century, 245
    among older people, contemporary
        period, 329–30
    in twelfth and thirteenth centuries,
        137–8
Shackle, The (Colette), 271
Shakespeare, William, 62, 195, 198, 203,
    217, 221, 225
    Antony and Cleopatra, 185
    As You Like It, 175–6, 210
    and beauty, 23, 180–1
    and boy actors, 222
    cuckoldry themes, 218
    goddess themes, 22–3, 62–3
    life-cycle definitions, 222
    Macbeth, 22, 62
    and male dress, 207, 209
    Merchant of Venice, 62
    Midsummer Night's Dream, A, 170, 186
    Much Ado About Nothing, 207, 209
    Othello, 199
    Romeo and Juliet, 187–8, 216
    sexuality in aging men, 199
    Winter's Tale, The, 180–1
Sheehy, Gail, *Passages*, 319, 326
Sibylline Books, 118
Sibyls, 59, 118–19, 121, 242–3
    and Michelangelo's depiction, 121
sixteenth and seventeenth centuries
    as ages of anxiety, 218
    and cuckoldry, 218
    and witchcraft persecutions, 190
Smith-Rosenberg, Carroll, 284, 294
Smollett, Tobias, *Adventures of Humphry
    Clinker*, 248
Song of Roland, The, 138
Song of Solomon (Morrison), 345
Sophia, 117, 119, 120
Spencer, Anna Garlin, 274, 275, 279,
    282, 288
spinsters, 243–4, 247–8, 249, 328; *see also*
    "old maid"
Staël, Germaine de, 8, 240, 244, 265
    Corinne, 240
    and John Rocca, 8, 272

Stanton, Elizabeth Cady, 7, 250, 282, 333
Steinach clinic, 291, 293, 309
Steinem, Gloria, 319
Stendhal, 244
  Red and the Black, The, 262, 266–7
stepmother, 136, 166, 173
  seduction of stepson motif, 10, 83, 173
Stone, Lawrence, 150, 173
Stopes, Marie, 294, 356
Stubbs, John, 169
Studies in the Psychology of Sex (Ellis), 286–7
subjectification, in art, of young men, 201; *see also* objectification, in art, of women
Sula (Morrison), 344, 345
Sunset Boulevard (film), 27–55, 305, 321, 331
  attitude toward fifties domesticity, 34, 42
  film noir themes in, 47
  as Gothic tale, 33–4
  heroism in, 43–8
  as Hollywood film, 36
  "novel of initation" theme in, 45
  older woman/younger man relationship in, 30–1, 37–8
  old world versus new world symbolism in, 46
  personifications of aging in, 32–3, 41
Sunset Boulevard (street)
  as metaphor for aging, 29
  and frontier mythology, 44
Sweet Bird of Youth (Williams), 50, 306
Symposium (Plato), 9, 11, 106, 107, 109

Tammuz, 63, 79; *see also* Ishtar
Tar Baby (Morrison), 345, 346
Taylor, Elizabeth, 318
Tea and Sympathy (Williams), 306
Telemachus, 88–9; *see also: Odyssey*
Tencin, Madame de, 227, 229
Their Eyes Were Watching God (Hurston), 349–52
"Theme of the Three Caskets" (Freud), 62
Theogeny (Hesiod), 77, 78, 98
thirteenth century, Europe
  decline of courtly love, 146

minority persecutions, 144–5
  as period of women's declining influence, 145–6
Thomas, Keith, 150
"throne of wisdom" sculptures, 141–2
Tilt, Edward, 278, 279, 281
Timaeus (Plato), 108, 118
Tom Jones (Fielding), 8, 221, 222, 246
Totem and Taboo (Freud), 298
Transcendentalists, 239–40
"transformation" tales, 134–5; *see also* Wife of Bath; folk and fairy tales
Treatise on Moral and Domestic Economy (Goodman of Paris), 165
Tristram and Isolde (Thomas of Britain), 141
Trotula of Salerno, 186
troubadours, 137, 141, 209
Trumbach, Randolph, 200
twelfth century, Europe
  as expansive age, 137–8, 144
  as period of greater influence for women, 138–44
Two Epistles to Two Women of Different Humours (Rabelais), 177, 178

univora, 111; *see also* Rome

Van de Velde, Theodoor, 292
Vaughan, John, 217
Ventadour, Bernard de, and Eleanor of Aquitaine, 142
Venus, *see* Aphrodite
Vestal Virgins, 110
Vickers, Nancy, 168
Victorianism, 17, 243–58
  beauty, 251–3, 255–7
  divisions among women, 247, 252, 257–8
  grandmother type, 253–5
  romantic love, 244
  sexuality, 246–7
  spinsters, 243, 247–8, 249
  witchcraft, 248–9
Vigeois, Geoffrey de, 208
Virgil, 118
  Aeneid, 119
Vitalis, Orderic, 208
von Eschenbach, Wolfram, *Parzifal*, 210

von Stroheim, Erich, 28, 39–40; *see also:*
       Sunset Boulevard

Walker, Alice, 316, 336–7, 340, 341, 343,
       344–8
   Color Purple, The, 346–7
   Temple of My Familiar, The, 347–8
Walpole, Horace, 228, 265
Warens, Madame de, 266
Warner, Marina, 21, 119
Wharton, Edith, 250
   Mother's Recompense, A, 289–90
   Old Maid, The, 250
widows
   as economic managers, 151, 158
   inheritance: in classical Athens, 103;
       in medieval and early modern
       Europe, 150–1, 156, 158; in Rome,
       111
   remarriage: in classical Athens, 103;
       in early modern Europe, 154,
       159–61; in nineteenth century, 257;
       in Rome, 111
   and sexuality, 261
Wife of Bath (Alison), 8, 21, 128–36,
       152, 159, 165, 171, 173, 186, 216–17;
       see also: Canterbury Tales
Wilder, Billy, 27, 28, 38–40, 43; *see also:*
       Sunset Boulevard
Williams, Tennessee, 50, 290, 306
   Night of the Iguana, The, 306
   Roman Spring of Mrs. Stone, The, 290
   Sweet Bird of Youth, 50, 306
   Tea and Sympathy, 306
Winkler, John, 108
Winter's Tale, The (Shakespeare), 180–1
wise woman, as role for aging women,
       52, 109, 116, 118, 121, 128, 134, 185
witchcraft, 18, 189–97, 248–9

Wolfe, A. Béran, 307
Wollstonecraft, Mary, 234
Woman in the Nineteenth Century
       (Fuller), 16, 238, 240–2, 249, 257
woman's rights movement, twentieth
       century, participation of aging
       women in, 282, 332
Wycherley, William, *Plain Dealer,* 154
Wylie, Philip, *Generation of Vipers,* 303,
       306
Wythorne, Thomas, 172, 173, 191

younger sons, as social group, 209–11;
       see also primogeniture
young gods, 63
   and castration, 81
   ceremonies surrounding, 79–80
   as dying and reviving vegetation gods,
       77–8
   and matrifocal imagination, 85
   as priests, 84
   and sacrifice, 78
youth, male
   eroticized, early modern Europe,
       198–223
   as hot-blooded, 197
   as life-stage for men, 198–231
   as powerful and powerless, early
       modern Europe, 209
   see also beauty, in young men;
       "lounge lizards"; primogeniture;
       young gods; younger sons
Yvain (Chrétien de Troyes), 141

Zeus (Jupiter), 355; *see also* Hera
Zola, Emile, 262
   Nana, 262

Lois Banner was born in Los Angeles, in 1939. She received her B.A. degree from the University of California at Los Angeles and her M.A. and Ph.D. from Columbia University. She has taught at Rutgers University, Princeton University, the University of Scranton, Hamilton College, the University of Maryland, and George Washington University. Currently she is Professor of History and the Program for the Study of Women and Men in Society at the University of Southern California. She has been a fellow of both the Bunting Institute of Radcliffe College and the Rockefeller Foundation. She is a Past President of the American Studies Association and is currently President-elect of the Pacific Coast Branch, American Historical Association. She is coeditor (with Mary S. Hartman) of Clio's Consciousness Raised: New Perspectives on the History of Women *(1974) and the author of* Women in Modern America: A Brief History *(1974),* Elizabeth Cady Stanton: A Radical for Woman's Rights *(1979), and* American Beauty *(1983).*

A NOTE ON THE TYPE

This book was set in Granjon, a type named in compliment to Robert Granjon but neither a copy of a classic face nor an entirely original creation. George W. Jones based his designs on the type used by Claude Garamond (c. 1480–1561) in his beautiful French books. Granjon more closely resembles Garamond's own type than do any of the various modern types that bear his name.

Robert Granjon began his career as a type cutter in 1523. The boldest and most original designer of his time, he was one of the first to practice the trade of type founder apart from that of printer. Between 1557 and 1562 Granjon printed about twenty books in types designed by himself, following, after the fashion, the cursive handwriting of the time. These types, usually known as caractères de civilité, he himself called lettres françaises, as especially appropriate to his own country.

Composed by Crane Typesetting Service, Inc.,
West Barnstable, Massachusetts
Printed and bound by the Courier Companies, Inc.,
Westford, Massachusetts
Designed by Mia Vander Els